CENSUS OF INDIA 1891

Census of India 1871-1951, 9 Sets In 384 Bindings (9788121258876) Rs. 700000

Census of India 1891, 28 Vols. In 49 Bindings (978-81-212-7129-5) Rs. 125000

1. General Report (9788121269834) Rs. 1450
2. General Tables For British Provinces And Feudatory States (9788121269810) Rs. 2710 (Vol. I)
3. General Tables For British Provinces And Feudatory States (9788121269797) Rs. 950 (Vol. II)
4. Assam - Report (9788121269773) Rs. 2390 (Vol. I, V.1)
5. Assam - Tables (9788121269759) Rs. 2210 (Vol. II, V.2)
6. Assam - Provincial Tables (9788121269735) Rs. 1310 (Vol. II, V.3)
7. The Lower Provinces of Bengal and their Feudatories - The Report (9788121269711) Rs. 1660 (Vol. III)
8. The Lower Provinces of Bengal and their feudatories - The Administrative Tables (9788121269698) Rs. 4200 (Vol. IV)
9. The Lower Provinces of Bengal and their feudatories - The Caste Tables (9788121269674) Rs. 2600 (Vol. V, Pt. 1)
10. Lower Provinces of Bengal - The Provincial Tables (9788121269650) Rs. 1980 (Vol. V, Pt. 2)
11. Berar or the Hyderabad Assigned Districts (9788121269636) Rs. 3360 (Vol. VI)
12. Bombay and Its Feudatories - Report (9788121269612) Rs. 4010 (Vol. VII, Pt. 1)
13. Bombay And Its Feudatories - Imperial Tables (9788121269599) Rs. 790 (Vol. VIII, Pt. 2)
14. Imperial Series - Burma Report (9788121269575) Rs. 2320 (Vol. IX-V.1)
15. Imperial Tables - Burma Report (9788121269551) Rs. 3360 (Vol. X-V.2)
16. Provincial Tables Burma Report (9788121269537) Rs. 3510 (Vol. X-V.3)
17. Provincial Tables Burma Report (9788121269513) Rs. 3630 (Vol. X-V.4)
18. The Central Provinces And Feudatories - The Report (9788121269490) Rs. 2290 (Vol. XI, Pt. 1)
19. The Central Provinces And Feudatories - Imperial tables and supplementary returns (9788121268936) Rs. 2010 (Vol. XII)
20. Madras The Report On The Census (9788121269476) Rs. 2870 (Vol. XIII)
21. Madras - Tables I to XVII-C, British Territory (9788121269452) Rs. 3490 (Vol. XIV)
22. Madras - Tables A TO E, British Territory. Tables for feudatory States and A Caste Index (9788121269438) Rs. 2820 (Vol. XV)
23. The North Western Provinces and Outh - Report and Provincial Tables (9788121268912) Rs. 3100 (Vol. XVI, Pt. 1)
24. The North - Western Provinces and Oudh- Imperial Tables (9788121269414) Rs. 2000 (Vol. XVII, Pt. 2)
25. The North - Western Provinces and Oudh- Imperial Caste Tables (9788121269391) Rs. 3020 (Vol. XVIII, Pt. 3)
26. Punjab and Its Feudatories - The Report on the Census (9788121269377) Rs. 2710 (Vol. XIX, Pt. 1)
27. Punjab and Its Feudatories - Imperial Tables and Supplementary Returns for the British Territory (9788121269353) Rs. 1370 (Vol. XX, Pt. 2)
28. Punjab and Its Feudatories - Imperial Tables and Supplementary Returns for the Native States, Together With A Caste Index (9788121269339) Rs. 4910 (Vol. XXI, Pt. 3)
29. Report on The Census of The Districts of Ajmere-Merwara (9788121269056) Rs. 720 (Vol. XXII)
30. His Highness The Nizam's Dominions - Report (9788121269315) Rs. 2240 (Vol. XXIII, Pt. 1)
31. His Highness The Nizam's Dominions - Report (9788121269292) Rs. 2410 (Vol. XXIII, Pt. 2)
32. His Highness The Nizam's Dominions - Imperial And Supplementry Tables and Caste Index (9788121269278) Rs. 3390 (Vol. XXIII, Pt. 3)
33. Baroda - Report (9788121269254) Rs. 3810 (Vol. XXIV, Pt. 1)
34. Baroda - Tables (9788121269230) Rs. 2620 (Vol. XXIV, Pt. 2)
35. Mysore - Report (9788121269216) Rs. 2590 (Vol. XXV, Pt. 1)
36. Mysore - Imperial Tables (9788121269193) Rs. 1600 (Vol. XXV, Pt. 2)
37. Mysore - Tables (9788121269179) Rs. 5320 (Vol. XXV, Pt. 3)
38. Mysore - Supplementary Tables (9788121269155) Rs. 3590 (Vol. XXV, Pt. 4)
39. Mysore- Supplement to the Mysore census report of 1891 being a list of villages in the Mysore province and : comparing the population as per Censuses of 1891, 1881 & 1871 (9788121279024) Rs. 5350 (Vol. XXV, Pt. 5)
40. Rajputana - The Report, Imperial Tables And Supplementary Returns (9788121269131) Rs. 2330 (Vol. XXVI, Pt. 1)
41. Rajputna - The Provincial Tables and Remarks (9788121269117) Rs. 550 (Vol. XXVI, Pt. 2)
42. Central India (9788121269094) Rs. 2000 (Vol. XXVII)
43. Kashmir State - The Report on the census and Imperial and supplementary Tables (9788121269070) Rs. 2290 (Vol. XXVIII)
44. The Census of Calcutta (9788121269032) Rs. 890
45. Report on the census of Cochin (9788121269018) Rs. 790 (Pt. 1)
46. Report on the census of Cochin - The Final Census Tables with Appendices (9788121268998) Rs. 910 (Pt. 2)
47. Report on the Census of Coorg (9788121268974) Rs. 730
48. Report on the census of Travancore -Report (9788121274029) Rs. 4220 (Vol. I)
49. Report on the census of Travancore -Appendix (9788121268950) Rs. 5300 (Vol. II)

Owing to the antiquity and rarity of this book, certain pages are regrettably absent, and readability is compromised due to the blurring of the original text. If you possess any insights regarding the availability of these missing sections, kindly inform us. Your assistance is crucial in ensuring the completion of this significant work for the benefit of future generations.

CENSUS OF INDIA, 1891

BOOK-49

REPORT

ON THE CENSUS OF TRAVANCORE

TAKEN

BY COMMAND OF

HIS HIGHNESS THE MAHARAJAH

ON THE

26TH FEBRUARY 1891— 16TH MASY 1066 M.E.

ALONG WITH THE

IMPERIAL CENSUS OF INDIA

VOL. II.—APPENDIX

Y. NAGAM AIYA

GYAN

Published by

Gyan Publishing House
5, Ansari Road
Daryaganj, New Delhi-110002
Phone: 011-47034999, 9811692060
E-mail: books@gyanbooks.com

Distribution Network
gyanbooks.com
India, USA, Canada, UK, Australia

ISBN: 978-81-212-7129-5 (Set) 28 Vols. In 49 Bindings
978-81-212-6895-0 (PB) Book-49, Pt. II

First Published, 1894

2nd Impression 2024

Printed at: Gyan Press, Delhi.

CENSUS OF INDIA 1891

REPORT

ON THE CENSUS OF TRAVANCORE,

TAKEN

BY COMMAND OF

HIS HIGHNESS THE MAHARAJAH

ON THE

26th February 1891—16th Masy 1066 M.E.

ALONG WITH THE

IMPERIAL CENSUS OF INDIA.

BY

Y. NAGAM AIYA, B.A., F.R. HIST. S.,
Dewan Peishcar—Census Commissioner.

VOL. II.—APPENDIX.

ADDISON & CO.,
158 & 188, Mount Road, Madras.

1894.

CONTENTS

OF

VOL. II.

Part I.—Statistics (Taluqwar).

Part II.—Statistics (Final Tables).

Part III.—Miscellaneous Information.

APPENDIX.

PART I.—STATISTICS (TALUQWAR).

TABLE
Area, Houses,

Number.	Taluq.	Area in square miles.	Number of		Occupied Houses.			
			Towns.	Villages.	Total.	Towns.	Villages.	Total.
1	2	3	4	5	6	7	8	9
1	Tovala ...	121	...	6	7,084		7,084	29,751
2	Agastiswaram ...	97	1	6	19,647	2,475	17,172	87,241
3	Eranial ...	142	...	8	22,208	...	22,208	105,098
4	Kalkulam ...	142	...	8	12,561	...	12,561	59,474
5	Vilavankodu ...	146	...	8	13,036	...	13,036	68,521
6	Neyattankara ...	213	...	10	22,266	...	22,266	110,755
7	Trivandram[1] ...	99	1	10	21,562	4,793	16,769	111,938
8	Nedumangadu ...	340	...	8	11,633	...	11,633	55,497
9	Sirayinkil ...	143	...	11	19,612	...	19,612	97,995
10	Kottarakkara ...	234	...	8	13,684	...	13,684	71,517
11	Pattanapuram ...	400	...	6	7,915	...	7,915	39,447
12	Shenkotta ...	65	1	8	7,693	2,121	5,572	32,088
13	Quilon[2] ...	154	1	7	22,816	2,895	19,921	121,935
14	Kunnattur ...	185	...	9	14,789	...	14,789	73,529
15	Karunagappalli ...	89	...	8	23,223	...	23,223	108,826
16	Kartigappalli ...	70	1	10	18,306	1,433	16,873	91,950
17	Mavellikkara ...	} 1,164	...	8	21,718	...	21,718	103,619
18	Chenganur ...		...	7	18,605	...	18,605	93,960
19	Tiruvalla ...	125	...	8	24,247	...	24,247	122,142
20	Ambalappula ...	121	1	12	18,720	4,505	14,215	94,745
21	Sherttala ...	129	...	7	28,571	...	28,571	117,261
22	Vykkam ...	88	1	7	17,579	1,493	16,086	80,628
23	Ettumanur ...	140	...	6	15,580	...	15,580	80,823
24	Kottayam ...	147	1	7	15,005	1,310	13,695	77,094
25	Changanachori ...	260	...	7	14,658	...	14,658	74,722
26	Meenachal ...	312	...	7	11,420	...	11,420	59,976
27	Muvattupula ...	516	...	8	20,387	...	20,387	103,009
28	Todupula ...	612	...	5	5,025	...	5,025	25,202
29	Kunnattunadu ...	221	...	11	20,702	...	20,702	114,049
30	Alangadu ...	208	...	7	13,183	...	13,183	70,958
31	Parur ...	47	...	6	10,729	...	10,729	59,278
	Cardamom Hills ..		...	1	1,754	...	1,754	11,413
	Periyar & Thekkadi.		...	2	618	...	618	3,295
	Total ...	6,730	8	247	516,536	21,025	495,511	2,557,736

1. Areas in British occupation included in the above, viz., Residency Escort. } Residency Escort...
2. Areas in British occupation included in the above, consisting of the Cantonment and Regimental lines. } Quilon Cantonment

I.
and Population.

POPULATION.							
TOTAL.		MALES.			FEMALES.		
Towns.	Villages.	Total.	Towns.	Villages.	Total.	Towns.	Villages.
10	11	12	13	14	15	16	17
...	29,751	14,489	...	14,489	15,262	...	15,262
11,187	76,054	43,226	5,335	37,891	44,015	5,852	38,163
...	105,098	52,883	...	52,883	52,215	...	52,215
...	59,474	29,834	...	29,834	29,640	...	29,640
...	68,521	35,202	...	35,202	33,319	...	33,319
...	110,755	56,953	...	56,953	53,802	...	53,802
27,887	84,051	56,909	14,707	42,202	55,029	13,180	41,849
...	55,497	27,857	...	27,857	27,640	...	27,640
...	97,995	48,271	...	48,271	49,724	...	49,724
...	71,517	36,055	...	36,055	35,462	...	35,462
..	39,447	19,858	...	19,858	19,589	...	19,589
8,727	23,361	15,700	4,202	11,498	16,388	4,525	11,863
15,375	106,560	60,832	7,871	52,961	61,103	7,504	53,599
...	73,529	37,397	...	37,397	36,132	..	36,132
...	108,826	52,862	...	52,862	55,964	...	55,964
6,890	85,060	45,216	3,448	41,768	46,734	3,442	43,292
...	103,619	52,494	...	52,494	51,125	...	51,125
...	93,960	48,443	...	48,443	45,517	...	45,517
...	122,142	62,514	...	62,514	59,628	...	59,628
22,768	71,977	46,909	11,286	35,623	47,836	11,482	36,354
...	117,261	58,448	...	58,448	58,813	...	58,813
7,769	72,859	40,947	4,113	36,834	39,681	3,656	36,025
...	80,823	41,536	...	41,536	39,287	...	39,287
7,090	70,004	39,229	3,539	35,690	37,865	3,551	34,314
...	74,722	38,596	...	38,596	36,126	...	36,126
...	59,976	30,830	...	30,830	29,146	...	29,146
...	103,009	51,595	...	51,595	51,414	...	51,414
...	25,202	12,786	...	12,786	12,416	..	12,416
...	114,049	57,216	...	57,216	56,833	...	56,833
...	70,958	35,944	...	35,944	35,014	...	35,014
...	59,278	30,082	...	30,082	29,196	...	29,196
..	11,413	6,714	...	6,714	4,699	...	4,699
...	3,295	2,588	...	2,588	707	...	707
107,693	2,450,043	1,290,415	54,501	1,235,914	1,267,321	53,192	1,214,129

	Occupied Houses.	Total Population.	Males.	Females.
... ...	81	226	127	99
and Regimental lines ...	636	2,539	1,357	1,182

TABLE

Variation in the Enumerated

Number.	Taluq.	Total. 1891.	Total. 1881.	Total. Variation.
1	2	3	4	5
1	Tovala	29,751	30,260	—509
2	Agastiswaram	87,241	78,979	+8,262
3	Eranial	105,098	112,116	—7,018
4	Kalkulam	59,474	60,908	—1,434
5	Vilavankodu	68,521	69,688	—1,167
6	Neyattankara	110,755	110,410	+345
7	Trivandram	111,938	102,986	+8,952
8	Nedumangadu	55,497	52,211	+3,286
9	Sirayinkil	97,995	87,072	+10,923
10	Kottarakkara	71,517	55,924	+15,593
11	Pattanapuram	39,447	37,064	+2,383
12	Shenkotta	32,088	30,477	+1,611
13	Quilon	121,935	108,469	+13,466
14	Kunnattur	73,529	62,700	+10,829
15	Karunagappalli	108,826	101,039	+7,787
16	Kartigappalli	91,950	81,969	+9,981
17	Mavellikkara	103,619	111,731	—8,112
18	Chenganur	93,960	81,301	+12,659
19	Tirûvalla	122,142	103,007	+19,135
20	Ambalappula	94,745	93,104	+1,641
21	Sherttala	117,261	113,704	+3,557
22	Vykkam	80,628	76,414	+4,214
23	Ettumanur	80,823	79,058	+1,765
24	Kottayam	77,094	64,958	+12,136
25	Changanacheri	74,722	74,154	+568
26	Meenachal	59,976	57,102	+2,874
27	Muvattupula	103,009	95,460	+7,549
28	Todupula	25,202	24,321	+881
29	Kunnattunadu	114,049	109,625	+4,424
30	Alangadu	70,958	66,753	+4,205
31	Parur	59,278	61,966	—2,688
	Cardamom Hills	11,413	6,228	+5,185
	Periyar and Thekkadi ...	3,295	...	+3,295
	Total ...	2,557,736	2,401,158	+156,578

II.

Population since last Census.

Males.			Females.		
1891.	1881.	Variation.	1891.	1881.	Variation.
6	7	8	9	10	11
14,489	14,830	—341	15,262	15,430	—168
43,226	37,741	+5,485	44,015	41,238	+2,777
52,883	55,124	—2,241	52,215	56,992	—4,777
29,834	30,341	—507	29,640	30,567	—927
35,202	35,101	+101	33,319	34,587	—1,268
56,953	55,318	+1,635	53,802	55,092	—1,290
56,909	51,633	+5,276	55,029	51,353	+3,676
27,857	26,465	+1,392	27,640	25,746	+1,894
48,271	42,193	+6,078	49,724	44,879	+4,845
36,055	28,253	+7,802	35,462	27,671	+7,791
19,858	18,594	+1,264	19,589	18,470	+1,119
15,700	14,688	+1,012	16,388	15,789	+599
60,832	53,027	+7,805	61,103	55,442	+5,661
37,397	31,358	+6,039	36,132	31,342	+4,790
52,862	48,815	+4,047	55,964	52,224	+3,740
45,216	40,009	+5,207	46,734	41,960	+4,774
52,494	55,604	—3,110	51,125	56,127	—5,002
48,443	41,375	+7,068	45,517	39,926	+5,591
62,514	52,719	+9,795	59,628	50,288	+9,340
46,909	46,957	—48	47,836	46,147	+1,689
58,448	56,204	+2,244	58,813	57,500	+1,313
40,947	38,448	+2,499	39,681	37,966	+1,715
41,536	39,446	+2,090	39,287	39,612	—325
39,229	33,008	+6,221	37,865	31,950	+5,915
38,596	38,169	+427	36,126	35,985	+141
30,830	29,120	+1,710	29,146	27,982	+1,164
51,595	47,395	+4,200	51,414	48,065	+3,349
12,786	12,335	+451	12,416	11,986	+430
57,216	54,625	+2,591	56,833	55,000	+1,833
35,944	33,407	+2,537	35,014	33,346	+1,668
30,082	31,487	—1,405	29,196	30,479	—1,283
6,714	3,345	+3,369	4,699	2,883	+1,816
2,588	...	+2,588	707	...	+707
1,290,415	1,197,134	+93,281	1,267,321	1,204,024	+63,297

TABLE

Towns and Villages

Number.	Taluq.	Total No. of Towns and Villages.	Total Population.	1–199. Number.	1–199. Population.	200–499. Number.	200–499. Population.	500–999. Number.	500–999. Population.	1,000-1,999. Number.	1,000-1,999. Population.
1	2	3	4	5	6	7	8	9	10	11	12
1	Tovala ...	6	29,751	...	...	...	...	...	...	...	...
2	Agastiswaram ...	7	87,241	...	...	...	...	...	...	...	...
3	Eranial ...	8	105,098	...	...	...	...	...	...	...	...
4	Kalkulam ...	8	59,474	...	...	...	...	...	...	...	...
5	Vilavankodu ...	8	68,521	...	...	...	...	...	...	...	...
6	Neyattankara ...	10	110,755	...	...	...	...	...	...	...	...
7	Trivandram ...	11	111,938	...	...	...	...	...	...	...	...
8	Nedumangadu ...	8	55,497	...	...	...	...	...	...	...	...
9	Sirayinkil ...	11	97,995	...	...	...	...	...	...	...	...
10	Kottarakkara ...	8	71,517	...	...	...	...	...	...	...	...
11	Pattanapuram ...	6	39,447	...	...	...	...	...	...	...	...
12	Shenkotta ...	9	32,088	...	...	...	...	...	...	3	4,150
13	Quilon ...	8	121,935	...	...	...	...	...	...	...	...
14	Kunnattur ...	9	73,529	...	...	...	...	...	...	...	...
15	Karunagappalli ...	8	108,826	...	...	...	...	...	...	...	...
16	Kartigappalli ...	11	91,950	...	...	...	...	...	...	...	...
17	Mavellikkara ...	8	103,619	...	...	...	...	...	...	...	...
18	Chenganur ...	7	93,960	...	...	...	...	...	...	...	...
19	Tiruvalla ...	8	122,142	...	...	...	...	...	...	...	...
20	Ambalappula ...	13	94,745	...	...	...	...	...	...	1	1,433
21	Sherttala ...	7	117,261	...	...	...	...	...	...	...	...
22	Vykkam ...	8	80,628	...	...	...	...	...	...	...	...
23	Ettumanur ...	6	80,823	...	...	...	...	...	...	...	...
24	Kottayam ...	8	77,094	...	...	...	...	...	...	...	...
25	Changanacheri ...	7	74,722	...	...	...	...	...	...	...	...
26	Meenachal ...	7	59,976	...	...	...	...	...	...	...	...
27	Muvattupula ...	8	103,009	...	...	...	...	...	...	...	...
28	Todupula ...	5	25,202	...	...	...	...	...	...	...	...
29	Kunnattunadu ...	11	114,049	...	...	...	...	...	...	...	...
30	Alangadu ...	7	70,958	...	...	...	...	...	...	...	...
31	Parur ...	6	59,278	...	...	...	...	...	...	...	...
	Cardamom Hills ...	1	11,413	...	...	...	...	...	...	...	...
	Periyar and Thekkadi.	2	3,295	...	...	...	...	1	716	...	..
	Total ...	255	2,557,736	...	...	...	...	1	716	4	5,583

III.

classified by Population.

2,000-2,999.		3,000-4,999.		5,000-9,999.		10,000-14,999.		15,000-19,999.		20,000-49,999.		50,000 & over.	
Number.	Population.	Number.	Population.	Number.	Population.	Number.	Population.	Number.	Population.	Number.	Population.	Number.	Population.
13	14	15	16	17	18	19	20	21	22	23	24	25	26
2	5,158	1	4,036	3	20,557	...	...	...	...	...	...	...	...
...	...	...	...	2	14,831	3	33,260	1	17,851	1	21,299	...	...
...	...	...	...	2	14,029	3	34,493	2	33,941	1	22,635	...	...
1	2,551	1	4,479	4	28,386	2	24,058	...	...	...	...	...	...
...	...	1	3,808	4	30,917	3	33,796	...	...	...	...	...	...
1	2,735	...	...	6	42,816	1	12,200	...	...	2	53,004	...	...
...	...	1	4,911	6	43,931	3	35,209	...	...	1	27,887	...	...
...	...	3	12,530	4	32,453	1	10,514	...	...	...	...	...	...
...	...	2	9,278	6	46,531	2	23,797	1	18,389	...	...	...	...
...	...	...	...	5	36,056	3	35,461	...	...	...	...	...	...
...	...	1	4,381	4	24,437	1	10,629	...	...	...	...	...	...
1	2,502	4	16,709	1	8,727	...	...	...	...	...	...	...	...
..	...	...	...	2	15,954	2	26,368	1	15,375	3	64,238	...	...
...	...	2	9,582	5	42,832	2	21,115	...	...	...	...	...	...
...	...	...	...	...	...	5	59,409	3	49,417	...	...	...	...
...	...	2	8,856	7	56,386	1	11,253	1	15,455	...	...	...	...
...	...	...	...	2	18,598	3	35,381	3	49,640	...	...	...	...
...	.	...	...	2	16,609	3	34,787	1	16,450	1	26,114	...	...
...	...	...	...	1	8,969	3	38,980	2	32,412	2	41,781	...	...
1	2,903	1	4,877	8	51,084	1	11,680	...	...	1	22,768	...	...
...	...	...	...	...	...	2	27,108	4	68,774	1	21,379	...	...
...	...	...	...	6	49,584	1	14,179	1	16,865	...	...	...	...
...	...	...	...	...	...	5	58,269	...	...	1	22,554	...	...
...	...	...	...	6	50,824	2	26,270	...	...	...	...	...	...
...	...	2	7,979	1	5,561	2	27,986	2	33,196	...	...	...	...
...	...	1	4,917	4	32,861	2	22,198	...	...	...	...	...	...
...	...	...	...	3	26,661	2	22,854	3	53,494	...	...	...	...
...	...	4	17,525	1	7,677	...	...	...	...	...	...	...	...
...	...	1	4,122	5	39,147	4	50,457	...	...	1	20,323	...	...
...	...	...	...	5	40,964	1	14,110	1	15,884	...	...	...	...
...	...	1	3,341	2	16,479	2	23,572	1	15,886	...	...	..	...
...	...	...	...	...	...	1	11,413	...	...	...	...	...	...
1	2,579	...	...	...	...	...	...	...	...	...	...	...	...
7	18,428	28	121,331	107	82[illegible],861	66	790,806	27	453,029	15	343,982	...	...

TABLE IV.

Towns according to Population compared with the preceding Census.

Town.	Municipality Suburbs or Cantonment.	Total Population.			Males.			Females.			Notes (Change in Areas, &c.)
		1891	1881	Variation.	1891	1881	Variation.	1891	1881	Variation.	
1	2	3	4	5	6	7	8	9	10	11	12
Trivandram..	...	27,661	...	...	14,580	...	...	13,081	...	...	Note.— The figures for 1881 are only approximate, for the towns were not then separately censused and their limits defined as on the present occasion: hence the large variation in the results.
...	Residency Escort.	226	...	...	127	...	...	99	...	...	
	Total ...	27,887	41,173	—13,286	14,707	...	...	13,180	...	...	
Alleppey ...	...	22,768	25,754	—2,986	11,286	...	...	11,482	...	...	
Quilon ...	...	12,836	...	...	6,514	...	...	6,322	...	...	
...	Cantonment ...	2,539	...	...	1,357	...	...	1,182	...	...	
	Total ...	15,375	13,588	+1,787	7,871	...	...	7,504	...	...	
Nagercoil ...	...	11,187	16,534	—5,347	5,335	...	...	5,852	...	...	
Shenkotta ...	...	8,727	7,882	+845	4,202	...	...	4,525	...	...	
Vykkam ...	...	7,769	13,053	—5,284	4,113	...	...	3,656	...	...	
Kottayam ...	...	7,090	11,293	—4,203	3,539	...	...	3,551	...	...	
Aripaud ...	...	6,890	...	...	3,448	...	...	3,442	...	...	Aripaud was not included as a town in the 1881 Census.

TABLE V.

Towns arranged territorially, with Population by Religion.

Town.		Total Population.			Hindu.			Mussalman.			Christian.			Jew.		
		Total.	Males.	Females.	Total.	Males.	Females.	Total.	Males.	Females.	Total.	Males.	Females.	Total.	Males.	Females.
1		2	3	4	5	6	7	8	9	10	11	12	13	14	15	16
Trivandram	...	27,887	14,707	13,180	24,804	13,243	11,561	1,610	817	793	1,473	647	826	...	...	...
Alleppey	...	22,768	11,286	11,482	11,304	5,583	5,721	7,470	3,441	4,029	3,994	2,262	1,732	...	...	...
Quilon	...	15,375	7,871	7,504	7,614	3,948	3,666	3,444	1,806	1,638	4,307	2,112	2,195	10	5	5
Nagercoil	...	11,187	5,335	5,852	9,632	4,618	5,014	57	33	24	1,498	684	814	...	...	...
Shenkotta	...	8,727	4,202	4,525	8,402	4,042	4,360	287	140	147	38	20	18	...	...	...
Vykkam	...	7,769	4,113	3,656	6,864	3,610	3,254	90	55	35	815	448	367	...	...	...
Kottayam	...	7,090	3,539	3,551	4,037	2,021	2,016	197	114	83	2,856	1,404	1,452	...	...	...
Aripaud	...	6,890	3,448	3,442	5,706	2,872	2,834	240	111	129	944	465	479	...	...	...

TABLE

Reli

Number.	TALUQ.	TOTAL POPULATION. Total.	Males.	Females.	HINDU. Total.	Males.	Females.
1	2	3	4	5	6	7	8
1	Tovala ...	29,751	14,489	15,262	26,822	13,107	13,715
2	Agastiswaram ...	87,241	43,226	44,015	68,634	33,920	34,714
3	Eranial ...	105,098	52,883	52,215	74,383	37,597	36,786
4	Kalkulam ...	59,474	29,834	29,640	47,117	23,607	23,510
5	Vilavankodu ...	68,521	35,202	33,319	56,718	29,108	27,610
6	Neyattankara ...	110,755	56,953	53,802	93,618	48,144	45,474
7	Trivandram ...	111,938	56,909	55,029	93,468	47,760	45,708
8	Nedumangadu ...	55,497	27,857	27,640	50,766	25,345	25,421
9	Sirayinkil ...	97,995	48,271	49,724	83,105	40,937	42,168
10	Kottarakkara ...	71,517	36,055	35,462	57,393	28,873	28,520
11	Pattanapuram ...	39,447	19,858	19,589	31,453	15,877	15,576
12	Shenkotta ...	32,088	15,700	16,388	30,033	14,603	15,430
13	Quilon ...	121,935	60,832	61,103	90,737	45,136	45,601
14	Kunnattur ...	73,529	37,397	36,132	61,948	31,606	30,342
15	Karunagappalli ...	108,826	52,862	55,964	86,968	41,679	45,289
16	Kartigappalli ...	91,950	45,216	46,734	76,849	37,693	39,156
17	Mavellikkara ...	103,619	52,494	51,125	85,000	42,881	42,119
18	Chenganur ...	93,960	48,443	45,517	65,795	33,894	31,901
19	Tiruvalla ...	122,142	62,514	59,628	77,711	39,751	37,960
20	Ambalappula ...	94,745	46,909	47,836	63,660	31,275	32,385
21	Sherttala ...	117,261	58,448	58,813	89,561	44,659	44,902
22	Vykkam ...	80,628	40,947	39,681	65,704	33,190	32,514
23	Ettumanur ...	80,823	41,536	39,287	49,356	25,423	23,933
24	Kottayam ...	77,094	39,229	37,865	49,756	25,300	24,456
25	Changanacheri ...	74,722	38,596	36,126	44,698	23,181	21,517
26	Meenachal ...	59,976	30,830	29,146	27,797	14,402	13,395
27	Muvattupula ...	103,009	51,595	51,414	52,923	26,341	26,582
28	Todupula ...	25,202	12,786	12,416	14,714	7,432	7,282
29	Kunnattunadu ...	114,049	57,216	56,833	66,116	33.037	33,079
30	Alangadu ...	70,958	35,944	35,014	38,056	18,967	19,089
31	Parur ...	59,278	30,082	29,196	38,216	19,427	18,789
	Cardamom Hills ...	11,413	6,714	4,699	10,235	5,877	4,358
	Periyar & Thekkadi.	3,295	2,588	707	2,554	1,966	588
	Total ...	2,557,736	1,290,415	1,267,321	1,871,864	941,995	929,869

VI.

gions.

Mussalman.			Christian.			Jain.			Parsi.			Jew.			None.		
Total.	Males.	Females.	Total.	Males.	Females.	Total.	Males.	Females.	Total.	Males.	Females.	Total.	Males.	Females.	Total.	Males.	Females.
9	10	11	12	13	14	15	16	17	18	19	20	21	22	23	24	25	26
1,184	550	634	1,745	832	913	...	...	...	...	...	...	...	...	...	...	...	...
3,387	1,709	1,678	15,220	7,597	7,623	...	...	...	...	...	...	...	...	...	...	...	...
4,065	2,115	1,950	26,650	13,171	13,479	...	...	...	...	...	...	...	...	...	...	...	...
2,420	1,222	1,198	9,937	5,005	4,932	...	...	...	...	...	...	...	...	...	...	...	...
2,087	1,064	1,023	9,716	5,030	4,686	...	...	...	...	...	...	...	...	...	...	...	...
5,143	2,589	2,554	11,994	6,220	5,774	...	...	...	...	...	...	...	...	...	...	...	...
9,506	4,718	4,788	8,963	4,430	4,533	...	...	...	1	1	...	...	...	...	...	...	...
3,308	1,718	1,590	1,423	794	629	...	...	...	...	...	...	...	...	...	...	...	...
13,050	6,434	6,616	1,840	900	940	...	...	...	...	...	...	...	...	...	...	...	...
4,550	2,376	2,174	9,574	4,806	4,768	...	...	...	...	...	...	...	...	...	...	...	...
4,169	2,063	2,106	3,825	1,918	1,907	...	...	...	...	...	...	...	...	...	...	...	...
1,611	864	747	444	233	211	...	...	...	...	...	...	...	...	...	...	...	...
13,650	6,995	6,655	17,538	8,696	8,842	...	...	...	...	...	...	10	5	5	...	...	...
2,759	1,426	1,333	8,822	4,365	4,457	...	...	...	...	...	...	...	...	...	...	...	...
13,061	6,884	6,177	8,797	4,299	4,498	...	...	...	...	...	...	...	...	...	...	...	...
7,075	3,549	3,526	8,026	3,974	4.052	...	...	...	...	...	...	...	...	...	...	...	...
4,134	2,188	1,946	14,485	7,425	7,060	...	...	...	...	...	...	...	...	...	...	...	...
2,843	1,485	1,358	25,322	13,064	12,258	...	...	...	...	...	...	...	...	...	...	...	...
2,175	1,158	1,017	42,256	21,605	20,651	...	...	...	...	...	...	...	...	...	...	...	...
10,133	4,789	5,344	20,952	10,845	10,107	...	...	...	...	...	...	...	...	...	...	...	...
2,787	1,363	1,424	24,913	12,426	12,487	...	...	...	...	...	...	...	...	...	...	...	...
3,423	1,767	1,656	11,501	5,990	5,511	...	...	...	...	...	...	...	...	...	...	...	...
483	313	170	30,984	15,800	15,184	...	...	...	...	...	...	...	...	...	...	...	...
1,151	637	514	26,187	13,292	12,895	...	...	...	...	...	...	...	...	...	...	...	...
3,420	1,795	1,625	26,604	13,620	12,984	...	...	...	...	...	...	...	...	...	...	...	...
1,084	631	453	31,095	15,797	15,298	...	...	...	...	...	...	...	...	...	...	...	...
6,442	3,348	3,094	43,644	21,906	21,738	...	...	...	...	...	...	...	...	...	...	...	...
2,676	1,409	1,267	7,812	3,945	3,867	...	...	...	...	...	...	...	...	...	...	...	...
11,386	5,884	5,502	36,547	18,295	18,252	...	...	...	...	...	...	...	...	...	...	...	...
11,386	5,994	5,392	21,513	10,980	10,533	3	3	...	...	...	...	...	...	...	...	...	...
3,632	1,874	1,758	17,315	8,721	8,594	...	...	...	...	...	...	115	60	55	...	...	...
345	221	124	833	616	217	...	...	...	...	...	...	...	...	...	...	...	...
298	243	55	434	372	62	7	5	2	...	...	...	...	...	...	2	2	...
158,823	81,375	77,448	526,911	266,969	259,942	10	8	2	1	1	...	125	65	60	2	2	...

TABLE

Ages, by Religions,

Number.	Taluq.	Total Population.		
		Total.	Males.	Females.
1	2	3	4	5
1	Tovala	29,751	14,489	15,262
2	Agastiswaram	87,241	43,226	44,015
3	Eranial	105,098	52,883	52,215
4	Kalkulam	59,474	29.834	29,640
5	Vilavankodu	68,521	35,202	33,319
6	Neyattankara	110,755	56,953	53,802
7	Trivandram	111,938	56,909	55,029
8	Nedumangadu	55,497	27,857	27,640
9	Sirayinkil	97,995	48,271	49,724
10	Kottarakkara	71,517	36,055	35,462
11	Pattanapuram	39,447	19,858	19,589
12	Shenkotta	32,088	15,700	16,388
13	Quilon	121,935	60,832	61,103
14	Kunnattur	73,529	37,397	36,132
15	Karunagappalli	108,826	52,862	55,964
16	Kartigappalli	91,950	45,216	46,734
17	Mavellikkara	103,619	52,494	51,125
18	Chenganur	93,960	48,443	45,517
19	Tiruvalla	122,142	62,514	59,628
20	Ambalappula	94,745	46,909	47,836
21	Sherttala	117,261	58,448	58,813
22	Vykkam	80,628	40,947	39,681
23	Ettumanur	80,823	41,536	39,287
24	Kottayam	77,094	39,229	37,865
25	Changanacheri	74,722	38,596	36,126
26	Meenachal	59,976	30,830	29,146
27	Muvattupula	103,009	51,595	51,414
28	Todupula	25,202	12,786	12,416
29	Kunnattunadu	114,049	57,216	56,833
30	Alangadu	70,958	35,944	35,014
31	Parur	59,278	30,082	29,196
	Cardamom Hills	11,413	6,714	4,699
	Periyar & Thekkadi... ...	3,295	2,588	707
	Total ...	2,557,736	1,290,415	1,267,321

VII.

Part (A)—Total Population.

Age Periods.							
Under 1 year.		1 year.		2 years.		3 years.	
Males.	Females.	Males.	Females.	Males.	Females.	Males.	Females.
6	7	8	9	10	11	12	13
161	188	426	524	392	406	480	482
627	640	1,050	1,184	1,123	1,317	1,333	1,419
848	970	1,258	1,458	1,387	1,569	1,778	1,969
323	470	808	855	741	772	1,004	1,107
561	852	697	829	686	807	1,090	1,282
934	1,215	849	1,047	1,101	1,360	1,520	1,691
870	1,035	1,128	1,311	1,286	1,390	1,565	1,596
659	768	581	622	663	741	857	808
839	1,030	1,134	1,239	1,377	1,446	1,598	1,605
509	630	825	1,001	1,155	1,228	1,186	1,220
294	340	398	473	586	674	559	663
421	426	392	404	443	475	478	494
967	1,125	1,356	1,481	1,717	1,798	1,981	1,985
655	751	925	944	1,146	1,195	1,100	1,140
942	1,064	1,407	1,596	1,583	1,609	1,685	1,747
605	762	1,153	1,396	1,267	1,404	1,380	1,397
556	635	1,134	1,237	1,446	1,443	1,514	1,513
717	707	1,200	1,190	1,337	1,354	1,417	1,457
1,051	1,135	1,268	1,466	1,547	1,641	1,798	2,010
795	1,336	1,378	1,671	1,288	1,473	1,411	1,647
732	780	1,149	1,528	1,413	1,483	1,760	2,061
437	521	821	875	1,001	1,001	1,165	1,275
569	670	856	1,044	989	1,130	1,324	1,596
669	821	921	972	1,034	1,108	1,173	1,260
682	745	759	908	1,027	1,057	1,180	1,174
370	490	921	1,061	994	1,054	915	947
588	786	1,240	1,410	1,380	1,674	1,648	1,956
361	362	412	369	439	409	363	394
682	820	1,227	1,446	1,470	1,761	1,765	2,102
631	698	867	869	896	995	990	978
420	589	826	967	977	1,094	1,004	1,080
42	69	131	136	126	146	149	153
9	15	8	9	22	17	20	22
19,526	23,445	29,500	33,522	34,039	37,031	39,140	42,180

TABLE

Ages, by Religions,

Number.	Taluq.	Age: 4 years. Males.	4 years. Females.	Total 0—4. Males.	Total 0—4. Females.	5—9. Males.	5—9. Females.
1	2	14	15	16	17	18	19
1	Tovala ...	398	410	1,857	2,010	1,633	1,792
2	Agastiswaram ...	1,227	1,325	5,360	5,885	5,352	5,475
3	Eranial ...	1,389	1,560	6,660	7,526	6,722	7,097
4	Kalkulam ...	760	787	3,636	3,991	3,622	3,855
5	Vilavankodu ...	856	840	3,890	4,560	4,251	4,264
6	Neyattankara ...	1,174	1,262	5,578	6,575	6,514	6,504
7	Trivandram ...	1,384	1,329	6,233	6,661	6,335	6,422
8	Nedumangadu ...	762	738	3,522	3,677	3,052	3,321
9	Sirayinkil ...	1,330	1,334	6,278	6,654	6,465	5,945
10	Kottarakkara ...	1,004	990	4,679	5,069	4,749	4,702
11	Pattanapuram ...	458	460	2,295	2,610	2,118	2,323
12	Shenkotta ...	433	426	2,167	2,225	1,919	1,970
13	Quilon ...	1,542	1,548	7,563	7,937	8,031	7,811
14	Kunnattur ...	1,052	870	4,878	4,900	4,598	4,365
15	Karunagappalli ...	1,337	1,441	6,904	7,457	6,843	6,670
16	Kartigappalli ...	1.126	1,240	5,531	6,199	5,397	5,515
17	Mavellikkara ...	1,232	1,266	5,882	6,094	6,119	6,069
18	Chenganur ...	1,099	1,144	5,770	5,852	5,966	5,607
19	Tiruvalla ...	1,341	1,435	7,005	7,687	7,591	7,436
20	Ambalappula ...	1,112	1,250	5,984	7,377	5,416	5,206
21	Sherttala ...	1,147	1,347	6,201	7,199	6,547	6,806
22	Vykkam ...	932	913	4,356	4,585	5,178	4,906
23	Ettumanur ...	963	1,096	4 701	5,536	5,244	5,041
24	Kottayam ...	820	876	4,617	5,037	5,014	5,014
25	Changanacheri ...	774	823	4,422	4,707	4,368	4,388
26	Meenachal ...	677	762	3,877	4,314	3,819	3,889
27	Muvattupula ...	1,139	1,163	5,995	6,989	7,175	7,043
28	Todupula ...	245	263	1,820	1,797	1,537	1,517
29	Kunnattunadu ...	1,399	1,592	6,543	7,721	7,731	7,759
30	Alangadu ...	1,074	1,100	4,458	4,640	4,819	4,654
31	Parur ...	844	902	4,071	4,632	4,112	3,945
	Cardamom Hills ...	142	138	590	642	587	593
	Periyar & Thekkadi.	22	9	76	72	77	56
	Total ...	31,194	32,639	153,399	168,817	158,901	157,960

VII.

Part (A)—Total Population—(*Continued*).

PERIODS—(*Continued*).

10—14.		15—19.		20—24.		25—29.	
Males.	Females.	Males.	Females.	Males.	Females.	Males.	Females.
20	21	22	23	24	25	26	27
1,545	1,409	1,223	1,346	1,201	1,427	1,343	1,490
4,818	4,438	3,932	3,998	3,500	3,999	3,667	4,232
5,668	5,047	4,847	4,523	4,166	4,508	4,688	5,221
3,416	3,044	3,171	3,058	2,514	2,833	2,743	2,864
4,110	3,645	3,751	3,647	3,017	3,232	3,277	3,364
6,339	5,985	5,725	6,655	4,862	5,320	5,566	5,450
6,817	5,941	5,522	6,128	5,555	5,796	5,313	5,120
3,197	3,072	2,554	3,174	2,368	2,856	2,567	2,515
5,828	5,303	4,387	5,319	3,898	4,713	4,132	4,538
4,155	3,910	3,267	3,439	2,769	3,053	3,228	3,265
2,087	2,044	1,892	2,033	1,603	1,809	2,003	1,958
1,802	1,746	1,393	1,453	1,300	1,419	1,276	1,506
7,273	6,815	5,737	6,422	5,038	5,264	5,333	5,556
4,298	3,752	3,236	3,299	2,922	3,153	3,337	3,377
6,143	6,041	4,654	5,401	4,165	4,991	5,008	5,519
5,299	4,954	4,091	4,740	3,766	4,391	4,429	4,847
5,875	5,400	4,917	5,052	4,177	4,706	4,915	5,020
5,950	5,356	4,767	4,527	4,151	4,010	4,375	4,224
7,478	6,848	5,715	5,820	5,280	5,547	5,830	5,668
5,340	4,810	4,462	4,677	4,141	4,580	4,294	4,466
5,882	5,887	4,865	5,831	4,845	5,986	6,073	6,704
4,633	4,132	3,733	3,972	3,388	3,810	3,904	4,166
4,920	4,241	3,688	3,749	3,458	3,523	3,691	3,548
4,835	4,396	3,785	3,743	3,260	3,358	3,425	3,497
4,592	4,053	3,331	3,385	3,043	3,512	3,158	3,521
3,832	3,269	3,025	3,087	2,872	2,830	2,767	2,519
6,783	6,183	4,521	4,621	3,999	4,449	4,672	4,866
1,706	1,590	1,269	1,413	1,097	1,131	1,081	1,083
6,927	6,303	5,002	5,222	4,468	5,129	5,040	5,462
4,393	4,306	3,266	3,617	2,714	3,126	3,185	3,606
3,679	3,400	2,762	2,781	2,594	2,765	2,523	2,643
684	496	787	523	796	507	998	527
122	68	281	72	400	102	518	106
149,926	137,884	119,558	126,727	107,327	117,835	118,359	122,448

TABLE

Ages, by Religions,

Number.	Taluq.	Age 30—34. Males.	30—34. Females.	35—39. Males.	35—39. Females.	40—44. Males.	40—44. Females.
1	2	28	29	30	31	32	33
1	Tovala ...	1,289	1,393	1,155	908	1,112	1,034
2	Agastiswaram ...	3,582	3,726	3,318	2,823	3,086	2,764
3	Eranial ...	4,300	4,291	4,142	3,343	3,505	2,910
4	Kalkulam ...	2,243	2,313	2,308	1,939	1,840	1,629
5	Vilavankodu ...	2,878	2,592	2,799	2,081	2,200	1,740
6	Neyattankara ...	4,441	4,049	4,720	3,544	3,847	2,919
7	Trivandram ...	4,562	4,079	4,250	3,487	3,839	3,135
8	Nedumangadu ...	2,075	2,023	2,159	1,661	1,516	1,418
9	Sirayinkil ...	3,364	3,711	3,505	2,951	2,682	2,709
10	Kottarakkara ...	2,489	2,487	2,693	2,303	2,070	1,827
11	Pattanapuram ...	1,619	1,569	1,901	1,384	1,218	974
12	Shenkotta ...	1,252	1,317	1,068	1,041	1,137	1,089
13	Quilon ...	4,335	4,423	4,334	3,866	3,598	3,506
14	Kunnattur ...	2,716	2,515	2,925	2,302	2,105	1,913
15	Karunagappalli ...	3,784	3,972	4,096	3,819	3,024	3,194
16	Kartigappalli ...	3,515	3,451	3,641	3,025	2,790	2,624
17	Mavellikkara ...	4,051	3,997	4,068	3,537	3,414	2,961
18	Chenganur ...	3,446	3,135	3,556	2,856	2,446	2,333
19	Tiruvalla ...	4,689	4,285	4,598	3,820	3,652	3,125
20	Ambalappula ...	3,551	3,469	3,379	3,041	2,938	2,817
21	Sherttala ...	5,244	5,115	5,533	4,082	4,301	2,994
22	Vykkam ...	3,431	3,228	3,341	2,750	2,782	2,374
23	Ettumanur ...	3,012	2,994	3,136	2,581	2,759	1,995
24	Kottayam ...	2,856	2,781	2,905	2,335	2,176	1,918
25	Changanacheri ...	3,494	3,092	3,310	2,212	2,339	1,809
26	Meenachal ...	2,276	1,977	2,208	1,695	1,705	1,378
27	Muvattupula ...	3,951	3,761	3,875	3,377	3,144	2,661
28	Todupula ...	897	839	922	765	732	603
29	Kunnattunadu ...	4,616	4,388	4,367	3,904	3,515	3,054
30	Alangadu ...	2,767	2,475	2,799	2,360	2,161	1,630
31	Parur ...	2,431	2,232	2,073	1,664	1,722	1,436
	Cardamom Hills ...	563	372	575	251	372	234
	Periyar & Thekkadi.	405	88	279	37	193	48
	Total ...	100,124	96,089	99,938	81,744	79,920	68,755

VII.

Part (A)—Total Population—(*Continued*).

PERIODS—(*Continued*).

45—49.		50—54.		55—59.		60 and over.	
Males.	Females.	Males.	Females.	Males.	Females.	Males.	Females.
34	35	36	37	38	39	40	41
659	537	593	690	307	347	572	879
2,055	1,574	1,801	1,860	920	895	1,835	2,346
2,317	1,803	1,885	2,028	1,297	1,333	2,686	2,585
1,396	1,158	1,076	1,053	690	558	1,179	1,845
1,727	1,192	1,189	976	712	554	1,401	1,472
2,836	1,857	2,156	1,642	1,479	954	2,890	2,348
2,792	2,140	2,311	2,058	1,483	1,424	2,397	2,638
1,349	1,041	1,226	941	829	657	1,443	1,284
2,114	1,841	1,904	1,833	1,315	1,161	2,399	3,046
1,583	1,303	1,433	1,424	882	823	2,058	1,857
1,036	750	778	726	513	374	795	1,035
692	622	746	818	369	395	579	787
2,654	2,276	2,368	2,459	1,519	1,535	3,049	3,233
1,669	1,474	1,565	1,588	1,048	1,149	2,100	2,345
2,326	2,118	2,084	2,221	1,309	1,404	2,522	3,157
2,033	1,668	1,697	1,790	1,120	1,083	1,907	2,447
2,570	2,024	2,227	1,994	1,393	1,313	2,886	2,958
2,242	1,830	1,943	1,837	1,285	1,187	2,546	2,763
2,786	2,407	2,681	2,340	1,872	1,533	3,337	3,162
2,087	2,078	1,900	1,845	1,352	1,301	2,065	2,169
3,033	2,188	2,150	1,989	1,380	1,296	2,394	2,736
1,913	1,420	1,634	1,500	891	857	1,763	1,981
1,849	1,522	1,825	1,596	1,115	1,004	2,138	1,957
1,874	1,573	1,580	1,443	1,035	891	1,867	1,879
1,809	1,384	1,638	1,308	1,073	823	2,019	1,932
1,211	1,042	1,137	957	710	718	1,391	1,471
2,185	2,032	2,113	1,930	1,127	1,074	2,055	2,428
524	414	431	449	292	282	478	538
2,581	2,259	2,462	1,955	1,348	1,297	2,616	2,380
1,510	1,309	1,324	1,114	914	801	1,684	1,376
1,217	984	1,031	921	652	651	1,215	1,142
263	148	159	121	149	90	191	195
92	15	71	20	37	6	37	17
58,984	47,983	51,118	47,426	32,417	29,770	60,444	63,883

TABLE

Ages, by Religions,

Number.	Taluq.	Total Hindu. Total.	Males.	Females.
1	2	3	4	5
1	Tovala	26,822	13,107	13,715
2	Agastiswaram	68,634	33,920	34,714
3	Eranial	74,383	37,597	36,786
4	Kalkulam	47,117	23,607	23,510
5	Vilavankodu	56,718	29,108	27,610
6	Neyattankara	93,618	48,144	45,474
7	Trivandram	93,468	47,760	45,708
8	Nedumangadu	50,766	25,345	25,421
9	Sirayinkil	83,105	40,937	42,168
10	Kottarakkara	57,393	28,873	28,520
11	Pattanapuram	31,453	15,877	15,576
12	Shenkotta	30,033	14,603	15,430
13	Quilon	90,737	45,136	45,601
14	Kunnattur	61,948	31,606	30,342
15	Karunagappalli	86,968	41,679	45,289
16	Kartigappalli	76,849	37,693	39,156
17	Mavellikkara	85,000	42,881	42,119
18	Chenganur	65,795	33,894	31,901
19	Tiruvalla	77,711	39,751	37,960
20	Ambalappula	63,660	31,275	32,385
21	Sherttala	89,561	44,659	44,902
22	Vykkam	65,704	33,190	32,514
23	Ettumanur	49,356	25,423	23,933
24	Kottayam	49,756	25,300	24,456
25	Changanacheri	44,698	23,181	21,517
26	Meenachal	27,797	14,402	13,395
27	Muvattupula	52,923	26,341	26,582
28	Todupula	14,714	7,432	7,282
29	Kunnattunadu	66,116	33,037	33,079
30	Alangadu	38,056	18,967	19,089
31	Parur	38,216	19,427	18,789
	Cardamom Hills	10,235	5,877	4,358
	Periyar and Thekkadi ...	2,554	1,966	588
	Total ...	1,871,864	941,995	929,869

VII.

Part (B)—Hindu.

Age Periods.							
Under 1 year.		1 year.		2 years.		3 years.	
Males.	Females.	Males.	Females.	Males.	Females.	Males.	Females.
6	7	8	9	10	11	12	13
141	163	385	458	342	356	432	423
506	515	796	902	831	1,008	1,029	1,065
640	734	895	1,019	950	1,083	1,290	1,399
262	395	633	664	559	580	770	847
468	703	591	711	544	658	896	1,032
801	1,061	707	889	916	1,150	1,298	1,419
756	905	911	1,042	1,067	1,124	1,267	1,266
614	700	547	583	599	684	784	738
713	880	964	1,035	1,154	1,208	1,366	1,370
383	488	655	780	916	946	956	934
217	263	325	368	458	543	440	507
396	394	368	376	393	442	435	459
675	797	1,013	1,089	1,227	1,305	1,405	1,435
515	609	767	769	946	978	913	923
713	821	1,083	1,250	1,224	1,252	1,267	1,387
480	618	972	1,167	1,067	1,148	1,126	1,147
416	457	875	973	1,150	1,162	1,225	1,206
492	490	766	772	892	867	936	965
619	663	748	859	913	1,000	1,080	1,175
514	667	903	939	844	901	909	1,028
519	551	823	1,115	1,046	1,088	1,329	1,524
361	428	646	693	782	774	947	1,022
342	399	524	622	616	658	790	954
444	558	546	589	656	686	763	787
380	414	411	481	568	565	675	606
160	232	408	427	446	457	409	429
315	412	607	675	644	800	787	989
210	215	230	223	248	242	191	215
420	481	725	796	829	1,003	999	1,196
451	517	467	457	481	500	507	508
294	385	500	600	638	691	652	688
33	61	124	130	117	137	141	146
9	13	2	9	19	12	15	20
14,268	16,989	20,917	23,462	24,082	26,008	28,029	29,809

TABLE

Ages, by Religions,

Number.	TALUQ.	AGE 4 years. Males.	4 years. Females.	Total 0—4. Males.	Total 0—4. Females.	5—9. Males.	5—9. Females.
1	2	14	15	16	17	18	19
1	Tovala ...	359	365	1,659	1,765	1,477	1,637
2	Agastiswaram ...	923	1,023	4,085	4,513	4,101	4,215
3	Eranial ...	993	1,094	4,768	5,329	4,739	4,987
4	Kalkulam ...	577	631	2,801	3,117	2,786	3,001
5	Vilavankodu ...	731	699	3,230	3,803	3,480	3,542
6	Neyattankara ...	978	1,040	4,700	5,559	5,509	5,362
7	Trivandram ...	1,140	1,062	5,141	5,399	5,164	5,217
8	Nedumangadu ...	703	673	3,247	3,378	2,777	3,060
9	Sirayinkil ...	1,144	1,115	5,341	5,608	5,377	4,984
10	Kottarakkara ...	753	783	3,663	3,931	3,682	3,658
11	Pattanapuram ...	370	369	1,810	2,050	1,691	1,847
12	Shenkotta ...	400	398	1,992	2,069	1,778	1,860
13	Quilon ...	1,106	1,090	5,426	5,716	5,729	5,692
14	Kunnattur ...	863	711	4,004	3,990	3,822	3,578
15	Karunagappalli ...	1,036	1,141	5,323	5,851	5,349	5,249
16	Kartigappalli ...	924	999	4,569	5,079	4,510	4,484
17	Mavellikkara ...	972	1,021	4,638	4,819	4,917	4,840
18	Chenganur ...	711	759	3,797	3,853	4,006	3,722
19	Tiruvalla ...	796	851	4,156	4,548	4,472	4,342
20	Ambalappula ...	688	700	3,858	4,235	3,567	3,543
21	Sherttala ...	833	1,000	4,550	5,278	4,765	5,058
22	Vykkam ...	751	724	3,487	3,641	4,162	3,942
23	Ettumanur ...	573	619	2,845	3,252	3,171	2,995
24	Kottayam ...	527	564	2,936	3,184	3,217	3,063
25	Changanacheri ...	428	463	2,471	2,529	2,432	2,385
26	Meenachal ...	270	335	1,693	1,880	1,663	1,697
27	Muvattupula ...	558	555	2,911	3,431	3,459	3,472
28	Todupula ...	128	153	1,007	1,048	850	837
29	Kunnattunadu ...	771	859	3,744	4,335	4,341	4,495
30	Alangadu ...	561	586	2,467	2,568	2,445	2,434
31	Parur ...	540	551	2,624	2,915	2,620	2,402
	Cardamom Hills ...	184	128	549	602	559	571
	Periyar & Thekkadi.	17	7	62	61	64	41
	Total ...	22,258	23,068	109,554	119,336	112,681	112,212

VII.

Part (B)—Hindu—(*Continued*).

PERIODS—(*Continued*).

10—14.		15—19.		20—24.		25—29.	
Males.	Females.	Males.	Females.	Males.	Females.	Males.	Females.
20	21	22	23	24	25	26	27
1,402	1,267	1,115	1,202	1,083	1,266	1,215	1,307
3,722	3,495	3,019	3,104	2,815	3,157	2,876	3,380
4,047	3,481	3,456	3,166	2,935	3,204	3,346	3,638
2,682	2,381	2,516	2,466	2,035	2,297	2,223	2,274
3,394	3,063	3,129	2,998	2,506	2,593	2,691	2,738
5,379	4,949	4,777	5,558	4,067	4,533	4,687	4,634
5,235	4,892	4,636	5,095	4,788	4,834	4,514	4,161
2,898	2,808	2,317	2,899	2,147	2,652	2,300	2,300
4,874	4,401	3,714	4,495	3,324	3,982	3,540	3,809
3,284	3,039	2,619	2,817	2,204	2,519	2,640	2,707
1,644	1,586	1,497	1,603	1,247	1,443	1,639	1,572
1,675	1,653	1,284	1,374	1,204	1,336	1,198	1,418
5,383	4,998	4,271	4,833	3,784	3,976	4,017	4,160
3,628	3,121	2,753	2,780	2,456	2,653	2,830	2,845
4,791	4,819	3,693	4,422	3,297	4,032	4,019	4,523
4,359	4,122	3,334	3,955	3,151	3,691	3,726	4,171
4,772	4,361	3,991	4,181	3,409	3,893	4,075	4,167
3,956	3,588	3,178	3,148	2,891	2,812	3,173	3,006
4,479	4,108	3,639	3,696	3,416	3,548	3,786	3,765
3,435	3,320	2,967	3,194	2,787	3,190	2,911	3,196
4,449	4,349	3,704	4,411	3,777	4,551	4,816	5,244
3,700	3,285	3,015	3,273	2,728	3,118	3,237	3,450
2,875	2,453	2,252	2,232	2,105	2,185	2,248	2,217
2,972	2,671	2,302	2,394	2,058	2,189	2,279	2,349
2,617	2,295	1,991	2,124	1,841	2,105	1,999	2,209
1,698	1,440	1,446	1,407	1,360	1,327	1,325	1,183
3,283	2,975	2,390	2,445	2,061	2,314	2,418	2,546
970	851	757	813	673	665	600	629
3,866	3,616	2,938	2,983	2,575	2,950	2,964	3,229
2,235	2,278	1,710	2,003	1,447	1,700	1,698	1,946
2,294	2,070	1,810	1,779	1,632	1,822	1,654	1,743
611	459	668	492	678	462	858	487
97	56	208	67	312	89	391	83
106,706	98,250	87,096	93,409	78,793	87,088	87,893	91,086

TABLE

Ages, by Religions,

Number.	Taluq.	Age 30—34. Males.	30—34. Females.	35—39. Males.	35—39. Females.	40—44. Males.	40—44. Females.
1	2	28	29	30	31	32	33
1	Tovala ...	1,153	1,261	1,017	792	1,010	955
2	Agastiswaram ...	2,873	2,976	2,631	2,230	2,487	2,213
3	Eranial ...	3,071	3,051	2,903	2,417	2,495	2,013
4	Kalkulam ...	1,764	1,807	1,832	1,567	1,477	1,304
5	Vilavankodu ...	2,380	2,114	2,328	1,750	1,788	1,434
6	Neyattankara ...	3,820	3,445	3,933	2,957	3,233	2,476
7	Trivandram ...	3,801	3,376	3,568	2,973	3,293	2,655
8	Nedumangadu ...	1,877	1,851	1,962	1,524	1,402	1,291
9	Sirayinkil ...	2,853	3,150	2,967	2,535	2,309	2,329
10	Kottarakkara ...	2,040	2,041	2,197	1,857	1,673	1,532
11	Pattanapuram ...	1,321	1,268	1,517	1,113	990	793
12	Shenkotta ...	1,153	1,249	1,002	971	1,056	1,026
13	Quilon ...	3,268	3,299	3,286	2,937	2,681	2,702
14	Kunnattur ...	2,310	2,119	2,518	1,984	1,803	1,651
15	Karunagappalli ...	3,073	3,268	3,284	3,124	2,432	2,683
16	Kartigappalli ...	2,997	2,973	3,070	2,585	2,341	2,257
17	Mavellikkara ...	3,369	3,339	3,367	2,963	2,875	2,527
18	Chenganur ...	2,513	2,325	2,614	2,055	1,801	1,761
19	Tiruvalla ...	3,128	2,847	3,041	2,518	2,458	2,119
20	Ambalappula ...	2,371	2,441	2,233	2,125	2,012	1,944
21	Sherttala ...	4,111	4,048	4,365	3,210	3,364	2,361
22	Vykkam ...	2,874	2,683	2,677	2,302	2,342	2,001
23	Ettumanur ...	1,921	1,903	1,906	1,666	1,798	1,264
24	Kottayam ...	1,961	1,937	1,887	1,527	1,460	1,306
25	Changanacheri ...	2,227	1,941	2,052	1,395	1,477	1,115
26	Meenachal ...	1,100	953	1,088	839	879	700
27	Muvattupula ...	2,065	1,994	1,996	1,802	1,708	1,489
28	Todupula ...	538	519	547	461	455	376
29	Kunnattunadu ...	2,724	2,606	2,594	2,366	2,046	1,814
30	Alangadu ...	1,525	1,401	1,482	1,288	1,143	898
31	Parur ...	1,610	1,495	1,333	1,091	1,138	978
	Cardamom Hills ...	465	327	471	220	304	214
	Periyar & Thekkadi.	304	69	210	28	142	44
	Total ...	74,555	72,076	73,878	61,172	59,872	52,225

VII.

Part (B)—Hindu—(*Continued*).

PERIODS—(*Continued*).

45—49.		50—54.		55—59.		60 and over.	
Males.	Females.	Males.	Females.	Males.	Females.	Males.	Females.
34	35	36	37	38	39	40	41
608	492	545	641	285	305	538	825
1,626	1,278	1,458	1,499	721	741	1,506	1,913
1,670	1,284	1,337	1,430	940	952	1,890	1,834
1,122	943	851	826	567	449	951	1,078
1,425	995	988	828	612	479	1,157	1,273
2,360	1,601	1,873	1,469	1,295	855	2,511	2,076
2,411	1,825	1,979	1,762	1,268	1,249	1,962	2,270
1,237	963	1,107	871	757	616	1,317	1,208
1,813	1,574	1,641	1,563	1,099	1,026	2,085	2,712
1,265	1,014	1,173	1,188	725	692	1,708	1,525
838	598	646	596	408	294	629	813
657	594	709	771	352	354	543	755
2,027	1,746	1,797	1,903	1,146	1,149	2,321	2,490
1,440	1,254	1,360	1,357	879	948	1,803	2,062
1,828	1,777	1,688	1,875	1,013	1,093	1,889	2,573
1,718	1,397	1,418	1,495	914	861	1,586	2,086
2,122	1,726	1,839	1,732	1,119	1,130	2,388	2,441
1,635	1,310	1,462	1,351	907	855	1,961	2,115
1,816	1,581	1,838	1,666	1,198	1,009	2,329	2,213
1,424	1,399	1,307	1,292	965	902	1,438	1,604
2,315	1,691	1,656	1,583	963	939	1,824	2,179
1,502	1,152	1,320	1,246	669	691	1,477	1,730
1,151	915	1,158	1,013	665	548	1,328	1,290
1,206	1,017	1,065	990	651	545	1,306	1,284
1,149	866	1,015	833	657	505	1,253	1,215
570	472	571	448	316	323	693	726
1,177	1,069	1,141	1,114	576	565	1,156	1,366
289	253	279	288	168	181	299	361
1,487	1,357	1,450	1,141	730	699	1,578	1,488
814	700	698	626	448	427	855	820
807	640	679	639	411	408	815	807
238	141	149	113	143	79	184	191
59	13	59	17	26	6	32	14
43,806	35,637	38 256	36,166	23,593	21,875	45,312	49,337

TABLE

Ages, by Religions,

Number.	Taluq.	Total Mussalman.			Age			
					Under 1 year.		1 year.	
		Total.	Males.	Females.	Males.	Females.	Males.	Females.
1	2	3	4	5	6	7	8	9
1	Tovala ...	1,184	550	634	5	9	17	23
2	Agastiswaram ...	3,387	1,709	1,678	25	21	50	47
3	Eranial ...	4,065	2,115	1,950	23	37	60	62
4	Kalkulam ...	2,420	1,222	1,198	5	5	21	34
5	Vilavankodu ...	2,087	1,064	1,023	13	33	15	12
6	Neyattankara ...	5,143	2,589	2,554	54	50	48	51
7	Trivandram ...	9,506	4,718	4,788	64	58	103	128
8	Nedumangadu ...	3,308	1,718	1,590	34	52	24	35
9	Sirayinkil ...	13,050	6,434	6,616	108	131	153	178
10	Kottarakkara ...	4,550	2,376	2,174	37	40	54	71
11	Pattanapuram ...	4,169	2,063	2,106	53	55	33	55
12	Shenkotta ...	1,611	864	747	17	28	18	20
13	Quilon ...	13,650	6,995	6,655	123	130	137	146
14	Kunnattur ...	2,759	1,426	1,333	52	43	50	38
15	Karunagappalli ...	13,061	6,884	6,177	147	153	191	208
16	Kartigappalli ...	7,075	3,549	3,526	66	64	77	101
17	Mavelikkara ...	4,134	2,188	1,946	29	35	57	48
18	Chenganur ...	2,843	1,485	1,358	20	22	37	47
19	Tiruvalla ...	2,175	1,158	1,017	17	19	23	27
20	Ambalappula ...	10,133	4,789	5,344	106	328	133	337
21	Sherttala ...	2,787	1,363	1,424	21	16	24	33
22	Vykkam ...	3,423	1,767	1,656	27	25	32	40
23	Ettumanur ...	483	313	170	2	4	4	6
24	Kottayam ...	1,151	637	514	7	8	11	19
25	Changanacheri ...	3,420	1,795	1,625	41	31	31	55
26	Meenachal ...	1,084	631	453	...	6	8	13
27	Muvattupula ...	6,442	3,348	3,094	60	83	90	87
28	Todupula ...	2,676	1,409	1,267	58	34	47	30
29	Kunnattunadu ...	11,386	5,884	5,502	82	104	122	167
30	Alangadu ...	11,386	5,994	5,392	50	60	155	139
31	Parur ...	3,632	1,874	1,758	32	42	64	67
	Cardamom Hills ...	345	221	124	4	4	3	5
	Periyar & Thekkadi.	298	243	55	...	1	1	...
	Total ...	158,823	81,375	77,448	1,382	1,731	1,893	2,329

VII.

Part (C)—Mussalman.

PERIODS.

2 years.		3 years.		4 years.		Total 0—4.		5—9.		10—14.	
Males.	Females.	Males.	Females.	Males.	Females.	Males.	Females.	Males.	Females.	Males.	Females.
10	11	12	13	14	15	16	17	18	19	20	21
16	21	19	22	9	19	66	94	63	67	56	54
40	44	54	58	58	54	227	224	242	230	178	159
55	60	73	70	53	48	264	277	285	278	212	178
30	33	36	46	33	32	125	150	183	169	147	125
26	17	30	27	30	29	114	118	137	135	188	119
63	66	79	87	76	68	320	322	310	360	255	290
107	140	133	152	120	127	527	605	575	622	579	545
47	44	52	47	47	47	204	225	195	192	201	195
196	208	206	207	158	196	821	920	947	832	822	772
81	88	71	101	62	82	305	382	334	328	256	245
74	72	62	88	61	47	283	317	232	245	252	219
38	24	37	32	28	19	138	123	112	83	96	68
205	209	260	220	175	202	900	907	1,029	890	842	742
42	51	43	57	46	37	233	226	189	160	157	146
216	200	218	209	188	165	960	935	899	829	846	713
98	119	97	116	100	109	438	509	412	446	437	386
69	52	59	63	58	46	272	244	272	242	240	226
39	41	40	38	38	31	174	179	165	134	157	162
31	25	35	43	25	22	131	136	163	131	132	119
139	231	159	236	147	229	684	1,361	529	368	531	357
21	48	39	46	22	29	127	172	159	178	122	156
40	49	34	62	37	58	170	234	218	233	182	203
5	7	6	4	4	8	21	29	30	24	31	22
19	16	18	17	18	20	73	80	64	55	92	72
37	67	46	56	40	44	195	253	194	191	169	182
9	14	6	8	15	17	38	58	80	47	64	42
93	108	184	142	71	82	448	502	482	441	420	344
53	44	48	52	38	27	244	187	159	184	202	161
156	194	209	254	185	185	754	904	860	824	797	624
159	168	143	142	227	206	734	715	846	693	676	642
62	64	72	71	52	77	282	321	285	235	242	206
6	3	5	8	5	8	23	18	13	8	22	9
1	...	1	1	2	1	5	3	8	6	12	4
2,273	2,527	2,524	2,777	2,228	2,366	10,300	11,730	10,671	9,860	9,565	8,487

TABLE

Ages, by Religions,

Number.	Taluq.	Age 15—19 Males.	15—19 Females.	20—24. Males.	20—24. Females.	25—29. Males.	25—29. Females.	30—34. Males.	30—34. Females.
1	2	22	23	24	25	26	27	28	29
1	Tovala ...	46	48	46	69	44	75	52	58
2	Agastiswaram ...	147	156	124	149	169	182	127	147
3	Eranial ...	214	189	185	162	156	191	170	175
4	Kalkulam ...	108	121	96	116	109	105	106	111
5	Vilavankodu ...	111	123	92	115	103	92	83	102
6	Neyattankara ...	238	305	214	238	276	263	189	203
7	Trivandram ...	469	555	429	488	417	468	364	364
8	Nedumangadu ...	167	197	159	146	168	147	125	110
9	Sirayinkil ...	598	721	500	631	530	634	446	484
10	Kottarakkara ...	224	192	194	171	212	210	179	140
11	Pattanapuram ...	193	204	167	182	170	209	154	169
12	Shenkotta ...	83	61	76	62	59	70	80	56
13	Quilon ...	691	710	592	543	585	599	515	471
14	Kunnattur ...	107	100	107	128	123	136	114	88
15	Karunagappalli ...	600	554	530	549	614	584	443	393
16	Kartigappalli ...	358	413	284	333	356	316	234	235
17	Mavellikkara ...	199	208	189	182	178	187	155	155
18	Chenganur ...	159	150	145	108	142	135	100	109
19	Tiruvalla ...	102	83	91	97	104	111	80	75
20	Ambalappula ...	459	482	450	491	444	503	373	394
21	Sherttala ...	106	134	110	123	121	142	117	124
22	Vykkam ...	176	165	152	187	144	169	152	107
23	Ettumanur ...	29	17	37	10	40	9	20	12
24	Kottayam ...	63	52	60	40	50	47	37	35
25	Changanacheri ...	143	124	123	169	135	184	172	163
26	Meenachal ...	70	53	56	43	58	46	47	29
27	Muvattupula ...	269	288	296	270	302	304	262	215
28	Todupula ...	131	144	107	132	124	115	85	82
29	Kunnattunadu ...	534	497	435	485	458	546	467	389
30	Alangadu ...	558	553	515	520	540	611	469	370
31	Parur ...	161	166	145	165	161	160	127	105
	Cardamom Hills ...	31	15	22	12	31	14	21	17
	Periyar & Thekkadi.	33	2	37	5	51	10	34	11
	Total ...	7,577	7,782	6,765	7,121	7,174	7,574	6,099	5,698

VII.

Part (C)—Mussalman—(*Continued*).

PERIODS—(*Continued*).

35—39.		40—44.		45—49.		50—54.		55—59.		60 and over.	
Males.	Females.	Males.	Females.	Males.	Females.	Males.	Females.	Males.	Females.	Males.	Females.
30	31	32	33	34	35	36	37	38	39	40	41
54	52	41	36	26	16	27	21	12	21	17	23
132	89	122	109	74	45	68	86	39	30	60	72
132	112	145	119	87	48	91	89	68	53	106	79
88	70	87	69	61	46	43	37	28	29	41	50
87	42	57	69	61	33	34	18	14	18	33	39
203	178	194	142	147	72	94	64	43	34	106	83
331	259	267	269	203	157	192	154	123	86	242	216
121	97	74	83	72	52	82	52	59	33	91	61
474	369	326	338	270	247	232	247	195	126	273	295
165	139	138	96	114	91	76	61	56	35	123	84
200	147	120	94	100	86	65	68	44	37	83	129
52	56	67	52	26	22	34	34	9	32	32	28
473	419	405	367	275	206	259	243	146	193	283	365
96	87	78	61	56	36	48	48	47	42	71	75
522	405	374	307	300	182	238	196	184	182	374	348
286	210	219	172	153	114	122	140	78	88	172	164
175	140	135	99	107	56	100	54	56	36	110	117
118	80	81	64	69	60	65	61	29	32	81	84
96	70	62	36	65	49	48	34	30	26	54	50
370	326	299	349	192	246	163	173	100	124	195	170
118	91	98	72	89	52	65	69	57	50	74	61
176	121	97	82	126	35	68	42	50	30	56	48
23	12	26	9	16	7	19	4	10	2	11	13
51	34	33	19	29	16	22	16	30	26	33	22
194	105	128	70	75	50	114	38	52	36	101	60
59	27	37	37	33	24	32	18	13	10	44	19
245	205	210	167	119	105	157	85	54	52	84	116
103	74	76	45	54	45	41	47	32	22	51	29
404	343	344	235	243	168	208	175	134	95	246	217
443	344	348	263	204	211	245	169	156	97	260	204
119	105	100	95	71	55	63	53	49	23	69	69
23	13	16	2	7	1	5	4	2	9	5	2
21	4	23	3	9	2	4	2	4	...	2	3
6,154	4,825	4,827	4,030	3,533	2,635	3,124	2,602	2,003	1,709	3,583	3,395

TABLE

Ages, by Religions,

Number.	TALUQ.	TOTAL CHRISTIAN.			AGE			
					Under 1 year.		1 year.	
		Total.	Males.	Females.	Males.	Females.	Males.	Females.
1	2	3	4	5	6	7	8	9
1	Tovala ...	1,745	832	913	15	16	24	43
2	Agastiswaram ...	15,220	7,597	7,623	96	104	204	235
3	Eranial ...	26,650	13,171	13,479	185	199	303	377
4	Kalkulam ...	9,937	5,005	4,932	56	70	154	157
5	Vilavankodu ...	9,716	5,030	4,686	80	116	91	106
6	Neyattankara ...	11,994	6,220	5,774	79	104	94	107
7	Trivandram ...	8,963	4,430	4,533	50	72	114	141
8	Nedumangadu ...	1,423	794	629	11	16	10	4
9	Sirayinkil ...	1,840	900	940	18	19	17	26
10	Kottarakkara ...	9,574	4,806	4,768	89	102	116	150
11	Pattanapuram ...	3,825	1,918	1,907	24	22	40	50
12	Shenkotta ...	444	233	211	8	4	6	8
13	Quilon ...	17,538	8,696	8,842	169	198	206	246
14	Kunnattur ...	8,822	4,365	4,457	88	99	108	137
15	Karunagappalli ...	8,797	4,299	4,498	82	90	133	138
16	Kartigappalli ...	8,026	3,974	4,052	59	80	104	128
17	Mavellikkara ...	14,485	7,425	7,060	111	143	202	216
18	Chenganur ...	25,322	13,064	12,258	205	195	397	371
19	Tiruvalla ...	42,256	21,605	20,651	415	453	497	580
20	Ambalappula ...	20,952	10,845	10,107	175	341	342	395
21	Sherttala ...	24,913	12,426	12,487	192	213	302	380
22	Vykkam ...	11,501	5,990	5,511	49	68	143	142
23	Ettumanur ...	30,984	15,800	15,184	225	267	328	416
24	Kottayam ...	26,187	13,292	12,895	218	255	364	364
25	Changanacheri ...	26,604	13,620	12,984	252	300	317	372
26	Meenachal ...	31,095	15,797	15,298	210	252	505	621
27	Muvattupula ...	43,644	21,906	21,738	213	291	543	648
28	Todupula ...	7,812	3,945	3,867	93	113	135	116
29	Kunnattunadu ...	36,547	18,295	18,252	180	235	380	483
30	Alangadu ...	21,513	10,980	10,533	130	121	245	273
31	Parur ...	17,315	8,721	8,594	94	162	261	299
	Cardamom Hills ...	833	616	217	5	4	4	1
	Periyar & Thekkadi.	434	372	62	...	1	...	...
	Total ...	526,911	266,969	259,942	3,876	4,725	6,689	7,730

VII.

Part (D)—Christian.

PERIODS.

2 years.		3 years.		4 years.		Total 0—4.		5—9.		10—14.	
Males.	Females.	Males.	Females.	Males.	Females.	Males.	Females.	Males.	Females.	Males.	Females.
10	11	12	13	14	15	16	17	18	19	20	21
34	29	29	37	30	26	132	151	93	88	87	88
252	265	250	296	246	248	1,048	1,148	1,009	1,030	918	784
382	426	415	500	343	418	1,628	1,920	1,698	1,832	1,409	1,388
152	159	198	214	150	124	710	724	653	685	587	538
116	132	164	173	95	112	546	639	634	587	578	463
122	144	143	185	120	154	558	694	695	782	705	746
112	126	165	178	124	140	565	657	596	583	503	504
17	13	21	23	12	18	71	74	80	69	98	69
27	30	26	28	28	23	116	126	141	129	132	130
158	194	159	185	189	125	711	756	733	716	615	626
54	59	57	68	27	44	202	243	195	231	191	239
12	9	6	3	5	9	37	33	29	27	31	25
285	284	315	330	261	256	1,236	1,314	1,273	1,228	1,048	1,075
158	166	144	160	143	122	641	684	587	627	513	485
143	157	150	151	118	135	621	671	595	592	506	509
102	137	157	134	102	132	524	611	475	585	503	446
227	229	230	244	202	199	972	1,031	930	987	863	813
406	446	441	454	350	354	1,799	1,820	1,795	1,751	1,837	1,606
603	616	683	792	520	562	2,718	3,003	2,956	2,963	2,867	2,621
305	341	343	383	277	321	1,442	1,781	1,320	1,295	1,374	1,133
346	347	392	491	292	318	1,524	1,749	1,623	1,570	1,311	1,382
179	178	184	191	144	131	699	710	798	731	751	644
368	465	528	638	386	469	1,835	2,255	2,043	2,022	2,014	1,766
359	406	392	456	275	292	1,608	1,773	1,733	1,896	1,771	1,653
422	425	459	512	306	316	1,756	1,925	1,742	1,812	1,806	1,576
539	583	500	510	392	410	2,146	2,376	2,076	2,145	2,070	1,787
643	766	727	825	510	526	2,636	3,056	3,284	3,130	3,080	2,864
138	123	124	127	79	83	569	562	528	496	534	578
485	564	557	652	443	548	2,045	2,482	2,530	2,440	2,264	2,063
256	327	340	328	286	308	1,257	1,357	1,528	1,527	1,482	1,386
274	338	279	320	249	271	1,157	1,390	1,198	1,301	1,139	1,115
3	6	3	4	3	7	18	22	15	14	51	28
2	5	4	1	3	1	9	8	5	9	13	8
7,681	8,495	8,585	9,593	6,705	7,202	33,536	37,745	35,540	35,880	33,651	31,138

TABLE

Ages, by Religions,

Number.	Taluq.		Age						
		15—19.		20—24.		25—29.		30—34.	
		Males.	Females.	Males.	Females.	Males.	Females.	Males.	Females.
1	2	22	23	24	25	26	27	28	29
1	Tovala ...	62	96	72	92	84	108	84	74
2	Agastiswaram ...	766	738	561	693	622	670	582	603
3	Eranial ...	1,177	1,168	1,046	1,142	1,186	1,392	1,059	1,065
4	Kalkulam ..	547	471	383	420	411	485	373	395
5	Vilavankodu ...	511	526	419	524	483	534	415	376
6	Neyattankara ...	710	792	581	549	603	553	432	401
7	Trivandram ...	417	478	338	474	382	491	897	339
8	Nedumangadu ...	70	78	62	58	99	68	73	62
9	Sirayinkil ...	75	103	74	100	62	95	65	77
10	Kottarakkara ...	424	430	371	363	376	348	270	306
11	Pattanapuram ...	202	226	189	184	194	177	144	132
12	Shenkotta ...	26	18	20	21	19	18	19	12
13	Quilon ...	774	879	662	745	731	795	552	653
14	Kunnattur ...	376	419	359	372	384	396	292	308
15	Karunagappalli ...	361	425	338	410	375	412	268	311
16	Kartigappalli ...	399	372	331	367	347	360	284	243
17	Mavellikkara ...	727	663	579	631	662	666	527	503
18	Chenganur ...	1,430	1,229	1,115	1,090	1,060	1,083	833	701
19	Tiruvalla ...	1,974	2,041	1,773	1,902	1,940	1,792	1,486	1,813
20	Ambalappula ...	1,036	1,001	904	899	939	767	807	634
21	Sherttala ...	1,055	1,286	958	1,312	1,136	1,318	1,016	943
22	Vykkam ...	542	534	508	505	523	547	405	438
23	Ettumanur ...	1,407	1,500	1,316	1,328	1,408	1,322	1,071	1,079
24	Kottayam ...	1,420	1,297	1,142	1,129	1,096	1,101	858	809
25	Changanacheri ...	1,197	1,137	1,079	1,238	1,024	1,128	1,095	988
26	Meenachal ...	1,509	1,627	1,456	1,460	1,384	1,290	1,129	995
27	Muvattupula ...	1,862	1,888	1,642	1,865	1,952	2,016	1,624	1,552
28	Todupula ...	381	456	317	334	357	339	274	238
29	Kunnattunadu ...	1,530	1,742	1,458	1,694	1,618	1,687	1,425	1,393
30	Alangadu ...	997	1,061	751	906	947	1,049	772	704
31	Parur ...	786	830	812	774	701	730	691	630
	Cardamom Hills ...	88	16	96	33	109	26	77	28
	Periyar & Thekkadi.	40	3	51	7	73	12	64	8
	Total ...	24,878	25,530	21,763	23,621	23,282	23,775	19,463	18,313

VII.

Part (D)—Christian—(*Continued*).

PERIODS—(*Continued*).

35—39.		40—44.		45—49.		50—54.		55—59.		60 and over.	
Males.	Females.	Males.	Females.	Males.	Females.	Males.	Females.	Males.	Females.	Males.	Females.
30	31	32	33	34	35	36	37	38	39	40	41
84	64	61	43	25	29	21	28	10	21	17	31
555	504	477	442	355	251	275	275	160	124	269	361
1,107	814	865	778	560	471	457	509	289	328	690	672
388	302	276	256	213	169	182	190	95	80	187	217
384	289	355	237	241	164	167	130	86	57	211	160
584	409	420	301	329	184	189	109	141	65	273	189
351	255	279	211	178	158	140	142	91	89	193	152
76	40	40	44	40	26	37	18	13	8	35	15
64	47	47	42	31	20	31	23	21	9	41	39
331	307	259	199	204	198	184	175	101	96	227	248
184	124	108	87	98	66	67	62	61	43	83	93
14	14	14	11	9	6	3	13	8	9	4	4
573	510	512	436	352	324	312	312	227	193	444	378
311	231	224	201	173	184	157	183	122	159	226	208
290	290	218	204	198	159	158	150	112	129	259	236
285	230	230	195	162	157	157	155	128	134	149	197
526	434	404	335	341	242	288	208	218	147	388	400
824	721	564	508	538	460	416	425	349	300	504	564
1,461	1,232	1,132	970	905	777	795	640	644	498	954	899
776	590	627	524	471	433	430	380	287	275	432	395
1,050	781	839	561	629	445	429	337	360	307	496	496
488	327	343	291	285	233	246	212	172	136	230	203
1,207	903	935	722	682	600	648	579	440	454	799	654
967	774	683	593	639	540	493	437	354	320	528	573
1,064	712	734	624	585	468	509	437	364	282	665	657
1,061	829	789	641	608	546	534	491	381	385	654	726
1,634	1,370	1,226	1,005	889	858	815	731	497	457	815	946
272	230	201	182	181	116	111	114	92	79	128	143
1,369	1,195	1,125	1,005	851	734	804	639	484	503	792	675
874	728	670	469	492	398	381	319	310	277	519	352
616	467	480	360	336	287	285	226	191	220	329	264
81	18	52	18	18	6	5	4	4	2	2	2
47	5	28	1	24	...	8	1	7	...	3	...
19,898	15,746	15,217	12,496	11,642	9,709	9,734	8,654	6,819	6,186	11,546	11,149

TABLE VII.
Ages, by Religions, Part (E)—Jain.

Number.	Taluq.	Total Jain.			Age Periods.															
					Under 1 year.		1 year.		2 years.		3 years.		4 years.		Total 0—4.		5—9.		10—14.	
		Total.	Males.	Females.	Males.	Females.	Males.	Females.	Males.	Females.	Males.	Females.	Males.	Females.	Males.	Females.	Males.	Females.	Males.	Females.
1	2	3	4	5	6	7	8	9	10	11	12	13	14	15	16	17	18	19	20	21
30	Alangadu ...	3	3	...	...	...	...	...	...	...	...	...	...	...	...	...	...	...	...	...
	Periyar and Thekkadi ...	7	5	2	...	...	...	...	...	...	...	...	...	...	...	...	...	...	...	...
	Total ...	10	8	2	...	...	...	...	...	...	...	...	...	...	...	...	...	...	...	...

Number.	Taluq.	Age Periods—(*Continued*).																			
		15—19.		20—24.		25—29.		30—34.		35—39.		40—44.		45—49.		50—54.		55—59.		60 and over.	
		Males.	Females.	Males.	Females.	Males.	Females.	Males.	Females.	Males.	Females.	Males.	Females.	Males.	Females.	Males.	Females.	Males.	Females.	Males.	Females.
1	2	22	23	24	25	26	27	28	29	30	31	32	33	34	35	36	37	38	39	40	41
30	Alangadu ...	1	...	1	...	...	...	1	...	...	...	...	...	...	...	...	...	...	...	...	...
	Periyar & Thekkadi.	...	...	...	1	2	1	2	...	1	...	...	...	...	...	...	...	...	...	...	...
	Total ...	1	...	1	1	2	1	3	...	1	...	...	...	...	...	...	...	...	...	...	...

TABLE VII.

Ages, by Religions, Part (F)—Parsi.

Number.	Taluq.	Total Parsi.			Age Periods.															
					Under 1 year.		1 year.		2 years.		3 years.		4 years.		Total 0—4.		5—9.		10—14.	
		Total.	Males.	Females.	Males.	Females.	Males.	Females.	Males.	Females.	Males.	Females.	Males.	Females.	Males.	Females.	Males.	Females.	Males.	Females.
1	2	3	4	5	6	7	8	9	10	11	12	13	14	15	16	17	18	19	20	21
7	Trivandram ...	1	1	...	...	...	...	...	...	...	...	...	...	...	...	...	...	...	...	...

Number.	Taluq.	Age Periods—(*Continued*).																			
		15—19.		20—24.		25—29.		30—34.		35—39.		40—44.		45—49.		50—54.		55—59.		60 and over.	
		Males.	Females.	Males.	Females.	Males.	Females.	Males.	Females.	Males.	Females.	Males.	Females.	Males.	Females.	Males.	Females.	Males.	Females.	Males.	Females.
1	2	22	23	24	25	26	27	28	29	30	31	32	33	34	35	36	37	38	39	40	41
7	Trivandram ...	...	...	...	...	...	...	...	...	...	...	...	...	...	..	...	...	1	...	...	...

TABLE VII.

Ages, by Religions, Part (G)—Jew.

Number.	Taluq.	Total Jew.			Age Periods.															
					Under 1 year.		1 year.		2 years.		3 years.		4 years.		Total 0—4.		5—9.		10—14.	
		Total.	Males.	Females.	Males.	Females.	Males.	Females.	Males.	Females.	Males.	Females.	Males.	Females.	Males.	Females.	Males.	Females.	Males.	Females.
1	2	3	4	5	6	7	8	9	10	11	12	13	14	15	16	17	18	19	20	21
13	Quilon	10	5	5	...	...	...	...	...	...	1	...	...	...	1	...	...	1	...	...
31	Parur	115	60	55	...	...	1	1	3	1	1	1	3	3	8	6	9	7	4	9
	Total ...	125	65	60	...	...	1	1	3	1	2	1	3	3	9	6	9	8	4	9

Number.	Taluq.	Age Periods—(*Continued*).																			
		15—19.		20—24.		25—29.		30—34.		35—39.		40—44.		45—49.		50—54.		55—59.		60 and over.	
		Males.	Females.	Males.	Females.	Males.	Females.	Males.	Females.	Males.	Females.	Males.	Females.	Males.	Females.	Males.	Females.	Males.	Females.	Males.	Females.
1	2	22	23	24	25	26	27	28	29	30	31	32	33	34	35	36	37	38	39	40	41
13	Quilon	1	...	...	...	...	2	...	...	2	...	...	1	...	...	...	1	...	...	1	...
31	Parur	5	6	5	4	7	10	3	2	5	1	4	3	3	2	4	3	1	...	2	2
	Total ...	6	6	5	4	7	12	3	2	7	1	4	4	3	2	4	4	1	...	3	2

TABLE VII.

Ages, by Religions, Part (H)—None.

Number.	Taluq.	Total None.			Age Periods.															
					Under 1 year.		1 year.		2 years.		3 years.		4 years.		Total 0—4.		5—9.		10—14.	
		Total.	Males.	Females.	Males.	Females.	Males.	Females.	Males.	Females.	Males.	Females.	Males.	Females.	Males.	Females.	Males.	Females.	Males.	Females.
1	2	3	4	5	6	7	8	9	10	11	12	13	14	15	16	17	18	19	20	21
	Periyar and Thekkadi ...	2	2	...	...	...	...	...	...	...	...	...	...	...	...	...	...	...	...	...

Number.	Taluq.	Age Periods—(Continued).																			
		15—19.		20—24.		25—29.		30—34.		35—39.		40—44.		45—49.		50—54.		55—59.		60 and over.	
		Males.	Females.	Males.	Females.	Males.	Females.	Males.	Females.	Males.	Females.	Males.	Females.	Males.	Females.	Males.	Females.	Males.	Females.	Males.	Females.
1	2	22	23	24	25	26	27	28	29	30	31	32	33	34	35	36	37	38	39	40	41
	Periyar & Thekkadi...	...	...	...	...	1	...	1	...	...	...	...	...	...	...	...	...	...	...	...	...

TABLE

Civil Condition by Religion and Age,

Number.	Taluq.	Total Unmarried. Total.	Total Unmarried. Males.	Total Unmarried. Females.	(1) UN — Age 0—4. Males.	0—4. Females.
1	2	3	4	5	6	7
1	Tovala ...	13,181	7,426	5,755	1,857	2,010
2	Agastiswaram ...	41,053	22,843	18,210	5,360	5,885
3	Eranial ...	52,011	28,655	23,356	6,660	7,522
4	Kalkulam ...	30,286	16,702	13,584	3,636	3,990
5	Vilavankodu ...	34,686	19,219	15,467	3,890	4,559
6	Neyattankara ...	55,407	30,245	25,162	5,578	6,575
7	Trivandram ...	57,769	31,850	25,919	6,233	6,648
8	Nedumangadu ...	29,955	15,980	13,975	3,522	3,672
9	Sirayinkil ...	52,143	27,527	24,616	6,278	6,654
10	Kottarakkara ...	36,760	19,773	16,987	4.679	5,068
11	Pattanapuram ...	17,823	9,439	8,384	2,295	2,610
12	Shenkotta ...	14,873	8,365	6,508	2,167	2,225
13	Quilon ...	64,922	34,806	30,116	7,561	7,936
14	Kunnattur ...	37,496	20,606	16,890	4,878	4,900
15	Karunagappalli ...	55,897	29,409	26,488	6,904	7,457
16	Kartigappalli ...	45,307	24,249	21,058	5,531	6,199
17	Mavellikkara ...	49,207	26,908	22,299	5,882	6,094
18	Chenganur ...	43,989	24,499	19,490	5,770	5,852
19	Tiruvalla ...	54,898	30,077	24,821	7,005	7,687
20	Ambalappula ...	47,147	24,886	22,261	5,984	7,377
21	Sherttala ...	55,425	29,014	26,411	6,201	7,199
22	Vykkam ...	36,723	20,431	16,292	4,356	4,585
23	Ettumanur ...	37,389	20,202	17,187	4,701	5,536
24	Kottayam ...	36,799	19,955	16,844	4,617	5,037
25	Changanacheri ...	33,978	18,647	15,331	4,422	4,707
26	Meenachal ...	27,009	14,843	12,166	3,877	4,314
27	Muvattupula ...	47,765	25,407	22,358	5,995	6,989
28	Todupula ...	12,122	6,628	5,494	1,820	1,797
29	Kunnattunadu ...	55,685	28,988	26,697	6,543	7,721
30	Alangadu ...	36,005	18,983	17,022	4,458	4,640
31	Parur ...	30,998	16,836	14,162	4,071	4,632
	Cardamom Hills ...	5,306	3,299	2,007	590	642
	Periyar and Thekkadi ...	1,126	915	211	76	72
	Total ...	1,251,140	677,612	573,528	153,397	168,791

VIII.

Part (A)—Total Population.

MARRIED.

PERIODS.

5—9.		10—14.		15—19.		20—24.	
Males.	Females.	Males.	Females.	Males.	Females.	Males.	Females.
8	9	10	11	12	13	14	15
1,627	1,763	1,517	1,205	1,102	404	658	82
5,337	5,405	4,753	4,031	3,522	1,755	1,972	359
6,702	7,038	5,581	4,643	4,431	2,046	2,500	519
3,609	3,808	3,366	2,808	2,921	1,388	1,525	349
4,246	4,219	4,056	3,303	3,355	1,602	1,728	395
6,505	6,442	6,268	5,252	5,115	2,780	2,958	1,045
6,314	6,309	6,216	5,204	4,987	2,785	3,506	1,258
3,042	3,310	3,159	2,800	2,396	1,562	1,613	653
6,445	5,906	5,798	4,989	4,043	2,882	2,371	1,137
4,742	4,677	4,080	3,477	2,812	1,736	1,470	607
2,117	2,310	2,065	1,841	1,545	908	617	245
1,918	1,941	1,756	1,494	1,247	507	697	105
7,995	7,748	7,188	6,333	5,271	3,831	3,225	1,332
4,587	4,346	4,240	3,452	2,866	1.813	1,648	812
6,836	6,658	6,098	5,733	4,265	3,110	2,440	1,133
5,393	5,494	5,260	4,579.	3,713	2,457	2,163	908
6,078	6,015	5,759	4,850	4,204	2,568	2,141	835
5,929	5,564	5,710	4,570	3,548	1,777	1,656	589
7,569	7,379	7,311	5,704	4,391	1,889	1,860	606
5,414	5,181	5,307	4,342	3,884	1,898	1,960	902
6,508	6,735	5,776	5,533	4,339	3,074	2,430	997
5,168	4,873	4,526	3,698	3,168	1,550	1,526	464
5,238	5,013	4,815	3,784	2,802	1,336	1,009	356
5,009	4,992	4,739	3,843	3,085	1,375	1,098	330
4,354	4,844	4,542	3,664	2,818	1,259	1,026	343
3,803	3,821	3,703	2,752	1,928	638	599	198
7,164	7,010	6,507	5,269	3,153	1,551	1,132	416
1,536	1,491	1,674	1,391	937	496	353	98
7,723	7,736	6,842	5,905	4,217	2,705	1,706	846
4,778	4,628	4,286	3,960	2,430	1,823	1,208	630
4,099	3,922	3,631	3,212	2,484	1,375	1,432	398
587	591	663	418	656	204	381	58
77	55	116	55	229	23	200	5
158,449	156,724	147,308	124,094	101,864	57,102	52,803	19,010

TABLE

Civil Condition by Religion and Age,

Number.	Taluq.	(1) UN Age 25—29. Males.	25—29. Females.	30—34. Males.	30—34. Females.	35—39. Males.	35—39. Females.
1	2	16	17	18	19	20	21
1	Tovala ...	352	59	106	39	65	33
2	Agastiswaram ...	923	181	358	151	185	105
3	Eranial ...	1,328	352	550	296	307	249
4	Kalkulam ...	778	229	312	201	174	170
5	Vilavankodu ...	892	325	381	225	259	173
6	Neyattankara ...	1,715	763	789	563	527	456
7	Trivandram ...	1,923	808	922	654	539	561
8	Nedumangadu ...	898	379	456	304	269	258
9	Sirayinkil ...	1,088	760	437	467	260	350
10	Kottarakkara ...	884	398	320	203	200	186
11	Pattanapuram ..	364	151	124	91	110	63
12	Shenkotta ...	288	50	122	35	64	25
13	Quilon ...	1,655	868	697	579	450	428
14	Kunnattur ...	1,031	486	427	262	336	266
15	Karunagappalli ...	1,514	839	593	533	423	514
16	Kartigappalli ...	1,226	656	531	329	278	265
17	Mavellikkara ...	1,290	571	460	365	388	300
18	Chenganur ...	855	343	316	225	237	146
19	Tiruvalla ...	810	370	319	254	238	219
20	Ambalappula ...	1,032	729	493	529	319	440
21	Sherttala ...	1,482	663	742	488	492	371
22	Vykkam ...	791	290	317	182	194	133
23	Ettumanur ...	544	260	314	184	188	133
24	Kottayam ...	487	199	223	194	138	129
25	Changanacheri ...	396	191	275	191	192	126
26	Meenachal ...	294	126	167	75	110	60
27	Muvattupula ...	547	251	307	210	188	144
28	Todupula ...	120	46	50	34	47	37
29	Kunnattunadu ...	875	465	401	317	223	249
30	Alangadu ...	688	429	332	248	272	179
31	Parur ...	578	209	236	150	127	86
	Cardamom Hills ..	242	27	68	16	50	11
	Periyar & Thekkadi...	131	...	42	...	20	1
	Total ...	28,021	12,468	12,187	8,594	7,869	6,866

VIII.

Part (A)—Total Population—(*Continued*).

MARRIED—(*Continued*).

PERIODS—(*Continued*).

40—44.		45—49.		50—54.		55—59.		60 and over.	
Males.	Females.	Males.	Females.	Males.	Females.	Males.	Females.	Males.	Females.
22	23	24	25	26	27	28	29	30	31
53	47	25	21	24	26	15	36	25	30
103	89	56	40	54	67	62	23	158	119
198	190	109	101	97	130	58	90	134	180
105	156	81	109	69	150	36	46	90	180
132	159	88	140	53	112	46	74	93	181
302	465	132	196	93	232	64	102	199	291
387	511	251	302	212	303	137	188	223	388
174	227	109	178	121	217	77	126	144	289
184	352	129	248	127	290	121	149	246	432
117	152	91	115	78	139	43	72	257	162
62	36	45	27	46	24	21	17	28	61
45	36	19	20	23	37	9	15	10	18
247	356	195	180	153	204	69	126	100	195
184	151	154	152	108	98	78	78	69	74
133	197	72	89	54	92	30	48	47	85
105	130	27	23	9	9	6	7	7	2
235	260	155	145	146	125	65	76	105	95
146	124	107	88	88	72	47	43	90	97
200	213	124	145	113	182	69	83	68	90
238	391	83	175	76	141	39	92	62	69
352	353	215	246	157	279	104	139	216	334
128	119	61	70	70	107	27	70	99	151
179	144	90	105	129	142	75	65	118	129
127	156	100	114	104	148	76	88	157	239
127	122	112	97	125	86	72	56	186	145
97	46	48	37	68	33	46	14	103	52
148	177	85	96	82	92	39	48	60	105
30	30	18	18	10	21	8	8	25	27
156	213	95	160	77	124	35	61	95	195
139	130	118	109	94	70	68	79	112	97
78	72	31	27	27	25	8	20	34	34
26	13	15	7	7	5	7	4	7	11
8	...	4	...	5	...	1	...	6	...
4,940	5,817	3,044	3,580	2,699	3,782	1,658	2,143	3,373	4,557

TABLE

Civil Condition by Religion and Age,

Number.	Taluq.	(2) Mar				
		Total Married.			Age	
					0—4.	
		Total.	Males.	Females.	Males.	Females.
1	2	3	4	5	6	7
1	Tovala	12,691	6,354	6,337	...	...
2	Agastiswaram	36,070	18,132	17,938	...	...
3	Eranial	42,691	21,673	21,018	...	4
4	Kálkulam	24,106	12,148	11,958	...	1
5	Vilavankodu	29,060	14,917	14,143	...	1
6	Neyattankara	49,792	25,470	24,322	...	...
7	Trivandram	46,017	23,009	23,008	...	13
8	Nedumangadu	22,838	11,326	11,512	...	5
9	Sirayinkil	39,826	19,743	20,083	...	...
10	Kottarakkara	30,556	15,448	15,108	...	1
11	Pattanapuram	19,229	9,890	9,339	...	...
12	Shenkotta	13,546	6,670	6,876	...	...
13	Quilon	47,055	23,901	23,154	2	1
14	Kunnattur	30,181	15,550	14,631	...	...
15	Karunagappalli ...	43,076	21,455	21,621	...	...
16	Kartigappalli	38,510	19,171	19,339	...	...
17	Mavellikkara	46,504	23,550	22,954	...	...
18	Chenganur	43,645	22,472	21,173	...	...
19	Tiruvalla	59,614	30,379	29,235	...	...
20	Ambalappula	40,459	20,170	20,289	...	...
21	Sherttala	53,126	27,091	26,035	...	...
22	Vykkam	37,899	18,881	19,018	...	...
23	Ettumanur	38,508	19,715	18,793	...	...
24	Kottayam	36,160	18,264	17,896	...	...
25	Changanacheri ...	36,213	18,505	17,708	...	...
26	Meenachal	28,991	14,842	14,149	...	...
27	Muvattupula	48,405	24,359	24,046	...	...
28	Todupula	11,354	5,717	5,637	...	...
29	Kunnattunadu	51,610	26,018	25,592	...	...
30	Alangadu	30,685	15,358	15,327	...	...
31	Parur	23,762	12,137	11,625	...	...
	Cardamom Hills ...	5,451	3,183	2,268	...	...
	Periyar and Thekkadi ...	1,972	1,590	382	...	...
	Total ...	1,119,602	567,088	552,514	2	26

VIII.

Part (A)—Total Population—(*Continued*).

RIED.

PERIODS.

5—9.		10—14.		15—19.		20—24.	
Males.	Females.	Males.	Females.	Males.	Females.	Males.	Females.
8	9	10	11	12	13	14	15
6	25	24	195	116	915	522	1,248
13	65	63	382	402	2,174	1,482	3,439
19	50	77	386	406	2,405	1,614	3,809
13	40	49	223	244	1,632	968	2,393
5	45	52	341	393	2,024	1,266	2,784
9	61	68	729	606	3,858	1,900	4,241
18	100	99	722	533	3,305	2,026	4,441
7	10	35	268	152	1,608	747	2,156
4	34	26	301	329	2,418	1,516	3,513
3	22	72	429	453	1,691	1,293	2,416
1	13	21	202	345	1,118	982	1,547
1	28	43	246	145	923	597	1,232
34	58	82	460	459	2,538	1,787	3,810
8	17	52	296	369	1,471	1,265	2,310
7	7	40	303	386	2,269	1,718	3,791
4	20	39	372	376	2,272	1,592	3,432
35	48	105	539	710	2,456	2,023	3,815
30	37	235	780	1,209	2,739	2,481	3,383
18	56	164	1,142	1,322	3,916	3,413	4,884
1	25	31	467	576	2,774	2,176	3,623
38	66	104	346	522	2,730	2,385	4,884
6	31	99	431	560	2,409	1,853	3,312
3	26	100	451	822	2,404	2,429	3,146
3	18	92	549	699	2,362	2,154	2,997
13	37	48	380	506	2,112	2,009	3,132
16	65	129	512	1,092	2,437	2,251	2,591
10	30	272	905	1,358	3,055	2,847	3,983
1	26	31	195	330	915	742	1,023
8	23	85	391	785	2,508	2,758	4,259
41	24	107	344	828	1,777	1,503	2,455
12	15	48	184	276	1,392	1,150	2,298
...	2	21	78	129	314	413	437
...	1	6	10	51	49	195	88
387	1,125	2,519	13,559	17,489	68,970	54,057	96,872

TABLE

Civil Condition by Religion and Age,

Number.	Taluq.	(2) MAR Age 25—29. Males.	Females.	30—34. Males.	Females.	35—39. Males.	Females.
1	2	16	17	18	19	20	21
1	Tovala ...	943	1,285	1,122	1,052	1,020	635
2	Agastiswaram ...	2,620	3,655	3,053	2,896	2,935	1,977
3	Eranial ...	3,270	4,508	3,581	3,379	3,656	2,428
4	Kalkulam ...	1,938	2,429	1,867	1,805	2,056	1,336
5	Vilavankodu ...	2,342	2,885	2,442	2,114	2,454	1,583
6	Neyattaukara ...	3,841	4,609	3,625	3,340	4,160	2,863
7	Trivandram ...	3,355	4,133	3,554	3,127	3,627	2,551
8	Nedumangadu ...	1,659	2,077	1,600	1,613	1,869	1,275
9	Sirayinkil ...	3,020	3,635	2,865	2,983	3,187	2,293
10	Kottarakkara ...	2,336	2,803	2,144	2,155	2,467	1,933
11	Pattanapuram ...	1,632	1,776	1,480	1,398	1,764	1,206
12	Shenkotta ...	972	1,316	1,100	996	967	747
13	Quilon ...	3,617	4,417	3,535	3,452	3,771	2,847
14	Kunnattur ...	2,289	2,808	2,250	2,086	2,525	1,780
15	Karunagappalli ...	3,457	4,514	3,152	3,136	3,596	2,869
16	Kartigappalli ...	3,184	4,040	2,940	2,852	3,296	2,422
17	Mavellikkara ...	3,605	4,338	3,543	3,409	3,609	2,925
18	Chengannur ...	3,495	3,796	3,089	2,758	3,265	2,444
19	Tiruvalla ...	4,995	5,201	4,319	3,801	4,282	3,363
20	Ambalappula ...	3,233	3,619	3,018	2,744	2,991	2,350
21	Sherttala ...	4,529	5,874	4,369	4,182	4,891	3,203
22	Vykkam ...	3,076	3,748	3,031	2,814	3,031	2,270
23	Ettumanur ...	3,120	3,221	2,647	2,697	2,869	2,241
24	Kottayam ...	2,906	3,221	2,598	2,452	2,717	2,032
25	Changanacheri ...	2,743	3,267	3,153	2,813	3,054	1,936
26	Meenachal ...	2,445	2,307	2,059	1,757	2,018	1,474
27	Muvattupula ...	4,072	4,466	3,578	3,322	3,582	2,950
28	Todupula ...	949	1,006	829	738	854	641
29	Kunnattunadu ...	4,155	4,946	4,183	3,939	4,075	3,446
30	Alangadu ...	2,471	3,092	2,392	2,127	2,460	2,020
31	Parur ...	1,920	2,298	2,154	1,838	1,863	1,306
	Cardamom Hills ...	738	471	471	322	503	215
	Periyar & Thekkadi.	375	99	357	62	242	29
	Total ...	89,302	105,860	86,100	80,159	89,656	65,590

VIII.

Part (A)—Total Population—(*Continued*).

RIED—(*Continued*).

PERIODS—(*Continued*).

40—44.		45—49.		50—54.		55—59.		60 and over.	
Males.	Females.	Males.	Females.	Males.	Females.	Males.	Females.	Males.	Females.
22	23	24	25	26	27	28	29	30	31
944	474	576	194	450	141	243	59	388	114
2,663	1,435	1,786	684	1,422	553	640	227	1,053	451
2,981	1,515	1,960	888	1,450	691	959	505	1,700	450
1,611	882	1,200	495	847	280	553	182	802	260
1,937	1,053	1,521	637	999	327	571	161	935	188
3,451	1,950	2,550	1,166	1,882	759	1,265	354	2,113	392
3,165	1,834	2,260	1,144	1,758	719	1,100	517	1,514	402
1,290	964	1,198	644	1,022	401	679	261	1,068	230
2,415	1,783	1,879	1,080	1,642	835	1,100	464	1,760	744
1,889	1,336	1,436	834	1,230	675	743	331	1,382	482
1,122	748	945	518	676	397	414	177	508	239
992	576	617	329	582	237	267	133	387	118
3,137	2,177	2,254	1,272	1,904	998	1,199	545	2,120	579
1,826	1,335	1,412	908	1,294	712	808	459	1,452	449
2,672	1,934	2,025	1,160	1,756	831	1,010	418	1,636	389
2,454	1,678	1,778	918	1,373	641	890	378	1,245	314
3,031	2,114	2,272	1,272	1,772	926	1,104	492	1,741	620
2,211	1,715	2,012	1,322	1,628	969	1,100	613	1,717	617
3,349	2,428	2,528	1,729	2,305	1,274	1,477	732	2,207	709
2,540	1,821	1,795	1,220	1,523	822	1,009	484	1,277	340
3,702	1,897	2,594	1,246	1,669	701	958	460	1,330	446
2,472	1,667	1,661	892	1,324	689	680	375	1,088	380
2,463	1,544	1,608	1,088	1,491	896	846	549	1,317	530
1,958	1,469	1,687	1,157	1,333	797	833	467	1,284	375
2,101	1,376	1,569	998	1,334	742	773	415	1,202	500
1,519	1,050	1,052	733	911	499	520	352	830	372
2,829	1,954	1,927	1,481	1,721	912	886	525	1,277	463
650	421	454	264	350	193	223	113	304	102
3,181	2,374	2,274	1,589	1,972	982	968	561	1,574	574
1,911	1,228	1,292	957	1,039	659	602	390	712	254
1,539	943	1,059	577	838	363	510	244	768	167
319	176	223	96	122	67	117	37	127	53
172	23	82	9	59	6	29	1	22	5
70,496	45,874	51,486	29,501	41,678	20,694	25,076	11,981	38,840	12,303

TABLE

Civil Condition by Religion and Age,

Number.	Taluq.	(3) Wi				
		Total Widowed.			Age	
					0—4.	
		Total.	Males.	Females.	Males.	Females.
1	2	3	4	5	6	7
1	Tovala ...	3,879	709	3,170	...	...
2	Agastiswaram ...	10,118	2,251	7,867	...	...
3	Eranial ...	10,396	2,555	7,841	...	...
4	Kalkulam ...	5,082	984	4,098	...	...
5	Vilavankodu ...	4,775	1,066	3,709	...	...
6	Neyattankara ...	5,556	1,238	4,318	...	..
7	Trivandram ...	8,152	2,050	6,102	...	...
8	Nedumangadu ...	2,704	551	2,153	...	...
9	Sirayinkil ...	6,026	1,001	5,025	...	...
10	Kottarakkara ...	4,201	834	3,367	...	...
11	Pattanapuram ...	2,395	529	1,866	...	...
12	Shenkotta ...	3,669	665	3,004	...	...
13	Quilon ...	9,958	2,125	7,833	...	...
14	Kunnattur ...	5,852	1,241	4,611	...	...
15	Karunagappalli ...	9,853	1,998	7,855	...	...
16	Kartigappalli ...	8,133	1,796	6,337	...	...
17	Mavellikkara ...	7,908	2,036	5,872	...	...
18	Chenganur ...	6,326	1,472	4,854	...	...
19	Tiruvalla ...	7,630	2,058	5,572	...	...
20	Ambalappula ...	7,139	1,853	5,286	...	...
21	Sherttala ...	8,710	2,343	6,367	...	...
22	Vykkam ...	6,006	1,635	4,371	...	...
23	Ettumanur ...	4,926	1,619	3,307	...	...
24	Kottayam ...	4,135	1,010	3,125	...	...
25	Changanacheri ...	4,531	1,444	3,087	..	...
26	Meenachal ...	3,976	1,145	2,831	...	...
27	Muvattupula ...	6,839	1,829	5,010	...	...
28	Todupula ...	1,726	441	1,285	...	...
29	Kunnattunadu ...	6,754	2,210	4,544	...	...
30	Alangadu ...	4,268	1,603	2,665	...	...
31	Parur ...	4,518	1,109	3,409	...	...
	Cardamom Hills ...	656	232	424	...	...
	Periyar & Thekkadi ...	197	83	114	...	...
	Total ...	186,994	45,715	141,279	...	...

VIII.

Part (A)—Total Population—(*Continued*).

DOWED.

PERIODS.

5—9.		10—14.		15—19.		20—24.	
Males.	Females.	Males.	Females.	Males.	Females.	Males.	Females.
8	9	10	11	12	13	14	15
...	4	4	9	5	27	21	97
2	5	2	25	8	69	46	201
1	9	10	18	10	72	52	180
...	7	1	13	6	38	21	91
...	...	2	1	3	21	23	53
...	1	3	4	4	17	4	34
3	13	2	15	2	38	23	97
3	1	3	4	6	4	8	47
16	5	4	13	15	19	11	63
4	3	3	4	2	12	6	30
...	...	1	1	2	7	4	17
...	1	3	6	1	23	6	82
2	5	3	22	7	53	26	122
3	2	6	4	1	15	9	31
...	5	5	5	3	22	7	67
...	1	...	3	2	11	11	51
6	6	11	11	3	28	13	56
7	6	5	6	10	11	14	38
4	1	3	2	2	15	7	57
1	...	2	1	2	10	5	55
1	5	2	8	4	27	30	105
4	2	8	3	5	13	9	34
3	2	5	6	64	9	20	21
2	4	4	4	1	6	13	31
1	7	2	9	7	14	8	37
...	3	...	5	5	12	22	41
1	3	4	9	10	15	20	50
...	...	1	4	2	2	2	10
...	...	...	7	...	9	4	24
...	2	...	2	8	17	3	41
1	8	...	4	2	14	12	69
...	...	...	...	2	5	2	12
...	...	...	3	1	...	5	9
65	111	99	231	205	655	467	1,953

TABLE

Civil Condition by Religion and Age,

Number.	Taluq.	(3) Widow Age 25—29. Males.	25—29. Females.	30—34. Males.	30—34. Females.	35—39. Males.	35—39. Females.
1	2	16	17	18	19	20	21
1	Tovala ...	48	146	61	302	70	240
2	Agastiswaram ...	124	396	171	679	198	741
3	Eranial ...	90	361	169	616	179	666
4	Kalkulam ...	27	206	64	307	78	433
5	Vilavankodu ...	43	154	55	253	86	325
6	Neyattankara ...	10	78	27	146	33	225
7	Trivandram ...	35	179	86	298	84	375
8	Nedumangadu ...	10	59	19	106	21	128
9	Sirayinkil ...	24	143	62	261	58	308
10	Kottarakkara ...	8	69	25	129	26	184
11	Pattanapuram ...	7	31	15	80	27	115
12	Shenkotta ...	16	140	30	286	37	269
13	Quilon ...	61	271	103	392	113	591
14	Kunnattur ...	17	83	39	167	64	256
15	Karunagappalli ...	37	166	39	303	77	436
16	Kartigappalli ...	19	151	44	270	67	338
17	Mavellikkara ...	20	111	48	223	71	312
18	Chenganur ...	25	85	41	152	54	266
19	Tiruvalla ...	25	97	51	180	78	238
20	Ambalappula ...	29	118	40	196	69	251
21	Sherttala ...	62	167	133	445	150	508
22	Vykkam ...	37	128	83	232	116	347
23	Ettumanur ...	27	67	51	113	79	207
24	Kottayam ...	32	77	35	135	50	174
25	Changanacheri ...	19	63	66	88	64	150
26	Meenachal ...	28	86	50	145	80	161
27	Muvattupula ...	53	149	66	229	105	283
28	Todupula ...	12	31	18	67	21	87
29	Kunnattunadu ...	10	51	32	132	69	209
30	Alangadu ..	26	85	43	100	67	161
31	Parur ...	25	136	41	244	83	272
	Cardamom Hills ...	18	29	24	34	22	25
	Periyar & Thekkadi.	12	7	6	26	17	7
	Total ...	1,036	4,120	1,837	7,336	2,413	9,288

VIII.

Part (A)—Total Population—(*Continued*).

ED—(*Continued*).

PERIODS—(*Continued*).

40—44.		45—49.		50—54.		55—59.		60 and over.	
Males.	Females.	Males.	Females.	Males.	Females.	Males.	Females.	Males.	Females.
22	23	24	25	26	27	28	29	30	31
115	513	58	322	119	523	49	252	159	735
320	1,240	213	850	325	1,240	218	645	624	1,776
326	1,205	248	814	338	1,207	280	738	852	1,955
124	591	115	554	160	623	101	330	287	905
131	528	118	415	137	537	95	319	373	1,103
94	504	154	495	181	651	150	498	578	1,665
287	790	281	694	341	1,036	246	719	660	1,848
52	227	42	219	83	323	73	270	231	765
83	574	106	513	135	708	94	548	393	1,870
64	339	56	354	125	610	96	420	419	1,213
34	190	46	205	56	305	78	180	259	735
100	477	56	273	141	544	93	247	182	656
214	973	205	824	311	1,257	251	864	829	2,459
95	427	103	414	163	778	162	612	579	1,822
219	1,063	229	869	274	1,298	269	938	839	2,683
231	816	228	727	315	1,140	224	698	655	2,131
148	587	143	607	309	943	224	745	1,040	2,243
89	494	123	420	227	796	138	531	739	2,049
103	484	134	533	263	884	326	718	1,062	2,363
165	605	209	683	301	882	304	725	726	1,760
247	744	224	696	324	1,009	318	697	848	1,956
182	588	191	458	240	704	184	412	576	1,450
117	307	151	329	205	558	194	390	703	1,298
91	293	87	302	143	498	126	336	426	1,265
111	311	128	289	179	480	228	352	631	1,287
89	282	111	272	158	425	144	352	458	1,047
167	530	173	455	310	926	202	501	718	1,860
52	152	52	132	71	235	61	161	149	404
178	467	212	510	413	849	345	675	947	1,611
111	272	100	243	191	385	244	332	810	1,025
105	421	127	380	166	533	134	387	413	941
27	45	25	45	30	49	25	49	57	131
13	25	6	6	7	14	7	5	9	12
4,484	17,064	4,454	14,902	6,741	22,950	5,683	15,646	18,231	47,023

TABLE

Civil Condition by Religion and Age,

Number.	TALUQ.		(1) UN			
		Total Unmarried.			AGE	
					0—4.	
		Total.	Males.	Females.	Males.	Females.
1	2	3	4	5	6	7
1	Tovala	11,850	6,724	5,126	1,659	1,765
2	Agastiswaram	31,426	17,528	13,898	4,085	4,513
3	Eranial	36,714	20,446	16,268	4,768	5,325
4	Kalkulam	23,712	13,148	10,564	2,801	3,116
5	Vilavankodu	28,949	16,034	12,915	3,230	3,802
6	Neyattankara	46,893	25,717	21,176	4,700	5,559
7	Trivandram	48,122	26,756	21,366	5,141	5,386
8	Nedumangadu	27,469	14,573	12,896	3,247	3,373
9	Sirayinkil	44,212	23,367	20,845	5,341	5,608
10	Kottarakkara	29,963	16,120	13,843	3,663	3,930
11	Pattanapuram	14,303	7,558	6,745	1,810	2,050
12	Shenkotta	13,833	7,725	6,108	1,992	2,069
13	Quilon	48,596	25,955	22,641	5,424	5,715
14	Kunnattur	32,286	17,804	14,482	4,004	3,990
15	Karunagappalli ..	44,889	23,331	21,558	5,323	5,851
16	Kartigappalli	38,231	20,445	17,786	4,569	5,079
17	Mavelikkara	40,892	22,334	18,558	4,638	4,819
18	Chenganur	31,310	17,430	13,880	3,797	3,853
19	Tiruvalla	35,241	19,383	15,858	4,156	4,548
20	Ambalappula	31,193	16,886	14,307	3,858	4,235
21	Sherttala	42,322	22,223	20,099	4,550	5,278
22	Vykkam	29,897	16,661	13,236	3,487	3,641
23	Ettumanur	23,193	12,595	10,598	2,845	3,252
24	Kottayam	23,895	13,040	10,855	2,936	3,184
25	Changanacheri	20,028	11,158	8,870	2,471	2,529
26	Meenachal	12,662	7,141	5,521	1,693	1,880
27	Muvattupula	24,780	13,239	11,541	2,911	3,431
28	Todupula	7,039	3,901	3,138	1,007	1,048
29	Kunnattunadu	32,477	16,968	15,509	3,744	4,335
30	Alangadu	19,807	10,344	9,463	2,467	2,568
31	Parur	19,587	10,821	8,766	2,624	2,915
	Cardamom Hills ...	4,823	2,935	1,888	549	602
	Periyar and Thekkadi ...	835	665	170	62	61
	Total ...	921,429	500,955	420,474	109,552	119,310

VIII.

Part (B)—Hindu.

MARRIED.

PERIODS.

5—9.		10—14.		15—19.		20—24.	
Males.	Females.	Males.	Females.	Males.	Females.	Males.	Females.
8	9	10	11	12	13	14	15
1,472	1,611	1,377	1,083	1,006	349	606	65
4,093	4,155	3,669	3,131	2,652	1,267	1,581	234
4,732	4,948	3,995	3,208	3,171	1,356	1,747	326
2,777	2,968	2,643	2,177	2,317	1,072	1,256	269
3,477	3,513	3,346	2,786	2,807	1,329	1,480	305
5,502	5,308	5,322	4,356	4,276	2,372	2,564	933
5,149	5,117	5,152	4,246	4,189	2,273	3,051	1,068
2,770	3,053	2,867	2,575	2,172	1,440	1,477	615
5,362	4,963	4,856	4,152	3,449	2,469	2,067	981
3,680	3,644	3,247	2,843	2,390	1,585	1,298	566
1,690	1,841	1,627	1,469	1,236	755	509	211
1,777	1,833	1,634	1,414	1,145	481	641	97
5,716	5,656	5,330	4,717	3,980	3,093	2,517	1,090
3,819	3,569	3,592	2,952	2,545	1,702	1,553	785
5,348	5,243	4,764	4,626	3,428	2,686	1,986	974
4,508	4,474	4,334	3,845	3,084	2,206	1,925	827
4,898	4,816	4,702	4,022	3,534	2,329	1,939	782
4,000	3,706	3,891	3,231	2,602	1,532	1,425	540
4,467	4,323	4,418	3,639	3,090	1,502	1,547	527
3,566	3,533	3,415	3,052	2.628	1,346	1,477	620
4,747	5,018	4,381	4,114	3,349	2,410	2,014	828
4,160	3,923	3,629	2,961	2,617	1,307	1,285	403
3,169	2,990	2,826	2,245	1,796	919	728	274
3,216	3,053	2,933	2,373	2,005	1,016	830	254
2,432	2,357	2,590	2,092	1,757	892	729	236
1,658	1,676	1,655	1,254	1,130	362	422	100
3,454	3,454	3,180	2,655	1,909	975	779	274
849	820	961	743	604	306	254	67
4,339	4,489	3,830	3,441	2,565	1,588	1,095	473
2,435	2,426	2,188	2,101	1,362	1,052	721	410
2,612	2,388	2,267	1,928	1,630	837	918	276
559	569	592	386	549	192	325	53
64	40	92	44	161	19	132	5
112,497	111,477	105,305	89,861	77,135	45,019	42,878	15,468

TABLE

Civil Condition by Religion and Age,

Number.	Taluq.	(1) UN — Age 25—29. Males.	25—29. Females.	30—34. Males.	30—34. Females.	35—39. Males.	35—39. Females.
1	2	16	17	18	19	20	21
1	Tovala ...	322	50	94	35	58	28
2	Agastiswaram ...	724	130	269	108	136	86
3	Eranial ...	978	227	401	207	226	185
4	Kalkulam ...	650	173	249	156	143	139
5	Vilavankodu ...	775	253	328	187	224	152
6	Neyattankara ...	1,514	681	689	490	471	385
7	Trivandram ...	1,666	686	824	564	493	513
8	Nedumangadu ...	800	355	412	282	238	237
9	Sirayinkil ...	952	648	393	401	215	315
10	Kottarakkara ...	809	366	303	185	191	170
11	Pattanapuram ...	315	135	102	88	99	56
12	Shenkotta ...	270	43	111	35	59	22
13	Quilon ...	1,347	715	600	457	387	346
14	Kunnattur ...	984	460	415	245	323	252
15	Karunagappalli ...	1,296	773	523	482	368	458
16	Kartigappalli ...	1,117	621	507	316	262	256
17	Mavellikkara ...	1,193	534	428	340	360	278
18	Chenganur ...	797	318	295	202	209	134
19	Tiruvalla ...	705	329	290	222	214	188
20	Ambalappula ...	855	470	409	313	271	259
21	Sherttala ...	1,251	569	621	407	428	329
22	Vykkam ...	693	249	288	157	163	122
23	Ettumanur ...	393	192	217	145	151	101
24	Kottayam ...	382	152	173	162	109	96
25	Changanacheri ...	310	142	225	144	151	90
26	Meenachal ...	207	70	98	37	70	35
27	Muvattupula ...	387	179	226	146	142	106
28	Todupula ...	81	34	38	27	37	28
29	Kunnattunadu ...	616	280	288	211	162	161
30	Alangadu ...	433	293	215	166	177	126
31	Parur ...	396	138	183	109	97	58
	Cardamom Hills ...	209	27	56	14	43	8
	Periyar & Thekkadi.	87	...	29	...	18	1
	Total ...	23,514	10,292	10,299	7,040	6,695	5,720

VIII.

Part (B)—Hindu—(*Continued*).

MARRIED—(*Continued*).

PERIODS—(*Continued*).

40—44.		45—49.		50—54.		55—59.		60 and over.	
Males.	Females.	Males.	Females.	Males.	Females.	Males.	Females.	Males.	Females.
22	23	24	25	26	27	28	29	30	31
45	44	24	19	22	21	14	32	25	24
67	76	31	31	35	55	43	14	143	98
140	122	72	68	75	97	41	55	100	144
82	114	67	88	49	117	36	35	78	140
119	133	74	131	47	102	41	67	86	155
257	395	110	163	81	191	58	93	173	250
359	450	225	273	196	265	117	163	194	362
161	208	102	170	114	203	76	117	137	268
168	317	118	225	121	243	103	133	222	390
110	134	84	97	73	129	38	64	234	130
49	30	34	22	43	19	18	14	26	55
41	32	17	19	20	34	8	12	10	17
220	298	173	150	126	181	57	79	78	144
178	146	151	144	103	96	73	72	64	69
119	187	67	83	47	79	22	42	40	74
98	123	23	23	7	8	6	6	5	2
213	243	149	139	136	117	59	67	85	72
131	110	94	70	78	61	41	34	70	89
181	182	102	119	102	147	56	66	55	66
196	251	70	71	65	78	27	47	49	32
300	313	180	211	135	237	86	100	181	285
113	109	51	58	58	97	25	66	92	143
143	123	77	90	100	113	61	55	89	99
104	127	77	89	79	121	65	64	131	164
100	91	88	72	97	70	61	48	147	107
58	33	30	13	40	20	21	9	59	32
93	119	55	58	43	57	23	20	37	67
23	20	14	12	7	14	7	5	19	14
114	152	68	112	61	84	25	51	61	132
92	85	80	75	61	48	46	47	67	66
50	49	17	18	12	15	3	13	12	22
20	12	14	6	6	4	7	4	6	11
7	...	3	...	5	...	1	...	4	...
4,151	4,828	2,541	2,919	2,244	3,123	1,365	1,694	2,779	3,723

TABLE

Civil Condition by Religion and Age,

Number.	Taluq.	(2) MAR				
		Total Married.			Age	
					0—4.	
		Total.	Males.	Females.	Males.	Females.
1	2	3	4	5	6	7
1	Tovala ...	11,396	5,728	5,668	...	...
2	Agastiswaram ...	28,926	14,563	14,363	...	...
3	Eranial ...	30,425	15,429	14,996	...	4
4	Kalkulam ...	19,258	9,652	9,606	...	1
5	Vilavankodu ..	23,812	12,207	11,605	...	1
6	Neyattankara ...	41,798	21,349	20,449	...	..
7	Trivandram ...	38,349	19,232	19,117	...	13
8	Nedumangadu ...	20,836	10,298	10,538	...	5
9	Sirayinkil ...	33,658	16,727	16,931	...	...
10	Kottarakkara ...	23,975	12,101	11,874	...	1
11	Pattanapuram ...	15,270	7,881	7,389	...	...
12	Shenkotta ...	12,709	6,251	6,458	...	...
13	Quilon ...	34,586	17,654	16,932	2	1
14	Kunnattur ..	24,593	12,749	11,844	...	...
15	Karunagappalli ...	34,099	16,862	17,237	...	...
16	Kartigappalli ...	31,741	15,743	15,998	...	...
17	Mavellikkara ...	37,479	18,908	18,571	...	...
18	Chenganur ...	29,784	15,394	14,390	...	...
19	Tiruvalla ...	37,398	19,046	18,352	...	...
20	Ambalappula ...	27,103	13,087	14,016	...	...
21	Sherttala ...	40,473	20,708	19,765	...	...
22	Vykkam ...	30,779	15,215	15,564	...	...
23	Ettumanur ...	23,025	11,836	11,189	...	...
24	Kottayam ...	23,127	11,613	11,514	...	...
25	Changanacheri ...	21,892	11,156	10,736	...	...
26	Meenachal ...	13,252	6,735	6,517	...	...
27	Muvattupula ...	24,455	12,167	12,288	...	...
28	Todupula ...	6,594	3,290	3,304	...	...
29	Kunnattunadu ...	29,740	14,858	14,882	...	...
30	Alangadu ...	15,986	7,829	8,157	...	...
31	Parur ...	15,443	7,836	7,607	...	...
	Cardamom Hills ...	4,799	2,720	2,079	...	...
	Periyar & Thekkadi ...	1,550	1,231	319	...	...
	Total ...	808,310	408,055	400,255	2	26

VIII.

Part (B)—Hindu—(*Continued*).

RIED.

PERIODS.

5—9.		10—14.		15—19.		20—24.	
Males.	Females.	Males.	Females.	Males.	Females.	Males.	Females.
8	9	10	11	12	13	14	15
5	22	21	176	105	828	457	1,113
7	56	51	345	360	1,782	1,211	2,749
7	31	49	264	282	1,766	1,154	2,761
9	28	39	194	194	1,361	764	1,949
3	29	46	276	321	1,649	1,006	2,246
7	53	57	591	501	3,174	1,502	3,570
15	87	82	631	446	2,795	1,719	3,679
6	6	31	231	141	1,457	664	1,993
1	17	15	238	256	2,009	1,248	2,946
2	11	36	193	228	1,222	904	1,929
1	6	16	116	259	844	734	1,221
1	27	40	235	138	873	558	1,161
12	33	53	266	286	1,715	1,255	2,809
3	.7	34	166	207	1,067	899	1,844
1	4	24	191	263	1,722	1,307	3,003
2	10	25	275	248	1,743	1,219	2,824
15	24	60	333	454	1,832	1,462	3,066
5	10	65	356	575	1,611	1,457	2,249
5	19	61	467	548	2,181	1,867	2,982
...	10	19	268	337	1,840	1,308	2,531
18	39	68	230	352	1,979	1,744	3,652
1	17	67	321	394	1,956	1,438	2,684
1	4	48	208	399	1,308	1,362	1,896
1	10	38	297	297	1,374	1,223	1,921
...	26	26	196	232	1,222	1,112	1,850
5	19	43	184	313	1,040	927	1,208
4	17	101	315	480	1,464	1,271	2,013
1	17	9	104	152	507	417	593
2	6	36	174	373	1,393	1,478	2,460
10	8	47	177	342	948	724	1,273
8	7	27	140	179	935	705	1,501
...	2	19	73	117	296	351	397
...	1	5	10	46	48	175	75
158	663	1,358	8,241	9,825	47,941	35,622	70,143

TABLE

Civil Condition by Religion and Age,

Number.	Taluq.	(2) MAR Age 25—29. Males.	Females.	30—34. Males.	Females.	35—39. Males.	Females.
1	2	16	17	18	19	20	21
1	Tovala ...	849	1,130	1,005	947	895	553
2	Agastiswaram ...	2,058	2,930	2,461	2,318	2,328	1,566
3	Eranial ...	2,300	3,156	2,561	2,424	2,561	1,767
4	Kalkulam ...	1,553	1,925	1,466	1,424	1,627	1,068
5	Vilavankodu ...	1,883	2,354	2,009	1,728	2,028	1,325
6	Neyattankara ...	3,167	3,889	3,114	2,836	3,437	2,378
7	Trivandram ...	2,818	3,339	2,907	2,577	3,002	2,137
8	Nedumangadu ...	1,491	1,897	1,451	1,474	1,705	1,171
9	Sirayinkil ...	2,569	3,038	2,415	2,531	2,702	1,962
10	Kottarakkara ...	1,825	2,284	1,721	1,757	1,986	1,543
11	Pattanapuram ...	1,318	1,417	1,206	1,125	1,396	977
12	Shenkotta ...	913	1,237	1,016	936	908	696
13	Quilon ...	2,626	3,248	2,603	2,568	2,829	2,149
14	Kunnattur ...	1,834	2,320	1,863	1,728	2,141	1,510
15	Karunagappalli ...	2,695	3,604	2,520	2,524	2,854	2,322
16	Kartigappalli ...	2,595	3,418	2,454	2,418	2,748	2,043
17	Mavellikkara ...	2,868	3,539	2,905	2,814	2,947	2,421
18	Chenganur ...	2,360	2,631	2,193	2,015	2,371	1,736
19	Tiruvalla ...	3,065	3,376	2,796	2,505	2,771	2,187
20	Ambalappula ...	2,040	2,652	1,933	1,982	1,920	1,691
21	Sherttala ...	3,520	4,540	3,386	3,281	3,830	2,473
22	Vykkam ...	2,514	3,087	2,516	2,325	2,418	1,883
23	Ettumanur ...	1,839	1,982	1,666	1,676	1,700	1,420
24	Kottayam ...	1,877	2,154	1,767	1,682	1,746	1,329
25	Changanacheri ...	1,676	2,029	1,970	1,747	1,863	1,224
26	Meenachal ...	1,107	1,081	977	854	985	729
27	Muvattupula ...	2,010	2,295	1,812	1,730	1,810	1,550
28	Todupula ...	512	574	490	446	502	378
29	Kunnattunadu ...	2,344	2,919	2,417	2,318	2,392	2,075
30	Alangadu ...	1,255	1,622	1,294	1,174	1,266	1,073
31	Parur ...	1,241	1,511	1,403	1,216	1,172	851
	Cardamom Hills ...	632	432	386	281	406	191
	Periyar & Thekkadi.	294	76	270	45	179	22
	Total ...	63,648	77,686	62,953	59,406	65,425	48,400

VIII.

Part (B)—Hindu—(*Continued*).

RIED—(*Continued*).

PERIODS—(*Continued*).

40—44.		45—49.		50—54.		55—59.		60 and over.	
Males.	Females.	Males.	Females.	Males.	Females.	Males.	Females.	Males.	Females.
22	23	24	25	26	27	28	29	30	31
854	438	531	177	418	133	225	44	368	107
2,148	1,122	1,424	547	1,164	428	506	179	845	341
2,126	1,056	1,419	623	1,032	469	707	368	1,231	307
1,301	707	960	394	665	213	443	144	631	198
1,564	889	1,259	529	831	269	489	142	768	168
2,889	1,643	2,111	986	1,627	692	1,106	321	1,831	316
2,674	1,539	1,931	953	1,471	607	941	443	1,226	317
1,197	880	1,100	596	924	366	618	245	970	217
2,077	1,508	1,600	899	1,402	706	923	395	1,519	682
1,508	1,104	1,142	647	1,003	543	612	257	1,134	383
911	614	769	419	557	327	323	134	391	189
924	540	587	312	554	224	254	111	358	106
2,327	1,646	1,702	937	1,442	736	909	395	1,608	429
1,540	1,129	1,207	749	1,115	591	672	365	1,234	368
2,134	1,583	1,566	942	1,416	689	785	335	1,297	318
2,049	1,430	1,490	755	1,146	526	737	299	1,030	257
2,538	1,768	1,852	1,075	1,458	782	879	409	1,470	508
1,611	1,265	1,445	933	1,206	702	779	430	1,327	452
2,217	1,609	1,627	1,129	1,571	917	965	486	1,553	494
1,702	1,238	1,204	793	1,028	509	730	308	866	194
2,894	1,450	1,964	927	1,274	537	659	312	999	345
2,075	1,390	1,298	722	1,072	548	515	306	907	325
1,594	934	981	627	943	540	495	271	808	323
1,294	977	1,074	748	900	530	514	254	882	238
1,314	844	981	620	806	461	449	238	727	279
782	531	492	337	455	239	230	152	419	148
1,537	1,097	1,033	773	918	511	451	275	740	248
408	257	251	167	228	120	127	69	193	72
1,833	1,373	1,311	952	1,180	580	551	292	941	340
998	657	690	495	533	367	310	225	360	138
1,011	623	705	358	551	227	319	143	515	95
261	164	200	92	115	64	111	37	122	50
123	23	51	8	51	6	18	1	19	4
52,415	34,028	37,957	21,221	31,051	15,159	18,352	8,385	29,289	8,956

TABLE

Civil Condition by Religion and Age,

(3) WI

Number.	Taluq.	Total Widowed. Total.	Males.	Females.	Age 0—4. Males.	Females.
1	2	3	4	5	6	7
1	Tovala	3,576	655	2,921	...	...
2	Agastiswaram	8,282	1,829	6,453	...	...
3	Eranial	7,244	1,722	5,522	...	...
4	Kalkulam	4,147	807	3,340	...	...
5	Vilavankodu	3,957	867	3,090	...	...
6	Neyattankara	4,927	1,078	3,849	...	...
7	Trivandram	6,997	1,772	5,225	...	...
8	Nedumangadu	2,461	474	1,987	...	...
9	Sirayinkil	5,235	843	4,392	...	...
10	Kottarakkara	3,455	652	2,803	...	...
11	Pattanapuram	1,880	438	1,442	...	...
12	Shenkotta	3,491	627	2,864	...	...
13	Quilon	7,555	1,527	6,028	...	...
14	Kunnattur	5,069	1,053	4,016	...	...
15	Karunagappalli ...	7,980	1,486	6,494	...	...
16	Kartigappalli	6,877	1,505	5,372	...	...
17	Mavellikkara	6,629	1,639	4,990	...	...
18	Chengannur	4,701	1,070	3,631	...	...
19	Tiruvalla	5,072	1,322	3,750	...	...
20	Ambalappula	5,364	1,302	4,062	...	...
21	Sherttala	6,766	1,728	5,038	...	...
22	Vykkam	5,028	1,314	3,714	...	...
23	Ettumanur	3,138	992	2,146	...	...
24	Kottayam	2,734	647	2,087	...	...
25	Changanacheri	2,778	867	1,911	...	...
26	Meenachal	1,883	526	1,357	...	...
27	Muvattupula	3,688	935	2,753	...	...
28	Todupula	1,081	241	840	...	...
29	Kunnattunadu	3,899	1,211	2,688	...	...
30	Alangadu	2,263	794	1,469	...	...
31	Parur	3,186	770	2,416	...	...
	Cardamom Hills ...	613	222	391	...	...
	Periyar and Thekkadi ...	169	70	99	...	...
	Total ...	142,125	32,985	109,140	...	...

VIII.

Part (B)—Hindu—(*Continued*).

DOWED.

PERIODS.

5—9.		10—14.		15—19.		20—24.		25—29.	
Males.	Females.	Males.	Females.	Males.	Females.	Males.	Females.	Males.	Females.
8	9	10	11	12	13	14	15	16	17
...	4	4	8	4	25	20	88	44	127
1	4	2	19	7	55	23	174	94	320
...	8	3	9	3	44	34	117	68	255
...	5	...	10	5	33	15	79	20	176
...	...	2	1	1	20	20	42	33	131
...	1	...	2	...	12	1	30	6	64
...	13	1	15	1	27	18	87	30	136
1	1	...	2	4	2	6	44	9	48
14	4	3	11	9	17	9	55	19	123
...	3	1	3	1	10	2	24	6	57
...	...	1	1	2	4	4	11	6	20
...	...	1	4	1	20	5	78	15	138
1	3	...	15	5	25	12	77	44	197
...	2	2	3	1	11	4	24	12	65
...	2	3	2	2	14	4	55	28	146
...	...	...	2	2	6	7	40	14	132
4	...	10	6	3	20	8	45	14	94
1	6	...	1	1	5	9	23	16	57
...	...	...	2	1	13	2	39	16	60
1	...	1	...	2	8	2	39	16	74
...	1	...	5	3	22	19	71	45	135
1	2	4	3	4	10	5	31	30	114
1	1	1	...	57	5	15	15	16	43
...	...	1	1	...	4	5	14	20	43
...	2	1	7	2	10	...	19	18	38
...	2	...	2	3	5	11	24	11	32
1	1	2	5	1	6	11	27	21	72
...	...	...	4	1	...	2	5	7	21
...	...	...	1	...	2	2	17	4	30
...	...	...	...	6	3	2	17	10	31
...	7	...	2	1	7	9	45	17	94
...	...	...	...	2	4	2	12	17	28
...	...	...	2	1	...	5	9	10	7
26	72	43	148	136	449	293	1,477	731	3,108

TABLE

Civil Condition by Religion and Age,

Number.	Taluq.	(3) Wi — Age — 30—34. Males.	30—34. Females.	35—39. Males.	35—39. Females.	40—44. Males.	40—44. Females.
1	2	18	19	20	21	22	23
1	Tovala ...	54	279	64	211	111	473
2	Agastiswaram ...	143	550	167	578	272	1,015
3	Eranial ...	109	420	116	465	229	835
4	Kalkulam ...	49	227	62	360	94	483
5	Vilavankodu ...	43	199	76	273	105	412
6	Neyattankara ...	17	119	25	194	87	438
7	Trivandram ...	70	235	73	323	260	666
8	Nedumangadu ...	14	95	19	116	44	203
9	Sirayinkil ...	45	218	50	258	64	504
10	Kottarakkara ...	16	99	20	144	55	294
11	Pattanapuram ...	13	55	22	80	30	149
12	Shenkotta ...	26	278	35	253	91	454
13	Quilon ...	65	274	70	442	134	758
14	Kunnattur ...	32	146	54	222	85	376
15	Karunagappalli ..	30	262	62	344	179	913
16	Kartigappalli ...	36	239	60	286	194	704
17	Mavellikkara ...	36	185	60	264	124	516
18	Chenganur ...	25	108	34	185	59	386
19	Tiruvalla ...	37	120	56	143	60	328
20	Ambalappula ...	29	146	42	175	114	455
21	Sherttala ...	104	360	107	408	170	598
22	Vykkam ...	70	201	96	297	154	502
23	Ettumanur ...	38	82	55	145	61	207
24	Kottayam ...	21	93	32	102	62	202
25	Changanacheri ...	32	50	88	81	63	180
26	Meenachal ...	25	62	33	75	39	136
27	Muvattupula ...	27	118	44	146	78	273
28	Todupula ...	10	46	8	55	24	99
29	Kunnattunadu ...	19	77	40	130	99	289
30	Alangadu ...	16	61	39	89	53	156
31	Parur ...	24	170	64	182	77	306
	Cardamom Hills ..	23	32	22	21	23	38
	Periyar & Thekkadi...	5	24	13	5	12	21
	Total ...	1,303	5,630	1,758	7,052	3,306	13,369

VIII.

Part (B)—Hindu—(*Continued*).

DOWED—(*Continued*).

PERIODS—(*Continued*).

45—49.		50—54.		55—59.		60 and over.	
Males.	Females.	Males.	Females.	Males.	Females.	Males.	Females.
24	25	26	27	28	29	30	31
53	296	110	487	46	229	145	694
171	700	259	1,016	172	548	518	1,474
179	593	230	864	192	529	559	1,383
95	461	137	496	88	270	242	740
92	335	110	457	82	270	303	950
139	452	165	586	131	441	507	1,510
255	599	312	890	210	643	542	1,591
35	197	69	302	63	254	210	723
95	450	118	614	73	498	344	1,640
39	270	97	516	75	371	340	1,012
35	157	46	250	67	146	212	569
53	263	135	513	90	231	175	632
152	659	229	986	180	675	635	1,917
82	361	142	670	134	511	505	1,625
195	752	225	1,107	206	716	552	2,181
205	619	265	961	171	556	551	1,827
121	512	245	833	181	654	833	1,861
96	307	178	588	87	391	564	1,574
87	333	165	602	177	457	721	1,653
150	535	214	705	208	547	523	1,378
171	553	247	809	218	527	644	1,549
153	372	190	601	129	319	478	1,262
93	198	115	360	109	222	431	868
55	180	86	339	72	227	293	882
80	174	112	302	147	219	379	829
48	122	76	189	65	162	215	546
89	238	180	546	102	270	379	1,051
24	74	44	154	34	107	87	275
108	293	209	477	154	356	576	1,016
44	130	104	211	92	155	428	616
85	264	116	397	89	252	288	690
24	43	28	45	25	38	56	130
5	5	3	11	7	5	9	10
3,308	11,497	4,961	17,884	3,876	11,796	13,244	36,658

TABLE

Civil Condition by Religion and Age,

(1) UN

Number.	Taluq.	Total Unmarried. Total.	Males.	Females.	Age 0—4. Males.	Females.
1	2	3	4	5	6	7
1	Tovala ...	527	271	256	66	94
2	Agastiswaram ...	1,612	931	681	227	224
3	Eranial ...	2,029	1,185	844	264	277
4	Kalkulam ...	1,277	690	587	125	150
5	Vilavankodu ...	1,051	605	446	114	118
6	Neyattankara ...	2,645	1,395	1,250	320	322
7	Trivandram ...	4,848	2,620	2,228	527	605
8	Nedumangadu ...	1,754	961	793	204	225
9	Sirayinkil ...	6,841	3,603	3,238	821	920
10	Kottarakkara ...	2,364	1,290	1,074	305	382
11	Pattanapuram ...	1,911	1,044	867	283	317
12	Shenkotta ...	814	503	311	138	123
13	Quilon ...	7,068	4,044	3,024	900	907
14	Kunnattur ...	1,347	760	587	233	226
15	Karunagappalli ...	6,651	3,815	2,836	960	935
16	Kartigappalli ...	3,467	1,905	1,562	438	509
17	Mavellikkara ...	1,942	1,124	818	272	244
18	Chenganur ...	1,278	758	520	174	179
19	Tiruvalla ...	973	563	410	131	136
20	Ambalappula ...	5,747	2,542	3,205	684	1,361
21	Sherttala ...	1,178	584	594	127	172
22	Vykkam ...	1,612	847	765	170	234
23	Ettumanur ...	212	131	81	21	29
24	Kottayam ...	573	350	223	73	80
25	Changanacheri ...	1,491	784	707	195	253
26	Meenachal ...	458	308	150	38	58
27	Muvattupula ...	3,208	1,756	1,452	448	502
28	Todupula ...	1,366	775	591	244	187
29	Kunnattunadu ...	6,121	3,272	2,849	754	904
30	Alangadu ...	5,823	3,176	2,647	734	715
31	Parur ...	1,959	1,068	891	282	321
	Cardamom Hills ...	141	107	34	23	18
	Periyar and Thekkadi ...	119	105	14	5	3
	Total ...	80,407	43,872	36,535	10,300	11,730

VIII.

Part (C)—Mussalman.

MARRIED.

Periods.

5—9.		10—14.		15—19.		20—24.	
Males.	Females.	Males.	Females.	Males.	Females.	Males.	Females.
8	9	10	11	12	13	14	15
63	67	55	53	41	17	24	8
242	229	175	143	141	52	73	8
285	276	210	158	197	85	124	16
181	167	141	117	101	61	56	28
137	135	138	105	105	53	51	18
308	359	255	245	214	115	128	33
573	612	572	480	424	218	271	89
193	189	200	164	159	85	92	27
942	815	810	711	522	340	251	112
334	327	250	216	207	64	104	20
232	245	251	189	168	71	66	19
112	82	94	60	79	19	45	6
1,025	881	831	666	637	282	375	86
188	160	154	128	94	35	48	8
898	826	839	654	549	222	305	69
412	440	432	362	330	167	166	46
268	234	231	190	155	75	87	23
162	133	155	131	145	49	74	10
161	127	131	106	78	16	31	8
528	368	529	319	420	190	212	156
154	164	116	136	88	50	45	19
217	283	180	192	159	77	79	17
30	23	30	19	23	8	13	1
64	54	91	64	59	9	29	...
194	191	169	171	133	54	46	16
79	47	64	29	57	12	31	2
481	440	410	305	221	110	99	23
159	183	197	128	99	50	44	14
858	819	788	581	484	282	214	106
822	681	650	592	450	323	235	122
282	231	242	200	141	90	85	25
13	8	21	4	25	1	11	...
8	6	12	3	31	2	28	...
10,605	9,752	9,423	7,621	6,736	3,284	3,542	1,135

TABLE

Civil Condition by Religion and Age,

(1) UN

Number.	Taluq.	Age 25—29. Males.	Age 25—29. Females.	Age 30—34. Males.	Age 30—34. Females.	Age 35—39. Males.	Age 35—39. Females.
1	2	16	17	18	19	20	21
1	Tovala ...	11	5	4	1	2	...
2	Agastiswaram ...	32	5	10	9	15	1
3	Eranial ...	58	11	19	6	8	5
4	Kalkulam ...	34	14	19	14	10	9
5	Vilavankodu ...	29	3	7	4	14	...
6	Neyattankara ...	78	32	32	39	16	22
7	Trivandram ...	137	69	46	53	18	21
8	Nedumangadu ...	53	16	21	16	16	15
9	Sirayinkil ...	113	98	38	54	40	30
10	Kottarakkara ...	53	16	11	7	5	13
11	Pattanapuram ...	23	9	9	...	3	4
12	Shenkotta ...	16	7	10	...	3	2
13	Quilon ...	164	50	41	39	24	32
14	Kunnattur ...	25	7	7	4	2	9
15	Karunagappalli ...	150	38	45	27	42	32
16	Kartigappalli ...	88	23	16	6	13	6
17	Mavellikkara ...	58	15	12	8	14	10
18	Chenganur ...	23	5	6	4	11	1
19	Tiruvalla ...	14	4	6	1	4	2
20	Ambalappula ...	95	200	32	164	16	147
21	Sherttala ...	29	12	13	9	6	10
22	Vykkam ...	28	5	3	1	4	1
23	Ettumanur ...	7	1	3	...	1	...
24	Kottayam ...	13	2	1	...	2	2
25	Changanacheri ...	21	6	9	8	10	2
26	Meenachal ...	11	2	2	...	5	...
27	Muvattupula ...	46	11	11	10	12	4
28	Todupula ...	18	7	4	3	5	4
29	Kunnattunadu ...	93	57	29	19	21	19
30	Alangadu ...	112	70	54	36	38	31
31	Parur ...	25	13	5	9	2	...
	Cardamom Hills ...	9	...	2	...	1	2
	Periyar & Thekkadi.	16	...	3	...	...	...
	Total ...	1,682	813	530	551	383	436

VIII.

Part (C)—Mussalman—(*Continued*).

MARRIED—(*Continued*).

PERIODS—(*Continued*).

40—44.		45—49.		50—54.		55—59.		60 and over.	
Males.	Females.	Males.	Females.	Males.	Females.	Males.	Females.	Males.	Females.
22	23	24	25	26	27	28	29	30	31
2	2	1	1	2	2	...	3	...	3
4	4	5	2	1	2	1	...	5	2
9	3	2	1	2	...	7	5	...	1
5	10	7	3	8	6	...	4	3	4
2	3	4	1	3	1	...	1	1	4
19	34	10	14	5	17	1	3	9	15
9	30	14	10	3	16	9	11	17	14
8	13	5	6	3	9	...	7	7	21
13	34	11	22	4	47	17	15	21	40
3	9	4	6	1	2	2	1	11	11
6	3	1	3	1	1	...	2	1	4
2	4	1	1	3	8	...	3	...	1
12	18	10	5	10	9	6	27	9	22
3	3	2	2	...	1	2	3	2	1
7	9	4	4	6	7	3	4	7	9
5	2	3	...	1	1	...	...	1	...
14	7	3	3	5	4	2	1	3	4
4	2	2	3	2	2	...	1	...	...
3	3	...	1	2	4	1	1	1	1
14	116	5	88	2	41	1	30	4	25
1	7	4	5	1	2	...	4	...	4
...	...	2	2	4	1	1	1	...	1
...	...	1	...	2	...	...	...	...	...
4	1	4	1	2	1	2	4	6	5
1	1	...	...	4	3	...	1	2	1
4	...	1	...	5	...	1	...	10	...
8	16	4	9	12	8	1	5	8	9
2	4	1	3	...	3	...	...	2	5
8	15	9	11	2	12	2	5	10	19
19	22	16	17	22	12	9	15	15	11
1	1	...	...	1	...	1	...	1	1
...	...	1	...	1	1	...	...	...	...
...	...	...	...	...	...	...	...	2	...
192	876	137	224	120	218	69	157	153	288

TABLE

Civil Condition by Religion and Age,

Number.	Taluq.	(2) MAR				
		Total Married.			Age	
					0—4.	
		Total.	Males.	Females.	Males.	Females.
1	2	3	4	5	6	7
1	Tovala	541	258	283	...	...
2	Agastiswaram	1,418	706	712	...	...
3	Eranial	1,605	811	794	...	...
4	Kalkulam	954	493	461	...	...
5	Vilavankodu	855	427	428	...	...
6	Neyattankara	2,260	1,141	1,119	...	...
7	Trivandram	4,030	1,963	2,067	...	...
8	Nedumangadu	1,410	718	692	...	...
9	Sirayinkil	5,548	2,701	2,847	...	...
10	Kottarakkara	1,949	1,019	930	...	...
11	Pattanapuram	1,939	973	966	...	...
12	Shenkotta	661	335	326	...	...
13	Quilon	5,445	2,710	2,735	...	...
14	Kunnattur	1,258	638	620	...	...
15	Karunagappalli ...	5,340	2,781	2,559	...	...
16	Kartigappalli	3,049	1,527	1,522	...	...
17	Mavellikkara	1,916	998	918	...	...
18	Chenganur	1,335	672	663	...	...
19	Tiruvalla	1,089	565	524	...	...
20	Ambalappula	3,929	2,081	1,848	...	...
21	Sherttala	1,353	679	674	...	...
22	Vykkam	1,606	852	754	...	...
23	Ettumanur	244	177	67	...	...
24	Kottayam	539	281	258	...	...
25	Changanacheri ...	1,732	933	799	...	...
26	Meenachal	527	286	241	...	...
27	Muvattupula	2,936	1,526	1,410	...	...
28	Todupula	1,163	593	570	...	...
29	Kunnattunadu	4,676	2,415	2,261	...	...
30	Alangadu	4,943	2,561	2,382	...	...
31	Parur	1,445	755	690	...	...
	Cardamom Hills ...	182	111	71	...	...
	Periyar and Thekkadi ...	168	136	32	...	...
	Total ...	68,045	34,822	33,223	...	...

VIII.

Part (C)—Mussalman—(*Continued*).

RIED.

PERIODS.

5—9.		10—14.		15—19.		20—24.	
Males.	Females.	Males.	Females.	Males.	Females.	Males.	Females.
8	9	10	11	12	13	14	15
...	...	1	1	5	30	22	59
...	...	3	13	6	99	51	136
...	2	1	17	13	98	61	135
2	2	6	8	7	58	38	85
...	...	...	14	6	69	41	90
2	1	...	43	24	187	85	202
...	10	6	65	44	333	155	395
...	3	1	29	8	112	66	117
3	17	11	59	70	379	247	518
...	1	5	29	17	127	87	149
...	...	1	30	25	131	101	158
...	1	2	8	4	41	30	52
4	9	10	71	52	414	210	438
...	...	3	18	13	65	58	118
1	2	5	56	50	327	222	471
...	5	5	23	28	242	116	282
4	5	9	32	44	126	102	155
...	1	1	31	11	99	71	98
1	4	1	13	24	67	60	87
1	...	2	38	39	290	238	331
5	12	6	19	17	83	57	100
1	...	2	11	17	87	73	170
...	...	1	2	6	9	24	9
...	1	1	8	4	43	31	39
...	...	...	11	9	70	77	148
1	...	0	11	13	41	24	41
1	1	9	39	47	178	196	246
...	1	5	33	32	92	63	117
2	5	9	43	50	212	221	378
24	10	26	49	108	225	279	391
3	4	...	6	20	75	60	137
...	...	1	5	6	13	11	12
...	...	...	...	2	...	9	5
55	97	133	835	821	4,422	3,186	5,864

TABLE

Civil Condition by Religion and Age,

Number.	Taluq.	(2) MAR — Age — 25—29. Males.	25—29. Females.	30—34. Males.	30—34. Females.	35—39. Males.	35—39. Females.
1	2	16	17	18	19	20	21
1	Tovala ...	33	67	45	49	51	44
2	Agastiswaram ...	130	155	107	109	116	64
3	Eranial ...	96	168	140	137	111	78
4	Kalkulam ..	73	84	84	80	76	54
5	Vilavankodu ...	72	81	71	82	69	32
6	Neyattankara ...	196	224	152	148	185	136
7	Trivandram ...	279	384	309	278	310	215
8	Nedumangadu ...	114	122	101	86	103	78
9	Sirayinkil ...	413	522	395	400	430	298
10	Kottarakkara ...	158	192	163	126	159	113
11	Pattanapuram ...	146	194	143	152	194	117
12	Shenkotta ...	42	61	66	48	47	42
13	Quilon ...	411	514	452	381	424	306
14	Kunnattur ...	95	126	106	79	92	73
15	Karunagappalli ...	458	534	393	348	472	330
16	Kartigappalli ...	266	283	214	211	271	172
17	Mavellikkara ...	119	170	141	137	160	117
18	Chenganur ...	117	123	90	94	105	66
19	Tiruvalla ...	89	107	74	72	90	63
20	Ambalappula ...	342	293	338	215	347	154
21	Sherttala ...	85	127	100	100	103	71
22	Vykkam ...	116	164	144	100	165	107
23	Ettumanur ...	33	8	17	11	22	10
24	Kottayam ...	37	45	36	30	48	31
25	Changanacheri ...	114	175	163	149	182	97
26	Meenachal ...	46	42	45	26	54	25
27	Muvattupula ...	254	288	247	199	230	191
28	Todupula ...	106	104	80	73	96	60
29	Kunnattunadu ...	363	482	437	357	376	305
30	Alangadu ...	424	523	407	326	398	294
31	Parur ...	135	141	121	82	115	87
	Cardamom Hills ...	22	14	19	16	22	7
	Periyar & Thekkadi .	34	10	31	11	21	4
	Total ...	5,418	6,527	5,431	4,712	5,644	3,841

VIII.

Part (C)—Mussalman—(*Continued*).

RIED—(*Continued*).

PERIODS—(*Continued*).

40—44.		45—49.		50—54.		55—59.		60 and over.	
Males.	Females.	Males.	Females.	Males.	Females.	Males.	Females.	Males.	Females.
22	23	24	25	26	27	28	29	30	31
37	16	25	6	19	4	12	6	8	1
109	60	62	17	56	30	30	7	36	22
118	73	78	23	77	27	46	26	70	10
68	39	53	26	32	10	24	11	30	4
54	31	53	13	25	7	12	6	24	3
172	82	133	43	79	23	39	9	74	21
247	166	179	97	175	58	94	25	165	41
64	58	66	36	70	29	54	12	71	10
296	248	253	165	215	118	160	67	208	61
133	69	102	51	71	33	46	19	78	21
113	64	96	48	57	29	40	17	57	26
60	30	23	12	27	8	7	17	27	6
371	240	249	133	212	98	112	72	203	59
74	45	52	28	46	22	39	22	60	24
343	212	278	125	199	81	152	43	208	30
194	110	140	72	98	58	65	37	130	27
121	80	101	39	80	25	52	9	65	23
75	47	63	44	51	28	25	15	63	17
58	30	63	35	40	23	22	9	43	14
270	202	172	117	133	91	68	61	131	56
87	44	79	34	51	44	42	27	47	13
92	62	118	18	52	20	38	6	34	9
25	6	14	3	17	...	10	2	8	7
29	13	25	13	19	10	26	18	25	7
122	58	72	42	93	19	45	16	56	14
28	25	30	12	24	9	7	6	14	3
195	114	108	77	136	30	47	27	56	20
65	28	48	30	35	18	24	10	39	4
313	186	215	115	178	79	91	46	160	53
310	203	174	170	194	98	120	54	97	39
96	72	70	44	51	22	36	7	48	13
15	...	6	1	3	1	2	...	4	2
22	...	9	1	4	...	4	...	...	1
4,376	2,713	3,209	1,690	2,619	1,152	1,591	709	2,339	661

TABLE

Civil Condition by Religion and Age,

Number.	Taluq.	(3) Wi				
		Total Widowed.			Age	
					0—4.	
		Total.	Males.	Females.	Males.	Females.
1	2	3	4	5	6	7
1	Tovala	116	21	95	...	...
2	Agastiswaram	357	72	285	...	...
3	Eranial	431	119	312	...	...
4	Kalkulam	189	39	150	...	...
5	Vilavankodu	181	32	149	...	...
6	Neyattankara	238	53	185	...	...
7	Trivandram	628	135	493	...	...
8	Nedumangadu	144	39	105	...	...
9	Sirayinkil	661	130	531	...	...
10	Kottarakkara	237	67	170	...	...
11	Pattanapuram	319	46	273	...	...
12	Shenkotta	136	26	110	...	...
13	Quilon	1,137	241	896	...	...
14	Kunnattur	154	28	126	...	...
15	Karunagappalli ...	1,070	288	782	...	...
16	Kartigappalli	559	117	442	...	...
17	Mavellikkara	276	66	210	...	...
18	Chenganur	230	55	175	...	...
19	Tiruvalla	113	30	83	...	...
20	Ambalappula	457	166	291	...	...
21	Sherttala	256	100	156	...	...
22	Vykkam	205	68	137	...	...
23	Ettumanur	27	5	22	..	...
24	Kottayam	39	6	33	...	...
25	Changanacheri ...	197	78	119	...	...
26	Meenachal	99	37	62	...	...
27	Muvattupula	298	66	232	...	...
28	Todupula	147	41	106	...	...
29	Kunnattunadu	589	197	392	...	...
30	Alangadu	620	257	363	...	...
31	Parur	228	51	177	...	...
	Cardamom Hills ...	22	3	19	...	...
	Periyar & Thekkadi ...	11	2	9	...	...
	Total ...	10,371	2,681	7,690	...	...

VIII.

Part (C)—Mussalman—(*Continued*).

DOWED.

PERIODS.

5—9.		10—14.		15—19.		20—24.	
Males.	Females.	Males.	Females.	Males.	Females.	Males.	Females.
8	9	10	11	12	13	14	15
...	...	...	...	...	1	...	2
...	1	...	3	...	5	...	5
...	...	1	3	4	6	...	11
...	...	...	...	...	2	2	3
...	...	...	...	...	1	...	7
...	...	...	2	...	3	1	3
2	...	1	...	1	4	3	4
2	...	...	2	...	...	1	2
2	...	1	2	6	2	2	6
...	...	1	...	...	1	3	2
...	...	...	...	...	2	...	5
...	...	...	...	...	1	1	4
...	...	1	5	2	14	7	19
1	...	...	...	...	...	1	2
...	1	2	3	1	5	3	9
...	1	...	1	...	4	2	5
...	3	...	4	...	7	...	4
3	...	1	...	3	2	...	...
1	...	...	...	...	...	...	2
...	...	...	...	...	2	...	4
...	2	...	1	1	1	8	4
...	...	...	...	...	1	...	...
...	1	...	1	...	...	...	...
...	...	...	...	...	...	...	1
...	...	...	...	1	...	...	5
...	...	...	2	...	...	1	...
...	...	1	...	1	...	1	1
...	...	...	...	...	2	...	1
...	...	...	...	...	3	...	1
...	2	...	1	...	5	1	7
...	...	...	...	...	1	...	3
...	...	...	...	...	1	...	...
...	...	...	1	...	...	...	...
11	11	9	31	20	76	37	122

TABLE

Civil Condition by Religion and Age,

Number.	Taluq.	(3) Wi Age 25—29. Males.	25—29. Females.	30—34. Males.	30—34. Females.	35—39. Males.	35—39. Females.
1	2	16	17	18	19	20	21
1	Tovala ...	...	3	3	8	1	8
2	Agastiswaram ...	7	22	10	29	1	24
3	Eranial ...	2	12	11	32	13	29
4	Kalkulam ...	2	7	3	17	2	7
5	Vilavankodu ...	2	8	5	16	4	10
6	Neyattankara ...	2	7	5	16	2	20
7	Trivandram ...	1	15	9	33	3	23
8	Nedumangadu ...	1	9	3	8	2	4
9	Sirayinkil ...	4	14	13	30	4	41
10	Kottarakkara ...	1	2	5	7	1	13
11	Pattanapuram ...	1	6	2	17	3	26
12	Shenkotta ...	1	2	4	8	2	12
13	Quilon ...	10	35	22	51	25	81
14	Kunnattur ...	3	3	1	5	2	5
15	Karunagappalli ...	6	12	5	18	8	43
16	Kartigappalli ...	2	10	4	18	2	32
17	Mavellikkara ...	1	2	2	10	1	13
18	Chenganur ...	2	7	4	11	2	13
19	Tiruvalla ...	1	...	...	2	2	5
20	Ambalappula ...	7	10	3	15	7	25
21	Sherttala ...	7	3	4	15	9	10
22	Vykkam ...	...	...	5	6	7	13
23	Ettumanur ...	...	...	...	1	...	2
24	Kottayam ...	...	...	...	5	1	1
25	Changanacheri ...	...	3	...	6	2	6
26	Meenachal ...	1	2	...	3	...	2
27	Muvattupula ...	2	5	4	6	3	10
28	Todupula ...	...	4	1	6	2	10
29	Kunnattunadu ...	2	7	1	13	7	19
30	Alangadu ...	4	18	8	8	7	19
31	Parur ...	1	6	1	14	2	18
	Cardamom Hills ...	...	...	...	1	...	4
	Periyar & Thekkadi.	1	...	...	...	...	...
	Total ...	74	234	138	435	127	548

VIII.

Part (C)—Mussalman—(*Continued*).

DOWED—(*Continued*).

PERIODS—(*Continued*).

40—44.		45—49.		50—54.		55—59.		60 and over.	
Males.	Females.	Males.	Females.	Males.	Females.	Males.	Females.	Males.	Females.
22	23	24	25	26	27	28	29	30	31
2	18	...	9	6	15	...	12	9	19
9	45	7	26	11	54	8	23	19	48
18	43	7	24	12	62	15	22	36	68
14	20	1	17	3	21	4	14	8	42
1	35	4	19	6	10	2	11	8	32
3	26	4	15	10	24	3	22	23	47
11	73	10	50	14	80	20	50	60	161
2	12	1	10	9	14	5	14	13	30
17	56	6	60	13	82	18	44	44	194
2	18	8	34	4	26	8	15	34	52
1	27	3	35	7	38	4	18	25	99
5	18	2	9	4	23	2	12	5	21
22	109	16	68	37	136	28	94	71	284
1	13	2	6	2	25	6	17	9	50
24	86	18	53	33	108	29	135	159	309
20	60	10	42	23	81	13	51	41	137
...	12	3	14	15	25	2	26	42	90
2	15	4	13	12	31	4	16	18	67
1	3	2	13	6	7	7	16	10	35
15	31	15	41	28	41	31	33	60	89
10	21	6	13	13	23	15	19	27	44
5	20	6	15	12	21	11	23	22	38
1	3	1	4	...	4	...	...	3	6
...	5	...	2	1	5	2	4	2	10
5	11	3	8	17	16	7	19	43	45
5	12	2	12	3	9	5	4	20	16
7	37	7	19	9	47	6	20	25	87
9	13	5	12	6	26	8	12	10	20
23	34	19	42	28	84	41	44	76	145
19	38	14	24	29	59	27	28	148	154
3	22	1	11	11	31	12	16	20	55
1	2	...	...	1	2	...	9	1	...
1	3	...	1	...	2	...	...	...	2
259	941	187	721	385	1,232	343	843	1,091	2,496

TABLE

Civil Condition by Religion and Age,

Number.	Taluq.	(1) UN				
		Total Unmarried.			Age	
					0—4.	
		Total.	Males.	Females.	Males.	Females.
1	2	3	4	5	6	7
1	Tovala ...	804	431	373	132	151
2	Agastiswaram ...	8,015	4,384	3,631	1,048	1,148
3	Eranial ...	13,268	7,024	6,244	1,628	1,920
4	Kalkulam ...	5,297	2,864	2,433	710	724
5	Vilavankodu ...	4,686	2,580	2,106	546	639
6	Neyattankara ...	5,869	3,133	2,736	558	694
7	Trivandram ...	4,799	2,474	2,325	565	657
8	Nedumangadu ...	732	446	286	71	74
9	Sirayinkil ..	1,090	557	533	116	126
10	Kottarakkara ...	4,433	2,363	2,070	711	756
11	Pattanapuram ...	1,609	837	772	202	243
12	Shenkotta ...	226	137	89	37	33
13	Quilon ...	9,253	4,804	4,449	1,236	1,314
14	Kunnattur ...	3,863	2,042	1,821	641	684
15	Karunagappalli ...	4,357	2,263	2,094	621	671
16	Kartigappalli ...	3,609	1,899	1,710	524	611
17	Mavellikkara ...	6,373	3,450	2,923	972	1,031
18	Chenganur ...	11,401	6,311	5,090	1,799	1,820
19	Tiruvalla ...	18,684	10,131	8,553	2,718	3,003
20	Ambalappula ...	10,207	5,458	4,749	1,442	1,781
21	Sherttala ...	11,925	6,207	5,718	1,524	1,749
22	Vykkam ...	5,214	2,923	2,291	699	710
23	Ettumanur ...	13,984	7,476	6,508	1,835	2,255
24	Kottayam ...	12,331	6,565	5,766	1,608	1,773
25	Changanacheri ..	12,459	6,705	5,754	1,756	1,925
26	Meenachal ...	13,889	7,394	6,495	2,146	2,376
27	Muvattupula ...	19,777	10,412	9,365	2,636	3,056
28	Todupula ...	3,717	1,952	1,765	569	562
29	Kunnattunadu ...	17,087	8,748	8,339	2,045	2,482
30	Alangadu ...	10,372	5,460	4,912	1,257	1,357
31	Parur ...	9,391	4,911	4,480	1,157	1,390
	Cardamom Hills ...	342	257	85	18	22
	Periyar and Thekkadi.	170	143	27	9	8
	Total ...	249,233	132,741	116,492	33,536	37,745

VIII.

Part (D)—Christian.

MARRIED.

PERIODS.

5—9.		10—14.		15—19.		20—24.	
Males.	Females.	Males.	Females.	Males.	Females.	Males.	Females.
8	9	10	11	12	13	14	15
92	85	85	69	55	38	28	9
1,002	1,021	909	757	729	436	318	117
1,685	1,814	1,376	1,277	1,063	605	629	177
651	673	582	514	503	255	213	52
632	571	572	412	443	220	197	72
695	775	691	651	625	293	266	79
592	580	492	478	374	294	184	101
79	68	92	61	65	37	44	11
141	128	132	126	72	73	53	44
728	706	583	418	215	87	68	21
195	224	187	183	141	82	42	15
29	26	28	20	23	7	11	2
1,254	1,210	1,027	950	653	456	333	156
580	617	494	372	227	76	47	19
590	589	495	453	288	202	149	90
473	580	494	372	299	84	72	35
912	965	826	638	515	164	115	30
1,767	1,725	1,664	1,208	801	196	157	39
2,941	2,929	2,762	1,959	1,223	371	282	71
1,320	1,280	1,363	971	836	357	271	126
1,607	1,553	1,279	1,283	902	614	371	150
791	717	717	545	392	166	162	44
2,039	2,000	1,959	1,520	983	409	268	81
1,729	1,885	1,715	1,406	1,021	350	234	76
1,728	1,796	1,783	1,401	928	313	251	91
2,066	2,098	1,984	1,469	741	264	146	96
3,229	3,116	2,917	2,309	1,023	466	254	119
528	488	516	520	234	140	55	17
2,526	2,428	2,224	1,883	1,168	835	397	267
1,521	1,521	1,448	1,267	617	448	251	98
1,196	1,296	1,118	1,076	708	445	425	96
15	14	50	28	82	11	45	5
5	9	12	8	37	2	40	...
35,338	35,487	32,576	26,604	17,986	8,796	6,378	2,406

TABLE

Civil Condition by Religion and Age,

(1) UN

AGE

Number.	Taluq.	25—29. Males.	25—29. Females.	30—34. Males.	30—34. Females.	35—39. Males.	35—39. Females.
1	2	16	17	18	19	20	21
1	Tovala ...	19	4	8	3	5	5
2	Agastiswaram ...	167	46	79	34	34	18
3	Eranial ...	292	114	130	83	73	59
4	Kalkulam ...	94	42	44	31	21	22
5	Vilavankodu ...	88	69	46	34	21	21
6	Neyattankara ...	123	50	68	34	40	49
7	Trivandram ...	120	53	52	37	28	27
8	Nedumangadu ...	45	8	23	6	15	6
9	Sirayinkil ...	23	14	6	12	5	5
10	Kottarakkara ...	22	11	6	11	4	3
11	Pattanapuram ...	26	7	13	3	8	3
12	Shenkotta ...	2	...	1	...	2	1
13	Quilon ...	144	102	56	83	38	50
14	Kunnattur ...	22	19	5	13	11	5
15	Karunagappalli ...	68	28	25	24	13	24
16	Kartigappalli ...	21	12	8	7	3	3
17	Mavellikkara ...	39	22	20	17	14	12
18	Chenganur ...	35	20	15	19	17	11
19	Tiruvalla ...	91	37	23	31	20	29
20	Ambalappula ...	82	59	52	52	32	34
21	Sherttala ...	202	82	108	72	58	32
22	Vykkam ...	70	36	26	24	27	10
23	Ettumanur ...	144	67	94	39	36	32
24	Kottayam ...	92	45	49	32	27	31
25	Changanachori ...	65	43	41	39	31	34
26	Meenachal ...	76	54	67	38	35	25
27	Muvattupula ...	114	61	70	54	34	34
28	Todupula ...	21	5	8	4	5	5
29	Kunnattunadu ...	166	128	84	87	40	69
30	Alangadu ...	143	66	62	46	57	22
31	Parur ...	151	58	48	32	28	28
	Cardamom Hills ...	24	...	10	2	6	1
	Periyar & Thekkadi.	27	...	9	...	2	...
	Total ...	2,818	1,362	1,356	1,003	790	710

VIII.

Part (D)—Christian—(*Continued*).

MARRIED—(*Continued*).

PERIODS—(*Continued*).

40—44.		45—49.		50—54.		55—59.		60 and over.	
Males.	Females.	Males.	Females.	Males.	Females.	Males.	Females.	Males.	Females.
22	23	24	25	26	27	28	29	30	31
6	1	...	1	...	3	1	1	...	3
32	9	20	7	18	10	18	9	10	19
49	65	35	32	20	33	10	30	34	35
18	32	7	18	12	27	...	7	9	36
11	23	10	8	3	9	5	6	6	22
26	36	12	19	7	24	5	6	17	26
19	31	12	19	13	22	11	14	12	12
5	6	2	2	4	5	1	2	...	...
3	1	...	1	2	...	1	1	3	2
4	9	3	12	4	8	3	7	12	21
7	3	10	2	2	4	3	1	1	2
2	...	1	...	...	...	1	...	...	...
15	40	12	25	17	14	6	20	13	29
3	2	1	6	5	1	3	3	3	4
7	1	1	2	1	6	5	2	...	2
2	5	1	...	1	...	...	1	1	...
8	10	3	3	5	4	4	8	17	19
11	12	11	15	8	9	6	8	20	8
16	28	22	25	9	31	12	16	12	23
23	24	8	16	9	22	11	15	9	12
51	33	31	30	21	40	18	35	35	45
15	10	8	10	8	9	1	3	7	7
36	21	12	15	27	29	14	10	29	30
19	28	19	24	23	26	9	20	20	70
26	30	24	25	24	13	11	7	37	37
35	13	17	24	23	13	24	5	34	20
47	42	26	29	27	27	15	23	20	29
5	6	3	3	3	4	1	3	4	8
34	46	18	37	14	28	8	5	24	44
28	23	22	17	11	10	13	17	30	20
27	22	14	9	14	10	4	7	21	11
6	1	...	1	...	...	...	...	1	...
1	...	1	...	...	...	...	...	...	...
597	613	366	437	335	441	224	292	441	596

TABLE

Civil Condition by Religion and Age,

Number.	Taluq.	(2) MAR				
		Total Married.			Age	
					0—4.	
		Total.	Males.	Females.	Males.	Females.
1	2	3	4	5	6	7
1	Tovala ...	754	368	386	...	...
2	Agastiswaram ...	5,726	2,863	2,863	...	...
3	Eranial ...	10,661	5,433	5,228	...	...
4	Kalkulam ...	3,894	2,003	1,891	...	...
5	Vilavankodu ...	4,393	2,283	2,110	...	...
6	Neyattankara ...	5,734	2,980	2,754	...	...
7	Trivandram ...	3,637	1,813	1,824	...	...
8	Nedumangadu ...	592	310	282	...	...
9	Sirayinkil ...	620	315	305	...	...
10	Kottarakkara ...	4,632	2,828	2,304	...	...
11	Pattanapuram ...	2,020	1,036	984	...	...
12	Shenkotta ...	176	84	92	...	...
13	Quilon ...	7,020	3,535	3,485	...	...
14	Kunnattur ...	4,330	2,163	2,167	...	...
15	Karunagappalli ...	3,637	1,812	1,825	...	...
16	Kartigappalli ...	3,720	1,901	1,819	...	...
17	Mavellikkara ...	7,109	3,644	3,465	...	...
18	Chenganur ...	12,526	6,406	6,120	...	...
19	Tiruvalla ...	21,127	10,768	10,359	...	...
20	Ambalappula ...	9,427	5,002	4,425	...	...
21	Sherttala ...	11,300	5,704	5,596	...	...
22	Vykkam ...	5,514	2,814	2,700	...	...
23	Ettumanur ...	15,239	7,702	7,537	...	...
24	Kottayam ...	12,494	6,370	6,124	...	...
25	Changanacheri ...	12,589	6,416	6,173	...	...
26	Meenachal ...	15,212	7,821	7,391	...	...
27	Muvattupula ...	21,014	10,666	10,348	...	...
28	Todupula ...	3,597	1,834	1,763	...	...
29	Kunnattunadu ...	17,194	8,745	8,449	...	...
30	Alangadu ...	9,756	4,968	4,788	...	...
31	Parur ...	6,828	3,523	3,305	...	...
	Cardamom Hills ...	470	352	118	...	...
	Periyar and Thekkadi.	247	218	29	...	...
	Total ...	243,189	124,180	119,009	...	...

VIII.

Part (D)—Christian—(*Continued*).

RIED.

PERIODS.

5—9.		10—14.		15—19.		20—24.	
Males.	Females.	Males.	Females.	Males.	Females.	Males.	Females.
8	9	10	11	12	13	14	15
1	3	2	18	6	57	43	76
6	9	9	24	36	293	220	554
12	17	27	105	111	541	399	913
2	10	4	21	43	213	166	359
2	16	6	51	66	306	219	448
...	7	11	95	81	497	313	469
3	3	11	26	43	177	152	367
1	1	3	8	3	39	17	46
...	...	...	4	3	30	21	54
1	10	31	207	208	342	302	338
...	7	4	56	61	143	147	168
...	...	1	3	3	9	9	19
18	16	19	123	121	409	322	563
5	10	15	112	149	339	308	348
5	1	11	56	73	220	189	317
2	5	9	74	100	287	257	326
16	19	36	174	212	498	459	594
25	26	169	393	623	1,029	953	1,036
12	33	102	662	750	1,668	1,486	1,815
...	15	10	161	200	644	630	761
15	15	30	97	153	668	584	1,132
4	14	30	99	149	366	342	458
2	22	51	241	417	1,087	1,043	1,241
2	7	53	244	398	945	900	1,037
13	11	22	173	265	820	820	1,134
10	46	86	317	766	1,356	1,300	1,347
5	12	162	551	831	1,413	1,380	1,724
...	8	17	58	146	316	262	313
4	12	40	174	362	903	1,059	1,421
7	6	34	118	378	604	500	791
1	4	21	37	77	379	384	657
...	...	1	...	6	5	51	28
...	...	1	...	3	1	11	7
174	365	1,028	4,482	6,843	16,604	15,248	20,861

TABLE

Civil Condition by Religion and Age,

Number.	Taluq.	(2) MAR Age 25—29. Males.	25—29. Females.	30—34. Males.	30—34. Females.	35—39. Males.	35—39. Females.
1	2	16	17	18	19	20	21
1	Tovala ...	61	88	72	56	74	38
2	Agastiswaram ...	432	570	485	469	491	347
3	Eranial ...	874	1,184	880	818	984	583
4	Kalkulam ...	312	420	317	301	353	214
5	Vilavankodu ...	387	450	362	304	357	226
6	Neyattankara ...	478	496	359	356	538	349
7	Trivandram ...	258	410	338	272	315	199
8	Nedumangadu ...	54	58	48	53	61	26
9	Sirayinkil ...	38	75	55	52	55	33
10	Kottarakkara ...	353	327	260	272	322	277
11	Pattanapuram ...	168	165	131	121	174	112
12	Shenkotta ...	17	18	18	12	12	9
13	Quilon ...	580	654	480	503	517	392
14	Kunnattur ..	360	362	281	279	292	197
15	Karunagappalli ...	304	376	239	264	270	217
16	Kartigappalli ...	323	339	272	223	277	207
17	Mavellikkara ...	618	629	497	458	502	387
18	Chenganur ...	1,018	1,042	806	649	789	642
19	Tiruvalla ...	1,841	1,718	1,449	1,224	1,421	1,113
20	Ambalappula ...	851	674	747	547	724	505
21	Sherttala ...	924	1,207	883	801	958	659
22	Vykkam ...	446	497	371	389	448	280
23	Ettumanur ...	1,248	1,231	964	1,010	1,147	811
24	Kottayam ...	992	1,022	795	740	923	672
25	Changanacheri ...	953	1,063	1,020	917	1,009	615
26	Meenachal ...	1,292	1,184	1,037	877	979	720
27	Muvattupula ...	1,808	1,883	1,519	1,393	1,542	1.209
28	Todupula ...	331	328	259	219	256	203
29	Kunnattunadu ...	1,448	1,545	1,329	1,264	1,307	1,066
30	Alangadu ...	792	947	691	627	796	653
31	Parur ...	544	637	627	539	571	367
	Cardamom Hills ...	84	25	66	25	75	17
	Periyar & Thekkadi.	45	12	54	6	41	3
	Total ...	20,234	21,636	17,711	16,040	18,580	13,348

VIII.

Part (D)—Christian—(*Continued*).

RIED—(*Continued*).

PERIODS—(*Continued*).

40—44.		45—49.		50—54.		55—59.		60 and over.	
Males.	Females.	Males.	Females.	Males.	Females.	Males.	Females.	Males.	Females.
22	23	24	25	26	27	28	29	30	31
53	20	20	11	18	4	6	9	12	6
406	253	300	120	202	95	104	41	172	88
737	386	463	242	341	195	206	111	399	133
242	136	187	75	150	57	86	27	141	58
319	133	209	95	143	51	70	13	143	17
390	225	306	137	176	44	120	24	208	55
244	129	150	94	112	54	64	49	128	44
29	26	32	12	28	6	7	4	27	3
42	27	26	16	25	11	17	2	33	1
248	163	192	136	156	99	85	55	170	78
98	70	80	51	62	41	51	26	60	24
8	6	7	5	1	5	6	5	2	1
439	291	303	202	250	163	178	78	308	91
212	161	153	131	133	99	97	72	158	57
195	139	181	93	141	61	73	40	131	41
211	138	148	91	129	57	88	42	85	30
372	266	319	158	234	119	173	74	206	89
525	403	504	345	371	239	296	168	327	148
1,074	789	838	565	694	334	490	237	611	201
568	381	419	310	362	222	211	115	280	90
721	403	551	285	344	120	257	121	284	88
305	215	245	152	200	121	127	63	147	46
844	604	613	458	531	356	341	276	501	200
635	479	588	396	414	257	293	195	377	130
665	474	516	336	435	262	279	161	419	207
709	494	530	384	432	251	283	194	397	221
1,097	743	786	631	667	371	388	223	481	195
177	136	155	67	87	55	72	34	72	26
1,035	815	748	522	614	323	326	223	473	181
603	368	428	292	312	194	172	111	255	77
428	245	281	173	232	114	154	94	203	59
43	12	17	3	4	2	4	...	1	1
27	...	22	...	4	...	7	...	3	...
13,701	9,130	10,317	6,588	8,004	4,382	5,131	2,887	7,209	2,686

TABLE

Civil Condition by Religion and Age,

Number.	Taluq.	(3) Wi — Total Widowed. Total.	Males.	Females.	Age 0—4. Males.	Females.
1	2	3	4	5	6	7
1	Tovala ...	187	33	154	...	...
2	Agastiswaram ...	1,479	350	1,129	...	...
3	Eranial ...	2,721	714	2,007	...	...
4	Kalkulam ...	746	138	608	...	...
5	Vilavankodu ...	637	167	470	...	...
6	Neyattankara ...	391	107	284	...	...
7	Trivandram ...	527	143	384	...	...
8	Nedumangadu ...	99	38	61	...	...
9	Sirayinkil ...	130	28	102	...	...
10	Kottarakkara ...	509	115	394	...	...
11	Pattanapuram ...	196	45	151	...	...
12	Shenkotta ...	42	12	30	...	...
13	Quilon ...	1,265	357	908	...	...
14	Kunnattur ...	629	160	469	...	...
15	Karunagappalli ...	803	224	579	..	...
16	Kartigappalli ...	697	174	523	...	...
17	Mavelikkara ...	1,003	331	672	...	...
18	Chenganur ...	1,395	347	1,048	...	...
19	Tiruvalla ...	2,445	706	1,739	...	...
20	Ambalappula ...	1,318	385	933	...	...
21	Sherttala ...	1,618	515	1,173	...	...
22	Vykkam ...	773	253	520	...	...
23	Ettumanur ...	1,761	622	1,139	...	...
24	Kottayam ...	1,362	357	1,005	...	...
25	Changanacheri ...	1,556	499	1,057	...	...
26	Meenachal ...	1,994	582	1,412	...	...
27	Muvattupula ...	2,853	828	2,025	...	...
28	Todupula ...	498	159	339	...	...
29	Kunnattunadu ...	2,266	802	1,464	...	...
30	Alangadu ...	1,385	552	833	...	...
31	Parur ...	1,096	287	809	...	...
	Cardamom Hills ...	21	7	14	...	...
	Periyar & Thekkadi ...	17	11	6	...	...
	Total ...	34,489	10,048	24,441	...	...

VIII.

Part (D)—Christian—(*Continued*).

DOWED.

PERIODS.

5—9.		10—14.		15—19.		20—24.	
Males.	Females.	Males.	Females.	Males.	Females.	Males.	Females.
8	9	10	11	12	13	14	15
...	...	...	1	1	1	1	7
1	...	...	3	1	9	28	22
1	1	6	6	3	22	18	52
...	2	1	3	1	3	4	9
...	...	...	...	2	...	3	4
...	...	3	...	4	2	2	1
1	...	...	...	...	7	2	6
...	...	3	...	2	2	1	1
...	1	...	...	...	...	...	2
4	...	1	1	1	1	1	4
...	...	...	...	...	1	...	1
...	1	2	2	...	2	...	...
1	2	2	2	...	14	7	26
2	...	4	1	...	4	4	5
...	2	...	...	...	3	...	3
...	...	...	...	...	1	2	6
2	3	1	1	...	1	5	7
3	...	4	5	6	4	5	15
3	1	3	...	1	2	5	16
...	...	1	1	...	...	8	12
1	2	2	2	...	4	3	30
3	...	4	...	1	2	4	3
2	...	4	5	7	4	5	6
2	4	3	3	1	2	3	16
1	5	1	2	4	4	3	13
...	1	...	1	2	7	10	17
...	2	1	4	8	9	8	22
...	...	1	...	1	...	...	4
...	...	...	6	...	4	2	6
...	...	...	1	2	9	...	17
1	1	...	2	1	6	3	21
...	...	...	...	...	...	...	...
...	...	...	...	...	...	...	...
28	28	47	52	49	130	137	354

TABLE

Civil Condition by Religion and Age,

Number.	Taluq.	(3) WI					
		Age					
		25—29.		30—34.		35—39.	
		Males.	Females.	Males.	Females.	Males.	Females.
1	2	16	17	18	19	20	21
1	Tovala ...	4	16	4	15	5	21
2	Agastiswaram ...	23	54	18	100	30	139
3	Eranial ...	20	94	49	164	50	172
4	Kalkulam ...	5	23	12	63	14	66
5	Vilavankodu ...	8	15	7	38	6	42
6	Neyattankara ...	2	7	5	11	6	11
7	Trivandram ...	4	28	7	30	8	29
8	Nedumangadu ...	...	2	2	3	...	8
9	Sirayinkil ...	1	6	4	13	4	9
10	Kottarakkara ...	1	10	4	23	5	27
11	Pattanapuram ...	...	5	...	8	2	9
12	Shenkotta ...	...	...	...	...	...	4
13	Quilon ...	7	39	16	67	18	68
14	Kunnattur ...	2	15	6	16	8	29
15	Karunagappalli ...	3	8	4	23	7	49
16	Kartigappalli ...	3	9	4	13	5	20
17	Mavellikkara ...	5	15	10	28	10	35
18	Chenganur ...	7	21	12	33	18	68
19	Tiruvalla ...	8	37	14	58	20	90
20	Ambalappula ...	6	34	8	35	20	51
21	Sherttala ...	10	29	25	70	34	90
22	Vykkam ...	7	14	8	25	13	37
23	Ettumanur ...	11	24	13	30	24	60
24	Kottayam ...	12	34	14	37	17	71
25	Changanacheri ...	6	22	34	32	24	63
26	Meenachal ...	16	52	25	80	47	84
27	Muvattupula ...	30	72	35	105	58	127
28	Todupula ...	5	6	7	15	11	22
29	Kunnattunadu ...	4	14	12	42	22	60
30	Alangadu ...	12	36	19	31	21	53
31	Parur ...	6	35	16	59	17	72
	Cardamom Hills ...	1	1	1	1	...	...
	Periyar & Thekkadi	1	...	1	2	4	2
	Total ...	230	777	396	1,270	528	1,688

VIII.

Part (D)—Christian—(*Continued*).

DOWED—(*Continued*).

PERIODS—(*Continued*).

40—44.		45—49.		50—54.		55—59.		60 and over.	
Males.	Females.	Males.	Females.	Males.	Females.	Males.	Females.	Males.	Females.
22	23	24	25	26	27	28	29	30	31
2	22	5	17	3	21	3	11	5	22
39	180	35	124	55	170	38	74	87	254
79	327	62	197	96	281	73	187	257	504
16	88	19	76	20	106	9	46	37	123
25	81	22	61	21	70	11	38	62	121
4	40	11	28	6	41	16	35	48	108
16	51	16	45	15	66	16	26	58	96
6	12	6	12	5	7	5	2	8	12
2	14	5	3	4	12	3	6	5	36
7	27	9	50	24	68	13	34	45	149
3	14	8	13	3	17	7	16	22	67
4	5	1	1	2	8	1	4	2	3
58	105	37	97	45	135	43	95	123	258
9	38	19	47	19	83	22	84	65	147
16	64	16	64	16	83	34	87	128	193
17	52	13	66	27	98	40	91	63	167
24	59	19	81	49	85	41	65	165	292
28	93	23	100	37	177	47	124	157	408
42	153	45	187	92	275	142	245	331	675
36	119	44	107	59	136	65	145	143	293
67	125	47	130	64	177	85	151	177	363
23	66	32	71	38	82	44	70	76	150
55	97	57	127	90	194	85	168	269	424
29	86	32	120	56	154	52	105	131	373
43	120	45	107	50	162	74	114	209	413
45	134	61	138	79	227	74	186	223	485
82	220	77	198	121	333	94	211	314	722
19	40	23	46	21	55	19	42	52	109
56	144	85	175	176	288	150	275	295	450
39	78	42	89	58	115	125	149	234	255
25	93	41	105	39	102	33	119	105	194
3	5	1	2	1	2	...	2	...	1
...	1	1	...	4	1	...	...	...	...
919	2,753	959	2,684	1,395	3,831	1,464	3,007	3,896	7,867

TABLE VIII.

Civil Condition by Religion and Age, Part (E)—Jain.

Number.	Taluq.	(1) UNMARRIED. Total Unmarried.			Age Periods. 0—4.		5—9.		10—14.		15—19.		20—24.	
		Total.	Males.	Females.	Males.	Females.	Males.	Females.	Males.	Females.	Males.	Females.	Males.	Females.
1	2	3	4	5	6	7	8	9	10	11	12	13	14	15
30	Alangadu	3	3	...	...	...	...	...	...	...	1	...	1	...

Number.	Taluq.	(1) UNMARRIED—(Continued). Age Periods—(Continued). 25—29.		30—34.		35—39.		40—44.		45—49.		50—54.		55—59.		60 and over.	
		Males.	Females.	Males.	Females.	Males.	Females.	Males.	Females.	Males.	Females.	Males.	Females.	Males.	Females.	Males.	Females.
1	2	16	17	18	19	20	21	22	23	24	25	26	27	28	29	30	31
30	Alangadu	...	...	1	...	...	...	...	...	...	..	...	...	...	...	...	...

TABLE VIII.

Civil Condition by Religion and Age, Part (E)—Jain—(*Continued*).

Number.	TALUQ.	(2) MARRIED.													
		TOTAL MARRIED.			AGE PERIODS.										
					0—4.		5—9.		10—14.		15—19.		20—24.		
		Total.	Males.	Females.	Males.	Females.	Males.	Females.	Males.	Females.	Males.	Females.	Males.	Females.	
1	2	3	4	5	6	7	8	9	10	11	12	13	14	15	
	Periyar and Thekkadi	7	5	2	...	...	...	...	...	...	...	...	...	1	

Number.	TALUQ.	(2) MARRIED—(*Continued*).															
		AGE PERIODS—(*Continued*).															
		25—29.		30—34.		35—39.		40—44.		45—49.		50—54.		55—59.		60 and over.	
		Males.	Females.	Males.	Females.	Males.	Females.	Males.	Females.	Males.	Females.	Males.	Females.	Males.	Females.	Males.	Females.
1	2	16	17	18	19	20	21	22	23	24	25	26	27	28	29	30	31
	Periyar and Thekkadi	2	1	2	...	1	...	...	...	...	...	...	...	...	...	...	...

TABLE VIII.
Civil Condition by Religion and Age, Part (F)—Parsi.

Number.	Taluq.	(2) Married.														
		Total Married.			Age Periods.											
					0—4.		5—9.		10—14.		15—19.		20—24.			
		Total.	Males.	Females.	Males.	Females.	Males.	Females.	Males.	Females.	Males.	Females.	Males.	Females.		
1	2	3	4	5	6	7	8	9	10	11	12	13	14	15		
7	Trivandram	1	1	...	...	...	...	...	...	...	...	...	...	...		

Number.	Taluq.	(2) Married—(Continued).															
		Age Periods—(Continued).															
		25—29.		30—34.		35—39.		40—44.		45—49.		50—54.		55—59.		60 and over.	
		Males.	Females.	Males.	Females.	Males.	Females.	Males.	Females.	Males.	Females.	Males.	Females.	Males.	Females.	Males.	Females.
1	2	16	17	18	19	20	21	22	23	24	25	26	27	28	29	30	31
7	Trivandram	...	...	...	...	...	...	...	...	...	...	...	...	1	...	...	...

TABLE VIII.

Civil Condition by Religion and Age, Part (G)—Jew.

Number.	Taluq.	(1) Unmarried. Total Unmarried.			Age Periods. 0—4.		5—9.		10—14		15—19.		20—24.	
		Total.	Males.	Females.	Males.	Females.	Males.	Females.	Males.	Females.	Males.	Females.	Males.	Females.
1	2	3	4	5	6	7	8	9	10	11	12	13	14	15
13	Quilon	5	3	2	1	...	...	1	...	...	1	...	...	...
31	Parur	61	36	25	8	6	9	7	4	8	5	3	4	1
	Total ...	66	39	27	9	6	9	8	4	8	6	3	4	1

TABLE VIII.

Civil Condition by Religion and Age, Part (G)—Jew—(*Continued*).

Number.	Taluq.	(1) UNMARRIED—(*Continued*). Age Periods—(*Continued*). 25—29. Males.	25—29. Females.	30—34. Males.	30—34. Females.	35—39. Males.	35—39. Females.	40—44. Males.	40—44. Females.	45—49. Males.	45—49. Females.	50—54. Males.	50—54. Females.	55—59. Males.	55—59. Females.	60 and over. Males.	60 and over. Females.
1	2	16	17	18	19	20	21	22	23	24	25	26	27	28	29	30	31
13	Quilon	...	1	...	...	1	...	...	...	...	...	...	...	...	...	...	...
31	Parur	6	...	...	...	...	...	...	...	...	...	...	...	...	...	...	...
	Total ...	6	1	...	...	1	...	...	...	...	...	...	...	...	...	...	...

TABLE VIII.

Civil Condition by Religion and Age, Part (G)—Jew—(*Continued*).

Number.	Taluq.	(2) Married.													
		Total Married.			Age Periods.										
					0—4.		5—9.		10—14.		15—19.		20—24.		
		Total.	Males.	Females.	Males.	Females.	Males.	Females.	Males.	Females.	Males.	Females.	Males.	Females.
1	2	3	4	5	6	7	8	9	10	11	12	13	14	15
13	Quilon	4	2	2	...	...	...	...	...	...	...	...	...	...
31	Parur	46	23	23	...	...	...	...	...	1	...	3	1	3
	Total ...	50	25	25	...	...	...	...	...	1	...	3	1	3

TABLE VIII.

Civil Condition by Religion and Age, Part (G)—Jew—(*Continued*).

Number.	Taluq.	(2) MARRIED—(*Continued*). Age Periods—(*Continued*). 25—29. Males.	25—29. Females.	30—34. Males.	30—34. Females.	35—39. Males.	35—39. Females.	40—44. Males.	40—44. Females.	45—49. Males.	45—49. Females.	50—54. Males.	50—54. Females.	55—59. Males.	55—59. Females.	60 & over. Males.	60 & over. Females.
1	2	16	17	18	19	20	21	22	23	24	25	26	27	28	29	30	31
13	Quilon	...	1	...	...	1	...	...	...	...	...	...	1	...	...	1	...
31	Parur	...	9	3	1	5	1	4	3	3	2	4	...	1	...	2	...
	Total ...	...	10	3	1	6	1	4	3	3	2	4	1	1	...	3	...

TABLE VIII.

Civil Condition by Religion and Age, Part (G)—Jew—(*Continued*).

Number.	Taluq.	(3) Widowed.													
		Total Widowed.			Age Periods.										
					0—4.		5—9.		10—14.		15—19.		20—24.		
		Total.	Males.	Females.	Males.	Females.	Males.	Females.	Males.	Females.	Males.	Females.	Males.	Females.
1	2	3	4	5	6	7	8	9	10	11	12	13	14	15
13	Quilon	1	...	1	...	...	...	...	...	...	...	...	...	...
31	Parur	8	1	7	...	...	...	...	...	...	...	...	...	...
	Total ...	9	1	8	...	...	...	...	...	...	...	...	...	...

TABLE VIII.

Civil Condition by Religion and Age, Part (G)—Jew—(*Continued*).

Number.	Taluq.	(3) WIDOWED—(*Continued*). Age Periods—(*Continued*). 25—29. Males.	25—29. Females.	30—34. Males.	30—34. Females.	35—39. Males.	35—39. Females.	40—44. Males.	40—44. Females.	45—49. Males.	45—49. Females.	50—54. Males.	50—54. Females.	55—59. Males.	55—59. Females.	60 & over. Males.	60 & over. Females.
1	2	16	17	18	19	20	21	22	23	24	25	26	27	28	29	30	31
13	Quilon	...	...	...	...	...	...	...	1	...	...	...	...	...	...	...	...
31	Parur	1	1	...	1	...	...	...	...	...	...	...	3	...	...	...	2
	Total ...	1	1	...	1	...	...	...	1	...	...	...	3	...	..	...	2

TABLE VIII.
Civil Condition by Religion and Age, Part (H)—None.

Number.	Taluq.	(1) Unmarried.												
		Total Unmarried.			Age Periods.									
					0—4.		5—9.		10—14.		15—19.		20—24.	
		Total.	Males.	Females.	Males.	Females.	Males.	Females.	Males.	Females.	Males.	Females.	Males.	Females.
1	2	3	4	5	6	7	8	9	10	11	12	13	14	15
	Periyar and Thekkadi	2	2	...	...	...	...	...	...	...	...	...	...	...

Number.	Taluq.	(1) Unmarried—(Continued).															
		Age Periods—(Continued).															
		25—29.		30—34.		35—39.		40—44.		45—49.		50—54.		55—59.		60 and over.	
		Males.	Females.	Males.	Females.	Males.	Females.	Males.	Females.	Males.	Females.	Males.	Females.	Males.	Females.	Males.	Females.
1	2	16	17	18	19	20	21	22	23	24	25	26	27	28	29	30	31
	Periyar and Thekkadi	1	...	1	...	...	...	...	...	...	...	...	...	...	...	...	...

TABLE

Education by Religion and Age,

Number.	Taluq.	Total Population. Total.	Males.	Females.	Total Learning. Males.	Females.
1	2	3	4	5	6	7
1	Tovala ...	29,751	14,489	15,262	612	35
2	Agastiswaram ...	87,241	43,226	44,015	1,730	459
3	Eranial ...	105,098	52,883	52,215	1,912	251
4	Kalkulam ...	59,474	29,834	29,640	756	111
5	Vilavankodu ...	68,521	35,202	33,319	903	111
6	Neyattankara ...	110,755	56,953	53,802	2,992	272
7	Trivandram ...	111,938	56,909	55,029	4,769	1,375
8	Nedumangadu ...	55,497	27,857	27,640	760	193
9	Sirayinkil ...	97,995	48,271	49,724	1,506	328
10	Kottarakkara ...	71,517	36,055	35,462	1,031	328
11	Pattanapuram ...	39,447	19,858	19,589	403	84
12	Shenkotta ...	32,088	15,700	16,388	674	60
13	Quilon ...	121.935	60,832	61,103	3,920	548
14	Kunnattur ...	73,529	37,397	36,132	575	65
15	Karunagappalli ...	108,826	52,862	55,964	1,470	308
16	Kartigappalli ...	91,950	45,216	46,734	1,669	520
17	Mavellikkara ...	103,619	52,494	51,125	1,863	180
18	Chenganur ...	93,960	48,443	45,517	3,694	246
19	Tiruvalla ...	122,142	62,514	59,628	3,893	429
20	Ambalappula ...	94,745	46,909	47,836	2,054	242
21	Sherttala ...	117,261	58,448	58,813	3,275	785
22	Vykkam ...	80,628	40,947	39,681	716	69
23	Ettumanur ...	80,823	41,536	39,287	1,002	170
24	Kottayam ...	77,094	39,229	37,865	1,676	180
25	Changanacheri ...	74,722	38,596	36,126	1,007	251
26	Meenachal ...	59,976	30,830	29,146	937	286
27	Muvattupula ...	103,009	51,595	51,414	836	168
28	Todupula ...	25,202	12,786	12,416	331	176
29	Kunnattunadu ...	114,049	57,216	56,833	2,178	578
30	Alangadu ...	70,958	35,944	35,014	1,255	642
31	Parur ...	59,278	30,082	29,196	1,456	232
	Cardamom Hills ...	11,413	6,714	4,699	98	2
	Periyar & Thekkadi	3,295	2,588	707	2	3
	Total ...	2,557,736	1,290,415	1,267,321	51,955	9,687

IX.

Part (A)—Total Population.

By Education.						Age Periods.	
Literate.		Illiterate.		Not stated.		0—14. Total.	
Males.	Females.	Males.	Females.	Males.	Females.	Males.	Females.
8	9	10	11	12	13	14	15
2,837	82	11,040	15,145	...	...	5,035	5,211
9,517	1,921	31,979	41,635	...	...	15,530	15,798
9,138	1,084	41,833	50,880	...	...	19,050	19,670
4,569	332	24,509	29,197	...	...	10,674	10,890
5,628	485	28,671	32,723	...	...	12,251	12,469
9,426	625	44,535	52,905	...	...	18,431	19,064
15,364	3,201	36,776	50,453	...	...	18,885	19,024
3,945	547	23,152	26,900	...	...	9,771	10,070
7,422	726	39,343	48,670	...	...	18,571	17,902
4,438	1,369	30,586	33,765	...	...	13,583	13,681
3,046	233	16,409	19,272	...	...	6,500	6,977
2,395	98	12,631	16,230	...	...	5,888	5,941
11,365	1,058	45,542	59,496	5	1	22,867	22,563
3,582	251	33,240	35,816	...	...	13,774	13,017
5,760	812	45,632	54,844	...	...	19,890	20,168
8,247	1,293	35,300	44,921	...	...	16,227	16,668
8,211	546	42,420	50,399	...	...	17,876	17,563
10,731	447	34,018	44,824	...	...	17,686	16,815
16,614	1,624	42,007	57,575	...	...	22,074	21,971
11,924	793	32,931	46,801	...	...	16,740	17,393
17,707	2,593	37,466	55,435	...	...	18,630	19,892
7,755	487	32,476	39,125	...	...	14,167	13,623
11,021	1,082	29,513	38,085	...	...	14,865	14,818
8,755	1,369	28,798	36,316	...	...	14,466	14,447
7,886	1,258	29,703	34,622	...	...	13,382	13,148
11,099	864	18,794	27,996	...	...	11,528	11,472
6,730	2,537	44,029	48,709	...	...	19,953	20,215
1,656	1,214	10,799	11,026	...	...	5,063	4,904
8,556	2,488	46,482	53,822	...	...	21,201	21,783
5,159	2,124	29,530	32,248	...	...	13,670	13,600
5,047	657	23,579	28,307	...	...	11,862	11,977
454	24	6,162	4,673	...	...	1,861	1,731
573	25	2,013	679	...	...	275	196
246,557	34,139	991,898	1,223,494	5	1	462,226	464,661

TABLE

Education by Religion and Age,

Number.	Taluq.	Age 0—14. Learning. Males.	Learning. Females.	Literate. Males.	Literate. Females.	Illiterate. Males.	Illiterate. Females.
1	2	16	17	18	19	20	21
1	Tovala ...	577	35	182	19	4,276	5,157
2	Agastiswaram ...	1,647	457	987	173	12,896	15,168
3	Eranial ...	1,724	232	443	101	16,883	19,337
4	Kalkulam ...	651	106	218	92	9,805	10,692
5	Vilavankodu ...	801	108	367	108	11,083	12,253
6	Neyattankara ...	2,741	257	127	77	15,563	18,730
7	Trivandram ...	3,883	1,247	769	421	14,233	17,356
8	Nedumangadu ...	661	154	313	146	8,797	9,770
9	Sirayinkil ...	1,289	309	647	125	16,635	17,468
10	Kottarakkara ...	803	202	733	603	12,047	12,876
11	Pattanapuram ...	328	47	210	39	5,962	6,891
12	Shenkotta ...	659	60	92	12	5,137	5,869
13	Quilon ...	3,418	424	770	236	18,677	21,903
14	Kunnattur ...	539	61	118	18	13,117	12,938
15	Karunagappalli ...	1,371	297	385	62	18,134	19,809
16	Kartigappalli ...	1,361	297	500	274	14,366	16,097
17	Mavellikkara ...	1,679	176	481	134	15,716	17,253
18	Chenganur ...	3,476	239	108	5	14,102	16,571
19	Tiruvalla ...	3,560	418	868	183	17,646	21,370
20	Ambalappula ...	1,791	235	596	84	14,353	17,074
21	Sherttala ...	2,925	750	1,025	253	14,680	18,889
22	Vykkam ...	642	65	364	40	13,161	13,518
23	Ettumanur ...	902	163	557	66	13,406	14,589
24	Kottayam ...	1,625	180	483	139	12,858	14,128
25	Changanacheri ...	914	231	631	162	11,837	12,755
26	Meenachal ...	901	279	790	107	9,837	11,086
27	Muvattupula ...	724	94	1,166	1,206	18,063	18,915
28	Todupula ...	239	68	394	356	4,430	4,480
29	Kunnattunadu ...	1,592	230	187	143	19,422	21,410
30	Alangadu ...	1,172	614	695	269	11,803	12,717
31	Parur ...	1,303	200	166	55	10,393	11,722
	Cardamom Hills ...	11	...	1	...	1,849	1,731
	Periyar & Thekkadi.	2	3	22	5	251	188
	Total ...	45,911	8,238	15,395	5,713	400,918	450,710

IX.

Part (A)—Total Population—(*Continued*).

PERIODS—(*Continued*).

Not stated.		15—24.					
		Total.		Learning.		Literate.	
Males.	Females.	Males.	Females.	Males.	Females.	Males.	Females.
22	23	24	25	26	27	28	29
...	...	2,424	2,773	35	...	692	42
...	...	7,432	7,997	83	2	2,439	507
...	...	9,013	9,031	188	15	2,057	193
...	...	5,685	5,891	98	5	1,183	104
...	...	6,768	6,879	92	1	1,357	158
...	...	10,587	11,975	216	9	2,788	252
...	...	11,077	11,924	849	112	3,934	1,209
...	...	4,922	6,030	75	28	981	134
...	...	8,285	10,032	153	6	1,827	253
...	...	6,036	6,492	102	72	976	129
...	...	3,495	3,842	33	12	706	67
...	...	2,693	2,872	11	...	629	31
2	...	10,775	11,686	357	28	3,224	431
...	...	6,158	6,452	25	...	769	33
...	...	8,819	10,392	95	11	1,562	341
...	...	7,857	9,131	162	210	1,947	296
...	...	9,094	9,758	182	4	2,060	195
...	...	8,918	8,537	218	7	3,357	161
...	...	10,995	11,367	332	11	4,420	484
...	...	8,603	9,257	229	4	2,928	261
...	...	9,710	11,817	337	31	3,860	940
...	...	7,121	7,782	58	3	1,781	151
...	...	7,146	7,272	93	7	2,616	243
...	...	7,045	7,101	49	...	2,354	724
...	...	6,374	6,897	98	20	1,658	295
...	...	5,897	5,917	36	5	3,038	345
...	...	8,520	9,070	19	11	895	218
...	...	2,366	2,544	15	28	322	209
...	...	9,470	10,351	39	27	1,809	281
...	...	5,980	6,743	38	9	1,127	498
.	...	5,356	5,546	130	11	1,264	192
...	...	1,583	1,080	18	...	120	2
...	...	681	174	...	...	166	7
2	...	226,885	244,562	4,455	689	60,846	9,381

TABLE

Education by Religion and Age,

Number.	Taluq.	Age 15—24. Illiterate. Males.	Illiterate. Females.	Not stated. Males.	Not stated. Females.	Total. Males.	Total. Females.
1	2	30	31	32	33	34	35
1	Tovala ...	1,697	2,731	...	...	7,030	7,278
2	Agastiswaram ...	4,910	7,488	...	...	20,264	20,220
3	Eranial ...	6,773	8,823	...	...	24,820	23,514
4	Kalkulam ...	4,404	5,782	...	...	13,475	12,859
5	Vilavankodu ...	5,319	6,720	...	...	16,183	13,971
6	Neyattankara ...	7,583	11,714	...	...	27,935	22,763
7	Trivandram ...	6,294	10,603	...	...	26,947	24,081
8	Nedumangadu ...	3,866	5,868	...	...	13,164	11,540
9	Sirayinkil ...	6,805	9,773	...	...	21,415	21,790
10	Kottarakkara ...	4,958	6,291	...	...	16,436	15,289
11	Pattanapuram ...	2,756	3,763	...	...	9,863	8,770
12	Shenkotta ...	2,053	2,841	...	...	7,119	7,575
13	Quilon ...	7,194	11,227	...	...	27,190	26,854
14	Kunnattur ...	5,364	6,419	...	...	17,465	16,663
15	Karunagappalli ...	7,162	10,040	...	...	24,153	25,404
16	Kartigappalli ...	5,748	8,625	...	...	21,132	20,935
17	Mavellikkara ...	6,852	9,559	...	...	25,524	23,804
18	Chenganur ...	5,343	8,369	...	...	21,839	20,165
19	Tiruvalla ...	6,243	10,872	...	...	29,445	26,290
20	Ambalappula ...	5,446	8,992	...	...	21,566	21,186
21	Sherttala ...	5,513	10,846	...	...	30,108	27,104
22	Vykkam ...	5,282	7,628	...	...	19,659	18,276
23	Ettumanur ...	4,437	7,022	...	...	19,525	17,197
24	Kottayam ...	4,642	6,377	...	...	17,718	16,317
25	Changanacheri ...	4,623	6,582	...	...	18,840	16,081
26	Meenachal ...	2,823	5,567	...	...	13,405	11,757
27	Muvattupula ...	7,606	8,846	...	...	23,122	22,129
28	Todupula ...	2,029	2,307	...	...	5,357	4,968
29	Kunnattunadu ...	7,622	10,043	...	...	26,545	24,699
30	Alangadu ...	4,815	6,236	...	...	16,294	14,671
31	Parur ...	3,962	5,343	...	...	12,864	11,673
	Cardamom Hills ...	1,445	1,028	...	...	3,270	1,938
	Periyar & Thekkadi.	515	167	...	...	1,632	337
	Total ...	161,584	234,492	...	...	601,304	558,098

IX.

Part (A)—Total Population—(*Continued*).

Periods—(*Continued*).

25 and over.

Learning.		Literate.		Illiterate.		Not stated.	
Males.	Females.	Males.	Females.	Males.	Females.	Males.	Females.
36	37	38	39	40	41	42	43
...	...	1,963	21	5,067	7,257	...	...
...	...	6,091	1,241	14,173	18,979	...	...
5	4	6,638	790	18,177	22,720	...	...
7	...	3,168	136	10,300	12,723	...	...
10	2	3,904	219	12,269	13,750	...	...
35	6	6,511	296	21,389	22,461	...	...
37	16	10,661	1,571	16,249	22,494	...	...
24	11	2,651	267	10,489	11,262	...	...
64	13	4,948	348	16,403	21,429	...	...
126	54	2,729	637	13,581	14,598	...	...
42	25	2,130	127	7,691	8,618	...	...
4	...	1,674	55	5,441	7,520	...	...
145	96	7,371	391	19,671	26,366	3	1
11	4	2,695	200	14,759	16,459	...	...
4	...	3,813	409	20,336	24,995	...	...
146	13	5,800	723	15,186	20,199	...	...
2	...	5,670	217	19,852	23,587	...	...
...	...	7,266	281	14,573	19,884	...	...
1	...	11,326	957	18,118	25,333	...	...
34	3	8,400	448	13,132	20,735	...	...
13	4	12,822	1,400	17,273	25,700	...	...
16	1	5,610	296	14,033	17,979	...	...
7	...	7,848	723	11,670	16,474	...	...
2	...	5,918	506	11,798	15,811	...	...
...	...	5,597	796	13,243	15,285	...	...
...	2	7,271	412	6,134	11,343	...	...
98	63	4,669	1,118	18,360	20,948	..	...
77	80	940	649	4,340	4,239	...	...
547	321	6,560	2,009	19,438	22,369	...	...
45	19	3,337	1,357	12,912	13,295	...	...
23	21	3,617	410	9,224	11,242	...	...
69	2	333	22	2,868	1,914	...	...
...	...	385	13	1,247	324	...	...
1,589	760	170,316	19,045	429,396	538,292	3	1

TABLE

Education by Religion and Age,

Number.	Taluq.	Total Hindu. Total.	Total Hindu. Males.	Total Hindu. Females.	Total — Learning. Males.	Total — Learning. Females.
1	2	3	4	5	6	7
1	Tovala	26,822	13,107	13,715	576	31
2	Agastiswaram	68,634	33,920	34,714	1,382	252
3	Eranial	74,383	37,597	36,786	1,521	173
4	Kalkulam	47,117	23,607	23,510	679	111
5	Vilavankodu	56,718	29,108	27,610	801	99
6	Neyattankara	93,618	48,144	45,474	2,584	207
7	Trivandram	93,468	47,760	45,708	4,229	1,113
8	Nedumangadu	50,766	25,345	25,421	728	175
9	Sirayinkil	83,105	40,937	42,168	1,376	304
10	Kottarakkara	57,393	28,873	28,520	840	268
11	Pattanapuram	31,453	15,877	15,576	333	67
12	Shenkotta	30,033	14,603	15,430	664	56
13	Quilon	90,737	45,136	45,601	2,983	332
14	Kunnattur	61,948	31,606	30,342	454	55
15	Karunagappalli ..	86,968	41,679	45,289	1,239	261
16	Kartigappalli	76,849	37,693	39,156	1,443	464
17	Mavellikkara	85,000	42,881	42,119	1,447	131
18	Chenganur	65,795	33,894	31,901	2,080	97
19	Tiruvalla	77,711	39,751	37,960	1,825	172
20	Ambalappula	63,660	31,275	32,385	1,346	170
21	Sherttala	89,561	44,659	44,902	2,483	527
22	Vykkam	65,704	33,190	32,514	618	64
23	Ettumanur	49,356	25,423	23,933	627	102
24	Kottayam	49,756	25,300	24,456	1,001	56
25	Changanacheri	44,698	23,181	21,517	573	105
26	Meenachal	27,797	14,402	13,395	323	78
27	Muvattupula	52,923	26,341	26,582	454	112
28	Todupula	14,714	7,432	7,282	229	132
29	Kunnattunadu	66,116	33,037	33,079	1,487	417
30	Alangadu	38,056	18,967	19,089	888	489
31	Parur	38,216	19,427	18,789	1,041	169
	Cardamom Hills ...	10,235	5,877	4,358	93	2
	Periyar and Thekkadi ...	2,554	1,966	588	2	...
	Total ...	1,871,864	941,995	929,869	38,349	6,791

IX.

Part (B)—Hindu.

BY EDUCATION.						Age Periods.	
Literate.		Illiterate.		Not stated.		0—14.	
						Total.	
Males.	Females.	Males.	Females.	Males.	Females.	Males.	Females.
8	9	10	11	12	13	14	15
2,655	66	9,876	13,618	...	...	4,538	4,669
7,810	1,116	24,728	33,346	...	...	11,908	12,223
6,887	757	29,189	35,856	...	...	13,554	13,797
3,820	302	19,108	23,097	...	...	8,269	8,499
4,769	407	23,538	27,104	...	...	10,104	10,408
8,096	484	37,464	44,783	...	...	15,588	15,870
13,439	2,677	30,092	41,918	...	...	15,540	15,508
3,695	511	20,922	24,735	...	...	8,922	9,246
6,651	667	32,910	41,197	...	...	15,592	14,993
3,530	1,101	24,503	27,151	...	...	10,629	10,628
2,423	192	13,121	15,317	...	...	5,145	5,483
2,343	90	11,596	15,284	...	...	5,445	5,582
9,119	584	33,031	44,684	3	1	16,538	16,406
2,942	216	28,210	30,071	...	...	11,454	10,689
4,800	694	35,640	44,334	...	...	15,463	15,919
6,649	1,223	29,601	37,469	...	...	13,438	13,685
6,421	460	35,013	41,528	...	...	14,327	14,020
6,704	266	25,110	31,538	...	...	11,759	11,163
9,124	968	28,802	36,820	...	...	13,107	12,998
7,823	474	22,106	31,741	...	...	10,860	11,098
13,701	1,688	28,475	42,687	...	...	13,764	14,685
6,004	352	26,568	32,098	...	...	11,349	10,868
6,379	578	18,417	23,253	...	...	8,891	8,700
5,250	765	19,049	23,635	...	...	9,125	8,918
4,380	670	18,228	20,742	...	...	7,520	7,209
4,315	191	9,764	13,126	...	...	5,054	5,017
3,759	1,537	22,128	24,933	...	...	9,653	9,878
1,175	837	6,028	6,313	...	...	2,827	2,736
5,577	1,782	25,973	30,880	...	...	11,951	12,446
3,336	1,635	14,743	16,965	...	...	7,147	7,280
3,350	528	15,036	18,092	...	...	7,538	7,387
248	9	5,536	4,347	...	...	1,719	1,632
300	9	1,664	579	...	...	223	158
177,474	23,836	726,169	899,241	3	1	328,941	329,798

TABLE

Education by Religion and Age,

Number.	Taluq.	Age 0—14. Learning. Males.	Learning. Females.	Literate. Males.	Literate. Females.	Illiterate. Males.	Illiterate. Females.
1	2	16	17	18	19	20	21
1	Tovala ...	544	31	172	19	3,822	4,619
2	Agastiswaram ...	1,311	252	751	98	9,846	11,873
3	Eranial ...	1,383	169	298	64	11,873	13,564
4	Kalkulam ...	587	106	185	85	7,497	8,308
5	Vilavankodu ...	722	96	310	98	9,072	10,214
6	Neyattankara ...	2,395	205	84	58	13,109	15,607
7	Trivandram ...	3,428	1,010	651	362	11,461	14,136
8	Nedumangadu ...	638	142	291	140	7,993	8,964
9	Sirayinkil ...	1,192	288	587	112	13,813	14,593
10	Kottarakkara ...	644	167	575	458	9,410	10,003
11	Pattanapuram ...	282	31	175	33	4,688	5,419
12	Shenkotta ...	649	56	91	12	4,705	5,514
13	Quilon ...	2,655	289	622	139	13,259	15,978
14	Kunnattur ...	430	51	88	6	10,936	10,632
15	Karunagappalli ...	1,152	251	306	50	14,005	15,618
16	Kartigappalli ...	1,175	257	430	263	11,833	13,165
17	Mavelikkara ...	1,295	128	348	116	12,684	13,776
18	Chenganur ...	1,944	94	55	3	9,760	11,066
19	Tiruvalla ...	1,674	172	495	97	10,938	12,729
20	Ambalappula ...	1,184	165	363	43	9,313	10,890
21	Sherttala ...	2,213	520	823	168	10,728	13,997
22	Vykkam ...	549	63	271	28	10,529	10,777
23	Ettumanur ...	598	96	316	35	7,977	8,569
24	Kottayam ...	960	56	279	67	7,886	8,795
25	Changanacheri ...	510	96	335	65	6,675	7,048
26	Meenachal ...	304	77	266	17	4,484	4,923
27	Muvattupula ...	379	39	577	625	8,697	9,214
28	Todupula ...	165	43	274	240	2,388	2,453
29	Kunnattunadu ...	1,049	184	95	76	10,807	12,186
30	Alangadu ...	845	484	449	194	5,853	6,602
31	Parur ...	934	143	97	35	6,507	7,209
	Cardamom Hills ...	9	...	1	...	1,709	1,632
	Periyar & Thekkadi.	2	...	9	2	212	156
	Total ...	33,801	5,761	10,669	3,808	284,469	320,229

IX.

Part (B)—Hindu—(*Continued*).

Periods—(*Continued*).

Not stated.		15—24.					
		Total.		Learning.		Literate.	
Males.	Females.	Males.	Females.	Males.	Females.	Males.	Females.
22	23	24	25	26	27	28	29
...	...	2,198	2,468	32	...	647	38
...	...	5,834	6,261	71	...	1,976	292
...	...	6,391	6,370	135	3	1,521	129
...	...	4,551	4,763	87	5	933	94
...	...	5,635	5,591	77	1	1,155	125
...	...	8,844	10,091	184	2	2,311	196
...	...	9,424	9,929	765	87	3,421	1,004
...	...	4,464	5,551	67	25	927	121
...	...	7,038	8,477	129	5	1,643	232
...	...	4,823	5,836	85	62	752	92
...	...	2,744	3,046	16	11	564	54
...	...	2,488	2,710	11	...	610	27
2	...	8,055	8,809	275	24	2,631	266
...	...	5,209	5,433	16	...	638	28
...	...	6,990	8,454	83	10	1,323	295
...	...	6,485	7,646	131	207	1,583	277
...	...	7,400	8,074	151	3	1,622	164
...	...	6,069	5,960	186	3	1,927	95
...	...	7,055	7,244	151	...	2,427	275
...	...	5,754	6,384	143	2	1,930	158
...	...	7,481	8,962	262	5	3,010	651
...	...	5,743	6,391	53	1	1,440	114
...	...	4,357	4,417	28	6	1,536	136
...	...	4,360	4,583	39	...	1,840	528
...	...	3,832	4,229	68	9	898	121
...	...	2,806	2,784	19	1	1,127	69
...	...	4,451	4,759	9	10	583	122
...	...	1,430	1,478	10	22	251	189
...	...	5,513	5,988	28	17	1,194	206
...	...	3,157	3,708	26	2	747	379
...	...	3,442	3,601	103	5	814	144
...	...	1,346	954	18	...	66	1
...	...	520	156	...	...	100	4
2	...	165,889	180,497	3,398	528	43,597	6,571

TABLE

Education by Religion and Age,

Number.	Taluq.	Age 15—24. Illiterate. Males.	Illiterate. Females.	Not stated. Males.	Not stated. Females.	Total. Males.	Total. Females.
1	2	30	31	32	33	34	35
1	Tovala ...	1,519	2,430	...	...	6,371	6,578
2	Agastiswaram ...	3,787	5,969	...	...	16,178	16,230
3	Eranial ...	4,735	6,238	...	...	17,652	16,619
4	Kalkulam ...	3,531	4,664	...	...	10,787	10,248
5	Vilavankodu ...	4,403	5,465	...	...	13,369	11,611
6	Neyattankara ...	6,349	9,893	...	...	23,712	19,513
7	Trivandram ...	5,238	8,838	...	...	22,796	20,271
8	Nedumangadu ...	3,470	5,405	...	...	11,959	10,624
9	Sirayinkil ...	5,266	8,240	...	...	18,307	18,698
10	Kottarakkara ...	3,986	5,182	...	...	13,421	12,556
11	Pattanapuram ...	2,164	2,981	...	...	7,988	7,047
12	Shenkotta ...	1,867	2,683	...	...	6,670	7,138
13	Quilon ...	5,149	8,519	...	...	20,543	20,386
14	Kunnattur ...	4,555	5,405	...	...	14,943	14,220
15	Karunagappalli ...	5,584	8,149	...	...	19,226	20,916
16	Kartigappalli ...	4,771	7,162	...	...	17,770	17,825
17	Mavellikkara ...	5,627	7,907	...	...	21,154	20,025
18	Chenganur ...	4,006	5,862	...	...	16,066	14,778
19	Tiruvalla ...	4,477	6,969	...	...	19,589	17,718
20	Ambalappula ...	3,681	6,224	...	...	14,661	14,903
21	Sherttala ...	4,209	8,306	...	...	23,414	21,255
22	Vykkam ...	4,250	6,276	...	...	16,098	15,255
23	Ettumanur ...	2,798	4,275	...	...	12,175	10,816
24	Kottayam ...	2,981	4,060	...	...	11,815	10,955
25	Changanacheri ...	2,871	4,099	...	...	11,829	10,079
26	Meenachal ...	1,660	2,664	...	...	6,542	5,644
27	Muvattupula ...	3,909	4,627	...	...	12,237	11,945
28	Todupula ...	1,169	1,317	...	...	3,175	3,068
29	Kunnattunadu ...	4,291	5,710	...	...	15,573	14,700
30	Alangadu ...	2,384	3,322	...	...	8,663	8,106
31	Parur ...	2,525	3,452	...	...	8,447	7,801
	Cardamom Hills ...	1,262	953	...	...	2,812	1,772
	Periyar & Thekkadi.	420	152	...	...	1,223	274
	Total ...	118,894	173,398	...	...	447,165	419,574

IX.

Part (B)—Hindu—(*Continued*).

Periods—(*Continued*).

25 and over.							
Learning.		Literate.		Illiterate.		Not stated.	
Males.	Females.	Males.	Females.	Males.	Females.	Males.	Females.
36	37	38	39	40	41	42	43
...	...	1,836	9	4,535	6,569	...	...
...	...	5,083	726	11,095	15,504	...	...
3	1	5,068	564	12,581	16,054	...	...,
5	..	2,702	123	8,080	10,125	...	...
2	2	3,304	184	10,063	11,425	...	...
5	...	5,701	230	18,006	19,283	...	...
36	16	9,367	1,311	13,393	18,944	...	...
23	8	2,477	250	9,459	10,366	...	...
55	11	4,421	323	13,831	18,364	...	...
111	39	2,203	551	11,107	11,966	...	...
35	25	1,684	105	6,269	6,917	..	...
4	...	1,642	51	5,024	7,087	...	...
53	19	5,866	179	14,623	20,187	1	1
8	4	2,216	182	12,719	14,034	...	...
4	...	3,171	349	16,051	20,567	...	...
137	...	4,636	683	12,997	17,142	...	...
1	...	4,451	180	16,702	19,845	...	...
...	...	4,722	168	11,344	14,610	...	...
...	...	6,202	596	13,387	17,122	...	...
19	3	5,530	273	9,112	14,627	...	...
8	2	9,868	869	13,538	20,384	...	...
16	...	4,293	210	11,789	15,045	...	...
6	...	4,527	407	7,642	10,409	...	...
2	...	3,631	175	8,182	10,780	...	...
...	...	3,147	484	8,682	9,595	...	...
...	...	2,922	105	3,620	5,539	...	...
66	63	2,649	790	9,522	11,092	...	...
54	67	650	458	2,471	2,543	...	...
410	216	4,288	1,500	10,875	12,984	...	...
17	3	2,140	1,062	6,506	7,041	...	...
4	21	2,439	349	6,004	7,431	...	...
66	2	181	8	2,565	1,762	...	...
...	...	191	3	1,032	271	..	...
1,150	502	123,208	13,457	322,806	405,614	1	1

TABLE

Education by Religion and Age,

Number.	Taluq.	Total Mussalman. Total.	Males.	Females.	Total — Learning. Males.	Females.
1	2	3	4	5	6	7
1	Tovala ...	1,184	550	634	13	...
2	Agastiswaram ...	3,387	1,709	1,678	46	25
3	Eranial ...	4,065	2,115	1,950	48	12
4	Kalkulam ...	2,420	1,222	1,198	23	...
5	Vilavankodu ...	2,087	1,064	1,023	28	1
6	Neyattankara ...	5,143	2,589	2,554	61	14
7	Trivandram ...	9,506	4,718	4,788	174	50
8	Nedumangadu ...	3,308	1,718	1,590	18	5
9	Sirayinkil ...	13,050	6,434	6,616	97	7
10	Kottarakkara ...	4,550	2,376	2,174	48	25
11	Pattanapuram ...	4,169	2,063	2,106	22	7
12	Shenkotta ...	1,611	864	747	3	...
13	Quilon ...	13,650	6,995	6,655	332	78
14	Kunnattur ...	2,759	1,426	1,333	4	...
15	Karunagappalli ...	13,061	6,884	6,177	66	8
16	Kartigappalli ...	7,075	3,549	3,526	89	15
17	Mavellikkara ...	4,134	2,188	1,946	48	1
18	Chenganur ...	2,843	1,485	1,358	32	1
19	Tiruvalla ...	2,175	1,158	1,017	37	7
20	Ambalappula ...	10,133	4,789	5,344	206	16
21	Sherttala ...	2,787	1,363	1,424	65	21
22	Vykkam ...	3,423	1,767	1,656	11	2
23	Ettumanur ...	483	313	170	4	5
24	Kottayam ...	1,151	637	514	22	...
25	Changanacheri ...	3,420	1,795	1,625	15	...
26	Meenachal ...	1,084	631	453	5	1
27	Muvattupula ...	6,442	3,348	3,094	41	1
28	Todupula ...	2,676	1,409	1,267	25	13
29	Kunnattunadu ...	11,386	5,884	5,502	62	17
30	Alangadu ...	11,386	5,994	5,392	111	35
31	Parur ...	3,632	1,874	1,758	35	7
	Cardamom Hills ...	345	221	124	3	...
	Periyar & Thekkadi ...	298	243	55	...	...
	Total ...	158,823	81,375	77,448	1,804	374

IX.

Part (C)—Mussalman.

BY EDUCATION.						AGE PERIODS.	
Literate.		Illiterate.		Not stated.		0—14.	
						Total.	
Males.	Females.	Males.	Females.	Males.	Females.	Males.	Females.
8	9	10	11	12	13	14	15
44	...	493	634	...	...	185	215
358	98	1,305	1,555	...	...	647	613
436	55	1,631	1,883	...	...	761	733
256	11	933	1,187	...	...	455	444
190	16	846	1,006	...	...	389	372
245	32	2,283	2,508	...	...	885	972
975	78	3,569	4,660	...	...	1,681	1,772
176	16	1,524	1,569	...	...	600	612
700	22	5,637	6,587	...	...	2,590	2,524
200	48	2,128	2,101	...	...	895	955
271	14	1,770	2,085	...	...	767	781
18	...	843	747	...	...	346	274
1,047	148	5,614	6,429	2	...	2,771	2,539
69	...	1,353	1,333	...	...	579	532
351	9	6,467	6,160	...	...	2,705	2,477
558	12	2,902	3,499	...	...	1,287	1,341
284	3	1,906	1,942	...	...	784	712
243	3	1,210	1,354	...	...	496	475
307	24	814	986	...	...	426	386
1,374	56	3,209	5,272	...	...	1,744	2,086
488	134	810	1,269	...	...	408	506
303	11	1,453	1,643	...	...	570	670
166	10	143	155	...	...	82	75
195	6	420	508	...	...	229	207
388	39	1,392	1,586	...	...	558	626
288	5	338	447	...	...	182	147
302	39	3,005	3,054	...	...	1,350	1,287
148	133	1,236	1,121	...	...	605	532
469	84	5,353	5,401	...	...	2,411	2,352
557	171	5,326	5,186	...	...	2,256	2,050
222	2	1,617	1,749	...	...	809	762
38	...	180	124	...	...	58	35
93	1	150	54	...	...	25	13
11,709	1,280	67,860	75,794	2	...	30,536	30,077

TABLE

Education by Religion and Age,

Number.	Taluq.	Age					
		0—14.					
		Learning.		Literate.		Illiterate.	
		Males.	Females.	Males.	Females.	Males.	Females.
1	2	16	17	18	19	20	21
1	Tovala ...	13	...	2	...	170	215
2	Agastiswaram ...	44	25	39	15	564	573
3	Eranial ...	43	9	18	...	700	724
4	Kalkulam ...	31	...	5	2	419	442
5	Vilavankodu ...	24	1	10	...	355	371
6	Neyattankara ...	48	8	17	7	820	957
7	Trivandram ...	151	49	61	4	1,469	1,719
8	Nedumangadu ...	15	3	16	3	569	606
9	Sirayinkil ...	72	5	55	8	2,463	2,511
10	Kottarakkara ...	34	10	14	34	847	911
11	Pattanapuram ..	14	6	20	...	733	775
12	Shenkotta ...	3	...	...	...	343	274
13	Quilon ...	282	30	45	43	2,444	2,466
14	Kunnattur ...	4	...	...	...	575	532
15	Karunagappalli ...	65	8	15	2	2,625	2,467
16	Kartigappalli ...	76	15	29	2	1,182	1,324
17	Mavellikkara ...	47	1	17	1	720	710
18	Chenganur ...	32	1	4	...	460	474
19	Tiruvalla ...	31	7	8	2	387	377
20	Ambalappula ...	182	15	65	2	1,497	2,069
21	Sherttala ...	62	21	25	11	321	474
22	Vykkam ...	10	2	9	1	551	667
23	Ettumanur ...	4	5	9	...	69	70
24	Kottayam ...	22	...	15	1	192	206
25	Changanacheri ...	13	...	24	...	521	626
26	Meenachal ...	5	1	23	...	154	146
27	Muvattupula ...	31	1	85	26	1,234	1,260
28	Todupula ...	10	5	50	49	545	478
29	Kunnattunadu ...	49	13	23	23	2,339	2,316
30	Alangadu ...	87	18	123	30	2,046	2,002
31	Parur ...	33	1	18	...	758	761
	Cardamom Hills ..	...	...	...	...	58	35
	Periyar & Thekkadi...	...	...	5	...	20	13
	Total ...	1,537	260	849	266	28,150	29,551

IX.

Part (C)—Mussalman—(*Continued*).

PERIODS—(*Continued*).

Not stated.		15—24.					
		Total.		Learning.		Literate.	
Males.	Females.	Males.	Females.	Males.	Females.	Males.	Females.
22	23	24	25	26	27	28	29
...	...	92	117	...	...	10	...
...	...	271	305	2	...	98	24
...	...	399	351	4	...	125	...
...	...	204	237	2	...	55	6
...	...	203	238	1	...	48	7
...	...	452	543	2	1	69	6
...	...	898	1,043	23	1	256	31
...	...	326	343	3	2	32	5
...	...	1,098	1,352	19	..	168	6
...	...	418	363	4	...	55	3
...	...	360	386	7	1	62	5
...	...	159	123	...	...	8	...
...	...	1,283	1,253	19	2	295	41
...	...	214	228	...	..	20	...
...	...	1,130	1,103	1	...	78	2
...	...	642	746	12	...	102	5
...	...	388	390	...	...	49	2
...	...	304	258	...	...	63	2
...	...	193	180	6	...	58	4
...	...	909	973	22	1	330	17
...	...	216	257	3	...	106	20
...	...	328	352	1	...	72	4
...	...	66	27	...	...	41	2
...	...	123	92	...	...	71	4
...	...	266	293	2	...	54	14
...	...	126	96	...	...	66	...
...	...	565	558	5	...	41	3
...	...	238	276	1	6	14	30
..	...	969	982	...	2	74	6
...	...	1,073	1,073	...	4	123	40
...	...	306	331	2	6	41	...
...	...	53	27	...	...	8	...
...	...	70	7	...	...	29	..
...	...	14,342	14,903	141	26	2,721	289

TABLE

Education by Religion and Age,

Number.	Taluq.	Age 15–24. Illiterate. Males.	Illiterate. Females.	Not stated. Males.	Not stated. Females.	Total. Males.	Total. Females.
1	2	30	31	32	33	34	35
1	Tovala ...	82	117	...	...	273	302
2	Agastiswaram ...	171	281	...	...	791	760
3	Eranial ...	270	351	...	...	955	866
4	Kalkulam ...	147	231	...	...	563	517
5	Vilavankodu ...	154	231	...	...	472	413
6	Neyattankara ...	381	536	...	...	1,252	1,039
7	Trivandram ...	619	1,011	...	...	2,139	1,973
8	Nedumangadu ...	291	336	...	...	792	635
9	Sirayinkil ...	911	1,346	...	...	2,746	2,740
10	Kottarakkara ...	359	360	...	...	1,063	856
11	Pattanapuram ...	291	380	...	...	936	939
12	Shenkotta ...	151	123	...	...	359	350
13	Quilon ...	969	1,210	...	...	2,941	2,863
14	Kunnattur ...	194	228	...	...	633	573
15	Karunagappalli ...	1,051	1,101	...	...	3,049	2,597
16	Kartigappalli ...	528	741	...	...	1,620	1,439
17	Mavellikkara ...	339	388	...	...	1,016	844
18	Chenganur ...	241	256	...	...	685	625
19	Tiruvalla ...	129	176	...	...	539	451
20	Ambalappula ...	557	955	...	...	2,136	2,285
21	Sherttala ...	107	237	...	...	739	661
22	Vykkam ...	255	348	...	...	869	634
23	Ettumanur ...	25	25	...	...	165	68
24	Kottayam ...	52	88	...	...	285	215
25	Changanacheri ...	210	279	...	...	971	706
26	Meenachal ...	60	96	...	...	323	210
27	Muvattupula ...	519	555	...	...	1,433	1,249
28	Todupula ...	223	240	...	...	566	459
29	Kunnattunadu ...	895	974	...	...	2,504	2,168
30	Alangadu ...	950	1,029	...	...	2,665	2,269
31	Parur ...	263	325	...	...	759	665
	Cardamom Hills ...	45	27	...	...	110	62
	Periyar & Thekkadi.	41	7	...	...	148	35
	Total ...	11,480	14,588	...	...	36,497	32,468

IX.

Part (C)—Mussalman—(*Continued*).

Periods—(*Continued*).

25 and over.							
Learning.		Literate.		Illiterate.		Not stated.	
Males.	Females.	Males.	Females.	Males.	Females.	Males.	Females.
36	37	38	39	40	41	42	43
...	...	32	...	241	302	...	...
...	...	221	59	570	701	...	...
1	3	293	55	661	808	...	...
...	...	196	3	367	514	...	...
3	...	132	9	337	404	...	...
11	5	159	19	1,082	1,015	...	...
...	...	658	43	1,481	1,930	...	...
...	...	128	8	664	627	...	...
6	2	477	8	2,263	2,730	...	...
10	15	131	11	922	830	...	...
1	...	189	9	746	930	...	...
...	...	10	...	349	350	...	...
31	46	707	64	2,201	2,753	2	...
...	...	49	...	584	573	...	...
...	...	258	5	2,791	2,592	...	...
1	...	427	5	1,192	1,434	...	...
1	...	168	...	847	844	...	...
...	...	176	1	509	624	...	...
...	...	241	18	298	433	...	...
2	...	979	37	1,155	2,248	...	...
...	...	357	103	382	558	...	...
...	...	222	6	647	628	...	...
...	...	116	8	49	60	...	...
...	...	109	1	176	214	...	...
...	...	310	25	661	681	...	...
...	...	199	5	124	205	...	...
5	...	176	10	1,252	1,239	...	...
14	2	84	54	468	403	...	...
13	2	372	55	2,119	2,111	...	...
24	13	311	101	2,330	2,155	...	...
...	...	163	2	596	663	...	...
3	...	30	...	77	62	...	...
...	...	59	1	89	34	...	...
126	88	8,139	725	28,230	31,655	2	...

TABLE

Education by Religion and Age,

Number.	Taluq.	Total Christians. Total.	Males.	Females.	Total Learning. Males.	Females.
1	2	3	4	5	6	7
1	Tovala ...	1,745	832	913	23	4
2	Agastiswaram ...	15,220	7,597	7,623	302	182
3	Eranial ...	26,650	13,171	13,479	343	66
4	Kalkulam ...	9,937	5,005	4,932	44	...
5	Vilavankodu ...	9,716	5,030	4,686	74	11
6	Neyattankara ...	11,994	6,220	5,774	347	51
7	Trivandram ...	8,963	4,430	4,533	366	212
8	Nedumangadu ...	1,423	794	629	14	13
9	Sirayinkil ...	1,840	900	940	33	17
10	Kottarakkara ...	9,574	4,806	4,768	143	35
11	Pattanapuram ...	3,825	1,918	1,907	48	10
12	Shenkotta ...	444	233	211	7	4
13	Quilon ...	17,538	8,696	8,842	605	137
14	Kunnattur ...	8,822	4,365	4,457	117	10
15	Karunagappalli ...	8,797	4,299	4,498	165	39
16	Kartigappalli ...	8,026	3,974	4,052	137	41
17	Mavellikkara ...	14,485	7,425	7,060	368	48
18	Chenganur ...	25,322	13,064	12,258	1,582	148
19	Tiruvalla ...	42,256	21,605	20,651	2,031	250
20	Ambalappula ...	20,952	10,845	10,107	502	56
21	Sherttala ...	24,913	12,426	12,487	727	237
22	Vykkam ...	11,501	5,990	5,511	87	3
23	Ettumanur ...	30,984	15,800	15,184	371	68
24	Kottayam ...	26,187	13,292	12,895	653	124
25	Changanacheri ...	26,604	13,620	12,984	419	146
26	Meenachal ...	31,095	15,797	15,298	609	207
27	Muvattupula ...	43,644	21,906	21,738	341	55
28	Todupula ...	7,812	3,945	3,867	77	31
29	Kunnattunadu ...	36,547	18,295	18,252	629	144
30	Alangadu ...	21,513	10,980	10,533	255	118
31	Parur ...	17,315	8,721	8,594	364	43
	Cardamom Hills ...	833	616	217	2	...
	Periyar and Thekkadi ...	434	372	62	...	3
	Total ...	526,911	266,969	259,942	11,785	2,508

IX.

Part (D)—Christian.

BY EDUCATION.						AGE PERIODS.	
Literate.		Illiterate.		Not stated.		0—14.	
						Total.	
Males.	Females.	Males.	Females.	Males.	Females.	Males.	Females.
8	9	10	11	12	13	14	15
138	16	671	893	...	...	312	327
1,349	707	5,946	6,734	...	...	2,975	2,962
1,815	272	11,013	13,141	...	...	4,735	5,140
493	19	4,468	4,913	..	...	1,950	1,947
669	62	4,287	4,613	...	...	1,758	1,689
1,085	109	4,788	5,614	...	...	1,958	2,222
950	446	3,114	3,875	...	...	1,664	1,744
74	20	706	596	...	...	249	212
71	37	796	886	...	...	389	385
708	220	3,955	4,513	...	...	2,059	2,098
352	27	1,513	1,870	...	...	588	713
34	8	192	199	...	...	97	85
1,195	323	6,896	8,382	...	...	3,557	3,617
571	85	3,677	4,412	...	...	1,741	1,796
609	109	3,525	4,350	...	...	1,722	1,772
1,040	58	2,797	3,953	...	...	1,502	1,642
1,556	83	5,501	6,929	...	...	2,765	2,831
3,784	178	7,698	11,932	...	...	5,431	5,177
7,183	632	12,391	19,769	...	...	8,541	8,587
2,727	263	7,616	9,788	...	...	4,136	4,209
3,518	771	8,181	11,479	...	...	4,458	4,701
1,448	124	4,455	5,384	...	...	2,248	2,085
4,476	444	10,953	14,677	...	...	5,892	6,043
3,310	598	9,329	12,173	...	...	5,112	5,322
3,118	544	10,083	12,294	...	...	5,304	5,313
6,496	668	8,692	14,423	...	...	6,292	6,308
2,669	961	18,896	20,722	...	...	8,950	9,050
333	244	3,535	3,592	...	...	1,631	1,636
2,510	567	15,156	17,541	...	...	6,839	6,985
1,264	318	9,461	10,097	...	...	4,267	4,270
1,445	94	6,912	8,457	...	...	3,494	3,806
168	15	446	202	...	...	84	64
177	15	195	44	...	...	27	25
57,335	8,987	197,849	248,447	...	...	102,727	104,763

TABLE

Education by Religion and Age,

Number.	Taluq.	Age 0—14. Learning. Males.	Learning. Females.	Literate. Males.	Literate. Females.	Illiterate. Males.	Illiterate. Females.
1	2	16	17	18	19	20	21
1	Tovala ...	20	4	8	...	284	323
2	Agastiswaram ..	292	180	197	60	2,486	2,722
3	Eranial ...	298	54	127	37	4,310	5,049
4	Kalkulam ...	33	...	28	5	1,889	1,942
5	Vilavankodu ...	55	11	47	10	1,656	1,668
6	Neyattankara ...	298	44	26	12	1,634	2,166
7	Trivandram ...	304	188	57	55	1,303	1,501
8	Nedumangadu ...	8	9	6	3	235	200
9	Sirayinkil ...	25	16	5	5	359	364
10	Kottarakkara ...	125	25	144	111	1,790	1,962
11	Pattanapuram ...	32	10	15	6	541	697
12	Shenkotta ...	7	4	1	...	89	81
13	Quilon ...	481	104	103	54	2,973	3,459
14	Kunnattur ...	105	10	30	12	1,606	1,774
15	Karunagappalli ...	154	38	64	10	1,504	1,724
16	Kartigappalli ...	110	25	41	9	1,351	1,608
17	Mavellikkara ...	337	47	116	17	2,312	2,767
18	Chenganur ...	1,500	144	49	2	3,882	5,031
19	Tiruvalla ...	1,855	239	365	84	6,321	8,264
20	Ambalappula ...	425	55	168	39	3,543	4,115
21	Sherttala ...	650	209	177	74	3,631	4,418
22	Vykkam ...	83	...	84	11	2,081	2,074
23	Ettumanur ...	300	62	232	31	5,360	5,950
24	Kottayam ...	643	124	189	71	4,280	5,127
25	Changanacheri ...	391	135	272	97	4,641	5,081
26	Meenachal ...	592	201	501	90	5,199	6,017
27	Muvattupula ...	314	54	504	555	8,132	8,441
28	Todupula ...	64	20	70	67	1,497	1,549
29	Kunnattunadu ...	494	33	69	44	6,276	6,908
30	Alangadu ...	240	112	123	45	3,904	4,113
31	Parur ...	321	43	51	17	3,122	3,746
	Cardamom Hills ...	2	...	...	...	82	64
	Periyar & Thekkadi.	...	3	8	3	19	19
	Total ...	10,558	2,203	3,877	1,636	88,292	100,924

IX.

Part (D)—Christian—(*Continued*).

PERIODS—(*Continued*).

Not stated.		15—24. Total.		Learning.		Literate.	
Males.	Females.	Males.	Females.	Males.	Females.	Males.	Females.
22	23	24	25	26	27	28	29
...	...	134	188	3	...	35	4
...	...	1,327	1,431	10	2	365	191
...	...	2,223	2,310	44	12	411	64
...	...	930	891	9	...	195	4
...	...	930	1,050	14	...	154	26
...	...	1,291	1,341	30	6	408	50
...	...	755	952	61	24	257	174
...	...	132	136	5	1	22	8
...	...	149	203	5	1	16	15
...	...	795	793	13	10	169	34
...	...	391	410	10	...	80	8
...	...	46	39	...	...	11	4
...	...	1,436	1,624	63	2	297	124
...	...	735	791	9	...	111	5
...	...	699	835	11	1	161	44
...	...	730	739	19	3	262	14
...	...	1,306	1,294	31	1	389	29
...	...	2,545	2,319	82	4	1,367	64
...	...	3,747	3,943	175	11	1,935	205
...	...	1,940	1,900	64	1	668	86
...	...	2,013	2,598	72	26	744	269
...	...	1,050	1,089	4	2	269	33
...	...	2,723	2,828	70	1	1,089	105
...	...	2,562	2,426	10	...	943	197
...	...	2,276	2,375	28	11	706	160
...	...	2,965	3,087	17	4	1,845	276
...	...	3,504	3,753	5	1	321	88
...	...	698	790	4	...	57	40
...	...	2,988	3,436	11	8	541	69
...	...	1,748	1,967	11	3	256	79
...	...	1,598	1,604	24	...	401	39
...	...	184	49	...	...	46	1
...	...	91	10	...	...	37	3
...	...	46,641	49,151	914	135	14,518	2,512

TABLE

Education by Religion and Age,

Number.	Taluq.	Age: 15—24. Illiterate. Males.	Illiterate. Females.	Not stated. Males.	Not stated. Females.	Total. Males.	Total. Females.
1	2	30	31	32	33	34	35
1	Tovala ...	96	184	...	...	386	398
2	Agastiswaram ...	952	1,238	...	...	3,295	3,230
3	Eranial ...	1,768	2,234	...	...	6,213	6,029
4	Kalkulam ...	726	887	...	...	2,125	2,094
5	Vilavankodu ...	762	1,024	...	...	2,342	1,947
6	Neyattankara ...	853	1,285	...	...	2,971	2,211
7	Trivandram ...	437	754	...	...	2,011	1,837
8	Nedumangadu ...	105	127	...	...	413	281
9	Sirayinkil ...	128	187	...	...	362	352
10	Kottarakkara ...	613	749	...	...	1,952	1,877
11	Pattanapuram ...	301	402	...	...	939	784
12	Shenkotta ...	35	35	...	...	90	87
13	Quilon ...	1,076	1,498	...	...	3,703	3,601
14	Kunnattur ...	615	786	...	...	1,889	1,870
15	Karunagappalli ...	527	790	...	...	1,878	1,891
16	Kartigappalli ...	449	722	...	...	1,742	1,671
17	Mavellikkara ...	886	1,264	...	...	3,354	2,935
18	Chenganur ...	1,096	2,251	...	...	5,088	4.762
19	Tiruvalla ...	1,637	3,727	...	...	9,317	8,121
20	Ambalappula ...	1,208	1,813	...	...	4,769	3,998
21	Sherttala ...	1,197	2,303	...	...	5,955	5,188
22	Vykkam ...	777	1,004	...	...	2,692	2,387
23	Ettumanur ...	1,614	2,722	...	...	7,185	6,313
24	Kottayam ...	1,609	2,229	...	...	5,618	5,147
25	Changanacheri ...	1,542	2,204	...	...	6,040	5,296
26	Meenachal ...	1,103	2,807	...	...	6,540	5,903
27	Muvattupula ...	3,178	3,664	...	...	9,452	8,935
28	Todupula ...	637	750	...	...	1,616	1,441
29	Kunnattunadu ...	2,436	3,359	...	...	8,468	7,831
30	Alangadu ...	1,481	1,885	...	...	4,965	4,296
31	Parur ...	1,173	1,565	...	...	3,629	3,184
	Cardamom Hills ...	138	48	...	...	348	104
	Periyar & Thekkadi.	54	7	...	...	254	27
	Total ...	31,209	46,504	...	...	117,601	106,028

IX.

Part (D)—Christian—(*Continued*).

Periods—(*Continued*).

25 and over.

Learning.		Literate.		Illiterate.		Not stated.	
Males.	Females.	Males.	Females.	Males.	Females.	Males.	Females.
36	37	38	39	40	41	42	43
...	...	95	12	291	386	...	...
...	...	787	456	2,508	2,774	...	...
1	...	1,277	171	4,935	5,858	...	...
2	...	270	10	1,853	2,084	...	...
5	...	468	26	1,869	1,921	...	...
19	1	651	47	2,301	2,168	...	...
1	...	636	217	1,374	1,620	...	...
1	3	46	9	366	269	...	...
3	...	50	17	309	335	...	...
5	...	395	75	1,552	1,802	...	...
6	...	257	13	676	771	...	...
...	...	22	4	68	83	...	...
61	31	795	145	2,847	3,425	...	...
3	...	430	18	1,456	1,852	...	...
...	...	384	55	1,494	1,836	...	...
8	13	737	35	997	1,623	...	...
...	...	1,051	37	2,303	2,898	...	...
...	...	2,368	112	2,720	4,650	...	...
1	...	4,883	343	4,433	7,778	...	...
13	...	1,891	138	2,865	3,860	...	...
5	2	2,597	428	3,353	4,758	...	...
...	1	1,095	80	1,597	2,306	...	...
1	...	3,205	308	3,979	6,005	...	...
...	...	2,178	330	3,440	4,817	...	...
...	...	2,140	287	3,900	5,009	...	...
...	2	4,150	302	2,390	5,599	...	...
22	...	1,844	318	7,586	8,617	...	...
9	11	206	137	1,401	1,293	...	...
124	103	1,900	454	6,444	7,274	...	...
4	3	885	194	4,076	4,099	...	...
19	...	993	38	2,617	3,146	...	...
...	...	122	14	226	90	...	...
...	...	132	9	122	18	...	...
313	170	38,940	4,839	78,348	101,019	...	...

TABLE IX.

Education by Religion and Age, Part (E)—Jain.

Number.	Taluq.	Total Jain.			Total by Education.								Age Periods. 0–14.									
					Learning.		Literate.		Illiterate.		Not stated.		Total.		Learning.		Literate.		Illiterate.		Not stated.	
		Total.	Males.	Females.	Males.	Females.	Males.	Females.	Males.	Females.	Males.	Females.	Males.	Females.	Males.	Females.	Males.	Females.	Males.	Females.	Males.	Females.
1	2	3	4	5	6	7	8	9	10	11	12	13	14	15	16	17	18	19	20	21	22	23
30	Alangadu ...	3	3	...	1	...	2	...	...	...	...	...	...	...	...	...	...	...	...	...	...	...
	Periyar & Thekkadi.	7	5	2	...	...	1	...	4	2	...	...	...	...	...	...	...	...	...	...	...	...
	Total ...	10	8	2	1	...	3	...	4	2	...	.	...	...	...	...	...	...	...	...	...	...

TABLE IX.

Education by Religion and Age, Part (E)—Jain—(*Continued*).

Number.	Taluq.	Age Periods—(*Continued*). 15—24. Total. Males.	Females.	Learning. Males.	Females.	Literate. Males.	Females.	Illiterate. Males.	Females.	Not stated. Males.	Females.	25 and over. Total. Males.	Females.	Learning. Males.	Females.	Literate. Males.	Females.	Illiterate. Males.	Females.	Not stated. Males.	Females.
1	2	24	25	26	27	28	29	30	31	32	33	34	35	36	37	38	39	40	41	42	43
30	Alangadu	2	...	1	...	1	...	...	...	...	...	1	...	...	...	1	...	...	...	...	...
	Periyar and Thekkadi.	...	1	...	...	...	...	...	1	...	...	5	1	...	...	1	...	4	1	...	...
	Total ...	2	1	1	...	1	...	...	1	...	...	6	1	...	...	2	...	4	1	...	...

TABLE IX.

Education by Religion and Age, Part (F)—Parsi.

Number.	Taluq.	Total Parsi.			Total by Education.								Age Periods. 0—14.									
					Learning.		Literate.		Illiterate.		Not stated.		Total.		Learning.		Literate.		Illiterate.		Not stated.	
		Total.	Males.	Females.	Males.	Females.	Males.	Females.	Males.	Females.	Males.	Females.	Males.	Females.	Males.	Females.	Males.	Females.	Males.	Females.	Males.	Females.
1	2	3	4	5	6	7	8	9	10	11	12	13	14	15	16	17	18	19	20	21	22	23
7	Trivandram ...	1	1	...	...	...	...	...	1	...	...	...	...	...	...	...	...	...	...	...	...	...

Number.	Taluq.	Age Periods—(*Continued*). 15—24.										25 and over.									
		Total.		Learning.		Literate.		Illiterate.		Not stated.		Total.		Learning.		Literate.		Illiterate.		Not stated.	
		Males.	Females.	Males.	Females.	Males.	Females.	Males.	Females.	Males.	Females.	Males.	Females.	Males.	Females.	Males.	Females.	Males.	Females.	Males.	Females.
1	2	24	25	26	27	28	29	30	31	32	33	34	35	36	37	38	39	40	41	42	43
7	Trivandram	...	...	...	...	...	...	...	...	...	...	1	...	...	...	...	...	1	...	...	...

TABLE IX.

Education by Religion and Age, Part (G)—Jew.

Number.	Taluq.	Total Jew.			Total by Education.								Age Periods. 0—14.									
					Learning.		Literate.		Illiterate.		Not stated.		Total.		Learning.		Literate.		Illiterate.		Not stated.	
		Total.	Males.	Females.	Males.	Females.	Males.	Females.	Males.	Females.	Males.	Females.	Males.	Females.	Males.	Females.	Males.	Females.	Males.	Females.	Males.	Females.
1	2	3	4	5	6	7	8	9	10	11	12	13	14	15	16	17	18	19	20	21	22	23
13	Quilon ...	10	5	5	...	1	4	3	1	1	...	...	1	1	...	1	...	...	1	...	...	...
31	Parur ...	115	60	55	16	13	30	33	14	9	...	...	21	22	15	13	...	3	6	6	...	...
	Total ...	125	65	60	16	14	34	36	15	10	...	...	22	23	15	14	...	3	7	6	...	...

TABLE IX.

Education by Religion and Age, Part (G)—Jew—(*Continued*).

Number.	Taluq.	15—24. Total. Males.	15—24. Total. Females.	15—24. Learning. Males.	15—24. Learning. Females.	15—24. Literate. Males.	15—24. Literate. Females.	15—24. Illiterate. Males.	15—24. Illiterate. Females.	15—24. Not stated. Males.	15—24. Not stated. Females.	25 and over. Total. Males.	25 and over. Total. Females.	25 and over. Learning. Males.	25 and over. Learning. Females.	25 and over. Literate. Males.	25 and over. Literate. Females.	25 and over. Illiterate. Males.	25 and over. Illiterate. Females.	25 and over. Not stated. Males.	25 and over. Not stated. Females.
1	2	24	25	26	27	28	29	30	31	32	33	34	35	36	37	38	39	40	41	42	43
18	Quilon	1	...	...	...	1	...	...	...	...	...	3	4	...	...	3	3	...	1	...	...
31	Parur	10	10	1	...	8	9	1	1	...	...	29	23	...	...	22	21	7	2	...	...
	Total ...	11	10	1	...	9	9	1	1	...	...	32	27	...	...	25	24	7	3	...	...

TABLE IX.

Education by Religion and Age, Part (H)—None.

Number.	Taluq.	Total None.			Total by Education.								Age Periods. 0—14.									
					Learning.		Literate.		Illiterate.		Not stated.		Total.		Learning.		Literate.		Illiterate.		Not stated.	
		Total.	Males.	Females.	Males.	Females.	Males.	Females.	Males.	Females.	Males.	Females.	Males.	Females.	Males.	Females.	Males.	Females.	Males.	Females.	Males.	Females.
1	2	3	4	5	6	7	8	9	10	11	12	13	14	15	16	17	18	19	20	21	22	23
	Periyar & Thekkadi.	2	2	...	...	...	2	...	...	...	...	...	...	...	...	...	...	...	...	...	...	...

Number.	Taluq.	Age Periods—(*Continued*). 15—24.										25 and over.									
		Total.		Learning.		Literate.		Illiterate.		Not stated.		Total.		Learning.		Literate.		Illiterate.		Not stated.	
		Males.	Females.	Males.	Females.	Males.	Females.	Males.	Females.	Males.	Females.	Males.	Females.	Males.	Females.	Males.	Females.	Males.	Females.	Males.	Females.
1	2	24	25	26	27	28	29	30	31	32	33	34	35	36	37	38	39	40	41	42	43
	Periyar and Thekkadi...	...	...	...	...	...	...	...	...	...	...	2	...	...	...	2	...	...	...	...	...

TABLE

Parent

Number.	Taluq.	Total Population. Total.	Males.	Females.
1	2	3	4	5
1	Tovala	29,751	14,489	15,262
2	Agastiswaram	87,241	43,226	44,015
3	Eranial	105,098	52,883	52,215
4	Kalkulam	59,474	29,834	29,640
5	Vilavankodu	68,521	35,202	33,319
6	Neyattankara	110,755	56,953	53,802
7	Trivandram	111,938	56,909	55,029
8	Nedumangadu	55,497	27,857	27,640
9	Sirayinkil	97,995	48,271	49,724
10	Kottarakkara	71,517	36,055	35,462
11	Pattanapuram	39,447	19,858	19,589
12	Shenkotta	32,088	15,700	16,388
13	Quilon	121.935	60,832	61,103
14	Kunnattur	73,529	37,397	36,132
15	Karunagappalli	108,826	52,862	55,964
16	Kartigappalli	91,950	45,216	46,734
17	Mavellikkara	103,619	52,494	51,125
18	Chenganur	93,960	48,443	45,517
19	Tiruvalla	122,142	62,514	59,628
20	Ambalappula	94,745	46,909	47,836
21	Sherttala	117,261	58,448	58,813
22	Vykkam	80,628	40,947	39,681
23	Ettumanur	80,823	41,536	39,287
24	Kottayam	77,094	39,229	37,865
25	Changanacheri	74,722	38,596	36,126
26	Meenachal	59,976	30,830	29,146
27	Muvattupula	103,009	51,595	51,414
28	Todupula	25,202	12,786	12,416
29	Kunnattunadu	114,049	57,216	56,833
30	Alangadu	70,958	35,944	35,014
31	Parur	59,278	30,082	29,196
	Cardamom Hills	11,413	6,714	4,699
	Periyar & Thekkadi	3,295	2,588	707
	Total ...	2,557,736	1,290,415	1,267,821

X.

Tongue.

Madras Languages.

Malayalam.			Tamil.			Konkan.		
Total.	Males.	Females.	Total.	Males.	Females.	Total.	Males.	Females.
6	7	8	9	10	11	12	13	14
108	61	47	29,405	14,305	15,100	...	...	...
596	299	297	84,649	41,923	42,726	...	...	...
8,845	4,365	4,480	96,128	48,431	47,697	...	...	...
11,979	5,934	6,045	47,190	23,713	23,477	...	...	...
17,560	8,874	8,686	50,868	26,261	24,607	...	...	...
95,565	48,983	46,582	15,108	7,921	7,187	...	...	...
85,481	43,042	42,439	21,821	11,392	10,429	176	95	81
50,052	25,054	24,998	5,344	2,741	2,603	8	5	3
89,991	44,224	45,767	7,718	3,861	3,857	6	5	1
67,665	34,059	33,606	3,721	1,919	1,802	29	16	13
35,327	17,667	17,660	3,984	2,106	1,878	11	7	4
20	16	4	30,923	15,118	15,805	...	...	...
112,537	55,756	56,781	6,399	3,444	2,955	224	114	110
71,876	36,485	35,391	1,595	878	717	28	15	13
106,393	51,646	54,747	1,786	912	874	370	167	203
87,256	42,827	44,429	2,192	1,153	1,039	2,196	1,079	1,117
101,138	51,172	49,966	2,262	1,206	1,056	117	59	58
90,911	46,801	44,110	2,995	1,607	1,388	...	...	...
119,377	61,045	58,332	2,481	1,322	1,159	186	90	96
87,284	43,002	44,282	4,347	2,204	2,143	1,967	1,057	910
113,398	56,403	56,995	1,225	641	584	1,741	973	768
77,217	39,106	38,111	2,448	1,293	1,155	594	344	250
79,240	40,676	38,564	1,318	713	605	187	98	89
74,887	38,065	36,822	1,564	828	736	284	140	144
70,405	36,323	34,082	4,063	2,144	1,919	207	99	108
59,065	30,331	28,734	895	489	406	...	...	...
101,623	50,834	50,789	1,350	737	613	10	5	5
23,664	11,960	11,704	1,519	818	701	...	...	...
112,715	56,509	56,206	1,072	538	534	4	3	1
70,273	35,557	34,716	545	299	246	27	17	10
52,100	26,278	25,822	2,963	1,605	1,358	2,325	1,283	1,042
4,377	2,687	1,690	6,688	3,835	2,853	...	...	...
346	330	16	1,756	1,311	445	...	...	...
2,079,271	1,046,371	1,032,900	448,322	227,668	220,654	10,697	5,671	5,026

TABLE

Parent

Number.	Taluq.	Madras — Telugu. Total.	Telugu. Males.	Telugu. Females.	Hindustani. Total.	Hindustani. Males.	Hindustani. Females.
1	2	15	16	17	18	19	20
1	Tovala ...	117	53	64	50	32	18
2	Agastiswaram ...	610	299	311	367	190	177
3	Eranial ...	35	19	16	35	26	9
4	Kalkulam ...	92	39	53	113	62	51
5	Vilavankodu ...	5	2	3	14	10	4
6	Neyattankara ...	15	11	4	6	2	4
7	Trivandram ...	1,252	638	614	1,207	653	554
8	Nedumangadu ...	19	9	10	38	26	12
9	Sirayinkil ...	...	...	...	93	69	24
10	Kottarakkara ...	27	15	12	6	3	3
11	Pattanapuram ...	57	34	23	31	19	12
12	Shenkotta ...	895	430	465	189	105	84
13	Quilon ...	944	490	454	923	505	418
14	Kunnattur ...	...	...	...	2	2	...
15	Karunagappalli ...	7	4	3	129	64	65
16	Kartigappalli ...	41	24	17	59	37	22
17	Mavellikkara ...	10	6	4	19	13	6
18	Chenganur ...	5	2	3	30	19	11
19	Tiruvalla ...	32	24	8	19	10	9
20	Ambalappula ...	118	60	58	303	178	125
21	Sherttala ...	54	26	28	110	53	57
22	Vykkam ...	11	10	1	26	20	6
23	Ettumanur ...	15	10	5	...	...	...
24	Kottayam ...	11	6	5	155	80	75
25	Changanacheri ...	...	...	...	38	21	17
26	Meenachal ...	...	...	...	...	...	...
27	Muvattupula ...	5	3	2	...	...	...
28	Todupula ...	...	...	...	8	2	6
29	Kunnattunadu ...	8	4	4	28	20	8
30	Alangadu ...	...	...	...	20	13	7
31	Parur ...	77	35	42	1,198	605	593
	Cardamom Hills ...	160	82	78	44	27	17
	Periyar & Thekkadi.	804	632	172	195	159	36
	Total ...	5,426	2,967	2,459	5,455	3,025	2,430

X.

Tongue—(*Continued*).

Languages—(*Continued*).

Tulu.			Canarese.			Patnul.		
Total.	Males.	Females.	Total.	Males.	Females.	Total.	Males.	Females.
21	22	23	24	25	26	27	28	29
20	16	4	10	3	7	...	...	...
58	44	14	14	11	3	816	389	427
34	27	7	2	2	...	...	...	...
70	64	6	10	10	...	...	...	...
39	33	6	25	14	11	...	...	...
36	21	15	20	12	8	...	...	...
252	193	59	222	121	101	...	..	...
6	3	3	6	4	2	...	...	...
6	6	...	99	54	45	...	...	...
26	19	7	37	18	19	...	...	...
2	2	...	1	1	...	...	...	...
...	...	...	32	16	16	...	...	...
35	27	8	50	33	17	...	...	...
13	6	7	4	4	...	...	...	...
7	5	2	20	7	13	7	5	2
106	52	54	10	5	5	...	...	...
1	1	...	17	11	6	...	...	...
8	6	2	3	3	...	...	...	...
6	3	3	7	7	...	...	...	...
...	...	...	16	8	8	...	...	...
34	25	9	40	26	14	...	...	...
24	20	4	37	27	10	...	...	...
35	22	13	9	5	4	...	...	...
12	9	3	35	17	18	...	...	...
...	...	...	6	6	...	...	...	...
8	3	5	...	...	...	...	...	...
3	3	...	12	10	2	...	...	...
...	...	...	...	...	...	...	...	...
35	25	10	43	33	10	...	...	...
2	2	...	6	3	3	...	...	...
15	15	...	1	1	...	...	...	...
...	...	...	34	16	18	...	...	...
...	...	...	63	46	17	...	...	...
893	652	241	891	534	357	823	394	429

TABLE

Parent

Number.	Taluq.	Madras Languages—(Continued). Total Madras Languages. Total.	Males.	Females.	Other Indian Mahrathi. Total.	Males.	Females.
1	2	30	31	32	33	34	35
1	Tovala ...	29,710	14,470	15,240	40	18	22
2	Agastiswaram ...	87,110	43,155	43,955	43	21	22
3	Eranial ...	105,079	52,870	52,209	1	1	...
4	Kalkulam ...	59,454	29,822	29,632	12	8	4
5	Vilavankodu ...	68,511	35,194	33,317	5	3	2
6	Neyattankara ...	110,750	56,950	53,800	2	2	...
7	Trivandram ...	110,411	56,134	54,277	450	214	236
8	Nedumangadu ...	55,473	27,842	27,631	...	...	...
9	Sirayinkil ...	97,913	48,219	49,694	2	2	...
10	Kottarakkara ...	71,511	36,049	35,462	...	...	...
11	Pattanapuram ...	39,413	19,836	19,577	...	...	...
12	Shenkotta ...	32,059	15,685	16,374	9	5	4
13	Quilon ...	121,112	60,369	60,743	355	206	149
14	Kunnattur ...	73,518	37,390	36,128	...	...	...
15	Karunagappalli ...	108,719	52,810	55,909	3	1	2
16	Kartigappalli ...	91,860	45,177	46,683	14	10	4
17	Mavellikkara ...	103,564	52,468	51,096	...	...	...
18	Chenganur ...	93,952	48,438	45,514	...	...	...
19	Tiruvalla ...	122,108	62,501	59,607	14	8	6
20	Ambalappula ...	94,035	46,509	47,526	103	67	36
21	Sherttala ...	116,602	58,147	58,455	533	253	280
22	Vykkam ...	80,357	40,820	39,537	173	82	91
23	Ettumanur ...	80,804	41,524	39,280	...	...	...
24	Kottayam ...	76,948	39,145	37,803	26	18	8
25	Changanacheri ...	74,719	38,593	36,126	...	...	...
26	Meenachal ...	59,968	30,823	29,145	4	3	1
27	Muvattupula ...	103,003	51,592	51,411	...	...	...
28	Todupula ...	25,191	12,780	12,411	...	...	...
29	Kunnattunadu ...	113,905	57,132	56,773	143	83	60
30	Alangadu ...	70,873	35,891	34,982	65	44	21
31	Parur ...	58,679	29,822	28,857	201	52	149
	Cardamom Hills ...	11,303	6,647	4,656	...	...	...
	Periyar & Thekkadi	3,164	2,478	686	7	5	2
	Total ...	2,551,778	1,287,282	1,264,496	2,205	1,106	1,099

X.

Tongue—(*Continued*).

LANGUAGES.

Guzeratti.			Cutchi.			Sindhi.		
Total.	Males.	Females.	Total.	Males.	Females.	Total.	Males.	Females.
36	37	38	39	40	41	42	43	44
...	...	...	...	...	...	...	...	...
..	...	...	...	...	...	...	...	...
...	...	...	...	...	...	...	...	...
...	...	...	...	...	...	...	...	...
...	...	...	...	...	...	...	...	...
...	...	...	...	...	...	...	...	...
15	12	3	132	68	64	...	...	...
...	...	...	...	...	...	...	...	...
9	8	1	...	...	...	...	...	...
2	2	...	...	...	...	...	...	...
...	...	...	...	...	...	...	...	...
...	...	...	...	...	...	...	...	...
73	59	14	5	3	2	...	..	...
...	...	...	...	..	...	11	7	4
8	7	1	...	...	...	...	...	...
...	...	...	...	...	...	...	...	...
...	...	...	...	...	...	...	...	...
...	...	...	...	...	...	...	...	...
...	...	...	...	...	...	...	...	...
316	153	163	22	12	10	...	...	...
...	...	...	...	...	...	...	...	...
...	...	...	...	...	...	...	...	...
4	4	...	...	...	...	...	...	...
...	...	...	...	...	...	...	...	...
...	...	...	...	...	...	...	...	...
..	...	...	...	...	...	...	...	...
..	...	...	1	1	...	...	...	...
...	...	...	...	...	...	...	...	...
...	...	...	...	...	...	...	...	...
...	...	...	...	...	...	...	...	...
...	...	...	...	...	...	...	...	...
...	...	...	...	...	...	...	...	...
...	...	...	...	...	...	...	...	...
427	245	182	160	84	76	11	7	4

TABLE

Parent

Number.	Taluq.	Other Indian Languages—(Continued). Bengali. Total.	Bengali. Males.	Bengali. Females.	Total other Indian Languages. Total.	Total other Indian Languages. Males.	Total other Indian Languages. Females.
1	2	45	46	47	48	49	50
1	Tovala ...	...	...	...	40	18	22
2	Agastiswaram ...	...	...	...	43	21	22
3	Eranial ...	...	...	...	1	1	...
4	Kalkulam ...	...	...	...	12	8	4
5	Vilavankodu ...	...	...	...	5	3	2
6	Neyattankara ...	...	...	...	2	2	...
7	Trivandram ...	4	3	1	601	297	304
8	Nedumangadu ...	...	...	...	...	...	...
9	Sirayinkil ...	...	...	...	11	10	1
10	Kottarakkara ...	...	...	...	2	2	...
11	Pattanapuram ...	...	...	...	...	...	...
12	Shenkotta ...	...	...	...	9	5	4
13	Quilon ...	...	...	...	433	268	165
14	Kunnattur ...	...	...	...	11	7	4
15	Karunagappalli ...	...	...	...	11	8	3
16	Kartigappalli ...	...	...	...	14	10	4
17	Mavellikkara ...	...	...	...	...	...	...
18	Chenganur ...	...	...	...	...	...	...
19	Tiruvalla ...	...	...	...	14	8	6
20	Ambalappula ...	...	...	...	441	232	209
21	Sherttala ...	...	...	...	533	253	280
22	Vykkam ...	1	1	...	174	83	91
23	Ettumanur ...	...	...	...	4	4	...
24	Kottayam ...	...	...	...	26	18	8
25	Changanacheri ...	...	...	...	...	...	...
26	Meenachal ...	...	...	...	4	3	1
27	Muvattupula ...	...	...	...	1	1	...
28	Todupula ...	...	...	...	...	...	...
29	Kunnattunadu ...	...	...	...	143	83	60
30	Alangadu ...	...	...	...	65	44	21
31	Parur ...	...	...	...	201	52	149
	Cardamom Hills ...	...	...	...	...	...	...
	Periyar & Thekkadi.	...	...	...	7	5	2
	Total ...	5	4	1	2,808	1,446	1,362

X.

Tongue—(*Continued*).

ASIATIC LANGUAGES.

Singalese.			Chinese.			Hebrew.			Syrian.		
Total.	Males.	Females.	Total.	Males.	Females.	Total.	Males.	Females.	Total.	Males.	Females.
51	52	53	54	55	56	57	58	59	60	61	62
...	...	...	...	...	...	...	...	...	...	...	...
...	...	...	...	...	...	...	...	...	...	...	...
...	...	...	...	...	...	...	...	...	...	...	...
...	...	...	...	...	...	...	...	...	...	...	...
...	...	...	...	...	...	...	...	...	...	...	...
...	...	...	...	...	...	...	...	...	...	...	...
...	...	...	...	...	...	...	...	...	...	...	...
...	...	...	...	...	...	...	...	...	...	...	...
...	...	...	...	...	...	...	...	...	...	...	...
...	...	...	...	...	...	...	...	...	...	...	...
...	...	...	...	...	...	...	...	...	...	...	...
...	...	...	...	...	...	...	...	...	...	...	...
...	...	...	...	...	...	9	5	4	...	...	...
...	...	...	...	...	...	...	...	...	...	...	...
...	...	...	...	...	...	...	...	...	...	...	...
...	...	...	...	...	...	...	...	...	...	...	...
...	...	...	...	...	...	...	...	...	...	...	...
...	...	...	...	...	...	...	...	...	...	...	...
...	...	...	...	...	...	...	...	...	...	...	...
...	...	...	...	...	...	...	...	...	...	...	...
...	...	...	...	...	...	...	...	...	...	...	...
...	...	...	...	...	...	4	1	3	...	...	...
...	...	...	...	...	...	...	...	...	...	...	...
...	...	...	...	...	...	...	...	...	...	...	...
...	...	...	...	...	...	...	...	...	...	...	...
...	...	...	...	...	...	...	...	...	2	2	...
...	...	...	...	...	...	...	...	...	...	...	...
...	...	...	...	...	...	...	...	...	...	...	...
...	...	...	...	...	...	...	...	...	...	...	...
...	...	...	...	...	...	4	2	2	...	...	...
...	...	...	...	...	...	121	64	57	...	...	...
8	8	...	...	...	...	...	...	...	...	...	...
...	...	...	1	1	...	...	...	...	...	...	...
8	8	...	1	1	...	138	72	66	2	2	...

TABLE

Parent

Number.	Taluq.	Asiatic Languages— Arabic. Total.	Arabic. Males.	Arabic. Females.	Persian. Total.	Persian. Males.	Persian. Females.
1	2	63	64	65	66	67	68
1	Tovala ...	...	...	...	...	...	...
2	Agastiswaram ...	3	2	1	1	1	...
3	Eranial ...	1	1	...	...	...	...
4	Kalkulam ...	...	...	...	...	...	...
5	Vilavankodu ...	...	...	...	...	...	...
6	Neyattankara ...	...	...	...	...	...	...
7	Trivandram ...	245	128	117	...	...	...
8	Nedumangadu ...	2	2	...	...	...	...
9	Sirayinkil ...	57	34	23	...	...	...
10	Kottarakkara ...	...	...	...	...	...	...
11	Pattanapuram ...	...	...	...	...	...	...
12	Shenkotta ...	...	...	...	...	...	...
13	Quilon ...	161	83	78	...	...	...
14	Kunnattur ...	...	...	...	...	...	...
15	Karunagappalli ...	10	7	3	...	...	...
16	Kartigappalli ...	76	29	47	...	...	...
17	Mavellikkara ...	...	...	...	...	...	...
18	Chenganur ...	6	3	3	...	...	...
19	Tiruvalla ...	17	4	13	...	...	...
20	Ambalappula ...	60	56	4	...	...	...
21	Sherttala ...	111	44	67	...	...	...
22	Vykkam ...	90	42	48	...	...	...
23	Ettumanur ...	11	4	7	...	...	...
24	Kottayam ...	75	43	32	...	...	...
25	Changanacheri ...	3	3	...	...	...	...
26	Meenachal ...	...	...	...	...	...	...
27	Muvattupula ...	4	1	3	...	...	...
28	Todupula ...	11	6	5	...	...	...
29	Kunnattunadu ...	1	1	...	...	...	...
30	Alangadu ...	10	4	6	...	...	...
31	Parur ...	71	30	41	...	...	...
	Cardamom Hills ...	3	3	...	...	...	...
	Periyar & Thekkadi.	1	1	...	...	...	...
	Total ..	1,029	531	498	1	1	...

X.

Tongue—(*Continued*).

(*Continued*). Total Asiatic Languages.			Non-Asiatic Languages. Italian.			Spanish.			Portuguese.		
Total.	Males.	Females.	Total.	Males.	Females.	Total.	Males.	Females.	Total.	Males.	Females.
69	70	71	72	73	74	75	76	77	78	79	80
...	...	...	...	...	...	...	...	...	...	...	...
4	3	1	...	...	...	...	...	...	6	4	2
1	1	...	1	1	...	1	1	...	...	...	...
...	...	...	...	...	...	...	...	...	...	...	...
...	...	...	1	1	...	...	...	...	...	...	...
...	...	...	...	...	...	...	...	...	...	...	...
245	128	117	...	...	...	6	3	3	18	12	6
2	2	...	...	...	...	...	...	...	...	...	...
57	34	23	...	...	...	...	...	...	1	1	...
...	...	...	...	...	...	...	...	...	...	...	...
...	...	...	...	...	...	...	...	...	...	...	...
...	...	...	...	...	...	...	...	...	...	...	...
170	88	82	3	3	...	...	...	...	...	...	...
...	...	...	...	...	...	...	...	...	...	...	...
10	7	3	...	...	...	...	...	...	48	22	26
76	29	47	...	...	...	...	...	...	...	...	...
...	...	...	...	...	...	...	...	...	47	21	26
6	3	3	...	...	...	...	...	...	...	...	...
17	4	13	...	...	...	...	...	...	...	...	...
60	56	4	...	...	...	...	...	...	50	21	29
111	44	67	...	...	...	...	...	...	1	1	...
94	43	51	...	...	...	...	...	...	...	...	...
11	4	7	...	...	...	...	...	...	4	4	...
75	43	32	...	...	...	1	1	...	23	12	11
3	3	...	...	...	...	...	...	...	...	...	...
2	2	...	...	...	...	...	...	...	...	...	...
4	1	3	...	...	...	...	...	...	...	...	...
11	6	5	...	...	...	...	...	...	...	...	...
1	1	...	...	...	...	...	...	...	...	...	...
14	6	8	...	...	...	...	...	...	...	...	...
192	94	98	3	3	...	3	3	...	194	102	92
6	6	...	...	...	...	...	...	...	7	7	...
2	2	...	...	...	...	...	...	...	61	58	3
1,174	610	564	8	8	...	11	8	3	460	265	195

TABLE

Parent

Number.	Taluq.	Non-Asiatic French. Total.	Males.	Females.	German. Total.	Males.	Females.
1	2	81	82	83	84	85	86
1	Tovala ...	...	...	...	...	...	...
2	Agastiswaram ...	...	...	...	...	...	...
3	Eranial ...	...	...	...	...	...	...
4	Kalkulam ...	...	...	...	...	...	...
5	Vilavankodu ...	...	...	...	...	...	...
6	Neyattankara ...	...	...	...	...	...	...
7	Trivandram ...	26	16	10	1	1	...
8	Nedumangadu ...	...	...	...	...	...	...
9	Sirayinkil ...	...	...	...	...	...	...
10	Kottarakkara ...	...	...	...	...	...	...
11	Pattanapuram ...	...	...	...	...	...	...
12	Shenkotta ...	1	...	1	...	...	...
13	Quilon ...	1	1	...	...	...	...
14	Kunnattur ...	...	...	...	...	...	...
15	Karunagappalli ...	...	...	...	...	...	...
16	Kartigappalli ...	...	...	...	...	...	...
17	Mavellikkara ...	...	...	...	...	...	...
18	Chenganur ...	...	...	...	...	...	...
19	Tiruvalla ...	...	...	...	...	...	...
20	Ambalappula ...	1	...	1	...	...	...
21	Sherttala ...	...	...	...	...	...	...
22	Vykkam ...	...	...	...	...	...	...
23	Ettumanur ...	...	...	...	...	...	...
24	Kottayam ...	...	...	...	...	...	...
25	Changanacheri ...	...	...	...	...	...	...
26	Meenachal ...	...	...	...	...	...	...
27	Muvattupula ...	...	...	...	...	...	...
28	Todupula ...	...	...	...	...	...	...
29	Kunnattunadu ...	...	...	...	...	...	...
30	Alangadu ...	...	...	...	...	...	...
31	Parur ...	1	1	...	...	...	...
	Cardamom Hills ...	...	...	...	1	1	...
	Periyar & Thekkadi.	...	...	...	...	...	...
	Total ...	30	18	12	2	2	...

X.

Tongue—(*Continued*).

LANGUAGES—(*Continued*).									Not stated.		
English.			Irish.			Total Non-Asiatic Languages.					
Total.	Males.	Females.	Total.	Males.	Females.	Total.	Males.	Females.	Total.	Males.	Females.
87	88	89	90	91	92	93	94	95	96	97	98
1	1	...	...	...	...	1	1	...	...	...	...
78	43	35	...	...	...	84	47	37	...	...	...
15	9	6	...	...	...	17	11	6	...	...	...
8	4	4	...	...	...	8	4	4	...	...	...
4	4	...	...	..	...	5	5	...	...	...	...
3	1	2	..	...	...	3	1	2	...	...	...
630	318	312	...	...	..	681	350	331	...	...	...
22	13	9	...	...	...	22	13	9	...	...	...
13	7	6	...	...	...	14	8	6	...	...	...
4	4	...	...	...	...	4	4	...	...	...	...
34	22	12	...	..	...	34	22	12	...	...	...
19	10	9	...	...	...	20	10	10	...	...	..
215	102	113	...	...	...	219	106	113	1	1	...
...	...	...	...	...	...	...	...	...	...	...	...
38	15	23	...	...	...	86	37	49	...	...	...
...	...	...	...	...	...	...	...	...	...	...	...
8	5	3	...	...	...	55	26	29	...	...	...
2	2	...	...	...	...	2	2	...	...	...	...
3	1	2	...	...	...	3	1	2	...	...	...
158	91	67	...	...	...	209	112	97	...	...	...
14	3	11	...	...	...	15	4	11	...	...	...
3	1	2	...	...	...	3	1	2	...	...	...
...	...	...	...	..	...	4	4	...	...	...	...
21	10	11	...	...	...	45	23	22	...	...	...
...	...	...	...	...	...	...	...	...	...	...	...
2	2	...	...	...	...	2	2	...	...	...	...
1	1	...	...	...	...	1	1	...	...	...	...
...	...	...	...	...	...	...	...	...	...	...	...
...	...	...	...	...	...	...	...	...	...	...	...
6	3	3	...	...	...	6	3	3	...	...	...
5	5	...	...	...	...	206	114	92	...	...	...
67	42	25	29	11	18	104	61	43	...	...	...
61	45	16	...	...	...	122	103	19	...	...	...
1,435	764	671	29	11	18	1,975	1,076	899	1	1	...

TABLE

Birth

District, State, Province or Country of Birth.	Total Population.		
	Total.	Males.	Females.
A. Within the Province.			
Travancore	2,540,758	1,279,321	1,261,437
Tinnevelly	7,785	4,831	2,954
Madura	2,113	1,464	649
Trichinopoly	499	340	159
Tanjore	507	314	193
South Arcot	69	62	7
Chingleput	28	18	10
Madras	508	296	212
Cochin	1,274	814	460
Malabar	362	258	104
South Canara	271	208	63
Nilgiris	1	1	...
Coimbatore	580	479	101
Salem	11	6	5
North Arcot	173	110	63
Nellore	53	29	24
Cuddappah	13	9	4
Kurnool	20	13	7
Bellary	6	4	2
Ceded Districts	2	1	1
Krishna	22	16	6
Godavari	36	21	15
Vizagapatam	395	209	186
Ganjam	164	118	46
Pondicherry	2	1	1
Total A. ...	2,555,652	1,288,943	1,266,709

XI.

place.

Taluqs.								
Tovala.			Agastiswaram.			Eranial.		
Total.	Males.	Females.	Total.	Males.	Females.	Total.	Males.	Females.
27,717	13,378	14,339	86,293	42,611	43,682	104,965	52,768	52,197
1,988	1,093	895	737	470	267	105	91	14
23	4	19	47	27	20	1	1	...
5	2	3	2	1	1	...	...	...
5	1	4	38	26	12	...	...	...
...	...	...	...	...	...	...	...	...
...	...	...	...	...	...	...	...	...
...	...	...	19	14	5	...	...	...
2	...	2	6	5	1	...	...	...
...	...	...	3	3	...	...	...	...
5	5	...	10	9	1	...	...	...
...	...	...	...	...	...	...	...	...
1	1	...	2	1	1	...	...	...
...	...	...	...	...	...	...	...	...
...	...	...	1	1	...	...	...	...
...	...	...	...	...	...	...	...	...
...	...	...	...	...	...	...	...	...
...	...	...	...	...	...	...	...	...
...	...	...	...	...	...	...	...	...
...	...	...	...	...	...	...	...	...
...	...	...	...	...	...	...	...	...
...	...	...	...	...	...	...	...	...
...	...	...	...	...	...	...	...	...
...	...	...	...	...	...	...	...	...
...	...	...	...	...	...	...	...	...
29,746	14,484	15,262	87,158	43,168	43,990	105,071	52,860	52,211

TABLE

Birth

District, State, Province or Country of Birth.	Taluq					
	Kalkulam.			Vilavankodu.		
	Total.	Males.	Females.	Total.	Males.	Females.
A. Within the Province.						
Travancore ...	59,308	29,704	29,604	68,442	35,127	33,315
Tinnevelly ...	107	83	24	35	31	4
Madura ...	2	2	...	..	...	...
Trichinopoly ...	3	3	...	...	...	...
Tanjore ...	1	1	...	...	...	...
South Arcot ...	2	2	...	...	...	...
Chingleput ...	..	...	...	...	...	...
Madras ...	...	...	...	2	2	...
Cochin ..	4	1	3	18	18	...
Malabar ...	...	...	...	...	...	...
South Canara ...	18	18	...	18	18	...
Nilgiris ...	...	...	...	...	...	...
Coimbatore ...	2	2	...	...	...	...
Salem ...	...	...	...	...	...	...
North Arcot ...	2	2	...	...	...	...
Nellore ...	...	...	...	...	...	...
Cuddappah ...	...	...	...	...	...	...
Kurnool ...	...	...	...	...	...	...
Bellary ...	...	...	...	...	...	...
Ceded Districts ...	...	...	...	...	...	...
Krishna ...	...	...	...	...	...	...
Godavari ...	...	...	...	...	...	...
Vizagapatam ...	...	...	...	...	...	...
Ganjam ...	...	...	...	...	...	...
Pondicherry ...	...	...	...	...	...	...
Total A. ...	59,449	29,818	29,631	68,515	35,196	33,319

XI.

place—(*Continued*).

—(*Continued*).

Neyattankara. Total.	Neyattankara. Males.	Neyattankara. Females.	Trivandram. Total.	Trivandram. Males.	Trivandram. Females.	Nedumangadu. Total.	Nedumangadu. Males.	Nedumangadu. Females.
110,661	56,864	53,797	109,523	55,445	54,078	55,495	27,856	27,639
66	63	3	1,390	826	564	...	...	...
10	9	1	53	40	13	...	...	...
...	...	...	30	19	11	...	...	...
...	...	...	118	70	48	...	...	...
...	...	...	...	...	...	...	...	...
...	...	...	4	2	2	...	...	...
...	...	...	42	25	17	...	...	...
4	4	...	72	44	28	...	...	...
...	...	...	86	59	27	...	...	...
8	8	...	108	60	48	...	...	...
...	...	...	...	...	...	...	...	...
...	...	...	133	107	26	...	...	...
...	...	...	...	...	...	...	...	...
...	...	...	18	13	5	...	...	...
...	...	...	7	3	4	...	...	...
...	...	...	1	1	...	...	...	...
...	...	...	1	1	...	...	...	...
...	...	...	2	1	1	...	...	...
...	...	...	...	...	...	...	...	...
...	...	...	2	2	...	...	...	...
...	...	...	4	3	1	...	...	...
...	...	...	61	29	32	...	...	...
...	...	...	12	3	9	...	...	...
...	...	...	...	...	...	...	...	...
110,749	56,948	53,801	111,667	56,753	54,914	55,495	27,856	27,639

TABLE
Birth

District, State, Province or Country of Birth.	Taluqs					
	Sirayinkil.			Kottarakkara.		
	Total.	Males.	Females.	Total.	Males.	Females.
A. Within the Province.						
Travancore ...	97,929	48,223	49,706	71,517	36,055	35,462
Tinnevelly ...	3	2	1	...	...	...
Madura ...	2	2	...	...	...	...
Trichinopoly ...	...	...	...	...	...	...
Tanjore ...	2	2	...	...	...	...
South Arcot ...	...	...	...	...	...	...
Chingleput ...	...	...	...	...	...	...
Madras ...	...	...	...	...	...	...
Cochin ...	4	4	...	...	...	...
Malabar ...	4	4	...	...	...	...
South Canara ...	...	...	...	...	...	...
Nilgiris ...	...	...	...	...	...	...
Coimbatore ...	...	...	...	...	...	...
Salem ...	...	...	...	...	...	...
North Arcot ...	...	...	...	...	...	...
Nellore ...	...	...	...	...	...	...
Cuddappah ...	...	...	...	...	...	...
Kurnool ...	...	...	...	...	...	...
Bellary ...	...	...	...	...	...	...
Ceded Districts ...	...	...	...	...	...	...
Krishna ...	4	3	1	...	...	...
Godavari ...	...	...	...	...	...	...
Vizagapatam ...	...	...	...	...	...	...
Ganjam ...	...	...	...	...	...	...
Pondicherry ...	...	...	...	...	...	...
Total A. ...	97,948	48,240	49,708	71,517	36,055	35,462

XI.

place—(*Continued*).

—(*Continued*).

Pattanapuram.			Shenkotta.			Quilon.		
Total.	Males.	Females.	Total.	Males.	Females.	Total.	Males.	Females.
39,439	19,851	19,588	30,612	14,863	15,749	119,535	59,379	60,156
...	...	...	1,441	814	627	270	141	129
...	...	...	10	7	3	52	34	18
...	...	...	...	...	...	180	87	93
...	...	...	1	...	1	142	86	56
...	...	...	...	...	...	56	55	1
...	...	...	...	...	...	4	2	2
...	...	...	8	4	4	280	148	132
...	...	...	...	...	...	59	36	23
...	...	...	...	...	...	31	18	13
...	...	...	2	2	...	11	9	2
...	...	...	...	...	...	1	1	...
...	...	...	...	...	...	...	...	...
...	...	...	...	...	...	8	6	2
...	...	...	...	...	...	145	89	56
...	...	...	...	...	...	16	7	9
...	...	...	...	...	...	7	4	3
...	...	...	...	...	...	6	4	2
...	...	...	...	...	...	2	2	...
...	...	...	...	...	...	2	1	1
...	...	...	...	...	...	9	4	5
...	...	...	...	...	...	19	9	10
...	...	...	...	...	...	333	180	153
...	...	...	...	...	...	152	115	37
...	...	...	...	...	...	1	...	1
39,439	19,851	19,588	32,074	15,690	16,384	121,321	60,417	60,904

TABLE
Birth

District, State, Province or Country of Birth.	Taluqs					
	Kunnattur.			Karunagappalli.		
	Total.	Males.	Females.	Total.	Males.	Females.
A. Within the Province.						
Travancore ...	73,510	37,378	36,132	108,810	52,851	55,959
Tinnevelly ...	14	14	...	2	2	...
Madura ..	4	4	...	...	...	...
Trichinopoly ...	...	...	...	...	...	...
Tanjore ...	...	...	...	...	...	...
South Arcot ...	...	...	...	...	...	...
Chingleput ...	...	...	...	...	...	...
Madras ...	...	...	...	...	...	...
Cochin ...	...	...	...	4	2	2
Malabar ...	...	...	...	...	...	...
South Canara ...	1	1	...	4	4	...
Nilgiris ...	...	...	...	...	...	...
Coimbatore ...	...	...	...	...	...	...
Salem ...	...	...	...	...	...	...
North Arcot ...	...	...	...	...	...	...
Nellore ...	...	...	...	...	...	...
Cuddappah ...	...	...	...	...	...	...
Kurnool ...	...	...	...	...	...	...
Bellary ...	...	...	...	...	...	...
Ceded Districts ...	...	...	...	...	...	...
Krishna ...	...	...	...	...	...	...
Godavari ...	...	...	...	...	...	...
Vizagapatam ...	...	...	...	...	...	...
Ganjam ...	...	...	...	...	...	...
Pondicherry ...	...	...	...	...	...	...
Total A. ...	73,529	37,397	36,132	108,820	52,859	55,961

XI.

place—(*Continued*).

—(*Continued*).

Kartigappalli.			Mavellikkara.			Chenganur.		
Total.	Males.	Females.	Total.	Males.	Females.	Total.	Males.	Females.
91,908	45,189	46,719	103,589	52,472	51,117	93,960	48,443	45,517
...	...	...	14	8	6	...	...	...
1	1	...	...	...	...	...	...	...
4	1	3	...	...	...	...	...	...
2	...	2	1	1	...	...	...	...
...	...	...	...	...	...	...	...	...
...	...	...	...	...	...	...	...	...
...	...	...	4	4	...	...	...	...
16	10	6	2	2	...	...	...	...
1	1	...	...	...	...	...	...	...
6	6	...	2	2	...	...	...	...
...	...	...	...	...	...	...	...	...
6	2	4	...	...	...	...	...	...
...	...	...	...	...	...	...	...	...
...	...	...	...	...	...	...	...	...
...	...	...	...	...	...	...	...	...
...	...	...	...	...	...	...	...	...
...	...	...	...	...	...	...	...	...
...	...	...	...	...	...	...	...	...
...	...	...	...	...	...	...	...	...
...	...	...	...	...	...	...	...	...
...	...	...	...	...	...	...	...	...
...	...	...	...	...	...	...	...	...
...	...	...	...	...	...	...	...	...
...	...	...	...	...	...	...	...	...
91,944	45,210	46,734	103,612	52,489	51,123	93,960	48,443	45,517

TABLE
Birth

District, State, Province or Country of Birth.	Taluqs					
	Tiruvalla.			Ambalappula.		
	Total.	Males.	Females.	Total.	Males.	Females.
A. Within the Province.						
Travancore ...	122,115	62,487	59,628	94,339	46,570	47,769
Tinnevelly ...	19	19	...	26	21	5
Madura ...	...	...	...	1	1	...
Trichinopoly ...	...	...	...	...	...	...
Tanjore ...	8	8	...	35	20	15
South Arcot ..	...	...	...	...	...	...
Chingleput ...	...	...	...	...	...	...
Madras ...	...	...	...	13	8	5
Cochin ...	...	...	...	66	47	19
Malabar ...	...	...	...	48	42	6
South Canara ...	...	...	...	3	3	...
Nilgiris ...	...	...	...	...	...	...
Coimbatore ...	...	...	...	...	...	...
Salem ...	...	...	...	...	...	...
North Arcot ...	...	...	...	...	...	...
Nellore ...	...	...	...	...	...	...
Cuddappah ...	...	...	...	...	...	...
Kurnool ...	...	...	...	...	...	...
Bellary ...	...	...	...	...	...	...
Ceded Districts ...	...	...	...	...	...	...
Krishna ...	...	...	...	...	...	...
Godavari ...	...	...	...	...	...	...
Vizagapatam ...	...	...	...	...	...	...
Ganjam ...	...	...	...	...	...	...
Pondicherry ...	...	...	...	...	...	...
Total A. ...	122,142	62,514	59,628	94,531	46,712	47,819

XI.

place—(*Continued*).

—(*Continued*).

Sherttala.			Vykkam.			Ettumanur.		
Total.	Males.	Females.	Total.	Males.	Females.	Total.	Males.	Females.
117,188	58,389	58,799	80,127	40,614	39,513	80,750	41,463	39,287
2	2	...	84	67	17	1	1	...
2	1	1	...	...	...	...	...	...
2	2	...	2	2	...	...	...	...
2	2	...	7	4	8	...	...	...
...	...	...	...	...	...	...	...	...
...	...	...	10	7	3	...	...	...
...	...	...	...	...	...	...	...	...
34	25	9	271	149	122	53	53	...
6	4	2	75	60	15	2	2	...
13	13	...	18	17	1	4	4	...
...	...	...	...	...	...	...	...	...
...	...	...	...	...	...	2	2	...
1	...	1	...	...	...	...	...	...
...	...	...	...	...	...	...	...	...
...	...	...	...	...	...	...	...	...
...	...	...	...	...	...	...	...	...
...	...	...	...	...	...	...	...	...
...	...	...	...	...	...	...	...	...
...	...	...	...	...	...	...	...	...
...	...	...	...	...	...	...	...	...
...	...	...	1	1	...	...	...	...
...	...	...	...	...	...	...	...	...
...	...	...	...	...	...	...	...	...
...	...	...	...	...	...	...	...	...
117,250	58,438	58,812	80,595	40,921	39,674	80,812	41,525	39,287

TABLE
Birth

District, State, Province or Country of Birth.	Taluqs					
	Kottayam.			Changanacheri.		
	Total.	Males.	Females.	Total.	Males.	Females.
A. Within the Province.						
Travancore ...	77,073	39,216	37,857	74,675	38,552	36,123
Tinnevelly ...	1	...	1	30	30	...
Madura ...	...	...	...	...	...	...
Trichinopoly ...	...	...	...	...	...	...
Tanjore ...	...	...	...	...	...	...
South Arcot ...	...	...	...	...	...	...
Chingleput ...	...	...	..	...	...	...
Madras ...	...	...	...	...	...	...
Cochin ...	5	5	...	...	...	...
Malabar ...	1	1	...	...	...	...
South Canara ...	...	...	...	...	...	...
Nilgiris ...	...	...	...	...	...	...
Coimbatore ...	...	...	...	...	...	...
Salem ...	...	...	...	...	...	...
North Arcot ...	...	...	...	...	...	...
Nellore ...	...	...	...	...	...	...
Cuddappah ...	...	...	...	...	...	...
Kurnool ...	...	...	...	...	...	...
Bellary ...	...	...	...	...	...	...
Ceded Districts ...	...	...	...	...	...	...
Krishna ...	...	...	...	...	...	...
Godavari ...	...	...	...	...	...	...
Vizagapatam ...	...	...	...	...	...	...
Ganjam ...	...	...	...	...	...	...
Pondicherry ...	...	...	...	...	...	...
Total A. ...	77,080	39,222	37,858	74,705	38,582	36,123

XI.

place—(*Continued*).

—(*Continued*).

Meenachal.			Mnvattnpula.			Todupula.		
Total.	Males.	Females.	Total.	Males.	Females.	Total.	Males.	Females.
59,966	30,822	29,144	102,898	51,529	51,369	25,200	12,784	12,416
8	6	2	...	...	...	...	...	...
...	...	...	...	...	...	...	...	...
...	...	...	5	3	2	...	...	...
...	...	...	1	1	...	...	...	...
...	...	...	...	...	...	...	...	...
...	...	...	...	...	...	...	...	...
...	...	...	...	...	...	...	...	...
...	...	...	96	53	43	2	2	...
...	...	...	...	...	...	...	...	...
...	...	...	...	...	...	...	...	...
...	...	...	...	...	...	...	...	...
...	...	...	...	...	...	...	...	...
...	...	...	...	...	...	...	...	...
...	...	...	...	...	...	...	...	...
...	...	...	...	...	...	...	...	...
...	...	...	...	...	...	...	...	...
...	...	...	...	...	...	...	...	...
...	...	...	...	...	...	...	...	...
...	...	...	...	...	...	...	...	...
...	...	...	...	...	...	...	...	...
...	...	...	...	...	...	...	...	...
...	...	...	...	...	...	...	...	...
...	...	...	...	...	...	...	...	...
...	...	...	...	...	...	...	...	...
59,974	30,828	29,146	103,000	51,586	51,414	25,202	12,786	12,416

TABLE
Birth

District, State, Province or Country of Birth.	Taluqs					
	Kunnattunadu.			Alangadu.		
	Total.	Males.	Females.	Total.	Males.	Females.
A. Within the Province.						
Travancore ...	113,949	57,120	56,829	70,910	35,900	35,010
Tinnevelly ...	1	1	...	9	8	1
Madura ...	...	...	...	...	...	...
Trichinopoly ...	...	...	...	...	...	...
Tanjore ...	...	...	...	...	...	...
South Arcot ...	...	...	...	...	...	...
Chingleput ...	...	...	...	...	...	...
Madras ...	...	...	...	...	...	...
Cochin ...	59	56	3	36	33	3
Malabar ...	...	...	...	...	...	...
South Canara ...	...	...	...	...	...	...
Nilgiris ...	...	...	...	...	...	...
Coimbatore ...	...	...	...	...	...	...
Salem ...	...	...	...	...	...	...
North Arcot ...	...	...	...	...	...	...
Nellore ...	...	...	...	...	...	...
Cuddappah ...	...	...	...	...	...	...
Kurnool ...	...	...	...	...	...	...
Bellary ...	...	...	...	...	...	...
Ceded Districts ...	...	...	...	...	...	...
Krishna ...	...	...	...	...	...	...
Godavari ...	...	...	...	...	...	...
Vizagapatam ...	...	...	...	...	...	...
Ganjam ...	...	...	...	...	...	...
Pondicherry ...	...	...	...	...	...	...
Total A. ...	114,009	57,177	56,832	70,955	35,941	35,014

XI.

place—(*Continued*).

—(*Continued*).

Parur.			Cardamom Hills.			Periyar and Thekkadi.		
Total.	Males.	Females.	Total.	Males.	Females.	Total.	Males.	Females.
58,714	29,815	28,899	9,397	5,375	4,022	244	228	16
45	29	16	1,095	755	340	292	254	38
...	...	...	317	197	120	1,588	1,134	454
...	...	...	38	31	7	228	189	39
47	33	14	41	25	16	56	34	22
...	...	...	1	...	1	10	5	5
...	...	...	...	...	...	10	7	3
...	...	...	41	26	15	99	65	34
245	56	189	50	48	2	166	161	5
90	52	38	6	4	2	9	8	1
39	28	11	1	1	...	...	...	...
...	...	...	...	...	...	...	...	...
...	...	...	69	37	32	365	327	38
...	...	...	...	...	...	2	...	2
...	...	...	1	1	...	6	4	2
...	...	...	...	...	...	30	19	11
...	...	...	...	...	...	5	4	1
...	...	...	...	...	...	13	8	5
...	...	...	...	...	...	2	1	1
...	...	...	...	...	...	...	...	...
...	...	...	...	...	...	7	7	...
...	...	...	...	...	...	12	8	4
...	...	...	...	...	...	1	...	1
...	...	...	...	...	...	...	...	...
...	...	...	...	...	...	1	1	...
59,180	30,013	29,167	11,057	6,500	4,557	3,146	2,464	682

TABLE
Birth

District, State, Province or Country of Birth.	Total Population.		
	Total.	Males.	Females.
B. In India beyond the Province.			
Mysore	154	88	66
Coorg	1	1	...
North Canara	27	25	2
Goa	11	11	...
Bijapur	3	3	...
Kolhapur	1	1	...
Ratnagiri	20	20	...
Bombay	182	162	20
Hyderabad	227	112	115
Nagpore	10	7	3
Jabbalpore	4	4	...
Central Provinces (Unspecified)	102	58	44
Bhopal	1	1	...
Malwa	55	48	7
Bundalkhand	1	1	...
Gwalior	1	1	...
Baroda	28	13	15
Guzerat	10	10	...
Cutch	66	41	25
Marwar	2	2	...
Jeypore	15	15	...
Delhi	22	20	2
Punjab	2	2	...
Agra	17	15	2
Allahabad	11	10	1
Benares	33	26	7
Oudh	44	40	4
Rohilkund	1	1	...
North-West Provinces (Unspecified) ...	15	14	1
Calcutta	10	8	2
Dacca	1	1	...
Bengal (Unspecified)	54	45	9
Orissa	10	4	6
Nepaul	2	2	...
British Burmah	2	...	2
British India (Unspecified)	539	342	197
Total B. ...	1,684	1,154	530

XI.

place—(*Continued*).

Taluqs.								
Tovala.			**Agastiswaram.**			**Eranial.**		
Total.	Males.	Females.	Total.	Males.	Females.	Total.	Males.	Females.
...	...	...	2	1	1	...	...	...
...	...	...	...	...	...	...	...	...
...	...	...	...	...	...	...	...	...
...	...	...	...	...	...	...	...	...
...	...	...	...	...	...	...	...	...
...	...	...	1	1	...	...	...	...
...	..	...	...	...	...	...	...	...
...	...	...	...	...	...	17	17	...
...	...	...	1	...	1	...	...	...
...	...	...	...	...	...	...	...	...
...	...	...	...	...	...	...	...	...
...	...	...	...	...	...	...	..	...
...	...	...	...	...	...	...	...	...
...	...	...	...	...	...	...	...	...
...	...	...	...	...	...	...	...	...
...	...	...	...	...	...	...	...	...
...	...	...	...	...	...	...	...	...
...	...	...	...	...	...	...	...	...
...	...	...	...	...	...	...	...	...
...	...	...	...	...	...	...	...	...
...	...	...	...	...	...	...	...	...
...	...	...	...	...	...	...	...	...
...	...	...	2	2	...	...	...	...
...	...	...	1	1	...	...	...	...
...	...	...	1	1	...	...	...	...
...	...	...	16	16	...	...	...	...
...	...	...	1	1	...	...	...	...
...	...	...	...	...	...	...	...	...
...	...	...	...	...	...	...	...	...
...	...	...	...	...	...	...	...	...
...	...	...	...	...	...	...	...	...
...	...	...	...	...	...	...	...	...
...	...	...	...	...	...	...	...	...
...	...	...	1	1	...	...	...	...
...	...	...	1	...	1	...	...	...
4	4	...	25	16	9	...	...	...
4	4	...	52	40	12	17	17	...

TABLE
Birth

District, State, Province or Country of Birth.	Taluqs					
	Kalkulam.			Vilavankodu.		
	Total.	Males.	Females.	Total.	Males.	Females.
B. In India beyond the Province.						
Mysore	2	2	...	...	...	...
Coorg	...	...	...	...	...	...
North Canara	...	...	...	2	2	...
Goa	...	...	...	...	...	...
Bijapur	...	...	...	...	...	...
Kolhapur	...	...	...	...	...	...
Ratnagiri	...	...	...	...	...	...
Bombay	...	...	...	...	...	...
Hyderabad	5	3	2	...	...	...
Nagpore	...	...	...	...	...	...
Jabbalpore	...	...	...	...	...	...
Central Provinces (Unspecified) ...	...	...	...	...	...	...
Bhopal	...	...	...	...	...	...
Malwa	5	5	...	...	...	...
Bundalkhand	...	...	...	...	...	...
Gwalior	...	...	...	...	...	...
Baroda	...	...	...	...	...	...
Guzerat	...	...	...	...	...	...
Cutch	...	...	...	...	...	...
Marwar	...	...	...	...	...	...
Jeypore	...	...	...	...	...	...
Delhi	...	...	...	...	...	...
Punjab	...	...	...	...	...	...
Agra	...	...	...	...	...	...
Allahabad	...	...	...	...	...	...
Benares	7	3	4	1	1	...
Oudh	...	...	...	...	...	...
Rohilkund	...	...	...	...	...	...
North-West Provinces (Unspecified).	...	...	...	...	...	...
Calcutta	...	...	...	...	...	...
Dacca	...	...	...	...	...	...
Bengal (Unspecified)	...	...	...	...	...	...
Orissa	...	...	...	...	...	...
Nepaul	...	...	...	...	...	...
British Burmah	...	...	...	...	...	...
British India (Unspecified) ...	2	1	1	...	...	...
Total B. ...	21	14	7	3	3	...

XI.

place—(*Continued*).

—(*Continued*).

Neyattankara.			Trivandram.			Nedumangadu.		
Total.	Males.	Females.	Total.	Males.	Females.	Total.	Males.	Females.
...	...	...	21	13	8	...	...	...
...	...	...	...	...	...	...	...	...
...	...	..	3	2	1	...	...	...
...	...	...	...	...	...	...	...	...
...	...	...	...	...	...	...	...	...
...	...	...	...	...	...	...	...	...
...	...	...	...	...	...	...	...	...
...	...	...	8	7	1	...	...	...
...	...	...	87	33	54	...	...	...
...	...	...	...	...	...	...	...	...
...	...	...	...	...	...	...	...	...
...	...	...	8	5	3	...	...	...
...	...	...	...	...	...	...	...	...
...	...	...	...	...	...	...	...	...
...	...	...	...	...	...	...	...	...
...	...	...	...	...	...	...	...	...
...	...	...	...	...	...	...	...	...
...	...	...	...	...	...	...	...	...
...	...	...	46	27	19	...	...	...
...	...	...	...	...	...	...	...	...
...	...	...	1	1	...	...	...	...
...	...	...	...	...	...	...	...	...
...	...	...	...	...	...	...	...	...
...	...	...	...	...	...	...	...	...
...	...	...	...	...	...	...	...	...
...	...	...	...	...	...	...	...	...
...	...	...	13	11	2	...	...	...
...	...	...	...	...	...	...	...	...
...	...	...	...	...	...	...	...	...
...	...	...	7	6	1	...	...	...
...	...	...	...	...	...	...	...	...
...	...	...	6	6	...	...	...	...
..	...	...	...	...	...	...	...	...
...	...	...	...	...	...	...	...	...
...	...	...	...	...	...	...	...	...
4	4	...	16	6	10	...	...	...
4	4	...	216	117	99	...	...	...

TABLE
Birth

District, State, Province or Country of Birth.	Taluqs					
	Sirayinkil.			Kottarakkara.		
	Total.	Males.	Females.	Total.	Males.	Females.
B. In India beyond the Province.						
Mysore	...	...	...	...	...	...
Coorg	...	...	...	...	...	...
North Canara	...	...	...	...	...	...
Goa	...	...	...	...	...	...
Bijapur	...	...	..	...	...	...
Kolhapur	...	...	...	...	...	...
Ratnagiri	...	...	...	...	...	...
Bombay	...	...	...	...	...	...
Hyderabad	...	...	...	...	...	...
Nagpore	2	2	...	...	...	...
Jabbalpore	2	2	...	...	...	...
Central Provinces (Unspecified) ...	...	...	...	...	...	...
Bhopal	1	1	...	...	...	...
Malwa	13	6	7	...	...	...
Bundalkhand	...	...	...	...	...	...
Gwalior	1	1	...	...	...	...
Baroda	...	...	...	...	...	...
Guzerat	...	...	...	...	...	...
Cutch	...	...	...	...	...	...
Marwar	2	2	...	...	...	...
Jeypore	5	5	...	...	...	...
Delhi	1	1	...	...	...	...
Punjab	...	...	...	...	...	...
Agra	4	4	...	...	...	...
Allahabad	4	4	...	...	...	...
Benares	...	...	...	...	...	...
Oudh	1	1	...	...	...	...
Rohilkund	1	1	...	...	...	...
North-West Provinces (Unspecified)...	...	...	...	...	...	...
Calcutta	...	...	...	...	...	...
Dacca	...	...	...	...	...	...
Bengal (Unspecified)	...	...	...	...	...	...
Orissa	...	...	...	...	...	...
Nepaul	...	...	...	...	...	...
British Burmah	...	...	...	...	...	...
British India (Unspecified) ...	10	1	9	...	...	...
Total **B.** ...	47	31	16	...	...	...

XI.

place—(*Continued*).

—(*Continued*).

Pattanapuram.			Shenkotta.			Quilon.		
Total.	Males.	Females.	Total.	Males.	Females.	Total.	Males.	Females.
...	...	...	...	...	...	85	41	44
...	...	...	...	...	...	...	...	...
...	...	...	...	...	...	...	...	...
...	...	...	...	...	...	8	8	...
...	...	...	...	...	...	...	...	...
...	...	...	...	...	...	...	...	...
...	...	...	...	...	...	...	...	...
...	...	...	...	...	...	84	76	8
...	...	...	...	...	...	131	74	57
...	...	...	...	...	...	...	...	...
...	...	...	...	...	...	...	...	...
...	...	...	...	...	...	94	53	41
...	...	...	...	...	...	...	...	...
...	...	...	...	...	...	...	...	...
...	...	...	...	...	...	...	...	...
...	...	...	...	...	...	...	...	...
...	...	...	...	...	...	28	13	15
...	...	...	...	...	...	10	10	...
...	...	...	...	...	...	4	2	2
...	...	...	...	...	...	...	...	...
...	...	...	...	...	...	...	...	...
...	...	...	...	...	...	...	...	...
...	...	...	...	...	...	...	...	...
...	...	...	...	...	...	2	2	...
...	...	...	...	...	...	...	...	...
...	...	...	...	...	...	...	...	...
...	...	...	...	...	...	...	...	...
...	...	...	...	...	...	...	...	...
...	...	...	...	...	...	2	2	...
...	...	...	...	...	...	...	...	...
...	...	...	...	...	...	...	...	...
...	...	...	...	...	...	4	3	1
...	...	...	...	...	...	10	4	6
...	...	...	...	...	...	1	1	...
...	...	...	...	...	...	1	...	1
2	2	...	9	8	1	9	6	3
2	2	...	9	8	1	473	295	178

TABLE
Birth

District, State, Province or Country of Birth.	Taluqs: Kunnattur. Total.	Kunnattur. Males.	Kunnattur. Females.	Karunagappalli. Total.	Karunagappalli. Males.	Karunagappalli. Females.
B. In India beyond the Province.						
Mysore	...	...	...	...	...	...
Coorg	...	...	...	...	...	...
North Canara	...	...	...	...	...	...
Goa	...	...	...	...	...	...
Bijapur	...	...	...	...	...	...
Kolhapur	...	...	...	...	...	...
Ratnagiri	...	...	...	...	...	...
Bombay	...	...	...	...	...	...
Hyderabad	...	...	...	...	...	...
Nagpore	...	...	...	...	...	...
Jabbalpore	...	...	...	...	...	...
Central Provinces (Unspecified) ...	...	...	...	...	...	...
Bhopal	...	...	...	...	...	...
Malwa	...	...	...	...	...	...
Bundalkhand	...	...	...	...	...	...
Gwalior	...	...	...	...	...	...
Baroda	...	...	...	...	...	...
Guzerat	...	...	...	...	...	...
Cutch	...	...	...	...	...	...
Marwar	...	...	...	...	...	...
Jeypore	...	...	...	...	...	...
Delhi	...	...	...	...	...	...
Punjab	...	...	...	...	...	...
Agra	...	...	...	...	...	...
Allahabad	...	...	...	...	...	...
Benares	...	...	...	2	...	2
Oudh	...	...	...	...	...	...
Rohilkund	...	...	...	...	...	...
North-West Provinces (Unspecified)...	...	...	...	3	2	1
Calcutta	...	...	...	...	...	...
Dacca	...	...	...	...	...	...
Bengal (Unspecified)	...	...	...	...	...	...
Orissa	...	...	...	...	...	...
Nepaul	...	...	...	...	...	...
British Burmah	...	...	...	...	...	...
British India (Unspecified) ...	...	...	...	...	...	...
Total B. ...	...	...	...	5	2	3

XI.

place—(*Continued*).

—(*Continued*).

Kartigappalli.			Mavellikkara.			Chenganur.		
Total.	Males.	Females.	Total.	Males.	Females.	Total.	Males.	Females.
...	...	...	...	...	...	...	...	...
...	...	...	...	...	...	...	...	...
...	...	...	...	...	...	...	...	...
...	...	...	...	...	...	...	...	...
...	...	...	...	...	...	...	...	...
...	...	...	...	...	...	...	...	...
...	...	...	...	...	...	...	...	...
...	...	...	...	...	...	...	...	...
...	...	...	...	...	...	...	...	...
...	...	...	...	...	...	...	...	...
...	...	...	...	...	...	...	...	...
...	...	...	...	...	...	...	...	...
...	...	...	...	...	...	...	...	...
...	...	...	...	...	...	...	...	...
...	...	...	...	...	...	...	...	...
...	...	...	...	...	...	...	...	...
...	...	...	...	...	...	...	...	...
...	...	...	...	...	...	...	...	...
...	...	...	...	...	...	...	...	...
...	...	...	...	...	...	...	...	...
...	...	...	...	...	...	...	...	...
...	...	...	...	...	...	...	...	...
...	...	...	...	...	...	...	...	...
...	...	...	...	...	...	...	...	...
...	...	...	...	...	...	...	...	...
...	...	...	...	...	...	...	...	...
6	6	...	7	5	2	...	...	...
...	...	...	...	...	...	...	...	...
...	...	...	...	...	...	...	...	...
...	...	...	...	...	...	...	...	...
...	...	...	...	...	...	...	...	...
...	...	...	...	...	...	...	...	...
...	...	...	...	...	...	...	...	...
...	...	...	...	...	...	...	...	...
...	...	...	...	...	...	...	...	...
...	...	...	...	...	...	...	...	...
6	6	...	7	5	2	...	...	...

TABLE
Birth

District, State, Province or Country of Birth.	Taluqs					
	Tiruvalla.			Ambalappula.		
	Total.	Males.	Females.	Total.	Males.	Females.
B. In India beyond the Province.						
Mysore	...	...	...	9	6	3
Coorg	...	...	...	...	...	...
North Canara	...	...	...	...	...	...
Goa	...	...	...	...	...	...
Bijapur	...	...	...	...	...	...
Kolhapur	...	...	...	...	...	...
Ratnagiri	...	...	...	20	20	...
Bombay	...	...	...	23	20	3
Hyderabad	...	...	...	1	1	...
Nagpore	...	...	...	...	...	...
Jabbalpore	...	...	...	1	1	...
Central Provinces (Unspecified) ...	...	...	...	...	...	...
Bhopal	...	...	...	...	...	...
Malwa	...	...	...	37	37	...
Bundalkhand	...	...	...	...	...	...
Gwalior	...	...	...	...	...	...
Baroda	...	...	...	...	...	...
Guzerat	...	...	...	...	...	...
Cutch	...	...	...	16	12	4
Marwar	...	...	...	...	...	...
Jeypore	...	...	...	4	4	...
Delhi	...	...	...	3	3	...
Punjab	...	...	...	...	...	...
Agra	...	...	...	...	...	...
Allahabad	...	...	...	...	...	...
Benares	...	...	...	5	5	...
Oudh	...	...	...	12	12	...
Rohilkund	...	...	...	...	...	...
North-West Provinces (Unspecified)...	...	...	...	1	1	...
Calcutta	...	...	...	...	...	...
Dacca	..	...	...	...	...	...
Bengal (Unspecified)	...	...	...	3	3	...
Orissa	...	...	...	...	...	...
Nepaul	...	...	...	...	...	...
British Burmah	...	...	...	...	...	...
British India (Unspecified) ...	...	...	...	12	11	1
Total B. ...	...	...	...	147	136	11

XI.

place—(*Continued*).

—(*Continued*).

Sherttala.			Vykkam.			Ettumanur.		
Total.	Males.	Females.	Total.	Males.	Females.	Total.	Males.	Females.
2	1	1	...	...	...	...	...	...
...	...	...	...	...	...	...	...	...
...	...	...	...	...	...	...	...	...
1	1	...	...	...	...	2	2	...
...	...	...	...	...	...	...	...	...
...	...	...	...	...	...	...	...	...
...	...	...	...	...	...	...	...	...
1	1	...	4	4	...	3	3	...
..	...	...	...	...	...	...	...	...
...	...	...	...	...	...	...	...	...
...	...	...	...	...	...	...	...	...
...	...	...	...	...	...	...	...	...
...	...	...	...	...	...	...	...	...
...	...	...	...	...	...	...	...	...
...	...	...	1	1	...	...	...	...
...	...	...	...	...	...	...	...	...
...	...	...	...	...	...	...	...	...
...	...	...	...	...	...	...	...	...
...	...	...	...	...	...	...	...	...
...	...	...	...	...	...	...	...	...
...	...	...	...	...	...	...	...	...
1	1	...	...	...	...	...	...	...
...	...	...	...	...	...	...	...	...
...	...	...	...	...	...	...	...	...
1	1	...	...	...	...	...	...	...
...	...	...	1	1	...	...	...	...
...	...	...	...	...	...	...	...	...
...	...	...	...	...	...	...	...	...
...	...	...	...	...	...	...	...	...
...	...	...	3	2	1	...	...	...
...	...	...	1	1	...	...	...	...
...	...	...	...	...	...	...	...	...
...	...	...	...	...	...	...	...	...
...	...	...	...	...	...	...	...	...
...	...	...	...	...	...	...	...	...
4	4	...	20	15	5	6	6	...
10	9	1	30	24	6	11	11	...

TABLE
Birth

District, State, Province or Country of Birth.	Taluqs					
	Kottayam.			Changanacheri.		
	Total.	Males.	Females.	Total.	Males.	Females.
B. In India beyond the Province.						
Mysore	...	...	...	...	...	...
Coorg	...	...	...	...	...	...
North Canara	...	...	...	...	...	...
Goa	...	...	...	...	...	...
Bijapur	...	...	...	...	...	...
Kolhapur	...	...	...	...	...	...
Ratnagiri	...	...	...	...	...	...
Bombay	...	...	...	...	...	...
Hyderabad	...	...	...	...	...	...
Nagpore	...	...	...	...	...	...
Jabbalpore	...	...	...	...	...	...
Central Provinces (Unspecified) ...	...	...	...	...	...	...
Bhopal	...	...	...	...	...	...
Malwa	...	...	...	...	...	...
Bundalkhand	...	...	...	...	...	...
Gwalior	...	...	...	...	...	...
Baroda	...	...	...	...	...	...
Guzerat	...	...	...	...	...	...
Cutch	...	...	...	...	...	...
Marwar	...	...	...	...	...	...
Jeypore	...	...	...	...	...	...
Delhi	...	...	...	...	...	...
Punjab	...	...	...	...	...	...
Agra	...	...	...	...	...	...
Allahabad	...	...	...	...	...	...
Benares	1	...	1	...	...	...
Oudh	...	...	...	...	...	...
Rohilkund	...	...	...	...	...	...
North-West Provinces (Unspecified)...	...	...	...	...	...	...
Calcutta	...	...	...	...	...	...
Dacca	...	...	...	...	...	...
Bengal (Unspecified)	...	...	...	...	...	...
Orissa	...	...	...	...	...	...
Nepaul	...	...	...	...	...	...
British Burmah	...	...	...	...	...	...
British India (Unspecified) ...	...	...	...	17	14	3
Total B. ...	1	...	1	17	14	3

XI.

place—(*Continued*).

—(*Continued*).

Meenachal.			Muvattupula.			Todupula.		
Total.	Males.	Females.	Total.	Males.	Females.	Total.	Males.	Females.
...	...	...	...	...	...	...	...	...
...	...	...	...	...	...	...	...	...
...	...	...	8	8	...	...	...	...
...	...	...	...	...	...	...	...	...
...	...	...	...	...	...	...	...	...
...	...	...	...	...	...	...	...	...
...	...	...	...	...	...	...	...	...
...	...	...	...	...	...	...	...	...
...	...	...	...	...	...	...	...	...
...	...	...	...	...	...	...	...	...
...	...	...	...	...	...	...	...	...
...	...	...	...	...	...	...	...	...
...	...	...	...	...	...	...	...	...
...	...	...	...	...	...	...	...	...
...	...	...	...	...	...	...	...	...
...	...	...	...	...	...	...	...	...
...	...	...	...	...	...	...	...	...
...	...	...	...	...	...	...	...	...
...	...	...	...	...	...	...	...	...
...	...	...	...	...	...	...	...	...
...	...	...	...	...	...	...	...	...
...	...	...	...	...	...	...	...	...
...	...	...	...	...	...	...	...	...
...	...	...	...	...	...	...	...	...
...	...	...	...	...	...	...	...	...
...	...	...	...	...	...	...	...	...
...	...	...	...	...	...	...	...	...
...	...	...	...	...	...	...	...	...
...	...	...	...	...	...	...	...	...
...	...	...	...	...	...	...	...	...
...	...	...	...	...	...	...	...	...
...	...	...	...	...	...	...	...	...
...	...	...	...	...	...	...	...	...
...	...	...	...	...	...	...	...	...
...	...	...	...	...	...	...	...	...
...	...	...	...	...	...	...	...	...
...	...	...	8	8	...	...	...	...

TABLE
Birth

District, State, Province or Country of Birth.	Taluqs — Kunnattunadu. Total.	Kunnattunadu. Males.	Kunnattunadu. Females.	Alangadu. Total.	Alangadu. Males.	Alangadu. Females.
B. In India beyond the Province.						
Mysore ...	...	...	...	...	...	...
Coorg	...	...	...	...	...	...
North Canara	12	11	1	...	...	...
Goa	...	...	...	...	...	...
Bijapur	...	...	...	...	...	...
Kolhapur	...	...	...	...	...	...
Ratnagiri	...	...	...	...	...	...
Bombay	...	...	...	...	...	...
Hyderabad	...	...	...	...	...	...
Nagpore	...	...	...	...	...	...
Jabbalpore	...	...	...	...	...	...
Central Provinces (Unspecified) ...	...	...	...	...	...	...
Bhopal	...	...	...	...	...	...
Malwa	...	...	...	...	...	...
Bundalkhand	...	...	...	...	...	...
Gwalior	...	...	...	...	...	...
Baroda	...	...	...	...	...	...
Guzerat	...	...	...	...	...	...
Cutch	...	...	...	...	...	...
Marwar	...	...	...	...	...	...
Jeypore	...	...	...	...	...	...
Delhi	...	...	...	...	...	...
Punjab	...	...	...	...	...	...
Agra	...	...	...	...	...	...
Allahabad	...	...	...	...	...	...
Benares	...	...	...	...	...	...
Oudh	...	...	...	...	...	...
Rohilkund	...	...	...	...	...	...
North-West Provinces (Unspecified).	...	...	...	...	...	...
Calcutta	...	...	...	...	...	...
Dacca	...	...	...	...	...	...
Bengal (Unspecified)	...	...	...	...	...	...
Orissa	...	...	...	...	...	...
Nepaul	...	...	...	...	...	...
British Burmah	...	...	...	...	...	...
British India (Unspecified) ...	28	28	...	1	1	...
Total B. ...	40	39	1	1	1	...

XI.

place—(*Continued*).

—(*Continued*).

Parur.			Cardamom Hills.			Periyar and Thekkadi.		
Total.	Males.	Females.	Total.	Males.	Females.	Total.	Males.	Females.
...	...	...	5	2	3	28	22	6
...	...	...	...	...	...	1	1	...
...	...	...	...	...	...	2	2	...
...	...	...	...	...	...	...	...	...
...	...	...	...	...	...	3	3	...
...	...	...	...	...	...	...	...	...
...	...	...	...	...	...	...	...	...
40	33	7	...	...	...	2	1	1
...	...	...	...	...	...	2	1	1
...	...	...	...	...	...	8	5	3
...	...	...	...	...	...	1	1	...
...	...	...	...	...	...	...	...	...
...	...	...	...	...	...	...	...	...
...	...	...	...	...	...	...	...	...
...	...	...	...	...	...	...	...	...
...	...	...	...	...	...	...	...	...
...	...	...	...	...	...	...	...	...
...	...	...	...	...	...	...	...	...
...	...	...	...	...	...	...	...	...
...	...	...	...	...	...	...	...	...
...	...	...	...	...	...	5	5	...
...	...	...	...	...	...	17	15	2
...	...	...	...	...	...	...	...	...
...	...	...	3	3	...	7	5	2
...	...	...	...	...	...	5	4	1
...	...	...	...	...	...	...	...	...
...	...	...	...	...	...	4	4	...
...	...	...	...	...	...	...	...	...
...	...	...	...	...	...	9	9	...
...	...	...	...	...	...	...	...	...
...	...	...	...	...	...	...	...	...
...	...	...	...	...	...	41	33	8
...	...	...	...	...	...	...	...	...
...	...	...	...	...	...	...	...	...
...	...	...	...	...	...	...	...	...
36	17	19	333	197	136	1	1	...
76	50	26	341	202	139	136	112	24

TABLE
Birth

District, State, Province or Country of Birth.	Total Population.		
	Total.	Males.	Females.
C. In Asia beyond India.			
Ceylon	131	107	24
Singapore	1	1	...
Java	1	1	...
China	3	3	...
Afghanistan	9	9	...
Persia	1	1	...
Arabia	93	86	7
Total **C.** ...	239	208	31
D. In Europe.			
Italy	9	9	...
Spain	9	6	3
France	2	1	1
Germany	3	3	...
Belgium	1	...	1
England	71	42	29
Scotland	16	11	5
Ireland	15	8	7
Wales	2	2	...
Holland	1	1	...
Europe (Unspecified)	21	16	5
Total **D.** ...	150	99	51
E. In Africa.			
Africa (Unspecified) **E.**	2	2	...
F. In America.			
The United States	2	2	...
Canada	5	5	...
America (Unspecified)	2	2	...
Total **F.** ...	9	9	...
Total ...	2,557,736	1,290,415	1,267,321

XI.

place—(*Continued*).

	Taluqs.								
	Tovala.			Agastiswaram.			Eranial.		
	Total.	Males.	Females.	Total.	Males.	Females.	Total.	Males.	Females.
	...	...	...	20	10	10	...	...	...
	...	...	...	...	...	...	...	...	...
	...	...	...	...	...	...	...	...	...
	...	...	...	...	...	...	...	...	...
	...	...	...	...	...	...	...	...	...
	...	...	...	...	...	...	...	...	...
	...	...	...	...	...	...	...	...	...
	...	...	...	20	10	10	...	...	...
	...	...	...	1	1	...	1	1	...
	...	...	...	...	...	...	1	1	...
	...	...	...	...	...	...	...	...	...
	...	...	...	...	...	...	...	...	...
	...	...	...	...	...	...	...	...	...
	1	1	...	4	3	1	5	1	4
	...	...	...	4	2	2	...	...	...
	...	...	...	...	...	...	...	...	...
	...	...	...	...	...	...	...	...	...
	...	...	...	...	...	...	...	...	...
	...	...	...	2	2	...	3	3	...
	1	1	...	11	8	3	10	6	4
	...	...	...	...	...	...	...	...	...
	...	...	...	...	...	...	...	...	...
	...	...	...	...	...	...	...	...	...
	...	...	...	...	...	...	...	...	...
	...	...	...	...	...	...	...	...	...
	29,751	14,489	15,262	87,241	43,226	44,015	105,098	52,883	52,215

TABLE

Birth

District, State, Province or Country of Birth.	Taluqs: Kalkulam. Total.	Kalkulam. Males.	Kalkulam. Females.	Vilavankodu. Total.	Vilavankodu. Males.	Vilavankodu. Females.
C. In Asia beyond India.						
Ceylon ...	2	1	1	...	...	...
Singapore ...	...	...	...	...	...	...
Java ...	...	...	...	...	...	...
China ...	...	...	...	...	...	...
Afghanistan ...	...	...	...	...	...	...
Persia ...	...	...	...	...	...	...
Arabia ...	...	...	...	...	...	...
Total C. ...	2	1	1	...	...	...
D. In Europe.						
Italy ...	...	...	...	1	1	...
Spain ...	...	...	...	...	...	...
France ...	...	...	...	...	...	...
Germany ...	...	...	...	...	...	...
Belgium ...	...	...	...	...	...	...
England ...	...	...	...	...	...	...
Scotland ...	...	...	...	...	...	...
Ireland ...	...	...	...	...	...	...
Wales ...	...	...	...	1	1	...
Holland ...	...	...	...	...	...	...
Europe (Unspecified) ...	2	1	1	1	1	...
Total D. ...	2	1	1	3	8	...
E. In Africa.						
Africa (Unspecified) E. ...	...	...	...	...	...	...
F. In America.						
The United States ...	...	...	...	...	...	...
Canada ...	...	...	...	...	...	...
America (Unspecified) ...	...	...	...	...	...	...
Total F. ...	...	...	...	...	...	...
Total ...	59,474	29,834	29,640	68,521	35,202	33,319

XI.

place—(*Continued*).

—(*Continued*).

Neyattankara.			Trivandram.			Nedumangadu.		
Total.	Males.	Females.	Total.	Males.	Females.	Total.	Males.	Females.
...	...	...	15	14	1	...	...	...
...	...	...	...	...	...	...	...	...
...	...	...	...	...	...	...	...	...
...	...	...	...	...	...	...	...	...
...	...	...	5	5	...	...	...	...
...	...	...	...	...	...	...	...	...
...	...	...	1	1	...	...	...	...
...	...	...	21	20	1	...	...	...
...	...	...	...	...	...	...	...	...
...	...	...	3	...	3	...	...	...
...	...	...	...	...	...	...	...	...
...	...	...	...	...	...	...	...	...
...	...	...	...	...	...	...	...	...
2	1	1	11	6	5	...	...	...
...	...	...	4	4	...	...	...	...
...	...	...	6	2	4	...	...	...
...	...	...	1	1	...	...	...	...
...	...	...	...	...	...	...	...	...
...	...	...	4	1	3	2	1	1
2	1	1	29	14	15	2	1	1
...	...	...	...	...	...	...	...	...
...	...	...	...	...	...	...	...	...
...	...	...	5	5	...	...	...	...
...	...	...	...	...	...	...	...	...
...	...	...	5	5	...	...	...	...
110,755	56,953	53,802	111,938	56,909	55,029	55,497	27,857	27,640

TABLE
Birth

District, State, Province or Country of Birth.	Taluqs					
	Sirayinkil.			Kottarakkara.		
	Total.	Males.	Females.	Total.	Males.	Females.
C. In Asia beyond India.						
Ceylon ...	...	...	...	...	...	...
Singapore ...	...	...	...	...	...	...
Java ...	...	...	...	...	...	...
China ...	...	...	...	...	...	...
Afghanistan ...	...	...	...	...	...	...
Persia ...	...	...	..	...	...	...
Arabia ...	...	...	...	...	...	...
Total C. ...	...	...	...	...	...	...
D. In Europe.						
Italy ...	...	...	...	...	...	...
Spain ...	...	...	...	...	...	...
France ...	...	...	...	...	...	...
Germany ...	...	...	...	...	...	...
Belgium ...	...	...	...	...	...	...
England ...	...	...	...	...	...	...
Scotland ...	...	...	...	...	...	...
Ireland ...	...	...	...	...	...	...
Wales ...	...	...	...	...	...	...
Holland ...	...	...	...	...	...	...
Europe (Unspecified) ...	...	...	...	...	...	...
Total D. ...	...	...	...	...	...	...
E. In Africa.						
Africa (Unspecified) E.	...	...	...	...	...	...
F. In America.						
The United States ...	...	...	...	...	...	...
Canada ...	...	...	...	...	...	...
America (Unspecified) ...	...	...	...	...	...	...
Total F. ...	...	...	...	...	...	...
Total ...	97,995	48,271	49,724	71,517	36,055	35,462

XI.

place—(*Continued*).

—(*Continued*).

Pattanapuram.			Shenkotta.			Quilon.		
Total.	Males.	Females.	Total.	Males.	Females.	Total.	Males.	Females.
...	...	...	...	...	...	76	67	9
...	...	...	...	...	...	...	...	...
...	...	...	...	...	...	1	1	...
...	...	...	...	...	...	...	...	...
...	...	...	...	...	...	...	...	...
...	...	...	...	...	...	...	...	...
...	...	...	...	...	...	38	37	1
...	...	..	...	...	...	115	105	10
1	1	...	...	...	...	2	2	...
...	...	...	...	...	...	...	...	...
...	...	...	...	...	...	...	...	...
...	...	...	...	...	...	...	...	...
...	...	...	1	...	1	...	...	...
2	2	...	4	2	2	15	6	9
3	2	1	...	...	...	2	1	1
...	...	...	...	...	...	2	1	1
...	...	...	...	...	...	...	...	...
...	...	...	...	...	...	...	...	...
...	...	...	...	...	...	5	5	...
6	5	1	5	2	3	26	15	11
...	...	...	...	...	...	...	...	...
...	...	...	...	...	...	...	...	...
...	...	...	...	...	...	...	...	...
...	...	...	...	...	...	...	...	...
...	...	...	..	...	...	...	...	...
39,447	19,858	19,589	32,088	15,700	16,388	121,935	60,832	61,103

TABLE

Birth

District, State, Province or Country of Birth.	Taluqs — Kunnattur. Total.	Kunnattur. Males.	Kunnattur. Females.	Karunagappalli. Total.	Karunagappalli. Males.	Karunagappalli. Females.
C. In Asia beyond India.						
Ceylon ...	...	...	...	1	1	...
Singapore ...	...	...	...	..	...	...
Java ...	...	...	...	...	...	...
China ...	...	...	...	...	...	...
Afghanistan ...	...	...	...	...	...	...
Persia ...	...	...	...	...	...	...
Arabia ..	...	...	...	...	...	...
Total C. ...	...	...	...	1	1	...
D. In Europe.						
Italy ...	...	...	...	...	...	...
Spain ...	...	...	...	...	...	...
France ...	...	...	...	...	...	...
Germany ...	...	...	...	...	...	...
Belgium ...	...	...	...	...	...	...
England ...	...	...	...	...	...	...
Scotland ...	...	...	...	...	...	...
Ireland ...	...	...	...	...	...	...
Wales ...	...	...	...	...	...	...
Holland ...	...	...	...	...	...	...
Europe (Unspecified) ...	...	...	...	...	...	...
Total D. ...	...	...	...	...	...	...
E. In Africa.						
Africa (Unspecified) E. ...	...	...	...	...	...	...
F. In America.						
The United States ...	...	...	...	...	...	...
Canada ...	...	...	...	...	...	...
America (Unspecified) ...	...	...	...	...	...	...
Total F. ...	...	...	...	...	...	...
Total ...	73,529	37,397	36,132	108,826	52,862	55,964

XI.

place—(*Continued*).

—(*Continued*).

Kartigappalli.			Mavellikkara.			Chenganur.		
Total.	Males.	Females.	Total.	Males.	Females.	Total.	Males.	Females.
...	...	...	...	...	...	...	...	...
...	...	...	...	...	...	...	...	...
...	...	...	...	...	...	...	...	...
...	...	...	...	...	...	...	...	...
...	...	...	...	...	...	...	...	...
...	...	...	...	...	...	...	...	...
...	...	...	...	...	...	...	...	...
...	...	...	...	...	...	...	...	...
...	...	...	...	...	...	...	...	...
...	...	...	...	...	...	...	...	...
...	...	...	...	...	...	...	...	...
...	...	...	...	...	...	...	...	...
...	...	...	...	...	...	...	...	...
...	...	...	...	...	...	...	...	...
...	...	...	...	...	...	...	...	...
...	...	...	...	...	...	...	...	...
...	...	...	...	...	...	...	...	...
...	...	...	...	...	...	...	...	...
...	...	...	...	...	...	...	...	...
...	...	...	...	...	...	...	...	...
...	...	...	...	...	...	...	...	...
...	...	...	...	...	...	...	...	...
...	...	...	...	...	...	...	...	...
...	...	...	...	...	...	...	...	...
...	...	...	...	...	...	...	...	...
91,950	45,216	46,734	103,619	52,494	51,125	93,960	48,443	45,517

TABLE
Birth

District, State, Province or Country of Birth.	Taluqs: Tiruvalla. Total.	Males.	Females.	Ambalappula. Total.	Males.	Females.
C. In Asia beyond India.						
Ceylon ...	...	...	...	6	6	...
Singapore ...	...	...	...	1	1	...
Java ...	...	...	...	...	...	...
China ...	...	...	...	...	.	...
Afghanistan ...	...	...	...	...	...	...
Persia ...	...	...	...	1	1	...
Arabia ...	...	...	...	43	40	3
Total **C.** ...	...	...	...	51	48	3
D. In Europe.						
Italy ...	...	...	...	...	...	...
Spain ...	...	...	...	1	1	...
France ...	...	...	...	1	...	1
Germany ...	...	...	...	...	...	...
Belgium ...	...	...	...	...	...	...
England ...	...	...	...	5	4	1
Scotland ...	...	...	...	3	2	1
Ireland ...	...	...	...	1	1	...
Wales ...	...	...	...	...	...	...
Holland ...	...	...	...	...	...	...
Europe (Unspecified) ...	...	...	...	...	...	...
Total **D.** ...	...	...	...	11	8	3
E. In Africa.						
Africa (Unspecified) **E.** ...	...	...	...	2	2	...
F. In America.						
The United States ...	...	...	...	2	2	...
Canada ...	...	...	...	...	...	...
America (Unspecified) ...	...	...	...	1	1	...
Total **F.** ...	...	...	...	3	3	...
Total ...	122,142	62,514	59,628	94,745	46,909	47,836

XI.

place—(*Continued*).

—(*Continued*).

Sherttala.			Vykkam			Ettumanur.		
Total.	Males.	Females.	Total.	Males.	Females.	Total.	Males.	Females.
...	...	...	...	...	...	...	...	...
...	...	...	...	...	...	...	...	...
...	...	..	...	...	...	...	...	...
...	...	...	...	...	...	...	...	...
1	1	...	...	...	...	...	...	...
...	...	..	...	...	...	...	...	...
...	...	...	...	...	...	...	...	...
1	1	...	...	...	...	...	...	...
...	...	...	...	...	...	...	...	...
...	...	...	...	...	...	...	...	...
...	...	...	...	...	...	...	...	...
...	...	...	...	...	...	...	...	...
...	...	...	...	...	...	...	...	...
...	...	...	...	...	...	...	...	...
...	...	...	...	...	...	...	...	...
...	...	...	3	2	1	...	...	...
...	...	...	...	...	...	...	...	...
...	...	...	...	...	...	...	...	...
...	...	...	...	...	...	...	...	...
...	...	...	3	2	1	...	...	...
...	...	...	...	...	...	...	...	...
...	...	...	...	...	...	...	...	...
...	...	...	...	...	...	...	...	...
...	...	...	...	...	...	...	...	...
...	...	...	...	...	...	...	...	...
117,261	58,448	58,813	80,628	40,947	39,681	80,823	41,536	39,287

TABLE

Birth

District, State, Province or Country of Birth.	Taluqs: Kottayam. Total.	Kottayam. Males.	Kottayam. Females.	Changanacheri. Total.	Changanacheri. Males.	Changanacheri. Females.
C. In Asia beyond India.						
Ceylon ...	2	...	2	...	...	...
Singapore ...	...	...	...	...	...	...
Java ...	...	...	...	...	...	...
China ...	...	...	...	...	...	...
Afghanistan ...	...	...	...	...	...	...
Persia ...	...	...	...	...	...	...
Arabia ...	...	...	...	...	...	...
Total C. ...	2	...	2	...	...	...
D. In Europe.						
Italy ...	...	...	...	...	...	...
Spain ...	1	1	...	...	...	...
France ...	...	...	...	...	...	...
Germany ...	...	...	...	...	...	...
Belgium ...	...	...	...	...	...	...
England ...	8	5	3	...	...	...
Scotland ...	...	...	...	...	...	...
Ireland ...	2	1	1	...	...	...
Wales ...	...	...	...	...	...	...
Holland ...	...	...	...	...	...	...
Europe (Unspecified) ...	...	...	...	...	...	...
Total D. ...	11	7	4	...	...	...
E. In Africa.						
Africa (Unspecified) E. ...	...	...	...	...	...	...
F. In America.						
The United States ...	...	...	...	...	...	...
Canada ...	...	...	...	...	...	...
America (Unspecified) ...	...	...	...	...	...	...
Total F. ...	...	...	...	...	...	...
Total ...	77,094	39,229	37,865	74,722	38,596	36,126

XI.

place—(*Continued*).

—(*Continued*).

Meenachal.			Muvattupula.			Todupula.		
Total.	Males.	Females.	Total.	Males.	Females.	Total.	Males.	Females.
...	...	...	...	...	...	...	...	...
...	...	...	...	...	...	...	...	...
...	...	...	...	...	...	...	...	...
...	...	...	...	...	...	...	...	...
...	...	...	...	...	...	...	...	...
...	...	...	...	...	...	...	...	...
...	...	...	...	...	...	...	...	...
...	...	...	...	...	...	...	...	...
...	...	...	...	...	...	...	...	...
...	...	...	...	...	...	...	...	...
...	...	...	...	...	...	...	...	...
...	...	...	...	...	...	...	...	...
...	...	...	...	...	...	...	...	...
...	...	...	1	1	...	...	...	...
...	...	...	...	...	...	...	...	...
...	...	...	...	...	...	...	...	...
...	...	...	...	...	...	...	...	...
...	...	...	...	...	...	...	...	...
2	2	...	...	...	...	...	...	...
2	2	...	1	1	...	...	...	...
...	...	...	...	...	...	...	...	...
...	...	...	...	...	...	...	...	...
...	...	...	...	...	...	...	...	...
...	...	...	...	...	...	...	...	...
...	...	...	...	...	...	...	...	...
59,976	30,830	29,146	103,009	51,595	51,414	25,202	12,786	12,416

TABLE
Birth

District, State, Province or Country of Birth.	Taluqs					
	Kunnattunadu.			Alangadu.		
	Total.	Males.	Females.	Total.	Males.	Females.
C. In Asia beyond India.						
Ceylon ...	...	...	...	...	...	...
Singapore ...	...	..	...	...	...	...
Java ...	...	...	...	...	...	...
China ...	...	...	...	...	...	...
Afghanistan ...	...	...	...	1	1	...
Persia ...	...	...	...	...	...	...
Arabia ...	...	...	...	...	...	...
Total C. ...	...	...	...	1	1	...
D. In Europe.						
Italy ...	...	...	...	...	...	...
Spain ...	...	...	...	...	...	...
France ...	...	...	...	...	...	...
Germany ...	...	...	...	...	...	...
Belgium ...	...	...	...	...	...	...
England ..	...	...	...	1	1	...
Scotland ...	...	...	...	...	...	...
Ireland ..	.	...	...	...	...	...
Wales ...	...	...	...	...	...	...
Holland ...	...	...	...	...	...	...
Europe (Unspecified) ...	...	...	...	...	...	...
Total D. ...	...	...	...	1	1	...
E. In Africa.						
Africa (Unspecified) E. ...	...	...	...	...	...	...
F. In America.						
The United States ...	...	...	...	...	...	...
Canada ...	...	...	...	...	...	...
America (Unspecified) ...	...	...	...	...	..	...
Total F. ...	...	...	...	...	...	..
Total ...	114,049	57,216	56,833	70,958	35,944	35,014

XI.

place—(*Continued*).

—(*Continued*).

Parur.			Cardamom Hills.			Periyar and Thekkadi.		
Total.	Males.	Females.	Total.	Males.	Females.	Total.	Males.	Females.
...	...	...	3	3	...	6	5	1
...	...	...	...	...	...	...	...	...
...	...	...	...	...	...	...	...	...
...	...	...	2	2	...	1	1	...
...	...	...	...	...	...	2	2	...
...	...	...	...	...	...	...	...	...
11	8	3	...	...	...	...	...	...
11	8	3	5	5	...	9	8	1
3	3	...	...	...	...	...	...	...
3	3	...	...	...	...	...	...	...
1	1	...	...	...	...	...	...	...
2	2	...	1	1	...	...	...	...
...	...	...	...	...	...	...	...	...
...	...	...	9	6	3	3	3	...
...	...	...	...	...	...	...	...	...
...	...	...	...	...	...	1	1	...
...	...	...	...	...	...	...	...	...
1	1	...	...	...	...	...	...	...
...	...	...	...	...	...	...	...	...
10	10	...	10	7	3	4	4	...
...	...	...	...	...	...	...	...	...
...	...	...	...	...	...	...	...	...
...	...	...	...	...	...	...	...	...
1	1	...	...	...	...	...	...	...
1	1	...	...	...	...	...	...	...
59,278	30,082	29,196	11,413	6,714	4,699	3,295	2,588	707

TABLE

Persons of Unsound Mind,

Number.	Taluq.	Total Insane. Total.	Males.	Females.
1	2	3	4	5
1	Tovala	5	5	...
2	Agastiswaram	22	10	12
3	Eranial	7	7	...
4	Kalkulam	6	3	3
5	Vilavankodu	3	1	2
6	Neyattankara	16	11	5
7	Trivandram	95	69	26
8	Nedumangadu	6	3	3
9	Sirayinkil	15	5	10
10	Kottarakkara	8	4	4
11	Pattanapuram	2	...	2
12	Shenkotta	2	2	...
13	Quilon	14	6	8
14	Kunnattur	5	1	4
15	Karunagappalli	21	15	6
16	Kartigappalli	15	11	4
17	Mavellikkara	16	10	6
18	Chenganur	8	6	2
19	Tiruvalla	16	9	7
20	Ambalappula	14	9	5
21	Sherttala	10	6	4
22	Vykkam	23	10	13
23	Ettumanur	4	3	1
24	Kottayam	9	6	3
25	Changanacheri	13	8	5
26	Meenachal	13	10	3
27	Muvattupula	7	5	2
28	Todupula	...	...	...
29	Kunnattunadu	3	1	2
30	Alangadu	6	5	1
31	Parur	7	5	2
	Cardamom Hills	3	3	...
	Periyar & Thekkadi	...	...	...
	Total ...	394	249	145

XII.

by Age.

Distribution by Age.

0—4.		5—9.		10—14.		15—19.		20—24.	
Males.	Females.	Males.	Females.	Males.	Females.	Males.	Females.	Males.	Females.
6	7	8	9	10	11	12	13	14	15
...	...	...	...	...	...	...	...	...	...
...	...	...	...	...	...	1	...	1	1
...	...	...	...	1	...	...	...	2	...
...	...	...	...	...	...	...	...	...	1
...	...	...	1	...	...	1	...	...	...
...	...	...	...	...	...	2	1	2	1
...	...	...	1	...	...	1	...	6	1
...	...	...	...	...	1	...	...	...	...
...	...	...	3	...	...	3	...	1	...
...	...	...	...	...	...	...	...	2	1
...	...	...	...	...	...	...	...	...	...
...	...	...	...	...	...	...	...	...	...
...	...	...	1	1	...	...	...	...	...
...	...	...	...	...	2	...	...	...	...
1	...	...	...	2	...	1	...	1	...
...	...	2	...	...	...	...	...	4	...
...	...	...	...	...	...	...	...	...	1
...	...	...	...	...	...	...	...	...	1
...	...	...	...	...	...	1	1	1	...
...	...	...	...	...	...	2	1	...	...
...	...	...	...	1	...	...	2	1	...
...	...	...	...	...	.	2	1	2	1
...	...	1	...	...	...	...	...	1	...
...	...	1	...	...	...	...	1	...	...
...	...	...	...	...	...	...	...	1	...
...	...	...	...	...	...	...	..	...	...
...	..	...	...	...	...	1	...	1	...
...	...	...	...	...	...	...	...	...	...
...	...	...	...	...	1	...	...	1	...
...	...	...	...	...	...	...	...	...	...
...	...	...	...	...	...	...	...	...	1
...	...	...	...	...	...	...	...	...	...
...	...	...	...	...	...	...	...	...	...
1	...	4	6	5	4	15	7	27	9

TABLE

Persons of Unsound Mind,

Number.	Taluq.	Distribution 25—29. Males.	25—29. Females.	30—34. Males.	30—34. Females.	35—39. Males.	35—39. Females.
1	2	16	17	18	19	20	21
1	Tovala ...	1	...	...	...	1	...
2	Agastiswaram ...	2	1	2	2	...	2
3	Eranial ...	2	...	1	...	1	...
4	Kalkulam ...	...	...	...	...	...	1
5	Vilavankodu ...	...	...	...	...	...	...
6	Neyattankara ...	1	...	1	1	2	1
7	Trivandram ...	13	1	10	5	10	4
8	Nedumangadu ...	1	...	...	...	1	1
9	Sirayinkil ...	...	2	...	1	...	...
10	Kottarakkara ...	1	...	...	1	...	...
11	Pattanapuram ...	...	...	...	1	...	...
12	Shenkotta ...	...	...	1	...	...	...
13	Quilon ...	2	2	2	...	...	2
14	Kunnattur ...	...	1	...	...	...	1
15	Karunagappalli ...	...	...	1	1	3	1
16	Kartigappalli ...	...	2	1	1	1	...
17	Mavellikkara ...	...	...	...	...	2	1
18	Chenganur ...	...	...	...	...	...	...
19	Tiruvalla ...	1	1	...	...	...	...
20	Ambalappula ...	1	1	1	...	1	...
21	Sherttala ...	1	...	1	1	1	...
22	Vykkam ...	1	...	...	1	...	2
23	Ettumanur ...	...	...	1	1	...	...
24	Kottayam ...	1	1	...	..	1	1
25	Changanacheri ...	3	...	...	...	1	...
26	Meenachal ...	...	...	1	...	1	1
27	Muvattupula ...	1	...	...	...	1	1
28	Todupula ...	...	...	...	...	...	...
29	Kunnattunadu ...	...	...	...	...	...	...
30	Alangadu ...	2	...	1	...	1	...
31	Parur ...	...	...	...	...	1	...
	Cardamom Hills ...	...	...	2	...	...	...
	Periyar & Thekkadi.	...	...	...	...	...	...
	Total ...	34	12	26	16	29	19

XII.

by Age—(*Continued*).

BY AGE—(*Continued*).

40—44.		45—49.		50—54.		55—59.		60 and over.	
Males.	Females.	Males.	Females.	Males.	Females.	Males.	Females.	Males.	Females.
22	23	24	25	26	27	28	29	30	31
2	...	1	...	...	...	...	...	...	...
2	3	2	1	...	...	...	2	...	...
...	...	...	...	...	...	...	...	...	...
2	...	...	1	...	...	...	..	1	...
...	...	...	...	...	...	...	1	...	...
1	...	...	...	1	...	...	...	1	1
12	4	8	4	6	2	2	1	1	3
1	...	...	1	...	...	...	...	...	...
...	...	1	2	...	1	...	...	...	1
...	...	...	1	...	1	...	...	1	...
...	1	...	...	...	...	...	...	...	...
...	...	1	...	...	...	...	...	...	...
...	1	...	1	1	...	...	...	...	1
...	...	...	...	1	...	...	...	...	...
2	...	2	2	1	2	1	...	...	...
1	...	...	...	1	...	...	...	1	1
1	1	3	...	1	1	3	2	...	...
1	...	...	...	2	1	2	...	1	...
1	2	2	...	1	...	1	2	1	1
...	2	3	...	...	...	...	1	1	...
...	...	...	1	1	...	...	...	...	...
1	3	2	1	1	1	...	...	1	3
...	...	...	...	...	...	...	...	...	...
1	...	1	...	...	...	1	...	...	...
2	2	1	...	...	...	...	1	...	2
4	...	...	1	2	1	...	...	2	...
...	...	...	1	...	...	1	...	...	...
...	...	...	...	...	...	...	...	...	...
...	...	...	...	...	...	...	...	...	1
..	...	1	...	...	...	...	1	...	...
1	...	1	1	...	...	...	...	2	...
...	...	1	...	...	...	...	...	...	...
...	...	...	...	...	...	...	...	...	...
35	19	30	18	19	10	11	11	13	14

TABLE

Deaf-Mutes,

Number.	Taluq.			Total Deaf-Mutes. Total.	Males.	Females.
1	2			3	4	5
1	Tovala	...	...	6	2	4
2	Agastiswaram	...	...	43	19	24
3	Eranial	...	...	20	14	6
4	Kalkulam	...	...	31	16	15
5	Vilavankodu	...	...	18	11	7
6	Neyattankara	...	...	56	38	18
7	Trivandram	...	...	27	15	12
8	Nedumangadu	...	...	22	15	7
9	Sirayinkil	...	...	46	20	26
10	Kottarakkara	...	...	23	15	8
11	Pattanapuram	...	...	9	3	6
12	Shenkotta	...	...	...	...	...
13	Quilon	...	...	50	33	17
14	Kunnattur	...	...	19	12	7
15	Karunagappalli	...	...	29	16	13
16	Kartigappalli	...	...	22	14	8
17	Mavellikkara	...	...	19	11	8
18	Chenganur	...	...	12	8	4
19	Tiruvalla	...	...	30	15	15
20	Ambalappula	...	...	29	17	12
21	Sherttala	...	...	28	18	10
22	Vykkam	...	...	43	23	20
23	Ettumanur	...	...	6	4	2
24	Kottayam	...	...	42	23	19
25	Changanacheri	...	...	29	16	13
26	Meenachal	...	..	29	20	9
27	Muvattupula	...	...	21	15	6
28	Todupula	...	...	8	4	4
29	Kunnattunadu	...	...	11	8	3
30	Alangadu	...	...	7	3	4
31	Parur	...	...	10	7	3
	Cardamom Hills	...	...	...	...	...
	Periyar & Thekkadi	...	...	...	...	...
		Total	...	745	435	310

XIII.

by Age.

Distribution by Age.

0—4.		5—9.		10—14.		15—19.		20—24.	
Males.	Females.	Males.	Females.	Males.	Females.	Males.	Females.	Males.	Females.
6	7	8	9	10	11	12	13	14	15
...	...	...	...	...	...	1	...	...	...
1	...	5	2	3	5	1	...	4	2
2	...	...	3	...	2	4	...	1	...
2	1	2	4	3	4	4	1	1	2
...	...	2	...	2	...	2	1	1	1
2	...	10	1	3	2	4	4	2	2
...	1	2	2	2	2	5	2	2	1
...	...	4	...	1	2	...	...	4	...
1	2	3	2	3	4	2	4	3	3
1	...	3	2	2	...	2	2	1	1
...	...	...	1	...	...	...	...	...	...
...	...	...	...	...	...	...	...	...	...
...	...	2	2	2	1	2	2	2	1
...	...	3	...	2	...	...	...	4	2
...	...	2	...	2	2	2	2	...	1
...	...	1	...	2	...	3	1	1	1
...	...	...	2	1	1	...	1	...	1
...	...	1	...	...	...	2	...	...	1
...	1	2	1	1	2	2	3	3	2
...	...	2	3	1	...	1	...	1	1
...	...	...	...	2	...	1	...	2	1
1	...	1	3	3	2	...	...	2	1
...	...	...	...	2	...	...	1	...	...
...	...	4	2	3	2	3	1	3	...
1	...	1	...	2	...	1	...	2	2
1	.	3	...	3	1	1	1	4	...
1	...	1	2	1	...	4	...	2	2
...	...	1	1	...	...	2	1	...	1
...	...	...	...	2	...	1	1	1	...
...	...	...	...	1	...	1	1	...	2
...	...	...	...	2	...	1	...	1	2
...	...	...	...	...	...	...	...	...	...
...	...	...	...	...	...	...	...	...	...
13	5	55	33	51	32	52	29	47	33

TABLE

Deaf-Mutes,

Number.	Taluq.	Distribution					
		25—29.		30—34.		35—39.	
		Males.	Females.	Males.	Females.	Males.	Females.
1	2	16	17	18	19	20	21
1	Tovala ...	...	...	...	...	1	...
2	Agastiswaram ...	1	5	2	2	...	1
3	Eranial ...	1	1	2	...	...	...
4	Kalkulam ...	1	...	2	1	...	...
5	Vilavankodu ...	1	...	...	2	2	1
6	Neyattankara ...	4	1	3	2	1	1
7	Trivandram ...	2	1	...	1	1	1
8	Nedumangadu ...	...	...	...	2	2	...
9	Sirayinkil ...	3	1	2	1	1	1
10	Kottarakkara ...	...	...	1	2	1	...
11	Pattanapuram ...	...	...	...	1	1	1
12	Shenkotta ...	...	...	...	...	...	...
13	Quilon ...	3	2	5	1	4	...
14	Kunnattur ...	1	...	2	1	...	2
15	Karunagappalli ..	1	1	3	3	2	...
16	Kartigappalli ...	...	1	...	2	...	1
17	Mavellikkara ...	1	...	...	1	3	1
18	Chenganur ...	...	1	...	...	1	...
19	Tiruvalla ...	2	1	1	1	1	...
20	Ambalappula ...	1	2	1	2	2	...
21	Sherttala ...	2	2	2	1	1	1
22	Vykkam ...	5	2	...	1	2	4
23	Ettumanur ...	...	...	1	...	...	1
24	Kottayam ...	3	...	1	2	...	2
25	Changanacheri ...	2	2	2	...	2	...
26	Meenachal ...	1	1	1	3	1	...
27	Muvattupula ...	1	1	...	...	1	...
28	Todupula ...	1	...	...	...	...	...
29	Kunnattunadu ...	...	1	1	...	...	...
30	Alangadu ...	1	1	...	...	...	...
31	Parur ...	...	...	1	...	...	...
	Cardamom Hills ...	...	...	...	...	...	...
	Periyar & Thekkadi.	...	...	...	...	...	...
	Total ...	38	27	33	32	30	18

XIII.

by Age—(*Continued*).

BY AGE—(*Continued*).

40—44.		45—49.		50—54.		55—59.		60 and over.	
Males.	Females.	Males.	Females.	Males.	Females.	Males.	Females.	Males.	Females.
22	23	24	25	26	27	28	29	30	31
...	1	...	...	...	...	...	...	...	3
...	3	...	...	...	1	1	...	1	3
1	...	2	...	1	...	...	...	...	...
...	1	1	...	...	1	...	...	...	...
...	1	...	...	...	1	1	...	...	...
1	2	2	...	...	1	3	...	3	2
...	...	...	1	...	...	...	...	1	...
1	1	...	...	...	1	1	...	2	1
...	1	...	3	1	2	...	...	1	2
1	...	...	1	1	...	...	...	2	...
1	1	...	1	...	1	...	...	1	...
...	...	...	...	...	...	...	...	...	...
3	3	1	...	3	3	1	1	5	1
...	1	...	1	...	...	...	...	...	...
...	2	2	...	1	2	...	...	1	...
3	1	1	...	2	...	...	...	1	1
1	...	1	1	3	...	...	...	1	...
...	...	...	1	1	...	2	...	1	1
...	1	1	...	1	...	...	...	1	3
3	...	1	...	...	2	...	...	4	2
1	2	1	...	1	1	1	1	4	1
4	1	1	2	1	1	...	1	3	2
...	...	...	...	...	...	...	...	1	...
1	2	1	1	...	1	...	3	4	3
...	3	1	1	...	1	1	...	1	4
2	...	...	3	2	...	...	...	1	...
3	...	...	...	1	1	...	...	...	...
...	...	...	...	...	...	...	...	...	1
1	...	1	...	...	...	...	1	1	...
...	...	...	...	...	...	...	...	...	...
...	...	...	...	1	...	...	...	1	1
...	...	...	...	...	...	...	...	...	...
...	...	...	...	...	...	...	...	...	...
27	27	17	16	20	20	11	7	41	31

TABLE
Blind,

Number.	Taluq.	Total Blind.		
		Total.	Males.	Females.
1	2	3	4	5
1	Tovala	11	4	7
2	Agastiswaram	49	27	22
3	Eranial	26	22	4
4	Kalkulam	20	14	6
5	Vilavankodu	23	9	14
6	Neyattankara	63	30	33
7	Trivandram	61	40	21
8	Nedumangadu	50	28	22
9	Sirayinkil	68	38	30
10	Kottarakkara	58	37	21
11	Pattanapuram	9	6	3
12	Shenkotta	...	...	...
13	Quilon	64	37	27
14	Kunnattur	21	14	7
15	Karunagappalli	29	19	10
16	Kartigappalli	44	22	22
17	Mavellikkara	35	25	10
18	Chenganur	25	17	8
19	Tiruvalla	33	20	13
20	Ambalappula	26	13	13
21	Sherttala	27	13	14
22	Vykkam	28	21	7
23	Ettumanur	12	4	8
24	Kottayam	22	15	7
25	Changanacheri	35	22	13
26	Meenachal	37	23	14
27	Muvattupula	65	38	27
28	Todupula	5	1	4
29	Kunnattunadu	18	9	9
30	Alangadu	15	10	5
31	Parur	38	20	18
	Cardamom Hills	...	...	...
	Periyar and Thekkadi	...	...	...
	Total ...	1,017	598	419

XIV.
by Age.

Distribution by Age.

0—4.		5—9.		10—14.		15—19.		20—24.	
Males.	Females.	Males.	Females.	Males.	Females.	Males.	Females.	Males.	Females.
6	7	8	9	10	11	12	13	14	15
...	1	...	...	1	...	...	...	1	...
...	1	...	...	...	...	1	1	1	1
1	...	...	...	...	...	1	...	1	...
1	...	1	...	...	...	1	...	2	1
...	...	...	...	..	1	...	...	1	...
1	...	1	..	3	2	...	2	1	2
...	1	...	1	2	..	2	2	4	2
...	2	3	1	3	1	5	2	3	2
1	1	2	2	3	...	4	1	...	2
4	1	2	1	4	2	...	...	1	1
1	...	1	...	1	...	...	...	1	...
...	...	...	...	...	...	...	...	...	...
1	...	4	2	1	5	3	...	4	1
2	...	1	1	1	...	...	...	1	1
1	...	1	...	...	...	1	...	2	1
...	...	2	1	2	...	2	2	...	1
...	...	1	1	...	...	2	1	5	...
...	...	3	...	3	...	...	2	2	1
...	...	2	2	1	...	...	...	2	...
1	...	2	...	...	...	...	...	...	1
...	1	...	...	...	1	1	...	1	2
2	1	1	...	2	1	4	1	1	1
...	...	...	2	1	...	...	...	1	...
...	...	1	...	1	...	3	...	1	1
1	...	2	...	1	1	2	...	1	...
2	...	1	1	2	1	5	1	3	...
...	...	1	...	2	2	3	...	2	3
...	...	..	...	1	2	...	...	...	1
...	...	1	1	1	1	...	...	...	1
...	1	1	...	..	...	...	...	...	1
1	...	1	...	...	...	...	2	3	2
...	...	...	...	...	...	...	...	...	...
...	. .	...	...	...	...	...	...	...	...
20	10	35	16	36	20	40	17	45	29

TABLE

Blind,

Number.	Taluq.	Distribution 25—29. Males.	25—29. Females.	30—34. Males.	30—34. Females.	35—39. Males.	35—39. Females.
1	2	16	17	18	19	20	21
1	Tovala ...	...	...	...	...	...	..
2	Agastiswaram ...	2	1	2	4	3	1
3	Eranial ...	2	...	1	...	3	...
4	Kalkulam ...	1	1	...	...	1	1
5	Vilavankodu ...	...	1	...	...	2	...
6	Neyattankara ...	2	5	2	2	3	4
7	Trivandram ...	1	1	3	2	2	2
8	Nedumangadu ...	1	3	1	1	...	2
9	Sirayinkil ...	2	2	3	4	4	3
10	Kottarakkara ...	...	3	2	2	4	1
11	Pattanapuram ...	1	1	...	...	...	...
12	Shenkotta ...	...	...	..	...	...	...
13	Quilon ...	1	...	1	2	3	1
14	Kunnattur ...	2	1	...	1	3	1
15	Karunagappalli ...	...	...	2	1	3	1
16	Kartigappalli ...	...	2	2	...	...	...
17	Mavellikkara ...	1	1	1	...	1	1
18	Chenganur ...	2	...	...	...	1	2
19	Tiruvalla ...	...	1	2	1	1	...
20	Ambalappula ...	2	...	...	2	2	...
21	Sherttala ...	1	1	3	1	4	1
22	Vykkam ...	2	1	1	...	2	...
23	Ettumanur ...	2	...	...	...	...	2
24	Kottayam ...	3	1	...	1	1	...
25	Changanacheri ...	1	...	1	1	2	...
26	Meenachal ...	1	2	2	2	2	1
27	Muvattupula ...	7	3	5	3	2	3
28	Todupula ...	...	...	...	...	...	1
29	Kunnattunadu ...	...	...	...	2	2	...
30	Alangadu ...	...	1	2	...	...	...
31	Parur ...	...	1	2	2	3	1
	Cardamom Hills ...	...	...	...	...	...	...
	Periyar & Thekkadi.	...	...	...	...	...	...
	Total ...	37	33	38	34	54	29

XIV.

by Age—(*Continued*).

BY AGE—(*Continued*).

40—44.		45—49.		50—54.		55—59.		60 and over.	
Males.	Females.	Males.	Females.	Males.	Females.	Males.	Females.	Males.	Females.
22	23	24	25	26	27	28	29	30	81
...	...	1	...	1	...	...	...	...	6
1	1	4	1	2	2	3	5	8	4
4	1	...	...	7	1	...	...	2	2
2	...	1	1	2	1	...	1	2	...
...	...	2	...	...	4	2	3	2	5
1	2	8	1	2	1	8	4	8	8
6	8	7	...	3	3	3	3	7	1
4	3	...	1	5	2	...	...	8	2
2	...	6	1	4	2	1	4	6	8
1	1	5	...	4	3	4	...	6	6
...	...	...	...	...	1	1	1	...	...
...	...	...	...	...	...	...	...	...	.
8	8	4	1	8	...	...	...	9	12
...	...	...	...	2	1	...	1	2	...
4	..	1	1	2	1	...	2	2	8
1	1	...	3	2	2	4	...	7	10
1	...	8	2	3	...	2	...	5	4
...	...	2	...	...	1	...	...	4	2
2	1	1	2	...	...	2	...	7	6
...	1	1	1	2	2	...	1	3	5
...	1	1	1	...	1	2	1	...	3
1	...	...	...	1	...	...	...	4	2
...	...	...	1	...	...	...	1	...	2
...	...	1	1	...	2	...	1	4	...
2	2	1	...	2	1	1	1	5	7
1	2	...	1	2	...	...	2	2	1
2	4	2	...	2	1	2	1	8	7
..	...	...	...	...	...	...	...	...	...
...	1	...	...	1	...	1	...	8	8
1	1	1	...	1	...	1	...	8	1
1	...	3	1	1	1	...	...	5	8
...	...	...	...	...	...	...	...	...	...
...	...	...	...	...	...	...	...	...	...
40	28	50	20	54	33	82	82	117	118

TABLE

Lepers,

Number.	Taluq.	Total Lepers. Total.	Males.	Females.
1	2	3	4	5
1	Tovala	6	6	...
2	Agastiswaram	14	13	1
3	Eranial	12	12	...
4	Kalkulam	9	6	3
5	Vilavankodu	15	7	8
6	Neyattankara	49	33	16
7	Trivandram	34	23	11
8	Nedumangadu	52	39	13
9	Sirayinkil	48	41	7
10	Kottarakkara	54	42	12
11	Pattanapuram	11	8	3
12	Shenkotta	...	...	...
13	Quilon	85	70	15
14	Kunnattur	29	22	7
15	Karunagappalli	65	42	23
16	Kartigappalli	117	79	38
17	Mavellikkara	18	11	7
18	Chenganur	10	7	3
19	Tiruvalla	25	16	9
20	Ambalappula	45	36	9
21	Sherttala	79	54	25
22	Vykkam	42	28	14
23	Ettumanur	11	4	7
24	Kottayam	11	5	6
25	Changanacheri	24	19	5
26	Meenachal	15	9	6
27	Muvattupula	15	8	7
28	Todupula	4	2	2
29	Kunnattunadu	19	12	7
30	Alangadu	20	11	9
31	Parur	22	12	10
	Cardamom Hills	8	7	1
	Periyar and Thekkadi	...	...	...
	Total ...	968	684	284

XV.

by Age.

Distribution by Age.

0—4.		5—9.		10—14.		15—19.		20—24.	
Males.	Females.	Males.	Females.	Males.	Females.	Males.	Females.	Males.	Females.
6	7	8	9	10	11	12	13	14	15
...	...	...	...	1	...	...	...	...	...
...	...	...	...	...	...	1	...	...	...
...	...	...	...	...	...	...	...	1	...
...	...	...	...	...	...	...	...	...	...
...	...	...	...	...	...	...	...	..	1
1	..	...	...	...	...	...	2	1	1
1	1	2	...	2	...	1	...	1	...
...	...	...	...	2	...	1	...	1	2
...	...	...	...	1	...	1	...	1	2
...	...	...	...	...	1	1	2	3	...
...	...	...	...	...	...	...	...	...	1
...	...	...	...	...	...	...	...	...	...
...	...	1	...	1	...	3	2	5	3
...	...	1	...	...	...	...	1	...	...
...	...	...	1	1	2	...	...	...	1
...	...	...	1	...	2	3	3	3	1
...	...	...	1	1	...	1	...	1	...
...	...	...	...	..	...	1	1	1	1
...	1	1	...	2	...	...	1	2	1
...	...	...	...	2	...	...	...	3	1
1	1	2	3	3	1	3	3	5	3
...	1	1	...	...	1	1	...	3	2
...	...	...	...	...	...	...	1	1	...
...	1	...	...	...	...	2	1	...	...
...	...	...	1	...	...	1	...	3	1
...	...	...	...	...	...	2	...	...	...
...	...	...	...	...	1	...	1	...	...
...	...	...	...	1	...	...	...	1	...
...	...	...	...	...	1	1	1	1	1
...	...	1	...	2	1	3	1	...	1
...	...	...	2	...	1	1	1	2	...
...	...	1	...	1	...	2	...	...	...
...	...	...	...	...	...	...	...	...	...
3	5	10	9	20	11	29	21	39	23

TABLE

Lepers,

Number.	Taluq.	Distribution					
		25—29.		30—34.		35—39.	
		Males.	Females.	Males.	Females.	Males.	Females.
1	2	16	17	18	19	20	21
1	Tovala ...	2	...	...	...	...	...
2	Agastiswaram ...	3	...	...	...	2	...
3	Eranial ...	1	...	4	...	2	...
4	Kalkulam ...	...	...	...	...	3	1
5	Vilavankodu ...	3	1	...	...	3	1
6	Neyattankara ...	5	2	2	1	4	1
7	Trivandram ...	4	...	1	1	...	4
8	Nedumangadu ...	2	...	4	2	4	...
9	Sirayinkil ...	2	1	4	1	7	1
10	Kottarakkara ...	5	2	3	1	4	3
11	Pattanapuram ...	...	...	1	...	2	1
12	Shenkotta ...	...	...	...	...	...	...
13	Quilon ...	2	1	7	2	11	1
14	Kunnattur ..	1	1	3	...	3	...
15	Karunagappalli ...	8	1	3	2	4	3
16	Kartigappalli ...	5	4	16	8	9	2
17	Mavellikkara ...	...	1	...	2	2	1
18	Chenganur ...	1	...	...	...	...	1
19	Tiruvalla ...	...	...	1	2	2	...
20	Ambalappula ...	1	2	6	...	8	1
21	Sherttala ...	4	...	4	4	9	1
22	Vykkam ...	7	...	5	2	3	2
23	Ettumanur ...	...	1	1	1	...	...
24	Kottayam ...	...	...	...	...	1	1
25	Changanacheri ...	...	...	...	...	4	1
26	Meenachal ...	1	1	1	1	...	1
27	Muvattupula ...	1	...	2	...	1	...
28	Todupula ...	...	1	...	1	...	...
29	Kunnattunadu ...	...	1	2	...	2	1
30	Alangadu ...	1	...	2	...	1	...
31	Parur ...	2	2	2	...	...	...
	Cardamom Hills ...	...	...	2	...	...	...
	Periyar & Thekkadi.	...	...	...	...	...	...
	Total ...	61	22	76	31	91	28

XV.

by Age—(*Continued*).

BY AGE—(*Continued*).

40—44.		45—49.		50—54.		55—59.		60 and over.	
Males.	Females.	Males.	Females.	Males.	Females.	Males.	Females.	Males.	Females.
22	23	24	25	26	27	28	29	30	31
1	...	2	...	...	...	...	...	...	...
3	...	...	..	1	...	1	...	2	1
...	...	2	...	...	...	...	...	2	...
...	...	...	1	1	1	...	...	2	...
1	1	...	...	...	1	...	2	...	1
8	...	2	5	4	1	2	2	4	1
2	1	5	3	3	...	...	...	1	1
8	1	5	2	6	4	4	...	2	2
6	1	7	...	4	1	3	...	5	...
6	...	6	2	3	1	2	...	9	...
2	1	3	...	...	...	...	...	...	...
...	...	...	...	...	...	...	...	...	...
12	1	5	1	7	2	3	...	13	2
1	2	3	1	4	2	2	...	4	...
5	3	8	4	3	4	4	2	6	...
11	3	15	4	9	5	6	2	2	3
4	2	1	...	...	...	1	...	...	...
1	...	...	...	...	...	...	...	3	...
4	...	2	...	...	1	1	...	1	3
6	...	2	3	2	...	1	...	5	2
4	2	5	2	7	2	2	1	5	2
3	2	...	2	1	1	1	...	3	1
...	...	...	...	2	1	...	...	...	3
...	2	1	...	...	...	1	...	...	1
1	1	2	1	2	...	1	...	5	...
2	1	1	...	2	1	...	1	...	...
2	3	...	1	...	...	...	...	2	1
...	...	...	...	...	...	...	...	...	...
...	...	1	...	2	...	2	...	1	2
1	2	...	1	...	1	...	1	...	1
2	3	1	...	...	1	1	...	1	...
...	1	...	...	1	...	...	...	...	...
...	...	...	...	...	...	...	...	...	...
96	33	79	33	64	30	38	11	78	27

TABLE

Castes, Tribes and Races, by

Class.	Group.	Caste, &c.	No. of recorded sub-divisions.	Religion.	Total.	Males.	Females.
1	2	3	4	5	6	7	8
A. Agricultural.	1. Military and Dominant.	1 Nair ...	75	Hindu...	*483,725*	241,598	242,127
		2 Ambalakāran...	...	" ...	*1*	1	...
		3 Kartāvu ...	...	" ...	*97*	55	42
		4 Koiltamburān...	...	" ...	*101*	58	43
		5 Kshatrya ...	7	" ...	*1,276*	653	623
		6 Mahratta ...	...	" ...	*93*	50	43
		7 Maravar ...	7	" ...	*5,642*	2,889	2,753
		8 Pandāla ...	...	" ...	71	36	35
		9 Rajaput ...	1	" ...	*20*	13	7
		10 Raju ...	1	" ...	*52*	30	22
		11 Sāmantakar ...	...	" ...	*188*	97	91
		12 Tampān ...	...	" ...	*286*	144	142
		13 Tirumulpād ...	...	" ...	*410*	232	178
		14 Unniyādiri ...	...	" ...	*94*	51	43
		15 Vellōdi ...	...	" ...	*44*	18	26
		Total Group 1 ...	...	...	492,100	245,925	246,175
	2(a). Other Agricultural land-holding classes.	1 Gavarulu ...	...	Hindu...	*12*	7	5
		2 Karayālar ...	...	" ...	*58*	27	31
		3 Kattāran ...	...	" ...	*5*	3	2
		4 Kodipattan ...	...	" ...	*423*	210	213
		5 Kurunni ...	...	" ...	*7*	7	...
		6 Lōti ...	...	" ...	*1*	1	...
		7 Mālli ...	...	" ...	*1*	1	...
		8 Mudali ...	5	" ...	*926*	437	489
		9 Pāndi Sudra ...	8	" ...	*5,144*	2,511	2,633
		10 Valamalu ...	...	" ...	*5*	2	3
		11 Vellāla ...	14	" ...	*44,886*	22,808	22,078
		Total Group 2(a)...	...	...	51,468	26,014	25,454

Name and Classification: columns 1–5. State Total: columns 6–8.

XVI.

Nationality or Traditional Occupation.

Taluqs.

Tovala.			Agastiswaram.			Eranial.		
Total.	Males.	Females.	Total.	Males.	Females.	Total.	Males.	Females.
9	10	11	12	13	14	15	16	17
822	156	166	1,578	797	781	4,848	2,422	2,426
...	...	...	...	...	...	...	...	...
...	...	...	...	...	...	...	...	...
...	...	...	...	...	...	...	...	...
38	18	20	29	19	10	12	5	7
...	...	...	...	...	...	3	1	2
831	415	416	965	502	463	60	20	40
...	...	...	...	...	...	...	...	...
...	...	...	...	...	...	...	...	...
...	...	...	8	4	4	...	...	...
...	...	...	...	...	...	...	...	...
...	...	...	...	...	...	...	...	...
...	...	...	...	...	...	...	...	...
...	...	...	...	...	...	...	...	...
...	...	...	...	...	...	...	...	...
1,191	589	602	2,580	1,322	1,258	4,923	2,448	2,475
...	...	...	...	...	...	...	...	...
...	...	...	...	...	...	...	...	...
...	...	...	...	...	...	...	...	...
...	...	...	...	...	...	...	...	...
...	...	...	...	...	...	...	...	...
...	...	...	...	...	...	...	...	...
...	...	...	...	...	...	...	...	...
23	7	16	486	245	241	35	18	17
1,008	443	565	645	322	323	83	36	47
...	...	...	...	...	...	...	...	...
7,219	3,490	3,729	11,021	5,428	5,593	1,648	784	864
8,250	3,940	4,310	12,152	5,995	6,157	1,766	838	928

TABLE

Castes, Tribes and Races, by

Class.	Group.	Caste, &c.	Taluqs: Kalkulam. Total.	Kalkulam. Males.	Kalkulam. Females.	Vilavankodu. Total.	Vilavankodu. Males.	Vilavankodu. Females.
1	2	3	18	19	20	21	22	23
A. Agricultural.	1. Military and Dominant.	1 Nair ...	8,266	4,144	4,122	13,213	6,873	6,340
		2 Ambalakāran...	...	...	...	...	...	...
		3 Kartāvu ...	...	...	...	...	...	...
		4 Koiltamburān...	...	...	...	...	...	...
		5 Kshatrya ..	...	...	...	...	...	...
		6 Mahratta ...	...	...	...	...	...	...
		7 Maravar ...	36	17	19	11	8	3
		8 Pandāla ...	...	...	...	...	...	...
		9 Rajaput ...	...	...	...	...	...	...
		10 Raju ...	...	...	...	...	...	...
		11 Sāmantakar ...	...	...	...	...	...	...
		12 Tampān ...	...	...	...	...	...	...
		13 Tirumulpād ...	...	...	...	...	...	...
		14 Unniyādiri ...	...	...	...	...	...	...
		15 Vollōdi ...	...	...	...	...	...	...
		Total Group 1 ...	8,302	4,161	4,141	13,224	6,881	6,343
	2 (a). Other Agricultural land-holding classes.	1 Gavarnlu ...	...	...	...	...	...	...
		2 Karayālar ...	...	...	...	...	...	...
		3 Kattāran ...	...	...	...	...	...	...
		4 Kodipattan ...	...	...	...	...	...	...
		5 Kuruni ...	...	...	...	...	...	...
		6 Lōti ...	...	...	...	...	...	...
		7 Mālli ...	...	...	...	...	...	...
		8 Mudali ...	29	13	16	51	26	25
		9 Pāndi Sudra ...	35	20	15	27	15	12
		10 Valamalu ...	...	...	...	...	...	...
		11 Vellāla ...	1,174	573	601	777	407	370
		Total Group 2 (a)..	1,238	606	632	855	448	407

XVI.

Nationality or Traditional Occupation—(*Continued*).

—(*Continued*).

Neyattankara.			Trivandram.			Nedumangadu.		
Total.	Males.	Females.	Total.	Males.	Females.	Total.	Males.	Females.
24	25	26	27	28	29	30	31	32
29,503	14,956	14,547	31,124	15,543	15,581	15,492	7,501	7,991
...	...	...	1	1	...	...	...	...
...	...	...	...	...	...	...	...	...
...	...	...	...	...	...	...	...	...
19	5	14	362	175	187	...	...	...
...	...	...	44	25	19	...	...	...
4	4	...	41	34	7	42	15	27
13	8	5	18	9	9	...	...	...
...	...	...	...	...	...	...	...	...
...	...	...	19	12	7	...	...	...
...	...	...	6	2	4	...	...	...
...	...	...	1	1	...	...	...	...
...	...	...	4	4	...	...	...	...
...	...	...	...	...	...	...	...	...
...	...	...	...	...	...	...	...	...
29,539	14,973	14,566	31,620	15,806	15,814	15,534	7,516	8,018
...	...	...	...	...	...	...	...	...
...	...	...	...	...	...	...	...	...
...	...	...	...	...	...	...	...	...
...	...	...	3	2	1	20	8	12
...	...	...	...	...	...	...	...	...
...	...	...	...	...	...	...	...	...
...	...	...	...	...	...	...	...	...
...	...	...	97	40	57	4	2	2
96	62	34	1,007	483	524	155	70	85
...	...	...	...	...	...	...	...	...
774	432	342	5,088	2,736	2,352	1,714	920	794
870	494	376	6,195	3,261	2,934	1,893	1,000	893

TABLE

Castes, Tribes and Races, by

Class.	Group.	Caste, &c.	Taluqs: Sirayinkil. Total.	Sirayinkil. Males.	Sirayinkil. Females.	Kottarakkara. Total.	Kottarakkara. Males.	Kottarakkara. Females.
1	2	3	33	34	35	36	37	38
A. Agricultural.	1. Military and Dominant.	1 Nair ...	23,833	11,868	11,965	16,690	8,459	8,231
		2 Ambalakāran...	...	...	...	...	...	...
		3 Kartāvu ...	...	...	...	...	...	...
		4 Koiltamburān...	61	34	27	...	...	...
		5 Kshatrya ...	2	2	...	...	...	...
		6 Mahratta ...	28	15	13	...	...	...
		7 Maravar ...	...	...	...	21	6	15
		8 Pandāla ...	...	...	...	...	...	...
		9 Rajaput ...	...	...	...	...	...	...
		10 Raju ...	...	...	...	...	...	...
		11 Sāmantakar ...	...	...	...	...	..	...
		12 Tampān ...	...	...	...	..	...	...
		13 Tirumulpād ...	...	...	...	...	...	...
		14 Unniyādiri ...	...	..	...	...	...	...
		15 Vellōdi ...	...	...	...	...	...	...
		Total Group 1 ...	23,924	11,919	12,005	16,711	8,465	8,246
	2 (a). Other Agricultural land-holding classes.	1 Gavarulu ...	...	...	...	...	...	...
		2 Karayālar ...	...	...	...	...	...	...
		3 Kattāran ...	...	...	...	...	...	...
		4 Kodipattan ...	...	...	...	...	...	...
		5 Kuruni ...	...	...	...	...	...	...
		6 Lōti ...	...	...	...	...	...	...
		7 Mālli ...	...	...	...	...	...	...
		8 Mudali ...	...	...	...	3	2	1
		9 Pāndi Sudra ...	12	7	5	20	11	9
		10 Valamalu ...	...	...	...	...	...	...
		11 Vellāla ...	518	264	254	532	267	265
		Total Group 2 (a).	530	271	259	555	280	275

XVI.

Nationality or Traditional Occupation—(*Continued*).

—(*Continued*).

Pattanapuram.			Shenkotta.			Quilon.		
Total.	Males.	Females.	Total.	Males.	Females.	Total.	Males.	Females.
39	40	41	42	43	44	45	46	47
9,330	4,642	4,688	112	52	60	31,410	15,558	15,852
...	...	...	...	...	...	...	...	...
...	...	...	...	..	...	...	...	...
...	...	...	...	...	...	...	...	...
5	3	2	11	3	8	...	...	...
...	...	...	...	...	...	18	9	9
2	2	...	3,271	1,637	1,634	28	18	10
...	...	...	...	...	...	...	...	...
...	...	...	...	...	...	8	4	4
..	...	...	7	2	5	18	12	6
...	...	...	...	...	...	...	...	...
...	...	...	...	...	...	...	...	...
...	...	...	...	...	...	12	12	...
...	...	...	...	...	..	...	...	...
...	...	...	...	...	...	...	...	...
9,337	4,647	4,690	3,401	1,694	1,707	31,494	15,613	15,881
...	...	...	...	...	...	12	7	5
...	...	...	2	2	...	...	...	...
...	...	...	...	...	...	...	...	...
...	...	...	...	...	...	...	...	...
...	...	...	...	...	...	...	...	...
...	...	...	...	...	...	...	...	...
...	...	...	...	...	...	...	...	...
2	2	...	99	33	66	62	29	33
55	30	25	611	278	333	200	103	97
...	...	...	...	...	...	5	2	3
749	423	326	3,369	1,644	1,725	708	406	302
806	455	351	4,081	1,957	2,124	987	547	440

TABLE
Castes, Tribes and Races, by

Class.	Group.	Caste, &c.	Taluqs — Kunnattur. Total.	Kunnattur. Males.	Kunnattur. Females.	Karunagappalli. Total.	Karunagappalli. Males.	Karunagappalli. Females.
1	2	3	48	49	50	51	52	53
A. Agricultural.	1. Military and Dominant.	1 Nair ...	20,113	10,765	9,348	25,687	12,229	13,458
		2 Ambalakāran...	...	...	...	...	...	...
		3 Kartāvu ...	...	...	...	...	...	...
		4 Koiltamburān...	...	...	...	...	...	...
		5 Kshatrya ...	34	14	20	36	14	22
		6 Mahratta ..	...	...	...	...	...	...
		7 Maravar ...	...	...	...	...	...	...
		8 Pandāla ...	...	...	...	...	...	...
		9 Rajaput ...	..	...	...	...	...	...
		10 Raju ...	...	...	...	...	...	...
		11 Sāmantakar ...	...	...	...	...	...	...
		12 Tampān ...	...	...	...	...	...	...
		13 Tirumulpād ...	...	...	...	28	12	16
		14 Unniyādiri ...	...	...	...	...	...	...
		15 Vellōdi ...	...	...	...	...	...	...
		Total Group 1 ...	20,147	10,779	9,368	25,751	12,255	13,496
	2(a). Other Agricultural land-holding classes.	1 Gavarulu ...	...	...	..	...	...	...
		2 Karayālar ...	...	...	...	...	...	...
		3 Kattāran ...	...	...	...	...	...	...
		4 Kodipattan ...	...	...	...	...	...	...
		5 Kuruni ...	...	...	...	...	...	...
		6 Lōti ...	...	..	...	...	...	...
		7 Mālli ...	..	...	...	...	...	...
		8 Mudali ...	...	...	..	...	...	...
		9 Pāndi Sudra ...	...	...	...	71	38	33
		10 Valamalu ...	...	...	...	...	...	...
		11 Vellāla ...	253	140	113	278	147	131
		Total Group 2 (a).	253	140	113	349	185	164

XVI.

Nationality or Traditional Occupation—(*Continued*).

—(*Continued*).

Kartigappalli.			Mavellikkara.			Changanur.		
Total.	Males.	Females.	Total.	Males.	Females.	Total.	Males.	Females.
54	55	56	57	58	59	60	61	62
22,979	11,168	11,811	30,800	15,509	15,291	22,150	11,265	10,885
...	...	...	...	...	...	...	...	...
...	...	...	...	...	...	...	...	...
...	...	...	10	6	4	13	8	5
79	42	37	107	71	36	109	51	58
...	...	...	...	...	...	...	...	...
...	...	...	...	...	...	...	...	...
13	5	8	16	8	8	1	1	...
...	...	...	...	...	...	...	...	...
...	...	...	...	...	...	...	...	...
...	...	...	...	...	...	...	...	...
...	...	...	25	12	13	...	...	...
2	1	1	54	33	21	...	...	...
...	...	...	...	...	...	..	...	...
...	...	...	...	...	...	...	....	...
23,073	11,216	11,857	31,012	15,639	15,373	22,273	11,325	10,948
...	...	...	...	...	...	...	...	...
...	...	...	56	25	31	...	...	...
...	...	...	...	...	...	...	...	...
...	...	...	...	...	...	...	...	...
...	...	...	...	...	...	...	...	...
...	...	...	...	...	...	...	...	...
...	...	...	...	...	...	...	...	...
..	...	...	...	...	...	..	...	...
128	58	70	60	31	29	18	10	8
...	...	...	...	...	...	...	...	...
616	330	286	264	124	140	867	433	434
744	388	356	380	180	200	885	443	442

TABLE

Castes, Tribes and Races, by

Class.	Group.	Caste, &c.	Taluqs: Tiruvalla. Total.	Tiruvalla. Males.	Tiruvalla. Females.	Ambalappula. Total.	Ambalappula. Males.	Ambalappula. Females.
1	2	3	63	64	65	66	67	68
A. Agricultural.	1. Military and Dominant.	1 Nair ...	28,842	14,472	14,370	17,388	8,438	8,950
		2 Ambalakāran ..	...	...	...	...	...	...
		3 Kartāvu ...	...	...	...	...	...	...
		4 Koiltamburān ..	...	...	...	...	...	...
		5 Kshatrya ...	141	73	68	73	35	38
		6 Mahratta ...	...	...	...	...	...	...
		7 Maravar ...	...	...	...	...	...	...
		8 Pandāla ...	...	...	...	...	...	...
		9 Rajaput ...	...	...	...	...	...	...
		10 Raju ...	...	...	...	...	...	...
		11 Sāmantakar ...	...	...	...	...	...	...
		12 Tampān ...	...	...	...	...	...	...
		13 Tirumulpād ...	78	42	36	38	30	8
		14 Unniyādiri ...	1	1	...	...	...	...
		15 Vellōdi ...	...	...	...	...	...	...
		Total Group 1 ...	29,062	14,588	14,474	17,499	8,503	8,996
	2 (a). Other Agricultural land-holding classes.	1 Gavarulu ...	...	...	...	...	...	...
		2 Karayālar ...	...	...	...	...	...	...
		3 Kattāran ...	...	...	...	...	...	...
		4 Kodipattan ...	...	...	...	...	...	...
		5 Kuruni ...	...	...	...	...	...	...
		6 Lōti ...	...	...	...	...	...	...
		7 Mālli ...	...	...	...	...	...	...
		8 Mudali ...	...	...	...	...	...	...
		9 Pāndi Sudra ...	348	200	148	100	52	48
		10 Valamalu ...	...	...	...	...	...	...
		11 Vellāla ...	218	116	102	1,049	539	510
		Total Group 2(a)..	566	316	250	1,149	591	558

XVI.

Nationality or Traditional Occupation—(*Continued*).

—(*Continued*).

Sherttala.			Vykkam.			Ettumanur.		
Total.	Males.	Females.	Total.	Males.	Females.	Total.	Males.	Females.
69	70	71	72	73	74	75	76	77
14,826	7,224	7,602	13,072	6,599	6,473	12,367	6,343	6,024
...	...	...	...	...	...	...	...	...
18	10	8	3	2	1	22	12	10
...	...	...	...	...	...	...	...	...
1	1	...	57	29	28	...	...	...
...	...	...	...	...	...	...	...	...
7	2	5	...	...	...	...	...	...
...	...	...	...	...	...	10	5	5
...	...	...	...	...	...	...	...	...
...	...	...	...	...	...	...	...	...
...	...	...	...	...	...	25	12	13
71	37	34	175	86	89	...	...	...
71	44	27	44	23	21	...	...	...
...	...	...	14	6	8	10	5	5
...	...	...	...	...	...	...	...	...
14,994	7,318	7,676	13,365	6,745	6,620	12,434	6,377	6,057
...	...	...	...	...	...	...	...	...
...	...	...	...	...	...	...	...	...
...	...	...	...	...	...	...	...	...
...	...	...	...	...	...	...	...	...
...	...	...	...	...	...	...	...	...
...	...	...	...	...	...	...	...	...
...	...	...	...	...	...	...	...	...
...	...	...	...	...	...	...	...	...
182	85	97	122	65	57	15	8	7
...	...	...	...	...	...	...	...	...
304	130	174	146	65	81	128	73	55
486	215	271	268	130	138	143	81	62

TABLE

Castes, Tribes and Races, by

Class.	Group.	Caste, &c.	Taluqs: Kottayam. Total.	Kottayam. Males.	Kottayam. Females.	Changanacheri. Total.	Changanacheri. Males.	Changanacheri. Females.
1	2	3	78	79	80	81	82	83
A. Agricultural.	1. Military and Dominant.	1 Nair ...	14,944	7,460	7,484	14,611	7,428	7,183
		2 Ambalakāran...	...	...	...	...	...	...
		3 Kartāvu ...	27	15	12	10	6	4
		4 Koiltamburān..	...	...	...	17	10	7
		5 Kshatrya ...	45	27	18	38	24	14
		6 Mahratta ...	...	...	...	...	...	...
		7 Maravar ...	...	...	...	...	...	...
		8 Pandāla ...	...	...	...	...	...	...
		9 Rajaput ...	...	...	...	...	...	...
		10 Raju ...	...	...	...	...	...	...
		11 Sāmantakar ...	19	10	9	36	19	17
		12 Tampān ...	...	...	...	...	...	...
		13 Tirumulpād ...	6	3	3	...	...	...
		14 Unniyādiri ...	33	16	17	12	8	4
		15 Vellōdi ...	...	...	...	...	...	...
		Total Group 1 ...	15,074	7,531	7,543	14,724	7,495	7,229
	2 (a). Other Agricultural land-holding classes.	1 Gavarulu ...	...	...	...	...	...	...
		2 Karayālar ...	...	...	...	...	...	...
		3 Kattāran ...	...	...	...	...	...	...
		4 Kodipattan ...	...	...	...	...	...	...
		5 Kuruni ...	...	...	...	...	...	...
		6 Lōti ...	...	...	...	...	...	...
		7 Mālli ...	...	...	...	...	...	...
		8 Mudali ...	...	...	...	...	...	...
		9 Pāndi Sudra ...	41	25	16	...	...	...
		10 Valamalu ...	...	...	...	...	...	...
		11 Vellāla ...	226	109	117	803	450	353
		Total Group 2(*a*)..	267	134	133	803	450	353

XVI.

Nationality or Traditional Occupation—(*Continued*).

—(*Continued*).

Meenachal.			Muvattuppula.			Todupula.		
Total.	Males.	Females.	Total.	Males.	Females.	Total.	Males.	Females.
84	85	86	87	88	89	90	91	92
8,917	4,531	4,386	13,572	6,524	7,048	2,995	1,527	1,468
...	...	...	...	...	...	...	...	...
...	...	...	7	4	3	...	...	...
...	...	...	...	...	...	...	...	...
44	26	18	...	...	...	...	...	...
...	...	...	...	...	...	...	...	...
2	2	...	...	...	...	...	...	...
...	...	...	...	...	...	...	...	...
...	...	...	...	...	...	...	...	...
...	...	...	...	...	...	...	...	...
54	25	29	...	...	...	...	...	...
...	...	...	...	...	...	...	...	...
...	...	...	47	15	32	...	...	...
13	9	4	...	...	...	...	...	...
...	...	...	...	...	...	...	...	...
9,030	4,593	4,437	13,626	6,543	7,083	2,995	1,527	1,468
...	...	...	...	...	...	...	...	...
...	...	...	...	...	...	...	...	...
...	...	...	...	...	...	...	...	...
...	...	...	...	...	...	...	...	...
...	...	...	...	...	...	...	...	...
...	...	...	...	...	...	...	...	...
...	...	...	...	...	...	...	...	...
...	...	...	...	...	...	...	...	...
7	4	3	15	6	9	18	7	11
...	...	...	...	...	...	...	...	...
128	84	44	107	55	52	1,715	873	842
135	88	47	122	61	61	1,733	880	853

TABLE

Castes, Tribes and Races, by

Class.	Group.	Caste, &c.	Taluqs: Kunnattunadu. Total.	Kunnattunadu. Males.	Kunnattunadu. Females.	Alangadu. Total.	Alangadu. Males.	Alangadu. Females.
1	2	3	93	94	95	96	97	98
A. Agricultural.	1. Military and Dominant.	1 Nair ...	16,907	8,269	8,638	10,314	4,989	5,325
		2 Ambalakāran ...	...	...	...	...	...	...
		3 Kartāvu ...	5	3	2	5	3	2
		4 Koiltamburān ..	...	...	...	...	...	...
		5 Kshatrya ...	...	...	...	...	...	...
		6 Mahratta ..	...	...	...	...	...	...
		7 Maravar ...	...	...	...	...	...	...
		8 Pandāla ...	...	...	...	...	...	...
		9 Rajaput ...	...	...	...	...	...	...
		10 Raju ...	...	...	...	...	...	...
		11 Sāmantakar ...	27	18	9	21	11	10
		12 Tampān ...	...	...	...	14	8	6
		13 Tirumulpād ...	26	13	13	...	...	...
		14 Unniyādiri ...	11	6	5	...	...	...
		15 Vellōdi ...	...	...	...	44	18	26
		Total Group 1 ...	16,976	8,309	8,667	10,398	5,029	5,369
	2 (a). Other Agricultural land-holding classes.	1 Gavarulu ..	...	...	...	...	...	...
		2 Karayālar ...	...	...	...	...	...	...
		3 Kattāran ...	...	...	...	...	...	...
		4 Kodipattan ...	31	15	16	...	...	..
		5 Kuruni ...	...	...	...	...	...	...
		6 Lōti ...	...	...	...	...	...	...
		7 Mālli ...	...	...	...	..	...	...
		8 Mudali ...	...	...	...	...	...	...
		9 Pāndi Sudra ...	54	37	17	...	...	...
		10 Valamalu ...	...	...	...	...	...	...
		11 Vellāla ...	98	47	51	117	59	58
		Total Group 2(a)...	183	99	84	117	59	58

XVI.

Nationality or Traditional Occupation—(*Continued*).

—(*Continued*).

Parur. Total.	Parur. Males.	Parur. Females.	Cardamom Hills. Total.	Cardamom Hills. Males.	Cardamom Hills. Females.	Periyar and Thokkadi. Total.	Periyar and Thokkadi. Males.	Periyar and Thokkadi. Females.
99	100	101	102	103	104	105	106	107
7,231	3,653	3,578	279	226	53	10	8	2
...	...	...	...	...	...	...	...	...
...	...	...	...	...	...	...	...	...
...	...	...	...	...	...	...	...	...
15	7	8	11	3	8	8	6	2
...	...	...	...	...	...	...	...	...
...	...	...	274	175	99	47	32	15
...	...	...	...	...	...	...	...	...
...	...	...	9	6	3	3	3	...
...	...	...	...	...	...	...	...	...
...	...	...	...	...	...	...	...	...
...	...	...	...	...	...	...	...	...
...	...	...	...	...	...	...	...	...
...	...	...	...	...	...	...	...	...
...	...	...	...	...	...	...	...	...
7,246	3,660	3,586	573	410	163	68	49	19
...	...	...	...	...	...	...	...	...
...	...	...	...	...	...	...	...	...
...	...	...	...	...	...	5	3	2
369	185	184	...	...	...	...	...	...
...	...	...	...	...	...	7	7	...
...	...	...	...	...	...	1	1	...
...	...	...	...	...	...	1	1	...
...	...	...	29	16	13	6	4	2
11	5	6	...	...	...	...	...	...
...	...	...	...	...	...	...	...	...
434	211	223	1,427	740	687	417	309	108
814	401	413	1,456	756	700	437	325	112

TABLE

Castes, Tribes and Races, by

Class.	Group.	Caste, &c.	No. of recorded sub-divisions.	Religion.	State Total. Total.	Males.	Females.
1	2	3	4	5	6	7	8
A. Agricultural—*Continued*.	2(c) Field-labouring classes.	1 Kanakkan ...	...	Hindu....	*192*	94	98
		2 Kurava ...	7	,, ...	*60,377*	29,660	30,717
		3 Padayāchi ...	...	,, ...	*4*	1	3
		4 Pallan ...	...	,, ...	*5,655*	2,811	2,844
		5 Pariah ...	9	{ Hindu Chris.	*71,847*	36,463	35,384
		6 Pulaya ...	5	Hindu....	*202,616*	103,153	99,463
		7 Udaya ...	...	,, ...	*7*	2	5
		8 Ullādan ...	...	,, ...	*2,873*	1,473	1,400
		9 Vettuvan ...	...	,, ...	*87*	39	48
		Total Group 2(c)...	...	...	343,658	173,696	169,962
	4 Forest and Hill tribes.	1 Iruler ...	...	Hindu....	*16*	7	9
		2 Kāttar ...	...	,, ...	*39*	23	16
		3 Kāttilaya ...	...	,, ...	*76*	40	36
		4 Kāttu Parisha (Forest tribe)..	...	,, ...	*34*	23	11
		5 Khond ...	1	,, ...	*10*	8	2
		6 Malayarien ...	1	,, ...	*4,809*	2,498	2,311
		7 Mariya ...	...	,, ...	*3*	3	...
		8 Muduvan ...	...	,, ...	*1,077*	545	532
		9 Mynāta ...	...	,, ...	*44*	24	20
		10 Nādipanikan ...	...	,, ...	*29*	9	20
		11 Pania ...	...	,, ...	*2*	...	2
		12 Vēlan ...	2	,, ...	*17,143*	8,660	8,483
		Total Group 4 ...	...	...	23,282	11,840	11,442
		Total Class A. ...	...	...	*910,508*	*457,475*	*453,033*

XVI.

Nationality or Traditional Occupation—(*Continued*).

TALUQS.

Tovala.			Agastiswaram.			Eranial.		
Total.	Males.	Females.	Total.	Males.	Females.	Total.	Males.	Females.
9	10	11	12	13	14	15	16	17
...	...	...	...	...	...	...	...	...
29	15	14	67	25	42	72	33	39
...	...	...	...	...	...	...	...	...
317	157	160	396	190	206	385	195	190
6,828	3,291	3,537	8,873	4,264	4,609	4,899	2,411	2,488
...	...	...	...	...	...	165	69	96
...	...	...	...	...	...	...	...	...
...	...	...	...	...	...	...	...	...
...	...	...	...	...	...	...	...	...
...	...	...	...	...	...	...	...	...
7,174	3,463	3,711	9,336	4,479	4,857	5,521	2,708	2,813
...	...	...	...	...	...	16	7	9
...	...	...	...	...	...	...	...	...
...	...	...	...	...	...	...	...	...
...	...	...	...	...	...	...	...	...
...	...	...	...	...	...	...	...	...
...	...	...	...	...	...	...	...	...
...	...	...	...	...	...	...	...	...
...	...	...	...	...	...	...	...	...
...	...	...	...	...	...	...	...	...
...	...	...	...	...	...	...	...	...
...	...	...	...	...	...	...	...	...
95	50	45	...	...	...	...	...	...
95	50	45	...	...	..	16	7	9
16,710	8,042	8,668	24,068	11,796	12,272	12,226	6,001	6,225

TABLE

Castes, Tribes and Races, by

Class.	Group.	Caste, &c.	Taluqs: Kalkulam. Total.	Kalkulam. Males.	Kalkulam. Females.	Vilavankodu. Total.	Vilavankodu. Males.	Vilavankodu. Females.
1	2	3	18	19	20	21	22	23
A. Agricultural.	2(c) Field-labouring classes.	1 Kanakkan ...	...	...	...	...	...	...
		2 Kurava ...	98	49	49	80	30	50
		3 Padayāchi ...	...	...	...	...	...	...
		4 Pallan ...	100	50	50	...	...	...
		5 Pariah ...	4,913	2,462	2,451	2,553	1,326	1,227
		6 Palaya ...	330	166	164	3,090	1,571	1,519
		7 Udaya ...	...	..	...	...	...	...
		8 Ullādan ...	...	...	...	...	...	...
		9 Vettuvan ...	...	...	...	...	...	...
		Total Group 2(c)...	5,441	2,727	2,714	5,723	2,927	2,796
	4. Forest and Hill tribes.	1 Iruler ...	...	...	...	...	...	...
		2 Kāttar ...	...	...	...	...	...	...
		3 Kāttilaya ...	...	..	...	...	...	...
		4 Kāttu Parisha (Forest tribe) .	...	...	...	...	...	...
		5 Khond ...	...	...	...	...	...	...
		6 Malayarien ...	1,023	519	504	...	...	...
		7 Mariya ...	...	...	...	...	...	...
		8 Muduvan ...	...	...	...	...	...	...
		9 Mynāta ...	...	...	...	...	...	...
		10 Nādipanikan ...	...	...	...	...	...	...
		11 Pania ...	...	...	...	...	...	...
		12 Vēlan ...	656	316	340	1,566	773	793
		Total Group 4 ...	1,679	835	844	1,566	773	793
		Total Class A. ...	16,660	8,329	8,331	21,368	11,029	10,339

XVI.

Nationality or Traditional Occupation—(*Continued*).

—(*Continued*).

Neyattankara.			Trivandram.			Nedumangadu.		
Total.	Males.	Females.	Total.	Males.	Females.	Total.	Males.	Females.
24	25	26	27	28	29	30	31	32
...	...	...	...	...	...	...	...	...
62	29	33	376	194	182	3,201	1,618	1,583
...	...	...	...	...	...	...	...	...
...	...	...	...	...	...	21	10	11
2,873	1,496	1,377	544	283	261	2,730	1,347	1,383
13,472	6,811	6,661	9,284	4,679	4,605	6,801	3,386	3,415
...	...	...	...	...	...	...	...	...
...	...	...	...	...	...	...	...	...
...	...	...	...	...	...	...	...	...
16,407	8,336	8,071	10,204	5,156	5,048	12,753	6,361	6,392
...	...	...	...	...	...	...	...	...
...	...	...	...	...	...	...	...	...
...	...	...	...	...	...	...	...	...
...	...	...	13	6	7	...	...	...
...	...	...	...	...	...	...	...	...
1,504	794	710	...	...	...	318	168	150
...	...	...	...	...	...	...	...	...
...	...	...	...	...	...	...	...	...
...	...	...	...	...	...	...	...	...
...	...	...	...	...	...	...	...	...
...	...	...	...	...	...	...	...	...
2,307	1,196	1,111	124	72	52	3,312	1,696	1,616
3,811	1,990	1,821	137	78	59	3,630	1,864	1,766
50,627	25,793	24,834	48,156	24,301	23,855	33,810	16,741	17,069

TABLE

Castes, Tribes and Races, by

CLASS.	GROUP.	CASTE, &c.	TALUQS: Sirayinkil. Total.	Sirayinkil. Males.	Sirayinkil. Females.	Kottarakkara. Total.	Kottarakkara. Males.	Kottarakkara. Females.
1	2	3	33	34	35	36	37	38
A. Agricultural.	2(c) Field-labouring classes.	1 Kanakkan ...	...	...	...	...	...	...
		2 Kurava ...	9,443	4,634	4,809	8,628	4,227	4,401
		3 Padayāchi ...	...	...	...	...	...	...
		4 Pallan ...	...	...	...	122	88	34
		5 Pariah ...	744	364	380	1,911	1,039	872
		6 Pulaya ...	2,928	1,416	1,512	5,207	2,649	2,558
		7 Udaya ...	...	...	...	...	...	...
		8 Ullādan ...	...	...	...	...	...	...
		9 Vettuvan ...	...	...	...	...	...	...
		Total Group 2(c)...	13,115	6,414	6,701	15,868	8,003	7,865
	4. Forest and Hill tribes.	1 Iruler ...	...	...	...	...	...	...
		2 Kāttar ...	...	...	...	...	...	...
		3 Kāttilaya ...	...	...	...	...	...	...
		4 Kāttu Parisha (Forest tribe).	...	...	...	...	...	...
		5 Khond ...	...	...	...	...	...	...
		6 Malayarien ...	...	...	...	227	98	129
		7 Mariya ...	...	...	...	...	...	...
		8 Muduvan ...	...	...	...	...	...	...
		9 Mynāta ...	...	...	...	...	...	...
		10 Nādipanikan ...	...	...	...	...	...	...
		11 Pania ...	...	...	...	...	...	...
		12 Vēlan ...	112	53	59	134	60	74
		Total Group 4 ...	112	53	59	361	158	203
		Total Class A. ...	37,681	18,657	19,024	33,495	16,906	16,589

XVI.

Nationality or Traditional Occupation—(*Continued*).

—(*Continued*).

	Pattanapuram.			Shenkotta.			Quilon.		
	Total.	Males.	Females.	Total.	Males.	Females.	Total.	Males.	Females.
	39	40	41	42	43	44	45	46	47
	...	...	...	...	...	...	...	...	...
	6,429	3,163	3,266	158	85	73	5,231	2,540	2,691
	...	...	...	...	...	...	4	1	3
	3	2	1	3,731	1,741	1,990	55	31	24
	1,797	925	872	1,874	889	985	1,197	586	611
	1,583	845	738	...	...	...	6,935	3,421	3,514
	...	...	...	...	...	...	7	2	5
	...	...	...	...	...	...	...	...	...
	...	...	...	...	...	...	...	...	...
	9,812	4,935	4,877	5,763	2,715	3,048	13,429	6,581	6,848
	...	...	...	...	...	...	...	...	...
	...	...	...	...	...	...	...	...	...
	...	...	...	...	...	...	...	...	...
	...	...	...	...	...	..	...	...	...
	...	...	...	...	...	...	...	...	...
	105	58	47	...	...	...	...	...	...
	...	...	...	...	...	...	...	...	...
	...	...	...	...	...	...	...	...	...
	...	...	...	...	...	...	...	...	...
	...	...	...	...	...	...	...	...	...
	...	...	...	...	...	...	2	..	2
	139	68	71	...	...	..	108	64	44
	244	126	118	...	...	...	110	64	46
	20,199	10,163	10,036	13,245	6,366	6,879	46,020	22,805	23,215

TABLE

Castes, Tribes and Races, by

Class.	Group.	Caste, &c.	Taluqs: Kunnattur. Total.	Kunnattur. Males.	Kunnattur. Females.	Karunagappalli. Total.	Karunagappalli. Males.	Karunagappalli. Females.
1	2	3	48	49	50	51	52	53
A. Agricultural.	2(c) Field-labouring classes.	1 Kanakkan ...	...	...	...	...	...	...
		2 Kurava ...	11,960	5,774	6,186	2,268	1,092	1,176
		3 Padayāchi ...	...	...	...	...	...	...
		4 Pallan ...	...	...	...	8	6	2
		5 Pariah ...	3,809	1,892	1,917	1,117	543	574
		6 Pulaya ...	6,178	3,104	3,074	4,268	1,887	2,381
		7 Udaya ...	...	...	...	...	...	...
		8 Ullādan ...	...	...	...	42	25	17
		9 Vettuvan ...	...	...	...	...	...	...
		Total Group 2(c)...	21,947	10,770	11,177	7,703	3,553	4,150
	4. Forest and Hill tribes.	1 Iruler ...	...	...	...	...	...	...
		2 Kāttar ...	...	...	...	...	...	...
		3 Kāttilaya ...	...	...	...	...	...	...
		4 Kāttu Parisha (Forest tribe).	..	...	...	...	...	...
		5 Khond ...	...	...	...	...	...	...
		6 Malayarien ...	...	...	...	...	...	...
		7 Mariya ...	...	...	...	...	...	...
		8 Muduvan ...	...	...	...	...	...	...
		9 Mynāta ...	...	...	...	...	...	...
		10 Nādipanikan....	...	...	...	...	...	...
		11 Pania ...	...	...	...	...	...	...
		12 Vēlan ...	146	59	87	182	99	83
		Total Group 4 ...	146	59	87	182	99	83
		Total Class A. ...	42,493	21,748	20,745	33,985	16,092	17,893

XVI.

Nationality or Traditional Occupation—(*Continued*).

—(*Continued*).

Kartigappalli.			Mavellikkara.			Changanur.		
Total.	Males.	Females.	Total.	Males.	Females.	Total.	Males.	Females.
54	55	56	57	58	59	60	61	62
...	...	...	...	...	...	...	...	...
423	221	202	6,076	3,012	3,064	4,354	2,186	2,168
...	...	...	...	...	...	...	...	...
...	...	...	...	...	...	...	...	...
731	347	384	1,947	1,039	908	2,646	1,342	1,304
5,098	2,569	2,529	10,904	5,528	5,376	10,934	5,818	5,116
...	...	...	...	...	...	...	...	...
151	89	62	...	...	...	56	30	26
...	...	...	...	...	...	...	...	...
6,403	3,226	3,177	18,927	9,579	9,348	17,990	9,376	8,614
...	...	...	...	...	...	...	...	...
...	...	...	...	...	...	15	10	5
...	...	...	...	...	...	...	...	...
...	...	...	...	...	...	...	...	...
...	...	...	...	...	...	...	...	...
...	...	...	...	...	...	61	48	13
...	...	...	...	...	...	...	...	...
...	...	...	...	...	...	...	...	...
...	...	...	...	...	...	...	...	...
...	...	...	...	...	...	...	...	...
...	...	...	...	...	...	...	...	...
490	243	247	193	96	97	274	132	142
490	243	247	193	96	97	350	190	160
30,710	15,073	15,637	50,512	25,494	25,018	41,498	21,334	20,164

TABLE

Castes, Tribes and Races, by

Class.	Group.	Caste, &c.	Taluqs: Tiruvalla. Total.	Tiruvalla. Males.	Tiruvalla. Females.	Ambalappula. Total.	Ambalappula. Males.	Ambalappula. Females.
1	2	3	63	64	65	66	67	68
A. Agricultural.	2(c) Field-labouring classes.	1 Kanakkan ...	...	...	...	...	...	...
		2 Kurava ...	746	377	369	53	26	27
		3 Padayāchi ...	...	...	...	...	...	...
		4 Pallan ...	...	...	...	...	...	...
		5 Pariah ...	2,782	1,392	1,390	1.015	533	482
		6 Pulaya ...	17,858	9,416	8,442	7,347	3,642	3,705
		7 Udaya ...	...	...	...	...	...	...
		8 Ulladan ...	188	109	79	37	18	19
		9 Vettuvan ...	87	39	48	...	...	...
		Total Group 2(c)..	21,661	11,333	10,328	8,452	4,219	4,233
	4. Forest and Hill tribes.	1 Iruler ...	...	...	...	...	...	...
		2 Kāttar ...	15	6	9	...	..	...
		3 Kāttilaya ...	...	...	...	...	...	...
		4 Kāttu Parisha (Forest tribe).	...	...	...	...	...	...
		5 Khond ...	...	...	...	...	...	...
		6 Malayarien ...	163	81	82	140	71	69
		7 Mariya ...	...	...	...	...	...	...
		8 Muduvan ...	...	...	...	...	...	...
		9 Mynāta ...	10	5	5	...	...	...
		10 Nādipanikan ...	...	...	...	...	...	...
		11 Pania ...	...	...	...	...	...	...
		12 Vēlan ...	205	108	97	119	60	59
		Total Group 4 ...	393	200	193	259	131	128
		Total Class A. ...	51,682	26,437	25,245	27,359	13,444	13,915

XVI.

Nationality or Traditional Occupation—(*Continued*).

—(*Continued*).

Sherttala.			Vykkam.			Ettumanur.		
Total.	Males.	Females.	Total.	Males.	Females.	Total.	Males.	Females.
69	70	71	72	73	74	75	76	77
...	...	...	...	...	...	...	...	...
111	59	52	71	36	35	27	12	15
...	...	...	...	...	...	...	...	...
...	...	...	...	...	...	...	...	...
141	73	68	373	182	191	1,372	752	620
5,480	2,759	2,721	9,041	4,522	4,519	11,966	6,221	5,745
...	...	...	...	...	...	...	...	...
275	137	138	70	32	38	76	34	42
...	...	...	...	...	...	...	...	...
6,007	3,028	2,979	9,555	4,772	4,783	13,441	7,019	6,422
...	...	...	...	...	...	...	...	...
...	...	...	...	...	...	...	...	...
...	...	...	...	...	...	...	...	...
...	...	...	...	...	...	...	...	...
...	...	...	...	...	...	...	...	...
...	...	...	...	...	...	...	...	...
...	...	...	...	...	...	...	...	...
...	...	...	...	...	...	...	...	...
34	19	15	...	...	...	...	...	...
...	...	...	...	...	...	...	...	...
...	...	...	...	...	...	...	...	...
1,922	910	1,012	1,160	638	522	421	245	176
1,956	929	1,027	1,160	638	522	421	245	176
23,443	11,490	11,953	24,348	12,285	12,063	26,439	13,722	12,717

TABLE

Castes, Tribes and Races, by

Class.	Group.	Caste, &c.	Taluqs: Kottayam. Total.	Kottayam. Males.	Kottayam. Females.	Changanacheri. Total.	Changanacheri. Males.	Changanacheri. Females.
1	2	3	78	79	80	81	82	83
A. Agricultural.	2(c) Field-labouring classes.	1 Kanakkan ...	...	...	..	1	1	...
		2 Kurava ...	25	10	15	3	2	1
		3 Padayāchi ...	...	...	...	...	...	...
		4 Pallan ...	...	...	...	3	3	...
		5 Pariah ...	3,112	1,646	1,466	3,448	1,820	1,628
		6 Pulaya ...	7,671	3,935	3,736	8,647	4,566	4,081
		7 Udaya ...	..	...	...	...	...	...
		8 Ullādan ...	206	102	104	309	147	162
		9 Vettuvan ...	...	...	...	...	...	...
		Total Group 2(c)....	11,014	5,693	5,321	12,411	6,539	5,872
	4. Forest and Hill tribes.	1 Iruler ...	...	...	...	...	...	...
		2 Kāttar ...	...	...	...	...	...	...
		3 Kāttilaya ..	...	..	...	...	...	...
		4 Kāttu Parisha (Forest tribe)..	...	...	...	10	6	4
		5 Khond ...	...	...	...	...	...	...
		6 Malayarien ...	85	66	19	155	78	77
		7 Mariya ...	...	...	...	...	...	...
		8 Muduvan ...	...	...	...	...	...	...
		9 Mynāta ...	...	...	...	...	...	...
		10 Nādipanikan ...	...	...	...	...	...	...
		11 Pania ...	...	...	...	...	...	...
		12 Vēlan ...	379	203	176	243	128	115
		Total Group 4 ...	464	269	195	408	212	196
		Total Class A. ...	26,819	13,627	13,192	28,346	14,696	13,650

XVI.

Nationality or Traditional Occupation—(*Continued*).

—(*Continued*).

Meenachal.			Muvattupula.			Todupula.		
Total.	Males.	Females.	Total.	Males.	Females.	Total.	Males.	Females.
84	85	86	87	88	89	90	91	92
...	...	...	...	...	...	...	...	...
8	3	5	126	75	51	...	...	...
...	...	...	...	...	...	...	...	...
...	...	...	...	...	...	...	...	...
237	126	111	1,177	633	544	128	55	73
4,107	2,155	1,952	12,641	6,399	6,242	2,187	1,107	1,080
..	...	...	...	...	...	...	...	...
788	393	395	220	112	108	154	86	68
...	...	...	...	...	...	...	...	...
5,140	2,677	2,463	14,164	7,219	6,945	2,469	1,248	1,221
...	...	...	...	...	...	...	...	...
...	...	...	9	7	2	...	...	...
...	...	...	76	40	36	...	...	...
...	...	...	11	11	...	...	...	...
...	...	...	...	..	...	...	...	...
46	29	17	...	...	...	...	...	...
...	...	...	...	...	...	..	...	...
...	...	...	...	...	...	...	...	...
...	...	..	...	...	...	...	...	...
...	...	...	...	...	...	...	...	...
...	...	...	...	...	...	...	...	...
382	182	200	982	481	501	99	50	49
428	211	217	1,078	539	539	99	50	49
14,733	7,569	7,164	28,990	14,362	14,628	7,296	3,705	3,591

TABLE

Castes, Tribes and Races, by

Class.	Group.	Caste, &c.	Taluqs: Kunnattunadu. Total.	Kunnattunadu. Males.	Kunnattunadu. Females.	Alangadu. Total.	Alangadu. Males.	Alangadu. Females.
1	2	3	93	94	95	96	97	98
A. Agricultural.	2(c) Field-labouring classes.	1 Kanakkan ...	92	45	47	26	10	16
		2 Kurava ...	111	61	50	61	29	32
		3 Padayāchi ...	...	...	...	...	...	...
		4 Pallan ...	...	...	...	...	...	...
		5 Pariah ...	3,155	1,589	1,566	1,127	554	573
		6 Pulaya ...	16,077	8,160	7,917	7,533	3,831	3,702
		7 Udaya ...	...	...	...	...	...	...
		8 Ullādan ...	29	18	11	88	47	41
		9 Vettuvan ...	...	...	...	...	...	...
		Total Group 2(c)...	19,464	9,873	9,591	8.835	4,471	4,364
	4. Forest and Hill tribes.	1 Iruler ...	...	...	...	...	...	...
		2 Kāttar ...	...	...	...	...	...	...
		3 Kāttilaya ...	...	...	...	...	...	...
		4 Kāttu Parisha (Forest tribe).	...	...	...	...	...	...
		5 Khond ...	...	...	...	...	...	...
		6 Malayarien ...	...	...	...	...	...	...
		7 Mariya ...	3	3	...	...	...	...
		8 Muduvan ...	...	...	...	...	...	...
		9 Mynāta ...	...	...	...	...	...	...
		10 Nādipanikan ...	29	9	20	...	...	...
		11 Pania ...	...	...	...	...	...	...
		12 Vēlan ...	766	367	399	436	218	218
		Total Group 4 ...	798	379	419	436	218	218
		Total Class A. ..	37,421	18,660	18,761	19,786	9,777	10,009

XVI.

Nationality or Traditional Occupation—(*Continued*).

—(*Continued*).

Parur.			Cardamom Hills.			Periyar & Thekkadi.		
Total.	Males.	Females.	Total.	Males.	Females.	Total.	Males.	Females.
99	100	101	102	103	104	105	106	107
73	38	35	...	...	...	...	...	...
25	11	14	55	32	23	...	...	...
...	...	...	...	...	...	...	...	...
...	...	...	427	264	163	87	74	13
139	75	64	1,078	730	348	577	457	120
3,317	1,709	1,608	1,567	812	755	...	...	...
...	...	..	...	...	..	...	...	...
153	78	75	31	16	15	...	...	...
...	...	...	..	...	...	...	...	...
3,707	1,911	1,796	3,158	1,854	1,304	664	531	133
...	...	...	...	...	...	...	...	...
...	...	...	...	...	...	...	...	...
...	...	...	...	...	...	...	...	...
...	...	...	...	...	...	...	...	...
...	...	...	...	...	...	10	8	2
207	108	99	775	380	395	...	...	...
...	...	...	...	...	...	...	...	...
...	...	..	1,077	545	532	...	...	...
...	...	...	...	...	...	...	...	...
...	...	...	...	...	...	...	...	...
...	...	...	...	...	...	...	...	...
187	93	94	4	...	4	..	...	...
394	201	193	1,856	925	931	10	8	2
12,161	6,173	5,988	7,043	3,945	3,098	1,179	913	266

TABLE

Castes, Tribes and Races, by

Class.	Group.	Caste, &c.	No. of recorded sub-divisions.	Religion.	Total.	Males.	Females.
1	2	3	4	5	6	7	8
B. Professional.	5. Priests.	1 Brahmin ...	...	Hindu...	*2,645*	1,423	1,222
		Foreign Brahmin ...	...	,, ..	*3,529*	1,961	1,568
		Aiyengar ...	...	,, ...	*898*	479	419
		Canarese Brahmin.	...	,, ...	*35*	18	17
		Gouda Brahmin ...	...	,, ...	*77*	66	11
		Hindustani Brahmin	...	,, ...	*6*	3	3
		Kannadasta ...	...	,, ...	*9*	4	5
		Kāsi Brahmin ...	...	,, ...	*59*	24	35
		Kēsiar ...	...	,, ...	*67*	34	33
		Mahratta Brahmin.	...	,, ...	*964*	525	439
		Nambiyān ...	..	,,	*214*	110	104
		Survēriya ...	..	,, ..	*1*	1	...
		Tamil Brahmin ...	...	,, ...	*21,899*	11,238	10,661
		Telugu Brahmin ...	...	,, ...	*797*	385	412
		Malayala Brahmin ..	...	,, ...	*3,451*	1,866	1,585
		Akkaradēsi ...	...	,, ...	*25*	25	...
		Bhattadiri ..	...	,, ...	*146*	74	72
		Embrān ...	...	,, ...	*1,938*	1,150	788
		Nambūdiri ...	...	,, ..	*3,750*	1,979	1,771
		Ponmany Gramom..	...	,, ..	*96*	55	41
		Pōtti ..	...	,, ...	*2,595*	1,421	1,174
		Tiruvalladēsi ...	...	,, ...	*328*	167	161
		Trippūnittoraidēsi..	..	,, ...	*66*	50	16
		2 Ariapattar ...	1	,, ...	*40*	21	19
		3 Ilayadu ...	4	,, ...	*3,260*	1,686	1,574
		4 Tangal ...	...	Mussalman.	*14*	9	5
		Total Group 5 ...	...	...	**46,909**	**24,774**	**22,135**

XVI.

Nationality or Traditional Occupation—(*Continued*).

TALUQS.

Tovala.			Agastiswaram.			Eranial.		
Total.	Males.	Females.	Total.	Males.	Females.	Total.	Males.	Females.
9	10	11	12	13	14	15	16	17
467	218	249	111	62	49	76	41	35
...	...	...	...	...	...	...	...	...
...	...	...	9	6	3	...	...	...
...	...	...	...	...	...	...	...	...
...	...	...	...	...	...	...	...	...
...	...	...	...	...	...	...	...	...
...	...	...	...	...	...	...	...	...
...	...	...	...	...	...	...	...	...
...	...	...	46	24	22	...	...	...
21	15	6	72	33	39	...	...	...
49	25	24	44	26	18	15	8	7
...	...	...	...	...	...	...	...	...
672	362	310	3,042	1,506	1,536	168	80	83
7	2	5	161	73	88	14	4	10
...	...	...	...	...	...	62	33	29
...	...	...	...	...	...	...	...	...
...	...	...	...	...	...	...	...	...
...	...	...	34	29	5	5	4	1
...	...	...	18	9	9	...	...	...
...	...	...	...	...	...	...	...	...
14	9	5	38	21	17	141	62	79
...	...	...	...	...	...	...	...	...
4	4	...	...	...	...	...	...	...
27	13	14	1	...	1	...	...	...
...	...	...	...	...	...	...	...	...
...	...	...	...	...	...	...	...	...
1,261	648	613	3,576	1,789	1,787	476	232	244

TABLE

Castes, Tribes and Races, by

Class.	Group.	Caste, &c.	Taluqs: Kalkulam. Total.	Kalkulam. Males.	Kalkulam. Females.	Vilavankodu. Total.	Vilavankodu. Males.	Vilavankodu. Females.
1	2	3	18	19	20	21	22	23
B. Professional.	5. Priests.	1 Brahmin ...	49	33	16	7	4	3
		Foreign Brahmin ...	...	...	...	...	...	...
		Aiyengar ...	58	22	36	...	...	...
		Canarese Brahmin.	...	...	...	...	...	...
		Gouda Brahmin ...	...	...	...	5	5	...
		Hindustani Brahmin	...	...	...	...	...	...
		Kannadasta ...	...	...	...	...	...	...
		Kāsi Brahmin ...	...	...	...	...	...	...
		Kēsiar ...	9	3	6	...	...	...
		Mahratta Brahmin.	51	28	23	5	3	2
		Nambiyān ...	24	11	13	..	...	...
		Survēriya ...	...	...	...	...	...	...
		Tamil Brahmin ...	1,340	662	678	483	225	258
		Telugu Brahmin ...	26	9	17	...	...	...
		Malayala Brahmin...	...	...	...	37	22	15
		Akkaradēsi ...	25	25	...	...	...	...
		Bhattadiri ...	...	...	...	...	...	...
		Embrān ...	...	...	...	30	18	12
		Nambūdiri ...	26	22	4	8	8	...
		Ponmany Gramom.	...	...	...	...	...	...
		Pōtti ...	121	87	34	30	13	17
		Tiruvallādēsi ...	...	...	...	...	...	...
		Trippūnittoraidēsi..	...	...	...	...	...	...
		2 Ariapattar ...	...	...	...	...	...	...
		3 Ilayadu ...	...	...	...	2	2	...
		4 Tangal ...	...	...	...	...	...	...
		Total Group 5 ...	1,729	902	827	607	300	307

XVI.

Nationality or Traditional Occupation—(*Continued*).

—(*Continued*).

Neyattankara.			Trivandram.			Nedumangadu.		
Total.	Males.	Females.	Total.	Males.	Females.	Total.	Males.	Females.
24	25	26	27	28	29	30	31	32
...	...	...	169	105	64	...	...	...
232	113	119	604	350	254	361	182	179
11	6	5	569	310	259	...	...	...
...	...	...	...	...	...	...	...	...
...	...	...	12	8	4	...	...	...
...	...	...	...	...	...	...	...	...
...	...	...	9	4	5	...	...	...
...	...	...	...	...	...	...	...	...
...	...	...	3	3	...	...	...	...
...	...	...	610	353	257	...	...	...
...	...	...	...	...	...	...	...	...
...	...	...	...	...	...	...	...	...
400	190	210	4,965	2,619	2,346	15	7	8
4	1	3	161	63	98	...	...	...
42	27	15	201	105	96	17	11	6
...	...	...	...	...	...	...	...	...
...	...	...	10	8	2	...	...	...
1	1	...	519	305	214	39	21	18
6	6	...	114	69	45	3	3	...
...	...	...	...	...	...	...	...	...
145	73	72	168	101	67	143	38	105
...	...	...	33	12	21	28	14	14
...	...	...	51	37	14	...	...	...
...	...	...	...	...	...	...	...	...
11	9	2	15	12	3	...	...	...
...	...	...	...	...	...	...	...	...
852	426	426	8,213	4,464	3,749	606	276	330

TABLE

Castes, Tribes and Races, by

Class.	Group.	Caste, &c.	Taluqs — Sirayinkil. Total.	Sirayinkil. Males.	Sirayinkil. Females.	Kottarakkara. Total.	Kottarakkara. Males.	Kottarakkara. Females.
1	2	3	33	34	35	36	37	38
B. Professional.	5. Priests.	1 Brahmin ...	...	...	...	...	...	...
		Foreign Brahmin ...	595	295	300	29	5	24
		Aiyengar ...	108	52	56	2	1	1
		Canarese Brahmin.	...	...	...	8	8	...
		Gouda Brahmin ...	9	8	1	...	...	...
		Hindustani Brahmin	...	...	...	...	...	...
		Kannadasta ...	...	...	...	...	...	...
		Kāsi Brahmin ...	2	2	...	...	...	...
		Kēsiar ...	...	...	...	...	..	...
		Mahratta Brahmin.	10	6	4	8	5	3
		Nambiyān ...	...	...	...	...	...	...
		Survēriya ...	...	...	...	...	...	...
		Tamil Brahmin ...	763	357	406	227	101	126
		Telugu Brahmin ..	...	...	...	...	...	...
		Malayala Brahmin...	28	15	13	126	67	59
		Akkaradēsi ...	...	...	...	...	...	...
		Bhattadiri ...	10	4	6	...	...	...
		Embrān ...	9	2	7	33	20	13
		Nambūdiri ...	91	51	40	31	20	11
		Ponmany Gramom.	...	...	...	80	47	33
		Pōtti ...	118	66	52	267	147	120
		Tiruvallādēsi ...	30	16	14	14	7	7
		Trippūnittoraidēsi..	...	...	...	...	...	...
		2 Ariapattar ...	...	...	...	...	...	..
		3 Ilayadu ...	33	17	16	85	54	31
		4 Tangal ...	...	...	...	...	...	...
		Total Group 5 ...	1,806	891	915	910	482	428

XVI.

Nationality or Traditional Occupation—(*Continued*).

—(*Continued*).

Pattanapuram.			Shenkotta.			Quilon.		
Total.	Males.	Females.	Total.	Males.	Females.	Total.	Males.	Females.
39	40	41	42	43	44	45	46	47
...	...	...	...	...	...	...	...	...
...	...	...	...	...	...	485	308	177
6	2	4	76	41	35	...	...	...
...	...	...	27	10	17	...	...	...
...	...	...	...	...	...	7	6	1
...	...	...	...	...	...	6	3	3
...	...	...	...	...	...	...	...	...
...	...	...	...	...	...	...	...	...
...	...	...	...	...	...	...	...	...
...	...	...	15	5	10	33	15	18
...	...	...	82	40	42	...	...	...
...	...	...	...	...	...	1	1	...
113	60	53	2,206	1,008	1,198	99	75	24
11	5	6	320	154	166	37	28	9
96	49	47	1	1	...	30	20	10
...	...	...	...	...	...	...	...	...
...	...	...	...	...	...	...	...	...
50	33	17	...	...	...	40	27	13
...	...	...	...	...	...	4	4	...
...	...	...	...	...	...	...	...	...
53	44	9	2	2	...	52	35	17
...	...	...	...	...	...	...	...	...
...	...	...	...	...	...	...	...	...
...	...	...	...	...	...	...	...	...
70	36	34	...	...	...	134	62	72
...	...	...	...	...	...	...	...	...
399	229	170	2,729	1,261	1,468	928	584	344

TABLE

Castes, Tribes and Races, by

Class.	Group.	Caste, &c.	Taluqs: Kunnattur. Total.	Kunnattur. Males.	Kunnattur. Females.	Karunagappalli. Total.	Karunagappalli. Males.	Karunagappalli. Females.
1	2	3	48	49	50	51	52	53
B. Professional.	5. Priests.	1 Brahmin ...	...	...	...	...	...	...
		Foreign Brahmin ...	18	18	...	59	30	29
		Aiyengar ...	...	...	...	...	...	...
		Canarese Brahmin.	...	...	...	...	...	...
		Gouda Brahmin ...	...	...	...	5	3	2
		Hindustani Brahmin	...	...	...	...	...	...
		Kannadasta ...	...	...	...	...	...	...
		Kāsi Brahmin ...	...	...	...	...	...	...
		Kēsiar ...	...	...	...	...	...	...
		Mahratta Brahmin.	...	...	...	...	...	...
		Nambiyān ...	...	...	...	...	...	...
		Survēriya ...	...	...	...	...	...	...
		Tamil Brahmin ...	124	69	55	217	108	109
		Telugu Brahmin ...	...	...	...	7	5	2
		Malayala Brahmin...	169	89	80	142	77	65
		Akkaradēsi ...	...	...	...	...	...	...
		Bhattadiri ...	15	10	5	...	...	...
		Embrān ..	...	...	...	4	4	...
		Nambūdiri ...	15	15	...	12	7	5
		Ponmany Gramom..	...	...	...	...	...	...
		Pōtti ...	108	56	52	140	68	72
		Tiruvallādēsi ...	...	...	...	...	...	...
		Trippūnittoraidēsi..	...	...	...	...	...	...
		2 Ariapattar ...	...	...	...	8	4	4
		3 Ilayadu ...	256	128	128	148	68	80
		4 Tangal ...	...	...	...	14	9	5
		Total Group 5 ...	705	385	320	756	383	373

XVI.

Nationality or Traditional Occupation—(*Continued*).

—(*Continued*).

Kartigappalli.			Mavellikkara.			Chenganur.		
Total.	Males.	Females.	Total.	Males.	Females.	Total.	Males.	Females.
54	55	56	57	58	59	60	61	62
...	...	...	...	...	...	...	...	...
...	...	...	271	144	127	140	123	17
6	4	2		...	...	...	...	...
...	...	...	...	...	...	...	...	...
...	...	...	...	...	...	...	...	...
...	...	...	...	...	...	...	...	...
...	...	...	...	...	...	...	...	...
...	...	...	...	...	...	...	...	...
...	...	...	...	...	...	...	...	..
7	4	3	...	...	...	...	...	...
...	...	...	...	...	...	...	...	...
...	...	...	...	...	...	...	...	...
1,158	672	486	278	158	120	264	137	127
23	16	7	...	...	...	5	5	...
214	118	96	50	30	20	264	151	113
...	...	...	...	...	...	...	...	...
20	12	8	...	...	...	...	...	..
...	...	...	2	1	1	158	95	63
35	20	15	17	13	4	11	6	5
...	...	...	...	...	...	16	8	8
177	92	85	301	167	134	43	22	21
...	...	...	...	...	...	73	38	35
...	...	...	...	...	..	...	...	...
4	4	...	...	...	...	...	...	...
117	53	64	309	162	147	102	60	42
...	...	...	...	...	...	...	...	...
1,761	995	766	1,228	675	553	1,076	645	431

TABLE

Castes, Tribes and Races, by

Class.	Group.	Caste, &c.	Taluqs: Tiruvalla. Total.	Tiruvalla. Males.	Tiruvalla. Females.	Ambalappula. Total.	Ambalappula. Males.	Ambalappula. Females.
1	2	3	63	64	65	66	67	68
B. Professional.	5. Priests.	1 Brahmin ...	..	...	...	...	...	...
		Foreign Brahmin ...	284	150	134	112	34	78
		Aiyengar ...	...	...	...	41	27	14
		Canarese Brahmin.	...	...	...	...	...	...
		Gouda Brahmin ...	...	...	...	33	30	3
		Hindustani Brahmin.	...	...	...	...	...	...
		Kannadasta ...	...	...	...	...	...	...
		Kāsi Brahmin ...	...	...	...	...	...	...
		Kēsiar ...	...	...	...	...	...	...
		Mahratta Brahmin.	...	...	...	20	10	10
		Nambiyān ...	...	...	...	...	...	...
		Survēriya ...	...	..	...	...	...	...
		Tamil Brahmin ...	261	155	106	1,384	659	725
		Telugu Brahmin ...	...	...	...	...	...	...
		Malayala Brahmin ...	586	326	260	99	64	35
		Akkaradēsi ...	...	...	...	...	...	...
		Bhattadiri ...	10	5	5	...	.	...
		Embrān ...	41	33	8	227	123	104
		Nambūdiri ...	102	59	43	89	41	48
		Ponmany Gramom..	...	...	...	...	...	...
		Pōtti ...	104	56	48	...	...	...
		Tiruvallādēsi ...	...	...	..	31	15	16
		Trippūnittoraidēsi...	...	...	...	...	...	...
		2 Ariapattar ...	...	...	...	...	...	...
		3 Ilayadu ...	105	54	51	38	14	24
		4 Tangal ...	...	...	...	...	...	...
		Total Group 5 ...	1,493	838	655	2,074	1,017	1,057

XVI.

Nationality or Traditional Occupation—(*Continued*).

—(*Continued*).

Sherttala.			Vykkam.			Ettumanur.		
Total.	Males.	Females.	Total.	Males.	Females.	Total.	Males.	Females.
69	70	71	72	73	74	75	76	77
119	71	48	254	172	82	16	16	...
75	40	35	45	27	18	...	...	...
...	...	...	4	2	2	...	...	...
...	...	...	...	...	...	...	...	...
...	...	...	6	6	...	...	...	...
...	...	...	...	...	...	...	...	...
...	...	...	...	...	...	...	...	...
...	...	...	52	22	30	5	...	5
9	4	5	...	..	...	...	...	...
...	...	...	26	12	14	18	8	10
...	...	...	...	...	...	...	...	..
...	...	...	...	...	...	...	...	...
207	126	81	855	461	394	397	202	195
...	...	...	...	...	...	21	20	1
61	35	26	37	19	18	283	136	147
...	...	...	...	...	...	...	...	...
...	...	...	17	6	11	18	9	9
103	57	46	91	50	41	124	68	56
29	22	7	381	204	177	617	308	309
...	...	...	...	...	...	...	...	...
...	...	...	1	1	...	...	...	...
18	11	7	7	5	2	71	37	34
..	...	...	...	...	...	11	9	2
...	...	...	...	...	...	...	...	...
64	36	28	159	87	72	259	143	116
...	...	...	...	...	...	...	...	...
685	402	283	1,935	1,074	861	1,840	956	884

TABLE

Castes, Tribes and Races, by

Class.	Group.	Caste, &c.	Taluqs: Kottayam. Total.	Kottayam. Males.	Kottayam. Females.	Changanacheri. Total.	Changanacheri. Males.	Changanacheri. Females.
1	2	3	78	79	80	81	82	83
B. Professional.	5. Priests.	1 Brahmin ...	...	...	...	4	4	...
		Foreign Brahmin ...	...	..	...	...	...	...
		Aiyengar ...	...	...	...	...	...	...
		Canarese Brahmin.	...	...	...	...	...	...
		Gouda Brahmin ...	...	...	...	...	...	...
		Hindustani Brahmin	...	...	...	...	...	...
		Kannadasta ...	...	...	...	...	...	...
		Kāsi Brahmin ...	...	...	..	...	...	...
		Kēsiar ...	...	...	...		...	...
		Mahratta Brahmin.	41	18	23	...	...	...
		Nambiyān ...	...	...	..	...	...	...
		Survēriya ...	...	...	...	...	...	...
		Tamil Brahmin ...	688	366	322	159	88	71
		Telugu Brahmin ...	...	...	...	...	...	...
		Malayala Brahmin...	184	86	98	26	14	12
		Akkaradēsi ...	...	...	...	...	...	...
		Bhattadiri ...	37	17	20	9	3	6
		Embrān ...	87	46	41	45	27	18
		Nambūdiri ...	319	176	143	150	89	61
		Ponmany Gramom.	...	...	...	...	...	...
		Pōtti ...	181	94	87	175	111	64
		Tiruvallādēsi ...	...	...	...	...	...	...
		Trippūnittoraidēsi..	...	...	...	...	...	...
		2 Ariapattar ...	...	...	...	...	...	...
		3 Ilayadu ...	253	120	133	200	103	97
		4 Tangal ...	...	...	...	...	...	...
		Total Group 5 ...	1,790	923	867	768	439	329

XVI.

Nationality or Traditional Occupation—(*Continued*).

—(*Continued*).

Meenachal.			Muvattupula.			Todupula.		
Total.	Males.	Females.	Total.	Males.	Females.	Total.	Males.	Females.
84	85	86	87	88	89	90	91	92
...	...	...	...	...	...	...	...	...
47	32	15	11	7	4	...	...	...
...	...	...	5	3	2	...	...	...
...	...	...	...	...	...	...	...	...
...	...	...	...	...	...	...	...	...
...	...	...	...	...	...	...	...	...
...	...	...	...	...	...	...	...	...
...	...	...	...	...	...	...	...	...
...	...	...	...	...	...	...	...	...
...	...	...	...	...	...	...	...	...
...	...	...	...	...	...	...	...	...
...	...	...	...	...	...	...	...	...
97	60	37	390	218	172	117	58	59
...	...	...	...	...	...	...	...	...
138	67	71	138	70	68	1	1	...
...	...	...	...	...	...	...	...	...
...	...	...	...	...	...	...	...	...
147	84	63	...	...	...	19	15	4
154	97	57	916	437	479	95	50	45
...	...	...	...	...	...	...	...	...
36	28	8	...	...	...	...	...	...
...	...	...	...	...	...	...	...	...
...	...	...	...	...	...	...	...	...
...	...	...	...	...	...	...	...	...
189	104	85	248	122	126	74	37	37
...	...	...	...	...	...	...	...	...
808	472	336	1,708	857	851	306	161	145

TABLE

Castes, Tribes and Races, by

Class.	Group.	Caste, &c.	Taluqs: Kunnattunadu. Total.	Kunnattunadu. Males.	Kunnattunadu. Females.	Alangadu. Total.	Alangadu. Males.	Alangadu. Females.
1	2	3	93	94	95	96	97	98
B. Professional.	5. Priests.	1 Brahmin ...	527	263	264	832	425	407
		Foreign Brahmin ...	36	29	7	...	...	...
		Aiyengar ...	...	...	...	...	...	...
		Canarese Brahmin..	...	...	...	...	...	...
		Gouda Brahmin ...	...	...	...	...	...	...
		Hindustani Brahmin	...	...	...	...	...	...
		Kannadasta ...	...	...	...	...	...	...
		Kāsi Brahmin ...	...	...	...	...	...	...
		Kēsiar ...	...	...	...	...	...	...
		Mahratta Brahmin..	...	...	...	...	...	...
		Nambiyān ...	...	...	...	...	...	...
		Survēriya ...	..	...	...	...	...	...
		Tamil Brahmin ...	357	177	180	7	4	3
		Telugu Brahmin ...	...	...	...	...	...	...
		Malayala Brahmin ...	257	131	126	109	67	42
		Akkaradēsi ...	...	...	...	...	...	...
		Bhattadiri ...	...	...	...	...	...	...
		Embrān ...	80	58	22	41	20	21
		Nambūdiri ...	414	203	211	63	28	35
		Ponmany Gramom.	...	...	...	...	...	...
		Pōtti ...	15	13	2	...	...	...
		Tiruvallādēsi ...	23	12	11	...	...	...
		Trippūnittoraidēsi..	...	...	...	...	...	...
		2 Ariapattar ...	...	...	...	...	...	...
		3 Ilayadu ...	134	68	66	191	99	92
		4 Tangal ...	...	...	...	...	...	...
		Total Group 5 ...	1,843	954	889	1,243	643	600

XVI.

Nationality or Traditional Occupation—(*Continued*).

—(*Continued*).

Parur.			Cardamom Hills.			Periyar & Thekkadi.		
Total.	Males.	Females.	Total.	Males.	Females.	Total.	Males.	Females.
99	100	101	102	103	104	105	106	107
...	...	...	14	9	5	...	...	...
125	74	51	...	...	...	...	...	...
...	...	...	...	...	...	3	3	...
...	...	...	...	...	...	...	...	...
...	...	...	...	...	...	...	...	...
...	...	...	...	...	...	...	...	...
...	...	...	...	...	...	...	...	...
...	...	...	...	...	...	...	...	...
...	...	...	...	...	...	...	...	...
19	8	11	...	...	...	8	2	6
...	...	...	...	...	...	...	...	...
...	...	...	...	...	...	...	...	...
440	260	180	1	1	...	10	7	3
...	...	...	...	...	...	...	...	...
51	33	18	...	...	...	2	2	...
...	...	...	...	...	...	...	...	...
...	...	...	...	...	...	...	...	...
...	...	...	...	...	...	9	9	...
30	12	18	...	...	...	...	...	...
...	...	...	...	...	...	...	...	...
22	15	7	...	...	...	...	...	...
...	...	...	...	...	...	...	...	...
...	...	...	...	...	...	...	...	...
...	...	...	...	...	...	...	...	...
64	36	28	...	...	...	...	...	...
...	...	...	...	...	...	...	...	...
751	438	313	15	10	5	32	23	9

TABLE

Castes, Tribes and Races, by

Class.	Group.	Caste, &c.	No. of recorded sub-divisions.	Religion.	Total.	Males.	Females.
1	2	3	4	5	6	7	8
B. Professional.	6. Devotees.	1 Fakkir ...	...	Mussalman.	*5*	4	1
		2 Gosains ...	1	Hindu...	*61*	40	21
		3 Sanniyāsi ...	...	,, ...	*9*	8	1
		4 Vyravi ...	2	,, ...	*712*	356	356
		Total Group 6 ...	...	...	**787**	**408**	**379**
	7. Temple servants.	1 Ambalavāsi ...	16	Hindu ...	*7,469*	3,890	3,579
		2 Krishnanvagai...	...	,, ...	*6,953*	3,394	3,559
		3 Pilāppalli ...	...	,, ...	*69*	33	36
		4 Sātāni ...	1	,, ...	*14*	7	7
		Total Group 7 ...	...	...	**14,505**	**7,324**	**7,181**
	8. Genealogists.	Tākur ...	...	Hindu...	*4*	3	1
	10. Astrologers and Quack-doctors.	1 Kaniyān ...	1	Hindu ...	*9,548*	4,846	4,702
		2 Pulluvan ...	...	,, ...	*274*	123	151
		Total Group 10 ...	...	...	**9,822**	**4,969**	**4,853**
		Total Class B. ...	...	...	*72,027*	*37,478*	*34,549*

Name and Classification: columns 1–5. State Total: columns 6–8.

XVI.

Nationality or Traditional Occupation—(*Continued*).

Taluqs.

Tovala.			Agastiswaram.			Eranial.		
Total.	Males.	Females.	Total.	Males.	Females.	Total.	Males.	Females.
9	10	11	12	13	14	15	16	17
...	...	...	...	...	...	...	...	...
...	...	...	9	9	...	...	...	...
...	...	...	1	1	...	...	...	...
71	23	48	215	112	103	120	58	62
71	23	48	225	122	103	120	58	62
7	4	3	56	22	34	102	42	60
9	5	4	42	20	22	5,175	2,516	2,659
...	...	...	...	...	...	...	...	...
...	...	...	...	...	...	...	...	...
16	9	7	98	42	56	5,277	2,558	2,719
...	...	...	...	...	...	...	...	...
28	17	11	44	20	24	52	24	28
...	...	...	...	...	...	...	...	...
28	17	11	44	20	24	52	24	28
1,376	697	679	3,943	1,973	1,970	5,925	2,872	3,058

TABLE

Castes, Tribes and Races, by

Class.	Group.	Caste, &c.	Taluqs: Kalkulam. Total.	Kalkulam. Males.	Kalkulam. Females.	Vilavankodu. Total.	Vilavankodu. Males.	Vilavankodu. Females.
1	2	3	18	19	20	21	22	23
B. Professional.	6. Devotees.	1 Fakkir ...	...	...	...	...	...	...
		2 Gosains ...	2	2	...	...	...	...
		3 Sanniyāsi ...	...	...	...	...	...	...
		4 Vyravi ...	64	32	32	...	...	...
		Total Group 6 ...	66	34	32	...	...	...
	7. Temple servants.	1 Ambalavāsi ...	91	54	37	68	46	22
		2 Krishnanvagai...	1,681	824	857	...	...	...
		3 Pilāppalli ...	...	...	...	...	...	...
		4 Sātāni ...	...	...	...	...	...	...
		Total Group 7 ...	1,772	878	894	68	46	22
	8. Genealogists.	Tākur ...	..	...	...	..	...	...
	10. Astrologers and Quack-doctors.	1 Kaniyān ...	77	42	35	250	122	128
		2 Pulluvan ...	...	...	...	...	...	...
		Total Group 10 ...	77	42	35	250	122	128
		Total Class B. ...	3,644	1,856	1,788	925	468	457

XVI.

Nationality or Traditional Occupation—(*Continued*).

—(*Continued*).

Neyattankara.			Trivandram.			Nedumangadu.		
Total.	Males.	Females.	Total.	Males.	Females.	Total.	Males.	Females.
24	25	26	27	28	29	30	31	32
...	...	...	...	...	...	...	...	...
...	...	...	21	13	8	...	...	...
...	...	...	...	...	...	...	...	...
...	...	...	...	...	...	67	33	34
...	...	...	21	13	8	67	33	34
181	87	94	328	173	155	76	34	42
31	19	12	5	5	...	10	5	5
...	...	...	...	...	...	...	...	...
...	...	...	...	...	..	...	...	...
212	106	106	333	178	155	86	39	47
...	...	...	...	...	...	...	...	...
271	134	137	214	119	95	215	104	111
...	...	...	...	...	...	...	...	...
271	134	137	214	119	95	215	104	111
1,335	666	669	8,781	4,774	4,007	974	452	522

TABLE

Castes, Tribes and Races, by

Class.	Group.	Caste, &c.	Taluqs: Sirayinkil. Total.	Sirayinkil. Males.	Sirayinkil. Females.	Kottarakkara. Total.	Kottarakkara. Males.	Kottarakkara. Females.
1	2	3	33	34	35	36	37	38
B. Professional.	6. Devotees.	1 Fakkir ...	...	...	...	...	...	...
		2 Gosains ...	1	1	...	...	...	...
		3 Sanniyāsi ...	...	...	...	...	...	...
		4 Vyravi ...	3	2	1	...	...	...
		Total Group 6 ...	4	3	1	...	...	...
	7. Temple servants.	1 Ambalavāsi ...	143	70	73	186	103	83
		2 Krishnanvagai...	...	...	...	...	...	...
		3 Pilāppalli ...	...	...	...	...	...	...
		4 Sātāni ...	...	...	...	...	...	...
		Total Group 7 ...	143	70	73	186	103	83
	8. Genealogists.	Tākur ...	...	...	...	...	...	...
	10. Astrologers and Quack-doctors.	1 Kaniyān ...	264	127	137	392	196	196
		2 Pulluvan ...	...	...	...	26	10	16
		Total Group 10 ...	264	127	137	418	206	212
		Total Class B. ...	2,217	1,091	1,126	1,514	791	723

XVI.

Nationality or Traditional Occupation—(*Continued*).

—(*Continued*).

Pattanapuram.			Shenkotta.			Quilon.		
Total.	Males.	Females.	Total.	Males.	Females.	Total.	Males.	Females.
39	40	41	42	43	44	45	46	47
...	...	...	...	...	...	...	...	...
...	...	...	...	...	...	...	...	...
...	...	...	...	...	...	7	6	1
9	9	...	154	85	69	...	...	...
9	9	...	154	85	69	7	6	1
121	65	56	25	15	10	138	66	72
...	...	...	...	...	...	...	...	...
...	...	...	...	...	...	...	...	...
...	...	...	...	...	...	5	2	3
121	65	56	25	15	10	143	68	75
...	...	...	...	...	...	..	...	...
191	102	89	...	...	...	444	200	244
...	...	...	13	7	6	33	2	31
191	102	89	13	7	6	477	202	275
720	405	315	2,921	1,368	1,553	1,555	860	695

TABLE

Castes, Tribes and Races, by

Class.	Group.	Caste, &c.	Taluqs: Kunnattur. Total.	Kunnattur. Males.	Kunnattur. Females.	Karunagappalli. Total.	Karunagappalli. Males.	Karunagappalli. Females.
1	2	3	48	49	50	51	52	53
B. Professional.	6. Devotees.	1 Fakkir ...	...	...	...	...	...	...
		2 Gosains ...	...	...	...	...	...	...
		3 Sanniyāsi ...	...	...	...	...	...	...
		4 Vyravi ...	...	...	...	...	...	...
		Total Group 6 ...	...	...	...	...	...	...
	7. Temple servants.	1 Ambalavāsi ...	154	89	65	345	170	175
		2 Krishnanvagai ..	...	...	...	...	...	...
		3 Pilāppalli ...	...	...	...	...	...	...
		4 Sātāni ...	...	...	...	...	...	...
		Total Group 7 ...	154	89	65	345	170	175
	8. Genealogists.	Tākur ...	...	...	...	...	...	...
	10. Astrologers and Quack-doctors.	1 Kaniyān ...	448	228	220	444	212	232
		2 Pulluvan ...	14	9	5	11	6	5
		Total Group 10 ...	462	237	225	455	218	237
		Total Class B. ...	1,321	711	610	1,556	771	785

XVI.

Nationality or Traditional Occupation—(*Continued*).

—(*Continued*).

Kartigappalli.			Mavellikkara.			Chenganur.		
Total.	Males.	Females.	Total.	Males.	Females.	Total.	Males.	Females.
54	55	56	57	58	59	60	61	62
...	...	...	...	...	...	...	...	...
...	...	...	...	...	...	...	...	...
...	...	...	...	...	...	...	...	...
...	...	...	9	2	7	...	...	...
...	...	...	9	2	7	...	...	...
309	173	136	442	230	212	261	131	130
...	...	...	...	...	...	...	...	...
...	...	...	...	...	...	...	...	...
...	...	...	...	...	...	...	...	...
309	173	136	442	230	212	261	131	130
...	...	...	...	...	...	...	...	...
451	216	235	536	301	235	564	302	262
...	...	...	1	1	...	...	...	...
451	216	235	537	302	235	564	302	262
2,521	1,384	1,137	2,216	1,209	1,007	1,901	1,078	823

TABLE

Castes, Tribes and Races, by

Class.	Group.	Caste, &c.	Taluqs: Tiruvalla. Total.	Tiruvalla. Males.	Tiruvalla. Females.	Ambalappula. Total.	Ambalappula. Males.	Ambalappula. Females.
1	2	3	63	64	65	66	67	68
B. Professional.	6. Devotees.	1 Fakkir ...	...	...	...	...	...	...
		2 Gosains ...	...	...	...	...	...	...
		3 Sanniyāsi ...	...	...	...	...	...	...
		4 Vyravi ...	...	...	...	...	...	...
		Total Group 6 ...	...	...	...	...	...	...
	7. Temple servants.	1 Ambalavāsi ...	364	187	177	293	163	130
		2 Krishnanvagai...	...	...	...	...	...	...
		3 Pilāppalli ...	...	...	...	69	33	36
		4 Sātāni ...	...	...	...	...	...	...
		Total Group 7 ...	364	187	177	362	196	166
	8. Genealogists.	Tākur ...	...	...	...	...	...	...
	10. Astrologers and Quack-doctors.	1 Kaniyān ...	647	331	316	400	205	195
		2 Pulluvan ...	11	7	4	10	2	8
		Total Group 10 ...	658	338	320	410	207	203
		Total Class B. ...	2,515	1,363	1,152	2.846	1,420	1,426

XVI.

Nationality or Traditional Occupation—(*Continued*).

—(*Continued*).

Sherttala.			Vykkam.			Ettumanur.		
Total.	Males.	Females.	Total.	Males.	Females.	Total.	Males.	Females.
69	70	71	72	73	74	75	76	77
...	...	...	5	4	1	...	...	...
...	...	...	17	7	10	...	...	...
...	...	...	...	...	...	...	...	...
...	...	...	...	...	...	...	...	...
...	...	...	22	11	11	...	...	...
601	321	280	279	151	128	429	230	199
...	...	...	...	...	...	...	...	...
...	...	...	...	...	...	...	...	...
...	...	...	...	...	...	...	...	...
601	321	280	279	151	128	429	230	199
...	...	...	...	...	...	...	...	...
258	127	131	289	155	134	329	153	176
4	2	2	...	...	...	...	...	...
262	129	133	289	155	134	329	153	176
1,548	852	696	2,525	1,391	1,134	2,598	1,339	1,259

TABLE

Castes, Tribes and Races, by

Class.	Group.	Caste, &c.	Taluqs: Kottayam. Total.	Kottayam. Males.	Kottayam. Females.	Changanacheri. Total.	Changanacheri. Males.	Changanacheri. Females.
1	2	3	78	79	80	81	82	83
B. Professional.	6. Devotees.	1 Fakkir ...	...	...	...	...	...	...
		2 Gosains ...	...	...	...	...	...	...
		3 Sanniyāsi ...	...	...	...	1	1	...
		4 Vyravi ...	...	...	...	...	...	...
		Total Group 6 ...	...	...	...	1	1	...
	7. Temple Servants.	1 Ambalavāsi ...	464	246	218	312	146	166
		2 Krishnanvagai...	...	...	...	...	...	...
		3 Pilāppalli ...	...	...	...	...	...	...
		4 Sātāni ...	...	...	...	...	...	...
		Total Group 7 ...	464	246	218	312	146	166
	8. Genealogists.	Tākur ...	...	...	...	...	...	...
	10. Astrologers and Quack-doctors.	1 Kaniyān ...	415	211	204	48	27	21
		2 Pulluvan ...	6	2	4	...	...	...
		Total Group 10 ...	421	213	208	48	27	21
		Total Class B. ...	2,675	1,382	1,293	1,129	613	516

XVI.

Nationality or Traditional Occupation—(*Continued*).

—(*Continued*).

Meenachal.			Muvattuppula.			Todupula.		
Total.	Males.	Females.	Total.	Males.	Females.	Total.	Males.	Females.
84	85	86	87	88	89	90	91	92
...	...	...	...	...	...	...	...	...
...	...	...	...	...	...	...	...	...
...	...	...	...	...	...	...	...	...
...	...	...	...	...	...	...	...	...
...	...	...	...	...	...	...	...	...
94	50	44	380	201	179	42	25	17
...	...	...	...	...	...	...	...	...
...	...	...	...	...	...	...	...	...
...	...	...	...	...	...	...	...	...
94	50	44	380	201	179	42	25	17
...	...	...	...	...	...	...	...	...
205	104	101	831	425	406	168	94	74
4	3	1	17	7	10	5	5	...
209	107	102	848	432	416	173	99	74
1,111	629	482	2,936	1,490	1,446	521	285	236

TABLE

Castes, Tribes and Races, by

Class.	Group.	Caste, &c.	Taluqs: Kunnattunadu. Total.	Kunnattunadu. Males.	Kunnattunadu. Females.	Alangadu. Total.	Alangadu. Males.	Alangadu. Females.
1	2	3	93	94	95	96	97	98
B. Professional.	6. Devotees.	1 Fakkir ...	...	...	...	...	...	...
		2 Gosains ...	...	...	...	...	...	...
		3 Sanniyāsi ...	...	...	...	...	...	...
		4 Vyravi ...	...	...	...	...	...	...
		Total Group 6 ...	...	...	...	...	...	...
	7. Temple servants.	1 Ambalavāsi ...	538	284	254	469	212	257
		2 Krishnanvagai...	...	...	...	...	...	...
		3 Pilāppalli ...	...	...	...	...	...	...
		4 Sātāni ...	...	...	...	...	...	...
		Total Group 7 ..	538	284	254	469	212	257
	8. Genealogists.	Tākur ...	...	...	...	...	...	...
	10. Astrologers and Quack-doctors.	1 Kaniyān ...	853	445	408	186	86	100
		2 Pulluvan ...	100	49	51	10	4	6
		Total Group 10 ...	953	494	459	196	90	106
		Total Class B. ...	3,334	1,732	1,602	1,908	945	963

XVI.

Nationality or Traditional Occupation—(*Continued*).

—(*Continued*).

Parur.			Cardamom Hills.			Periyar and Thekkadi.		
Total.	Males.	Females.	Total.	Males.	Females.	Total.	Males.	Females.
99	100	101	102	103	104	105	106	107
...	...	...	...	...	...	...	...	...
11	8	3	...	...	...	...	...	...
...	...	...	...	...	...	...	...	...
...	...	...	...	...	...	...	...	...
11	8	3	...	...	...	...	...	...
171	100	71	...	...	...	...	...	...
...	...	...	...	...	...	...	...	...
...	...	...	...	...	...	...	...	...
...	...	...	...	...	...	9	5	4
171	100	71	...	...	...	9	5	4
...	...	...	...	...	...	4	3	1
30	14	16	4	3	1	...	...	...
...	...	...	...	...	...	9	7	2
30	14	16	4	3	1	9	7	2
963	560	403	19	13	6	54	38	16

TABLE

Castes, Tribes and Races, by

Class.	Group.	Caste, &c.	No. of recorded sub-divisions.	Religion.	State Total. Total.	State Total. Males.	State Total. Females.
1	2	3	4	5	6	7	8
C. Commercial.	14. Traders.	1 Balija ...	11	Hindu....	*449*	249	200
		2 Baniya ...	...	Hindu / Jain	*62*	53	9
		3 Chetti ...	28	Hindu....	*17,769*	9,089	8,680
		4 Ilavaniyan ...	...	„ ...	*3,311*	1,647	1,664
		5 Jonaka ...	1	Muslmn.	*51,791*	26,568	25,223
		6 Labbai ...	...	„ ...	*361*	213	148
		7 Mēttan ..	1	„ ...	*54,086*	27,523	26,563
		8 Rāwut ...	...	„ ...	*57*	30	27
		9 Vaduka ...	13	Hindu....	*2,696*	1,427	1,269
		10 Vaisya ...	...	„ ...	*474*	259	215
		Total Group 14 ...	...	...	131,056	67,058	63,998
	15. Pedlars.	1 Balukar ...	...	Hindu....	*6*	6	...
		2 Manikār ...	...	„ ...	*36*	22	14
		Total Group 15 ...	...	...	42	28	14
		Total Class C. ...	...	...	*131,098*	*67,086*	*64,012*

XVI.

Nationality or Traditional Occupation—(*Continued*).

TALUQS.

Tovala.			Agastiswaram.			Eraniel.		
Total.	Males.	Females.	Total.	Males.	Females.	Total.	Males.	Females.
9	10	11	12	13	14	15	16	17
...	...	...	...	...	...	...	...	...
...	...	...	...	...	...	...	...	...
134	44	90	842	400	442	2,560	1,243	1,317
171	82	89	163	88	75	149	67	82
...	...	...	...	...	...	...	...	...
...	...	...	...	...	...	...	...	...
...	...	...	2,333	1,127	1,206	1,387	739	648
...	...	...	17	9	8	...	...	...
371	194	177	264	127	137	8	7	1
27	20	7	...	...	...	22	11	11
703	340	363	3,619	1,751	1,868	4,126	2,067	2,059
...	...	...	...	...	...	...	...	...
...	...	...	...	...	...	...	...	...
...	...	...	...	...	...	...	...	...
703	340	363	3,619	1,751	1,868	4,126	2,067	2,059

TABLE

Castes, Tribes and Races, by

Class.	Group.	Caste, &c.	Taluqs: Kalkulam. Total.	Kalkulam. Males.	Kalkulam. Females.	Vilavankodu. Total.	Vilavankodu. Males.	Vilavankodu. Females.
1	2	3	18	19	20	21	22	23
C. Commercial.	14. Traders.	1 Balija ...	...	...	...	...	...	...
		2 Baniya ...	...	...	...	...	...	...
		3 Chetti ...	541	278	263	505	283	222
		4 Ilavaniyan ...	48	24	24	...	...	...
		5 Jonaka ...	...	...	...	...	...	...
		6 Labbai ...	...	...	...	...	...	...
		7 Mēttan ...	2,232	1,124	1,108	925	490	435
		8 Rāwut ...	...	...	...	...	...	...
		9 Vaduka ...	98	66	32	...	...	...
		10 Vaisya ...	...	...	...	...	...	...
		Total Group 14 ...	2,919	1,492	1,427	1,430	773	657
	15. Pedlars.	1 Balukar ...	...	...	...	...	...	...
		2 Manikār ...	...	...	...	...	...	...
		Total Group 15 ...	...	...	...	...	...	...
		Total Class C. ...	2,919	1,492	1,427	1,430	773	657

XVI.

Nationality or Traditional Occupation—(*Continued*).

—(*Continued*).

Neyattankara.			Trivandram.			Nedumangadu.		
Total.	Males.	Females.	Total.	Males.	Females.	Total.	Males.	Females.
24	25	26	27	28	29	30	31	32
...	...	...	56	33	23	...	...	...
...	...	...	...	...	...	...	...	...
225	118	107	1,210	591	619	156	88	68
6	6	...	292	138	154	16	6	10
...	...	...	7	2	5	...	...	...
...	...	...	...	...	...	...	...	...
3,056	1,454	1,602	3,289	1,631	1,658	2,028	1,073	955
...	...	...	34	15	19	...	...	...
14	12	2	1,220	592	628	55	31	24
...	...	...	21	14	7	...	...	...
3,301	1,590	1,711	6,129	3,016	3,113	2,255	1,198	1,057
...	...	...	...	...	...	...	...	...
...	...	...	...	...	...	...	...	...
...	...	...	...	...	...	...	...	...
3,301	1,590	1,711	6,129	3,016	3,113	2,255	1,198	1,057

TABLE

Castes, Tribes and Races, by

Class.	Group.	Caste, &c.	Taluqs: Sirayinkil. Total.	Sirayinkil. Males.	Sirayinkil. Females.	Kottarakkara. Total.	Kottarakkara. Males.	Kottarakkara. Females.
1	2	3	33	34	35	36	37	38
C. Commercial.	14. Traders.	1 Balija ...	...	...	...	...	...	...
		2 Baniya ...	...	...	...	...	...	...
		3 Chetti ...	473	237	236	877	463	414
		4 Ilavaniyan ...	...	...	...	12	12	...
		5 Jonaka ...	769	353	416	...	...	...
		6 Labbai ...	...	...	...	...	...	...
		7 Mēttan ...	9,478	4,696	4,782	3,026	1,575	1,451
		8 Rāwut ...	...	...	...	...	...	...
		9 Vaduka ...	...	...	...	6	5	1
		10 Vaisya ...	...	...	...	...	...	...
		Total Group 14 ...	10,720	5,286	5,434	3,921	2,055	1,866
	15. Pedlars.	1 Balukar ...	...	...	...	...	...	...
		2 Manikār ...	...	...	...	...	...	...
		Total Group 15 ...	...	...	...	...	...	...
		Total Class C. ...	10,720	5,286	5,434	3,921	2,055	1,866

XVI.

Nationality or Traditional Occupation—(Continued).

—(Continued).

Pattanapuram.			Shenkotta.			Quilon.		
Total.	Males.	Females.	Total.	Males.	Females.	Total.	Males.	Females.
39	40	41	42	43	44	45	46	47
...	...	...	...	...	...	393	216	177
...	...	...	...	...	...	...	...	...
647	312	335	313	159	154	1,524	777	747
...	...	...	2,423	1,204	1,219	23	13	10
85	62	23	...	...	...	...	...	...
...	...	...	...	...	...	267	138	129
3,980	1,948	2,032	...	...	...	10,380	5,172	5,208
...	...	...	...	...	...	...	...	...
58	28	30	6	4	2	267	131	136
...	...	...	...	...	...	...	...	...
4,770	2,350	2,420	2,742	1,367	1,375	12,854	6,447	6,407
...	...	...	...	...	...	1	1	...
...	...	...	...	...	...	...	...	...
...	...	...	...	...	...	1	1	...
4,770	2,350	2,420	2,742	1,367	1,375	12,855	6,448	6,407

TABLE

Castes, Tribes and Races, by

Class.	Group.	Caste, &c.	Taluqs: Kunnattur. Total.	Kunnattur. Males.	Kunnattur. Females.	Karunagappalli. Total.	Karunagappalli. Males.	Karunagappalli. Females.
1	2	3	48	49	50	51	52	53
C. Commercial.	14. Traders.	1 Balija ...	...	...	...	...	...	...
		2 Baniya ...	...	...	...	...	...	...
		3 Chetti ...	249	134	115	133	77	56
		4 Ilavaniyan ...	...	...	...	...	...	...
		5 Jonaka ...	725	327	398	10,543	5,487	5,056
		6 Labbai ...	...	...	...	...	...	...
		7 Mēttan ...	2,016	1,086	930	1,616	966	650
		8 Rāwut ...	...	...	...	...	...	...
		9 Vaduka ...	...	...	...	5	3	2
		10 Vaisya ...	...	...	...	...	...	...
		Total Group 14 ...	2,990	1,547	1,443	12,297	6,533	5,764
	15. Pedlars.	1 Balukar ...	...	...	...	...	...	...
		2 Manikār ...	...	...	...	...	...	...
		Total Group 15 ...	...	...	...	...	...	...
		Total Class C. ...	2,990	1,547	1,443	12,297	6,533	5,764

XVI.

Nationality or Traditional Occupation—(*Continued*).

—(*Continued*).

Kartigappalli.			Mavellikkara.			Chenganur.		
Total.	Males.	Females.	Total.	Males.	Females.	Total.	Males.	Females.
54	55	56	57	58	59	60	61	62
...	...	...	...	...	...	...	...	...
...	...	...	...	...	...	...	...	...
96	48	48	220	107	113	12	6	6
...	...	...	...	...	...	...	...	...
6,396	3,222	3,174	...	...	...	...	...	...
...	...	...	...	...	...	...	...	...
449	218	231	1,641	905	736	2,089	1,080	1,009
...	...	...	...	...	...	...	...	...
...	...	...	...	...	...	...	...	...
...	...	...	...	...	...	1	...	1
6,941	3,488	3,453	1,861	1,012	849	2,102	1,086	1,016
...	...	...	...	...	...	...	...	...
...	...	...	...	...	...	...	...	...
...	...	...	...	...	...	...	...	...
6,941	3,488	3,453	1,861	1,012	849	2,102	1,086	1,016

TABLE

Castes, Tribes and Races, by

Class.	Group.	Caste, &c.	Taluqs: Tiruvalla. Total.	Tiruvalla. Males.	Tiruvalla. Females.	Ambalappula. Total.	Ambalappula. Males.	Ambalappula. Females.
1	2	3	63	64	65	66	67	68
C. Commercial.	14. Traders.	1 Balija ...	...	...	...	...	...	...
		2 Baniya ...	...	...	...	54	47	7
		3 Chetti ...	776	404	372	853	447	406
		4 Ilavaniyan ...	...	...	...	8	7	1
		5 Jonaka ...	...	...	...	429	224	205
		6 Labbai ...	...	...	...	...	...	...
		7 Mēttan ...	1,334	734	600	341	174	167
		8 Rāwut ...	...	...	...	...	...	...
		9 Vaduka ...	2	1	1	98	47	51
		10 Vaisya ...	34	26	8	25	10	15
		Total Group 14 ...	2,146	1,165	981	1,808	956	852
	15. Pedlars.	1 Balukar ...	...	...	...	...	...	...
		2 Manikār ...	...	...	...	...	...	...
		Total Group 15 ...	...	...	...	...	...	...
		Total Class C. ...	2,146	1,165	981	1,808	956	852

XVI.

Nationality or Traditional Occupation—(*Continued*).

—(*Continued*).

Sherttala.			Vykkam.			Ettumanur.		
Total.	Males.	Females.	Total.	Males.	Females.	Total.	Males.	Females.
69	70	71	72	73	74	75	76	77
...	...	...	...	...	...	...	...	...
...	...	...	...	...	...	...	...	...
1,043	543	500	346	178	168	189	95	94
...	...	...	...	...	...	...	...	...
1,505	700	805	2,746	1,384	1,362	...	...	...
...	...	...	...	...	...	...	...	...
653	363	290	205	98	107	...	...	...
...	...	...	...	...	...	...	...	...
6	4	2	15	10	5	...	...	...
35	12	23	...	...	...	12	7	5
3,242	1,622	1,620	3,312	1,670	1,642	201	102	99
...	...	...	...	...	...	...	...	...
...	...	...	...	...	.	...	...	...
...	...	...	...	...	...	...	...	...
3,242	1,622	1,620	3,312	1,670	1,642	201	102	99

TABLE

Castes, Tribes and Races, by

Class.	Group.	Caste, &c.	Taluqs: Kottayam. Total.	Kottayam. Males.	Kottayam. Females.	Changanacheri. Total.	Changanacheri. Males.	Changanacheri. Females.
1	2	3	78	79	80	81	82	83
C. Commercial.	14. Traders.	1 Balija ...	...	...	...	...	...	...
		2 Baniya ...	...	...	...	...	...	...
		3 Chetti ...	122	84	38	229	138	91
		4 Ilavaniyan ...	...	...	...	...	...	...
		5 Jonaka ...	345	193	152	30	19	11
		6 Labbai ...	...	...	...	...	...	...
		7 Mēttan ...	454	250	204	...	...	...
		8 Rāwut ...	...	...	...	...	...	...
		9 Vaduka ...	...	...	...	4	4	...
		10 Vaisya ...	...	...	...	...	...	...
		Total Group 14 ...	921	527	394	263	161	102
	15. Pedlars.	1 Balukar ...	...	...	...	...	...	...
		2 Manikār ...	...	..	...	...	...	...
		Total Group 15 ...	...	...	...	...	...	...
		Total Class C. ...	921	527	394	263	161	102

XVI.

Nationality or Traditional Occupation—(*Continued*).

—(*Continued*).

Meenachal.			Muvattupula.			Todupula.		
Total.	Males.	Females.	Total.	Males.	Females.	Total.	Males.	Females.
84	85	86	87	88	89	90	91	92
...	...	...	...	...	...	...	...	...
...	...	...	...	...	...	...	...	...
182	104	78	23	16	7	24	11	13
...	...	...	...	...	...	...	...	...
...	...	...	5,690	2,909	2,781	910	442	468
...	...	..	...	...	...	...	...	...
6	6	...	49	31	18	...	...	...
...	...	...	..	...	...	...	...	...
22	14	8	...	...	...	...	...	...
3	1	2	...	...	...	...	...	...
213	125	88	5,762	2,956	2,806	934	453	481
...	...	...	...	...	...	..	...	...
...	...	...	...	...	...	...	...	...
...	...	...	...	...	...	...	...	...
213	125	88	5,762	2,956	2,806	934	453	481

TABLE

Castes, Tribes and Races, by

Class.	Group.	Caste, &c.	Taluqs: Kunnattunadu. Total.	Kunnattunadu. Males.	Kunnattunadu. Females.	Alangadu. Total.	Alangadu. Males.	Alangadu. Females.
1	2	3	93	94	95	96	97	98
C. Commercial.	14. Traders.	1 Balija ...	...	...	...	...	...	...
		2 Baniya ...	...	...	...	...	...	...
		3 Chetti ..	479	253	226	39	11	28
		4 Ilavaniyan ...	...	...	...	...	...	...
		5 Jonaka ...	10,158	5,249	4,909	8,129	4,268	3,861
		6 Labbai ...	...	...	...	...	...	...
		7 Mēttan ...	1,041	514	527	...	...	...
		8 Rāwut ...	...	...	...	...	...	...
		9 Vaduka ...	...	...	...	...	...	...
		10 Vaisya ...	294	158	136	...	...	...
		Total Group 14 ...	11,972	6,174	5,798	8,168	4,279	3,889
	15. Pedlars.	1 Balukar ...	...	...	...	...	...	...
		2 Manikār ...	...	...	...	...	...	...
		Total Group 15 ...	...	...	...	...	...	...
		Total Class C. ...	11,972	6,174	5.798	8,168	4,279	3,889

XVI.

Nationality or Traditional Occupation—(*Continued*).

—(*Continued*).

Parur.			Cardamom Hills.			Periyar & Thekkadi.		
Total.	Males.	Females.	Total.	Males.	Females.	Total.	Males.	Females.
99	100	101	102	103	104	105	106	107
...	...	...	...	...	...	...	...	...
...	...	...	...	...	...	8	6	2
2,448	1,263	1,185	118	65	53	181	112	69
...	...	...	...	...	...	...	...	...
3,324	1,727	1,597	...	...	...	...	...	...
...	...	...	12	7	5	82	68	14
...	...	...	...	...	...	78	69	9
...	...	...	...	...	...	6	6	...
12	6	6	53	47	6	112	94	18
...	...	...	...	...	...	...	...	...
5,784	2,996	2,788	183	119	64	467	355	112
...	...	...	...	...	...	5	5	...
...	...	...	7	5	2	29	17	12
...	...	...	7	5	2	34	22	12
5,784	2,996	2,788	190	124	66	501	377	124

TABLE

Castes, Tribes and Races, by

NAME AND CLASSIFICATION.					STATE	
CLASS.	GROUP.	CASTE, &c.	No. of recorded sub-divisions.	Religion.	Total.	Males.
1	2	3	4	5	6	7
D. Artisans and Village Menials.	17. Goldsmiths.	Tattan ...	4	Hindu...	*24,698*	12,506
	17(*a*). Artisans (general).	1 Kammāla ...	4	Hindu...	*1,982*	985
		2 Kamsāla ...	...	„ ..	*13*	7
		Total Group 17(*a*).	...	...	1,995	992
	18. Barbers.	1 Īlavāti ...	...	Hindu...	*2,869*	1,360
		2 Kāvadi ...	2	„ ...	*5,267*	2,677
		3 Kōmaram ...	...	„ ...	*257*	138
		4 Kshourakan ...	9	„ ...	*16,130*	7,987
		5 Mārān ...	12	„ ...	*15,228*	7,456
		6 Ostta ...	2	Muslmn.	*66*	22
		7 Taravan ...	...	Hindu...	*455*	226
		Total Group 18 ...	...	...	40,272	19,866
	19. Black-smiths.	1 Kollan ...	3	Hindu...	*26,982*	13,903
		2 Lōhar ...	..	„ ...	*3*	3
		Total Group 19 ...	..	...	26,985	13,906
	20. Carpenters, Masons and Turners.	1 Āsāri ...	5	Hindu...	*33,641*	16,932
		2 Tachan ...	...	„ ...	*4,066*	2,014
		Total Group 20 ...	...	...	37,707	18,946
	21. Brass and Coppersmiths.	1 Chembutatti ...	...	Hindu...	*98*	56
		2 Kannān ...	3	„ ...	*5,697*	2,894
		Total Group 21 ...	...	...	5,795	2,950
	22. Tailors.	Pānān ...	3	Hindu...	*2,708*	1,409

XVI.

Nationality or Traditional Occupation—(*Continued*).

TOTAL.	TALUQS.								
	Tovala.			Agastiswaram.			Eranial.		
Females.	Total.	Males.	Females.	Total.	Males.	Females.	Total.	Males.	Females.
8	9	10	11	12	13	14	15	16	17
12,192	177	94	83	1,409	716	693	553	272	281
997	11	7	4	114	59	55	172	88	84
6	...	...	...	...	...	...	...	...	...
1,003	11	7	4	114	59	55	172	88	84
1,509	...	...	...	...	...	...	...	...	...
2,590	...	...	...	339	141	198	2,664	1,389	1,275
119	...	...	...	...	...	...	...	...	...
8,143	333	143	190	691	357	334	473	224	249
7,772	128	61	67	124	61	63	139	74	65
44	...	...	...	...	...	...	...	...	...
229	...	...	...	...	...	...	...	...	...
20,406	461	204	257	1,154	559	595	3,276	1,687	1,589
13,079	267	135	132	707	359	348	509	258	251
...	...	...	...	...	...	...	...	...	...
13,079	267	135	132	707	359	348	509	258	251
16,709	201	112	89	681	333	348	489	242	247
2,052	406	202	204	483	240	243	104	52	52
18,761	607	314	293	1,164	573	591	593	294	299
42	...	...	...	...	...	...	...	...	...
2,803	25	15	10	658	324	334	220	111	109
2,845	25	15	10	658	324	334	220	111	109
1,299	22	9	13	126	66	60	43	21	22

TABLE

Castes, Tribes and Races, by

Class.	Group.	Caste, &c.	Taluqs: Kalkulam. Total.	Kalkulam. Males.	Kalkulam. Females.	Vilavankodu. Total.	Vilavankodu. Males.	Vilavankodu. Females.
1	2	3	18	19	20	21	22	23
D. Artisans and Village Menials.	17. Goldsmiths.	Tattan ...	474	240	234	632	323	309
	17(a). Artisans (general).	1 Kammāla ...	50	18	32	151	66	85
		2 Kamsāla ...	...	...	...	...	...	...
		Total Group 17(a).	50	18	32	151	66	85
	18. Barbers.	1 Īlavāti ...	...	...	...	...	...	...
		2 Kāvadi ...	562	277	285	1,228	632	596
		3 Kōmaram ...	...	...	...	...	...	...
		4 Kshourakan ...	378	185	193	503	250	253
		5 Mārān ...	284	141	143	215	106	109
		6 Ostta ...	...	...	...	...	...	...
		7 Taravan ...	...	...	...	...	...	...
		Total Group 18 ...	1.224	603	621	1,946	988	958
	19. Blacksmiths.	1 Kollan ...	574	288	286	537	284	253
		2 Lōhar ...	...	...	...	...	...	...
		Total Group 19 ...	574	288	286	537	284	253
	20. Carpenters, Masons and Turners.	1 Āsāri ...	489	214	275	1,148	589	559
		2 Tachan ...	94	46	48	...	...	...
		Total Group 20 ...	583	260	323	1,148	589	559
	21. Brass and Coppersmiths.	1 Chembutatti ...	...	...	...	...	...	...
		2 Kannān ...	75	35	40	17	9	8
		Total Group 21 ...	75	35	40	17	9	8
	22. Tailors.	Pānān ...	24	14	10	...	...	...

XVI.

Nationality or Traditional Occupation—(*Continued*).

—(*Continued*).

Neyattankara.			Trivandram.			Nedumangadu.		
Total.	Males.	Females.	Total.	Males.	Females.	Total.	Males.	Females.
24	25	26	27	28	29	30	31	32
474	248	226	2,038	1,014	1,024	732	384	348
161	85	76	...	...	...	...	...	...
...	...	...	...	...	...	...	...	...
161	85	76	...	...	...	...	...	...
77	50	27	8	5	3	284	143	141
454	226	228	...	...	...	...	...	...
...	...	...	...	...	...	...	...	...
962	489	473	1,017	503	514	764	379	385
277	135	142	662	320	342	1,036	525	511
...	...	...	57	16	41	...	...	...
116	55	61	194	99	95	...	...	...
1,886	955	931	1,938	943	995	2,084	1,047	1,037
951	503	448	731	398	333	388	203	185
...	...	...	...	...	..	...	...	...
951	503	448	731	398	333	388	203	185
2,223	1,131	1,092	3,102	1,583	1,519	2,011	1,042	969
...	...	...	...	...	...	...	.	...
2,223	1,131	1,092	3,102	1,583	1,519	2,011	1,042	969
5	2	3	71	41	30	...	...	...
39	14	25	677	346	331	89	39	50
44	16	28	748	387	361	89	39	50
49	28	21	251	131	120	108	54	54

TABLE

Castes, Tribes and Races, by

Class.	Group.	Caste, &c.	Taluqs: Sirayinkil. Total.	Sirayinkil. Males.	Sirayinkil. Females.	Kottarakkara. Total.	Kottarakkara. Males.	Kottarakkara. Females.
1	2	3	33	34	35	36	37	38
D. Artisans and Village Menials.	17. Goldsmiths.	Tattan ...	978	482	496	606	291	315
	17(*a*). Artisans (general).	1 Kammāla ...	203	93	110	...	...	...
		2 Kamsāla ...	...	...	...	...	...	...
		Total Group 17(*a*).	203	93	110	...	...	...
	18. Barbers.	1 Īlavāti ...	356	148	208	187	85	102
		2 Kāvadi ...	20	12	8	...	...	...
		3 Kōmaram ...	...	...	...	...	...	...
		4 Kshourakan ...	702	326	376	546	298	248
		5 Mārān ...	942	465	477	999	485	514
		6 Ostta ...	...	...	...	4	3	1
		7 Taravan ...	145	72	73	...	...	...
		Total Group 18 ...	2,165	1,023	1,142	1,736	871	865
	19. Blacksmiths.	1 Kollan ...	769	383	386	1,098	544	554
		2 Lōhar ...	...	...	...	...	...	...
		Total Group 19 ...	769	383	386	1,098	544	554
	20. Carpenters, Masons and Turners.	1 Āsāri ...	2,391	1,201	1,190	1,136	597	539
		2 Tachan ...	...	...	...	36	21	15
		Total Group 20 ...	2,391	1,201	1,190	1,172	618	554
	21. Brass and Coppersmiths.	1 Chembutatti ...	...	...	...	...	...	...
		2 Kannān ...	125	62	63	144	69	75
		Total Group 21 ...	125	62	63	144	69	75
	22. Tailors.	Pānān ...	172	71	101	120	62	58

XVI.

Nationality or Traditional Occupation—(*Continued*).

—(*Continued*).

Pattanapuram.			Shenkotta.			Quilon.		
Total.	Males.	Females.	Total.	Males.	Females.	Total.	Males.	Females.
39	40	41	42	43	44	45	46	47
505	242	263	526	247	279	922	465	457
...	...	...	448	230	218	30	15	15
...	..	...	...	...	...	13	7	6
...	...	...	448	230	218	43	22	21
132	71	61	...	...	...	165	82	83
...	...	...	...	...	...	...	...	...
...	...	...	...	...	...	...	...	...
262	125	137	405	199	206	626	304	322
450	216	234	121	63	58	709	327	382
...	...	...	...	...	...	...	...	...
...	...	...	...	...	...	...	...	...
844	412	432	526	262	264	1,500	713	787
530	284	246	699	345	354	1,547	781	766
...	...	...	...	...	...	...	...	...
530	284	246	699	345	354	1,547	781	766
564	272	292	487	255	232	2,048	1,010	1,038
142	71	71	179	83	96	343	169	174
706	343	363	666	338	328	2,391	1,179	1,212
...	...	...	...	...	...	...	...	...
113	51	62	133	72	61	167	94	73
113	51	62	133	72	61	167	94	73
106	64	42	381	198	183	178	90	88

TABLE

Castes, Tribes and Races, by

Class.	Group.	Caste, &c.	Taluqs: Kunnattur. Total.	Kunnattur. Males.	Kunnattur. Females.	Karunagappalli. Total.	Karunagappalli. Males.	Karunagappalli. Females.
1	2	3	48	49	50	51	52	53
D. Artisans and Village Menials.	17. Goldsmiths.	Tattan ...	511	266	245	732	362	370
	17(*a*). Artisans (general).	1 Kammāla ...	10	6	4	...	...	...
		2 Kamsāla ...	..	...	...	...	...	...
		Total Group 17(*a*).	10	6	4	...	...	...
	18. Barbers.	1 Īlavāti ...	101	50	51	290	130	160
		2 Kāvadi ...	...	..	...	...	...	...
		3 Kōmaram ...	...	...	...	...	...	...
		4 Kshourakan ...	443	222	221	450	207	243
		5 Mārān ...	786	371	415	820	408	412
		6 Ostta ...	...	...	...	...	...	...
		7 Taravan ...	...	...	...	...	...	...
		Total Group 18 ...	1,330	643	687	1,560	745	815
	19. Black-smiths.	1 Kollan ...	750	375	375	1,033	528	505
		2 Lōhar ...	...	...	...	...	...	...
		Total Group 19 ...	750	375	375	1,033	528	505
	20. Carpenters, Masons and Turners.	1 Āsāri ...	1,021	504	517	1,223	628	595
		2 Tachan ...	210	106	104	320	162	158
		Total Group 20 ...	1,231	610	621	1,543	790	753
	21. Brass and Coppersmiths.	1 Chembutatti ...	...	...	...	20	11	9
		2 Kannān ...	39	27	12	160	84	76
		Total Group 21 ...	39	27	12	180	95	85
	22. Tailors.	Pānān ...	152	78	74	120	67	53

XVI.

Nationality or Traditional Occupation—(*Continued*).

—(*Continued*).

Kartigappalli.			Mavellikkara.			Chenganur.		
Total.	Males.	Females.	Total.	Males.	Females.	Total.	Males.	Females.
54	55	56	57	58	59	60	61	62
908	462	446	554	305	249	655	390	265
...	...	...	...	...	...	...	...	...
...	...	...	...	...	...	...	...	...
...	...	...	...	...	...	...	...	...
415	145	270	130	67	63	165	82	83
...	...	...	...	...	...	...	...	...
...	...	...	...	...	...	...	...	...
423	213	210	631	322	309	697	325	372
1,234	605	629	638	307	331	431	213	218
...	...	...	...	...	...	..	...	...
...	...	...	...	...	...	...	...	...
2,072	963	1,109	1,399	696	703	1,293	620	673
1,072	527	545	747	381	366	1,107	576	531
...	...	...	...	...	...	...	...	...
1,072	527	545	747	381	366	1,107	576	531
1,661	835	826	1,661	844	817	637	327	310
201	100	101	378	192	186	302	149	153
1,862	935	927	2,039	1,036	1,003	939	476	463
...	...	...	...	...	...	...	...	...
180	95	85	62	19	43	308	160	148
180	95	85	62	19	43	308	160	148
113	56	57	103	59	44	146	84	62

TABLE

Castes, Tribes and Races, by

Class.	Group.	Caste, &c.	Taluqs: Tiruvalla. Total.	Tiruvalla. Males.	Tiruvalla. Females.	Ambalappula. Total.	Ambalappula. Males.	Ambalappula. Females.
1	2	3	63	64	65	66	67	68
D. Artisans and Village Menials.	17. Goldsmiths.	Tattan ...	1,054	539	515	1,157	508	649
	17(*a*). Artisans (general).	1 Kammāla ...	...	...	...	...	...	...
		2 Kamsāla ...	...	...	...	...	...	...
		Total Group 17(*a*).	...	...	...	...	...	...
	18. Barbers.	1 Īlavāti ...	227	120	107	...	...	...
		2 Kāvadi ...	...	...	...	...	...	...
		3 Kōmaram ...	...	...	...	51	29	22
		4 Kshourakan ...	817	424	393	486	255	231
		5 Mārān ...	467	229	238	571	281	290
		6 Ostta ...	5	3	2	...	...	...
		7 Taravan ...	...	...	...	...	...	...
		Total Group 18 ...	1,516	776	740	1,108	565	543
	19. Blacksmiths.	1 Kollan ...	975	513	462	708	359	349
		2 Lōhar ...	...	...	...	...	...	...
		Total Group 19 ...	975	513	462	708	359	349
	20. Carpenters, Masons and Turners.	1 Āsāri ...	977	481	496	1,202	615	587
		2 Tachan ...	76	35	41	...	...	...
		Total Group 20 ...	1,053	516	537	1,202	615	587
	21. Brass and Coppersmiths.	1 Chembutatti ...	...	...	...	...	...	...
		2 Kannān ...	300	154	146	199	100	99
		Total Group 21 ...	300	154	146	199	100	99
	22. Tailors.	Pānān ...	116	51	65	39	27	12

XVI.

Nationality or Traditional Occupation—(*Continued*).

— *Continued*).

Sherttala.			Vykkam.			Ettumanur.		
Total.	Males.	Females.	Total.	Males.	Females.	Total.	Males.	Females.
69	70	71	72	73	74	75	76	77
1,065	586	479	1,702	829	873	428	203	225
...	...	...	...	...	...	632	318	314
...	...	...	...	...	...	...	...	...
...	...	...	...	...	...	632	318	314
92	53	39	...	...	..	...	...	...
...	...	...	...	...	...	...	...	...
11	4	7	20	13	7	28	15	13
281	141	140	198	95	103	759	336	423
429	214	215	355	175	180	412	209	203
...	...	...	..	...	...	...	...	...
...	...	...	...	...	...	...	...	...
813	412	401	573	283	290	1,199	560	639
615	307	308	791	400	391	1,029	554	475
...	...	...	...	...	...	...	...	...
615	307	308	791	400	391	1,029	554	475
497	240	257	215	100	115	968	482	486
20	9	11	...	...	...	312	155	157
517	249	268	215	100	115	1,280	637	643
...	...	...	...	...	...	...	...	...
115	56	59	116	59	57	153	79	74
115	56	59	116	59	57	153	79	74
...	...	...	14	8	6	...	...	...

TABLE

Castes, Tribes and Races, by

Class.	Group.	Caste, &c.	Taluqs: Kottayam. Total.	Kottayam. Males.	Kottayam. Females.	Changanacheri. Total.	Changanacheri. Males.	Changanacheri. Females.
1	2	3	78	79	80	81	82	83
D. Artisans and Village Menials.	17. Goldsmiths.	Tattan ...	893	462	431	921	472	449
	17(*a*). Artisans (general).	1 Kammāla ...	...	...	...	...	...	...
		2 Kamsāla ...	...	...	...	...	...	...
		Total Group 17(*a*).	...	...	...	...	...	...
	18. Barbers.	1 Īlavāti ...	14	6	8	17	9	8
		2 Kāvadi ...	...	...	...	...	...	...
		3 Kōmaram ...	95	50	45	17	12	5
		4 Kshourakan ...	648	339	309	722	371	351
		5 Mārān ...	481	236	245	410	207	203
		6 Ostta ...	...	...	...	...	...	...
		7 Taravan ...	...	...	...	..	...	...
		Total Group 18 ...	1,238	631	607	1,166	599	567
	19. Blacksmiths.	1 Kollan ...	1,149	618	531	1,175	624	551
		2 Lōhar ...	...	...	...	...	...	...
		Total Group 19 ...	1,149	618	531	1,175	624	551
	20. Carpenters, Masons and Turners.	1 Āsāri ...	856	414	442	191	94	97
		2 Tachan ...	288	135	153	51	25	26
		Total Group 20 ...	1,144	549	595	242	119	123
	21. Brass and Coppersmiths.	1 Chembutatti ...	2	2	...	...	...	...
		2 Kannān ...	192	93	99	334	185	149
		Total Group 21 ...	194	95	99	334	185	149
	22. Tailors.	Pānān .	22	11	11	68	33	35

XVI.

Nationality or Traditional Occupation—(*Continued*).

—(*Continued*).

Meenachal.			Muvattupula.			Todupula.		
Total.	Males.	Females.	Total.	Males.	Females.	Total.	Males.	Females.
84	85	86	87	88	89	90	91	92
693	354	339	1,105	572	533	299	147	152
...	...	...	...	...	...	...	...	...
...	...	...	...	...	...	...	...	...
...	...	...	...	...	...	...	...	...
62	33	29	...	...	...	...	...	...
...	...	...	...	...	...	...	...	...
35	15	20	...	...	...	...	...	...
381	203	178	564	284	280	126	57	69
441	217	224	569	274	295	145	74	71
...	...	...	...	...	...	...	...	...
...	..	...	...	..	...	...	...	...
919	468	451	1,133	558	575	271	131	140
644	342	302	2,118	1,077	1,041	217	127	90
...	...	...	...	...	...	...	...	...
644	342	302	2,118	1,077	1,041	217	127	90
268	130	138	843	441	402	281	124	157
62	30	32	21	7	14	...	...	...
330	160	170	864	448	416	281	124	157
...	...	...	...	...	...	...	...	...
150	77	73	355	187	168	...	...	...
150	77	73	355	187	168	...	...	...
86	38	48	29	14	15	2	2	...

TABLE

Castes, Tribes and Races, by

Class.	Group.	Caste, &c.	Taluqs: Kunnattunadu. Total.	Kunnattunadu. Males.	Kunnattunadu. Females.	Alangadu. Total.	Alangadu. Males.	Alangadu. Females.
1	2	3	93	94	95	96	97	98
D. Artisans and Village Menials.	17. Goldsmiths.	Tattan ...	960	509	451	559	270	289
	17(*a*). Artisans (general).	1 Kammāla ...	...	...	...	...	...	...
		2 Kamsāla ...	...	...	...	...	...	...
		Total Group 17(*a*)	...	...	...	...	...	...
	18. Barbers.	1 Īlavāti ...	41	24	17	19	12	7
		2 Kāvadi ...	...	...	...	...	...	...
		3 Kōmrama ...	...	...	...	..	...	...
		4 Kshourakan ..	392	193	199	250	121	129
		5 Mārān ...	531	250	281	127	61	66
		6 Ostta ...	...	...	...	...	...	...
		7 Taravan ...	...	...	...	...	...	...
		Total Group 18 ...	964	467	497	396	194	202
	19. Blacksmiths.	1 Kollan ...	2,116	1,091	1,025	870	445	425
		2 Lōhar ...	...	...	...	...	...	...
		Total Group 19 ...	2,116	1,091	1,025	870	445	425
	20. Carpenters, Masons and Turners.	1 Āsāri ...	1,902	949	953	1,968	991	977
		2 Tachan ...	24	15	9	5	3	2
		Total Group 20 ...	1,926	964	962	1,973	994	979
	21. Brass and Coppersmiths.	1 Chembutatti ...	...	...	...	...	...	...
		2 Kannān ...	298	144	154	122	62	60
		Total Group 21 ...	298	144	154	122	62	60
	22. Tailors.	Pānān ...	63	43	20	55	30	25

XVI.

Nationality or Traditional Occupation—(*Continued*).

—(*Continued*).

Parur.			Cardamom Hills.			Periyar & Thekkadi.		
Total.	Males.	Females.	Total.	Males.	Females.	Total.	Males.	Females.
99	100	101	102	103	104	105	106	107
440	228	212	23	15	8	13	9	4
...	...	...	...	...	...	...	...	...
...	...	...	...	...	...	...	...	...
...	...	...	...	...	...	...	...	...
87	45	42	...	...	...	...	...	...
...	...	...	...	...	...	...	...	...
...	...	...	...	...	...	...	...	...
135	68	67	51	20	31	14	9	5
291	143	148	4	3	1	...	...	...
...	...	...	...	...	...	...	...	...
...	...	...	...	...	...	...	...	...
513	256	257	55	23	32	14	9	5
537	273	264	7	6	1	15	15	...
...	...	...	...	...	...	3	3	...
537	273	264	7	6	1	18	18	...
171	71	100	98	52	46	31	29	2
4	2	2	5	5	...	...	...	...
175	73	102	103	57	46	31	29	2
...	...	...	...	...	...	...	...	...
132	72	60	...	...	...	...	...	...
132	72	60	...	...	...	...	...	...
...	...	...	...	...	...	...	...	...

TABLE

Castes, Tribes and Races, by

NAME AND CLASSIFICATION.					STATE	
CLASS.	GROUP.	CASTE, &c.	No. of recorded sub-divisions.	Religion.	Total.	Males.
1	2	3	4	5	6	7
D. Artisans and Village Menials.	22 (*a*). Grain parchers and confectioners.	1 Idiyar ...	...	Hindu...	*1,266*	660
		2 Mudayar ...	...	,, ...	*1*	1
		Total Group 22(*a*).	...	...	**1,267**	**661**
	23. Weavers, calenderers and dyers.	1 Kōri ...	...	Hindu ...	*7*	5
		2 Patnūl ...	...	,, ...	*854*	393
		3 Sālē ...	5	,, ...	*7,289*	3,580
		Total Group 23 ...	...	...	**8,150**	**3,978**
	24. Washermen.	1 Ainuttar ...	...	Hindu...	*2*	1
		2 Dōbi ...	...	,, ...	*138*	65
		3 Mannān ...	2	,, ...	*7,082*	3,509
		4 Velutadan ...	6	,, ...	*13,826*	6,993
		Total Group 24 ...	...	...	**21,048**	**10,568**
	26. Shepherds and Wool-weavers.	1 Āttidaya ...	...	Hindu ...	*217*	109
		2 Gollalu ...	1	,, ...	*67*	36
		3 Idaya ...	9	,, ...	*5,848*	2,863
		4 Kāngaya ...	...	,, ...	*125*	67
		5 Kūttidaya ...	...	,, ...	*105*	58
		Total Group 26 ...	...	...	**6,362**	**3,133**
	27. Oil pressers.	1 Chekkāla ...	3	Hindu...	*11,592*	5,739
		2 Vānian ...	3	,, ...	*13,758*	7,031
		Total Group 27 ...	...	...	**25,350**	**12,770**

XVI.

Nationality or Traditional Occupation—(*Continued*).

TOTAL.	TALUQS.								
	Tovala.			Agastiswaram.			Eranial.		
Females.	Total.	Males.	Females.	Total.	Males.	Females.	Total.	Males.	Females.
8	9	10	11	12	13	14	15	16	17
606	...	...	...	...	...	...	...	...	...
...	...	...	...	...	..	...	...	...	...
606	..	...	...	...	...	...	...	...	...
2	...	...	...	...	...	...	...	...	...
461	...	...	...	803	374	429	...	...	...
3,709	3	1	2	3,213	1,557	1,656	869	461	408
4,172	3	1	2	4,016	1,931	2,085	869	461	408
1	...	...	...	...	...	...	...	...	...
73	...	...	...	...	...	...	...	...	...
3,573	..	...	...	...	...	...	279	141	138
6,833	289	153	136	832	422	410	248	118	130
10,480	289	153	136	832	422	410	527	259	268
108	...	...	...	...	...	...	50	26	24
31	...	...	...	...	...	...	...	...	...
2,985	1,032	554	478	1,457	651	806	272	149	123
58	...	...	...	...	...	...	9	5	4
47	..	...	...	...	...	...	...	...	...
3,229	1,032	554	478	1,457	651	806	331	180	151
5,853	35	18	17	23	11	12	939	410	529
6,727	261	120	141	1,909	957	952	527	265	262
12,580	296	138	158	1,932	968	964	1,466	675	791

TABLE

Castes, Tribes and Races, by

Class.	Group.	Caste, &c.	Taluqs: Kalkulam. Total.	Kalkulam. Males.	Kalkulam. Females.	Vilavankodu. Total.	Vilavankodu. Males.	Vilavankodu. Females.
1	2	3	18	19	20	21	22	23
D. Artisans and Village Menials.	22 (a). Grain parchers and confectioners.	1 Idiyar ...	...	...	...	...	...	...
		2 Mudayar ...	...	...	...	...	...	...
		Total Group 22(a).	...	...	...	...	...	...
	23. Weavers, calenderers and dyers.	1 Kōri ..	...	...	...	...	...	...
		2 Patnūl ...	...	...	...	...	...	...
		3 Sālē ..	14	10	4	363	198	165
		Total Group 23 ...	14	10	4	363	198	165
	24. Washermen.	1 Ainuttar ...	...	...	...	...	...	...
		2 Dōbi ...	...	...	...	...	...	...
		3 Mannān ...	243	124	119	304	152	152
		4 Velutadan ...	216	120	96	190	97	93
		Total Group 24 ...	459	244	215	494	249	245
	26. Shepherds and Wool-weavers.	1 Āttidaya ...	29	14	15	16	8	8
		2 Gollalu ...	...	...	...	...	...	...
		3 Idaya ...	207	95	112	76	40	36
		4 Kāngaya ...	95	51	44	14	8	6
		5 Kūttidaya ..	...	...	...	...	...	...
		Total Group 26 ...	331	160	171	106	56	50
	27. Oil pressers.	1 Chekkāla ..	456	208	248	1,375	703	672
		2 Vānian ...	357	170	187	86	49	37
		Total Group 27 ...	813	378	435	1,461	752	709

XVI.

Nationality or Traditional Occupation—(*Continued*).

—(*Continued*).

Neyattankara.			Trivandram.			Nedumangadu.		
Total.	Males.	Females.	Total.	Males.	Females.	Total.	Males.	Females.
24	25	26	27	28	29	30	31	32
...	...	...	113	63	50	...	...	...
...	...	...	...	...	...	...	...	...
...	...	...	113	63	50	...	...	...
...	...	...	...	...	...	...	...	...
...	...	...	25	8	17	...	...	...
463	251	212	136	66	70	...	...	...
463	251	212	161	74	87	...	...	...
...	...	...	...	...	...	...	...	...
...	...	...	...	...	...	...	...	...
286	142	144	84	42	42	40	21	19
436	223	213	913	457	456	461	243	218
722	365	357	997	499	498	501	264	237
16	7	9	...	...	...	...	...	...
...	...	...	5	3	2	...	...	...
103	55	48	343	181	162	80	40	40
...	...	...	7	3	4	...	...	...
...	...	...	..	...	...	...	...	...
119	62	57	355	187	168	80	40	40
1,311	691	620	530	240	290	452	230	222
650	393	257	1,765	969	796	297	147	150
1,961	1,084	877	2,295	1,209	1,086	749	377	372

TABLE

Castes, Tribes and Races, by

Class.	Group.	Caste, &c.	Taluqs: Sirayinkil. Total.	Sirayinkil. Males.	Sirayinkil. Females.	Kottarakkara. Total.	Kottarakkara. Males.	Kottarakkara. Females.
1	2	3	33	34	35	36	37	38
D. Artisans and Village Menials.	22 (*a*). Grain parchers and confectioners.	1 Idiyar ...	...	...	...	...	...	...
		2 Mudayar ...	...	...	...	...	...	...
		Total Group 22(*a*).	...	...	...	...	...	...
	23. Weavers, calenderers and dyers.	1 Kōri ...	...	...	...	...	...	...
		2 Patnūl ...	...	...	...	...	...	...
		3 Sālē ...	...	...	...	12	12	...
		Total Group 23 ...	...	...	...	12	12	...
	24. Washermen.	1 Ainuttar ...	...	...	...	...	...	...
		2 Dōbi ...	...	...	...	...	...	...
		3 Mannān ...	83	43	40	134	58	76
		4 Velutadan ...	836	439	397	550	288	262
		Total Group 24 ...	919	482	437	684	346	338
	26. Shepherds and Wool-weavers.	1 Āttidaya ...	...	...	...	89	45	44
		2 Gollalu ...	...	...	...	...	...	...
		3 Idaya ...	41	18	23	...	...	...
		4 Kāngaya ...	...	...	...	...	...	...
		5 Kūttidaya ...	...	...	...	...	...	...
		Total Group 26 ...	41	18	23	89	45	44
	27. Oil pressers.	1 Chekkāla ...	918	436	482	841	420	421
		2 Vānian ...	1,898	930	968	68	37	31
		Total Group 27 ...	2,816	1,366	1,450	909	457	452

XVI.

Nationality or Traditional Occupation—(*Continued*).

—(*Continued*).

Pattanapuram.			Shenkotta.			Quilon.		
Total.	Males.	Females.	Total.	Males.	Females.	Total.	Males.	Females.
39	40	41	42	43	44	45	46	47
...	...	...	...	...	...	105	55	50
...	...	...	..	...	...	...	...	...
...	...	...	...	...	...	105	55	50
...	...	...	...	...	...	...	...	...
...	...	...	...	...	...	26	11	15
...	...	...	...	...	...	5	3	2
...	...	...	...	...	..	31	14	17
...	...	...	...	...	...	2	1	1
...	...	...	...	...	...	136	63	73
82	36	46	316	149	167	199	91	108
472	240	232	71	36	35	511	260	251
554	276	278	387	185	202	848	415	433
...	...	...	17	9	8	...	...	...
...	...	...	...	...	...	60	31	29
29	16	13	1,770	843	927	70	35	35
...	...	...	...	...	...	...	...	...
...	...	...	...	...	...	...	...	...
29	16	13	1,787	852	935	130	66	64
...	...	...	...	...	...	338	206	132
92	43	49	928	457	471	559	287	272
92	43	49	928	457	471	897	493	404

TABLE

Castes, Tribes and Races, by

Class.	Group.	Caste, &c.	Taluqs: Kunnattur. Total.	Kunnattur. Males.	Kunnattur. Females.	Karunagappalli. Total.	Karunagappalli. Males.	Karunagappalli. Females.
1	2	3	48	49	50	51	52	53
D. Artisans and Village Menials.	22 (*a*). Grain parchers and confectioners.	1 Idiyar ...	...	...	...	...	...	...
		2 Mudayar ...	...	...	...	...	...	...
		Total Group 22(*a*).	...	...	...	...	...	...
	23. Weavers, calenderers and dyers.	1 Kōri ...	...	...	...	...	...	...
		2 Patnūl ...	...	...	...	...	...	...
		3 Sālē ...	...	...	...	...	...	...
		Total Group 23 ...	...	...	...	...	...	...
	24. Washermen.	1 Ainuttar ...	...	...	...	...	...	...
		2 Dōbi ...	...	...	...	...	...	...
		3 Mannān ...	111	48	63	416	190	226
		4 Velutadan ...	518	261	257	567	272	295
		Total Group 24 ...	629	309	320	983	462	521
	26. Shepherds and Wool-weavers.	1 Āttidaya ...	...	...	...	...	...	...
		2 Gollalu ...	...	...	...	...	...	...
		3 Idaya ...	3	3	...	...	...	...
		4 Kāngaya ...	...	...	...	...	...	...
		5 Kūttidaya ...	...	...	...	...	...	...
		Total Group 26 ...	3	3	...	...	...	...
	27. Oil pressers.	1 Chekkāla ...	466	232	234	1,824	843	981
		2 Vānian ...	198	102	96	768	335	433
		Total Group 27 ...	664	334	330	2,592	1,178	1,414

XVI.

Nationality or Traditional Occupation—(*Continued*).

—(*Continued*).

Kartigappalli.			Mavellikkara.			Chenganur.		
Total.	Males.	Females.	Total.	Males.	Females.	Total.	Males.	Females.
54	55	56	57	58	59	60	61	62
372	183	189	...	...	...	...	...	...
...	...	...	...	...	...	...	...	...
372	183	189	...	...	...	...	...	...
...	...	...	...	...	...	...	...	...
...	...	...	...	...	...	...	...	...
5	2	3	64	29	35	...	...	...
5	2	3	64	29	35	...	...	...
...	...	...	...	...	...	...	...	...
...	...	...	...	...	...	...	...	...
524	270	254	217	112	105	141	64	77
412	197	215	611	322	289	865	473	392
936	467	469	828	434	394	1,006	537	469
...	...	...	...	...	...	...	...	...
...	...	...	...	...	...	...	...	...
...	...	...	...	...	...	...	...	...
...	...	...	...	...	...	...	...	...
...	...	...	...	...	...	...	...	...
...	...	...	...	...	...	...	...	...
381	236	145	...	...	...	...	...	...
399	189	210	200	104	96	646	345	301
780	425	355	200	104	96	646	345	301

TABLE

Castes, Tribes and Races, by

Class.	Group.	Caste, &c.	Taluqs: Tiruvalla. Total.	Tiruvalla. Males.	Tiruvalla. Females.	Ambalappula. Total.	Ambalappula. Males.	Ambalappula. Females.
1	2	3	63	64	65	66	67	68
D. Artisans and Village Menials.	22 (*a*). Grain parchers and confectioners.	1 Idiyar ...	72	39	33	4	2	2
		2 Mudayar ...	...	...	...	...	...	...
		Total Group 22(*a*).	72	39	33	4	2	2
	23. Weavers, calenderers and dyers.	1 Kōri ...	...	...	...	...	...	...
		2 Patnūl ...	...	...	...	...	...	...
		3 Sālē ...	67	36	31	...	...	...
		Total Group 23 ...	67	36	31	...	...	...
	24. Washermen.	1 Ainuttar ...	...	...	...	...	...	...
		2 Dōbi ...	...	...	...	...	...	..
		3 Mannān ...	1,394	695	699	790	371	419
		4 Velutadan ...	669	319	350	764	376	388
		Total Group 24 ...	2,063	1,014	1,049	1,554	747	807
	26. Shepherds and Wool-weavers.	1 Āttidaya ...	...	...	...	...	...	...
		2 Gollalu ...	...	...	...	...	...	...
		3 Idaya ...	...	...	...	151	72	79
		4 Kāngaya ...	...	...	...	...	...	...
		5 Kūttidaya ...	...	...	...	...	...	...
		Total Group 26 ...	...	...	...	151	72	79
	27. Oil pressers.	1 Chekkāla ...	...	...	...	7	4	3
		2 Vānian ...	51	37	14	332	179	153
		Total Group 27 ...	51	37	14	339	183	156

XVI.

Nationality or Traditional Occupation—(*Continued*).

—(*Continued*).

Sherttala.			Vykkam.			Ettumanur.		
Total.	Males.	Females.	Total.	Males.	Females.	Total.	Males.	Females.
69	70	71	72	73	74	75	76	77
511	267	244	77	45	32	...	...	...
...	...	...	...	...	...	...	...	...
511	267	244	77	45	32	...	...	...
...	...	...	...	...	...	...	...	...
...	...	...	...	...	...	...	...	...
620	299	321	892	405	487	...	...	...
620	299	321	892	405	487	...	...	...
...	...	...	...	...	...	...	...	...
...	...	...	...	...	...	...	...	...
559	318	241	11	8	3	57	26	31
261	112	149	268	128	140	393	187	206
820	430	390	279	136	143	450	213	237
...	...	...	...	...	...	...	...	...
...	...	...	...	...	...	...	...	...
...	...	...	9	4	5	...	...	...
...	...	...	...	...	...	...	...	...
...	...	...	...	...	...	...	...	...
...	...	...	9	4	5	...	...	...
...	...	...	...	...	...	...	...	...
330	144	186	371	201	170	63	28	35
330	144	186	371	201	170	63	28	35

TABLE

Castes, Tribes and Races, by

Class.	Group.	Caste, &c.	Taluqs					
			Kottayam.			Changanacheri.		
			Total.	Males.	Females.	Total.	Males.	Females.
1	2	3	78	79	80	81	82	83
D. Artisans and Village Menials.	22 (*a*). Grain parchers and confectioners.	1 Idiyar ...	...	...	...	...	...	...
		2 Mudayar ...	...	...	...	...	...	...
		Total Group 22(*a*).	...	...	...	...	...	...
	23. Weavers, calenderers and dyers.	1 Kōri ...	...	...	...	...	...	...
		2 Patnūl ...	...	...	...	...	...	...
		3 Sālē ...	...	...	...	...	...	...
		Total Group 23 ...	...	...	...	...	...	...
	24. Washermen.	1 Ainuttar ...	...	...	...	...	...	...
		2 Dōbi ...	...	...	..	...	...	...
		3 Mannān ...	10	4	6	251	126	125
		4 Velutadan ...	498	250	248	550	285	265
		Total Group 24 ...	508	254	254	801	411	390
	26. Shepherds and Wool-weavers.	1 Āttidaya ...	...	...	...	...	...	...
		2 Gollalu ...	...	...	...	...	..	...
		3 Idaya ...	2	1	1	...	...	...
		4 Kāngaya ...	...	...	...	...	...	...
		5 Kūttidaya ...	...	...	...	...	...	...
		Total Group 26 ...	2	1	1	...	...	...
	27. Oil pressers.	1 Chekkāla ...	98	55	43	...	...	...
		2 Vānian ...	313	167	146	217	129	88
		Total Group 27 ...	411	222	189	217	129	88

Nationality or Traditional Occupation—(*Continued*).

—(*Continued*).

Meenachal.			Muvattupula.			Todupula.		
Total.	Males.	Females.	Total.	Males.	Females.	Total.	Males.	Females.
84	85	86	87	88	89	90	91	92
12	6	6	...	...	...	...	...	...
...	...	...	...	...	...	...	...	...
12	6	6	...	...	...	...	...	...
...	...	...	...	...	...	...	...	...
...	...	...	...	...	...	...	...	...
...	...	...	2	1	1	4	3	1
...	...	...	2	1	1	4	3	1
...	...	...	...	...	...	...	...	...
...	...	...	...	...	...	...	...	...
10	3	7	117	59	58	42	20	22
325	177	148	297	139	158	93	50	43
335	180	155	414	198	216	135	70	65
...	...	...	...	...	...	...	...	...
...	...	...	...	...	...	...	...	...
2	2	...	13	...	13	...	...	...
...	...	...	...	...	...	...	...	...
...	...	...	105	58	47	...	...	...
2	2	...	118	58	60	...	...	...
272	130	142	559	274	285	356	162	194
7	3	4	60	40	20	...	...	...
279	133	146	619	314	305	356	162	194

TABLE

Castes, Tribes and Races, by

Class.	Group.	Caste, &c.	Taluqs: Kunnattunadu. Total.	Kunnattunadu. Males.	Kunnattunadu. Females.	Alangadu. Total.	Alangadu. Males.	Alangadu. Females.
1	2	3	93	94	95	96	97	98
D. Artisans and Village Menials.	22 (*a*). Grain parchers and confectioners.	1 Idiyar ...	...	...	...	...	...	...
		2 Mudayar ...	...	...	...	...	...	...
		Total Group 22 (*a*).	...	...	...	...	...	...
	23. Weavers, calenderers and dyers.	1 Kōri ...	...	...	...	...	...	...
		2 Patnūl ...	...	...	...	...	...	...
		3 Sālē ...	134	63	71	263	102	161
		Total Group 23 ...	134	63	71	263	102	161
	24. Washermen.	1 Ainuttar ...	...	...	...	...	...	...
		2 Dōbi ...	...	...	...	...	...	..
		3 Mannān ...	341	165	176	4	3	1
		4 Velutadan ...	344	167	177	265	132	133
		Total Group 24 ...	685	332	353	269	135	134
	26. Shepherds and Wool-weavers.	1 Attidaya ...	...	...	...	...	...	...
		2 Gollain ...	...	...	...	...	...	..
		3 Idaya ...	4	1	3	75	46	29
		4 Kāngaya ...	...	...	...	...	...	...
		5 Kūttidaya ...	...	...	...	...	...	...
		Total Group 26 ...	4	1	3	75	46	29
	27. Oil pressers.	1 Chekkāla ...	243	141	102	61	33	28
		2 Vānian ..	...	...	...	...	...	...
		Total Group 27 ...	243	141	102	61	33	28

XVI.

Nationality or Traditional Occupation—(*Continued*).

—(*Continued*).

Parur.			Cardamom Hills.			Periyar and Thekkadi.		
Total.	Males.	Females.	Total.	Males.	Females.	Total.	Males.	Females.
99	100	101	102	103	104	105	106	107
...	...	...	...	...	...	...	...	...
...	...	...	...	...	...	1	1	...
...	...	...	...	...	...	1	1	...
...	...	...	...	...	...	7	5	2
...	...	...	...	...	...	...	...	...
160	81	79	...	...	...	...	...	...
160	81	79	...	...	...	7	5	2
...	...	...	...	..	...	...	...	...
...	...	...	...	...	...	2	2	...
11	8	3	20	15	5	6	5	1
101	50	51	...	...	...	...	...	...
112	58	54	20	15	5	8	7	1
...	...	...	...	...	...	...	...	...
...	...	...	...	...	...	2	2	...
...	...	...	88	41	47	21	16	5
...	...	...	...	...	...	...	...	...
...	...	...	...	...	...	...	...	...
...	...	...	88	41	47	23	18	5
107	56	51	...	...	...	...	...	...
406	204	202	...	...	...	...	...	...
513	260	253	...	...	...	...	...	...

TABLE

Castes, Tribes and Races, by

Class.	Group.	Caste, &c.	No. of recorded sub-divisions.	Religion.	Total.	Males.
1	2	3	4	5	6	7
D. Artisans and Village Menials.	28. Potters.	Kosava ...	5	Hindu....	*6,395*	**3,269**
	30. Salt, &c., workers.	Alava ...	1	Hindu....	*394*	**206**
	31. Lime-burners.	Paravan ...	1	Hindu....	*8,172*	**3,983**
	35. Fishermen, Boatmen, Palki-bearers, Water-bearers, Cooks, &c.	1 Chaluppan ...	...	Hindu....	*921*	**471**
		2 Kāhar ...	...	,, ...	*1*	**1**
		3 Marakkan ...	2	{ Musln. / Christ.	*5,491*	**2,639**
		4 Mukkuva ...	5	Hindu...	*30,354*	**15,082**
		5 Pōndan ...	...	,, ...	*1,139*	**617**
		Total Group 35 ...	...	...	**37,906**	**18,810**
	35 (*a*). Personal service.	Chākkār ...	...	Hindu...	*565*	**306**
	36. Distillers and Toddy-drawers.	1 Īluva ...	7	Hindu...	*414,217*	**206,528**
		2 Pashi ...	...	,, ...	*3*	**3**
		3 Chānnān ...	11	,, ...	*136,611*	**70,001**
		4 Tandān ...	3	,, ...	*22,614*	**11,158**
		Total Group 36 ...	...	...	**573,445**	**287,690**
	38. Leather-workers.	Chemmān ...	6	Hindu...	*2,156*	**1,094**
	39. Scavengers.	1 Dāss ...	...	Hindu...	*10*	**5**
		2 Valluvan ...	1	,, ...	*113*	**56**
		Total Group 39 ...	..	...	**123**	**61**
		Total Class D. ...	...	...	*831,493*	*417,104*

XVI.

Nationality or Traditional Occupation—(*Continued*).

TOTAL.	TALUQS.								
	Tovala.			Agastiswaram.			Eranial.		
Females.	Total.	Males.	Females.	Total.	Males.	Females.	Total.	Males.	Females.
8	9	10	11	12	13	14	15	16	17
3,126	200	105	95	365	179	186	450	239	211
188	...	...	...	282	143	139	50	29	21
4,189	39	18	21	239	97	142	425	211	214
450	...	...	...	29	15	14	...	...	...
...	...	...	...	...	...	...	...	...	...
2,852	...	...	...	...	...	...	...	...	...
15,272	415	198	217	409	198	211	181	83	98
522	...	...	...	22	9	13	...	...	...
19,096	415	198	217	460	222	238	181	83	98
259	...	..	...	...	...	...	...	...	...
207,689	661	319	342	619	307	312	629	332	297
...	...	...	...	...	...	...	...	...	...
66,610	3,133	1,593	1,540	21,963	11,002	10,961	42,128	21,638	20,490
11,456	...	...	...	...	...	...	91	47	44
285,755	3,794	1,912	1,882	22,582	11,309	11,273	42,848	22,017	20,831
1,062	13	6	7	346	180	166	52	29	23
5	...	...	...	...	...	...	...	...	...
57	6	2	4	...	...	...	...	...	...
62	6	2	4	...	...	...	...	...	...
414,389	7,657	3,865	3,792	37,843	18,758	19,085	52,565	26,914	25,651

TABLE

Castes, Tribes and Races, by

Class.	Group.	Caste, &c.	Kalkulam. Total.	Kalkulam. Males.	Kalkulam. Females.	Vilavankodu. Total.	Vilavankodu. Males.	Vilavankodu. Females.
1	2	3	18	19	20	21	22	23
D. Artisans and Village Menials.	28. Potters.	Kosava ...	170	85	85	237	117	120
	30. Salt, &c., workers.	Alava ...	57	32	25	...	...	...
	31. Lime-burners.	Paravan ...	46	25	21	187	94	93
	35. Fishermen, Boatmen, Palki-bearers, Water-bearers, Cooks, &c.	1 Chaluppan ...	20	13	7	...	...	...
		2 Kāhar ...	...	...	...	...	...	...
		3 Marakkān ...	...	...	...	...	...	...
		4 Mukkuva ...	31	12	19	111	52	59
		5 Pōndan ...	172	82	90	...	...	...
		Total Group 35 ...	223	107	116	111	52	59
	35 (a). Personal service.	Chākkār ...	...	...	...	...	...	...
	36. Distillers and Toddy-drawers.	1 Īluva ...	882	420	462	2,299	1,099	1,200
		2 Pāshi ...	...	...	...	...	...	...
		3 Chānnān ...	19,378	9,741	9,637	22,917	11,773	11,144
		4 Tandān ...	123	57	66	804	413	391
		Total Group 36 ...	20,383	10,218	10,165	26,020	13,285	12,735
	38. Leather-workers.	Chemmān ...	18	12	6	5	2	3
	39. Scavengers.	1 Dāss ...	...	...	...	...	...	...
		2 Valluvan ...	...	...	...	...	...	...
		Total Group 39 ...	...	...	...	...	...	...
		Total Class D. ...	25,518	12,729	12,789	33,415	17,064	16,351

XVI.

Nationality or Traditional Occupation—(*Continued*).

—(*Continued*).

Neyattankara.			Trivandram.			Nedumangadu.		
Total.	Males.	Females.	Total.	Males.	Females.	Total.	Males.	Females.
24	25	26	27	28	29	30	31	32
731	399	332	414	209	205	44	21	23
...	...	...	5	2	3	...	...	...
204	104	100	674	311	363	272	140	132
...	...	...	561	297	264	...	...	...
...	...	...	...	...	...	...	...	...
...	...	...	394	79	315	...	...	...
10	5	5	373	200	173	...	...	...
14	6	8	34	22	12	10	5	5
24	11	13	1,362	598	764	10	5	5
...	...	..	...	...	...	...	...	...
10,832	5,611	5,221	13,295	6,794	6,501	4,551	2,293	2,258
...	...	...	...	...	...	...	...	...
17,640	9,156	8,484	1,836	1,020	816	1,195	604	591
945	495	450	1,692	849	843	36	16	20
29,417	15,262	14,155	16,823	8,663	8,160	5,782	2,913	2,869
42	22	20	170	81	89	200	104	96
...	...	...	...	...	...	...	...	...
...	...	...	5	4	1	...	...	...
...	...	...	5	4	1	...	...	...
39,471	20,526	18,945	32,182	16,356	15,826	13,050	6,633	6,417

TABLE

Castes, Tribes and Races, by

Class.	Group.	Caste, &c.	Taluqs: Sirayinkil. Total.	Sirayinkil. Males.	Sirayinkil. Females.	Kottarakkara. Total.	Kottarakkara. Males.	Kottarakkara. Females.
1	2	3	33	34	35	36	37	38
D. Artisans and Village Menials.	28. Potters.	Kosava ...	161	74	87	378	186	192
	30. Salt, &c., workers.	Alava ...	...	...	...	...	...	...
	31. Lime-burners.	Paravan ...	815	312	503	20	9	11
	35. Fishermen, Boatmen, Palki-bearers, Water-bearers, Cooks, &c.	1 Chaluppan ...	...	...	...	28	11	17
		2 Kāhar ...	...	...	...	...	...	...
		3 Marakkān ...	149	65	84	...	...	...
		4 Mukkuva ...	12	6	6	...	...	...
		5 Pōndan ...	145	68	77	120	63	57
		Total Group 35 ...	306	139	167	148	74	74
	35 (*a*). Personal service.	Chākkār ...	...	...	...	...	...	...
	36. Distillers and Toddy-drawers.	1 Īluva ...	26,383	13,044	13,339	10,199	5,069	5,130
		2 Pāshi ...	...	...	...	...	...	...
		3 Chānnān ...	583	289	294	300	154	146
		4 Tandān ...	2,416	1,120	1,296	488	249	239
		Total Group 36 ...	29,382	14,453	14,929	10,987	5,472	5,515
	38 Leather-workers.	Chemmān ...	57	30	27	95	38	57
	39. Scavengers.	1 Dāss ...	...	...	...	...	...	...
		2 Valluvan ...	...	...	...	...	...	...
		Total Group 39 ...	...	...	...	...	...	...
		Total Class D. ...	41,300	20,189	21,111	18,198	9,094	9,104

XVI.

Nationality or Traditional Occupation—(*Continued*).

—(*Continued*).

Pattanapuram.			Shenkotta.			Quilon.		
Total.	Males.	Females.	Total.	Males.	Females.	Total.	Males.	Females.
39	40	41	42	43	44	45	46	47
158	85	73	362	184	178	93	45	48
...	...	...	...	...	...	...	...	...
8	8	...	28	16	12	56	28	28
...	...	...	250	120	130	33	15	18
...	...	...	...	...	...	...	...	...
18	13	5	...	...	...	1,070	538	532
...	...	...	317	157	160	172	85	87
99	48	51	14	12	2	118	74	44
117	61	56	581	289	292	1,393	712	681
...	...	...	...	...	...	...	...	...
4,375	2,238	2,137	716	325	391	25,371	12,492	12,879
...	...	...	...	...	...	...	...	...
277	144	133	2,192	1,118	1,074	889	477	412
212	104	108	...	...	...	3,535	1,744	1,791
4,864	2,486	2,378	2,908	1,443	1,465	29,795	14,713	15,082
27	10	17	297	152	145	176	92	84
...	...	...	...	...	...	...	...	...
...	...	...	...	...	...	22	12	10
...	...	...	...	...	...	22	12	10
8,653	4,381	4,272	10,657	5,270	5,387	40,294	19,989	20,305

TABLE

Castes, Tribes and Races, by

Class.	Group.	Caste, &c.	Taluqs: Kunnattur. Total.	Kunnattur. Males.	Kunnattur. Females.	Karunagappalli. Total.	Karunagappalli. Males.	Karunagappalli. Females.
1	2	3	48	49	50	51	52	53
D. Artisans and Village Menials.	28. Potters.	Kosava ...	179	98	81	26	14	12
	30. Salt, &c., workers.	Alava ...	...	...	...	...	...	...
	31. Lime burners.	Paravan ...	102	49	53	...	...	...
	35. Fishermen, Boatmen, Palki-bearers, Water-bearers, Cooks, &c.	1 Chaluppan ...	...	...	...	...	...	...
		2 Kāhar ...	...	...	...	...	...	...
		3 Marakkān ...	337	159	178	750	367	383
		4 Mukkuva ...	...	..	...	5,728	2,737	2,991
		5 Pōndan ...	7	5	2	64	33	31
		Total Group 35 ...	344	164	180	6,542	3,137	3,405
	35 (*a*). Personal service.	Chākkār ...	...	...	...	...	...	...
	36. Distillers and Toddy-drawers.	1 Iluva ...	10,181	5,146	5,035	30,628	14,805	15,823
		2 Pāshi ...	...	...	..	...	...	...
		3 Chānnān ...	299	150	149	91	48	43
		4 Tandān ..	752	393	359	4,669	2,233	2,436
		Total Group 36 ...	11,232	5,689	5,543	35,388	17,086	18,302
	38. Leather-workers.	Chemmān ...	20	10	10	141	68	73
	39. Scavengers.	1 Dāss ...	...	...	...	...	...	...
		2 Valluvan ...	...	...	...	...	...	...
		Total Group 39 ...	...	...	...	...	...	...
		Total Class D. ...	17,196	8,661	8,535	50,840	24,532	26,308

XVI.

Nationality or Traditional Occupation—(*Continued*).

—(*Continued*).

Kartigappalli.			Mavellikkara.			Cheuganur.		
Total.	Males.	Females.	Total.	Males.	Females.	Total.	Males.	Females.
54	55	56	57	58	59	60	61	62
120	59	61	72	37	35	80	46	34
...	..	...	...	...	...	...	...	...
...	...	...	42	17	25	239	126	113
...	...	...	...	...	...	...	...	...
...	...	...	...	...	...	...	...	...
...	...	...	12	9	3	...	...	...
1,828	955	873	...	...	...	58	31	27
142	73	69	21	12	9	50	29	21
1,970	1,028	942	33	21	12	108	60	48
...	...	...	...	...	...	107	62	45
28,169	13,535	14,634	22,655	11,246	11,409	14,059	7,158	6,901
...	...	...	...	...	...	...	...	...
474	230	244	...	...	...	417	219	198
2,886	1,393	1,493	1,880	977	903	49	26	23
31,529	15,158	16,371	24,535	12,223	12,312	14,525	7,403	7,122
7	2	5	97	50	47	27	16	11
...	...	...	...	...	...	...	...	..
...	...	...	...	...	...	...	...	...
...	...	...	...	...	...	...	...	...
41,926	20,362	21,564	30,775	15,411	15,364	21,186	10,901	10,285

TABLE

Castes, Tribes and Races, by

Class.	Group.	Caste, &c.	Taluqs: Tiruvalla. Total.	Tiruvalla. Males.	Tiruvalla. Females.	Ambalappula. Total.	Ambalappula. Males.	Ambalappula. Females.
1		3	63	64	65	66	67	68
D. Artisans and Village Menials.	28. Potters.	Kosava ...	13	7	6	54	29	25
	30. Salt, &c., workers.	Alava ...	...	...	..	...	...	...
	31. Lime-burners.	Paravan ...	8	4	4	72	31	41
	34. Fishermen, Boatmen, Palki-bearers, Water-bearers, Cooks, &c.	1 Chaluppan ...	...	...	...	...	...	...
		2 Kābar ...	...	...	...	...	...	...
		3 Marakkān ...	825	419	406	...	...	...
		4 Mukkuva ...	55	21	34	4,678	2,310	2,368
		5 Pōndan ..	...	...	...	...	...	...
		Total Group 35 ...	880	440	440	4,678	2,310	2,368
	35 (*a*). Personal service.	Chākkar ...	458	244	214	...	...	...
	36. Distillers and Toddy-drawers.	1 Īluva ...	13,403	6,770	6,633	19,388	9,399	9,989
		2 Pāshi ...	...	...	...	...	...	...
		3 Chānnān ...	...	.	...	3	2	1
		4 Tandān ...	351	197	154	109	64	45
		Total Group 36 ...	13,754	6,967	6,787	19,500	9,465	10,035
	38. Leather-workers.	Chemmān ..	24	9	15	71	35	36
	39. Scavengers.	1 Dāss ...	...	...	...	10	5	5
		2 Valluvan ...	...	...	...	...	...	...
		Total Group 39 ...	...	...	...	10	5	5
		Total Class D. ...	22,404	11,346	11,058	30,846	15,053	15,793

XVI.

Nationality or Traditional Occupation—(*Continued*).

—(*Continued*).

Sherttala.			Vykkam.			Ettumanur.		
Total.	Males.	Females.	Total.	Males.	Females.	Total.	Males.	Females.
69	70	71	72	73	74	75	76	77
96	51	45	183	85	98	246	111	135
...	...	...	...	...	...	...	...	...
145	75	70	767	392	375	1,047	545	502
... ... 1,936 2,906 ...	... ... 990 1,501 ...	... ... 946 1,405 ...	... ... 6,019 23	... ... 3,051 11	... ... 2,968 12	... ... 502 ...	... ... 255 ...	... ... 247 ...
4,842	2,491	2,351	6,042	3,062	2,980	502	255	247
...	...	...	...	...	...	...	...	...
52,896 48	26,302 20	26,594 28	25,604	12,873	12,731	12,057	6,253	5,804 ... ...
52,944	26,322	26,622	25,604	12,873	12,731	12,057	6,253	5,804
...	...	...	12	10	2	4	2	2
... ...	... ...	... ...	... ...	... ...	... ...	... ...	... ...	... ...
...	...	...	...	...	...	...	...	...
63,433	31,689	31,744	37,647	18,892	18,755	19,090	9758	9,332

TABLE

Castes, Tribes and Races, by

Class.	Group.	Caste, &c.	Kottayam. Total.	Kottayam. Males.	Kottayam. Females.	Changanacheri. Total.	Changanacheri. Males.	Changanacheri. Females.
1	2	3	78	79	80	81	82	83
D. Artisans and Village Menials.	28. Potters.	Kosava ...	47	31	16	124	66	58
	30. Salt, &c., workers.	Alava ...	...	...	...	...	...	...
	31. Lime-burners.	Paravan ...	1,139	582	557	222	96	126
	35. Fishermen, Boatmen, Palki-bearers, Water-bearers, Cooks, &c.	1 Chaluppan ...	...	...	...	...	...	...
		2 Kāhar ...	...	...	...	...	...	...
		3 Marakkān ...	...	...	...	...	...	...
		4 Mukkuva ..	96	44	52	57	28	29
		5 Pōndan ...	...	...	...	...	...	...
		Total Group 35 ...	96	44	52	57	28	29
	35 (*a*). Personal services.	Chākkār ...	...	...	...	...	...	...
	36. Distillers and Toddy-drawers.	1 Īluva ...	12,475	6,262	6,213	8,649	4,475	4,174
		2 Pāshi ...	...	...	...	...	...	...
		3 Chānnān ...	87	59	28	...	...	...
		4 Tandān ...	18	10	8	302	142	160
		Total Group 36 ...	12,580	6,331	6,249	8,951	4,617	4,334
	38. Leather-workers.	Chemmān ...	18	10	8	9	5	4
	39. Scavengers.	1 Dāss ...	...	...	...	...	...	...
		2 Valluvan ...	80	38	42	...	...	...
		Total Group 39 ...	80	38	42	...	..	...
		Total Class B. ...	19,521	9,879	9,642	14,287	7,384	6,903

XVI.

Nationality or Traditional Occupation—(*Continued*).

—(*Continued*).

Meenachal.			Muvattupula.			Todupula.		
Total.	Males.	Females.	Total.	Males.	Females.	Total.	Males.	Females.
84	85	86	87	88	89	90	91	92
34	21	13	154	76	78	...	...	...
...	...	...	...	...	...	...	...	...
402	194	208	627	314	313	275	137	138
... ... 1,049 ...	... ... 522 ...	... ... 527 ...	... ... 523 ...	... ... 259 ...	... ... 264 ...	... ... 1,227 ...	... ... 622 ...	... ... 605 ...
1,049	522	527	523	259	264	1,227	622	605
...	...	...	...	...	...	...	...	...
6,431 41	3,389 29	3,042 12	11,495	5,669	5,826	3,565	1,783	1,782 ... ...
6,472	3,418	3,054	11,495	5,669	5,826	3,565	1,783	1,782
...	...	...	4	3	1	...	...	...
... ...	... ...	... ...	... ...	... ...	... ...	... ...	... ...	... ...
...	...	...	...	...	...	...	...	...
11,407	5,915	5,492	19,560	9,748	9,812	6,632	3,308	3,324

TABLE

Castes, Tribes and Races, by

Class.	Group.	Caste.	Taluqs: Kunnattunadu. Total.	Kunnattunadu. Males.	Kunnattunadu. Females.	Alangadu. Total.	Alangadu. Males.	Alangadu. Females.
1	2	3	93	94	95	96	97	98
D. Artisans and Village Menials.	28. Potters.	Kosava ...	532	284	248	628	309	319
	30. Salt, &c., workers.	Alava ...	...	...	...	...	...	...
	31. Lime-burners.	Paravan ...	64	40	24	...	...	...
	35. Fishermen, Boatmen, Palki-bearers, Water-bearers, Cooks, &c.	1 Chaluppan ...	...	...	...	...	...	...
		2 Kāhar ...	...	...	...	...	...	...
		3 Marakkan ...	...	...	...	...	...	...
		4 Mukkuva ...	496	244	252	293	144	149
		5 Pōndan ...	...	...	...	...	...	...
		Total Group 35 ...	496	244	252	293	144	149
	35 (*a*). Personal service.	Chākkār ...	...	...	...	...	...	...
	36. Distillers and Toddy-drawers.	1 Īluva ..	14,880	7,323	7,557	9,968	5,073	4,895
		2 Pāshi ...	...	...	...	...	...	...
		3 Chānnān ...	...	...	...	...	...	...
		4 Tandān ...	29	16	13	...	...	...
		Total Group 36 ..	14,909	7,339	7,570	9,968	5,073	4,895
	38. Leather workers.	Chemmān ...	31	20	11	...	...	...
	39. Scavengers.	1 Dāss ...	...	...	...	...	...	...
		2 Valluvan ...	...	...	...	...	...	...
		Total Group 39 ...	...	...	..	...	...	...
		Total Class D. ...	23,425	11,682	11,748	15,532	7,837	7,695

XVI.

Nationality or Traditional Occupation—(*Continued*).

—(*Continued*).

Parur.			Cardamom Hills.			Periyar and Thekkadi.		
Total.	Males.	Females.	Total.	Males.	Females.	Total.	Males.	Females.
99	100	101	102	103	104	105	106	107
28	11	17	16	6	10	...	...	...
...	...	...	...	...	...	...	...	...
...	...	...	8	8	...	...	...	...
...	...	...	...	...	...	...	...	...
...	...	...	...	...	...	1	1	...
...	...	...	...	...	...	...	...	...
2,799	1,353	1,446	9	9	...	...	...	...
...	...	...	...	...	...	84	65	19
2,799	1,353	1,446	9	9	...	85	66	19
...	...	...	...	...	...	...	...	...
16,459	8,395	8,064	405	294	111	38	35	3
...	...	...	...	...	...	3	3	...
...	...	...	785	569	216	24	15	9
...	...	...	1,138	564	574	...	...	...
16,459	8,395	8,064	2,328	1,427	901	65	53	12
...	...	...	154	76	78	39	20	19
...	...	...	...	...	...	...	...	...
...	...	...	...	...	...	...	...	...
...	...	...	...	...	...	...	...	...
21,868	11,060	10,808	2,811	1,683	1,128	304	235	69

TABLE

Castes, Tribes and Races, by

Class.	Group.	Caste, &c.	No. of recorded sub-divisions.	Religion.	Total.	Males.
		Name and Classification.			State	
1	2	3	4	5	6	7
E. Vagrant minor Artisans and Performers.	40. Grind-stone makers and stone-quarriers.	Kallāsāri ...	3	Hindu...	*8,138*	**4,079**
	41. Earth-workers & stone-dressers.	1 Ottan ...	...	Hindu...	*377*	**292**
		2 Ottiya ...	...	" ...	*25*	**10**
		Total Group 41 ...	...	...	**402**	**302**
	43. Mat-makers, cane-splitters, grass-cutters, &c.	Nolayan ...	1	Hindu...	*2,323*	**1,260**
	44. Hunters, Fowlers, &c.	1 Talavan ...	...	Hindu...	*756*	**371**
		2 Vēdan ...	1	" ...	*6,809*	**3,498**
		3 Vettāran ...	...	" ...	*349*	**178**
		Total Group 44 ...	...	...	**7,914**	**4,047**
	45. Miscellaneous and disreputable vagrants.	1 Kākkālan ...	1	Hindu...	*897*	**422**
		2 Passiavan ...	...	" ...	*64*	**35**
		Total Group 45 ...	...	...	**961**	**457**
	45(*a*). Beggars.	1 Panisivan ...	...	Hindu...	*58*	**32**
		2 Sangampandāram ...	10	" ...	*10,724*	**5,416**
		Total Group 45 (*a*).	...	...	**10,782**	**5,448**
	46. Tumblers and Acrobats.	1 Gopāl ...	...	Hindu...	*4*	**3**
		2 Kūttādi ...	...	" ...	*38*	**17**
		Total Group 46 ...	...	...	**42**	**20**
	47. Jugglers, snake charmers and animal exhibitors.	Kuluvan ...	1	Hindu...	*73*	**42**
		Total Class E. ...	...	...	*30,635*	*15,655*

XVI.

Nationality or Traditional Occupation—(*Continued*).

Total.	Taluqs.								
	Tovala.			Agastiswaram.			Eranial.		
Females.	Total.	Males.	Females.	Total.	Males.	Females.	Total.	Males.	Females.
8	9	10	11	12	13	14	15	16	17
4,059	65	35	30	406	204	202	251	116	135
85 15	... ...	... ...	... ...	... ...	... ...	... ...	... ...	... ...	... ...
100	...	...	...	...	...	...	...	...	...
1,063	...	...	...	21	21	...	139	73	66
385 3,311 171	... 2 ...	... 1 ...	... 1 ...	 327	 166	 161	 21	 11	 10
3,867	2	1	1	327	166	161	21	11	10
475 29	... 9	... 3	... 6	... 55	... 32	... 23	... ...	... ...	... ...
504	9	3	6	55	32	23	...	...	...
26	...	...	...	11	8	3	...	...	...
5,308	300	124	176	567	283	284	506	271	235
5,334	300	124	176	578	291	287	506	271	235
1 21	... ...	... ...	... ...	... 38	... 17	... 21	... ...	... ...	... ...
22	...	...	...	38	17	21	...	...	...
31	...	...	...	36	20	16	3	3	...
14,980	376	163	213	1,461	751	710	920	474	446

TABLE

Castes, Tribes and Races, by

Class.	Group.	Caste, &c.	Taluqs Kalkulam. Total.	Kalkulam. Males.	Kalkulam. Females.	Vilavankodu. Total.	Vilavankodu. Males.	Vilavankodu. Females.
1	2	3	18	19	20	21	22	23
E. Vagrant minor Artisans and Performers.	40. Grind-stone makers and stone-quarriers.	Kallāsāri ...	229	123	106	66	32	34
	41. Earth-workers & stone-dressers.	1 Ottan ...	...	...	...	...	...	...
		2 Ottiya ...	...	...	...	...	...	...
		Total Group 41 ...	...	...	...	...	...	...
	43. Mat-makers, cane-splitters, grass-cutters, &c.	Nolayan ...	26	14	12	269	135	134
	44. Hunters, Fowlers, &c.	1 Talavan ...	...	...	...	...	...	...
		2 Vēdan ...	40	18	22	...	...	...
		3 Vettāran ...	...	...	...	...	...	...
		Total Group 44 ...	40	18	22	...	...	...
	45. Miscellaneous and disreputable vagrants.	1 Kākkālan ...	...	...	...	...	...	...
		2 Passiavan ...	...	...	...	...	...	...
		Total Group 45 ...	...	...	...	...	...	...
	45(*a*). Beggars.	1 Panisivan ...	22	13	9	...	...	...
		2 Sangampandāram ...	240	135	105	168	95	73
		Total Group 45(*a*).	262	148	114	168	95	73
	46. Tumblers and Acrobats.	1 Gopāl ...	...	.	...	...	...	...
		2 Kūttādi ...	...	...	..	...	...	...
		Total Group 46 ...	...	...	...	...	...	...
	47. Jugglers, snake charmers and animal exhibitors.	Kuluvan ...	10	7	3	...	...	...
		Total Class E. ...	567	310	257	503	262	241

XVI.

Nationality or Traditional Occupation—(*Continued*).

—(*Continued*).

Neyattankara.			Trivandram.			Nedumangadu.		
Total.	Males.	Females.	Total.	Males.	Females.	Total.	Males.	Females.
24	25	26	27	28	29	30	31	32
159	76	83	399	201	198	280	136	144
...	...	...	103	49	54	19	11	8
...	...	...	...	...	...	...	...	...
...	...	...	103	49	54	19	11	8
952	521	431	718	377	341	...	...	...
16	10	6	...	...	...	87	46	41
212	106	106	4	2	2	1,153	603	550
...	...	...	1	1	...	...	...	...
228	116	112	5	3	2	1,240	649	591
...	...	...	...	...	...	...	...	...
...	...	...	...	...	...	...	...	...
...	...	...	...	...	...	...	...	...
...	...	...	...	...	...	25	11	14
601	310	291	592	327	265	1,135	585	550
601	310	291	592	327	265	1,160	596	564
...	...	...	4	3	1	...	...	...
...	...	...	...	...	...	...	...	...
...	...	...	4	3	1	...	...	...
...	...	...	12	2	10	...	...	...
1,940	1,023	917	1,833	962	871	2,699	1,392	1,307

TABLE

Castes, Tribes and Races, by

Class.	Group.	Caste, &c.	Taluqs: Sirayinkil. Total.	Males.	Females.	Kottarakkara. Total.	Males.	Females.
1	2	3	33	34	35	36	37	38
E. Vagrant minor Artisans and Performers.	40. Grind-stone makers and stone-quarriers.	Kallāsāri ...	39	20	19	104	42	62
	41. Earth-workers & stone-dressers.	1 Ottan ...	...	...	...	...	...	...
		2 Ottiya ...	...	...	...	...	...	...
		Total Group 41 ...	...	...	...	...	...	...
	43. Mat-makers, cane-splitters, grass-cutters, &c.	Nolayan ...	198	119	79	...	...	...
	44. Hunters, Fowlers, &c.	1 Talavan ...	...	...	...	382	188	194
		2 Vēdan ...	972	516	456	2,125	1,033	1,092
		3 Vettāran ...	...	...	...	...	...	...
		Total Group 44 ..	972	516	456	2,507	1,221	1,286
	45. Miscellaneous and disreputable vagrants.	1 Kākkālan ...	...	...	...	99	54	45
		2 Passiavan ...	...	...	...	...	...	...
		Total Group 45 ...	...	...	...	99	54	45
	45(*a*). Beggars.	1 Panisivan ...	...	...	...	...	...	...
		2 Saugampandāram ...	296	130	166	550	272	278
		Total Group 45(*a*).	296	130	166	550	272	278
	46. Tumblers and Acrobats.	1 Gopāl ...	...	...	...	...	...	...
		Kūttādi ...	...	...	...	...	...	...
		Total Group 46 ...	...	...	...	...	...	...
	47. Jugglers, snake charmers and animal exhibitors.	Kuluvan ...	...	...	...	...	...	...
		Total Class E. ...	1,505	785	720	3,260	1,589	1,671

XVI.

Nationality or Traditional Occupation—(*Continued*).

—(*Continued*).

Pattanapuram.			Shenkotta.			Quilon.		
Total.	Males.	Females.	Total.	Males.	Females.	Total.	Males.	Females.
39	40	41	42	43	44	45	46	47
246	120	126	299	158	141	413	200	213
...	...	...	...	...	...	...	...	...
...	...	...	...	...	...	...	...	...
...	...	...	...	...	...	...	...	..
...	...	...	...	...	...	...	...	...
182	82	100	...	...	...	...	...	...
511	263	248	...	...	...	878	464	414
...	...	...	...	...	...	...	...	...
693	345	348	...	...	...	878	464	414
20	13	7	...	...	...	54	22	32
...	...	...	...	...	...	...	..	...
20	13	7	...	...	...	54	22	32
...	...	...	...	...	...	...	...	...
224	116	108	169	74	95	156	83	73
224	116	108	169	74	95	156	83	73
...	...	...	...	...	...	...	...	...
...	...	...	...	...	...	...	...	...
...	...	...	...	...	...	...	...	...
...	...	...	...	..	...	12	10	2
1,183	594	589	468	232	236	1,513	779	734

TABLE

Castes, Tribes and Races, by

Class.	Group.	Caste, &c.	Taluqs: Kunnattur. Total.	Kunnattur. Males.	Kunnattur. Females.	Karunagappalli. Total.	Karunagappalli. Males.	Karunagappalli. Females.
1	2	3	48	49	50	51	52	53
E. Vagrant minor Artisans and Performers.	40. Grind-stone makers and stone-quarriers.	Kallāsāri ...	194	93	101	448	217	231
	41. Earth-workers & stone-dressers.	1 Ottan ...	...	...	...	...	...	...
		2 Ottiya ...	...	...	...	...	...	...
		Total Group 41 ...	...	...	...	...	...	...
	43. Mat-makers, cane splitters, grass-cutters, &c.	Nolayan ...	...	...	...	...	...	...
	44. Hunters, Fowlers, &c.	1 Talavan ...	89	45	44	...	...	...
		2 Vēdan ...	140	75	65	46	22	24
		3 Vettāran ...	...	...	...	...	...	...
		Total Group 44 ...	229	120	109	46	22	24
	45. Miscellaneous and disreputable vagrants.	1 Kākkālan ...	89	43	46	118	53	65
		2 Passiavan ...	...	...	...	...	...	...
		Total Group 45 ...	89	43	46	118	53	65
	45(*a*). Beggars.	1 Panisivan ...	...	...	...	...	...	...
		2 Sangampandāram ...	467	228	239	489	235	254
		Total Group 45(*a*).	467	228	239	489	235	254
	46. Tumblers and Acrobats.	1 Gopāl ...	...	...	...	...	...	...
		2 Kūttādi ...	...	...	...	...	...	...
		Total Group 46 ...	...	...	...	...	...	...
	47. Jugglers, snake charmers and animal exhibitors.	Kuluvan ...	...	...	...	...	...	...
		Total Class E. ...	979	484	495	1,101	527	574

XVI.

Nationality or Traditional Occupation—(*Continued*).

—(*Continued*).

Kartigappalli.			Mavellikkara.			Chenganur.		
Total.	Males.	Females.	Total.	Males.	Females.	Total.	Males.	Females.
54	55	56	57	58	59	60	61	62
96	50	46	132	86	46	624	306	318
...	...	...		...	...	...	...	...
..	...	...			...	6	2	4
...	...	...	...	.	..	6	2	4
...	...	..	.	...	..	...	...	...
...	...	...	...	...	...	...	...	...
...	...	...	16	5	11	122	53	69
...	...	...	...	..	...	..	...	...
...	...	...	16	5	11	122	53	69
65	31	34	105	41	64	48	26	22
...	...	...	...	...	...	...	...	...
65	31	34	105	41	64	48	26	22
...	...	...	...	...	.	...	...	...
592	304	288	806	431	375	394	186	208
592	304	288	806	431	375	394	186	208
...	...	..	...	...	...	...	..	...
...	...	...	...	...	...	...	...	...
...	...	...	...	...	.		...	...
...	...	...	...	...	...	...	...	...
753	385	368	1,059	563	496	1,194	573	621

TABLE

Castes, Tribes and Races, by

Class.	Group.	Caste, &c.	Taluqs: Tiruvalla. Total.	Tiruvalla. Males.	Tiruvalla. Females.	Ambalappula. Total.	Ambalappula. Males.	Ambalappula. Females.
1	2	3	63	64	65	66	67	68
E. Vagrant minor Artisans and Performers.	40. Grind-stone makers and stone-quarriers.	Kallāsāri ...	338	175	163	256	124	132
	41. Earth-workers & stone-dressers.	1 Ottan ...	...	...	...	...	...	...
		2 Ottiya ...	19	8	11	...	..	...
		Total Group 41 ..	19	8	11	...	...	...
	43. Mat-makers, cane-splitters, grass-cutters, &c.	Nolayan ...	...	...	...	...	...	...
	44. Hunters, Fowlers, &c.	1 Talavan ...	...	...	...	...	...	...
		2 Vēdan ...	138	66	72	...	...	...
		3 Vettāran ..	...	...	...	...	..	...
		Total Group 44 ...	138	66	72	...	...	...
	45. Miscellaneous and disreputable vagrants.	1 Kākkālan ...	114	60	54	8	4	4
		2 Passiavan ...	...	...	...	...	...	...
		Total Group 45 ...	114	60	54	8	4	4
	45(*a*). Beggars.	1 Panisivan ...	...	...	...	...	...	...
		2 Sangampandāram ...	317	171	146	11	6	5
		Total Group 45(*a*).	317	171	146	11	6	5
	46. Tumblers and Acrobats.	1 Gopāl ...	...	...	...	...	...	...
		2 Kūttādi ...	...	...	...	...	...	...
		Total Group 46 ...	...	...	...	...	...	...
	47. Jugglers, snake charmers and animal exhibitors.	Kuluvan ...	...	...	...	...	...	...
		Total Class E. ...	926	480	446	275	134	141

XVI.

Nationality or Traditional Occupation—(*Continued*).

—(*Continued*).

Sherttala.			Vykkam.			Ettumanur.		
Total.	Males.	Females.	Total.	Males.	Females.	Total.	Males.	Females.
69	70	71	72	73	74	75	76	77
...	...	...	198	104	94	340	168	172
... ...	... ...	... ...	... ...	... ...	... ...	... ...	... ...	... ...
...	...	...	...	...	...	...	...	...
...	...	...	...	...	...	...	...	...
... 5 ...	... 1 ...	... 4 ...	... 14 ...	... 8 ...	... 6 ...	... 23 ...	... 14 ...	... 9 ...
5	1	4	14	8	6	23	14	9
... ...	... ...	... ...	... ...	... ...	... ...	32 ...	13 ...	19 ...
...	...	...	...	...	...	32	13	19
... 7	... 6	... 1	... 57	... 26	... 31	... 275	... 118	... 157
7	6	1	57	26	31	275	118	157
... ...	... ...	... ...	... ...	... ...	... ...	... ...	... ...	... ...
...	...	...	...	...	...	...	...	...
...	...	...	...	...	...	...	...	...
12	7	5	269	138	131	670	313	357

TABLE

Castes, Tribes and Races, by

Class.	Group.	Caste, &c.	Taluqs: Kottayam. Total.	Kottayam. Males.	Kottayam. Females.	Changanacheri. Total.	Changanacheri. Males.	Changanacheri. Females.
1	2	3	78	79	80	81	82	83
E. Vagrant minor Artisans and Performers.	40. Grind-stone makers and stone-quarriers.	Kallāsāri ...	311	163	148	292	158	134
	41. Earth-workers & stone-dressers.	1 Ottan ...	1	1	...	...	...	...
		2 Ottiya ...	...		...	...	...	...
		Total Group 41 ...	1	1	...	...	...	...
	43. Mat-makers, cane-splitters, grass-cutters, &c.	Nolayan ...	...	...	...	...	...	...
	44. Hunters, Fowlers, &c.	1 Talavan ...	..	...	...	...	...	...
		2 Vēdan ...	...	...	...	80	35	45
		3 Vettāran ...	...	...	...	...	...	...
		Total Group 44 ...	...	...	...	80	35	45
	45. Miscellaneous and disreputable vagrants.	1 Kākkālan ...	45	16	29	22	12	10
		2 Passiavan ...	...	...	...	...	...	...
		Total Group 45 ...	45	16	29	22	12	10
	45(a). Beggars.	1 Panisivan ...	...	...	...	...	..	...
		2 Sangampandāram ...	161	96	65	53	19	34
		Total Group 45(a).	161	96	65	53	19	34
	46. Tumblers and Acrobats.	1 Gopāl ...	...	...	...	...	...	...
		2 Kūttādi ...	...	...	...	...	...	...
		Total Group 46 ...	...	...	...	...	..	...
	47. Jugglers, snake charmers and animal exhibitors.	Kuluvan ...	...	...	...	...	...	...
		Total Class E. ...	518	276	242	447	224	223

XVI.

Nationality or Traditional Occupation—(*Continued*).

—(*Continued*).

Meenachal.			Muvattupula.			Todupula.		
Total.	Males.	Females.	Total.	Males.	Females.	Total.	Males.	Females.
84	85	86	87	88	89	90	91	92
132	69	63	698	345	353	157	72	85
...	...	...	...	...	...	...	...	...
...	...	...	...	...	...	...	...	...
...	...	...	...	...	...	...	...	...
...	...	...	...	...	...	...	...	...
...	...	...	...	...	...	...	...	...
43	25	18	13	8	5	...	...	...
...	...	...	...	...	...	...	...	...
43	25	18	13	8	5	...	...	...
4	3	1	19	10	9	2	1	1
...	...	...	...	...	...	...	...	...
4	3	1	19	10	9	2	1	1
...	...	...	...	...	...	...	...	...
118	59	59	610	314	296	52	29	23
118	59	59	610	314	296	52	29	23
...	...	...	...	...	...	...	...	...
...	...	...	...	...	...	...	...	...
...	...	...	...	...	...	...	...	...
...	...	...	...	...	...	...	...	...
297	156	141	1,340	677	663	211	102	109

TABLE

Castes, Tribes and Races, by

Class.	Group.	Caste, &c.	Taluqs: Kunnattunadu. Total.	Kunnattunadu. Males.	Kunnattunadu. Females.	Alangadu. Total.	Alangadu. Males.	Alangadu. Females.
1	2	3	93	94	95	96	97	98
E. Vagrant minor Artisans and Performers.	40. Grind-stone makers and stone-quarriers.	Kallāsāri ...	287	138	149	369	175	194
	41. Earth-workers & stone-dressers.	1 Ottan ...	...	...	...	...	...	...
		2 Ottiya ...	...	...	...	...	...	...
		Total Group 41 ..	..	...	...	...	...	...
	43. Mat-makers, cane-splitters, grass-cutters, &c.	Nolayan ...	...	...	...	...	...	...
	44. Hunters, Fowlers, &c.	1 Talavan ...	...	...	...	...	...	...
		2 Vēdan ...	...	...	...	7	7	...
		3 Vettāran ...	...	...	...	...	...	...
		Total Group 44 ...	...	...	...	7	7	...
	45. Miscellaneous and disreputable vagrants.	1 Kākkālan ...	46	16	30	...	...	...
		2 Passiavan ...	...	...	...	...	...	...
		Total Group 45 ...	46	16	30	...	...	...
	45(*a*). Beggars.	1 Panisivan ...	...	...	...	...	...	...
		2 Sangampandāram ...	404	176	228	275	138	137
		Total Group 45(*a*).	404	176	228	275	138	137
	46. Tumblers and Acrobats.	1 Gopāl ...	...	...	...	...	...	...
		2 Kūttādi ...	...	...	...	...	...	...
		Total Group 46 ...	...	...	...	...	...	...
	47. Jugglers, snake charmers and animal exhibitors.	Kuluvan ...	...	...	...	...	...	...
		Total Class E. ...	737	330	407	651	320	331

XVI.

Nationality or Traditional Occupation—(*Continued*).

—(*Continued*).

Parur.			Cardamom Hills.			Periyar & Thekkadi.		
Total.	Males.	Females.	Total.	Males.	Females.	Total.	Males.	Females.
99	100	101	102	103	104	105	106	107
105	56	49	125	71	54	80	46	34
... ...	... ...	... ...	... ...	... ...	... ...	254 ...	231 ...	23 ...
...	...	...		...	...	254	231	23
...	...	...	...	...	...	...	...	...
... 164 ...	... 80 ...	... 84 ...	... ...	... ...	... ...	... 101 ...	... 93 ...	... 8 ...
164	80	84	...	...	...	101	93	8
7 ...	4 ..	3 ...	... ..	... ...	... ...	... ...	... ...	... ...
7	4	3	...	...	...	...	...	...
...	...	...	...	...	...	...	...	...
55	8	47	34	31	3	43	30	13
55	8	47	34	31	3	43	30	13
... ...	... ...	... ...	... ...	... ...	... ...	... ..	... ...	... ...
...	...	...	...	...	...	...	...	...
...	...	...	...	...	...	...	...	...
331	148	183	159	102	57	478	400	78

TABLE

Castes, Tribes and Races, by

Class.	Group.	Caste, &c.	No. of recorded sub-divisions.	Religion.	State Total.	Males.
1	2	3	4	5	6	7
F. Races and Nationalities.	48. Asiatic races of reputed non-Indian descent.	1 Arabs ...	2	Muslmn..	*446*	260
		2 Chinese ...	...	Christn..	*1*	1
		3 Jew ...	...	Jew ...	*125*	65
		4 Kābūl ...	...	Muslmn.	*129*	84
		5 Mughal ...	...	,, ...	*582*	317
		6 Parsi ...	...	Parsi ...	*1*	1
		7 Pathān ..	...	Muslmn..	*4,353*	2,508
		8 Sheik ...	...	,, ..	*414*	240
		9 Singhalese ...	...	Hindu ...	*29*	17
		10 Syed ...	...	Muslmn.	*232*	117
		Total Group 48 ...	...	...	6,312	3,610
	50 Non-Asiatic races.	European ...	10	{ Christn. None ..	*361*	210
	51. Eurasians.	1 East Indian ...	...	Christn..	*2,072*	995
		2 Eurasian ...	...	,, ...	*532*	285
		Total Group 51 ...	...	...	2,604	1,280
	52. Christian converts.	1 Native ...	3	Christn..	*221,006*	112,489
		2 Syrian ...	5	,, ...	*297,795*	150,395
		Total Group 52 ...	...	...	518,801	262,884
		Total Class F. ...	...	...	*528,078*	*267,984*

XVI.

Nationality or Traditional Occupation—(*Continued*).

TOTAL.	TALUQS.								
	Tovala.			Agastiswaram.			Eranial.		
Females.	Total.	Males.	Females.	Total.	Males.	Females.	Total.	Males.	Females.
8	9	10	11	12	13	14	15	16	17
186	...	...	...	...	...	...	...	...	...
...	...	...	...	...	...	...	...	...	...
60	...	...	...	...	...	...	...	...	...
45	...	...	...	...	...	...	...	...	...
265	...	...	...	...	...	...	...	...	...
...	...	...	...	...	...	...	...	...	...
1,845	...	...	...	144	77	67	28	12	16
174	...	...	...	...	...	...	...	...	...
12	...	...	...	...	...	...	...	...	...
115	...	...	...	...	...	...	...	...	...
2,702	...	...	...	144	77	67	28	12	16
151	1	1	...	30	16	14	11	5	6
1,077	11	5	6	24	10	14	16	8	8
247	1	1	...	58	42	16	...	...	...
1,324	12	6	6	82	52	30	16	8	8
1,08,517	1,732	825	907	14,917	7,437	7,480	26,187	12,927	13,260
1,47,400	...	...	...	191	92	99	436	231	205
2,55,917	1,732	825	907	15,108	7,529	7,579	26,623	13,158	13,465
2,60,094	1,745	832	913	15,364	7,674	7,690	26,678	13,183	13,495

TABLE

Castes, Tribes and Races, by

Class.	Group.	Caste, &c.	Taluqs: Kalkulam. Total.	Kalkulam. Males.	Kalkulam. Females.	Vilavankodu. Total.	Vilavankodu. Males.	Vilavankodu. Females
1	2	3	18	19	20	21	22	23
F. Races and Nationalities.	48. Asiatic races of reputed non-Indian descent.	1 Arabs ...	...	...	...	...	...	...
		2 Chinese ...	...	...	...	...	...	...
		3 Jew ...	...	...	...	...	...	...
		4 Kābūl ...	...	...	...	...	...	...
		5 Mughal ...	...	...	...	...	...	...
		6 Parsi ...	...	...	...	...	...	...
		7 Pathān ...	...	...	..	...	...	...
		8 Sheik ...	...	...	...	...	...	...
		9 Singhalese ...	...	...	...	...	...	...
		10 Syed ...	14	2	12	...	...	...
		Total Group 48 ..	14	2	12	...	...	...
	50. Non-Asiatic races.	European ...	8	4	4	1	1	...
	51. Eurasians.	1 East Indian ...	7	3	4	15	7	8
		2 Eurasian ...	2	1	1	...	...	...
		Total Group 51 ...	9	4	5	15	7	8
	52. Christian converts.	1 Native ...	9,739	4,903	4,836	9,642	4,991	4,651
		2 Syrian ...	181	94	87	58	31	27
		Total Group 52 ...	9,920	4,997	4,923	9,700	5,022	4,678
		Total Class F. ...	9,951	5,007	4,944	9,716	5,030	4,686

XVI.

Nationality or Traditional Occupation—(*Continued*).

—(*Continued*).

Neyattankara.			Trivandram.			Nedumangadu.		
Total.	Males.	Females.	Total.	Males.	Females.	Total.	Males.	Females.
24	25	26	27	28	29	30	31	32
...	...	...	...	...	...	...	...	...
...	...	...	...	...	...	...	...	...
...	...	...	...	...	...	...	...	...
...	...	...	...	...	...	...	...	...
...	...	...	14	14	...	...	...	...
...	...	...	1	1	...	...	...	...
6	3	3	907	544	363	47	28	19
...	...	...	57	26	31	...	...	...
...	...	...	...	...	...	...	...	...
...	...	...	114	56	58	...	...	...
6	3	3	1,093	641	452	47	28	19
2	1	1	119	66	53	5	4	1
7	4	3	353	174	179	18	8	10
2	1	1	136	65	71	...	...	...
9	5	4	489	239	250	18	8	10
11,958	6,200	5,758	7,079	3,466	3,613	1,384	772	612
25	14	11	1,276	659	617	16	10	6
11,983	6,214	5,769	8,355	4,125	4,230	1,400	782	618
12,000	6,223	5,777	10,056	5,071	4,985	1,470	822	648

TABLE

Castes, Tribes and Races, by

Class.	Group.	Caste, &c.	Taluqs: Sirayinkil. Total.	Sirayinkil. Males.	Sirayinkil. Females.	Kottarakkara. Total.	Kottarakkara. Males.	Kottarakkara. Females.
1	2	3	33	34	35	36	37	38
F. Races and Nationalities.	48. Asiatic races of reputed non-Indian descent.	1 Arabs ...	...	...	...	...	...	...
		2 Chinese ...	...	...	...	...	...	...
		3 Jew ...	...	...	...	...	...	...
		4 Kābūl ...	...	...	...	...	...	...
		5 Mughal ...	...	...	...	23	19	4
		6 Parsi ...	...	...	...	...	...	...
		7 Pathān ...	56	44	12	157	88	69
		8 Sheik ...	...	...	...	...	...	...
		9 Singhalese ...	...	...	...	...	...	...
		10 Syed ...	...	...	...	...	...	...
		Total Group 48 ...	56	44	12	180	107	73
	50. Non-Asiatic races.	European ...	...	...	...	...	...	...
	51. Eurasians.	1 East Indian ...	7	4	3	87	40	47
		2 Eurasian ...	21	12	9	3	3	...
		Total Group 51 ...	28	16	12	90	43	47
	52. Christian converts.	1 Native ...	1,632	786	846	1,862	973	889
		2 Syrian ...	38	17	21	7,622	3,790	3,832
		Total Group 52 ...	1,670	803	867	9,484	4,763	4,721
		Total Class F. ...	1,754	863	891	9,754	4,913	4,841

XVI.

Nationality or Traditional Occupation —(*Continued*).

—(*Continued*).

Pattanapuram.			Shenkotta.			Quilon.		
Total.	Males.	Females.	Total.	Males.	Females.	Total.	Males.	Females.
39	40	41	42	43	44	45	46	47
...	...	...	...	...	...	...	...	...
...	...	...	...	...	...	...	...	...
...	...	...	...	...	...	10	5	5
...	...	...	7	7	...	122	77	45
...	...	...	...	...	...	263	126	137
...	...	...	...	...	...	...	...	...
77	44	33	105	49	56	1,047	623	424
...	...	...	...	...	...	240	157	83
...	...	...	...	...	...	...	...	...
...	...	...	...	...	...	82	43	39
77	44	33	112	56	56	1,764	1,031	733
7	4	3	12	3	9	36	21	15
19	10	9	...	...	...	276	123	153
14	8	6	5	...	5	89	52	37
33	18	15	5	...	5	365	175	190
319	176	143	427	230	197	7,934	3,812	4,122
3,448	1,707	1,741	...	...	...	8,072	4,126	3,946
3,767	1,883	1,884	427	230	197	16,006	7,938	8,068
3,884	1,949	1,935	556	289	267	18,171	9,165	9,006

TABLE

Castes, Tribes and Races, by

Class.	Group.	Caste, &c.	Kunnattur. Total.	Kunnattur. Males.	Kunnattur. Females.	Karunagappalli. Total.	Karunagappalli. Males.	Karunagappalli. Females.
1	2	3	48	49	50	51	52	53
F. Races and Nationalities.	48. Asiatic races of reputed non-Indian descent.	1 Arabs ...	...	...	...	...	...	...
		2 Chinese ...	...	...	...	...	...	...
		3 Jew ...	...	...	...	...	...	...
		4 Kābūl ...	...	...	...	...	...	...
		5 Mughal ...	...	...	...	...	...	...
		6 Parsi ...	...	...	...	...	...	...
		7 Pathān ...	18	13	5	134	73	61
		8 Sheik ...	...	...	...	...	...	...
		9 Singhalese ...	...	...	...	...	...	...
		10 Syed ...	...	...	...	...	...	...
		Total Group 48 ...	18	13	5	134	73	61
	50. Non-Asiatic races.	European ...	...	...	...	...	...	...
	51. Eurasians.	1 East Indian ...	26	9	17	59	28	31
		2 Eurasian ...	...	...	...	15	5	10
		Total Group 51 ...	26	9	17	74	33	41
	52. Christian converts.	1 Native ...	535	261	274	3,526	1,638	1.888
		2 Syrian ...	7,924	3,936	3,988	4,447	2,261	2,186
		Total Group 52 ...	8,459	4,197	4,262	7,973	3,899	4,074
		Total Class F. ...	8,503	4,219	4,284	8,181	4,005	4,176

XVI.

Nationality or Traditional Occupation—(*Continued*).

—(*Continued*).

Kartigappalli.			Mavellikkara.			Chenganur.		
Total.	Males.	Females.	Total.	Males.	Females.	Total.	Males.	Females.
54	55	56	57	58	59	60	61	62
...	...	...	...	...	...	...	...	...
...	...	...	...	...	...	...	...	...
...	...	...	...	...	...	...	...	...
...	...	...	...	...	...	...	...	...
...	...	...	201	106	95	56	33	23
...	...	...	...	...	...	...	...	...
16	5	11	36	20	16	48	30	18
...	...	...	117	57	60	...	...	...
...	...	...	...	...	...	...	...	...
...	...	...	...	...	...	...	...	...
16	5	11	354	183	171	104	63	41
...	...	...	...	...	...	...	...	...
94	43	51	41	18	23	9	5	4
6	4	2	...	...	...	...	...	...
100	47	53	41	18	23	9	5	4
534	261	273	589	295	294	2,915	1,491	1,424
7,392	3,666	3,726	13,843	7,103	6,740	22,398	11,568	10,830
7,926	3,927	3,999	14,432	7,398	7,034	25,313	13,059	12,254
8,042	3,979	4,063	14,827	7,599	7,228	25,426	13,127	12,299

TABLE

Castes, Tribes and Races, by

Class.	Group.	Caste, &c.	Taluqs: Tiruvalla. Total.	Tiruvalla. Males.	Tiruvalla. Females.	Ambalappula. Total.	Ambalappula. Males.	Ambalappula. Females.
1	2	3	63	64	65	66	67	68
F. Races and Nationalities.	48. Asiatic races of reputed non-Indian descent.	1 Arabs ...	...	...	...	157	84	73
		2 Chinese ...		...	...	...	...	...
		3 Jew ...	...	...	...	...	...	...
		4 Kābūl ...	...	...	...	...	...	...
		5 Mughal ...	...	...	...	...	...	...
		6 Parsi ...	...	...	...	...	...	...
		7 Pathān ..	81	29	52	171	99	72
		8 Sheik ...	...	...	...	...	...	...
		9 Singhalese ...	...	...	...	...	...	...
		10 Syed ...	...	...	...	...	...	...
		Total Group 48 ...	81	29	52	328	183	145
	50. Non-Asiatic races.	European ...	...	...	...	27	15	12
	51. Eurasians.	1 East Indian ...	13	7	6	443	204	239
		2 Eurasian ...	...	...	...	83	39	44
		Total Group 51 ...	13	7	6	526	243	283
	52. Christian converts.	1 Native ...	1,529	750	779	9,916	5,536	4,380
		2 Syrian ...	39,889	20,429	19,460	10,483	5,051	5,432
		Total Group 52 ...	41,418	21,179	20,239	20,399	10,587	9,812
		Total Class F. ...	41,512	21,215	20,297	21,280	11,028	10,252

XVI.

Nationality or Traditional Occupation—(*Continued*).

—(*Continued*).

Sherttala.			Vykkam.			Ettumanur.		
Total.	Males.	Females.	Total.	Males.	Females	Total.	Males.	Females.
69	70	71	72	73	74	75	76	77
...	...	...	...	...	...	...	...	...
...	...	...	...	...	...	...	...	...
...	...	...	...	...	...	...	...	...
...	...	...	...	...	...	...	...	...
...	...	...	...	...	...	9	4	5
...	...	...	...	...	...	...	...	...
44	23	21	341	190	151	...	...	...
...	...	...	...	...	...	...	...	...
...	...	...	...	...	...	...	...	...
..	...	...	...	...	...	...	...	...
44	23	21	341	190	151	9	4	5
...	...	...	4	2	2	1	1	...
21	9	12	9	5	4	4	3	1
...	...	...	...	...	...	...	...	...
21	9	12	9	5	4	4	3	1
12,376	6,145	6,231	2,528	1,308	1,220	12,305	6,366	5,939
10,586	5,287	5,299	8,960	4,675	4,285	18,674	9,430	9,244
22,962	11,432	11,530	11,488	5,983	5,505	30,979	15,796	15,183
23,027	11,464	11,563	11,842	6,180	5,662	30,993	15,804	15,189

TABLE

Castes, Tribes and Races, by

Class.	Group.	Caste, &c.	Taluqs: Kottayam. Total.	Kottayam. Males.	Kottayam. Females.	Changanacheri. Total.	Changanacheri. Males.	Changanacheri. Females.
1	2	3	78	79	80	81	82	83
F. Races and Nationalities.	48. Asiatic races of reputed non-Indian descent.	1 Arabs ...	...	...	...	...	...	...
		2 Chinese ...	...	...	...	...	...	...
		3 Jew ...	...	...	...	...	...	...
		4 Kābūl ...	...	...	...	...	...	...
		5 Mughal ...	...	...	...	...	...	...
		6 Parsi ...	...	...	...	...	...	...
		7 Pathān ...	307	168	139	32	22	10
		8 Sheik ...	...	...	...	...	...	...
		9 Singhalese ...	...	...	...	...	...	...
		10 Syed ...	...	...	...	...	...	...
		Total Group 48 ...	307	168	139	32	22	10
	50. Non-Asiatic races.	European ...	17	7	10	...	...	...
	51. Eurasians.	1 East Indian ...	81	36	45	90	41	49
		2 Eurasian ...	31	16	15	8	2	6
		Total Group 51 ...	112	52	60	98	43	55
	52. Christian converts.	1 Native ...	8,843	4,682	4,161	10,176	5,467	4,709
		2 Syrian ...	17,215	8,551	8,664	16,330	8,110	8,220
		Total Group 52 ...	26,058	13,233	12,825	26,506	13,577	12,929
		Total Class F. ...	26,494	13,460	13,034	26,636	13,642	12,994

XVI.

Nationality or Traditional Occupation—(*Continued*).

—(*Continued*).

Meenachal.			Muvattupula.			Todupula.		
Total.	Males.	Females.	Total.	Males.	Females.	Total.	Males.	Females.
84	85	86	87	88	89	90	91	92
...	...	...	...	...	...	...	...	...
...	...	...	...	...	...	...	...	...
...	...	...	...	...	...	...	...	...
...	...	...	...	...	...	...	...	...
...	...	...	...	...	...	...	...	...
..	...	...	...	...	...	...	...	...
6	3	3	23	13	10	117	61	56
...	...	...	...	...	...	...	...	...
...	...	...	...	...	...	...	...	...
...	...	...	...	...	...	...	...	...
6	3	3	23	13	10	117	61	56
2	2	...	1	1	...	..	...	...
65	27	38	40	19	21	9	4	5
...	...	...	...	...	...	...	...	...
65	27	38	40	19	21	9	4	5
15,470	8,018	7,452	8,993	4,399	4,594	2,928	1,520	1,408
15,558	7,750	7,808	34,610	17,487	17,123	4,875	2,421	2,454
31,028	15,768	15,260	43,603	21,886	21,717	7,803	3,941	3,862
31,101	15,800	15,301	43,667	21,919	21,748	7,929	4,006	3,923

TABLE

Castes, Tribes and Races, by

Class.	Group.	Caste, &c.	Taluqs: Kunnattunadu. Total.	Kunnattunadu. Males.	Kunnattunadu. Females.	Alangadu. Total.	Alangadu. Males.	Alangadu. Females.
1	2	3	93	94	95	96	97	98
F. Races and Nationalities.	48. Asiatic races of reputed non-Indian descent.	1 Arabs ...	...	...	...	...	...	...
		2 Chinese ...	...	...	...	...	...	...
		3 Jew ...	...	...	...	...	...	...
		4 Kābūl ...	...	...	...	...	...	...
		5 Mughal ...	...	...	...	...	...	...
		6 Parsi ...	...	...	...	...	...	...
		7 Pathān ...	29	28	1	18	9	9
		8 Sheik ...	...	...	...	...	...	...
		9 Singhalese ...	...	...	...	...	...	...
		10 Syed ...	...	...	...	...	...	...
		Total Group 48 ...	29	28	1	18	9	9
	50. Non-Asiatic races.	European ...	...	...	...	1	1	...
	51. Eurasians.	1 East Indian ...	50	26	24	16	9	7
		2 Eurasian ...	...	...	...	...	...	...
		Total Group 51 ...	50	26	24	16	9	7
	52. Christian converts.	1 Native ...	18,020	8,785	9,235	6,770	3,568	3,202
		2 Syrian ...	18,477	9,484	8,993	14,726	7,402	7,324
		Total Group 52 ...	36,497	18,269	18,228	21,496	10,970	10,526
		Total Class F.	36,576	18,323	18,253	21,531	10,989	10,542

XVI.

Nationality or Traditional Occupation—(*Continued*).

—(*Continued*).

Parur.			Cardamom Hills.			Periyar and Thekkadi.		
Total.	Males.	Females.	Total.	Males.	Females.	Total.	Males.	Females.
99	100	101	102	103	104	105	106	107
...	...	...	281	171	110	8	5	3
...	...	...	...	...	...	1	1	...
115	60	55	...	...	...	...	...	...
...	...	...	...	...	...	...	...	...
6	6	...	...	...	...	10	9	1
...	...	...	...	...	...	...	...	...
237	120	117	29	20	9	92	70	22
...	...	...	...	...	...	...	...	...
...	...	...	...	...	...	29	17	12
...	...	...	...	...	...	22	16	6
358	186	172	310	191	119	162	118	44
6	6	...	56	37	19	14	12	2
57	27	30	52	27	25	53	52	1
13	4	9	4	3	1	41	27	14
70	31	39	56	30	26	94	79	15
7,279	3,736	3,543	647	493	154	315	272	43
9,960	4,948	5,012	74	56	18	11	9	2
17,239	8,684	8,555	721	549	172	326	281	45
17,673	8,907	8,766	1,143	807	336	596	490	106

TABLE

Castes, Tribes and Races, by

Class.	Group.	Caste, &c.	No. of recorded sub-divisions.	Religion.	Total.	Males.	Females.
		Name and Classification.			**State Total.**		
1	2	3	4	5	6	7	8
G. Undefined.	54. Linguistic, territorial and religious names.	1 Bengalese ...	...	Hindu...	*3*	3	...
		2 Guzerāti ...	...	,, ..	*48*	28	20
		3 Jain ...	...	Jain ...	*3*	3	...
		4 Kannadiyan ...	...	Hindu...	*41*	19	22
		5 Ḳonkani ...	3	,, ...	*7,070*	3,681	3,389
		6 Kutch ...	3	Muslmn.	*316*	147	169
		7 Mussalman ...	1	,, ...	*14,750*	7,203	7,547
		8 Tamil ...	...	Hindu...	*3*	3	...
		9 Telugu ...	...	,, ...	*20*	10	10
		10 Tulukken ...	..	Muslmn.	*29,770*	15,555	14,215
		Total Group 54 ...	..	...	52,024	26,652	25,372
	55. Unknown.	1 Bālāji ...	1	Hindu...	*97*	77	20
		2 Bhavarāsi ...	...	,, ...	*11*	7	4
		3 Bhujār ...	...	,, ...	*1*	1	...
		4 Bhujavar ...	...	,, ...	*1*	1	...
		5 Chilambātti ...	...	,, ...	*9*	6	3
		6 Heathen ...	...	,, ..	*1*	1	...
		7 Kadiyan ...	...	,, ...	*3*	2	1
		8 Kāmuvar ...	...	,, ...	*2*	2	...
		9 Kodayan ...	...	,, ...	*15*	3	12
		10 Kūch ...	...	,, ...	*2*	1	1
		11 Malayānkāran..	...	,, ...	*246*	146	100
		12 Mustān ...	...	Muslmn.	*4*	1	3
		13 Nāgamom ...	...	Hindu...	*13*	5	8

XVI.

Nationality or Traditional Occupation—(*Continued*).

Taluqs.								
Tovala.			Agastiswaram.			Eranial.		
Total.	Males.	Females.	Total.	Males.	Females.	Total.	Males.	Females.
9	10	11	12	13	14	15	16	17
...	...	...	...	...	...	...	...	...
...	...	...	...	...	...	...	...	...
...	...	...	...	...	...	...	...	...
...	...	...	...	...	...	...	...	...
...	...	...	...	...	...	8	8	...
...	...	...	...	...	...	...	...	...
...	...	...	5	4	1	...	...	...
...	...	...	...	...	...	...	...	...
...	...	...	...	...	...	...	...	...
1,159	536	623	888	492	396	2,650	1,364	1,286
1,159	536	623	893	496	397	2,658	1,372	1,286
...	...	...	...	...	...	...	...	...
...	...	...	...	...	...	...	...	...
...	...	...	...	...	...	...	...	...
...	...	...	...	...	...	...	...	...
...	...	...	...	...	...	...	...	...
...	...	...	...	...	...	...	...	...
...	...	...	...	...	...	...	...	...
...	...	...	...	...	...	...	...	...
...	...	...	...	...	...	...	...	...
...	...	...	...	...	...	...	...	...
...	...	...	6	3	3	...	...	...
...	...	...	...	...	...	...	...	...
...	...	...	...	...	...	...	...	...

TABLE

Castes, Tribes and Races, by

Class.	Group.	Caste, &c.	Taluqs: Kalkulam. Total.	Kalkulam. Males.	Kalkulam. Females.	Vilavankodu. Total.	Vilavankodu. Males.	Vilavankodu. Females.
1	2	3	18	19	20	21	22	23
G. Undefined.	54. Linguistic, territorial and religious names.	1 Bengalese ...	...	...	...	...	...	...
		2 Guzerāti ...	...	...	...	...	...	...
		3 Jain ...	...	...	...	...	...	...
		4 Kannadiyan ...	...	...	...	...	...	...
		5 Konkani ...	...	...	...	...	...	...
		6 Kutch ...	...	...	...	...	...	...
		7 Mussalman ...	...	...	...	625	313	312
		8 Tamil ...	...	...	...	...	...	...
		9 Telugu ...	...	...	...	...	...	...
		10 Tulukken ...	55	34	21	537	261	276
		Total Group 54 ...	55	34	21	1,162	574	588
	55. Unknown.	1 Bālāji ...	...	...	...	...	...	...
		2 Bhavarāsi ...	...	...	...	...	...	...
		3 Bhujār ...	...	...	...	...	...	...
		4 Bhujavar ...	...	...	...	...	...	...
		5 Chilambātti ...	...	...	...	...	...	...
		6 Heathen ...	...	...	...	...	...	...
		7 Kadiyan ...	...	...	...	...	...	...
		8 Kāmuvar ...	...	...	...	2	2	...
		9 Kodayan ...	...	...	...	...	...	...
		10 Kūch ..	...	...	...	...	...	...
		11 Malayānkāran.	...	...	...	...	...	...
		12 Mustān ...	...	...	...	...	..	...
		13 Nāgamom ...	13	5	8	...	...	...

XVI.

Nationality or Traditional Occupation—(*Continued*).

—(*Continued*).

Neyattankara.			Trivandram.			Nedumangadu.		
Total.	Males.	Females.	Total.	Males.	Females.	Total.	Males.	Females.
24	25	26	27	28	29	30	31	32
...	...	...	...	...	...	...	...	...
...	...	...	...	...	...	...	...	...
...	...	...	...	...	...	...	...	...
...	...	...	4	2	2	...	...	...
...	...	...	163	91	72	6	2	4
...	...	...	184	75	109	...	...	...
7	2	5	1,387	719	668	...	...	...
...	...	...	...	...	...	...	...	...
...	...	...	...	...	...	...	...	...
2,074	1,130	944	3,062	1,541	1,521	1,233	617	616
2,081	1,132	949	4,800	2,428	2,372	1,239	619	620
...	...	...	...	...	...	...	...	...
...	...	...	...	...	...	...	...	...
...	...	...	...	...	...	...	...	...
...	...	...	...	...	...	...	...	...
...	...	...	...	...	...	...	...	...
...	...	...	1	1	...	...	...	...
...	...	...	...	...	...	...	...	...
...	...	...	...	...	...	...	...	...
...	...	...	...	...	...	...	...	...
...	...	...	...	...	...	...	...	...
...	...	...	...	...	...	...	...	...
...	...	...	...	...	...	...	...	...
...	...	...	...	...	...	...	...	...

TABLE

Castes, Tribes and Races, by

Class.	Group.	Caste, &c.	Taluqs: Sirayinkil. Total.	Sirayinkil. Males.	Sirayinkil. Females.	Kottarakkara. Total.	Kottarakkara. Males.	Kottarakkara. Females.
1	2	3	33	34	35	36	37	38
G. Undefined.	54. Linguistic, territorial and religious names.	1 Bengalese ...	...	...	...	...	...	...
		2 Guzerāti ...	...	...	...	...	...	...
		3 Jain ...	...	...	...	...	...	...
		4 Kannadiyan ...	...	...	...	...	...	...
		5 Konkani ...	78	43	35	35	16	19
		6 Kutch ...	...	...	...	...	...	...
		7 Mussalman ...	...	...	...	...	...	...
		8 Tamil ...	...	...	...	...	...	...
		9 Telugu ...	...	...	...	..	...	...
		10 Tulukken ...	2,598	1,276	1,322	1,340	691	649
		Total Group 54 ...	2,676	1,319	1,357	1,375	707	668
	55. Unknown.	1 Bālāji ...	...	...	...	...	...	...
		2 Bhavarāsi ...	...	...	...	...	...	...
		3 Bhujār ...	...	...	...	...	...	...
		4 Bhujavar ...	...	...	...	...	...	...
		5 Chilambātti ...	...	...	...	...	...	...
		6 Heathen ...	...	...	...	...	...	...
		7 Kadiyan ...	...	...	...	...	...	...
		8 Kāmuvar ...	...	...	...	...	...	...
		9 Kodayan ...	...	...	...	...	...	...
		10 Kūch ...	...	...	...	...	...	...
		11 Malayānkāran..	...	...	...	...	...	...
		12 Mustān ...	...	...	...	...	...	...
		13 Nāgamom ...	...	...	...	...	...	...

XVI.

Nationality or Traditional Occupation—(*Continued*).

—(*Continued*).

Pattanapuram.			Shenkotta.			Quilon.		
Total.	Males.	Females.	Total.	Males.	Females.	Total.	Males.	Females.
39	40	41	42	43	44	45	46	47
...	...	...	...	...	...	...	...	...
...	...	...	...	...	...	21	11	10
...	...	...	...	...	...	...	...	...
...	...	...	...	...	...	14	2	12
11	7	4	...	...	...	208	95	113
...	...	...	...	...	...	54	43	11
...	...	...	...	...	...	172	96	76
...	...	...	...	...	...	3	3	...
...	...	...	...	...	...	20	10	10
27	9	18	1,499	808	691	1,023	520	503
38	16	22	1,499	808	691	1,515	780	735
...	...	...	...	...	...	...	...	...
...	...	...	...	...	...	...	...	...
...	...	...	...	...	...	...	...	...
...	...	...	...	...	...	...	...	...
...	...	...	...	...	...	...	...	...
...	...	...	...	...	...	...	...	...
...	...	...	...	...	...	...	...	...
...	...	...	...	...	...	...	...	...
...	...	...	...	...	...	...	...	...
...	...	...	...	...	...	...	...	...
...	...	...	...	...	...	...	...	...
...	...	...	...	...	...	...	...	...
...	...	...	...	...	...	...	...	...

TABLE

Castes, Tribes and Races, by

Class.	Group.	Caste, &c.	Kunnattur. Total.	Kunnattur. Males.	Kunnattur. Females.	Karunagappalli. Total.	Karunagappalli. Males.	Karunagappalli. Females.
			Taluqs					
1	2	3	48	49	50	51	52	53
G. Undefined.	54. Linguistic, territorial and religious names.	1 Bengalese ...	...	...	...	...	...	...
		2 Guzerāti ...	...	...	...	...	...	...
		3 Jain ...	...	...	...	...	...	...
		4 Kannadiyan ...	...	...	...	...	...	...
		5 Konkani ...	47	27	20	109	51	58
		6 Kutch ...	...	...	...	...	...	...
		7 Mussalman ..	...	...	...	...	...	...
		8 Tamil ...	...	...	...	...	...	...
		9 Telugu ...	...	...	...	...	...	...
		10 Tulukken ...	...	...	...	...	...	...
		Total Group 54 ...	47	27	20	109	51	58
	55. Unknown.	1 Bālāji ...	...	...	...	...	...	...
		2 Bhavarāsi ...	...	...	...	...	...	...
		3 Bhujār ...	...	...	...	...	...	...
		4 Bhujavar ...	...	...	...	...	...	...
		5 Chilambātti ...	...	...	...	...	...	...
		6 Heathen ...	...	...	...	...	...	...
		7 Kadiyan ...	...	...	...	3	2	1
		8 Kāmuvar ...	...	...	...	...	...	...
		9 Kodayan ...	...	...	...	...	...	...
		10 Kūch ...	...	...	...	...	...	...
		11 Malayānkāran.	...	...	...	...	..	...
		12 Mustān ...	...	...	...	...	...	...
		13 Nāgamom ...	...	...	...	...	...	...

XVI.

Nationality or Traditional Occupation—(*Continued*).

—(*Continued*).

Kartigappalli.			Mavellikkara.			Chenganur.		
Total.	Males.	Females.	Total.	Males.	Females.	Total.	Males.	Females.
54	55	56	57	58	59	60	61	62
...	...	...	...	...	...	...	...	...
...	...	...	...	...	...	...	...	...
...	...	...	...	...	...	...	...	...
...	...	...	...	...	...	...	...	...
843	441	402	230	106	124	3	2	1
78	29	49	...	...	...	...	...	...
136	75	61	...	...	...	...	...	...
...	...	...	...	...	...	...	...	...
...	...	...	...	...	...	...	...	...
...	...	...	2,139	1,100	1,039	650	342	308
1,057	545	512	2,369	1,206	1,163	653	344	309
...	...	...	...	...	...	...	...	...
...	...	...	...	...	...	...	...	...
...	...	...	...	...	...	...	...	...
...	...	...	...	...	...	...	...	...
...	...	...	...	...	...	...	...	...
...	...	...	...	...	...	...	...	...
...	...	...	...	...	...	...	...	...
...	...	...	...	...	...	...	...	...
...	...	...	...	...	...	...	...	...
...	...	...	...	...	...	...	...	...
...	...	...	...	...	...	...	...	...
...	...	...	...	...	...	...	...	...
...	...	...	...	...	...	...	...	...

TABLE

Castes, Tribes and Races, by

Class.	Group.	Caste, &c.	Taluqs: Tiruvalla. Total.	Tiruvalla. Males.	Tiruvalla. Females.	Ambalappula. Total.	Ambalappula. Males.	Ambalappula. Females.
1	2	3	63	64	65	66	67	68
G. Undefined.	54. Linguistic, territorial and religious names.	1 Bengalese ...	...	...	...	...	...	...
		2 Guzerāti ...	...	...	...	...	...	...
		3 Jain ...	...	...	...	...	...	...
		4 Kannadiyan ...	...	...	...	...	...	...
		5 Konkani ...	187	108	79	1,296	666	630
		6 Kutch ...	...	...	...	...	...	...
		7 Mussalman ...	...	...	...	9,026	4,203	4,823
		8 Tamil ...	...	...	...	...	...	...
		9 Telugu ...	...	...	...	...	...	...
		10 Tulukken ...	755	392	363	5	4	1
		Total Group 54 ...	942	500	442	10,327	4,873	5,454
	55. Unknown.	1 Bālāji ...	...	...	...	...	...	...
		2 Bhavarāsi ...	...	...	...	...	...	...
		3 Bhujār ...	...	...	...	...	...	...
		4 Bhujavar ...	...	...	...	...	...	...
		5 Chilambātti ...	...	...	...	...	...	...
		6 Heathen ...	...	...	...	...	...	...
		7 Kadiyan ...	...	...	...	...	...	...
		8 Kāmuvar ...	...	...	...	..	...	...
		9 Kodayan ...	...	...	...	...	...	...
		10 Kūch ...	...	...	...	...	...	...
		11 Malayānkāran	...	...	...	...	...	...
		12 Mustān ...	...	...	...	4	1	3
		13 Nāgamom ...	...	...	...	...	...	...

XVI.

Nationality or Traditional Occupation—(*Continued*).

—(*Continued*).

Sherttala.			Vykkam.			Ettumanur.		
Total.	Males.	Females.	Total.	Males.	Females.	Total.	Males.	Females.
69	70	71	72	73	74	75	76	77
..	...	...	...	...	...	...	...	...
...	...	...	...	...	...	...	...	...
...	...	...	...	...	...	...	...	...
...	...	...	...	...	...	...	...	...
1,898	987	911	544	297	247	229	132	97
...	...	...	...	...	..	...	...	...
151	74	77	6	4	2	...	...	...
...	...	...	...	...	...	...	...	...
...	...	...	...	...	...	...	...	...
428	198	230	120	87	33	474	309	165
2,477	1,259	1,218	670	388	282	703	441	262
...	...	...	...	...	...	...	...	...
...	...	...	...	...	...	...	...	...
...	...	...	...	..	...	...	...	...
...	...	...	...	...	...	...	...	...
...	...	...	...	...	...	...	...	...
...	...	...	...	...	...	...	...	...
...	...	...	...	...	...	...	...	...
...	...	...	...	...	...	...	...	...
...	...	...	15	3	12	...	...	...
...	...	...	...	...	...	...	...	...
79	65	14	...	...	...	129	57	72
...	...	...	...	...	...	...	...	...
...	...	...	...	...	...	...	...	...

TABLE

Castes, Tribes and Races, by

Class.	Group.	Caste, &c.	Taluqs: Kottayam. Total.	Kottayam. Males.	Kottayam. Females.	Changanacheri. Total.	Changanacheri. Males.	Changanacheri. Females.
1	2	3	78	79	80	81	82	83
G. Undefined.	54. Linguistic, territorial and religious names.	1 Bengalese ...	...	...	...	...	...	...
		2 Guzerāti ...	...	...	..	...	...	...
		3 Jain ...	...	...	...	...	...	..
		4 Kannadiyan ...	...	...	...	...	...	...
		5 Konkani ...	101	52	49	143	68	75
		6 Kutch ...	...	...	...	...	...	...
		7 Mussalman ...	...	...	...	...	...	...
		8 Tamil ...	...	...	...	...	...	...
		9 Telugu ...	...	...	...	...	...	...
		10 Tulukken ...	45	26	19	3,358	1,754	1,604
		Total Group 54 ...	146	78	68	3,501	1,822	1,679
	55. Unknown.	1 Bālāji ...	...	...	...	...	...	...
		2 Bhavarāsi ...	...	...	...	...	...	...
		3 Bhujār ...	...	...	...	...	...	...
		4 Bhujavar ...	...	...	...	...	...	..
		5 Chilambātti ...	...	...	...	...	...	...
		6 Heathen ...	...	...	...	..	...	...
		7 Kadiyan ...	...	...	...	...	...	...
		8 Kāmuvar ...	...	...	..	...	...	...
		9 Kodayan ...	...	...	...	...	...	...
		10 Kūch ...	...	...	...	...	...	...
		11 Malayānkāran.	...	...	...	...	...	...
		12 Mustān ...	...	...	...	...	...	...
		13 Nāgamom ...	...	...	...	...	...	...

XVI.

Nationality or Traditional Occupation—(*Continued*).

—(*Continued*).

Meenachal.			Muvattupula.			Todupula.		
Total.	Males.	Females.	Total.	Males.	Females.	Total.	Males.	Females.
84	85	86	87	88	89	90	91	92
...	...	...	...	...	...	...	...	...
...	...	...	...	...	...	...	...	...
...	..	...	...	...	...	...	...	...
...	...	...	...	...	...	...	...	...
...	...	...	42	27	15	...	...	...
...	...	...	...	...	...	...	...	...
...	...	...	...	...	...	...	...	...
...	...	...	...	...	...	...	...	...
...	..	...	...	..	...	...	...	...
1,072	622	450	680	395	285	1,649	906	743
1,072	622	450	722	422	300	1,649	906	743
...	...	...	...	...	...	...	...	...
...	...	...	...	...	...	...	...	...
...	...	...	...	...	...	...	...	...
...	...	...	...	...	...	...	...	...
...	...	...	...	...	...	...	...	...
...	...	...	...	...	...	...	...	...
...	...	...	...	...	...	...	...	...
...	...	...	...	...	...	...	...	...
...	...	...	...	...	...	...	...	...
...	...	...	...	...	...	...	...	...
...	...	...	...	..	...	...	...	...
..	...	...	...	...	...	...	...	...
...	...	...	...	...	...	...	...	...

TABLE

Castes, Tribes and Races, by

Class.	Group.	Caste, &c.	Taluqs: Kunnattunadu. Total.	Kunnattunadu. Males.	Kunnattunadu. Females.	Alangadu. Total.	Alangadu. Males.	Alangadu. Females.
1	2	3	93	94	95	96	97	98
G. Undefined.	54. Linguistic, territorial and religious names.	1 Bengalese ...	...	...	...	...	...	...
		2 Guzerāti ...	...	...	...	...	...	...
		3 Jain ...	...	...	...	3	3	...
		4 Kannadiyan ..	...	...	...	...	...	...
		5 Konkani ...	316	161	155	140	77	63
		6 Kutch ...	...	...	...	...	...	...
		7 Mussalman ...	...	...	...	3,235	1,713	1,522
		8 Tamil ...	...	...	...	...	...	...
		9 Telugu ...	...	...	...	...	...	...
		10 Tulukken ...	158	93	65	4	4	...
		Total Group 54...	474	254	220	3,382	1,797	1,585
	55. Unknown.	1 Bālāji ...	...	...	...	...	...	...
		2 Bhavarāsi ...	...	...	...	...	...	...
		3 Bhujār ...	...	...	...	...	...	...
		4 Bhujavar ...	...	...	...	...	...	...
		5 Chilambātti ...	9	6	3	...	...	...
		6 Heathen ...	...	...	...	...	...	...
		7 Kadiyan ...	...	...	...	...	...	...
		8 Kāmuvar ...	...	...	...	...	...	...
		9 Kodayan ...	...	...	...	...	...	...
		10 Kuch ...	...	...	...	...	...	...
		11 Malayānkāran	...	...	.	...	...	...
		12 Mustān ...	...	...	...	...	...	...
		13 Nagamom ...	...	...	...	...	...	...

XVI.

Nationality or Traditional Occupation—(*Continued*).

—(*Continued*).

Parur.			Cardamom Hills.			Periyar & Thekkadi.		
Total.	Males.	Females.	Total.	Males.	Females.	Total.	Males.	Females.
99	100	101	102	103	104	105	106	107
...	...	...	3	3	...	...	...	...
...	...	...	...	...	...	27	17	10
...	...	...	...	...	...	...	...	...
...	...	...	22	14	8	1	1	...
433	217	216	...	...	...	...	...	...
...	...	...	...	...	...	...	...	...
...	...	...	...	...	...	...	...	...
...	...	...	...	...	...	..	...	...
...	...	...	...	...	...	...	...	...
65	21	44	23	23	...	...	...	...
498	238	260	48	40	8	28	18	10
...	...	...	...	...	...	97	77	20
...	...	...	...	...	...	11	7	4
...	...	...	...	...	...	1	1	...
...	...	...	...	...	...	1	1	...
...	...	...	...	...	...	...	...	...
...	...	...	...	...	...	...	...	...
..	...	...	...	...	...	...	...	...
...	...	...	...	...	...	...	...	...
...	...	...	...	...	...	...	...	...
...	...	...	...	...	...	2	1	1
...	...	...	...	...	...	32	21	11
...	...	...	...	...	...	...	...	...
...	...	...	...	...	...	...	...	...

TABLE

Castes, Tribes and Races, by

Class.	Group.	Caste, &c.	No. of recorded sub-divisions.	Religion.	Total.	Males.
		Name and Classification.			**State**	
1	2	3	4	5	6	7
G. Undefined.	55. Unknown.	14 Nālikan ...	...	Hindu ...	*187*	104
		15 Naralavelu ...	...	„ ...	*1*	1
		16 Neriyan ...	...	„ ...	*145*	63
		17 Nodiyan ...	...	„ ...	*13*	10
		18 Not stated ...	...	{ „ ... Christian None ...	*192*	108
		19 Pani ...	...	Muslmn....	*898*	425
		20 Pattōl ...	...	Hindu ...	*10*	5
		21 Sahabiti ...	...	„ ...	*5*	1
		22 Tāli ...	...	„ ...	*1*	1
		23 Tāttedam ...	...	„ ...	*10*	6
		24 Tolar ...	...	„ ...	*6*	4
		Total Group 55 ...	...	...	**1,873**	**981**
		Total Class G. ...	...	...	*53,897*	*27,633*
		Grand Total ...	...	...	*2,557,736*	*1,290,415*

XVI.

Nationality or Traditional Occupation—(*Continued*).

Total.	Taluqs.								
	Tovala.			Agastiswaram.			Eranial.		
Females.	Total.	Males.	Females.	Total.	Males.	Females.	Total.	Males.	Females.
8	9	10	11	12	13	14	15	16	17
83	...	...	...	...	...	...	...	...	...
...	...	...	...	...	...	...	...	...	...
82	...	...	...	...	...	...	...	...	...
3	...	...	...	...	...	...	...	...	...
84	...	...	...	44	24	20	...	...	...
473	25	14	11	...	...	...	...	...	...
5	..	...	...	...	...	...	...	...	...
4	...	...	...	...	...	...	...	...	...
...	...	...	...	...	...	...	...	...	...
4	...	...	...	...	...	...	...	...	...
2	..	...	...	...	...	...	...	...	...
892	25	14	11	50	27	23	...	...	...
26,264	1,184	550	634	943	523	420	2,658	1,372	1,286
1,267,321	29,751	14,489	15,262	87,241	43,226	44,015	105,098	52,883	52,215

TABLE

Castes, Tribes and Races, by

Class.	Group.	Caste, &c.	Kalkulam. Total.	Kalkulam. Males.	Kalkulam. Females.	Vilavankodu. Total.	Vilavankodu. Males.	Vilavankodu. Females.
1	2	3	18	19	20	21	22	23
G. Undefined.	55. Unknown.	14 Nālikan ...	28	10	18	...	...	...
		15 Naralavelu ...	...	...	...	...	...	...
		16 Neriyan ...	...	...	...	...	...	...
		17 Nodiyan ...	...	...	...	...	...	...
		18 Not stated ...	...	...	...	...	...	...
		19 Pani ...	119	62	57	...	...	...
		20 Pattōl ...	...	...	...	...	...	..
		21 Sahabiti ...	...	...	...	...	...	...
		22 Tāli ...	...	...	...	...	...	...
		23 Tāttedam ...	...	...	...	...	...	...
		24 Tolar ...	...	...	...	...	...	...
		Total Group 55 ...	160	77	83	2	2	...
		Total Class G. ...	215	111	104	1,164	576	588
		Grand Total ...	59,474	29,834	29,640	68,521	35,202	33,319

Taluqs

XVI.

Nationality or Traditional Occupation—(*Continued*).

—(*Continued*).

Neyattankara.			Trivandram.			Nedumangadu.		
Total.	Males.	Females.	Total.	Males.	Females.	Total.	Males.	Females.
24	25	26	27	28	29	30	31	32
...	...	...	...	...	...	...	...	...
...	...	...	...	...	...	...	...	...
...	...	...	...	...	...	...	...	...
...	...	...	...	...	...	...	...	...
...	...	...	...	...	...	...	...	...
...	...	...	...	...	...	...	...	...
...	...	...	...	...	...	...	...	...
...	...	...	...	...	...	...	...	...
...	...	...	...	...	...	...	...	...
...	...	...	...	...	...	...	...	...
...	...	...	...	...	...	...	...	...
...	...	...	1	1	...	...	...	...
2,081	1,132	949	4,801	2,429	2,372	1,239	619	620
110,755	56,953	53,802	111,938	56,909	55,029	55,497	27,857	27,640

TABLE

Castes, Tribes and Races, by

Class.	Group.	Caste, &c.	Taluqs: Sirayinkil. Total.	Sirayinkil. Males.	Sirayinkil. Females.	Kottarakkara. Total.	Kottarakkara. Males.	Kottarakkara. Females.
1	2	3	33	34	35	36	37	38
G. Undefined.	55. Unknown.	14 Nālikan ...	...	...	...	...	...	...
		15 Naralavelu ...	...	...	...	...	...	...
		16 Neriyan ...	...	...	...	...	...	...
		17 Nodiyan ...	...	...	...	...	...	...
		18 Not stated ...	142	81	61	...	...	...
		19 Pani ...	...	...	...	...	...	...
		20 Pattōl ...	...	...	...	...	...	...
		21 Sahabiti ...	...	...	...	...	...	...
		22 Tāli ...	...	...	...	...	...	...
		23 Tāttedam ...	...	...	...	...	...	...
		24 Tolar ...	...	...	...	...	...	...
		Total Group 55 ...	142	81	61	...	...	...
		Total Class G. ...	2,818	1,400	1,418	1,375	707	668
		Grand Total ...	97,995	48,271	49,724	71,517	36,055	35,462

XVI.

Nationality or Traditional Occupation—(*Continued*).

—(*Continued*).

Pattanapuram.			Shenkotta.			Quilon.		
Total.	Males.	Females.	Total.	Males.	Females.	Total.	Males.	Females.
39	40	41	42	43	44	45	46	47
...	...	...	...	...	...	...	...	...
...	...	...	..	...	...	1	1	...
...	...	...	...	...	...	...	...	...
...	...	...	...	...	...	...	...	...
...	...	...	...	...	...	...	...	...
...	...	...	...	...	...	...	...	...
...	...	...	...	...	...	...	...	...
...	...	...	...	...	...	5	1	4
...	...	...	...	...	...	...	...	...
...	...	...	...	...	...	...	...	...
...	...	...	...	...	...	6	4	2
...	...	...	...	...	...	12	6	6
38	16	22	1,499	808	691	1,527	786	741
39,447	19,858	19,589	32,088	15,700	16,388	121,935	60,832	61,103

TABLE

Castes, Tribes and Races, by

Class.	Group.	Caste, &c.	Taluqs Kunnattur. Total.	Males.	Females.	Karunagappalli. Total.	Males.	Females.
1	2	3	48	49	50	51	52	53
G. Undefined.	55. Unknown.	14 Nālikan ...	...	...	...	...	...	...
		15 Naralavelu ...	...	...	...	...	...	...
		16 Neriyan ...	...	...	...	...	...	...
		17 Nodiyan ...	...	...	...	...	...	...
		18 Not stated ...	...	...	...	...	...	...
		19 Pani ...	...	...	...	754	349	405
		20 Pattōl ...	...	...	...	...	...	...
		21 Sahabiti ...	...	...	...	...	...	...
		22 Tāli ...	...	...	...	...	...	...
		23 Tāttedam ...	...	...	...	...	...	...
		24 Tolar ...	...	...	...	...	...	...
		Total Group 55 ...	...	...	...	757	351	406
		Total Class G. ...	47	27	20	866	402	464
		Grand Total ...	73,529	37,397	36,132	108,826	52,862	55,964

XVI.

Nationality or Traditional Occupation—(*Continued*).

—(*Continued*).

Kartigappalli.			Mavellikkara.			Chenganur.		
Total.	Males.	Females.	Total.	Males.	Females.	Total.	Males.	Females.
54	55	56	57	58	59	60	61	62
...	...	...	...	...	...	...	...	...
...	...	...	...	...	...	...	...	...
...	...	...	...	...	...	...	...	...
...	...	...	...	...	...	...	...	...
...	...	...	...	...	...	...	...	...
...	...	...	...	...	...	...	...	...
...	...	...	...	...	...	...	...	...
...	...	...	...	...	...	...	...	...
...	...	...	...	...	...	...	...	...
...	...	...	...	...	...	...	...	...
...	...	...	...	...	...	...	...	...
...	...	...	...	...	...	...	...	...
1,057	545	512	2,369	1,206	1,163	653	344	309
91,950	45,216	46,734	103,619	52,494	51,125	93,960	48,443	45,517

TABLE

Castes, Tribes and Races, by

Class.	Group.	Caste, &c.	Taluqs: Tiruvalla. Total.	Tiruvalla. Males.	Tiruvalla. Females.	Ambalappula. Total.	Ambalappula. Males.	Ambalappula. Females.
1	2	3	63	64	65	66	67	68
G. Undefined.	55. Unknown.	14 Nālikan ...	...	...	...	...	...	...
		15 Naralavelu ...	...	...	...	...	...	...
		16 Neriyan ...	...	...	...	...	...	...
		17 Nodiyan ...	...	...	...	...	...	...
		18 Not stated ...	5	2	3	...	...	...
		19 Pani ...	...	...	...	...	...	...
		20 Pattōl ...	...	...	...	...	...	...
		21 Sahabiti ...	...	...	...	...	...	...
		22 Tāli ...	...	...	...	...	...	...
		23 Tāttedam ...	10	6	4	...	...	...
		24 Tolar ...	...	...	...	...	...	...
		Total Group 55 ...	15	8	7	4	1	3
		Total Class G. ...	957	508	449	10,331	4,874	5,457
		Grand Total ...	122,142	62,514	59,628	94,745	46,909	47,836

XVI.

Nationality or Traditional Occupation—(*Continued*).

—, *Continued*).

Sherttala.			Vykkam.			Ettumanur.		
Total.	Males.	Females.	Total.	Males.	Females.	Total.	Males.	Females.
69	70	71	72	73	74	75	76	77
...	...	...	...	...	...	...	...	...
...	...	...	...	...	...	...	...	...
...	...	...	...	...	...	...	...	...
...	...	...	...	...	...	...	...	...
...	...	...	...	...	...	...	...	...
...	...	...	...	...	...	...	...	...
...	...	...	...	...	...	...	...	...
...	...	...	...	...	...	...	...	...
...	...	...	...	...	...	...	...	...
...	...	...	...	...	...	...	...	...
...	...	...	...	...	...	...	...	...
79	65	14	15	3	12	129	57	72
2,556	1,324	1,232	685	391	294	832	498	334
117,261	58,448	58,813	80,628	40,947	39,681	80,823	41,536	39,287

TABLE

Castes, Tribes and Races, by

Class.	Group.	Caste, &c.	Taluqs: Kottayam. Total.	Kottayam. Males.	Kottayam. Females.	Changanacheri. Total.	Changanacheri. Males.	Changanacheri. Females.
1	2	3	78	79	80	81	82	83
G. Undefined.	55. Unknown.	14 Nālikan ...	...	...	...	...	...	...
		15 Naralavelu ...	...	...	...	...	...	...
		16 Neriyan ...	...	...	...	113	54	59
		17 Nodiyan ...	...	...	...	...	...	...
		18 Not stated ...	...	...	...	...	...	...
		19 Pani ...	...	...	...	...	...	...
		20 Pattōl ...	...	...	...	...	...	...
		21 Sahabiti ...	...	...	...	...	...	...
		22 Tāli ...	...	...	...	...	...	...
		23 Tāttedam ...	...	...	...	...	...	...
		24 Tolar ...	...	...	...	...	...	...
		Total Group 55 ...	...	...	...	113	54	59
		Total Class G. ...	146	78	68	3,614	1,876	1,738
		Grand Total ...	77,094	39,229	37,865	74,722	38,596	36,126

XVI.

Nationality or Traditional Occupation—(*Continued*).

—(*Continued*).

Meenachal.			Muvattupula.			Todupula.		
Total.	Males.	Females.	Total.	Males.	Females.	Total.	Males.	Females.
84	85	86	87	88	89	90	91	92
...	...	...	27	16	11	22	16	
...	...	...	...	...	...	...	...	...
32	9	23	...	...	...	...	...	...
...	...	...	5	5	...	8	5	3
...	...	...	...	...	...	...	...	...
...	...	...	...	...	...	...	...	...
10	5	5	...	...	...	...	...	...
...	...	...	...	...	...	...	...	...
...	...	...	...	...	...	...	...	...
...	...	...	...	...	...	...	...	...
...	...	...	...	...	...	...	...	...
42	14	28	32	21	11	30	21	9
1,114	636	478	754	443	311	1,679	927	752
59,976	30,830	29,146	103,009	51,595	51,414	25,202	12,786	12,416

TABLE

Castes, Tribes and Races, by

Class.	Group.	Caste, &c.	Taluqs: Kunnattunadu. Total.	Kunnattunadu. Males.	Kunnattunadu. Females.	Alangadu. Total.	Alangadu. Males.	Alangadu. Females.
1	2	3	93	94	95	96	97	98
G. Undefined.	55. Unknown.	14 Nālikan ...	101	55	46	...	...	...
		15 Naralavelu ...	...	...	...	...	...	...
		16 Neriyan ...	...	...	...	...	...	...
		17 Nodiyan ...	...	...	...	...	...	...
		18 Not stated ...	...	...	...	...	...	...
		19 Pani ...	...	...	...	...	...	...
		20 Pattōl ..	...	...	..	...	...	...
		21 Sahabiti ...	...	...	...	...	...	...
		22 Tāli ...	...	...	...	...	...	...
		23 Tāttedam ...	...	...	...	...	...	...
		24 Tolar ...	...	...	...	...	...	...
		Total Group 55 ...	110	61	49	...	...	...
		Total Class G. ...	584	315	269	3,382	1,797	1,585
		Grand Total ...	114,049	57,216	56,833	70,958	35,944	35,014

XVI.

Nationality or Traditional Occupation—(*Continued*).

—(*Continued*).

Parur.			Cardamom Hills.			Periyar and Thekkadi.		
Total.	Males.	Females.	Total.	Males.	Females.	Total.	Males.	Females.
99	100	101	102	103	104	105	106	107
...	...	...	...	...	...	9	7	2
...	...	...	...	...	...	...	...	...
...	...	...	...	...	...	...	...	...
...	...	...	...	...	...	...	...	...
...	...	...	...	...	...	1	1	...
...	...	...	...	...	...	...	...	...
...	...	...	...	...	...	...	...	...
...	...	...	...	...	...	...	...	...
...	...	...	...	...	...	1	1	...
...	...	...	...	...	...	...	...	...
...	...	...	...	...	...	...	...	...
...	...	...	...	...	...	155	117	38
498	238	260	48	40	8	183	135	48
59,278	30,082	29,196	11,413	6,714	4,699	3,295	2,588	707

TABLE

Occupations, Part B.—

Class.	Group.	Occupation.	State Total. Total.	Males.	Females.
1	2	3	4	5	6
A. Government.	1	British Resident of Travancore and Cochin ...	2	1	1
		Officers ...	8	5	3
		Office Superintendents and Clerical Establishments ...	198	144	54
		Menials, Peons, &c. ...	7	7	...
		Total Sub-order 1 ...	**215**	**157**	**58**
	4	Officers ...	34	23	11
		Non-Commissioned Officers and Privates ...	915	646	269
		Followers ...	54	35	19
		Clerks ...	1	1	...
		Total Sub-order 4 ...	**1,004**	**705**	**299**
	6	H. H. The Maharajah of Travancore, G.C.S.I. ...	1	1	...
		Officers ...	957	540	417
		Clerical Establishments ...	6,741	3,667	3,074
		Menials, &c. ...	40,936	23,369	17,567
		Total Sub-order 6 ...	**48,635**	**27,577**	**21,058**
	7	Officers ...	104	44	60
		Privates, &c. ...	1,163	765	398
		Total Sub-order 7 ...	**1,267**	**809**	**458**
		Total Class A. ...	*51,121*	*29,248*	*21,873*

XVII.

(State Distribution).

Taluqs.								
Tovala.			Agastiswaram.			Eranial.		
Total.	Males.	Females.	Total.	Males.	Females.	Total.	Males.	Females.
7	8	9	10	11	12	13	14	15
...	...	...	...	...	...	...	...	...
...	...	...	...	...	...	...	...	...
...	...	...	...	...	...	...	...	...
...	...	...	...	...	...	...	...	...
...	...	...	...	...	...	...	...	...
...	...	...	...	...	...	...	...	...
...	...	...	...	...	...	...	...	...
...	...	...	...	...	...	...	...	...
...	...	...	...	...	...	...	...	...
...	...	...	...	...	...	...	...	...
...	...	...	...	...	...	...	...	...
7	4	3	48	26	22	16	4	12
153	88	65	268	139	129	176	97	79
1,288	730	558	1,624	925	699	1,549	836	713
1,448	822	626	1,940	1,090	850	1,741	937	804
...	...	...	...	...	...	...	...	...
...	...	...	...	...	...	...	...	...
...	...	...	...	...	...	...	...	...
1,448	822	626	1,940	1,090	850	1,741	937	804

TABLE

Occupations, Part B.—

Class.	Group.	Occupation.	Taluqs: Kalkulam. Total.	Kalkulam. Males.	Kalkulam. Females.	Vilavankodu. Total.	Vilavankodu. Males.	Vilavankodu. Females.
1	2	3	16	17	18	19	20	21
A. Government.	1	British Resident of Travancore and Cochin ...	...	...	...	...	...	...
		Officers ...	...	...	...	...	...	...
		Office Superintendents and Clerical Establishments ...	...	...	...	...	...	...
		Menials, Peons, &c. ...	...	...	...	...	...	...
		Total Sub-order 1 ...	...	...	...	...	...	...
	4	Officers ...	...	...	...	...	...	...
		Non-Commissioned Officers and Privates ...	...	...	...	...	...	...
		Followers ...	...	...	...	...	...	...
		Clerks ...	...	...	...	...	...	...
		Total Sub-order 4 ...	...	...	...	...	...	...
	6	H. H. The Maharajah of Travancore, G.C.S.I. ...	...	...	...	...	...	...
		Officers ...	20	11	9	12	7	5
		Clerical Establishments ..	208	116	92	174	89	85
		Menials, &c. ...	1,274	749	525	810	493	317
		Total Sub-order 6 ...	1,502	876	626	996	589	407
	7	Officers ...	...	...	...	...	...	...
		Privates, &c. ...	...	...	...	...	...	...
		Total Sub-order 7 ...	...	...	...	...	...	...
		Total Class A. ...	1,502	876	626	996	589	407

XVII.

(State Distribution)—(*Continued*).

—(*Continued*).

Neyattankara.			Trivandram.			Nedumangadu.		
Total.	Males.	Females.	Total.	Males.	Females.	Total.	Males.	Females.
22	23	24	25	26	27	28	29	30
...	...	...	2	1	1	...	...	...
...	...	...	8	5	3	...	...	...
...	...	...	39	31	8	...	...	...
...	...	...	...	...	...	...	...	...
...	...	..	49	37	12	...	...	...
...	...	...	11	8	3	...	...	...
...	...	...	183	105	78	...	...	...
...	...	...	6	4	2	...	...	...
...	...	...	...	...	...	...	...	...
...	...	...	200	117	83	...	..	...
...	...	...	1	1	...	...	...	...
12	8	4	296	154	142	10	7	3
240	117	123	794	465	329	152	94	58
1,503	884	619	11,432	7,103	4,329	644	368	276
1,755	1,009	746	12,523	7,723	4,800	806	469	337
...	...	...	104	44	60	...	...	...
...	...	...	1,163	765	398	...	...	...
...	...	...	1,267	809	458	...	...	...
1,755	1,009	746	14,039	8,686	5,353	806	469	337

TABLE

Occupations, Part B.—

Class.	Group.	Occupation.	Taluqs: Sirayinkil. Total.	Sirayinkil. Males.	Sirayinkil. Females.	Kottarakkara. Total.	Kottarakkara. Males.	Kottarakkara. Females.
1	2	3	31	32	33	34	35	36
A. Government.	1	British Resident of Travancore and Cochin ...	...	...	...	...	...	...
		Officers ...	...	...	...	...	...	...
		Office Superintendents and Clerical Establishments ...	...	...	...	...	...	...
		Menials, Peons, &c. ...	...	...	...	...	...	...
		Total Sub-order 1 ...	...	...	...	...	...	...
	4	Officers ...	...	...	...	...	...	...
		Non-Commissioned Officers and Privates ...	...	...	...	...	...	...
		Followers ...	...	...	...	...	...	...
		Clerks ...	...	...	...	...	...	...
		Total Sub-order 4 ...	...	...	...	...	...	...
	6	H. H. The Maharajah of Travancore, G.C.S.I. ...	...	...	...	...	...	...
		Officers ...	18	6	12	11	7	4
		Clerical Establishments ...	166	97	69	163	79	84
		Menials, &c. ...	1,718	1,180	538	874	618	256
		Total Sub-order 6 ...	1,902	1,283	619	1,048	704	344
	7	Officers ...	...	...	...	...	...	...
		Privates, &c. ...	...	...	...	...	...	...
		Total Sub-order 7 ...	...	...	...	...	...	...
		Total Class A ...	1,902	1,283	619	1,048	704	344

XVII.

(State Distribution)—(Continued).

—(Continued).

Pattanapuram.			Shenkotta.			Quilon.		
Total.	Males.	Females.	Total.	Males.	Females.	Total.	Males.	Females.
37	38	39	40	41	42	43	44	45
...	...	...	...	...	...	...	...	...
...	...	...	...	...	...	...	...	...
...	...	...	...	...	...	13	9	4
...	...	...	...	...	...	...	...	...
...	...	...	...	...	...	13	9	4
...	...	...	...	...	...	23	15	8
...	...	...	...	...	...	732	541	191
...	...	...	...	...	...	48	31	17
...	...	...	...	...	...	1	1	...
...	...	...	...	...	...	804	588	216
...	...	...	...	...	...	...	...	...
8	6	2	13	8	5	85	48	37
113	55	58	162	79	83	343	204	139
599	212	387	650	438	212	2,237	938	1,299
720	273	447	825	525	300	2,665	1,190	1,475
...	...	...	...	...	...	...	...	...
...	...	...	...	...	...	...	...	...
...	...	...	...	...	...	...	...	...
720	273	447	825	525	300	3,482	1,787	1,695

TABLE

Occupations, Part B.—

Class.	Group.	Occupation.	Taluqs: Kunnattur. Total.	Kunnattur. Males.	Kunnattur. Females.	Karunagappalli. Total.	Karunagappalli. Males.	Karunagappalli. Females.
1	2	3	46	47	48	49	50	51
A. Government.	1	British Resident of Travancore and Cochin ...	...	...	...	...	...	...
		Officers ...	...	...	...	...	...	...
		Office Superintendents and Clerical Establishments ...	...	...	...	...	...	...
		Menials, Peons, &c. ...	...	...	...	...	...	...
		Total Sub-order 1 ...	...	...	...	...	...	...
	4	Officers ...	...	...	...	...	...	...
		Non-Commissioned Officers and Privates ...	...	...	...	...	...	...
		Followers ...	...	...	...	...	...	...
		Clerks ...	...	...	...	...	...	...
		Total Sub-order 4 ...	...	...	...	...	...	...
	6	H. H. The Maharajah of Travancore, G.C.S.I. ...	...	...	...	...	...	...
		Officers ...	13	7	6	19	7	12
		Clerical Establishments ...	169	83	86	182	94	88
		Menials, &c. ...	837	324	513	784	478	306
		Total Sub-order 6 ...	1,019	414	605	985	579	406
	7	Officers ...	...	...	...	...	...	...
		Privates, &c. ...	...	...	...	...	...	...
		Total Sub-order 7 ...	...	...	...	...	...	...
		Total Class A. ...	1,019	414	605	985	579	406

XVII.

(State Distribution)—(*Continued*).

—(*Continued*).

Kartigappalli.			Mavellikkara.			Chenganur.		
Total.	Males.	Females.	Total.	Males.	Females.	Total.	Males.	Females.
52	53	54	55	56	57	58	59	60
...	...	...	...	...	...	...	...	...
...	...	...	...	...	...	...	...	...
...	...	...	...	...	...	...	...	...
...	...	...	...	...	...	...	...	...
...	...	...	...	...	...	...	...	...
...	...	...	...	...	...	...	...	...
...	...	...	...	...	...	...	...	...
...	...	...	...	...	...	...	...	...
...	...	...	...	...	...	...	...	...
...	...	...	...	...	...	...	...	...
...	...	...	...	...	...	...	...	...
26	12	14	14	8	6	14	11	3
229	108	121	183	104	79	154	76	78
700	385	315	801	378	423	825	499	326
955	505	450	998	490	508	993	586	407
...	...	...	...	...	...	...	...	...
...	...	...	...	...	...	...	...	...
...	...	...	...	...	...	...	...	...
955	505	450	998	490	508	993	586	407

TABLE

Occupations, Part B.—

Class.	Group.	Occupation.	Taluqs: Tiruvalla. Total.	Tiruvalla. Males.	Tiruvalla. Females.	Ambalappula. Total.	Ambalappula. Males.	Ambalappula. Females.
1	2	3	61	62	63	64	65	66
A. Government.	1	British Resident of Travancore and Cochin ...	...	...	...	...	...	...
		Officers ...	...	...	...	...	...	...
		Office Superintendents and Clerical Establishments ...	...	...	...	...	...	...
		Menials, Peons, &c. ...	...	...	...	...	...	...
		Total Sub-order 1 ...	...	...	...	...	...	...
	4	Officers ...	...	...	...	...	...	...
		Non-Commissioned Officers and Privates ...	...	...	...	...	...	...
		Followers ...	...	...	...	...	...	...
		Clerks ...	...	...	...	...	...	...
		Total Sub-order 4 ..	...	..	...	...	...	...
	6	H. H. The Maharajah of Travancore, C.G.S.I. ...	...	...	...	...	...	...
		Officers ...	17	12	5	46	23	23
		Clerical Establishments ...	217	120	97	344	186	158
		Menials, &c. ...	635	317	318	3,222	1,859	1,363
		Total Sub-order 6 ...	869	449	420	3,612	2,068	1,544
	7	Officers ...	...	...	...	...	...	...
		Privates, &c. ...	...	...	...	...	...	...
		Total Sub-order 7 ...	...	...	...	...	...	...
		Total Class A. ...	869	449	420	3,612	2,068	1,544

XVII.

(State Distribution)—(*Continued*).

—(*Continued*).

Sherttala.			Vykkam.			Ettumanur.		
Total.	Males.	Females.	Total.	Males.	Females.	Total.	Males.	Females.
67	68	69	70	71	72	73	74	75
...	...	...	...	...	...	...	...	...
...	...	...	...	...	...	...	...	...
...	...	...	...	...	...	...	...	...
...	...	...	...	...	...	...	...	...
...	...	...	...	...	...	...	...	...
...	...	...	...	...	...	...	...	...
...	...	...	...	...	...	...	...	...
...	...	...	...	...	...	...	...	...
...	...	...	...	...	...	...	...	...
..	...	...	...	...	...	...	...	...
...	...	...	...	...	...	...	...	...
13	9	4	23	14	9	29	12	17
192	103	89	222	126	96	161	94	67
806	489	317	625	336	289	544	258	286
1,011	601	410	870	476	394	734	364	370
...	...	...	...	...	...	...	...	...
...	...	...	...	...	...	...	...	...
...	...	...	...	...	...	...	...	...
1,011	601	410	870	476	394	734	364	370

TABLE

Occupations, Part B.—

Class.	Group.	Occupation.	Kottayam. Total.	Kottayam. Males.	Kottayam. Females.	Changanacheri. Total.	Changanacheri. Males.	Changanacheri. Females.
1	2	3	76	77	78	79	80	81
A. Government.	1	British Resident of Travancore and Cochin ...	...	...	...	...	...	...
		Officers ...	...	...	...	...	...	...
		Office Superintendents and Clerical Establishments ...	...	...	...	...	...	...
		Menials, Peons, &c. ...	...	...	...	..	...	..
		Total Sub-order 1 ...	...	...	.	...	...	...
	4	Officers ...	...	...	...	...	...	...
		Non-Commissioned Officers and Privates ...	...	...	...	...	...	...
		Followers ...	...	...	...	...	...	...
		Clerks ...	...	...	...	...	...	...
		Total Sub-order 4 ...	...	...	...	...	...	...
	6	H. H. The Maharajah of Travancore, G.C.S.I. ...	...	...	...	...	...	...
		Officers	52	39	13	35	31	4
		Clerical Establishments ...	311	176	135	197	118	79
		Menials, &c. ...	1,148	662	486	776	418	358
		Total Sub-order 6 ...	1,511	877	634	1,008	567	441
		Officers ...	...	...	...	...	...	...
		Privates, &c. ...	...	...	...	...	...	...
		Total Sub-order 7 ...	...	..	...	...	...	...
		Total Class A. ...	1,511	877	634	1,008	567	441

XVII.

(State Distribution)—(*Continued*).

—(*Continued*).

Meenachal.			Muvattupula.			Todupula.		
Total.	Males.	Females.	Total.	Males.	Females.	Total.	Males.	Females.
82	83	84	85	86	87	88	89	90
...	...	...	...	...	...	...	...	...
...	...	...	...	...	...	...	...	...
...	...	...	..	...	...	...	...	...
...	...	...	...	...	...	...	...	...
...	...	...	...	...	...	...	...	...
...	...	...	...	...	...	...	...	...
...	...	...	...	...	...	...	...	...
...	...	...	...	..	...	...	...	...
...	...	...	...	...	...	...	...	...
...	...	...	...	...	...	...	...	...
...	..	...	...	...	...	...	...	...
7	5	2	10	7	3	23	7	16
123	64	59	206	111	95	80	44	36
410	213	197	431	243	188	359	134	225
540	282	258	647	361	286	462	185	277
								...
...	...	...	...	...	...	...	...	...
...	...	...	...	...	...	...	...	...
...	...	...	...	...	...	...	...	...
540	282	258	647	361	286	462	185	277

TABLE

Occupations, Part B.—

Class.	Group.	Occupation.	Kunnattunadu. Total.	Kunnattunadu. Males.	Kunnattunadu. Females.	Alangadu. Total.	Alangadu. Males.	Alangadu. Females.
1	2	3	91	92	93	94	95	96
A. Government.	1	British Resident of Travancore and Cochin ...	...	...	...	...	...	...
		Officers ...	...	...	...	...	...	...
		Office Superintendents and Clerical Establishments ...	...	...	...	...	...	...
		Menials, Peons, &c. ...	...	...	...	...	...	...
		Total Sub-order 1 ...	...	...	...	...	...	...
	4	Officers ...	...	...	...	...	...	...
		Non-Commissioned Officers and Privates ...	...	...	...	...	...	...
		Followers ...	...	...	...	...	...	...
		Clerks ...	...	...	..	...	...	..
		Total Sub-order 4 ..	...	...	...	...	...	...
	6	H. H. The Maharajah of Travancore, G.C.S.I. ...	...	...	...	...	...	...
		Officers ...	12	8	4	9	6	3
		Clerical Establishments ...	219	117	102	176	87	89
		Menials, &c. ...	704	339	365	413	215	198
		Total Sub-order 6 ...	935	464	471	598	308	290
	7	Officers ...	...	...	...	...	...	...
		Privates, &c. ...	...	...	...	...	...	...
		Total Sub-order 7 ...	...	...	...	...	...	...
		Total Class A. ...	935	464	471	598	308	290

XVII.

(State Distribution)—(*Continued*).

—(*Continued*).

Parur.			Cardamom Hills.			Periyar and Thekkadi.		
Total.	Males.	Females.	Total.	Males.	Females.	Total.	Males.	Females.
97	98	99	100	101	102	103	104	105
...	...	...	...	...	...	...	...	...
...	...	...	...	...	...	...	...	...
...	...	...	...	...	...	146	104	42
...	...	...	...	...	...	7	7	...
...	...	...	...	...	...	153	111	42
...	...	...	...	...	...	...	...	...
...	...	...	...	...	...	...	...	...
...	...	...	...	...	...	...	...	...
...	...	...	...	...	...	...	...	...
...	...	...	...	...	...	...	...	...
...	...	...	...	...	...	...	...	...
34	23	11	5	3	2	...	...	...
220	113	107	44	24	20	...	...	...
709	346	363	5	2	3	...	...	...
963	482	481	54	29	25	...	...	...
...	...	...	...	...	...	...	...	...
...	...	...	...	...	...	...	...	...
...	...	...	...	...	...	...	...	...
963	482	481	54	29	25	153	111	42

TABLE

Occupations, Part B.—

Class.	Group.	Occupation.	Total.	Males.	Females.
1	2	3	4	5	6
B. Pasture and Agriculture.	8(*a*)	Horse dealers ...	*4*	4	...
		Cattle dealers ...	*8*	8	..
		Herdsmen ...	*740*	507	233
		Buffalo breeders and dealers ...	*34*	16	18
		Total Sub-order 8(*a*) ...	**786**	**535**	**251**
	8(*b*)	Elephant catchers ...	*2*	2	...
	8(*c*)	Sheep and goat breeders and dealers.	*795*	547	248
	9(*a*)	Veterinary Surgeons ...	*23*	13	10
		Farriers ...	*21*	10	11
		Horse and elephant breakers and trainers ...	*321*	211	110
		Total Sub-order 9(*a*) ...	**365**	**234**	**131**
	10	Land-occupants, not cultivating ...	*1,697*	695	1,002
		Land-occupants, cultivating ...	*37*	15	22
		Tenants, not cultivating ...	*48*	30	18
		Tenants, cultivating ...	*3,610*	1,712	1,898
		Total Sub-order 10 ...	**5,392**	**2,452**	**2,940**
	11	Field-labourers and crop-watchers ...	*1,046,071*	543,540	502,531

XVII.

(State Distribution)—(*Continued*).

TALUQS.

Tovala.			Agastiswaram.			Eranial.		
Total.	Males.	Females.	Total.	Males.	Females.	Total.	Males.	Females.
7	8	9	10	11	12	13	14	15
...	...	...	...	...	...	...	...	...
...	...	...	...	...	...	4	4	...
100	67	33	21	13	8	190	136	54
25	12	13	6	2	4	3	2	1
125	79	46	27	15	12	197	142	55
...	...	...	...	...	...	...	...	...
188	125	63	198	137	61	37	25	12
5	3	2	9	4	5	5	2	3
...	...	...	5	3	2	...	...	...
...	...	...	...	...	...	...	...	...
5	3	2	14	7	7	5	2	3
53	18	35	80	33	47	88	37	51
...	...	...	22	9	13	...	...	...
...	...	...	21	13	8	...	...	...
76	35	41	276	124	152	295	137	158
129	53	76	399	179	220	383	174	209
10,769	5,452	5,317	34,222	16,746	17,476	34,204	17,408	16,796

TABLE

Occupations, Part B.—

Class.	Group.	Occupation.	Taluqs: Kalkulam. Total.	Kalkulam. Males.	Kalkulam. Females.	Vilavankodu. Total.	Vilavankodu. Males.	Vilavankodu. Females.
1	2	3	16	17	18	19	20	21
B. Pasture and Agriculture.	8(a)	Horse dealers ...	...	...	...	...	...	...
		Cattle dealers ...	...	...	...	...	...	...
		Herdsmen ...	35	24	11	23	16	7
		Buffalo breeders and dealers..	...	...	...	...	...	...
		Total Sub-order 8(a) ...	35	24	11	23	16	7
	8(b)	Elephant catchers ...	...	...	...	...	...	...
	8(c)	Sheep and goat breeders and dealers ...	4	4	...	27	19	8
	9(a)	Veterinary Surgeons ...	1	1	...	...	...	...
		Farriers ...	...	...	...	...	...	...
		Horse and elephant breakers and trainers ...	...	...	...	5	5	...
		Total Sub-order 9(a) ...	1	1	...	5	5	...
	10	Land-occupants, not cultivating ...	91	43	48	76	37	39
		Land-occupants, cultivating..	...	...	...	...	...	...
		Tenants, not cultivating ...	...	...	...	...	...	...
		Tenants, cultivating ...	173	84	89	113	55	58
		Total Sub-order 10 ..	264	127	137	189	92	97
	11	Field-labourers and crop-watchers ...	25,030	12,012	13,018	22,262	11,177	11,085

XVII.

(State Distribution)—(*Continued*).

—(*Continued*).

Neyattankara.			Trivandram.			Nedumangadu.		
Total.	Males.	Females.	Total.	Males.	Females.	Total.	Males.	Females.
22	23	24	25	26	27	28	29	30
...	...	...	3	3	...	...	...	...
...	...	...	2	2	...	...	...	...
21	16	5	27	17	10	37	23	14
...	...	...	...	...	...	...	...	...
21	16	5	32	22	10	37	23	14
...	...	...	...	...	...	...	...	...
42	29	13	26	17	9	19	14	5
...	...	...	3	3	...	...	...	...
...	...	...	7	2	5	...	...	...
...	...	...	40	22	18	13	8	5
...	...	...	50	27	23	13	8	5
99	43	56	177	74	103	33	14	19
...	...	..	...	...	...	...	...	...
...	...	...	9	4	5	...	...	...
129	60	69	250	118	132	182	88	94
228	103	125	436	196	240	215	102	113
51,760	27,496	24,264	21,914	11,670	10,244	26,542	13,948	12,594

TABLE

Occupations, Part B.—

Class.	Group.	Occupation.	Taluqs: Sirayinkil. Total.	Sirayinkil. Males.	Sirayinkil. Females.	Kottarakkara. Total.	Kottarakkara. Males.	Kottarakkara. Females.
1.	2	3	31	32	33	34	35	36
B. Pasture and Agriculture.	8(*a*)	Horse dealers ...	...	...	...	...	...	...
		Cattle dealers ...	...	...	...	...	...	...
		Herdsmen ...	22	14	8	26	17	9
		Buffalo breeders and dealers.	...	...	...	...	...	...
		Total Sub-order 8(*a*) ...	22	14	8	26	17	9
	8(*b*)	Elephant catchers ...	...	...	...	...	...	...
	8(*c*)	Sheep and goat breeders and dealers ...	20	13	7	...	...	...
	9(*a*)	Veterinary Surgeons ...	...	...	...	...	...	...
		Farriers ...	...	...	...	...	...	...
		Horse and elephant breakers and trainers ...	...	...	...	...	...	...
		Total Sub-order 9(*a*) ...	...	...	...	...	...	...
	10	Land-occupants, not cultivating ...	78	30	48	23	10	13
		Land-occupants, cultivating..	...	...	...	...	...	...
		Tenants, not cultivating ...	...	...	...	...	...	...
		Tenants, cultivating ...	192	93	99	125	58	67
		Total Sub-order 10 ...	270	123	147	148	68	80
	11	Field-labourers and crop-watchers ...	43,602	21,253	22,349	35,757	18,802	16,955

XVII.

(State Distribution)—(*Continued*).

—(*Continued*).

Pattanapuram.			Shenkotta.			Quilon.		
Total.	Males.	Females.	Total.	Males.	Females.	Total.	Males.	Females.
37	38	39	40	41	42	43	44	45
...	...	...	...	...	...	1	1	...
...	...	...	...	...	...	...	...	...
...	...	...	41	28	13	27	18	9
...	...	...	...	...	...	...	...	...
...	...	...	41	28	13	28	19	9
...	...	...	...	...	...	...	...	...
16	12	4	13	8	5	...	...	...
...	...	...	...	...	...	...	...	...
...	...	...	...	...	...	9	5	4
18	14	4	...	...	...	36	20	16
18	14	4	...	...	...	45	25	20
36	17	19	16	7	9	89	33	56
...	...	...	...	...	...	...	...	...
...	...	...	3	3	...	10	10	...
170	79	91	99	46	53	142	74	68
206	96	110	118	56	62	241	117	124
18,773	9,589	9,184	12,221	5,790	6,431	48,804	24,741	24,063

TABLE

Occupations, Part B.—

Class.	Group.	Occupation.	Taluqs: Kunnattur. Total.	Kunnattur. Males.	Kunnattur. Females.	Karunagappalli. Total.	Karunagappalli. Males.	Karunagappalli. Females.
1	2	3	46	47	48	49	50	51
B. Pasture and Agriculture.	8(*a*)	Horse dealers ...	...	...	...	...	...	...
		Cattle dealers ...	...	...	...	...	...	...
		Herdsmen ...	...	...	...	3	3	...
		Buffalo breeders and dealers..	...	...	...	...	...	...
		Total Sub-order 8(*a*) ...	...	...	...	3	3	...
	8(*b*)	Elephant catchers ...	...	...	...	...	...	...
	8(*c*)	Sheep and goat breeders and dealers ...	19	13	6	...	...	...
	9(*a*)	Veterinary Surgeons ...	...	...	...	...	...	...
		Farriers ...	...	...	...	...	...	...
		Horse and elephant breakers and trainers ...	7	4	3	20	9	11
		Total Sub-order 9(*a*) ...	7	4	3	20	9	11
	10	Land-occupants, not cultivating ...	83	31	52	81	38	43
		Land-occupants, cultivating...	...	...	...	...	...	...
		Tenants, not cultivating ...	...	...	...	...	...	...
		Tenants, cultivating ...	40	17	23	35	17	18
		Total Sub-order 10 ...	123	48	75	116	55	61
	11	Field-labourers and crop-watchers ...	38,127	19,395	18,732	47,678	23,514	24,164

XVII.

(State Distribution)—(*Continued*).

—(*Continued*).

Kartigappalli.			Mavellikkara.			Chenganur.		
Total.	Males.	Females.	Total.	Males.	Females.	Total.	Males.	Females.
52	53	54	55	56	57	58	59	60
...	...	...	...	...	...	...	...	...
...	...	...	...	...	...	...	...	...
7	5	2	...	...	...	22	14	8
...	...	...	...	...	...	...	...	...
7	5	2	...	...	...	22	14	8
...	...	...	...	...	...	...	...	...
20	13	7	20	14	6	17	12	5
...	...	...	...	...	...	...	...	...
...	...	...	...	...	...	...	...	...
26	14	12	19	15	4	...	...	...
26	14	12	19	15	4	...	...	...
92	37	55	29	12	17	90	34	56
15	6	9	...	...	...	...	...	...
5	...	5	...	...	...	...	...	...
48	24	24	60	28	32	112	55	57
160	67	93	89	40	49	202	89	113
32,084	16,877	15,207	48,019	25,854	22,165	51,992	28,130	23,862

TABLE

Occupations, Part B.—

Class.	Group.	Occupation.	Taluc Tiruvalla. Total.	Tiruvalla. Males.	Tiruvalla. Females.	Ambalappula. Total.	Ambalappula. Males.	Ambalappula. Females.
1	2	3	61	62	63	64	65	66
B. Pasture and Agriculture.	8(*a*)	Horse dealers ...	...	...	...	...	...	...
		Cattle dealers ...	...	...	...	...	...	...
		Herdsmen ...	20	13	7	...	...	...
		Buffalo breeders and dealers.	...	...	...	...	...	...
		Total Sub-order 8(*a*) ...	20	13	7	...	...	...
	8(*b*)	Elephant catchers ...	...	...	...	...	...	...
	8(*c*)	Sheep and goat breeders and dealers ...	22	14	8	9	7	2
	9(*a*)	Veterinary Surgeons ...	...	...	...	...	...	...
		Farriers ...	...	...	...	...	...	...
		Horse and elephant breakers and trainers ...	...	...	...	22	14	8
		Total Sub-order 9(*a*) ...	...	...	...	22	14	8
	10	Land-occupants not cultivating ...	90	31	59	55	24	31
		Land-occupants, cultivating...	...	...	...	...	...	...
		Tenants, not cultivating ...	...	...	...	...	...	...
		Tenants, cultivating ...	95	46	49	183	89	94
		Total Sub-order 10 ...	185	77	108	238	113	125
	11	Field-labourers and crop-watchers ...	59,579	31,813	27,766	18,913	9,216	9,697

XVII.

(State Distribution)—(*Continued*).

—(*Continued*).

Sherttala.			Vykkam.			Ettumanur.		
Total.	Males.	Females.	Total.	Males.	Females.	Total.	Males.	Females.
67	68	69	70	71	72	73	74	75
...	...	...	...	...	...	...	...	...
...	...	...	...	...	...	...	...	...
...	...	...	26	17	9	17	12	5
...	...	...	...	...	...	...	...	...
...	...	...	26	17	9	17	12	5
...	...	...	...	...	...	...	...	...
31	24	7	17	11	6	...	...	...
...	...	...	...	...	...	...	...	...
...	...	...	...	...	...	...	...	...
...	...	...	18	13	5	...	...	..
...	...	...	18	13	5	...	...	...
27	9	18	30	13	17	...	...	...
...	...	...	...	...	...	...	...	...
...	...	...	...	...	...	...	...	...
194	96	98	111	52	59	101	48	53
221	105	116	141	65	76	101	48	53
32,845	17,435	15,410	21,870	12,784	9,086	33,701	18,622	15,079

TABLE

Occupations, Part B.—

Class.	Group.	Occupation.	Taluqs: Kottayam. Total.	Kottayam. Males.	Kottayam. Females.	Changanacheri. Total.	Changanacheri. Males.	Changanacheri. Females.
1	2	3	76	77	78	79	80	81
B. Pasture and Agriculture.	8(*a*)	Horse dealers ...	...	...	...	...	...	...
		Cattle dealers ...	...	...	...	2	2	...
		Herdsmen ...	...	...	...	20	14	6
		Buffalo breeders and dealers.	...	...	...	...	...	...
		Total Sub-order 8(*a*) ...	...	...	...	22	16	6
	8(*b*)	Elephant catchers ...	...	...	...	...	...	...
	8(*c*)	Sheep and goat breeders and dealers ...	...	...	...	...	...	...
	9(*a*)	Veterinary Surgeons ...	...	...	...	...	...	...
		Farriers ...	...	...	...	...	...	...
		Horse and elephant breakers and trainers ...	...	...	...	...	...	...
		Total Sub-order 9(*a*) ...	...	...	...	...	...	...
	10	Land-occupants and cultivating ...	37	14	23	24	8	16
		Land-occupants, cultivating...	...	...	...	...	...	...
		Tenants, not cultivating ...	...	...	...	...	...	...
		Tenants, cultivating ...	115	56	59	56	24	32
		Total Sub-order 10 ...	152	70	82	80	32	48
	11	Field-labourers and crop-watchers ...	27,279	14,455	12,824	26,275	14,956	11,319

XVII.

(State Distribution)—(*Continued*).

—(*Continued*).

Meenachal.			Muvattupula.			Todupula.		
Total.	Males.	Females.	Total.	Males.	Females.	Total.	Males.	Females.
82	83	84	85	86	87	88	89	90
...	...	...	...	...	...	...	...	...
...	...	...	...	...	...	...	...	...
11	8	3	...	...	...	10	7	3
...	...	...	...	...	...	...	...	...
11	8	3	...	...	...	10	7	3
...	...	...	...	...	...	...	...	...
25	19	6	...	...	...	3	3	...
...	...	...	...	...	...	...	...	...
...	...	...	...	...	...	...	..	...
...	...	...	47	34	13	...	...	...
...	...	...	47	34	13	...	...	...
21	9	12	28	14	14	...	...	...
...	...	...	...	...	...	...	...	...
...	...	...	...	...	...	...	...	...
72	34	38	36	15	21	10	4	6
93	43	50	64	29	35	10	4	6
37,639	19,982	17,657	59,350	30,067	29,283	15,093	8,146	6,947

TABLE

Occupations, Part B.—

Class.	Group.	Occupation.	Taluqs: Kunnattunadu. Total.	Kunnattunadu. Males.	Kunnattunadu. Females.	Alangadu. Total.	Alangadu. Males.	Alangadu. Females.
1	2	3	91	92	93	94	95	96
B. Pasture and Agriculture.	8(*a*)	Horse dealers ...	...	...	...	...	...	...
		Cattle dealers ...	...	...	...	...	..	...
		Herdsmen ...	...	...	...	...	...	...
		Buffalo breeders and dealers.	...	...	...	...	...	...
		Total Sub-order 8(*a*) ...	...	...	...	...	...	...
	8(*b*)	Elephant catchers ...	...	...	...	...	...	...
	8(*c*)	Sheep and goat breeders and dealers ...	22	14	8	...	...	...
	9(*a*)	Veterinary Surgeons ...	...	...	...	...	...	...
		Farriers ...	...	...	...	...	...	...
		Horse and elephant breakers and trainers ...	46	36	10	...	...	...
		Total Sub-order 9(*a*) ...	46	36	10	...	...	...
	10	Land-occupants, not cultivating ...	37	13	24	...	...	...
		Land-occupants, cultivating...	...	...	...	...	...	...
		Tenants, not cultivating ...	...	...	...	...	...	...
		Tenants, cultivating ...	16	7	9	43	20	23
		Total Sub-order 10 ...	53	20	33	43	20	23
	11	Field-labourers and crop-watchers ...	61,011	30,412	30,599	34,809	18,777	16,032

XVII.

(State Distribution)—(*Continued*).

—(*Continued*).

Parur.			Cardamom Hills.			Periyar and Thekkadi.		
Total.	Males.	Females.	Total.	Males.	Females.	Total.	Males.	Females.
97	98	99	100	101	102	103	104	105
...	...	...	...	...	...	...	...	...
...	...	...	...	...	...	...	...	...
10	7	3	24	18	6	...	...	...
...	...	...	...	...	...	...	...	...
10	7	3	24	18	6	...	...	...
...	...	...	...	...	...	2	2	...
...	...	...	...	...	...	...	...	...
...	...	...	...	...	...	...	...	...
...	...	...	...	...	...	...	...	...
...	...	...	4	3	1	...	...	...
...	...	...	4	3	1	...	..	...
19	7	12	11	4	7	4	1	3
...	...	...	...	...	...	...	...	...
...	...	...	...	...	...	...	...	...
61	29	32	...	...	...	...	...	...
80	36	44	11	4	7	4	1	3
8,927	4,178	4,749	4,974	2,810	2,164	46	33	13

TABLE

Occupations, Part B.—

Class.	Group.	Occupation.	Total.	Males.	Females.
1	2	3	4	5	6
B. Pasture and Agriculture.	12	Tea and coffee planters, managers and assistants ...	*232*	150	82
		Cocoanut growers ...	*27*	12	15
		Betel-vine growers ...	*204*	95	109
		Cardamom and pepper growers ...	*127*	66	61
		Market gardeners (vegetable growers) ...	*3,793*	3,220	573
		Gardeners, &c. ...	*127*	92	35
		Manure preparers and sellers ...	*78*	41	37
		Forest officers ...	*11*	10	1
		Forest guards and peons ...	*253*	109	144
		Total Sub-order 12 ...	**4,852**	**3,795**	**1,057**
	13	Agents and managers of landed estates ...	*285*	169	116
		Total Class B. ...	*1,058,548*	*551,274*	*507,274*

XVII.

(State Distribution)—(*Continued*).

TALUQS.

Tovala.			Agastiswaram.			Eranial.		
Total.	Males.	Females.	Total.	Males.	Females.	Total.	Males.	Females.
7	8	9	10	11	12	13	14	15
25	16	9	6	4	2	...	...	...
...	...	...	...	...	...	...	...	...
...	...	...	...	...	...	22	8	14
...	...	...	...	...	...	...	...	...
222	186	36	162	134	28	191	178	13
34	23	11	9	7	2	12	9	3
...	...	...	...	...	...	...	...	...
...	...	...	...	...	...	...	...	...
...	...	...	11	4	7	...	...	...
281	225	56	188	149	39	225	195	30
...	...	...	...	...	...	...	...	...
11,497	5,937	5,560	35,048	17,233	17,815	35,051	17,946	17,105

TABLE

Occupations, Part B.—

Class.	Group.	Occupation.	Taluqs: Kalkulam. Total.	Kalkulam. Males.	Kalkulam. Females.	Vilavankodu. Total.	Vilavankodu. Males.	Vilavankodu. Females.
1	2	3	16	17	18	19	20	21
B. Pasture and Agriculture.	12	Tea and coffee planters, managers and assistants ...	2	2	...	1	1	...
		Cocoanut growers ...	...	...	...	...	...	...
		Betel-vine growers ...	11	4	7	31	13	18
		Cardamom & pepper growers.	...	...	...	...	...	...
		Market gardeners (vegetable growers) ...	165	136	29	158	141	17
		Gardeners, &c. ...	9	5	4	...	...	...
		Manure preparers and sellers	78	41	37	...	...	...
		Forest officers ...	...	...	...	...	...	...
		Forest guards and peons ...	...	...	...	8	3	5
		Total Sub-order 12 ...	265	188	77	198	158	40
	13	Agents and managers of landed estates ...	13	8	5	...	...	...
		Total Class B. ...	25,612	12,364	13,248	22,704	11,467	11,237

XVII.

(State Distribution)—(*Continued*).

—(*Continued*).

Neyattankara.			Trivandram.			Nedumangadu.		
Total.	Males.	Females.	Total.	Males.	Females.	Total.	Males.	Females.
22	23	24	25	26	27	28	29	30
...	...	...	7	4	3	21	13	8
...	...	...	...	...	...	...	...	...
...	...	...	30	13	17	...	...	...
...	...	...	...	...	...	13	7	6
151	132	19	80	67	13	93	79	14
...	...	...	...	...	...	...	...	...
...	...	...	...	...	...	...	...	...
...	...	...	6	6	...	...	...	...
...	...	...	32	13	19	20	9	11
151	132	19	155	103	52	147	108	39
...	...	...	21	13	8	...	...	...
52,202	27,776	24,426	22,634	12,048	10,586	26,973	14,203	12,770

TABLE

Occupations, Part B.—

Class.	Group.	Occupation.	Taluqs: Sirayinkil. Total.	Sirayinkil. Males.	Sirayinkil. Females.	Kottarakkara. Total.	Kottarakkara. Males.	Kottarakkara. Females.
1	2	3	31	32	33	34	35	36
B. Pasture and Agriculture.	12	Tea and coffee planters, managers and assistants ...	...	...	...	...	...	...
		Cocoanut growers ...	...	...	...	...	...	...
		Betel-vine growers ...	11	4	7	...	...	...
		Cardamom & pepper growers.	..	...	...	...	...	...
		Market gardeners (vegetable growers) ...	104	79	25	58	47	11
		Gardeners, &c. ...	...	...	...	...	...	...
		Manure preparers and sellers.	...	...	...	...	...	...
		Forest officers ...	...	...	...	...	..	...
		Forest guards and peons ...	...	...	...	...	...	...
		Total Sub-order 12 ...	115	83	32	58	47	11
	13	Agents and managers of landed estates ...	36	22	14	...	...	...
		Total Class B. ...	44,065	21,508	22,557	35,989	18,934	17,055

XVII.

(State Distribution)—(*Continued*).

—(*Continued*).

Pattanapuram.			Shenkotta.			Quilon.		
Total.	Males.	Females.	Total.	Males.	Females.	Total.	Males.	Females.
37	38	39	40	41	42	43	44	45
13	8	5	...	...	..	...	...	...
...	...	...	...	...	...	...	...	...
...	...	...	...	...	...	28	13	15
7	4	3	...	...	...	...	...	...
80	73	7	127	103	24	103	74	29
...	...	...	...	...	.	...	...	...
...	...	...	...	...	...	.. .	...	...
...	...	...	...	...	...	3	2	1
16	8	8	...	...	...	41	17	24
116	93	23	127	103	24	175	106	69
...	...	...	...	...	...	...	...	...
19,129	9,804	9,325	12,520	5,985	6,535	49,293	25,008	24,285

TABLE

Occupations, Part B.—

CLASS.	GROUP.	OCCUPATION.	TALUQS — Kunnattur. Total.	Kunnattur. Males.	Kunnattur. Females.	Karunagappalli. Total.	Karunagappalli. Males.	Karunagappalli. Females.
1	2	3	46	47	48	49	50	51
B. Pasture and Agriculture.	12	Tea and coffee planters, managers and assistants ...	...	...	...	...	...	...
		Cocoanut growers ...	...	...	...	27	12	15
		Betel-vine growers ...	..	...	...	9	3	6
		Cardamom & pepper growers.	...	...	...	...	...	...
		Market gardeners (vegetable growers) ...	160	143	17	150	138	12
		Gardeners, &c. ...	...	...	...	37	29	8
		Manure preparers and sellers.	..	...	...	...	...	...
		Forest officers ...	...	...	...	...	...	...
		Forest guards and peons ...	...	...	...	...	...	...
		Total Sub-order 12 ...	160	143	17	223	182	41
	13	Agents and managers of landed estates ...	...	...	...	24	13	11
		Total Class B. ...	38,436	19,603	18,833	48,064	23,776	24,288

XVII.

(State Distribution)—(*Continued*).

—(*Continued*).

Kartigappalli.			Mavellikkara.			Chenganur.		
Total.	Males.	Females.	Total.	Males.	Females.	Total.	Males.	Females.
52	53	54	55	56	57	58	59	60
...	...	...	...	...	...	...	...	...
...	...	...	...	...	...	...	...	...
...	...	...	12	7	5	2	2	...
...	...	...	...	...	...	9	5	4
135	114	21	154	139	15	139	132	7
...	...	...	...	..	...	...	...	...
...	...	...	...	...	...	...	...	...
...	...	...	...	...	...	...	...	...
...	...	...	12	7	5	41	17	24
135	114	21	178	153	25	191	156	35
...	...	...	16	9	7	...	..	...
32,432	17,090	15,342	48,341	26,085	22,256	52,424	28,401	24,023

TABLE

Occupations, Part B.—

Class.	Group.	Occupation.	Taluqs: Tiruvalla. Total.	Tiruvalla. Males.	Tiruvalla. Females.	Ambalapula. Total.	Ambalapula. Males.	Ambalapula. Females.
1	2	3	61	62	63	64	65	66
B. Pasture and Agriculture.	12	Tea and coffee planters, managers and assistants ...	...	...	...	...	...	...
		Cocoanut growers ...	...	...	...	...	...	...
		Betel-vine growers ...	17	8	9	...	...	...
		Cardamom & pepper growers.	...	...	...	...	...	...
		Market gardeners (vegetable growers) ...	96	87	9	108	89	19
		Gardeners, &c. ...	...	...	...	...	...	...
		Manure preparers and sellers.	...	...	...	...	...	...
		Forest officers ...	...	...	...	...	...	...
		Forest guards and peons ...	...	...	...	10	4	6
		Total Sub-order 12 ...	113	95	18	118	93	25
	13	Agents and managers of landed estates ...	...	...	...	...	...	...
		Total Class B. ...	59,919	32,012	27,907	19,300	9,443	9,857

XVII.

(State Distribution)—(*Continued*).

—(*Continued*).

Sherttala.			Vykkam.			Ettumanur.		
Total.	Males.	Females.	Total.	Males.	Females.	Total.	Males.	Females.
67	68	69	70	71	72	73	74	75
...	...	...	...	...	...	...	...	...
...	...	...	...	...	...	...	...	...
...	...	...	11	7	4	...	...	...
...	...	...	...	...	...	...	...	...
154	137	17	85	72	13	145	139	6
25	18	7	...	...	...	...	...	...
...	...	...	...	...	..	...	...	...
...	...	...	...	...	...	...	...	...
...	..	...	...	...	...	...	...	...
179	155	24	96	79	17	145	139	6
...	...	...	22	13	9	...	...	...
33,276	17,719	15,557	22,190	12,982	9,208	33,964	18,821	15,143

TABLE

Occupations, Part B.—

Class.	Group.	Occupation.	Taluqs: Kottayam. Total.	Kottayam. Males.	Kottayam. Females.	Changanacheri. Total.	Changanacheri. Males.	Changanacheri. Females.
1	2	3	76	77	78	79	80	81
B. Pasture and Agriculture.	12	Tea and coffee planters, managers and assistants ...	...	...	...	19	12	7
		Cocoanut growers ...	...	...	...	...	...	...
		Betel-vine growers ...	...	...	...	...	...	...
		Cardamom & pepper growers.	...	...	...	26	14	12
		Market gardeners (vegetable growers) ..	134	117	17	176	153	23
		Gardeners, &c. ...	...	...	...	...	...	...
		Manure preparers and sellers.	...	...	...	...	...	...
		Forest officers ...	...	...	...	...	...	...
		Forest guards and peons ...	...	...	...	...	...	...
		Total Sub-order 12 ...	134	117	17	221	179	42
	13	Agents and managers of landed estates ...	...	...	...	31	18	13
		Total Class B. ...	27,565	14,642	12,923	26,629	15,201	11,428

XVII.

(State Distribution)—(*Continued*).

—(*Continued*).

Meenachal.			Muvattupula.			Todupula.		
Total.	Males.	Females.	Total.	Males.	Females.	Total.	Males.	Females.
82	83	84	85	86	87	88	89	90
3	2	1	...	...	...	2	2	...
...	...	...	...	...	...	...	...	...
20	13	7	...	...	...	...	...	...
9	4	5	...	...	...	...	...	...
85	74	11	126	94	32	69	46	23
...	...	...	...	...	...	...	...	...
...	...	...	...	...	...	...	...	...
...	...	...	...	...	...	...	...	...
1	1	...	52	22	30	...	...	...
118	94	24	178	116	62	71	48	23
...	...	...	...	...	...	...	...	...
37,886	20,146	17,740	59,639	30,246	29,393	15,187	8,208	6,979

TABLE

Occupations, Part B.—

Class.	Group.	Occupation.	Taluqs: Kunnattunadu. Total.	Kunnattunadu. Males.	Kunnattunadu. Females.	Alangadu. Total.	Alangadu. Males.	Alangadu. Females.
1	2	3	91	92	93	94	95	96
B. Pasture and Agriculture.	12	Tea and coffee planters, managers and assistants ...	...	...	...	..	...	...
		Cocoanut growers ...	...	...	...	...	...	...
		Betel-vine growers ...	...	...	...	...	...	...
		Cardamom & pepper growers..	...	...	...	...	...	...
		Market gardeners (vegetable growers) ..	48	37	11	...	...	...
		Gardeners, &c. ...	...	...	...	...	...	...
		Manure preparers and sellers.	...	...	...	...	...	...
		Forest officers ...	...	...	...	...	...	...
		Forest guards and peons ...	..	...	...	...	...	...
		Total Sub-order 12 ...	48	37	11	...	...	...
	13	Agents and managers of landed estates ...	91	50	41	...	...	...
		Total Class B. ...	61,271	30,569	30,702	34,852	18,797	16,055

XVII.

(State Distribution)—(Continued).

—(*Continued*).

Parur.			Cardamom Hills.			Periyar & Thekkadi.		
Total.	Males.	Females.	Total.	Males.	Females.	Total.	Males.	Females.
97	98	99	100	101	102	103	104	105
...	...	...	133	86	47	..	...	...
...	...	...	...	...	...	...	...	...
...	...	...	...	...	...	...	...	...
...	...	...	63	32	31	...	...	...
74	43	31	61	37	24	...	...	...
...	...	...	...	...	...	1	1	...
...	...	...	...	...	...	...	...	...
...	...	...	2	2	...	...	...	...
...	...	...	9	4	5	...	...	...
74	43	31	268	161	107	1	1	...
31	23	8	..	...	...	...	...	...
9,122	4,287	4,835	5,281	2,996	2,285	53	37	16

TABLE

Occupations, Part B.—

Class.	Group.	Occupation and Class. — Occupation.	State Total. — Total.	Males.	Females.
1	2	3	4	5	6
C. Personal Services.	14	Barbers ...	*17,395*	8,604	8,791
		Ear-pickers ...	*18*	11	7
		Washermen ...	*21,631*	9,472	12,159
		Water-carriers ...	*172*	79	93
		Cooks ...	*473*	159	314
		In-door servants ...	*38,842*	10,048	28,794
		Grooms, coachmen, dog-boys, &c. ...	*526*	343	183
		Door-keepers, &c. ...	*14*	10	4
		Total Sub-order 14 ...	**79,071**	**28,726**	**50,345**
	15	Hotel-keepers, &c. ...	*735*	254	481
		Rest-house keepers ...	*2*	2	...
		Club Secretaries ...	*11*	11	...
		Total Sub-order 15 ...	**748**	**267**	**481**
	16	Sanitary officers of Government ...	*51*	17	34
		Sweepers and scavengers ...	*408*	219	189
		Total Sub-order 16 ...	**459**	**236**	**223**
		Total Class C. ...	*80,278*	*29,229*	*51,049*

XVII.

(State Distribution)—(*Continued*).

TALUQS.

Tovala.			Agastiswaram.			Eranial.		
Total.	Males.	Females.	Total.	Males.	Females.	Total.	Males.	Females.
7	8	9	10	11	12	13	14	15
280	137	143	483	238	245	869	423	446
...	...	...	...	...	...	...	...	...
266	109	157	849	350	499	1,873	886	987
...	...	...	7	4	3	...	...	...
...	...	...	58	19	39	35	13	22
473	125	348	1,639	360	1,279	4,079	836	3,243
...	...	...	16	11	5	10	7	3
...	...	...	...	...	...	...	...	...
1,019	371	648	3,052	982	2,070	6,866	2,165	4,701
6	4	2	8	3	5	8	2	6
...	...	...	...	...	...	...	...	...
...	...	...	...	...	...	...	...	...
6	4	2	8	3	5	8	2	6
...	...	...	5	2	3	...	...	...
...	...	...	32	17	15	...	...	...
...	...	...	37	19	18	...	...	...
1,025	375	650	3,097	1,004	2,093	6,874	2,167	4,707

TABLE
Occupations, Part B.—

Class.	Group.	Occupation.	Taluqs: Kalkulam. Total.	Kalkulam. Males.	Kalkulam. Females.	Vilavankodu. Total.	Vilavankodu. Males.	Vilavankodu. Females.
1	2	3	16	17	18	19	20	21
C. Personal Services.	14	Barbers ...	295	146	149	580	283	297
		Ear-pickers ...	...	...	...	...	...	...
		Washermen ...	449	201	248	419	221	198
		Water-carriers ...	...	...	...	...	...	...
		Cooks ...	...	...	...	...	...	...
		In-door servants ..	757	242	515	902	224	678
		Grooms, coachmen, dog-boys, &c. ...	5	3	2	...	...	...
		Door-keepers, &c. ...	3	2	1	...	...	...
		Total Sub-order 14 ...	1,509	594	915	1,901	728	1,173
	15	Hotel-keepers, &c. ...	16	7	9	8	3	5
		Rest-house keepers ...	...	...	...	...	...	...
		Club Secretaries ...	...	...	...	...	...	...
		Total Sub-order 15 ...	16	7	9	8	3	5
	16	Sanitary officers of Government ...	...	...	...	...	...	...
		Sweepers and scavengers ...	...	...	...	...	...	...
		Total Sub-order 16 ...	...	...	...	...	...	...
		Total Class C. ...	1,525	601	924	1,909	731	1,178

XVII.

(State Distribution)—(*Continued*).

—(*Continued*).

Neyattankara.			Trivandram.			Nedumangadu.		
Total.	Males.	Females.	Total.	Males.	Females.	Total.	Males.	Females.
22	23	24	25	26	27	28	29	30
872	429	443	1,338	660	678	534	245	289
...	...	...	18	11	7	...	...	...
870	374	496	1,386	561	825	371	174	197
...	...	...	96	42	54	...	...	...
...	...	...	179	54	125	...	...	...
1,320	386	934	3,406	972	2,434	504	186	318
...	...	...	308	198	110	...	...	...
...	...	...	6	3	3	...	...	...
3,062	1,189	1,873	6,737	2,501	4,236	1,409	605	804
10	4	6	317	84	233	...	...	...
1	1	...	...	...	...	1	1	...
...	...	...	...	...	...	...	...	...
11	5	6	317	84	233	1	1	...
...	...	...	23	8	15	...	...	...
...	...	...	215	114	101	...	...	...
...	...	...	238	122	116	...	...	...
3,073	1,194	1,879	7,292	2,707	4,585	1,410	606	804

TABLE
Occupations, Part B.—

Class.	Group.	Occupation.	Talugs: Sirayinkil. Total.	Sirayinkil. Males.	Sirayinkil. Females.	Kottarakkara. Total.	Kottarakkara. Males.	Kottarakkara. Females.
1	2	3	31	32	33	34	35	36
C. Personal Services.	14	Barbers ...	944	411	533	164	79	85
		Ear-pickers ...	...	...	...	...	...	...
		Washermen ...	758	362	396	239	102	137
		Water-carriers ...	...	..	...	...	...	...
		Cooks ...	...	...	...	...	...	...
		In-door servants ...	1,360	343	1,017	942	217	725
		Grooms, coachmen, dog-boys, &c. ...	...	...	...	...	..	...
		Door-keepers, &c. ...	...	...	...	...	...	...
		Total Sub-order 14 ...	3,062	1,116	1,946	1,345	398	947
	15	Hotel-keepers, &c. ...	10	3	7	6	2	4
		Rest-house keepers ...	...	...	...	...	...	...
		Club Secretaries ...	...	...	...	...	...	...
		Total Sub-order 15 ...	10	3	7	6	2	4
	16	Sanitary officers of Government ...	...	...	...	...	...	...
		Sweepers and scavengers ...	...	...	...	...	...	...
		Total Sub-order 16 ...	...	...	...	...	...	...
		Total Class C. ...	3,072	1,119	1,953	1,351	400	951

XVII.

(State Distribution)—(*Continued*).

—(*Continued*).

Pattanapuram.			Shenkotta.			Quilon.		
Total.	Males.	Females.	Total.	Males.	Females.	Total.	Males.	Females.
37	38	39	40	41	42	43	44	45
439	222	217	468	219	249	848	461	387
...	...	...	...	...	...	...	...	...
205	87	118	537	200	337	779	316	463
...	...	...	...	...	...	20	8	12
15	4	11	11	3	8	50	21	29
453	98	355	1,045	214	831	2,269	531	1,738
...	...	...	...	...	...	75	47	28
...	...	...	...	...	...	...	...	...
1,112	411	701	2,061	636	1,425	4,041	1,384	2,657
7	4	3	4	2	2	113	43	70
...	...	...	...	...	...	...	...	...
...	...	...	...	...	...	11	11	...
7	4	3	4	2	2	124	54	70
...	...	...	...	...	...	8	3	5
...	...	...	...	...	...	48	29	19
...	...	...	...	...	...	56	32	24
1,119	415	704	2,065	638	1,427	4,221	1,470	2,751

TABLE
Occupations, Part B.—

Class.	Group.	Occupation.	Taluqs: Kunnattur. Total.	Kunnattur. Males.	Kunnattur. Females.	Karunagappalli. Total.	Karunagappalli. Males.	Karunagappalli. Females.
1	2	3	46	47	48	49	50	51
C. Personal Services.	14	Barbers ...	554	256	298	674	311	363
		Ear-pickers ...	...	...	...	...	...	...
		Washermen ...	599	284	315	1,319	502	817
		Water-carriers ...	...	...	...	...	...	...
		Cooks ...	...	...	...	...	...	...
		In-door servants ...	992	279	713	1,550	514	1,036
		Grooms, coachmen, dog-boys, &c. ...	...	...	...	...	...	...
		Door-keepers, &c. ...	...	...	...	2	2	...
		Total Sub-order 14 ...	2,145	819	1,326	3,545	1,329	2,216
	15	Hotel-keepers, &c. ...	...	...	...	16	7	9
		Rest-house keepers ...	...	...	...	...	...	...
		Club Secretaries ...	...	...	...	...	...	...
		Total Sub-order 15 ...	...	...	...	16	7	9
	16	Sanitary officers of Government ...	...	...	...	...	...	...
		Sweepers and scavengers ...	...	...	...	...	...	...
		Total Sub-order 16 ...	...	...	...	...	...	...
		Total Class C. ...	2,145	819	1,326	3,561	1,336	2,225

XVII.

(State Distribution)—(*Continued*).

—(*Continued*).

Kartigappalli.			Mavellikkara.			Chenganur.		
Total.	Males.	Females.	Total.	Males.	Females.	Total.	Males.	Females.
52	53	54	55	56	57	58	59	60
386	217	169	1,004	510	494	1,021	516	505
...	...	...	...	...	...	...	...	...
772	356	416	846	359	487	942	403	539
...	...	...	..	...	...	...	...	...
...	...	...	...	...	...	...	...	...
1,385	417	968	1,255	368	887	1,580	486	1,094
...	...	...	...	...	...	...	...	...
...	...	...	2	2	...	...	...	...
2,543	990	1,553	3,107	1,239	1,868	3,543	1,405	2,138
...	...	...	22	9	13	...	...	...
...	...	...	...	...	...	...	...	...
...	...	...	...	...	...	...	...	...
...	...	...	22	9	13	...	..	...
...	...	...	...	...	...	...	...	...
...	...	...	...	...	...	...	...	...
...	...	...	...	...	...	...	...	...
2,543	990	1,553	3,129	1,248	1,881	3,543	1,405	2,138

TABLE

Occupations, Part B.—

Class.	Group.	Occupation.	Taluqs Tiruvalla. Total.	Tiruvalla. Males.	Tiruvalla. Females.	Ambalappula. Total.	Ambalappula. Males.	Ambalappula. Females.
1	2	3	61	62	63	64	65	66
C. Personal Services.	14	Barbers ...	821	422	399	753	405	348
		Ear-pickers ...	...	...	...		...	...
		Washermen ...	1,075	481	594	742	329	413
		Water-carriers ...	...	...	...	16	7	9
		Cooks ...	...	...	...	48	13	35
		In-door servants ...	1,856	543	1,313	2,447	698	1,749
		Grooms, coachmen, dog-boys, &c. ...	...	...	...	45	30	15
		Door-keepers, &c. ...	...	...	...	...	...	...
		Total Sub-order 14 ...	3,752	1,446	2,306	4,051	1,482	2,569
	15	Hotel-keepers, &c. ...	..	...	...	60	28	32
		Rest-house keepers ...	...	...	...	...	...	...
		Club Secretaries ...	...	...	..	...	...	...
		Total Sub-order 15 ...	...	...	...	60	28	32
	16	Sanitary officers of Government ...	...	...	...	10	3	7
		Sweepers and scavengers ...	...	...	...	79	43	36
		Total Sub-order 16 ..	...	...	...	89	46	43
		Total Class C. ...	3,752	1,446	2,306	4,200	1,556	2,644

XVII.

(State Distribution)—(*Continued*).

—(*Continued*).

Sherttala.			Vykkam.			Ettumanur.		
Total.	Males.	Females.	Total.	Males.	Females.	Total.	Males.	Females.
67	68	69	70	71	72	73	74	75
422	225	197	354	166	188	543	274	269
...	...	...	...	...	...	...	...	...
362	176	186	1,375	578	797	647	310	337
...	...	...	...	...	...	...	...	...
...	...	..	...	...	...	...	...	...
815	176	639	711	143	568	687	189	498
...	...	...	...	...	...	...	...	...
...	...	...	...	...	...	...	...	...
1,599	577	1,022	2,440	887	1,553	1,877	773	1,104
...	...	...	20	7	13	6	2	4
...	...	...	...	...	...	...	..	...
...	...	...	...	...	...	...	...	...
...	...	...	20	7	13	6	2	4
...	...	...	...	...	...	...	...	...
...	...	...	...	...	...	...	...	...
...	...	...	...	...	...	...	...	...
1,599	577	1,022	2,460	894	1,566	1,883	775	1,108

TABLE

Occupations, Part B.—

Class.	Group.	Occupation.	Kottayam. Total.	Kottayam. Males.	Kottayam. Females.	Changanacheri. Total.	Changanacheri. Males.	Changanacheri. Females.
1	2	3	76	77	78	79	80	81
C. Personal Services.	14	Barbers ...	399	202	197	870	401	469
		Ear-pickers ...	...	...	...	...	...	...
		Washermen ...	501	232	269	653	262	391
		Water-carriers ...	19	10	9	...	...	...
		Cooks ...	37	12	25	...	...	...
		In-door servants ...	2,683	547	2,136	526	109	417
		Grooms, coachmen, dog-boys, &c. ...	25	18	7	...	...	...
		Door-keepers, &c. ...	...	...	...	...	...	...
		Total Sub-order 14 ...	3,664	1,021	2,643	2,049	772	1,277
	15	Hotel-keepers, &c. ...	52	23	29	...	...	...
		Rest-house keepers ...	...	...	...	...	...	...
		Club Secretaries ...	...	...	...	...	...	...
		Total Sub-order 15 ...	52	23	29	...	...	...
	16	Sanitary officers of Government ...	5	1	4	...	...	...
		Sweepers and scavengers ...	34	16	18	...	...	...
		Total Sub-order 16 ...	39	17	22	...	..	...
		Total Class C. ...	3,755	1,061	2,694	2,049	772	1,277

Taluqs: Kottayam, Changanacheri.

XVII.

(State Distribution)—(*Continued*).

—(*Continued*).

Meenachal.			Muvattupula.			Todupula.		
Total.	Males.	Females.	Total.	Males.	Females.	Total.	Males.	Females.
82	83	84	85	86	.87	88	89	90
270	139	131	271	137	134	124	68	56
...	...	...	...	...	...	...	...	...
355	156	199	405	188	217	155	68	87
...	...	...	...	...	...	...	...	...
...	...	...	...	...	...	...	...	...
387	88	299	611	166	445	580	153	427
...	...	...	...	...	...	...	...	...
...	...	...	...	...	...	...	...	...
1,012	383	629	1,287	491	796	859	289	570
12	4	8	...	...	...	...	...	...
...	...	...	...	...	...	..	...	...
...	...	...	...	...	...	...	...	...
12	4	8	...	...	...	...	...	...
...	...	...	...	...	...	...	...	...
...	...	...	...	...	...	...	...	...
...	...	...	..	...	...	...	...	...
1,024	387	637	1,287	491	796	859	289	570

TABLE

Occupations, Part B.—

Class.	Group.	Occupation.	Taluqs: Kunnattunadu. Total.	Kunnattunadu. Males.	Kunnattunadu. Females.	Alangadu. Total.	Alangadu. Males.	Alangadu. Females.
1	2	3	91	92	93	94	95	96
C. Personal Services.	14	Barbers ...	517	215	302	93	62	31
		Ear-pickers ...	...	...	...	...	...	...
		Washermen ...	801	363	438	895	384	511
		Water-carriers ...	...	...	...	...	...	...
		Cooks ...	...	...	...	...	...	...
		In-door servants ...	653	185	468	475	121	354
		Grooms, coachmen, dog-boys, &c. ..	...	...	...	...	...	...
		Door-keepers, &c. ...	...	...	...	...	...	...
		Total Sub-order 14 ...	1,971	763	1,208	1,463	567	896
	15	Hotel-keepers, &c. ...	11	4	7	...	...	...
		Rest-house keepers ...	...	...	...	...	...	...
		Club Secretaries ...	...	...	...	...	...	...
		Total Sub-order 15 ...	11	4	7	...	...	...
	16	Sanitary officers of Government ...	...	...	...	...	...	...
		Sweepers and scavengers ...	...	...	...	...	...	...
		Total Sub-order 16 ...	...	...	...	...	...	...
		Total Class C. ...	1,982	767	1,215	1,463	567	896

XVII.

(State Distribution)—(*Continued*).

—(*Continued*).

Parur.			Cardamom Hills.			Periyar and Thekkadi.		
Total.	Males.	Females.	Total.	Males.	Females.	Total.	Males.	Females.
97	98	99	100	101	102	103	104	105
177	109	68	27	15	12	1	1	...
...	...	...	...	...	...	...	...	...
180	94	86	1	1	...	5	3	2
...	...	...	...	...	...	14	8	6
...	...	...	14	8	6	26	12	14
314	35	279	106	42	64	80	55	25
10	7	3	21	14	7	11	8	3
1	1	...	...	...	...	...	...	...
682	246	436	169	80	89	137	87	50
22	9	13	...	...	...	1	...	1
...	...	...	...	...	...	...	...	...
...	...	...	...	...	...	...	...	...
22	9	13	...	...	...	1	...	1
...	...	...	...	...	...	...	...	...
...	...	...	...	...	...	...	...	...
...	...	...	...	...	...	...	...	...
704	255	449	169	80	89	138	87	51

TABLE

Occupations, Part B.—

Class.	Group.	Occupation.	Total.	Males.	Females.
1	2	3	4	5	6
D. Preparation and supply of material substances.	17	Cow and buffalo keepers and milk and butter sellers ...	*709*	**224**	**485**
		Ghee preparers and sellers ...	*56*	**37**	**19**
		Butchers ...	*646*	**388**	**258**
		Fowl and egg sellers ...	*47*	**29**	**18**
		Fishermen and fish-curers ...	*28,885*	**19,132**	**9,753**
		Fish dealers ...	*26,807*	**10,314**	**16,493**
		Total Sub-order 17 ...	**57,150**	**30,124**	**27,026**
	18	Grain dealers ...	*1,084*	**725**	**359**
		Flour preparers and sellers ...	*53*	**29**	**24**
		Bakers ...	*17*	**13**	**4**
		Bran sellers ...	*49*	**10**	**39**
		Vegetable sellers ...	*351*	**149**	**202**
		Fruit sellers ...	*9*	**6**	**3**
		Cocoanut dealers ...	*1,230*	**727**	**503**
		Confectioners and sweet-meat makers and sellers and cooks (publique) ...	*3,051*	**1,393**	**1,658**
		Sweet-meat pedlars ...	*16*	**13**	**3**
		Total Sub-order 18 ...	**5,860**	**3,065**	**2,795**

XVII.

(State Distribution)—(*Continued*).

TALUQS.

Tovala.			Agastiswaram.			Eranial.		
Total.	Males.	Females.	Total.	Males.	Females.	Total.	Males.	Females.
7	8	9	10	11	12	13	14	15
12	3	9	70	18	52	26	7	19
...	...	...	3	2	1	...	...	...
...	...	...	56	37	19	30	14	16
...	...	...	6	4	2	...	...	...
...	...	...	...	...	...	1,112	734	378
201	107	94	1,538	705	833	4,134	1,889	2,245
213	110	103	1,673	766	907	5,302	2,644	2,658
19	14	5	57	38	19	68	42	26
...	...	...	13	8	5	...	...	...
...	...	...	...	...	...	...	...	...
...	...	...	2	...	2	...	...	...
8	3	5	36	14	22	14	8	6
...	...	...	...	...	...	...	...	...
...	...	...	...	...	...	77	41	36
26	14	12	234	109	125	36	17	19
...	...	...	...	...	...	...	...	...
53	31	22	342	169	173	195	108	87

TABLE

Occupations, Part B.—

Class.	Group.	Occupation.	Taluqs: Kalkulam. Total.	Kalkulam. Males.	Kalkulam. Females.	Vilavankodu. Total.	Vilavankodu. Males.	Vilavankodu. Females.
1	2	3	16	17	18	19	20	21
D. Preparation and supply of material substances.	17	Cow and buffalo keepers and milk and butter sellers ...	22	9	13	...	...	...
		Ghee preparers and sellers ...	...	...	...	...	...	...
		Butchers ...	16	7	9	...	...	..
		Fowl and egg sellers ...	...	...	...	...	...	...
		Fishermen and fish-curers ...	...	...	...	1,661	925	736
		Fish dealers ...	55	10	45	2,485	1,127	1 358
		Total Sub-order 17 ...	93	26	67	4,146	2,052	2,094
	18	Grain dealers ...	...	...	...	28	17	11
		Flour preparers and sellers...	...	...	...	...	...	...
		Bakers ...	...	...	...	...	...	...
		Bran sellers ...	...	...	...	...	...	...
		Vegetable sellers ...	9	3	6	...	...	...
		Fruit sellers ...	...	...	...	...	...	...
		Cocoanut dealers ...	...	...	...	...	...	...
		Confectioners and sweet-meat makers and sellers and cooks (publique) ...	101	47	54	67	31	36
		Sweet-meat pedlars ...	...	...	...	...	...	...
		Total Sub-order 18 ...	110	50	60	95	48	47

XVII.

(State Distribution)—(*Continued*).

—(*Continued*).

Neyattankara.			Trivandram.			Nedumangadu.		
Total.	Males.	Females.	Total.	Males.	Females.	Total	Males.	Females.
22	23	24	25	26	27	28	29	30
46	14	32	227	48	179	...	...	...
...	...	...	20	13	7	...	...	...
9	4	5	123	69	54	...	...	...
...	...	...	22	13	9	...	...	...
1,715	1,147	568	2,210	1,360	850	...	...	...
1,376	431	945	3,624	1,543	2,081	90	34	56
3,146	1,596	1,550	6,226	3,046	3,180	90	34	56
56	31	25	180	124	56	...	...	...
...	...	...	26	14	12	...	...	...
...	...	...	12	8	4	...	...	...
...	...	...	28	7	21	...	...	...
...	...	...	74	30	44	...	...	...
...	...	...	9	6	3	...	...	...
67	38	29	98	52	46	...	...	...
61	28	33	599	268	331	31	14	17
...	...	...	11	8	3	...	...	...
184	97	87	1,037	517	520	31	14	17

TABLE

Occupations, Part B.—

Class.	Group.	Occupation.	Taluqs: Sirayinkil. Total.	Sirayinkil. Males.	Sirayinkil. Females.	Kottarakkara. Total.	Kottarakkara. Males.	Kottarakkara. Females.
1	2	3	31	32	33	34	35	36
D. Preparation and supply of material substances.	17	Cow and buffalo keepers and milk and butter sellers ...	53	14	39	...	...	...
		Ghee preparers and sellers ...	8	4	4	...	...	...
		Butchers .	25	14	11	...	...	...
		Fowl and egg sellers ...	...	...	...	...	...	...
		Fishermen and fish-curers ...	1,898	1,142	756	...	...	...
		Fish dealers ...	1,873	638	1,235	48	17	31
		Total Sub-order 17 ...	3,857	1,812	2,045	48	17	31
	18	Grain dealers ...	31	18	13	...	...	...
		Flour preparers and sellers ...	...	...	...	...	...	...
		Bakers ...	...	...	...	...	...	...
		Bran sellers ...	...	...	...	...	...	...
		Vegetable sellers ...	...	...	...	...	...	...
		Fruit sellers ...	...	...	...	...	...	...
		Cocoanut dealers ...	59	34	25	...	...	...
		Confectioners and sweet-meat makers and sellers and cooks (publique) ...	95	41	54	73	34	39
		Sweet-meat pedlars ...	...	...	...	...	...	...
		Total Sub-order 18 ...	185	93	92	73	34	39

XVII.

(State Distribution)—(*Continued*).

—(*Continued*).

Pattanapuram.			Shenkotta.			Quilon.		
Total.	Males.	Females.	Total.	Males.	Females.	Total.	Males.	Females.
37	38	39	40	41	42	43	44	45
...	...	...	30	13	17	39	21	18
...	...	...	5	3	2	12	7	5
22	13	9	15	8	7	67	42	25
...	...	...	...	...	...	11	7	4
...	...	...	...	...	...	2,712	1,814	898
26	14	12	45	24	21	1,083	215	868
48	27	21	95	48	47	3,924	2,106	1,818
...	...	...	28	19	9	216	149	67
...	...	...	4	2	2	...	...	...
...	...	...	...	...	...	...	...	...
...	...	...	...	...	...	18	3	15
...	...	...	...	...	...	31	14	17
...	...	...	...	...	...	...	...	...
...	...	...	...	...	...	170	109	61
12	5	7	101	47	54	386	189	197
...	...	...	...	...	...	5	5	...
12	5	7	133	68	65	826	469	357

TABLE

Occupations, Part B.—

Class.	Group.	Occupation	Kunnattur. Total.	Kunnattur. Males.	Kunnattur. Females.	Karunagappalli. Total.	Karunagappalli. Males.	Karunagappalli. Females.
1	2	3	46	47	48	49	50	51
D. Preparation and supply of material substances.	17	Cow aud buffalo keepers and milk and butter sellers ...	...	...	...	53	27	26
		Ghee preparers and sellers ...	...	...	...	...	...	...
		Butchers ...	...	...	...	...	...	...
		Fowl and egg sellers ...	...	...	...	...	...	...
		Fishermen and fish-curers ...	433	205	228	2,008	1,352	656
		Fish dealers ...	446	217	229	610	241	369
		Total Sub-order 17 ...	879	422	457	2,671	1,620	1,051
	18	Grain dealers ...	46	34	12	25	11	14
		Flour preparers and sellers...	...	...	...	...	...	...
		Bakers ...	...	...	...	...	...	...
		Bran sellers ...	...	...	...	...	...	...
		Vegetable sellers ...	21	8	13	41	19	22
		Fruit sellers ...	...	...	...	...	...	...
		Cocoanut dealers ...	...	...	...	165	107	58
		Confectioners and sweet-meat makers and sellers and cooks (publique) ...	69	31	38	33	14	19
		Sweet-meat pedlars ...	...	...	...	...	...	...
		Total Sub-order 18 ...	136	73	63	264	151	113

(Header above district columns: TALUQS)

XVII.

(State Distribution)—(*Continued*).

—(*Continued*).

Kartigappalli.			Mavellikkara.			Chenganur.		
Total.	Males.	Females.	Total.	Males.	Females.	Total.	Males.	Females.
52	53	54	55	56	57	58	59	60
...	...	...	...	...	...	...	...	...
...	...	...	...	...	...	...	...	...
24	14	10	...	...	...	26	17	9
...	...	...	...	...	...	...	...	...
1,606	793	813	35	14	21	...	...	...
841	352	489	396	138	258	222	117	105
2,471	1,159	1,312	431	152	279	248	134	114
32	17	15	...	...	...	...	...	...
...	...	...	...	...	...	...	...	...
...	...	...	...	...	...	...	...	..
...	...	...	...	...	...	...	...	...
23	13	10	...	...	...	...	...	...
...	...	...	...	...	...	...	...	...
77	41	36	...	...	...	..	...	...
237	104	133	105	49	56	40	18	22
...	...	...	...	...	...	...	...	...
369	175	194	105	49	56	40	18	22

TABLE

Occupations, Part B.—

Class.	Group.	Occupation.	Taluqs: Tiruvalla. Total.	Tiruvalla. Males.	Tiruvalla. Females.	Ambalappula. Total.	Ambalappula. Males.	Ambalappula. Females.
1	2	3	61	62	63	64	65	66
D. Preparation and supply of material substances.	17	Cow and buffalo keepers and milk and butter sellers ...	...	...	...	84	31	53
		Ghee preparers and sellers ...	...	...	...	4	4	...
		Butchers ...	...	..	...	36	23	13
		Fowl and egg sellers ...	...	...	...	...	...	...
		Fishermen and fish-curers ...	...	...	...	2,559	1,994	565
		Fish dealers ...	321	194	127	1,674	498	1,176
		Total Sub-order 17 ...	321	194	127	4,357	2,550	1,807
	18	Grain dealers ..	...	...	...	203	145	58
		Flour preparers and sellers...	...	...	..	6	3	3
		Bakers ...	...	...	...	2	2	...
		Bran sellers ...	...	...	...	1	...	1
		Vegetable sellers ...	...	...	...	10	4	6
		Fruit sellers ...	...	...	...	...	...	...
		Cocoanut dealers ...	...	...	...	190	116	74
		Confectioners and sweet-meat makers and sellers and cooks (publique) ...	31	14	17	123	54	69
		Sweet-meat pedlars ...	...	...	...	...	...	...
		Total Sub-order 18 ...	31	14	17	535	324	211

XVII.

(State Distribution)—(*Continued*).

—(*Continued*).

Sherttala.			Vykkam.			Ettumanur.		
Total.	Males.	Females.	Total.	Males.	Females.	Total.	Males.	Females.
67	68	69	70	71	72	73	74	75
...	...	...	31	14	17	...	...	...
...	...	...	...	...	...	...	...	...
...	...	...	26	14	12	...	...	...
...	...	...	...	...	...	...	...	...
7,550	5,597	1,953	293	197	96	578	319	259
2,602	437	2,165	337	148	189	282	123	159
10,152	6,034	4,118	687	373	314	860	442	418
...	...	...	...	...	...	...	...	...
...	...	...	...	...	...	...	...	...
...	...	...	...	...	...	...	...	...
...	...	...	...	...	...	...	...	...
...	...	...	...	...	...	...	...	...
...	...	...	...	...	...	...	...	...
72	41	31	..	...	...	32	17	15
21	8	13	206	93	113	31	14	17
...	...	...	...	...	...	...	...	...
93	49	44	206	93	113	63	31	32

TABLE

Occupations, Part B.—

Class.	Group.	Occupation.	Taluqs: Kottayam. Total.	Kottayam. Males.	Kottayam. Females.	Changanacheri. Total.	Changanacheri. Males.	Changanacheri. Females.
1	2	3	76	77	78	79	80	81
D. Preparation and supply of material substances.	17	Cow and buffalo keepers and milk and butter sellers ...	16	5	11	...	...	...
		Ghee preparers and sellers ...	3	3	...	...	...	...
		Butchers ...	66	47	19	...	...	...
		Fowl and egg sellers ...	...	...	...	...	...	...
		Fishermen and fish-curers ...	1,417	874	543	579	314	265
		Fish dealers ...	318	131	187	1,135	538	597
		Total Sub-order 17 ...	1,820	1,060	760	1,714	852	862
	18	Grain dealers ...	69	48	21	...	...	...
		Flour preparers and sellers...	4	2	2	...	...	...
		Bakers ...	...	...	...	...	...	...
		Brain sellers ...	...	...	...	...	...	...
		Vegetable sellers ...	...	...	...	84	33	51
		Fruit sellers ...	...	...	...	...	...	...
		Cocoanut dealers ...	...	...	...	85	46	39
		Confectioners and sweet-meat makers and sellers and cooks (publique) ...	106	50	56	16	7	9
		Sweet-meat pedlars ...	...	...	...	...	...	...
		Total Sub-order 18 ...	179	100	79	185	86	99

XVII.

(State Distribution)—(*Continued*).

—(*Continued*).

Meenachal.			Muvattupula.			Todupula.		
Total.	Males.	Females.	Total.	Males.	Females.	Total.	Males.	Females.
82	83	84	85	86	87	88	89	90
...	...	...	...	...	...	...	...	...
...	...	...	...	...	...	...	...	...
...	...	...	22	14	8	...	...	...
...	...	...	...	...	...	...	...	...
...	...	...	...	...	...	...	...	...
84	39	45	318	145	173	33	14	19
84	39	45	340	159	181	33	14	19
...	...	...	...	...	...	...	...	...
...	...	...	...	...	...	...	...	...
...	...	...	...	...	...	...	...	...
...	...	...	...	...	...	...	...	...
...	...	...	...	...	...	...	...	...
...	...	...	...	...	...	...	...	...
...	...	...	...	...	...	...	...	...
...	...	...	32	14	18	...	...	...
...	...	...	...	...	...	...	...	...
...	...	...	32	14	18	...	...	...

TABLE

Occupations, Part B.—

Class.	Group.	Occupation.	Taluqs: Kunnattunadu. Total.	Kunnattunadu. Males.	Kunnattunadu. Females.	Alangadu. Total.	Alangadu. Males.	Alangadu. Females.
1	2	3	91	92	93	94	95	96
D. Preparation and supply of material substances.	17	Cow and buffalo keepers and milk and butter sellers ...	...	...	...	...	...	...
		Ghee preparers and sellers ...	...	...	...	...	...	...
		Butchers ...	...	...	...	13	8	5
		Fowl and egg sellers ...	...	...	...	...	...	...
		Fishermen and fish-curers ...	...	...	...	...	...	...
		Fish dealers ...	102	49	53	84	38	46
		Total Sub-order 17 ...	102	49	53	97	46	51
	18	Grain dealers ...	20	14	6	...	...	...
		Flour preparers and sellers...	...	...	...	...	...	...
		Bakers ...	...	...	...	...	...	...
		Bran sellers ...	...	...	...	...	...	...
		Vegetable sellers ...	...	...	...	...	...	...
		Fruit sellers ...	...	...	...	...	...	...
		Cocoanut dealers ...	...	...	...	...	...	...
		Confectioners and sweet-meat makers and sellers and cooks (publique) ...	...	...	...	30	12	18
		Sweet-meat pedlars ...	...	...	...	...	...	...
		Total Sub-order 18 ...	20	14	6	30	12	18

XVII.

(State Distribution)—(*Continued*).

—(*Continued*).

Parur.			Cardamom Hills.			Periyar & Thekkadi.		
Total.	Males.	Females.	Total.	Males.	Females.	Total.	Males.	Females.
97	98	99	100	101	102	103	104	105
...	...	...	...	...	...	...	...	...
...	...	...	...	...	...	1	1	...
44	27	17	20	12	8	6	4	2
8	5	3	..	...	...	...	...	...
511	343	168	5	5	...	3	3	...
416	138	278	...	...	...	8	3	5
979	513	466	25	17	8	18	11	7
...	...	...	...	..	...	6	4	2
...	...	...	...	...	...	...	...	...
...	...	...	...	...	...	3	3	...
...	...	...	...	...	...	...	...	...
...	...	...	...	...	...	...	...	...
...	...	...	...	...	...	...	...	...
138	85	53	...	...	...	...	...	...
141	62	79	5	3	2	3	2	1
...	...	...	...	...	...	...	...	...
279	147	132	5	3	2	12	9	3

TABLE

Occupations, Part B.—

Occupation and Class.			State Total.		
Class.	Group.	Occupation.	Total.	Males.	Females.
1	2	3	4	5	6
D. Preparation and supply of material substances.	19	Sharbat preparers and sellers ...	*6*	6	...
		Country-spirits distillers and sellers...	*1,581*	469	1,112
		Toddy drawers and sellers ...	*75,746*	40,675	35,071
		Foreign wine and spirit dealers ...	*2*	2	...
		Tea sellers ...	*7*	7	...
		Coffee preparers and sellers ...	*131*	70	61
		Sugar sellers ...	*24*	16	8
		Molasses (jaggery, gur, &c.) makers and sellers ...	*68,395*	38,075	30,320
		Salt preparers and sellers ...	*1,207*	688	519
		Grocers and general condiment dealers ...	*508*	423	85
		Betel-leaf and arecanut sellers ...	*1,222*	585	637
		Tobacco and snuff manufacturers and sellers ...	*4,026*	2,385	1,641
		Opium, &c., sellers ...	*9*	5	4
		Total Sub-order 19 ..	**152,864**	**83,406**	**69,458**
	20	Oil-pressers and sellers ..	*14,071*	7,874	6,197
		Oil sellers ...	*2,987*	1,325	1,662
		Oil-cake dealers ..	*677*	526	151
		Kerosine oil dealers ...	*35*	22	13
		Matches sellers ...	*12*	8	4
		Lamp and lantern makers and sellers.	*25*	15	10
		Lamp lighting ...	*22*	14	8
		Total Sub-order 20 ...	**17,829**	**9,784**	**8,045**

XVII.

(State Distribution)—(*Continued*).

Taluqs.								
Tovala.			Agastiswaram.			Eranial.		
Total.	Males.	Females.	Total.	Males.	Females.	Total.	Males.	Females.
7	8	9	10	11	12	13	14	15
...	...	...	...	...	...	...	...	...
30	17	13	161	22	139	34	7	27
...	...	...	...	...	...	...	...	...
...	...	...	...	...	...	...	...	...
...	...	...	...	...	...	...	...	...
...	...	...	...	...	...	...	...	...
...	...	...	...	...	...	...	...	...
461	273	188	10,604	5,745	4,859	23,188	12,501	10,687
24	14	10	337	194	143	418	234	184
19	19	...	52	43	9	42	31	11
...	...	...	23	8	15	31	14	17
13	8	5	308	179	129	237	159	78
...	...	...	...	...	...	...	...	...
547	331	216	11,485	6,191	5,294	23,950	12,946	11,004
...	...	...	83	48	35	27	11	16
64	26	38	298	126	172	134	66	68
...	...	...	48	33	15	27	18	9
...	...	...	...	...	...	...	...	...
...	...	...	...	...	...	...	...	...
...	...	...	...	...	...	...	...	...
...	...	...	...	...	...	...	...	...
64	26	38	429	207	222	188	95	93

TABLE

Occupations, Part B.—

Class.	Group.	Occupation.	Kalkulam. Total.	Kalkulam. Males.	Kalkulam. Females.	Vilavankodu. Total.	Vilavankodu. Males.	Vilavankodu. Females.
1	2	3	16	17	18	19	20	21
D. Preparation and supply of material substances.	19	Sharbat preparers and sellers.	...	...	...	...	...	...
		Country-spirits distillers and sellers ...	17	4	13	17	6	11
		Toddy drawers and sellers ...	...	...	...	36	20	16
		Foreign wine and spirit dealers ...	...	...	...	...	...	...
		Tea sellers ...	...	...	...	...	...	...
		Coffee preparers and sellers...	...	...	...	...	...	...
		Sugar sellers ...	...	...	...	...	...	...
		Molasses (jaggery, gur, &c.) makers and sellers ...	7,490	4,512	2,978	20,493	11,325	9,168
		Salt preparers and sellers ...	39	18	21	26	14	12
		Grocers and general condiment dealers ...	4	4	...	...	...	...
		Betel-leaf and arecanut sellers.	55	33	22	52	19	33
		Tobacco and snuff manufacturers and sellers ...	141	88	53	78	33	45
		Opium, &c., sellers ...	...	...	...	...	...	...
		Total Sub-order 19 ...	7,746	4,659	3,087	20,702	11,417	9,285
	20	Oil-pressers and sellers ...	73	31	42	101	48	53
		Oil sellers ...	62	25	37	267	122	145
		Oil-cake dealers ...	39	31	8	...	...	...
		Kerosine oil dealers ...	...	...	...	...	...	...
		Matches sellers ...	...	...	...	...	...	...
		Lamp and lantern makers and sellers ...	...	...	...	...	...	...
		Lamp lighting ...	...	...	...	...	...	...
		Total Sub-order 20 ...	174	87	87	368	170	198

Taluqs: Kalkulam (cols 16–18), Vilavankodu (cols 19–21).

XVII.

(State Distribution)—(*Continued*).

—(*Continued*).

Neyattankara.			Trivandram.			Nedumangadu.		
Total.	Males.	Females.	Total.	Males.	Females.	Total.	Males.	Females.
22	23	24	25	26	27	28	29	30
...	...	...	3	3	...	2	2	...
112	44	68	185	43	142	39	14	25
397	172	225	2,011	1,043	968	93	54	39
...	...	...	2	2	...	...	...	...
...	...	...	3	3	...	...	...	...
...	...	...	67	32	35	...	...	...
...	...	...	...	...	...	..	...	...
4,732	3,001	1,731	176	98	78	3	3	...
40	23	17	82	47	35	22	14	8
22	22	...	71	49	22	10	8	2
21	7	14	231	89	142	66	31	35
56	22	34	437	248	189	61	39	22
...	...	...	9	5	4	...	..	...
5,380	3,291	2,089	3,277	1,662	1,615	296	165	131
656	370	286	673	360	313	122	68	54
60	31	29	123	55	68	176	89	87
...	...	...	...	...	...	...	...	...
...	...	...	20	14	6	...	...	...
...	...	...	12	8	4	...	...	...
...	...	...	9	4	5	...	...	...
..	...	...	14	8	6	...	...	...
716	401	315	851	449	402	298	157	141

TABLE

Occupations, Part B.—

Class.	Group.	Occupation.	Taluqs: Sirayinkil. Total.	Sirayinkil. Males.	Sirayinkil. Females.	Kottarakkara. Total.	Kottarakkara. Males.	Kottarakkara. Females.
1	2	3	31	32	33	34	35	36
D. Preparation and supply of material substances.	19	Sharbat preparers and sellers.	...	...	...	...	...	...
		Country-spirits distillers and sellers ...	151	52	99	40	13	27
		Toddy drawers and sellers ...	1,840	975	865	433	200	233
		Foreign wine and spirit dealers ...	...	...	...	...	...	...
		Tea sellers ...	...	...	...	...	...	...
		Coffee preparers and sellers...	...	...	...	...	...	...
		Sugar sellers ...	...	...	...	...	...	...
		Molasses (jaggery, gur, &c.) makers and sellers ...	37	20	17	...	...	...
		Salt preparers and sellers ...	...	...	...	23	18	5
		Grocers and general condiment dealers ...	17	14	3	9	9	...
		Betel-leaf and arecanut sellers.	55	18	37	32	13	19
		Tobacco and snuff manufacturers and sellers ...	83	47	36	158	89	69
		Opium, &c., sellers ...	...	...	...	...	...	...
		Total Sub-order 19 ...	2,183	1,126	1,057	695	342	353
	20	Oil-pressers and sellers ...	468	290	178	64	39	25
		Oil sellers ...	678	285	393	167	88	79
		Oil-cake dealers ...	...	...	...	...	...	...
		Kerosine oil dealers ...	...	...	...	...	...	...
		Matches sellers ...	...	...	...	...	...	...
		Lamp and lantern makers and sellers ...	...	...	...	...	...	...
		Lamp lighting ...	...	...	...	...	...	...
		Total Sub-order 20 ...	1,146	575	571	231	127	104

XVII.

(State Distribution)—*(Continued)*.

—*(Continued)*.

Pattanapuram.			Shenkotta.			Quilon.		
Total.	Males.	Females.	Total.	Males.	Females.	Total.	Males.	Females.
37	38	39	40	41	42	43	44	45
...	...	...	...	...	...	...	...	...
43	12	31	75	27	48	95	36	59
493	229	264	60	24	36	5,553	2,922	2,631
...	...	...	...	...	...	...	...	...
...	...	...	...	...	...	2	2	...
...	...	...	...	...	...	33	18	15
...	...	...	...	...	...	...	...	...
...	...	...	...	...	...	...	...	...
...	...	...	22	13	9	...	...	...
...	...	...	...	...	...	37	28	9
49	31	18	...	...	...	69	45	24
71	33	38	42	17	25	314	188	126
...	...	...	...	...	...	...	...	...
656	305	351	199	81	118	6,103	3,239	2,864
17	11	6	99	56	43	645	358	287
15	9	6	27	12	15	22	13	9
...	...	...	...	...	...	51	35	16
...	...	...	...	...	...	6	3	3
...	...	...	...	...	...	...	...	...
...	...	...	...	...	...	6	3	3
...	...	...	...	...	...	4	2	2
32	20	12	126	68	58	734	414	320

TABLE

Occupations, Part B.—

Class.	Group.	Occupation.	Taluqs: Kunnattur. Total.	Kunnattur. Males.	Kunnattur. Females.	Karunagappalli. Total.	Karunagappalli. Males.	Karunagappalli. Females.
1	2	3	46	47	48	49	50	51
D. Preparation and supply of material substances.	19	Sharbat preparers and sellers.	...	...	...	...	...	...
		Country-spirits distillers and sellers ...	39	14	25	44	13	31
		Toddy drawers and sellers ...	960	580	380	5,477	2,741	2,736
		Foreign wine and spirit dealers ...	...	...	...	...	...	...
		Tea sellers ...	...	...	...	...	...	...
		Coffee preparers and sellers...	...	...	...	...	...	...
		Sugar sellers ...	...	...	...	...	...	...
		Molasses (jaggery, gur, &c.) makers and sellers ...	...	...	...	...	...	...
		Salt preparers and sellers ...	...	...	...	34	19	15
		Grocers and general condiment dealers ...	...	...	...	20	17	3
		Betel-leaf and arecanut sellers.	7	7	...	26	11	15
		Tobacco and snuff manufacturers and sellers ...	77	36	41	147	94	53
		Opium, &c., sellers ...	...	...	...	...	...	...
		Total Sub-order 19 ...	1,083	637	446	5,748	2,895	2,853
	20	Oil-pressers and sellers ...	43	25	18	670	372	298
		Oil sellers ...	26	7	19	69	31	38
		Oil-cake dealors ...	...	...	...	406	327	79
		Kerosine oil dealers ...	...	...	...	...	...	...
		Matches sellers ...	...	...	...	...	...	...
		Lamp and lantern makers and sellers ...	...	...	...	...	...	...
		Lamp lighting ...	...	...	...	...	...	...
		Total Sub-order 20 ...	69	32	37	1,145	730	415

XVII.

(State Distribution)—(*Continued*).

—(*Continued*).

Kartigappalli.			Mavellikkara.			Chengannur.		
Total.	Males.	Females.	Total.	Males.	Females.	Total.	Males.	Females.
52	53	54	55	56	57	58	59	60
...	...	...	...	...	...	...	...	...
...	...	...	79	31	48	30	13	17
2,270	1,274	996	2,174	1,161	1,013	746	378	368
...	...	...	...	...	...	...	...	...
...	...	...	...	...	...	...	...	...
...	...	...	...	...	...	...	...	...
...	...	...	...	...	...	6	4	2
...	...	...	...	...	...	313	145	168
...	...	...	...	...	...	...	...	...
25	19	6	7	7	...	...	...	...
21	9	12	45	27	18	...	...	...
152	87	65	146	89	57	153	87	66
...	...	...	...	...	...	...	...	...
2,468	1,389	1,079	2,451	1,315	1,136	1,248	627	621
439	260	179	600	317	283	253	139	114
15	6	9	54	20	34	39	14	25
...	...	...	...	...	...	...	...	...
...	...	...	...	...	...	...	...	...
...	...	...	...	...	...	...	...	...
...	...	...	...	...	...	...	...	...
...	...	...	...	...	...	...	...	...
454	266	188	654	337	317	292	153	139

TABLE

Occupations, Part B.—

Class.	Group.	Occupation.	Taluqs: Tiruvalla. Total.	Tiruvalla. Males.	Tiruvalla. Females.	Ambalappula. Total.	Ambalappula. Males.	Ambalappula. Females.
1	2	3	61	62	63	64	65	66
D. Preparation and supply of material substances.	19	Sharbat preparers and sellers.	...	...	...	1	1	...
		Country-spirits distillers and sellers ...	16	7	9	...	...	...
		Toddy drawers and sellers ...	2,869	1,715	1,154	3,814	2,083	1,731
		Foreign wine and spirit dealers ...	...	...	...	...	...	...
		Tea sellers ...	...	...	...	2	2	...
		Coffee preparers and sellers...	...	...	...	21	13	8
		Sugar sellers ...	...	...	...	...	...	...
		Molasses (jaggery, gur, &c.) makers and sellers ...	...	...	...	271	134	137
		Salt preparers and sellers ...	15	8	7	27	16	11
		Grocers and general condiment dealers ...	12	12	...	46	43	3
		Betel-leaf and arecanut sellers	19	13	6	72	27	45
		Tobacco and snuff manufacturers and sellers ...	205	119	86	288	183	105
		Opium, &c., sellers ...	...	...	...	...	...	...
		Total Sub-order 19 ...	3,136	1,874	1,262	4,542	2,502	2,040
	20	Oil-pressers and sellers ...	829	443	386	692	399	293
		Oil sellers ...	58	27	31	319	133	186
		Oil-cake dealers ...	...	...	...	...	...	...
		Kerosine oil dealers ...	...	...	...	7	3	4
		Matches sellers ...	...	...	...	...	...	...
		Lamp and lantern makers and sellers ...	...	...	...	10	8	2
		Lamp lighting ...	...	...	...	2	2	...
		Total Sub-order 20 ...	887	470	417	1,030	545	485

XVII.

(State Distribution)—(*Continued*).

—(*Continued*).

Sherttala.			Vykkam.			Ettumanur.		
Total.	Males.	Females.	Total.	Males.	Females.	Total.	Males.	Females.
67	68	69	70	71	72	73	74	75
...	...	...	...	...	...	...	...	...
...	...	...	...	...	...	95	14	81
13,082	7,164	5,918	7,475	3,850	3,625	2,132	1,145	987
...	...	...	...	...	...	...	...	...
...	...	...	...	...	...	...	...	...
...	...	...	...	...	...	...	...	...
...	...	...	8	4	4	10	8	2
...	...	...	...	...	...	162	84	78
...	...	...	...	...	...	32	13	19
...	...	...	11	11	...	...	...	...
71	39	32	78	41	37	38	18	20
74	48	26	61	43	18	62	37	25
...	...	...	...	...	...	...	...	...
13,227	7,251	5,976	7,633	3,949	3,684	2,531	1,319	1,212
3,733	2,147	1,586	2,175	1,213	962	488	263	225
117	41	76	86	39	47	21	12	9
15	10	5	...	...	...	...	...	...
...	...	...	...	...	...	...	...	...
...	...	...	...	...	...	...	...	...
...	...	...	...	...	...	...	...	...
..	...	...	2	2	...	...	...	...
3,865	2,198	1,667	2,263	1,254	1,009	509	275	234

TABLE

Occupations, Part B.—

Class.	Group.	Occupation.	Taluqs: Kottayam. Total.	Kottayam. Males.	Kottayam. Females.	Changanacheri. Total.	Changanacheri. Males.	Changanacheri. Females.
1	2	3	76	77	78	79	80	81
D. Preparation and supply of material substances.	19	Sharbat preparers and sellers.	...	...	...	...	...	...
		Country-spirits distillers and sellers ...	46	19	27	...	...	...
		Toddy drawers and sellers ...	5,732	3,043	2,689	2,550	1,436	1,114
		Foreign wine and spirit dealers ...	...	...	...	...	...	...
		Tea sellers ...	...	...	...	...	...	...
		Coffee preparers and sellers...	10	7	3	...	...	...
		Sugar sellers ...	...	...	...	...	...	...
		Molasses (jaggery, gur, &c.) makers and sellers ...	...	...	...	...	...	...
		Salt preparers and sellers ...	...	...	...	15	9	6
		Grocers and general condiment dealers ...	55	44	11	14	13	1
		Betel-leaf and arecanut sellers.	36	21	15	59	31	28
		Tobacco and snuff manufacturers and sellers ...	128	87	41	49	31	18
		Opium, &c., sellers ...	...	...	...	...	...	...
		Total Sub-order 19 ...	6,007	3,221	2,786	2,687	1,520	1,167
	20	Oil-pressers and sellers ...	147	91	56	398	181	217
		Oil sellers ...	5	5	...	12	8	4
		Oil-cake dealers ...	81	62	19	...	...	...
		Kerosine oil dealers ...	...	...	...	...	...	...
		Matches sellers ...	...	...	...	...	...	...
		Lamp and lantern makers and sellers ...	...	...	...	...	...	...
		Lamp lighting ...	...	...	...	...	...	...
		Total Sub-order 20 ...	233	158	75	410	189	221

XVII.

(State Distribution)—(*Continued*).

—(*Continued*).

Meenachal.			Muvattupula.			Todupula.		
Total.	Males.	Females.	Total.	Males.	Females.	Total.	Males.	Females.
82	83	84	85	86	87	88	89	90
...	...	...	...	...	...	...	...	...
83	14	69	...	...	...	51	12	39
3,982	2,086	1,896	4,783	2,552	2,231	689	392	297
...	...	...	...	...	...	...	...	...
...	...	...	...	...	...	...	...	...
...	...	...	...	...	...	...	...	...
...	...	...	...	...	...	...	...	...
86	47	39	...	...	...	...	...	...
...	...	...	12	7	5	...	...	...
15	12	3	...	...	...	...	...	...
15	9	6	8	3	5	9	7	2
31	18	13	213	117	96	19	14	5
...	...	...	...	...	...	...	...	...
4,212	2,186	2,026	5,016	2.679	2,337	768	425	343
44	28	16	47	25	22	...	...	...
10	7	3	26	14	12	9	3	6
...	...	...	...	...	...	...	...	...
...	...	...	...	...	...	...	...	...
...	...	...	...	...	...	...	...	...
...	...	...	...	...	....	...	...	...
...	...	...	...	...	...	...	...	...
54	35	19	73	39	34	9	3	6

TABLE

Occupations, Part B.—

Class.	Group.	Occupation.	Taluqs: Kunnattunadu. Total.	Kunnattunadu. Males.	Kunnattunadu. Females.	Alangadu. Total.	Alangadu. Males.	Alangadu. Females.
1	2	3	91	92	93	94	95	96
D. Preparation and supply of material substances.	19	Sharbat preparers and sellers.	...	...	...	...	...	...
		Country-spirits distillers and sellers ...	58	13	45	21	8	13
		Toddy drawers and sellers ...	...	...	...	...	...	...
		Foreign wine and spirit dealers ...	...	...	...	...	...	...
		Tea sellers ..	...	...	...	...	...	...
		Coffee preparers and sellers...	...	...	...	...	...	...
		Sugar sellers ...	...	...	...	...	...	..
		Molasses (jaggery, gur, &c.) makers and sellers ...	...	...	...	379	187	192
		Salt preparers and sellers ...	27	19	8	...	...	...
		Grocers and general condiment dealers ...	...	...	...	...	...	...
		Betel-leaf and arecanut sellers.	7	3	4	15	8	7
		Tobacco and snuff manufacturers and sellers ...	28	19	9	136	87	49
		Opium, &c., sellers ...	...	...	...	...	...	...
		Total Sub-order 19 ...	120	54	66	551	290	261
	20	Oil-pressers and sellers ..	200	111	89	...	...	...
		Oil sellers ...	22	9	13	6	2	4
		Oil-cake dealers ...	...	...	...	...	...	...
		Kerosine oil dealers ...	...	...	...	...	...	...
		Matches sellers ...	...	...	...	...	...	...
		Lamp and lantern makers and sellers ...	...	...	...	...	...	...
		Lamp lighting ...	...	...	...	...	...	...
		Total Sub-order 20 ...	222	120	102	6	2	4

XVII.

(State Distribution)—(*Continued*).

—(*Continued*).

Parur.			Cardamom Hills.			Periyar and Thekkadi.		
Total.	Males.	Females.	Total.	Males.	Females.	Total.	Males.	Females.
97	98	99	100	101	102	103	104	105
...	...	...	...	...	...	...	...	..
20	14	6	...	...	...	...	...	...
6,095	3,436	2,659	...	...	...	...	...	...
...	...	...	...	...	...	...	...	...
...	...	...	...	...	...	...	...	...
...	...	...	...	...	...	...	...	...
...	...	...	...	...	...	...	...	...
...	...	...	...	...	...	...	...	...
8	5	3	...	...	...	4	3	1
10	10	...	...	...	...	10	8	2
12	3	9	...	...	...	...	...	...
50	34	16	3	2	1	5	3	2
...	...	...	...	...	...	...	...	...
6,195	3,502	2,693	3	2	1	19	14	5
285	170	115	...	...	...	...	...	...
...	...	...	...	...	...	...	...	...
10	10	...	...	...	...	...	...	...
2	2	...	...	...	...	...	...	...
...	...	...	...	...	...	...	...	...
...	...	...	...	...	...	...	...	...
...	...	...	...	...	...	...	...	...
297	182	115	...	...	...	...	...	...

TABLE

Occupations, Part B.—

Class.	Group.	Occupation.	Total.	Males.	Females.
1	2	3	4	5	6
D. Preparation and supply of material substances.	21	Fire-wood and grass gatherers and sellers ...	*71*	8	63
		Fire-wood contractors and dealers ...	*389*	122	267
		Charcoal burners and dealers ...	*50*	19	31
		Hay dealers ...	*23*	13	10
		Total Sub-order 21 ...	**533**	**162**	**371**
	22	Brick and tile burners and sellers ...	*56*	30	26
		Lime, chunam and shell burners and sellers ...	*1,265*	642	623
		Thatch dealers and thatchers ...	*174*	81	93
		Total Sub-order 22 ...	**1,495**	**753**	**742**
	23	Building contractors ...	*378*	219	159
		Stone workers ...	*5,839*	1,171	4,668
		Masons ...	*1,783*	624	1,159
		Mud-wall and roof builders ...	*162*	88	74
		Glaziers ...	*41*	26	15
		Tilers ...	*124*	15	109
		Total Sub-order 23 ...	**8,327**	**2,143**	**6,184**
	25	Cart makers and sellers ...	*3*	2	1
		Palki-makers ...	*3*	2	1
		Total Sub-order 25 ...	**6**	**4**	**2**
	26	Shipwrights and boat-builders, &c. ...	*142*	79	63
		Canoe diggers, &c. ...	*603*	143	460
		Total Sub-order 26 ...	**745**	**222**	**523**

XVII.

(State Distribution)—(*Continued*).

TALUQS.

Tovala.			Agastiswaram.			Eranial.		
Total.	Males.	Females.	Total.	Males.	Females.	Total.	Males.	Females.
7	8	9	10	11	12	13	14	15
...	...	...	3	...	3	...	...	...
2	...	2	23	4	19	...	...	...
...	...	...	15	6	9	...	...	...
...	...	..	...	...	...	...	...	...
2	...	2	41	10	31	...	...	...
...	...	...	...	...	...	9	4	5
52	27	25	66	32	34	84	46	38
...	...	...	...	...	...	30	14	16
52	27	25	66	32	34	123	64	59
...	...	...	22	13	9	14	8	6
...	...	...	190	34	156	362	67	295
58	17	41	117	41	76	81	39	42
...	...	...	...	...	...	17	9	8
...	...	...	...	...	...	...	...	...
...	...	...	9	...	9	...	...	...
58	17	41	338	88	250	474	123	351
...	...	...	...	...	...	...	...	...
...	...	...	...	...	...	...	...	...
...	...	...	...	...	...	...	...	...
...	...	...	...	...	...	...	...	...
...	...	...	...	...	...	...	...	...
...	...	...	...	...	...	...	...	...

TABLE

Occupations, Part B.—

Class.	Group.	Occupation.	Taluqs: Kalkulam: Total.	Kalkulam: Males.	Kalkulam: Females.	Vilavankodu: Total.	Vilavankodu: Males.	Vilavankodu: Females.
1	2	3	16	17	18	19	20	21
D. Preparation and supply of material substances.	21	Fire-wood and grass gatherers and sellers ...	...	...	...	1	...	1
		Fire-wood contractors and dealers ...	5	...	5	10	3	7
		Charcoal burners and dealers.	21	8	13	7	2	5
		Hay dealers ...	...	...	...	...	..	...
		Total Sub-order 21 ...	26	8	18	18	5	13
	22	Brick and tile burners and sellers ...	15	8	7	...	...	...
		Lime, chunam and shell burners and sellers ..	...	...	...	54	29	25
		Thatch dealers and thatchers.	..	...	...	...	...	...
		Total Sub-order 22 ..	15	8	7	54	29	25
	23	Building contractors ...	20	13	7	14	9	5
		Stone workers ..	203	34	169	37	...	37
		Masons ...	189	71	118	52	16	36
		Mud-wall and roof builders...	25	11	14	...	...	...
		Glaziers ...	...	...	...	...	...	...
		Tilers ...	13	...	13	...	...	...
		Total Sub-order 23 ...	450	129	321	103	25	78
	25	Cart makers and sellers ...	...	...	...	...	...	...
		Palki-makers ...	...	...	...	...	...	...
		Total Sub-order 25 ...	...	...	...	...	...	...
	26	Shipwrights and boat-builders, &c. ...	...	...	...	...	...	...
		Canoe diggers, &c. ...	...	...	...	...	...	...
		Total Sub-order 26 ...	...	...	...	...	...	...

XVII.

(State Distribution)—(*Continued*).

—(*Continued*).

Neyattankara.			Trivandram.			Nedumangadu.		
Total.	Males.	Females.	Total	Males.	Females.	Total.	Males.	Females.
22	23	24	25	26	27	28	29	30
...	...	...	33	8	25	...	...	...
...	...	...	129	43	86	...	...	...
...	...	...	...	...	...	7	3	4
10	8	2	13	5	8	...	...	...
10	8	2	175	56	119	7	3	4
...	...	...	15	8	7	...	...	...
101	48	53	68	37	31	...	...	...
...	...	...	24	13	11	...	...	...
101	48	53	107	58	49	...	...	...
...	...	...	51	23	28	...	...	...
204	33	171	485	89	396	87	33	54
47	19	28	382	117	265	26	8	18
...	...	...	30	17	13	...	...	...
...	...	...	26	16	10	...	...	...
...	...	...	46	8	38	...	...	...
251	52	199	1,020	270	750	113	41	72
...	...	...	...	...	...	...	...	...
...	...	...	3	2	1	...	...	...
...	...	...	3	2	1	...	...	...
...	...	...	...	...	...	...	...	...
...	...	...	...	...	...	...	...	...
...	...	...	...	...	...	...	...	...

TABLE

Occupations, Part B.—

Class.	Group.	Occupation.	Sirayinkil. Total.	Sirayinkil. Males.	Sirayinkil. Females.	Kottarakkara. Total.	Kottarakkara. Males.	Kottarakkara. Females.
1	2	3	31	32	33	34	35	36
D. Preparation and supply of material substances.	21	Fire-wood and grass gatherers and sellers ...	...	...	...	...	...	...
		Fire-wood contractors and dealers ...	...	...	...	...	...	...
		Charcoal burners and dealers.	...	...	...	...	...	...
		Hay dealers ...	...	...	...	...	...	...
		Total Sub-order 21 ...	...	...	...	...	...	...
	22	Brick and tile burners and sellers ...	...	...	...	...	...	...
		Lime, chunam and shell burners and sellers ...	69	41	28	...	...	...
		Thatch dealers and thatchers.	...	...	...	...	...	...
		Total Sub-order 22 ...	69	41	28	...	...	...
	23	Building contractors ...	16	7	9	...	...	...
		Stone workers ...	...	...	...	177	24	153
		Masons ...	108	34	74	...	...	...
		Mud-wall and roof builders ...	...	...	...	...	...	...
		Glaziers ...	...	...	...	...	...	...
		Tilers ...	...	...	...	...	...	...
		Total Sub-order 23 ...	124	41	83	177	24	153
	25	Cart makers and sellers ...	...	...	...	...	...	...
		Palki-makers ...	...	...	...	...	...	...
		Total Sub-order 25 ...	...	...	..	...	...	...
	26	Shipwrights and boat-builders, &c. ...	67	40	27	...	...	...
		Canoe diggers, &c. ...	...	...	...	...	...	...
		Total Sub-order 26 ...	67	40	27	...	...	...

XVII.

(State Distribution)—(Continued).

—(Continued).

Pattanapuram.			Shenkotta.			Quilon.		
Total.	Males.	Females.	Total.	Males.	Females.	Total.	Males.	Females.
37	38	39	40	41	42	43	44	45
...	...	...	5	...	5	18	...	18
...	...	...	23	9	14	46	23	23
...	...	...	...	...	...	...	...	...
...	...	...	...	...	...	...	...	...
...	...	...	28	9	19	64	23	41
...	...	...	...	...	...	13	8	5
...	...	...	...	...	...	181	82	99
...	...	...	...	...	...	40	18	22
...	...	...	...	...	...	234	108	126
...	...	...	...	...	..	49	28	21
21	8	13	24	9	15	488	99	389
39	14	25	25	8	17	112	39	73
...	...	...	...	...	...	41	19	22
...	...	...	...	...	...	...	...	...
...	...	...	...	...	...	56	7	49
60	22	38	49	17	32	746	192	554
...	...	...	...	...	...	3	2	1
...	...	...	...	...	...	...	...	...
...	...	...	...	...	...	3	2	1
...	...	...	...	...	...	75	39	36
65	16	49	...	...	...	69	18	51
65	16	49	...	...	...	144	57	87

TABLE

Occupations, Part B.—

Class.	Group.	Occupation.	Kunnattur. Total.	Kunnattur. Males.	Kunnattur. Females.	Karunagappalli. Total.	Karunagappalli. Males.	Karunagappalli. Females.
1	2	3	46	47	48	49	50	51
D. Preparation and supply of material substances.	21	Fire-wood and grass gatherers and sellers ...	...	...	...	...	...	...
		Fire-wood contractors and dealers ...	...	...	...	...	...	...
		Charcoal burners and dealers.	...	...	...	...	...	...
		Hay dealers ...	...	...	...	...	...	...
		Total Sub-order 21 ...	...	...	...	...	...	...
	22	Brick and tile burners and sellers ...	...	...	...	...	...	...
		Lime, chunam and shell burners and sellers ...	...	...	...	99	53	46
		Thatch dealers and thatchers.	27	14	13	30	13	17
		Total Sub-order 22 ...	27	14	13	129	66	63
	23	Building contractors ...	...	...	...	11	7	4
		Stone workers ...	236	46	190	242	89	153
		Masons ...	...	...	...	...	...	...
		Mud-wall and roof builders...	...	...	...	14	8	6
		Glaziers ...	...	...	...	...	...	...
		Tilers ...	...	...	...	...	...	...
		Total Sub-order 23 ...	236	46	190	267	104	163
	25	Cart makers and sellers ...	...	...	...	...	...	...
		Palki-makers ...	...	...	...	...	...	...
		Total Sub-order 25 ...	...	...	...	...	...	...
	26	Shipwrights and boat-builders, &c. ...	...	...	...	...	...	...
		Canoe diggers, &c. ...	59	23	36	...	...	...
		Total Sub-order 26 ...	59	23	36	...	...	...

XVII.

(State Distribution)—(*Continued*).

—(*Continued*).

Kartigappalli.			Mavellikkara.			Chenganur.		
Total.	Males.	Females.	Total.	Males.	Females.	Total.	Males.	Females.
52	53	54	55	56	57	58	59	60
...	...	...	...	...	...	...	...	..
...	...	...	...	...	...	...	...	...
...	...	...	...	...	...	...	...	...
...	...	...	...	...	...	...	...	...
...	...	...	...	...	...	...	...	...
...	...	...	...	...	...	...	...	...
56	31	25	...	...	...	...	...	...
...	...	...	...	...	...	...	...	...
56	31	25	...	...	...	...	...	...
8	5	3	17	9	8	7	3	4
213	37	176	264	86	178	278	89	189
49	17	32	...	...	...	41	16	25
...	...	...	...	...	...	...	...	...
...	...	...	...	...	...	...	...	...
...	...	...	...	...	...	...	...	...
270	59	211	281	95	186	326	108	218
...	...	...	...	...	...	...	...	...
...	...	...	...	...	...	...	...	...
...	...	...	...	...	...	...	...	...
...	...	...	...	...	...	...	...	...
...	...	...	...	...	...	55	14	41
...	...	...	...	...	...	55	14	41

TABLE
Occupations, Part B.—

Class.	Group.	Occupation.	Taluqs: Tiruvalla. Total.	Tiruvalla. Males.	Tiruvalla. Females.	Ambalappula. Total.	Ambalappula. Males.	Ambalappula. Females.
1	2	3	61	62	63	64	65	66
D. Preparation and supply of material substances.	21	Fire-wood and grass gatherers and sellers ...	...	...	...	6	...	6
		Fire-wood contractors and dealers ...	13	...	13	41	13	28
		Charcoal burners and dealers.	...	...	...	...	...	...
		Hay dealers ...	...	...	...	...	...	...
		Total Sub-order 21 ...	13	...	13	47	13	34
	22	Brick and tile burners and sellers ...	4	2	2	...	...	...
		Lime, chunam and shell burners and sellers ...	...	...	...	165	84	81
		Thatch dealers and thatchers.	..	...	...	...	...	...
		Total Sub-order 22 ...	4	2	2	165	84	81
	23	Building contractors ..	18	8	10	...	...	..
		Stone workers ...	653	117	536	340	43	297
		Masons ...	81	34	47	61	25	36
		Mud-wall and roof builders...	...	...	...	14	8	6
		Glaziers ...	...	...	...	15	10	5
		Tilers ...	...	...	...	...	...	...
		Total Sub-order 23 ...	752	159	593	430	86	344
	25	Cart makers and sellers ...	...	...	...	...	...	...
		Palki-makers ...	...	...	...	...	...	...
		Total Sub-order 25 ...	...	...	...	...	...	...
	26	Shipwrights and boat-builders, &c. ...	...	...	...	...	...	...
		Canoe diggers, &c. ...	33	8	25	...	...	...
		Total Sub-order 26 ...	33	8	25	...	...	...

XVII.

(State Distribution)—(*Continued*).

—(*Continued*).

Sherttala.			Vykkam.			Ettumanur.		
Total.	Males.	Females.	Total.	Males.	Females.	Total.	Males.	Females.
67	68	69	70	71	72	73	74	75
2	...	2	3	...	3	...	...	...
15	8	7	22	9	13	...	...	...
...	...	...	...	...	...	...	...	...
...	...	...	...	...	...	...	...	...
17	8	9	25	9	16	...	...	...
...	...	...	...	...	...	...	...	...
151	78	73	...	...	...	...	...	...
23	9	14	...	...	...	...	...	...
174	87	87	...	...	...	...	...	...
9	7	2	14	9	5	...	...	...
...	...	...	211	36	175	225	39	186
...	...	...	41	14	27	...	...	...
...	...	...	5	3	2	...	...	...
...	...	...	...	...	...	...	...	...
...	...	...	...	...	...	...	...	...
9	7	2	271	62	209	225	39	186
...	...	...	...	...	...	...	...	...
...	...	...	...	...	...	...	...	...
...	...	...	...	...	...	...	...	...
...	...	...	...	...	...	...	...	...
20	2	18	...	...	...	...	...	...
20	2	18	...	...	...	...	...	...

TABLE

Occupations, Part B.—

Class.	Group.	Occupation.	Kottayam. Total.	Kottayam. Males.	Kottayam. Females.	Changanacheri. Total.	Changanacheri. Males.	Changanacheri. Females.
1	2	3	76	77	78	79	80	81
D. Preparation and supply of material substances.	21	Fire-wood and grass gatherers and sellers ...	...	...	...	...	...	...
		Fire-wood contractors and dealers ...	41	10	31	...	...	...
		Charcoal burners and dealers.	...	...	...	...	...	...
		Hay dealers ...	...	...	...	...	...	...
		Total Sub-order 21 ...	41	10	31	...	...	...
	22	Brick and tile burners and sellers ...	...	...	...	...	...	...
		Lime, chunam and shell burners and sellers ...	...	...	...	...	...	...
		Thatch dealers and thatchers.	...	...	...	...	...	...
		Total Sub-order 22 ...	...	...	...	...	...	...
	23	Building contractors ...	31	19	12	27	18	9
		Stone workers ...	...	...	...	79	43	36
		Masons ...	48	13	35	...	...	...
		Mud-wall and roof builders ...	...	...	...	...	...	...
		Glaziers ...	...	...	...	...	...	...
		Tilers ...	...	...	...	...	...	...
		Total Sub-order 23 ...	79	32	47	106	61	45
	25	Cart makers and sellers ...	...	...	...	...	...	...
		Palki-makers ...	...	...	...	...	...	...
		Total Sub-order 25 ...	...	...	...	...	...	...
	26	Shipwrights and boat-builders, &c. ...	...	...	...	...	...	...
		Canoe diggers, &c. ...	49	8	41	...	...	...
		Total Sub-order 26 ...	49	8	41	...	...	...

XVII.

(State Distribution)—(*Continued*).

—(*Continued*).

Meenachal.			Muvattupula.			Todupula.		
Total.	Males.	Females.	Total.	Males.	Females.	Total.	Males.	Females.
82	83	84	85	86	87	88	89	90
...	...	...	...	...	...	...	...	...
...	...	...	...	...	...	...	...	...
...	...	...	...	...	...	...	...	...
...	...	...	...	...	...	...	...	...
...	...	...	...	...	...	...	...	...
...	...	...	...	...	...	...	...	...
...	...	...	...	...	...	...	...	...
...	...	...	...	...	...	...	...	...
...	...	...	...	...	...	...	...	...
21	13	8	12	8	4	...	...	...
171	17	154	45	13	32	...	...	...
38	14	24	...	...	...	15	4	11
...	...	...	...	...	...	7	5	2
...	...	...	...	...	...	...	...	...
...	...	...	...	...	...	...	...	...
230	44	186	57	21	36	22	9	13
...	...	...	...	...	...	...	...	...
..	...	...	...	...	...	...	...	...
...	...	...	...	...	...	...	...	...
...	...	...	...	...	...	...	...	...
...	...	...	102	23	79	...	...	..
...	...	...	102	23	79	...	...	...

TABLE

Occupations, Part B.—

Class.	Group.	Occupation.	Taluqs					
			Kunnattunadu.			Alangadu.		
			Total.	Males.	Females.	Total.	Males.	Females.
1	2	3	91	92	93	94	95	96
D. Preparation and supply of material substances.	21	Fire-wood and grass gatherers and sellers ...	...	...	...	...	...	...
		Fire-wood contractors and dealers ...	...	...	...	16	...	16
		Charcoal burners and dealers.	...	...	...	...	...	...
		Hay dealers ...	...	...	...	...	...	...
		Total Sub-order 21 ...	...	...	...	16	...	16
	22	Brick and tile burners and sellers ...	...	...	...	...	...	...
		Lime, chunam and shell burners and sellers ...	...	...	...	...	...	...
		Thatch dealers and thatchers.	...	...	...	...	...	...
		Total Sub-order 22 ...	...	...	...	...	...	...
	23	Building contractors ...	7	4	3	...	...	...
		Stone workers ...	33	8	25	142	31	111
		Masons ...	58	19	39	77	23	54
		Mud-wall and roof builders...	...	...	...	9	8	1
		Glaziers ..	...	...	...	...	...	...
		Tilers ...	...	...	...	...	...	...
		Total Sub-order 23 ...	98	31	67	228	62	166
	25	Cart makers and sellers ...	...	...	...	...	...	...
		Palki-makers ...	...	...	...	...	...	...
		Total Sub-order 25 ...	...	...	...	...	...	...
	26	Shipwrights and boat-builders, &c. ...	..	...	...	..	...	...
		Canoe diggers, &c. ...	...	...	...	151	31	120
		Total Sub-order 26 ...	...	...	...	151	31	120

XVII.

(State Distribution)—(*Continued*).

—(*Continued*).

Parur.			Cardamom Hills.			Periyar and Thekkadi.		
Total.	Males.	Females.	Total.	Males.	Females.	Total.	Males.	Females.
97	98	99	100	101	102	103	104	105
...	...	...	...	...	...	...	...	...
3	...	3	...	...	...	...	...	...
...	...	...	...	...	...	...	...	...
...	...	...	...	...	...	...	...	...
3	...	3	...	...	...	...	...	...
...	...	...	...	...	...	...	...	...
119	54	65	...	...	...	...	...	...
...	...	...	...	...	...	...	...	...
119	54	65	...	...	...	...	...	...
...	...	...	...	..	...	10	8	2
424	46	378	...	...	...	5	1	4
19	8	11	...	...	...	19	14	5
...	...	...	...	...	...	...	...	...
...	...	...	...	...	...	...	...	...
...	...	...	...	...	...	...	...	...
443	54	389	...	...	...	34	23	11
...	...	...	...	...	...	...	...	...
...	...	...	...	...	...	...	...	...
...	...	...	...	...	...	...	...	...
...	...	...	...	...	...	...	...	...
...	...	...	...	...	...	...	...	...
...	...	...	...	...	...	...	...	...

TABLE

Occupations, Part B.—

Class.	Group.	Occupation.	Total.	Males.	Females.
1	2	3	4	5	6
D. Preparation and supply of material substances.	27	Paper makers and palm-leaf binders..	*26*	17	9
		Stationers ...	*27*	19	8
		Total Sub-order 27 ...	**53**	**36**	**17**
	28	Press proprietors and printers ...	*214*	103	111
		Book-binders ..	*90*	57	33
		Book-sellers ...	*26*	71	9
		Newspaper proprietors ...	*1*	1	...
		Picture dealers ...	*1*	1	...
		Total Sub-order 28 ...	**332**	**179**	**153**
	29	Watch and clock makers ...	*34*	18	16
	30	Wood and ebony carvers ...	*2*	2	...
		Ivory carvers ...	*168*	66	102
		Turners ...	*1,239*	733	506
		Engravers ...	*99*	50	49
		Total Sub-order 30 ...	**1,508**	**851**	**657**
	31	Toy and kite makers and sellers ...	*8*	5	3
	32	Conch dealers and drum makers ...	*3*	3	...
	33	Bangle-sellers in lac ...	*16*	16	...
		Flower garland makers and sellers ...	*60*	36	24
		Sacred thread makers and sellers ..	*44*	22	22
		Total Sub-order 33 ...	**120**	**74**	**46**

XVII.

(State Distribution)—(*Continued*).

TALUQS.

Tovala.			Agastiswaram.			Eranial.		
Total.	Males.	Females.	Total.	Males.	Females.	Total.	Males.	Females.
7	8	9	10	11	12	13	14	15
...	...	...	...	...	...	...	...	...
...	...	...	...	...	...	8	5	3
...	...	...	...	...	...	8	5	3
...	...	...	...	...	...	...	...	...
...	...	...	6	3	3	...	...	...
...	...	...	...	...	...	...	...	...
...	...	...	1	1	...	...	...	...
...	...	...	...	...	...	...	...	...
...	...	...	7	4	3	...	...	...
...	...	...	7	3	4	...	...	...
...	...	...	...	...	...	...	...	...
...	...	...	...	...	...	19	6	13
...	...	...	56	34	22	63	33	30
...	...	...	...	...	...	10	4	6
...	...	...	56	34	22	92	43	49
...	...	...	...	...	...	...	...	...
...	...	...	...	...	...	...	...	...
...	...	...	3	3	...	...	...	...
20	11	9	21	13	8	...	...	...
...	...	...	...	...	...	...	...	...
20	11	9	24	16	8	...	...	...

TABLE

Occupations, Part B.—

Class.	Group.	Occupation.	Taluqs: Kalkulam. Total.	Kalkulam. Males.	Kalkulam. Females.	Vilavankodu. Total.	Vilavankodu. Males.	Vilavankodu. Females.
1	2	3	16	17	18	19	20	21
D. Preparation and supply of material substances.	27	Paper makers and palm-leaf binders ...	...	...	...	...	...	...
		Stationers ...	...	...	...	...	...	...
		Total Sub-order 27 ...	...	...	...	...	...	...
	28	Press proprietors and printers ...	...	...	...	...	...	...
		Book-binders ...	6	4	2	...	...	...
		Book-sellers ...	...	...	...	...	...	...
		Newspaper proprietors ...	...	...	...	...	...	...
		Picture dealers ...	...	...	...	...	...	...
		Total Sub-order 28 ...	6	4	2	...	..	...
	29	Watch and clock makers ...	...	...	..	...	...	...
	30	Wood and ebony carvers ...	...	...	...	...	...	...
		Ivory carvers ...	...	...	...	...	...	...
		Turners ...	...	...	...	...	...	...
		Engravers ...	...	...	...	...	...	...
		Total Sub-order 30 ...	...	...	...	...	...	...
	31	Toy and kite makers and sellers ..	...	...	...	...	...	...
	32	Conch dealers and drum makers ...	...	...	...	...	...	...
	33	Bangle-sellers in lac ...	3	3	..	...	...	...
		Flower garland makers and sellers ...	...	...	...	..	...	...
		Sacred thread makers and sellers ...	...	...	...	...	...	...
		Total Sub-order 33 ...	3	3	...	...	...	...

XVII.

(State Distribution)—(*Continued*).

—(*Continued*).

Neyattankara.			Trivandram.			Nedumangadu.		
Total.	Males.	Females.	Total.	Males.	Females.	Total.	Males.	Females.
22	23	24	25	26	27	28	29	30
...	...	...	13	8	5	...	...	...
...	...	...	19	14	5	...	...	...
...	...	...	32	22	10	...	...	...
...	...	...	175	84	91	...	...	...
...	...	...	27	18	9	...	...	...
...	...	...	10	6	4	...	...	...
...	...	...	...	...	...	...	...	...
...	...	...	1	1	...	...	...	...
...	...	...	213	109	104	...	...	...
...	...	...	17	9	8	...	...	...
...	...	...	2	2	...	...	...	...
...	...	...	93	39	54	...	...	...
...	...	...	293	168	125	...	...	...
...	...	...	40	18	22	...	...	...
...	...	...	428	227	201	...	...	...
...	...	...	2	2	...	...	...	...
...	...	...	3	3	...	...	...	...
...	...	...	5	5	...	...	...	...
...	...	...	12	9	3	...	...	...
...	...	...	30	16	14	...	...	...
...	...	...	47	30	17	...	...	...

TALBE

Occupations, Part B.—

Class.	Group.	Occupation.	Taluqs: Sirayinkil. Total.	Sirayinkil. Males.	Sirayinkil. Females.	Kottarakkara. Total.	Kottarakkara. Males.	Kottarakkara. Females.
1	2	3	31	32	33	34	35	36
D. Preparation and supply of material substances.	27	Paper makers and palm-leaf binders ...	...	...	...	...	...	...
		Stationers ...	...	...	...	...	...	...
		Total Sub-order 27 ...	...	...	...	...	...	...
	28	Press proprietors and printers ...	...	...	...	...	...	...
		Book-binders ...	...	...	...	...	...	...
		Book-sellers ...	...	...	...	...	...	...
		Newspaper proprietors ...	...	...	...	...	...	...
		Picture dealers ...	...	...	...	...	...	..
		Total Sub-order 28 ...	...	...	...	...	...	...
	29	Watch and clock makers ...	...	...	...	...	...	...
	30	Wood and ebony carvers ...	...	...	...	...	...	...
		Ivory carvers ...	...	...	...	...	...	...
		Turners ...	...	...	...	...	...	...
		Engravers ...	...	...	...	...	...	...
		Total Sub-order 30 ...	...	...	...	...	...	...
	31	Toy and kite makers and sellers ...	...	...	...	...	...	...
	32	Conch dealers and drum makers ...	...	...	...	...	...	...
	33	Bangle-sellers in lac ...	...	..	...	...	...	...
		Flower garland-makers and sellers ...	...	...	...	...	...	...
		Sacred thread makers and sellers ...	...	...	...	...	...	...
		Total Sub-order 33 ...	...	...	...	...	...	...

XVII.

(State Distribution)—(*Continued*).

—(*Continued*).

Pattanapuram.			Shenkotta.			Quilon.		
Total.	Males.	Females.	Total.	Males.	Females.	Total.	Males.	Females.
37	38	39	40	41	42	43	44	45
13	9	4	...	...	...	..	...	...
...	...	...	...	...	...	.	...	...
13	9	4	...	...	...	.	...	...
...	...	...	...	...	...	18	9	9
...	...	...	...	...	...	13	8	5
...	...	...	...	...	...	7	4	3
...	...	...	...	...	...	...	...	...
...	...	...	...	...	...	...	...	...
...	...	...	...	..	...	38	21	17
...	...	...	...	...	...	...	...	...
...	...	...	...	...	...	...	...	...
...	...	...	...	...	...	38	13	25
...	...	...	...	...	...	205	131	74
...	...	...	...	...	...	...	...	...
...	...	...	...	...	...	243	144	99
...	...	...	...	...	...	6	3	3
...	...	...	...	...	...	...	...	...
...	...	...	...	...	...	...	...	...
...	...	...	6	2	4	1	1	...
...	...	...	...	...	...	...	...	...
...	...	...	6	2	4	1	1	...

TABLE

Occupations, Part B.—

Class.	Group.	Occupation.	Kunnattur. Total.	Kunnattur. Males.	Kunnattur. Females.	Karunagappalli. Total.	Karunagappalli. Males.	Karunagappalli. Females.
1	2	3	46	47	48	49	50	51
D. Preparation and supply of material substances.	27	Paper makers and palm-leaf binders ...	...	...	...	...	...	...
		Stationers ...	...	...	...	...	...	...
		Total Sub-order 27 ...	...	...	...	...	...	...
	28	Press proprietors and printers ...	...	...	...	...	...	...
		Book-binders ...	...	...	...	...	...	...
		Book-sellers ...	...	...	...	...	...	...
		Newspaper proprietors ...	...	...	...	...	...	...
		Picture dealers ...	...	...	...	...	...	...
		Total Sub-order 28 ...	...	...	...	...	...	...
	29	Watch and clock makers ...	...	...	...	...	...	...
	30	Wood and ebony carvers ...	...	...	...	...	...	...
		Ivory carvers ...	...	...	...	...	...	...
		Turners ...	...	...	...	...	...	...
		Engravers ...	...	...	...	...	...	...
		Total Sub-order 30 ...	...	...	...	...	...	...
	31	Toy and kite makers and sellers ...	...	...	...	...	...	...
	32	Conch dealers and drum makers ...	...	...	...	...	...	...
	33	Bangle-sellers in lac ...	...	...	...	...	...	...
		Flower garland makers and sellers ...	...	...	...	...	...	...
		Sacred thread makers and sellers ...	...	..	...	...	...	...
		Total Sub-order 33 ...	...	...	...	...	...	...

XVII.

(State Distribution)—(*Continued*).

—(*Continued*).

Kartigappalli.			Mavellikkara.			Chenganur.		
Total.	Males.	Females.	Total.	Males.	Females.	Total.	Males.	Females.
52	53	54	55	56	57	58	59	60
...	...	...	..	...	...	...	...	...
...	...	...	...	.	...	...	...	...
...	...	...	...	...	...	...	...	...
...	...	..	...	...	...	...	..	...
...	...	...	...	...	...	...	...	...
...	...	...	...	..	...	...	...	...
...	...	...	...	...	...	...	...	...
...	...	...	...	...	...	...	...	...
...	..	...	...	...	...	...	...	...
...	...	...	...	...	...	...	..	...
...	...	...	...	...	...	...	...	...
...	...	...	18	8	10	...	...	...
146	87	59	156	98	58	...	...	...
...	...	...	...	...	...	...	...	...
146	87	59	174	106	68	...	...	..
...	...	...	...	...	...	...	...	...
...	...	...	...	...	...	...	...	...
...	...	...	3	3	...	...	...	...
..	...	...	...	...	...	...	...	...
...	...	...	...	...	...	...	...	...
...	...	...	... 3	3	...	...	...	...

TABLE

Occupations, Part B.—

Class.	Group.	Occupation.	Tiruvalla. Total.	Tiruvalla. Males.	Tiruvalla. Females.	Ambalappula. Total.	Ambalappula. Males.	Ambalappula. Females.
1	2	3	61	62	63	64	65	66
D. Preparation and supply of material substances.	27	Paper makers and palm-leaf binders ...	...	...	...	...	...	...
		Stationers ...	...	...	...	...	...	...
		Total Sub-order 27 ...	...	...	...	...	...	...
	28	Press proprietors and printers ...	...	...	...	...	...	...
		Book-binders ...	...	...	...	15	9	6
		Book-sellers ...	...	...	...	3	3	...
		Newspaper proprietors ...	...	...	...	...	...	...
		Picture dealers ...	.	...	...	...	...	...
		Total Sub-order 28 ...	...	...	...	18	12	6
	29	Watch and clock makers ...	...	...	...	10	6	4
	30	Wood and ebony carvers ...	...	...	...	...	...	...
		Ivory carvers ...	..	...	...	...	...	...
		Turners ...	...	...	...	161	86	75
		Engravers ...	...	...	...	...	...	...
		Total Sub-order 30 ...	...	...	...	161	86	75
	31	Toy and kite makers and sellers ...	...	...	...	...	...	...
	32	Conch dealers and drum makers ...	...	...	...	...	...	...
	33	Bangle-sellers in lac ...	...	...	...	2	2	...
		Flower garland makers and sellers ...	...	...	...	...	...	...
		Sacred thread makers and sellers ...	...	...	...	14	6	8
		Total Sub-order 33 ...	...	...	...	16	8	8

XVII.

(State Distribution)—(*Continued*).

—(*Continued*).

Sherttala.			Vykkam.			Ettumanur.		
Total.	Males.	Females.	Total.	Males.	Females.	Total.	Males.	Females.
67	68	69	70	71	72	73	74	75
...	...	...	...	...	...	...	...	...
...	...	...	...	...	...	...	...	...
...	...	...	...	...	...	...	...	...
...	...	...	...	...	...	...	...	..
...	...	...	...	...	...	...	...	...
...	...	...	...	...	...	...	...	...
...	...	...	...	...	...	...	...	...
...	...	...	...	...	...	...	...	...
...	...	...	...	...	...	...	...	...
...	...	...	...	...	...	...	...	...
...	...	...	...	...	...	...	...	...
...	...	...	...	...	...	...	...	...
...	...	...	...	...	...	...	...	...
...	...	...	...	...	...	49	28	21
...	...	...	...	...	...	49	28	21
...	...	...	...	...	...	...	...	...
...	...	...	...	...	...	...	...	...
...	...	...	...	...	...	...	...	...
...	...	...	...	...	...	...	...	...
..	...	...	...	...	...	...	...	...
...	...	...	...	...	...	...	...	...

TABLE

Occupations, Part B.—

Class.	Group.	Occupation.	Taluqs: Kottayam. Total.	Kottayam. Males.	Kottayam. Females.	Changanacheri. Total.	Changanacheri. Males.	Changanacheri. Females.
1	2	3	76	77	78	79	80	81
D. Preparation and supply of material substances.	27	Paper makers and palm-leaf binders ...	...	...	...	...	...	...
		Stationers ...	...	...	...	...	...	...
		Total Sub-order 27 ...	...	...	...	...	...	...
	28	Press proprietors and printers ...	21	10	11	...	...	...
		Book-binders ...	17	9	8	...	...	...
		Book-sellers ...	6	4	2	...	...	...
		Newspaper proprietors ...	...	...	...	...	...	...
		Picture dealers ...	...	...	...	...	...	...
		Total Sub-order 28 ...	44	23	21	...	...	...
	29	Watch and clock makers ...	...	...	...	...	...	...
	30	Wood and ebony carvers ...	...	...	...	...	...	...
		Ivory carvers ...	...	...	...	...	...	...
		Turners ...	147	87	60	...	...	...
		Engravers ...	...	...	...	...	...	...
		Total Sub-order 30 ...	147	87	60	...	...	...
	31	Toy and kite makers and sellers ...	...	...	...	...	...	...
	32	Conch dealers and drum makers ...	...	...	...	...	...	...
	33	Bangle-sellers in lac ...	...	...	...	...	...	...
		Flower garland makers and sellers ...	...	...	...	...	...	...
		Sacred thread makers and sellers ...	...	...	...	...	...	...
		Total Sub-order 33 ...	...	...	...	...	...	...

XVII.

(State Distribution)—(*Continued*).

—(*Continued*).

Meenachal.			Muvattupula.			Todupula.		
Total.	Males.	Females.	Total.	Males.	Females.	Total.	Males.	Females.
82	83	84	85	86	87	88	89	90
...	...	...	...	...	...	...	...	...
...	...	...	...	...	...	...	...	...
...	...	...	...	...	...	...	...	...
...	...	...	...	...	...	...	...	...
...	...	...	...	...	...	...	...	...
...	...	...	...	...	...	...	...	...
...	...	...	...	...	...	...	...	...
...	...	...	...	...	...	...	...	...
...	...	...	...	...	...	...	...	...
...	...	...	...	...	...	...	...	...
...	...	...	...	...	...	...	...	...
...	...	...	...	...	...	...	...	...
...	...	...	...	...	...	...	...	...
...	...	...	...	...	...	...	...	...
...	...	...	...	...	...	...	...	...
...	...	...	...	...	...	...	...	...
...	...	...	...	...	...	...	...	...
...	...	...	...	...	...	...	...	...
...	...	...	...	...	...	...	...	...
...	...	...	...	...	...	...	...	...
...	...	...	...	...	...	...	...	...

TABL

Occupations, Part B.—

Class.	Group.	Occupation.	Taluqs Kunnattunadu. Total.	Kunnattunadu. Males.	Kunnattunadu. Females.	Alangadu. Total.	Alangadu. Males.	Alangadu. Females.
1	2	3	91	92	93	94	95	96
D. Preparation and supply of material substances.	27	Paper makers and palm-leaf binders ...	...	...	...	...	...	...
		Stationers ...	...	...	...	...	...	...
		Total Sub-order 27 ...	...	...	...	...	...	...
	28	Press proprietors and printers ...	...	...	...	...	...	...
		Book-binders ...	...	...	...	...	...	...
		Book-sellers ...	...	...	...	...	...	...
		Newspaper proprietors ...	...	...	...	...	...	...
		Picture dealers ...	...	...	...	...	...	...
		Total Sub-order 28 ...	...	...	...	...	...	...
	29	Watch and clock makers ...	...	...	...	...	...	...
	30	Wood and ebony carvers ...	...	...	...	...	...	...
		Ivory carvers ...	...	...	...	...	...	...
		Turners ...	...	...	...	...	...	...
		Engravers ...	...	...	...	...	...	...
		Total Sub-order 30 ...	...	...	...	...	...	...
	31	Toy and kite makers and sellers ...	...	...	...	...	...	...
	32	Conch dealers and drum makers ...	...	...	...	...	...	...
	33	Bangle-sellers in lac ...	...	...	...	...	...	...
		Flower garland makers and sellers ...	...	...	...	...	...	...
		Sacred thread makers and sellers ...	...	...	...	...	...	...
		Total Sub-order 33 ...	...	...	...	...	...	...

XVII.

(State Distribution)—(*Continued*).

—(*Continued*).

Parur.			Cardamom Hills.			Periyar and Thekkadi.		
Total.	Males.	Females.	Total.	Males.	Females.	Total.	Males.	Females.
97	98	99	100	101	102	103	104	105
...	...	...	...	...	...	...	...	...
...	...	...	...	...	...	...	...	...
...	...	...	...	...	...	...	...	...
...	...	..	...	...	...	...	...	...
6	6	...	...	...	...	...	...	...
...	...	...	...	..	...	...	...	...
...	...	...	...	...	...	...	...	...
...	...	...	...	...	...	...	...	...
6	6	...	...	...	...	...	...	...
...	...	...	..	...	...	...	...	...
...	...	..	...	...	...	...	...	...
...	...	...	...	...	...	...	...	...
12	9	3	...	...	...	...	...	...
...	...	...	.	..	...	...	...	...
12	9	3	...	...	...	...	...	...
...	...	...	...	...	...	...	...	...
...	...	...	...	...	...	...	...	...
...	...	...	...	...	...	...	...	...
...	...	...	...	...	...	...	...	...
...	...	...	...	...	...	...	...	...
...	.	...	...	...	...	... ...	...	...

TABLE

Occupations, Part B.—

Class.	Group.	Occupation.	Total.	Males.	Females.
		Occupation and Class.	**State Total.**		
1	2	3	4	5	6
D. Preparation and supply of material substances.	34	Upholsterers ...	*11*	5	6
		Furniture makers ...	*48*	23	25
		Looking-glass sellers ..	*3*	2	1
		Total Sub-order 34 ...	**62**	**30**	**32**
	35	Whip, goad, &c., makers ...	*9*	7	2
	36	Knife and tool makers ...	*16*	12	4
		Knife and tool grinders ...	*39*	26	13
		Mechanic (not Railway) ...	*22*	18	4
		Total Sub-order 36 ...	**77**	**56**	**21**
	37	Gun makers ...	*4*	3	1
		Ammunition and cap dealers ...	*7*	7	...
		Gunpowder makers and sellers ...	*6*	6	..
		Fire-work makers ...	*82*	43	39
		Sword makers and sellers ...	*5*	3	2
		Total Sub-order 37 ...	**104**	**62**	**42**
	38	Woollen-cloth dealers ...	*6*	4	2
	39	Silk dealers ...	*8*	5	3
	40	Cotton cleaners and pressers ...	*11*	6	5
		Cotton-carpet sellers ...	*3*	3	...
		Cotton spinners, &c. ...	*3,963*	1,009	2,954
		Cotton weavers, mill-owners and managers ...	*32,074*	17,664	14,410
		Cotton Factory hands ...	*325*	158	167
		Tape and cotton sellers ...	*316*	126	190
		Total Sub-order 40 ..	**36,692**	**18,966**	**17,726**

XVII.

(State Distribution)—(*Continued*).

Taluqs.								
Tovala.			Agastiswaram.			Eranial.		
Total.	Males.	Females.	Total.	Males.	Females.	Total.	Males.	Females.
7	8	9	10	11	12	13	14	15
...	...	...	...	...	...	...	...	...
...	...	...	...	...	...	...	...	...
...	...	...	...	...	...	...	...	...
...	...	...	...	...	...	...	...	...
...	...	...	...	...	...	...	...	...
...	...	...	...	...	...	3	2	1
...	...	...	...	...	...	10	6	4
...	...	...	...	...	...	...	...	...
...	...	...	...	...	..	13	8	5
...	...	...	...	...	...	...	...	...
...	...	...	..	...	...	...	...	...
...	...	...	...	...	...	...	...	...
...	...	...	...	...	...	16	7	9
...	...	...	...	...	...	...	...	...
...	...	...	...	...	...	16	7	9
...	...	...	...	...	...	...	...	...
...	...	...	...	...	...	...	...	...
...	...	...	...	...	..	...	...	...
...	...	...	3	3	...	...	...	...
17	1	16	452	139	313	...	...	...
167	88	79	4,322	2,313	2,009	3,418	1,881	1,537
...	...	...	...	...	...	...	...	...
...	...	...	...	...	...	...	...	...
184	89	95	4,777	2,455	2,322	3,418	1,881	1,537

TABLE

Occupations, Part B.—

Class.	Group.	Occupation.	Taluqs: Kalkulam. Total.	Kalkulam. Males.	Kalkulam. Females.	Vilavankodu. Total.	Vilavankodu. Males.	Vilavankodu. Females.
1	2	3	16	17	18	19	20	21
D. Preparation and supply of material substances.	34	Upholsterers ...	...	...	...	...	...	...
		Furniture makers ...	...	...	...	...	...	...
		Looking-glass sellers ...	...	...	...	...	...	...
		Total Sub-order 34 ...	...	...	...	...	...	...
	35	Whip, goad, &c., makers ...	5	3	2	...	...	...
	36	Knife and tool makers ...	...	...	...	...	...	...
		Knife and tool grinders ...	...	...	...	...	...	...
		Mechanic (not Railway) ...	...	...	...	...	...	...
		Total Sub-order 36 ...	...	...	...	...	...	...
	37	Gun makers ...	...	...	...	...	...	...
		Ammunition and cap dealers.	...	...	...	...	...	...
		Gunpowder makers and sellers ...	...	...	...	...	...	...
		Fire-work makers ...	9	3	6	...	...	...
		Sword makers and sellers	...	...	...	...	...	...
		Total Sub-order 37 ...	9	3	6	...	...	..
	38	Woollen-cloth dealers ...	...	...	...	...	...	...
	39	Silk dealers ...	...	...	...	...	...	...
	40	Cotton cleaners and pressers.	...	...	...	...	...	...
		Cotton-carpet sellers ...	...	...	...	...	...	...
		Cotton spinners, &c. ...	...	...	...	...	...	...
		Cotton weavers, mill-owners and managers .	1,126	590	536	1,290	666	624
		Cotton Factory hands ...	...	...	...	...	...	..
		Tape and cotton sellers ...	...	...	...	45	18	27
		Total Sub-order 40 ...	1,126	590	536	1,335	684	651

XVII.

(State Distribution)—(*Continued*).

—(*Continued*).

Neyattankara.			Trivandram.			Nedumangadu.		
Total.	Males.	Females.	Total.	Males.	Females.	Total.	Males.	Females.
22	23	24	25	26	27	28	29	30
...	...	...	6	2	4	...	...	...
...	...	...	24	13	11	...	...	...
...	...	...	...	...	...	...	...	...
...	...	...	30	15	15	...	...	...
...	...	...	4	4	...	...	...	...
...	...	...	3	3	...	...	...	...
...	...	...	6	4	2	...	...	...
...	...	...	...	...	...	...	...	...
...	...	...	9	7	2	...	...	...
...	...	...	...	...	...	...	...	...
...	...	...	3	3	...	...	...	...
...	...	...	3	3	...	...	...	...
...	...	...	21	13	8	...	...	...
...	...	...	3	1	2	...	...	...
...	...	...	30	20	10	...	...	...
...	...	...	6	4	2	...	...	...
...	...	...	...	...	...	...	...	...
...	...	...	...	...	...	...	...	...
...	...	...	...	...	...	...	...	...
...	...	...	...	...	...	...	...	...
3,796	1,984	1,812	1,170	632	538	14	8	6
...	...	...	...	...	...	...	...	...
...	...	...	33	12	21	...	...	...
3,796	1,984	1,812	1,203	644	559	14	8	6

TABLE

Occupations, Part B.—

Class.	Group.	Occupation.	Taluqs: Sirayinkil. Total.	Sirayinkil. Males.	Sirayinkil. Females.	Kottarakkara. Total.	Kottarakkara. Males.	Kottarakkara. Females.
1	2	3	31	32	33	34	35	36
D. Preparation and supply of material substances.	34	Upholsterers ..	...	...	...	...	...	...
		Furniture makers .	...	...	...	...	...	...
		Looking-glass sellers ...	...	...	...	...	...	...
		Total Sub-order 34 ...	...	...	...	...	...	...
	35	Whip, goad, &c., makers ...	...	...	...	...	...	...
	36	Knife and tool makers ...	...	...	..		...	...
		Knife and tool grinders ...	...	...	...	...	...	...
		Mechanic (not Railway) ...	...	...	...	...	...	...
		Total Sub-order 36 ...	...	...	...	...	...	...
	37	Gun makers ...	...	...	...	...	...	...
		Ammunition and cap dealers.	...	...	...	...	...	...
		Gunpowder makers and sellers ...	...	...	...	...	...	...
		Fire-work makers ...	...	...	...	...	...	...
		Sword makers and sellers ...	...	...	...	...	...	...
		Total Sub-order 37 ...	...	...	...	...	...	...
	38	Woollen-cloth dealers ...	...	...	...	..	...	...
	39	Silk dealers ...	...	...	...	...	...	...
	40	Cotton cleaners and pressers.	...	...	...	...	...	...
		Cotton-carpet sellers ...	...	...	...	...	...	...
		Cotton spinners, &c. ...	...	...	...	...	...	...
		Cotton weavers, mill-owners and managers ...	4,778	2,621	2,157	800	438	362
		Cotton Factory hands ...	...	...	...	..	...	...
		Tape and cotton sellers ...	...	...	...	...	...	...
		Total Sub-order 40 ...	4,778	2,621	2,157	800	438	362

XVII.

(State Distribution)—(*Continued*).

—(*Continued*).

Pattanapuram.			Shenkotta.			Quilon.		
Total.	Males.	Females.	Total.	Males.	Females.	Total.	Males.	Females.
37	38	39	40	41	42	43	44	45
...	...	...	...	...	...	...	...	...
...	...	...	...	...	...	24	10	14
...	...	...	...	...	...	3	2	1
...	...	...	...	...	...	27	12	15
...	...	...	...	...	...	...	...	...
...	...	...	...	...	...	2	2	...
...	...	...	...	..	...	7	3	4
...	...	...	...	...	...	6	3	3
...	...	...	...	...	...	15	8	7
...	...	...	...	...	...	...	...	...
...	...	...	...	...	...	...	...	...
...	...	...	1	1	...	...	...	...
...	...	..	15	9	6	...	..	...
...	..	...	...	...	...	...	..	...
...	...	...	16	10	6	...	...	...
...	...	...	...	...	...	...	...	...
...	...	...	...	...	...	...	...	...
...	...	...	...	...	...	11	6	5
...	...	...	...	...	...	...	...	...
...	...	...	...	...	...	176	28	148
8	5	3	306	177	129	5,359	3,064	2,295
...	...	...	...	...	...	325	158	167
...	...	...	...	...	...	33	17	16
8	5	3	306	177	129	5,904	3,273	2,631

TABLE

Occupations, Part B.—

Class.	Group.	Occupation.	Taluqs: Kunnattur. Total.	Kunnattur. Males.	Kunnattur. Females.	Karunagappalli. Total.	Karunagappalli. Males.	Karunagappalli. Females.
1	2	3	46	47	48	49	50	51
D. Preparation and supply of material substances.	34	Upholsterers ...	...	...	...	...	...	...
		Furniture makers ...	...	...	...	...	...	...
		Looking-glass sellers ...	...	...	...	...	...	...
		Total Sub-order 34 ...	...	...	...	...	...	...
	35	Whip, goad, &c., makers ...	...	...	...	...	...	...
	36	Knife and tool makers ...	...	...	...	...	...	...
		Knife and tool grinders ...	...	...	...	...	...	...
		Mechanic (not Railway) ..	...	...	...	...	...	...
		Total Sub-order 36 ...	...	...	...	...	...	...
	37	Gun makers ...	...	...	...	...	...	...
		Ammunition and cap dealers.	...	...	...	...	...	...
		Gunpowder makers and sellers ...	...	...	...	...	...	...
		Fire-work makers ...	...	...	...	...	...	...
		Sword makers and sellers ...	.	...	...	...	...	...
		Total Sub-order 37 ...	...	...	...	...	...	...
	38	Woollen-cloth dealers ...	...	...	...	...	...	...
	39	Silk dealers ..	...	...	...	...	...	...
	40	Cotton cleaners and pressers..	...	...	...	...	...	...
		Cotton-carpet sellers ...	...	...	...	...	...	...
		Cotton spinners, &c. ...	...	...	...	...	...	...
		Cotton weavers, mill-owners and managers ..	51	15	36	263	146	117
		Cotton Factory hands ...	...	...	...	...	...	...
		Tape and cotton sellers ...	..	...	...	16	9	7
		Total Sub-order 40 ...	51	15	36	279	155	124

XVII.

(State Distribution)—(*Continued*).

—(*Continued*).

Kartigappalli.			Maveilikkara.			Chenganur.		
Total.	Males.	Females.	Total.	Males.	Females.	Total.	Males.	Females.
52	53	54	55	56	57	58	59	60
...	...	...	...	...	...	...	...	...
...	...	...	...	...	...	...	...	...
...	...	...	...	...	...	...	...	...
...	...	...	...	...	...	...	...	...
...	..	...	...	...	...	...	...	...
...	...	...	8	5	3	...	...	...
...	...	...	11	8	3	...	...	..
...	...	...	...	...	...	...	...	...
...	...	...	19	13	6	...	...	...
...	...	...	...	...	...	...	...	...
...	...	..	...	...	...	...	...	...
...	...	...	...	...	...	...	...	...
...	...	...	...	...	...	...	...	...
...	...	...	...	...	...	..	...	...
...	...	...	...	...	...	...	...	...
...	...	...	...	...	...	...	...	...
...	...	...	...	...	...	...	...	...
...	...	...	...	...	...	...	...	...
...	...	...	...	...	...	...	...	...
...	...	...	...	...	...	...	...	...
43	19	24	20	8	12	...	...	...
...	...	...	...	...	...	...	...	...
...	...	...	...	...	...	...	...	...
43	19	24	20	8	12	...	...	...

TABLE

Occupations, Part B.—

Class.	Group.	Occupation.	Taluqs: Tiruvalla. Total.	Tiruvalla. Males.	Tiruvalla. Females.	Ambalappula. Total.	Ambalappula. Males.	Ambalappula. Females.
1	2	3	61	62	63	64	65	66
D. Preparation and supply of material substances.	34	Upholsterers ...	...	..	..	4	2	2
		Furniture makers ...	...	...	...	...	...	...
		Looking-glass sellers ...	...	...	...	...	...	...
		Total Sub-order 34 ...	...	...	...	4	2	2
	35	Whip, goad, &c., makers ...	...	...	...	...	...	...
	36	Knife and tool makers ...	...	...	...	...	...	...
		Knife and tool grinders ...	...	...	...	...	...	...
		Mechanic (not Railway) ...	...	...	...	...	...	...
		Total Sub-order 36 ...	...	...	...	...	...	...
	37	Gun makers ...	...	...	...	4	3	1
		Ammunition and cap dealers.	...	...	...	4	4	...
		Gunpowder makers and sellers ...	...	...	...	2	2	...
		Fire-work makers ...	...	...	...	13	7	6
		Sword makers and sellers ...	...	...	...	2	2	...
		Total Sub-order 37 ...	...	...	...	25	18	7
	38	Woollen-cloth dealers ...	...	...	...	...	...	...
	39	Silk dealers ...	...	...	...	8	5	3
	40	Cotton cleaners and pressers.	...	...	...	...	...	...
		Cotton-carpet sellers ...	...	...	...	...	...	...
		Cotton spinners, &c. ...	...	...	...	...	...	...
		Cotton-weavers, mill-owners and managers ...	1,004	490	514	374	241	133
		Cotton Factory hands ...	...	...	...	...	...	..
		Tape and cotton sellers .	...	...	...	21	12	9
		Total Sub-order 40 ...	1,004	490	514	395	253	142

XVII.

(State Distribution)—(*Continued*).

—(*Continued*).

Sherttala.			Vykkam.			Ettumanur.		
Total.	Males.	Females.	Total.	Males.	Females.	Total.	Males.	Females.
67	68	69	70	71	72	73	74	75
...	...	...	...	...	...	...	...	...
...	...	...	...	...	...	...	...	...
...	...	...	...	...	...	...	...	...
...	...	...	...	...	...	...	...	...
...	...	...	...	...	...	...	...	...
...	...	...	...	...	...	...	...	...
...	...	...	...	...	...	...	...	...
...	...	...	...	...	...	...	...	...
...	...	...	...	...	...	...	...	...
...	...	...	...	...	...	...	...	...
...	...	...	...	...	...	...	...	...
...	...	...	...	...	...	...	...	...
...	...	...	...	...	...	...	...	...
...	...	...	...	...	...	...	...	...
...	...	...	...	...	...	...	...	...
...	...	...	...	...	...	...	...	...
...	...	...	...	...	...	...	...	...
...	...	...	...	...	...	...	...	...
...	...	...	...	...	...	...	...	...
2,366	675	1,691	951	165	786	...	...	...
218	136	82	67	39	28	284	167	117
...	...	...	...	...	...	...	...	...
39	14	25	...	...	...	...	...	...
2,623	825	1,798	1,018	204	814	284	167	117

TABLE

Occupations, Part B.—

Class.	Group.	Occupation.	Kottayam. Total.	Kottayam. Males.	Kottayam. Females.	Changanacheri. Total.	Changanacheri. Males.	Changanacheri. Females.
1	2	3	76	77	78	79	80	81
D. Preparation and supply of material substances.	34	Upholsterers ...	1	1	...	...	...	...
		Furniture makers ...	...	...	...	...	...	...
		Looking-glass sellers ...	...	...	...	...	...	...
		Total Sub-order 34 ...	1	1	...	...	...	...
	35	Whip, goad, &c., makers ...	...	...	...	...	...	...
	36	Knife and tool makers ...	...	...	...	...	...	...
		Knife and tool grinders ...	...	...	...	5	5	...
		Mechanic (not Railway) ...	...	...	...	...	...	...
		Total Sub-order 36 ...	...	...	...	5	5	...
	37	Gun makers ...	...	...	...	...	...	...
		Ammunition and cap dealers	...	...	...	...	...	...
		Gunpowder makers and sellers ...	...	...	...	...	...	...
		Fire-work makers ...	8	4	4	...	...	...
		Sword makers and sellers ...	...	...	...	...	...	...
		Total Sub-order 37 ...	8	4	4	...	...	...
	38	Woollen-cloth dealers ...	...	...	...	...	...	...
	39	Silk dealers ...	...	...	...	...	...	...
	40	Cotton cleaners and pressers.	...	...	...	...	...	...
		Cotton-carpet sellers ..	...	...	...	...	...	...
		Cotton spinners, &c. ...	1	1	...	...	...	...
		Cotton weavers, mill-owners and managers ...	222	143	79	481	332	149
		Cotton Factory hands ...	...	...	...	...	...	...
		Tape and cotton sellers ...	57	21	36	72	23	49
		Total Sub-order 40 ...	280	165	115	553	355	198

TALUQS

XVII.

(State Distribution)—(*Continued*).

—(*Continued*).

Meenachal.			Muvattupula.			Todupula.		
Total.	Males.	Females.	Total.	Males.	Females.	Total.	Males.	Females.
82	83	84	85	86	87	88	89	90
...	...	...	...	...	...	...	...	...
...	...	...	...	...	...	...	...	...
...	...	...	...	...	...	...	...	...
...	...	...	...	...	...	...	...	...
...	...	...	...	...	...	...	...	...
...	...	...	...	...	...	...	...	...
...	...	...	...	...	...	...	...	...
...	...	...	...	...	...	...	...	...
...	...	...	...	...	...	...	...	...
...	...	...	...	...	...	...	...	...
...	...	...	...	...	...	...	...	...
...	...	...	...	...	...	...	...	...
...	...	...	...	...	...	...	...	...
...	...	...	...	...	...	...	...	...
...	...	...	...	...	...	...	...	...
...	...	...	...	...	...	...	...	...
...	...	...	...	...	...	...	...	...
...	...	...	...	...	...	...	...	...
...	...	...	...	...	...	...	...	...
...	...	...	...	...	...	...	...	...
...	...	...	535	319	216	...	...	...
...	...	...	...	...	...	...	...	...
...	...	...	...	...	...	...	...	...
...	...	...	535	319	216	...	...	...

TABLE

Occupations, Part B.—

Class.	Group.	Occupation.	Taluqs: Kunnattunadu. Total.	Kunnattunadu. Males.	Kunnattunadu. Females.	Alangadu. Total.	Alangadu. Males.	Alangadu. Females.
1	2	3	91	92	93	94	95	96
D. Preparation and supply of material substances.	34	Upholsterers ...	...	...	...	...	...	...
		Furniture makers ...	...	...	...	...	...	...
		Looking-glass sellers ...	...	...	...	...	...	...
		Total Sub-order 34 ...	...	...	...	...	...	...
	35	Whip, goad, &c., makers ...	...	...	...	...	..	...
	36	Knife and tool makers ...	...	...	..	...	...	...
		Knife and tool grinders ...	...	...	...	...	...	...
		Machanic (not Railway) ...	...	...	...	...	...	...
		Total Sub-order 36 ...	...	...	...	...	...	...
	37	Gun makers ...	...	...	...	...	...	...
		Ammunition and cap dealers.	...	...	...	...	...	...
		Gunpowder makers and sellers ...	...	...	...	...	...	...
		Fire-work makers ...	...	...	...	...	...	...
		Sword makers and sellers ...	...	...	...	...		...
		Total Sub-order 37 ...	...	...	...	...	...	...
	38	Woollen-cloth dealers ...	...	...	...	...	...	...
	39	Silk dealers ...	...	...	...	...	...	...
	40	Cotton cleaners and pressers.	...	...	...	...	...	...
		Cotton-carpet sellers ...	...	...	...	...	..	...
		Cotton spinners, &c. ..	...	...	...	...	...	...
		Cotton weavers, mill-owners and managers ...	780	456	324	625	327	298
		Cotton Factory hands ...	...	...	...	...	...	...
		Tape and cotton sellers ...	...	...	...	...	...	...
		Total Sub-order 40 ...	780	456	324	625	327	298

XVII.

(State Distribution)—(*Continued*).

—(*Continued*).

Parur.			Cardamom Hills.			Periyar and Thekkadi.		
Total.	Males.	Females.	Total.	Males.	Females.	Total.	Males.	Females.
97	98	99	100	101	102	103	104	105
...	...	...	...	...	...	...	...	...
...	...	...	...	...	...	...	...	...
...	...	...	...	...	...	...	...	...
...	...	...	...	...	...	...	...	...
...	...	...	...	...	...	...	...	...
...	...	...	...	...	...	...	...	...
...	...	...	...	...	...	...	...	...
...	...	...	...	...	...	16	15	1
...	...	...	...	...	...	16	15	1
...	...	...	...	...	...	...	...	...
...	...	...	...	...	...	...	...	...
...	...	...	...	...	...	...	...	...
...	...	...	...	...	...	...	...	...
...	...	...	...	...	...	...	...	...
...	...	...	...	...	...	...	...	...
...	...	...	...	...	...	...	...	...
...	...	...	...	...	...	...	...	...
...	...	...	...	...	...	...	...	...
...	...	...	...	...	...	...	...	...
...	...	...	...	...	...	...	...	...
553	359	194	...	...	...	...	...	...
...	...	...	...	...	...	...	...	...
...	...	...	...	...	...	...	...	...
553	359	194	...	...	...	...	...	...

TABLE

Occupations, Part B.—

Class.	Group.	Occupation.	Total.	Males.	Females.
1	2	3	4	5	6
D. Preparation and supply of material substances.	41	Flax spinners, weavers and sellers ...	*148*	87	61
		Hemp-rope makers and sellers ...	*79*	65	14
		Net makers and sellers ..	*1,766*	923	843
		Coir preparers, manufacturers and sellers ...	*26,713*	7,368	19,345
		Total Sub-order 41 ...	**28,706**	**8,443**	**20,263**
	42	Tailors ...	*5,559*	2,466	3,093
		Hat, cap and turban makers and sellers ...	*14*	6	8
		Turban-binders ...	*12*	4	8
		Umbrella makers and sellers ...	*6,471*	3,434	3,037
		Lace sellers ...	*3*	2	1
		Button sellers ...	*1*	1	...
		Piece-goods dealers ...	*2,859*	1,941	918
		Total Sub-order 42 ...	**14,919**	**7,854**	**7,065**
	43	Gold and silver dealers ...	*346*	251	95
		Gold and silver workers ...	*19,140*	10,001	9,139
		Goldsmiths' dust washers ...	*46*	25	21
		Enamellers ...	*5*	2	3
		Gold and silver braid makers ...	*17*	10	7
		Diamond polishers and sellers ...	*2*	2	...
		Ruby workers ..	*39*	20	19
		Ruby and emerald, &c., dealers ...	*3*	3	...
		Pearls and other precious stones dealers ...	*21*	12	9
		Coral dealers ...	*32*	24	8
		Total Sub-order 43 ...	**19,651**	**10,350**	**9,301**

Occupation and Class. — State Total.

XVII.

(State Distribution)—(*Continued*).

Taluqs.								
Tovala.			Agastiswaram.			Eranial.		
Total.	Males.	Females.	Total.	Males.	Females.	Total.	Males.	Females.
7	8	9	10	11	12	13	14	15
...	...	...	43	25	18	49	24	25
...	...	...	...	...	...	32	18	14
...	...	...	52	34	18	304	145	159
...	...	...	...	...	...	69	17	52
...	...	...	95	59	36	454	204	250
8	3	5	404	179	225	309	131	178
...	...	...	...	...	...	...	...	...
...	...	...	...	...	...	...	...	...
...	...	...	...	...	...	32	19	13
...	...	...	...	...	...	...	...	...
...	...	...	...	...	...	...	...	...
28	19	9	309	187	122	206	132	74
36	22	14	713	366	347	547	282	265
...	...	...	34	26	8	20	18	2
274	133	141	1,080	599	481	675	333	342
...	...	...	11	5	6	6	3	3
...	...	...	...	...	...	...	...	...
...	...	...	...	...	...	...	...	...
...	...	...	...	...	...	...	...	...
...	...	...	8	3	5	...	...	...
...	...	...	...	...	...	...	...	...
...	...	...	6	2	4	...	...	...
...	...	...	7	4	3	...	...	...
274	133	141	1,146	639	507	701	354	347

TABLE

Occupations, Part B.—

Class.	Group.	Occupation.	Taluqs: Kalkulam. Total.	Kalkulam. Males.	Kalkulam. Females.	Vilavankodu. Total.	Vilavankodu. Males.	Vilavankodu. Females.
1	2	3	16	17	18	19	20	21
D. Preparation and supply of material substances.	41	Flax spinners, weavers and sellers ...	...	...	...	...	...	...
		Hemp-rope makers and sellers ...	7	7	...	...	...	...
		Net makers and sellers ...	...	...	...	161	78	83
		Coir preparers, manufacturers and sellers ...	...	...	...	58	19	39
		Total Sub-order 41 ...	7	7	...	219	97	122
	42	Tailors ...	52	18	34	...	...	...
		Hat, cap and turban makers and sellers ..	...	...	...	...	...	...
		Turban-binders ...	...	...	...	...	...	...
		Umbrella makers and sellers .	79	37	42	412	199	213
		Lace sellers ...	...	...	...	...	...	...
		Button sellers ...	...	...	...	...	...	...
		Piece-goods dealers ...	116	83	33	109	57	52
		Total Sub-order 42 ...	247	138	109	521	256	265
	43	Gold and silver dealers ...	...	...	...	...	...	...
		Gold and silver workers ...	386	215	171	384	216	168
		Goldsmiths' dust washers ...	2	2	...	...	...	...
		Enamellers ...	...	...	...	...	...	...
		Gold and silver braid makers.	7	2	5	...	...	...
		Diamond polishers and sellers ...	...	...	...	...	...	...
		Ruby workers ...	...	...	...	...	...	...
		Ruby and emerald, &c., dealers ...	...	...	...	...	...	...
		Pearls and other precious stones dealers ...	...	...	...	...	...	...
		Coral dealers ...	...	...	...	...	...	...
		Total Sub-order 43 ...	395	219	176	384	216	168

XVII.

(State Distribution)—(*Continued*).

—(*Continued*).

Neyattankara.			Trivandram.			Nedumangadu.		
Total.	Males.	Females.	Total.	Males.	Females.	Total.	Males.	Females.
22	23	24	25	26	27	28	29	30
..	...	...	19	13	6	...	...	...
...	...	...	9	9	...	...	...	...
330	163	167	123	59	64	...	...	...
310	89	221	1,434	435	999	...	...	...
640	252	388	1,585	516	1,069	...	...	...
52	19	33	860	336	524	...	...	...
...	...	...	8	3	5	...	...	...
...	...	...	12	4	8	...	...	...
262	138	124	173	95	78	259	128	131
...	...	...	3	2	1	...	...	...
...	...	...	1	1	...	...	...	...
119	88	31	359	236	123	153	115	38
433	245	188	1,416	677	739	412	243	169
...	...	..	95	66	29	...	...	...
604	310	294	1,983	998	985	387	211	176
...	...	...	15	8	7	...	...	...
...	...	...	5	2	3	...	...	...
..	...	...	5	5	...	...	...	...
...	...	...	1	1	...	...	...	...
...	...	...	7	4	3	...	...	...
...	...	...	3	3	...	...	...	...
...	...	...	8	6	2	...	...	...
...	...	...	10	9	1	...	...	...
604	310	294	2,132	1,102	1,030	387	211	176

TABLE

Occupations, Part B.—

Class.	Group.	Occupation.	Taluqs					
			Sirayinkil.			Kottarakkara.		
			Total.	Males.	Females.	Total.	Males.	Females.
1	2	3	31	32	33	34	35	36
D. Preparation and supply of material substances.	41	Flax spinners, weavers and sellers ...	...	...	...	...	...	...
		Hemp-rope makers and sellers ...	7	7	...	...	...	...
		Net makers and sellers ...	58	36	22	...	...	...
		Coir preparers, manufacturers and sellers .	1,239	374	865	...	...	...
		Total Sub-order 41 ...	1,304	417	887	...	...	...
	42	Tailors ...	39	18	21	...	...	...
		Hat, cap and turban makers and sellers ...	...	...	...	...	...	...
		Turban-binders	...	...	...	...	...	...
		Umbrella makers and sellers.	215	116	99	305	141	164
		Lace sellers ...	...	...	...	...	...	..
		Button sellers ..	...	...	...	...	...	...
		Piece-goods dealers ...	129	98	31	25	10	15
		Total Sub-order 42 ...	383	232	151	330	151	179
	43	Gold and silver dealers ...	21	17	4	..	...	...
		Gold and silver workers ..	679	411	268	418	205	213
		Goldsmith's dust washers ...	...	...	...	...	...	...
		Enamellers ..	...	...	...	...	...	...
		Gold and silver braid makers.	...	...	...	...	...	...
		Diamond polishers and sellers ...	...	...	...	...	...	...
		Ruby workers ..	...	..	...	...	...	...
		Ruby and emerald, &c., dealers ...	...	...	...	...	...	...
		Pearls and other precious stones dealers ...	...	...	...	...	...	...
		Coral dealers ..	...	...	...	...	...	...
		Total Sub-order 43 ...	700	428	272	418	205	213

XVII.

(State Distribution)—(*Continued*).

—(*Continued*).

Pattanapuram.			Shenkotta.			Quilon.		
Total.	Males.	Females.	Total.	Males.	Females.	Total.	Males.	Females.
37	38	39	40	41	42	43	44	45
...	...	...	...	...	...	12	8	4
...	...	...	...	...	...	8	8	...
...	...	...	...	...	...	179	117	62
...	...	...	...	...	...	2,453	768	1,685
...	...	...	...	...	...	2,652	901	1,751
..	...	...	36	17	19	762	268	494
...	...	...	...	...	...	6	3	3
...	...	...	...	...	...	...	...	...
242	129	113	37	16	21	297	198	99
...	...	...	...	...	...	...	...	...
...	...	...	...	...	...	...	...	...
40	31	9	24	18	6	184	143	41
282	160	122	97	51	46	1,249	612	637
...	...	...	25	18	7	53	39	14
174	80	94	407	242	165	1,117	598	519
	...	...	...	..	...	7	5	2
...	...	...	...	...	...	...	...	...
...	...	...	...	...	...	...	...	...
...	...	...	...	.	...	1	1	...
...	...	...	...	...	...	5	2	3
...	...	...	...	...	...	...	...	...
...	...	...	...	...	...	7	4	3
...	...	...	...	...	...	10	8	2
174	80	94	432	260	172	1,200	657	543

TABLE

Occupations, Part B.—

Class.	Group.	Occupation.	Kunnattur. Total.	Kunnattur. Males.	Kunnattur. Females.	Karunagappalli. Total.	Karunagappalli. Males.	Karunagappalli. Females.
1	2	3	46	47	48	49	50	51
D. Preparation and supply of material substances.	41	Flax spinners, weavers and sellers ...	...	...	...	...	...	...
		Hemp-rope makers and sellers ...	...	...	...	...	...	..
		Netmakers and sellers ...	...	...	...	287	143	144
		Coir preparers, manufacturers and sellers ...	...	...	...	4,412	1,238	3,174
		Total Sub-order 41 ...	...	..	...	4,699	1,381	3,318
	42	Tailors ...	...	...	...	395	136	259
		Hat, cap and turban makers and sellers ...	...	...	...	...	...	...
		Turban-binders ..	...	...	...	..	...	...
		Umbrella makers and sellers..	...	...	...	247	145	102
		Lace sellers ...	...	...	...	...	...	...
		Button sellers ...	...	...	...	...	...	...
		Piece-goods dealers ...	...	...	...	96	73	23
		Total Sub-order 42 ...	...	...	...	738	354	384
	43	Gold and silver dealers ...	...	..	...	...	...	...
		Gold and silver workers ...	397	210	187	607	314	293
		Goldsmiths' dust washers ...	...	...	...	...	...	...
		Enamellers ...	...	...	...	...	...	...
		Gold and silver braid makers.	...	...	...	...	...	...
		Diamond polishers and sellers ...	...	...	...	...	...	...
		Ruby workers ...	...	...	...	...	...	...
		Ruby and emerald, &c., dealers ...	...	...	...	...	...	...
		Pearls and other precious stones dealers ...	...	...	...	...	...	...
		Coral dealers ...	...	...	...	...	...	...
		Total Sub-order 43 ...	397	210	187	607	314	293

XVII.

(State Distribution)—(*Continued*).

—(*Continued*).

Kartigappalli.			Mavellikkara.			Chenganur.		
Total.	Males.	Females.	Total.	Males.	Females.	Total.	Males.	Females.
52	53	54	55	56	57	58	59	60
...	...	...	...	...	...	...	...	...
6	6	...	...	...	...	...	...	...
143	69	74	...	...	...	...	...	...
3,877	978	2,899	...	...	...	...	...	...
4,026	1,053	2,973	...	...	...	..	...	...
76	39	37	209	68	141	...	...	...
...	...	...	...	...	...	...	...	...
...	...	...	...	...	...	...	...	...
210	124	86	290	141	149	225	137	88
...	...	...	...	...	...	...	...	...
...	...	...	...	...	...	...	...	...
166	127	39	86	54	32	...	...	...
452	290	162	585	263	322	225	137	88
21	19	2	...	...	...	...	...	...
504	242	262	574	292	282	413	214	199
...	...	...	...	...	...	...	...	...
...	...	...	...	...	...	...	...	...
...	...	...	...	...	...	...	...	...
...	...	...	...	...	...	...	...	...
...	...	...	...	...	...	...	...	...
...	...	...	...	...	...	...	...	...
...	...	...	...	...	...	...	...	...
...	...	...	...	...	...	...	...	...
525	261	264	574	292	282	413	214	199

TABLE

Occupations, Part B.—

Class.	Group.	Occupation.	Tiruvalla. Total.	Tiruvalla. Males.	Tiruvalla. Females.	Ambalappula. Total.	Ambalappula. Males.	Ambalappula. Females.
1	2	3	61	62	63	64	65	66
D. Preparation and supply of material substances.	41	Flax spinners, weavers and sellers ...	...	...	...	20	12	8
		Hemp-rope makers and sellers ...	...	...	...	7	7	...
		Net makers and sellers ...	...	...	...	64	48	16
		Coir preparers, manufacturers and sellers ..	...	...	...	5,027	1,343	3,684
		Total Sub-order 41 ...	...	...	...	5,118	1,410	3,708
	42	Tailors ...	53	32	21	695	376	319
		Hat, cap and turban makers and sellers ...	..	...	...	...	...	...
		Turban-binders ...	..	...	...	...	...	...
		Umbrella makers and sellers.	372	210	162	419	228	191
		Lace sellers ...	...	...	...	...	...	...
		Button sellers ...	...	...	...	...	..	...
		Piece-goods dealers ...	74	46	28	231	168	63
		Total Sub-order 42 ...	499	288	211	1,345	772	573
	43	Gold and silver dealers ...	...	...	...	39	27	12
		Gold and silver workers ...	501	252	249	869	444	425
		Goldsmiths' dust washers ...	...	...	...	5	2	3
		Enamellers ...	...	...	...	...	...	...
		Gold and silver braid makers.	...	...	...	5	3	2
		Diamond polishers and sellers ...	...	...	...	...	...	...
		Ruby workers ...	...	...	...	10	6	4
		Ruby and emerald, &c., dealers ...	...	...	...	...	...	...
		Pearls and other precious stones dealers ...	...	...	...	...	...	...
		Coral dealers ...	...	...	...	5	3	2
		Total Sub-order 43 ...	501	252	249	933	485	448

XVII.

(State Distribution)—(*Continued*).

—(*Continued*).

Sherttala.			Vykkam.			Ettumanur.		
Total.	Males.	Females.	Total.	Males.	Females.	Total.	Males.	Females.
67	68	69	70	71	72	73	74	75
...	...	...	...	...	...	...	...	...
...	...	...	...	...	...	3	3	...
65	31	34	...	...	...	...	...	...
4,093	1,148	2,945	1,068	347	721	...	...	...
4,158	1,179	2,979	1,068	347	721	3	3	...
142	68	74	67	39	28	...	...	...
...	...	...	...	...	...	...	...	...
...	...	...	...	...	...	...	...	...
224	128	96	447	172	275	172	98	74
...	...	...	...	...	...	...	...	...
...	...	...	...	...	...	...	...	...
...	...	...	90	54	36	3	3	...
366	196	170	604	265	339	175	101	74
...	...	...	...	...	...	...	...	...
967	499	468	727	387	340	585	319	266
...	...	...	...	...	...	...	...	...
...	...	...	...	...	...	...	...	...
...	...	...	...	...	...	...	...	...
...	...	...	...	...	...	...	...	...
...	...	...	...	...	...	...	...	...
...	...	...	...	...	...	...	...	...
...	...	...	...	...	...	...	...	...
...	...	...	...	...	...	...	...	...
967	499	468	727	387	340	585	319	266

TABLE

Occupations, Part B.—

Class.	Group.	Occupation.	Taluqs: Kottayam. Total.	Kottayam. Males.	Kottayam. Females.	Changanacheri. Total.	Changanacheri. Males.	Changanacheri. Females.
1	2	3	76	77	78	79	80	81
D. Preparation and supply of material substances.	41	Flax spinners, weavers and sellers ...	...	...	...	...	...	...
		Hemp-rope makers and sellers ...	...	...	...	...	...	...
		Net makers and sellers ...	...	...	...	...	...	...
		Coir preparers, manufacturers and sellers ...	457	143	314	167	58	109
		Total Sub-order 41 ...	457	143	314	167	58	109
	42	Tailors ...	506	263	243	408	186	222
		Hat, cap and turban makers and sellers ...	...	..	...	...	...	...
		Turban-binders ...	...	...	...	...	...	...
		Umbrella makers and sellers..	480	268	212	239	134	105
		Lace sellers ...	...	...	...	...	...	...
		Button sellers ...	...	...	...	...	...	...
		Piece-goods dealers ...	123	81	42	65	38	27
		Total Sub-order 42 ...	1,109	612	497	712	358	354
	43	Gold and silver dealers ...	20	13	7	...	...	...
		Gold and silver workers ...	782	486	296	588	278	310
		Goldsmiths' dust washers ...	...	...	...	...	...	...
		Enamellers ...	...	...	...	...	...	...
		Gold and silver braid makers.	...	...	...	...	...	...
		Diamond polishers and sellers ...	...	...	...	...	...	...
		Ruby workers ...	6	2	4	...	...	...
		Ruby and emerald, &c., dealers ...	...	...	...	...	...	...
		Pearls and other precious stones dealers ...	...	...	...	...	...	...
		Coral dealers ...	...	...	...	...	...	...
		Total Sub-order 43 ...	808	501	307	588	278	310

XVII.

(State Distribution)—(*Continued*).

—(*Continued*).

Meenachal.			Muvattupula.			Todupula.		
Total.	Males.	Females.	Total.	Males.	Females.	Total.	Males.	Females.
82	83	84	85	86	87	88	89	90
...	...	...	...	...	...	..	...	...
...	...	...	...	...	...	...	...	...
...	...	...	...	...	...	...	...	...
...	...	...	...	...	...	...	...	...
...	...	...	...	...	...	...	...	...
...	...	...	...	...	...	...	...	...
...	...	...	...	...	...	...	...	...
...	...	...	...	...	...	...	...	...
...	...	...	241	146	95	34	15	19
...	...	...	...	...	...	...	...	...
...	...	...	...	...	...	...	...	...
...	...	...	21	16	5	11	9	2
...	...	...	262	162	100	45	24	21
...	...	...	...	...	...	...	...	...
587	299	288	540	286	254	260	115	145
...	...	...	...	...	...	...	...	...
...	...	...	...	...	...	...	...	...
...	...	...	...	...	...	...	...	...
...	...	...	...	...	...	...	...	...
...	...	...	...	...	...	...	...	...
...	...	...	...	...	...	...	...	...
...	...	...	...	...	...	...	...	...
...	...	...	...	...	...	...	...	...
587	299	288	540	286	254	260	115	145

TABLE

Occupations, Part B.—

Class.	Group.	Occupation.	Taluqs: Kunnattunadu. Total.	Males.	Females.	Alangadu. Total.	Males.	Females.
1	2	3	91	92	93	94	95	96
D. Preparation and supply of material substances.	41	Flax spinners, weavers and sellers ...	...	...	...	...	...	...
		Hemp-rope makers and sellers ...	...	...	...	...	...	...
		Net makers and sellers ...	...	...	...	...	...	...
		Coir preparers, manufacturers and sellers ...	...	...	...	...	...	...
		Total Sub-order 41 ...	...	...	...	...	...	...
	42	Tailors ...	84	38	46	...	...	...
		Hat, cap and turban makers and sellers ...	...	...	...	...	...	...
		Turban-binders ...	...	...	...	...	...	...
		Umbrella makers and sellers.	385	163	222	21	12	9
		Lace sellers ...	...	...	...	...	...	...
		Button sellers ...	...	...	...	...	...	...
		Piece-goods dealers ...	...	...	...	13	6	7
		Total Sub-order 42 ...	469	201	268	34	18	16
	43	Gold and silver dealers ...	...	...	...	...	...	...
		Gold and silver workers ...	599	278	321	471	217	254
		Goldsmiths' dust washers ...	...	...	...	...	...	...
		Enamellers ...	...	...	...	...	...	...
		Gold and silver braid makers.	...	...	...	...	...	...
		Diamond polishers and sellers ...	...	...	...	...	...	...
		Ruby workers ...	...	...	...	...	...	...
		Ruby and emerald, &c., dealers ...	...	...	...	...	...	...
		Pearls and other precious stones dealers ...	...	...	...	...	...	...
		Coral dealers ...	...	...	...	...	...	...
		Total Sub-order 43 ...	599	278	321	471	217	254

XVII.

(State Distribution)—(*Continued*).

—(*Continued*).

Parur.			Cardamom Hills.			Periyar & Thekkadi.		
Total.	Males.	Females.	Total.	Males.	Females.	Total.	Males.	Females.
97	98	99	100	101	102	103	104	105
5	5	...	...	...	...	...	...	...
...	...	...	...	...	...	...	...	...
...	...	...	...	...	...	...	...	...
2,049	411	1,638	...	...	...	...	...	...
2,054	416	1,638	...	...	...	...	...	...
379	216	163	12	9	3	11	7	4
...	...	...	...	...	...	...	...	...
...	...	...	...	...	...	...	...	...
152	97	55	...	...	...	...	...	...
...	...	...	...	...	...	...	...	...
...	...	...	...	...	...	...	...	...
73	43	30	2	2	...	4	4	...
604	356	248	14	11	3	15	11	4
18	8	10	...	...	...	...	...	...
551	284	267	42	29	13	8	5	3
...	...	...	...	...	...	...	...	...
...	...	...	...	...	...	...	...	...
...	...	...	...	...	...	...	...	...
...	...	...	...	...	...	...	...	...
3	3	...	...	...	...	...	...	...
...	...	...	...	...	...	...	...	...
...	...	...	...	...	...	...	...	...
...	...	...	...	...	...	...	...	...
572	295	277	42	29	13	8	5	3

TABLE
Occupations, Part B.—

Class.	Group.	Occupation.	Total.	Males.	Females.
1	2	3	4	5	6
D. Preparation and supply of material substances.	44	Brass workers and sellers ...	*23*	15	8
		Copper workers and sellers ...	*134*	107	27
		Bell-metal workers and sellers ...	*2,634*	1,458	1,176
		General workers in brass, copper and bell-metal ...	*87*	58	29
		Brass and copper dealers ...	*3*	3	...
		Total Sub-order 44 ...	**2,881**	**1,641**	**1,240**
	45	Tin workers and sellers ...	*60*	39	21
		Tinfoil sellers ...	*6*	4	2
		Zinc workers and sellers ...	*13*	5	8
		Lead and quicksilver workers and sellers ...	*91*	21	70
		General workers in lead and zinc ...	*27*	18	9
		Total Sub-order 45 ...	**197**	**87**	**110**
	46	Iron and steel sellers ...	*91*	74	17
		Blacksmiths ...	*19,308*	10,239	9,069
		Iron and hardware dealers ...	*84*	55	29
		Lock makers and sellers ...	*4*	4	...
		Total Sub-order 46 ...	**19,487**	**10,372**	**9,115**
	47	Bottle dealers ...	*9*	5	4
		Glass and china-ware dealers ...	*30*	14	16
		Total Sub-order 47 ...	**39**	**19**	**20**
	48	Potters and pot makers and sellers...	*5,504*	2,718	2,786
		Grind-stone, mill-stone, &c., makers and sellers ...	*6*	4	2
		Pestle and mortar makers and sellers.	*6*	4	2
		Total Sub-order 48 ...	**5,516**	**2,726**	**2,790**

XVII.

(State Distribution)—(*Continued*).

Taluqs.								
Tovala.			Agastiswaram.			Eranial.		
Total.	Males.	Females.	Total.	Males.	Females.	Total.	Males.	Females.
7	8	9	10	11	12	13	14	15
...	...	...	7	3	4	...	...	...
...	...	...	20	17	3	...	...	...
12	5	7	139	74	65	293	177	116
...	...	...	21	12	9	...	...	...
...	...	...	...	...	...	...	...	...
12	5	7	187	106	81	293	177	116
...	...	...	8	3	5	...	...	...
...	...	...	...	...	...	...	...	...
...	...	...	...	...	...	...	...	...
...	...	...	12	3	9	...	...	...
...	...	...	3	3	...	...	...	...
...	...	...	23	9	14	...	...	...
...	...	...	13	9	4	...	...	...
188	100	88	712	387	325	819	441	378
...	...	...	1	1	...	14	9	5
...	...	...	...	...	...	...	...	...
188	100	88	726	397	329	833	450	383
...	...	...	...	...	...	...	...	...
...	...	...	1	1	...	...	...	...
...	...	...	1	1	...	...	...	...
60	28	32	180	86	94	385	230	155
...	...	...	6	4	2	...	...	...
...	...	...	...	...	...	...	...	...
60	28	32	186	90	96	385	230	155

TABLE

Occupations, Part B.—

Class.	Group.	Occupation.	Taluqs: Kalkulam. Total.	Kalkulam. Males.	Kalkulam. Females.	Vilavankodu. Total.	Vilavankodu. Males.	Vilavankodu. Females.
1	2	3	16	17	18	19	20	21
D. Preparation and supply of material substances.	44	Brass workers and sellers ...	...	...	...	...	...	...
		Copper workers and sellers ...	...	...	...	...	...	...
		Bell-metal workers and sellers ...	66	34	32	32	13	19
		General workers in brass, copper and bell-metal ...	...	...	...	...	...	...
		Brass and copper dealers ...	...	...	...	...	...	...
		Total Sub-order 44 ...	66	34	32	32	13	19
	45	Tin workers and sellers ...	...	...	...	...	...	...
		Tinfoil sellers ...	...	...	...	...	...	...
		Zinc workers and sellers ...	...	...	...	...	...	...
		Lead and quicksilver workers and sellers ...	...	...	...	...	...	...
		General workers in lead & zinc.	...	...	...	...	...	...
		Total Sub-order 45 ...	...	...	...	...	...	...
	46	Iron and steel sellers ...	...	...	...	...	...	...
		Blacksmiths ...	524	250	274	571	275	296
		Iron and hardware dealers ...	...	...	...	...	...	..
		Lock makers and sellers ...	...	...	...	...	...	...
		Total Sub-order 46 ...	524	250	274	571	275	296
	47	Bottle dealers ...	...	...	...	...	...	...
		Glass and china-ware dealers.	...	...	...	...	...	...
		Total Sub-order 47 ...	...	...	...	...	...	...
	48	Potters and pot makers and sellers ...	255	113	142	312	147	165
		Grind-stone, mill-stone, &c., makers and sellers ...	...	...	...	...	...	...
		Pestle and mortar makers and sellers ...	...	...	...	...	...	...
		Total Sub-order 48 ...	255	113	142	312	147	165

XVII.

(State Distribution)—(*Continued*).

—(*Continued*).

Neyattankara.			Trivandram.			Nedumangadu.		
Total.	Males.	Females.	Total.	Males.	Females.	Total	Males.	Females.
22	23	24	25	26	27	28	29	30
...	...	...	12	8	4	...	...	...
...	...	...	45	36	9	...	...	...
2	2	...	418	181	237	20	12	8
...	...	...	25	19	6	...	...	...
...	...	...	3	3	...	...	...	...
2	2	...	503	247	256	20	12	8
...	...	...	21	14	7	...	...	...
...	...	...	2	2	...	...	...	...
...	...	...	...	...	...	...	...	...
...	...	...	30	9	21	...	...	...
...	...	...	6	4	2	...	...	...
...	...	...	59	29	30	...	...	...
...	...	...	38	29	9	...	...	...
564	251	313	1,867	1,073	794	418	220	198
...	...	...	23	15	8	...	...	...
...	...	...	1	1	...	...	...	...
564	251	313	1,929	1,118	811	418	220	198
...	...	...	2	2	...	...	...	...
...	...	...	9	5	4	...	...	...
...	...	...	11	7	4	...	...	...
773	379	394	275	148	127	177	82	95
...	...	...	...	...	...	...	...	...
...	...	..	6	4	2	...	...	...
773	379	394	281	152	129	177	82	95

TABLE

Occupations, Part B.—

Class.	Group.	Occupation.	Taluqs. Sirayinkil. Total.	Males.	Females.	Kottarakkara. Total.	Males.	Females.
1	2	3	31	32	33	34	35	36
D. Preparation and supply of material substances.	44	Brass workers and sellers ...	...	...	...	...	...	...
		Copper workers and sellers...	...	...	...	...	...	...
		Bell-metal workers and sellers ...	20	14	6	65	36	29
		General workers in brass, copper and bell-metal ...	...	...	...	...	...	...
		Brass and copper dealers ..	...	...	...	...	...	...
		Total Sub-order 44 ...	20	14	6	65	36	29
	45	Tin workers and sellers ...	...	...	...	...	...	...
		Tinfoil sellers ...	...	...	...	...	...	...
		Zinc workers and sellers ...	...	...	...	...	...	...
		Lead and quicksilver workers and sellers ...	...	...	...	...	...	...
		General workers in lead & zinc	...	...	...	...	...	...
		Total Sub-order 45 ...	...	...	...	...	...	...
	46	Iron and steel sellers ...	...	...	...	...	...	...
		Blacksmiths ...	595	321	274	515	247	268
		Iron and hardware dealers ...	...	...	...	...	...	...
		Lock makers and sellers ...	...	...	...	...	...	...
		Total Sub-order 46 ...	595	321	274	515	247	268
	47	Bottle dealers ..	...	...	...	...	...	...
		Glass and china-ware dealers..	...	...	...	...	...	...
		Total Sub-order 47 ...	...	...	...	...	...	...
		Potters and pot makers and sellers ...	396	202	194	425	228	197
		Grind-stone, mill-stone, &c., makers and sellers ...	...	...	...	...	...	...
		Pestle and mortar makers and sellers ...	...	...	...	...	...	...
		Total Sub-order 48 ...	396	202	194	425	228	197

XVII.

(State Distribution)—(*Continued*).

—(*Continued*).

Pattanapuram.			Shenkotta.			Quilon.		
Total.	Males.	Females.	Total.	Males.	Females.	Total.	Males.	Females.
37	38	39	40	41	42	43	44	45
...	...	...	...	...	...	...	...	...
...	...	...	...	...	...	14	9	5
39	21	18	28	15	13	57	30	27
...	...	...	...	...	...	12	8	4
...	...	...	...	...	...	...	...	...
39	21	18	28	15	13	83	47	36
...	...	...	...	...	...	12	8	4
...	...	...	...	...	...	...	...	...
...	...	...	...	...	...	...	...	...
...	...	...	...	...	...	24	6	18
...	...	...	...	...	...	10	8	2
...	...	...	...	...	...	46	22	24
...	...	...	...	...	...	13	13	...
335	148	187	321	167	154	1,320	782	538
...	...	...	17	11	6	6	4	2
...	...	...	...	...	...	3	3	...
335	148	187	338	178	160	1,342	802	540
...	...	...	...	...	...	7	3	4
...	...	...	...	...	...	9	3	6
...	...	...	...	...	...	16	6	10
191	87	104	47	15	32	251	95	156
...	..	...	...	...	...	...	...	...
...	...	...	...	...	...	...	...	...
191	87	104	47	15	32	251	95	156

TABLE

Occupations, Part B.—

Class.	Group.	Occupation.	Kunnattur. Total.	Kunnattur. Males.	Kunnattur. Females.	Karunagappalli. Total.	Karunagappalli. Males.	Karunagappalli. Females.
1	2	3	46	47	48	49	50	51
D. Preparation and supply of material substances.	44	Brass workers and sellers ...	...	...	...	...	...	...
		Copper workers and sellers...	...	...	...	...	...	...
		Bell-metal workers and sellers ...	77	45	32	23	15	8
		General workers in brass, copper and bell-metal ...	...	...	...	...	...	...
		Brass and copper dealers ...	...	...	...	...	...	...
		Total Sub-order 44 ...	77	45	32	23	15	8
	45	Tin workers and sellers ...	...	...	...	...	...	...
		Tinfoil sellers ...	...	...	...	...	...	...
		Zinc workers and sellers ...	...	...	...	...	...	...
		Lead and quicksilver workers and sellers ...	...	...	...	...	...	...
		General workers in lead & zinc.	...	...	...	...	...	...
		Total Sub-order 45 ...	...	...	...	...	...	...
	46	Iron and steel sellers ...	...	...	...	2	2	...
		Blacksmiths ...	459	216	243	825	471	354
		Iron and hardware dealers ...	...	...	...	...	...	...
		Lock makers and sellers ...	...	...	...	...	...	...
		Total Sub-order 46 ...	459	216	243	827	473	354
	47	Bottle dealers ...	...	...	...	...	...	...
		Glass and china-ware dealers.	...	...	...	...	...	...
		Total Sub-order 47 ...	...	...	...	...	...	...
	48	Potters and pot makers and sellers ...	139	74	65	...	..	...
		Grind-stone, mill-stone, &c., makers and sellers ...	...	...	...	...	...	...
		Pestle and mortar makers and sellers ...	...	...	...	...	...	...
		Total Sub-order 48 ...	139	74	65	...	...	...

XVII.

(State Distribution)—(*Continued*).

—(*Continued*).

Kartigappalli.			Mavellikkara.			Chenganur.		
Total.	Males.	Females.	Total.	Males.	Females.	Total.	Males.	Females.
52	53	54	55	56	57	58	59	60
...	...	...	...	..	...	...	...	...
...	...	...	...	...	...	...	...	...
29	18	11	186	110	76	116	62	54
...	...	...	...	...	...	...	...	...
...	...	...	...	...	...	...	...	...
29	18	11	186	110	76	116	62	54
...	...	...	...	...	...	...	...	...
...	...	...	...	...	...	...	...	...
...	...	...	...	...	...	...	...	...
...	...	...	...	...	...	...	...	...
...	...	...	...	...	...	...	...	...
...	...	...	...	...	...	...	...	...
...	...	...	...	...	...	...	...	...
486	223	263	487	269	218	369	207	162
9	5	4	...	...	...	...	...	...
...	...	...	...	...	...	...	...	...
495	228	267	487	269	218	369	207	162
...	...	...	...	...	...	...	...	...
...	...	...	...	...	...	...	...	...
...	...	...	...	...	...	...	...	...
301	134	167	104	40	64	165	76	89
...	...	...	...	...	...	...	...	...
...	...	...	...	...	...	...	...	...
301	134	167	104	40	64	165	76	89

TABLE
Occupations, Part B.—

Class.	Group.	Occupation.	Taluqs: Tiruvalla. Total.	Tiruvalla. Males.	Tiruvalla. Females.	Ambalappula. Total.	Ambalappula. Males.	Ambalappula. Females.
1	2	3	61	62	63	64	65	66
D. Preparation and supply of material substances.	44	Brass workers and sellers ...	...	...	...	4	4	...
		Copper workers and sellers...	...	...	...	29	23	6
		Bell-metal workers and sellers ...	238	140	98	190	111	79
		General workers in brass, copper and bell-metal ...	...	...	...	21	13	8
		Brass and copper dealers ..	...	...	...	...	...	...
		Total Sub-order 44 ...	238	140	98	244	151	93
	45	Tin workers and sellers ...	...	...	...	11	9	2
		Tinfoil sellers ...	...	...	...	4	2	2
		Zinc workers and sellers ...	...	...	...	13	5	8
		Lead and quicksilver workers and sellers ...	...	...	...	25	3	22
		General workers in lead & zinc..	...	...	...	8	3	5
		Total Sub-order 45 ...	...	...	...	61	22	39
	46	Iron and steel sellers ...	...	...	...	16	12	4
		Blacksmiths ...	634	353	281	1,296	741	555
		Iron and hardware dealers ...	...	...	...	8	5	3
		Lock makers and sellers ...	...	...	...	...		...
		Total Sub-order 46 ...	634	353	281	1,320	758	562
	47	Bottle dealers ..	...	...	...	...	...	...
		Glass and china-ware dealers.	...	...	...	9	3	6
		Total Sub-order 47 ...	...	...	...	9	3	6
	48	Potters and pot makers and sellers ...	285	133	152	61	24	37
		Grand-stone, mill-stone, &c., makers and sellers ...	...	...	...	...	...	...
		Pestle and mortar makers and sellers ...	...	...	...	...	...	...
		Total Sub-order 48 ...	285	133	152	61	24	37

XVII.

(State Distribution)—(*Continued*).

—(*Continued*).

Sherttala.			Vykkam.			Ettumanur.		
Total.	Males.	Females.	Total.	Males.	Females.	Total.	Males.	Females.
67	68	69	70	71	72	73	74	75
...	...	...	...	...	...	...	...	...
...	...	...	...	...	...	...	...	...
124	71	53	32	20	12	18	10	8
...	...	...	...	...	...	...	...	...
...	...	...	...	...	...	...	...	...
124	71	53	32	20	12	18	10	8
...	...	...	...	...	...	...	...	...
...	...	...	...	...	...	...	...	...
...	...	...	...	...	...	...	...	...
...	...	...	...	...	...	...	...	...
...	...	...	...	...	...	...	...	...
...	...	...	...	...	...	...	...	...
...	...	...	...	...	...	...	...	...
603	284	319	551	247	304	332	178	154
...	...	...	6	5	1	...	...	...
...	...	...	...	...	...	...	...	...
603	284	319	557	252	305	332	178	154
...	...	...	...	...	...	...	...	...
...	...	...	...	...	...	...	...	...
...	...	...	...	...	...	...	...	...
...	...	...	...	...	...	75	46	29
...	...	...	...	...	...	...	...	...
...	...	...	...	...	...	...	...	...
...	...	...	...	...	...	75	46	29

TABLE

Occupations, Part B.—

Class.	Group.	Occupation.	Kottayam. Total.	Kottayam. Males.	Kottayam. Females.	Changanacheri. Total.	Changanacheri. Males.	Changanacheri. Females.
			TALUQS					
1	2	3	76	77	78	79	80	81
D. Preparation and supply of material substances.	44	Brass workers and sellers ...	...	...	...	...	...	...
		Copper workers and sellers...	12	12	...	...	...	...
		Bell-metal workers and sellers ...	206	113	93	59	33	26
		General workers in brass, copper and bell-metal ...	7	5	2	...	...	...
		Brass and copper dealers ...	...	...	...	...	...	...
		Total Sub-order 44 ...	225	130	95	59	33	26
	45	Tin workers and sellers ...	8	5	3	...	...	...
		Tinfoil sellers ...	...	...	...	...	...	...
		Zinc workers and sellers ..	...	...	...	...	...	...
		Lead and quicksilver workers and sellers ...	...	...	...	...	...	...
		General workers in lead & zinc	...	...	...	...	...	...
		Total Sub-order 45 ...	8	5	3	...	...	...
	46	Iron and steel sellers ...	3	3	...	...	...	...
		Blacksmiths ...	1,194	638	556	606	289	317
		Iron and hardware dealers ...	...	...	...	...	...	...
		Lock makers and sellers ...	..	...	...	...	...	...
		Total Sub-order 46 ...	1,197	641	556	606	289	317
	47	Bottle dealers ...	...	...	...	...	...	...
		Glass and china-ware dealers.	2	2	...	...	...	...
		Total Sub-order 47 ...	2	2	...	...	...	...
	48	Potters and pot makers and sellers ...	...	...	...	25	17	8
		Grind-stone, mill-stone, &c., makers and sellers ...	...	...	...	...	...	...
		Pestle and mortar makers and sellers ...	...	...	...	...	...	...
		Total Sub-order 48 ...	...	...	...	25	17	8

XVII.

(State Distribution)—(*Continued*).

—(*Continued*).

Meenachal.			Muvattupula.			Todupula.		
Total.	Males.	Females.	Total.	Males.	Females.	Total.	Males.	Females.
82	83	84	85	86	87	88	89	90
...	...	...	...	...	...	...	...	...
...	...	...	...	...	...	...	...	...
43	28	15	7	4	3	2	2	...
...	...	...	...	...	...	...	...	..
...	...	...	...	...	...	...	...	...
43	28	15	7	4	3	2	2	...
...	...	...	...	...	...	...	...	...
...	...	...	...	...	...	...	...	...
...	...	...	...	..	..	...	...	...
...	...	..	...	...	...	...	...	...
...	...	...	...	...	...	...	...	...
...	...	...	...	...	...	...	...	...
...	...	...	..	...	...	...	...	...
514	236	278	365	200	165	211	122	89
...	...	...	...	...	...	...	...	...
...	...	...	...	...	...	...	...	...
514	236	278	365	200	165	211	122	89
...	...	...	...	..	...	...	...	...
...	...	...	...	...	...	...	...	...
...	...	...	...	...	...	...	...	...
...	...	...	...	...	...	100	64	36
...	...	...	...	...	..	...	...	...
...	...	...	...	...	...	...	...	...
...	...	...	...	...	...	100	64	36

TABLE

Occupations, Part B.—

Class.	Group.	Occupation.	Taluqs: Kunnattunadu. Total.	Kunnattunadu. Males.	Kunnattunadu. Females.	Alangadu. Total.	Alangadu. Males.	Alangadu. Females.
1	2	3	91	92	93	94	95	96
D. Preparation and supply of material substances.	44	Brass workers and sellers ...	...	...	...	...	...	...
		Copper workers and sellers ...	...	...	...	...	...	...
		Bell-metal workers and sellers ...	5	5	...	20	12	8
		General workers in brass, copper and bell-metal ...	...	...	...	...	...	...
		Brass and copper dealers ...	...	...	..	...	...	...
		Total Sub-order 44 ...	5	5	...	20	12	8
	45	Tin workers and sellers ...	...	...	...	...	...	...
		Tinfoil sellers ...	...	...	...	...	...	...
		Zinc workers and sellers ...	...	...	...	...	...	..
		Lead and quicksilver workers and sellers ...	...	...	...	...	...	...
		General workers in lead & zinc.	..	...	...	...	...	...
		Total Sub-order 45 ...	...	...	..	...	...	...
	46	Iron and steel sellers ...	...	...	..	...	...	
		Blacksmiths ...	408	227	181	377	203	174
		Iron and hardware dealers ...	...	...	..	...	...	...
		Lock makers and sellers ...	...	...	...	...	...	..
		Total Sub-order 46 ...	408	227	181	377	203	174
	47	Bottle dealers ...	...	...	...	...	...	...
		Glass and china-ware dealers.	...	...	...	...	...	...
		Total Sub-order 47 ...	...	...	...	...	...	...
	48	Potters and pot makers and sellers ...	...	...	...	472	249	223
		Grind-stone, mill-stone, &c., makers and sellers ...	...	...	...	...	..	...
		Pestle and mortar makers and sellers ...	..	...	...	...	...	...
		Total Sub-order 48 ...	...	...	...	472	249	223

XVII.

(State Distribution)—(*Continued*).

—(*Continued*).

Parur.			Cardamom Hills.			Periyar & Thekkadi.		
Total.	Males.	Females.	Total.	Males.	Females.	Total.	Males.	Females.
97	98	99	100	101	102	103	104	105
...	...	...	...	...	...	...	...	...
14	10	4	...	...	...	...	...	...
68	45	23	...	...	...	...	...	...
1	1	...	...	...	...	...	...	...
...	...	...	...	...	...	...	...	...
83	56	27	...	...	...	..	...	...
...	...	...	...	...	...	...	...	...
...	...	...	...	...	...	...	...	...
...	...	...	...	...	...	...	...	...
...	...	...	...	...	...	...	...	...
...	...	...	...	...	...	...	...	...
...	...	...	...	...	...	...	...	...
6	6	...	...	...	...	...	...	...
741	415	326	93	50	43	8	8	...
..	...	...	...	...	...	...	...	...
...	...	...	...	...	...	...	...	...
747	421	326	93	50	43	8	8	...
...	...	...	...	...	...	...	...	...
...	...	..	...	...	...	...	...	...
...	...	...	...	...	...	...	...	...
50	21	29	...	...	...	...	...	...
...	...	...	...	...	...	...	...	...
...	...	...	...	...	...	...	...	...
50	21	29	..	...	...	...	...	...

TABLE

Occupations, Part B.—

Class.	Group.	Occupation.	Total.	Males.	Females.
1	2	3	4	5	6
D. Preparation and supply of material substances.	49	Timber and bamboo dealers ...	*693*	464	229
		Wood-cutters and sawyers ...	*4,888*	2,227	2,661
		Carpenters ...	*39,534*	20,674	18,860
		Box makers and sellers ...	*241*	43	198
		Total Sub-order 49 ...	**45,356**	**23,408**	**21,948**
	50	Rattan workers and sellers ...	*140*	60	80
		Basket-weavers and winnowing-pan makers and sellers ...	*7,913*	4,002	3,911
		Mat makers and sellers ...	*1,145*	665	480
		Leaf-plate sellers ...	*77*	40	37
		Leaf-fan makers and sellers ...	*98*	60	38
		Comb makers and sellers ...	*50*	26	24
		Broom sellers ...	*23*	7	16
		Total Sub-order 50 ...	**9,446**	**4,860**	**4,586**
	51	Wax, honey and general forest produce collectors and sellers ...	*39*	29	10
	52	Druggists ...	*131*	119	12
		Kanku or red-powder preparers and sellers ...	*12*	1	11
		Perfume sellers ...	*6*	3	3
		Total Sub-order 52 ...	**149**	**123**	**26**
	53	Tanners, &c. ...	*302*	180	122
		Shoe and boot makers and sellers ...	*168*	132	36
		Leather dyers ...	*11*	3	8
		Hide dealers ...	*46*	16	30
		Grease preparers and sellers ...	*18*	12	6
		Total Sub-order 53 ...	**545**	**343**	**202**
		Total Class D. ...	*430,756*	*220,214*	*210,542*

XVII.

(State Distribution)—(*Continued*).

TALUQS.

Tovala.			Agastiswaram.			Eranial.		
Total.	Males.	Females.	Total.	Males.	Females.	Total.	Males.	Females.
7	8	9	10	11	12	13	14	15
...		...	66	48	18	21	14	7
36	14	22	131	47	84	55	20	35
381	194	187	1,144	625	519	1,348	643	705
...	...	...	33	8	25	...	...	...
417	208	209	1,374	728	646	1,424	677	747
...	...	...	...	...	...	...	...	...
116	55	61	261	136	125	305	156	149
...	...	...	56	31	25	25	16	9
...	...	...	...	...	...	...	...	...
...	...	...	...	...	...	...	...	...
...	...	...	...	...	...	...	...	...
...	...	...	...	...	..	...	...	...
116	55	61	317	167	150	330	172	158
...	...	...	...	...	...	...	...	...
...	...	...	...	...	...	...	...	...
...	...	...	...	...	...	...	...	...
...	...	...	...	...	...	...	...	...
...	...	...	...	...	...	...	...	...
...	...	...	25	16	9	26	14	12
...	...	...	21	15	6	...	...	...
...	...	...	...	...	...	...	...	...
..	...	...	17	5	12	...	...	...
...	...	...	9	4	5	...	...	...
...	...	...	72	40	32	26	14	12
2,296	1,193	1,103	24,085	12,577	11,508	38,772	20,484	18,288

TABLE

Occupations, Part B.—

Class.	Group.	Occupation.	Taluqs: Kalkulam. Total.	Kalkulam. Males.	Kalkulam. Females.	Vilavankodu. Total.	Vilavankodu. Males.	Vilavankodu. Females.
1	2	3	16	17	18	19	20	21
D. Preparation and supply of material substances.	49	Timber and bamboo dealers...	...	...	...	...	...	...
		Wood-cutters and sawyers ...	105	48	57	125	52	73
		Carpenters ...	365	222	143	643	391	252
		Box makers and sellers ...	...	...	...	...	...	...
		Total Sub-order 49 ...	470	270	200	768	443	325
	50	Rattan workers and sellers ...	...	...	...	...	...	...
		Basket-weavers and winnowing-pan makers and sellers .	91	53	38	385	209	176
		Mat makers and sellers ..	41	19	22	83	39	44
		Leaf-plate sellers ...	...	...	...	28	12	16
		Leaf-fan makers and sellers...	...	...	...	13	8	5
		Comb makers and sellers ...	...	...	...	...	...	...
		Broom sellers ...	..	...	...	...	...	...
		Total Sub-order 50 ...	132	72	60	509	268	241
	51	Wax, honey and general forest produce collectors and sellers ...	15	13	2	8	5	3
	52	Druggists ...	...	...	...	...	...	...
		Kanku or red-powder preparers and sellers ...	4	...	4	...	...	...
		Perfume sellers ...	...	...	...	...	...	...
		Total Sub-order 52 ...	4	...	4	...	...	...
	53	Tanners, &c.	35	20	15	7	5	2
		Shoe and boot makers and sellers ...	...	...	...	...	...	...
		Leather dyers ...	...	...	...	...	...	...
		Hide dealers ...	...	...	...	...	...	...
		Grease preparers and sellers..	...	...	...	...	...	...
		Total Sub-order 53 ...	35	20	15	7	5	2
		Total Class D. ...	11,913	6,706	5,207	30,152	16,155	13,997

XVII.

(State Distribution)—(*Continued*).

—(*Continued*).

Neyattankara.			Trivandram.			Nedumangadu.		
Total.	Males.	Females.	Total.	Males.	Females.	Total.	Males.	Females.
22	23	24	25	26	27	28	29	30
38	17	21	148	96	52	24	16	8
460	143	317	416	162	254	105	56	49
1,703	969	734	2,419	1,213	1,206	1,235	647	588
...	...	...	67	13	54	...	...	...
2,201	1,129	1,072	3,050	1,484	1,566	1,364	719	645
...	...	...	22	8	14	14	5	9
274	136	138	201	99	102	517	263	254
168	106	62	72	43	29	136	86	50
...	...	...	...	...	...	...	...	...
17	9	8	29	18	11	...	...	...
...	...	...	29	16	13	...	...	...
...	...	...	23	7	16	...	...	...
459	251	208	376	191	185	667	354	313
...	..	...	...	...	...	13	8	5
41	33	8	18	16	2	...	...	...
...	...	...	8	1	7	...	...	...
...	...	...	6	3	3	...	...	...
41	33	8	32	20	12	...	...	...
...	...	...	45	28	17	...	...	...
...	...	...	43	34	9	...	...	...
...	...	...	...	...	...	...	...	...
...	...	...	10	4	6	...	...	...
...	...	...	9	8	1	...	...	...
...	...	...	107	74	33	...	...	...
19,301	10,329	8,972	26,201	12,773	13,428	4,307	2,271	2,086

TABLE

Occupations, Part B.—

Class.	Group.	Occupation.	Sirayinkil. Total.	Sirayinkil. Males.	Sirayinkil. Females.	Kottarakkara. Total.	Kottarakkara. Males.	Kottarakkara. Females.
1	2	3	31	32	33	34	35	36
D. Preparation and supply of material substances.	49	Timber and bamboo dealers ...	...	...	...	33	21	12
		Wood-cutters and sawyers ...	322	168	154	152	77	75
		Carpenters ...	2,059	1,013	1,046	1,618	786	832
		Box makers and sellers ...	...	...	...	..	...	...
		Total Sub-order 49 ...	2,381	1,181	1,200	1,803	884	919
	50	Rattan-workers and sellers ...	61	24	37	...	...	...
		Basket-weavers and winnowing-pan makers and sellers ..	221	113	108	162	86	76
		Mat makers and sellers ...	...	...	...	27	18	9
		Leaf-plate sellers ...	...	...	...	...	...	...
		Leaf-fan makers and sellers ...	8	5	3	...	...	...
		Comb makers and sellers ...	...	...	...	...	...	...
		Broom sellers ...	...	...	...	...	...	...
		Total Sub-order 50 ...	290	142	148	189	104	85
	51	Wax, honey and general forest produce collectors and sellers ...	...	...	...	...	...	...
	52	Druggists ...	...	...	...	...	...	...
		Kanku or red-powder preparers and sellers ...	...	...	...	...	...	...
		Perfume sellers ...	...	...	..	...	...	...
		Total Sub-order 52 ...	...	...	...	...	...	...
	53	Tanners, &c. ...	...	...	...	...	...	...
		Shoe and boot makers and sellers ...	...	...	...	...	...	...
		Leather dyers ...	...	...	...	...	...	...
		Hide dealers ...	...	...	...	...	...	...
		Grease preparers and sellers ..	...	...	...	...	...	...
		Total Sub-order 53 ...	...	...	..	...	...	...
		Total Class D. ...	18,478	9,286	9,192	5,769	2,837	2,932

XVII.

(State Distribution)—(*Continued*).

—(*Continued*).

Pattanapuram.			Shenkotta.			Quilon.		
Total.	Males.	Females.	Total.	Males.	Females.	Total.	Males.	Females.
37	38	39	40	41	42	43	44	45
...	...	...	...	...	...	59	42	17
62	33	29	45	27	18	359	190	169
770	451	319	650	387	263	2,062	1,021	1,041
...	...	...	..	...	...	56	12	44
832	484	348	695	414	281	2,536	1,265	1,271
13	8	5	...	...	...	21	12	9
258	123	135	79	36	43	235	131	104
30	19	11	...	...	...	71	44	27
...	...	...	...	...	...	...	...	...
...	...	...	...	...	...	31	20	11
...	...	...	..	...	...	15	8	7
...	...	...	...	..	...	...	...	...
301	150	151	79	36	43	373	215	158
...	...	...	...		...	...	...	...
...	...	...	...	..	...	20	18	2
...	...	...	...	...	...	...	..	...
...	...	...	...	...	...	...	...	...
...	...	...	...	...	...	20	18	2
...	...	...	...	...	...	65	31	34
..	...	...	...	...	...	45	38	7
...	..	...	...	...	...	11	3	8
...	...	...	10	3	7	...	..	...
..,	..	...	...	...	...	...	...	...
...	...	...	10	3	7	121	72	49
3,048	1,539	1,509	2,684	1,452	1,232	28,901	14,784	14,117

TABLE

Occupations, Part B.—

Class.	Group.	Occupation.	Taluqs: Kunnattur. Total.	Kunnattur. Males.	Kunnattur. Females.	Karunagappalli. Total.	Karunagappalli. Males.	Karunagappalli. Females.
1	2	3	46	47	48	49	50	51
D. Preparation and supply of material substances.	49	Timber and bamboo dealers ...	...	...	...	24	16	8
		Wood-cutters and sawyers ...	133	59	74	263	104	159
		Carpenters ...	1,527	795	732	1,714	895	819
		Box makers and sellers ...	...	...	...	...	...	...
		Total Sub-order 49 ...	1,660	854	806	2,001	1,015	986
	50	Rattan workers and sellers .	...	...	...	...	...	...
		Basket-weavers and winnowing-pan makers and sellers.	338	186	152	232	113	119
		Mat makers and sellers ...	55	26	29	93	59	34
		Leaf-plate sellers ...	...	...	...	49	28	21
		Leaf-fan makers and sellers ...	...	...	...	...	...	...
		Comb makers and sellers ...	...	...	...	...	...	...
		Broom sellers ...	...	...	...	...	...	...
		Total Sub-order 50 ...	393	212	181	374	200	174
	51	Wax, honey and general forest produce collectors and sellers ...	...	...	...	...	...	...
	52	Druggists ...	...	...	...	...	...	...
		Kanku or red-powder preparers and sellers ...	...	...	...	...	...	...
		Perfume sellers ...	...	...	...	...	...	...
		Total Sub-order 52 ...	...	...	...	...	...	...
	53	Tanners, &c. ...	...	...	...	...	...	...
		Shoe and boot makers and sellers ...	...	...	...	...	...	...
		Leather dyers ...	...	...	...	...	...	...
		Hide dealers ...	...	...	...	...	...	...
		Grease preparers and sellers.	...	...	...	...	...	...
		Total Sub-order 53 ...	...	...	...	...	...	...
		Total Class D ...	5,665	2,873	2,792	19,772	9,473	10,299

XVII.

(State Distribution)—(*Continued*).

—(*Continued*).

Kartigappalli.			Mavellikkara.			Chenganur.		
Total.	Males.	Females.	Total.	Males.	Females.	Total.	Males.	Females.
52	53	54	55	56	57	58	59	60
...	...	...	...	...	...	33	21	12
126	50	76	447	198	249	179	92	87
832	478	354	1,364	786	578	1,214	693	521
...	...	...	...	...	...	...	...	...
958	528	430	1,811	984	827	1,426	806	620
...	...	...	..	...	...	9	3	6
282	134	148	254	129	125	532	273	259
8	5	3	...	...	...	74	46	28
...	...	...	...	...	...	...	...	...
...	...	...	...	...	...	...	...	...
...	...	...	...	...	...	...	...	...
...	...	...	...	...	...	...	...	...
290	139	151	254	129	125	615	322	293
...	...	...	...	...	...	3	3	...
...	...	...	...	...	...	.	...	...
...	...	...	...	...	...	...	...	...
...	...	...	...	...	...	...	...	...
...	...	...	...	...	...	...	...	...
..	...	...	...	...	...	...	...	...
...	...	...	.	...	...	...	...	...
...	...	...	...	...	...	...	...	...
...	...	...	...	...	...	...	...	...
...	...	...	...	...	...	...	...	...
...	..	...	...	...	...	...	...	...
13,353	5,836	7,517	8,139	4,165	3,974	5,541	2,881	2,660

TABLE

Occupations, Part B.—

Class.	Group.	Occupation.	Taluqs: Tiruvalla. Total.	Males.	Females.	Ambalappula. Total.	Males.	Females.
1	2	3	61	62	63	64	65	66
D. Preparation and supply of material substances.	49	Timber and bamboo dealers...	13	8	5	52	36	16
		Wood-cutters and sawyers ...	321	145	176	147	78	69
		Carpenters ...	1,193	674	519	1,686	889	797
		Box makers and sellers ...	...	...	...	44	5	39
		Total Sub-order 49 ...	1,527	827	700	1,929	1,008	921
	50	Rattan workers and sellers ...	...	...	...	...	...	...
		Basket-weavers and winnowing-pan makers and sellers.	400	174	226	321	164	157
		Mat makers and sellers ...	...	...	...	65	31	34
		Leaf-plate sellers ...	...	...	...	...	...	...
		Leaf-fan makers and sellers...	...	...	...	...	...	...
		Comb makers and sellers ...	...	...	...	6	2	4
		Broom sellers ...	...	...	...	...	...	...
		Total Sub-order 50 ...	400	174	226	392	197	195
	51	Wax, honey and general forest produce collectors and sellers ...	...	...	...	...	...	...
	52	Druggists ...	...	...	...	8	8	...
		Kanku or red-powder preparers and sellers ...	...	...	...	...	...	...
		Perfume sellers ...	...	...	...	...	...	...
		Total Sub-order 52 ...	...	...	...	8	8	...
	53	Tanners, &c. ...	...	...	...	44	25	19
		Shoe and boot makers and sellers ...	...	...	...	33	24	9
		Leather dyers ...	...	...	...	...	...	...
		Hide dealers ...	...	...	...	9	4	5
		Grease preparers and sellers..	...	...	...	...	...	...
		Total Sub-order 53 ...	...	...	...	86	53	33
		Total Class D. ...	10,265	5,378	4,887	23,249	11,385	11,864

XVII.

(State Distribution.—(*Continued*).

—(*Continued*).

Sherttala.			Vykkam.			Ettumanur.		
Total.	Males.	Females.	Total.	Males.	Females.	Total.	Males.	Females.
67	68	69	70	71	72	73	74	75
...	...	...	23	14	9	...	...	...
68	33	35	82	35	47	42	19	23
1,148	564	584	1,417	628	789	725	373	352
...	...	...	...	...	...	41	5	36
1,216	597	619	1,522	677	845	808	397	411
...	...	...	...	...	...	..	...	
142	74	68	137	65	72	207	94	113
...	...	...	33	16	17	22	14	8
...	...	...	...	...	...	...	...	...
...	...	...	...	...	...	...	...	...
...	...	...	...	...	...	...	...	...
...	...	...	...	...	...	...	...	...
142	74	68	170	81	89	229	108	121
...	...	...	...	...	...	...	...	...
...	...	...	...	...	...	...	...	...
...	...	...	...	...	...	...	...	...
...	...	...	...	...	...	...	...	...
...	...	...	...	...	...	...	...	...
...	...	...	...	...	...	...	...	...
...	...	...	...	...	...	...	...	...
...	...	...	...	...	...	...	...	...
...	...	...	...	...	...	...	...	...
...	...	...	...	...	...	...	...	...
...	...	...	...	...	...	...	...	...
37,756	19,361	18,395	16,783	7,973	8,810	6,746	3,463	3,283

TABLE

Occupations, Part B.—

Class.	Group.	Occupation.	Kottayam. Total.	Kottayam. Males.	Kottayam. Females.	Changanacheri. Total.	Changanacheri. Males.	Changanacheri. Females.
1	2	3	76	77	78	79	80	81
D. Preparation and supply of material substances.	49	Timber and bamboo dealers...	54	38	16	17	12	5
		Wood-cutters and sawyers ...	162	73	89	18	13	5
		Carpenters ...	691	386	305	1,039	552	487
		Box makers and sellers ...	...	...	...	...	...	...
		Total Sub-order 49 ...	907	497	410	1,074	577	497
	50	Rattan workers and sellers ...	...	...	...	...	...	...
		Basket-weavers and winnowing-pan makers and sellers..	282	137	145	418	199	219
		Mat makers and sellers ...	28	15	13	25	13	12
		Leaf-plate sellers ...	...	...	...	...	...	...
		Leaf-fan makers and sellers...	...	...	...	...	...	...
		Comb makers and sellers ...	...	...	...	...	...	...
		Broom sellers ...	...	...	...	...	...	...
		Total Sub-order 50 ...	310	152	158	443	212	231
	51	Wax, honey and general forest produce collectors and sellers ...	...	...	...	...	...	...
	52	Druggists ...	31	31	...	...	..	...
		Kanku or red-powder preparers and sellers ...	...	...	...	...	...	...
		Perfume sellers ...	...	...	...	...	...	...
		Total Sub-order 52 ...	31	31	...	...	...	...
	53	Tanners, &c. ...	25	16	9	10	5	5
		Shoe and boot makers and sellers ...	26	21	5	...	...	...
		Leather dyers ..	...	...	...	...	...	...
		Hide dealers ...	...	...	...	...	...	...
		Grease preparers and sellers..	...	...	...	...	...	..
		Total Sub-order 53 ...	51	37	14	10	5	5
		Total Class D. ...	13,993	7,620	6,373	9,344	4,895	4,449

XVII.

(State Distribution)—(*Continued*).

—(*Continued*).

Meenachal.			Muvattupula.			Todupula.		
Total.	Males.	Females.	Total.	Males.	Females.	Total.	Males.	Females.
82	83	84	85	86	87	88	89	90
...	...	...	27	19	8	...	...	...
62	28	34	37	20	17	28	19	9
322	168	154	2,458	1,213	1,245	102	48	54
...	...	...	...	...	...	...	...	...
384	196	188	2,522	1,252	1,270	130	67	63
...	...	...	...	...	...	...	...	...
261	137	124	365	188	177	68	36	32
...	...	...	33	19	14	...	...	...
...	...	...	...	...	...	...	...	...
...	...	...	...	...	...	...	...	...
...	...	...	...	...	...	...	...	...
...	...	...	...	...	...	...	...	...
261	137	124	398	207	191	68	36	32
...	...	...	...	...	...	...	...	...
...	...	...	...	...	...	...	...	...
...	...	...	...	...	...	...	...	...
...	...	...	...	...	...	...	...	...
...	...	...	...	...	...	...	...	...
...	...	...	...	...	...	...	...	...
...	...	...	...	...	...	...	...	...
...	...	...	...	...	...	...	...	...
...	...	...	...	...	...	...	...	...
...	...	...	...	...	...	...	...	...
...	...	...	...	...	...	...	...	...
...	...	...	...	...	...	...	...	...
6,369	3,200	3,169	10,249	5,365	4,884	1,648	881	767

TABLE

Occupations, Part B.—

Class.	Group.	Occupation.	Taluqs: Kunnattunadu. Total.	Kunnattunadu. Males.	Kunnattunadu. Females.	Alangadu. Total.	Alangadu. Males.	Alangadu. Females.
1	2	3	91	92	93	94	95	96
D. Preparation and supply of material substances.	49	Timber and bamboo dealers...	20	16	4	...	...	...
		Wood-cutters and sawyers ...	39	25	14	288	149	139
		Carpenters ...	1,883	921	962	1,867	953	914
		Box makers and sellers ...	...	...	...	...	...	...
		Total Sub-order 49 ...	1,942	962	980	2,155	1,102	1,053
	50	Rattan workers and sellers ...	...	...	...	...	...	...
		Basket weavers and winnowing-pan makers and sellers..	269	136	133	165	89	76
		Mat makers and sellers ...	...	...	...	...	...	...
		Leaf-plate sellers ...	...	...	...	...	...	...
		Leaf-fan makers and sellers...	...	...	...	...	...	...
		Comb makers and sellers ...	...	...	...	...	...	...
		Broom sellers ...	...	...	...	...	...	...
		Total Sub-order 50 .	269	136	133	165	89	76
	51	Wax, honey and general forest produce collectors and sellers ...	...	...	...	...	...	..
	52	Druggists ...	...	...	...	13	13	...
		Kanku or red-powder preparers and sellers ...	...	...	...	...	...	...
		Perfume sellers ...	...	...	...	...	...	...
		Total Sub-order 52 ..	...	...	...	13	13	...
	53	Tanners, &c. ...	...	...	.	5	5	...
		Shoe and boot makers and sellers ...	...	...	...	...	...	...
		Leather dyers ...	...	...	...	...	...	...
		Hide dealers ...	..	...	...	...	...	...
		Grease preparers and sellers..	...	...	...	...	...	...
		Total Sub-order 53 ...	...		...	5	5	...
		Total Class D. ...	5,034	2,533	2,501	5,416	2,678	2,738

XVII.

(State Distribution)—(*Continued*).

—(*Continued*).

Parur.			Cardamom Hills.			Periyar and Thekkadi.		
Total.	Males.	Females.	Total.	Males.	Females.	Total.	Males.	Females.
97	98	99	100	101	102	103	104	105
36	25	11	5	5	...	...	...	...
12	7	5	29	17	12	32	26	6
1,736	947	789	116	57	59	103	92	11
...	...	...	...	...	...	...	...	...
1,784	979	805	150	79	71	135	118	17
...	...	...	...	...	...	...	...	...
121	69	52	14	9	5	...	...	...
...	...	...	...	...	...	...	...	...
...	...	...	...	...	...	...	...	...
...	...	...	...	...	...	...	...	...
...	...	...	...	...	...	...	...	...
...	...	...	...	...	...	...	...	...
121	69	52	14	9	5	...	...	...
...	...	...	...	...	...	...	...	...
...	...	...	...	...	...	...	...	...
...	...	...	...	...	...	...	...	...
...	...	...	...	...	...	...	...	...
...	...	...	...	...	...	...	...	...
15	15	...	...	...	...	...	...	...
...	...	...	...	...	...	...	...	...
...	...	...	...	...	...	...	...	...
...	...	...	...	...	...	...	...	...
...	...	...	...	...	...	...	...	...
15	15	...	...	...	...	...	...	...
14,916	7,454	7,462	346	200	146	265	214	51

TABLE

Occupations, Part B.—

Class.	Group.	Occupation and Class. — Occupation.	State Total. — Total.	Males.	Females.
1	2	3	4	5	6
E. Commerce, Transport and Storage.	54	Money-lenders and pawn-brokers ...	*271*	137	134
		Bill-discounters ...	*43*	41	2
		Money changers and testers ...	*156*	146	10
		Total Sub-order 54 ...	**470**	**324**	**146**
	55	General merchants ...	*119,907*	58,722	61,185
		Merchants' clerks, accountants, &c...	*885*	496	389
		Total Sub-order 55 ...	**120,792**	**59,218**	**61,574**
	56	Shopkeepers' clerks ...	*10*	8	2
		Shopkeepers' servants ...	*30*	18	12
		Shopkeepers unspecified ...	*31,845*	15,099	16,746
		Total Sub-order 56 ..	**31,885**	**15,125**	**16,760**
	57*a*	Brokers, agents and dubash ...	*52*	36	16
		Auctioneers and Appraisers ...	*53*	25	28
		Total Sub-order 57(*a*) ...	**105**	**61**	**44**
	57*b*	Farmers of tolls ...	*2*	1	1
		Farmers of liquor ...	*178*	133	45
		Contractors unspecified ...	*49*	28	21
		Total Sub-order 57(*b*) ...	**229**	**162**	**67**

XVII.

(State Distribution)—(*Continued*).

Taluqs.								
Tovala.			Agastiswaram.			Eranial.		
Total.	Males.	Females.	Total.	Males.	Females.	Total.	Males.	Females.
7	8	9	10	11	12	13	14	15
...	...	...	41	19	22	...	...	...
...	...	...	8	8	...	...	...	...
...	...	...	19	13	6	19	19	...
...	...	...	68	40	28	19	19	...
995	452	543	4,808	2,194	2,614	5,026	2,589	2,437
...	...	...	60	31	29	26	14	12
995	452	543	4,868	2,225	2,643	5,052	2,603	2,449
...	...	...	...	...	...	...	...	...
...	...	...	...	...	...	...	...	...
260	112	148	823	386	437	788	389	399
260	112	148	823	386	437	788	389	399
3	3	...	11	7	4	...	...	...
...	...	...	...	...	...	...	...	...
3	3	...	11	7	4	...	...	...
...	...	...	...	...	...	...	...	...
...	...	...	19	14	5	...	...	...
...	...	...	11	6	5	8	4	4
...	...	...	30	20	10	8	4	4

TABLE

Occupations, Part B.—

Class.	Group.	Occupation.	Taluqs: Kalkulam. Total.	Kalkulam. Males.	Kalkulam. Females.	Vilavankodu. Total.	Vilavankodu. Males.	Vilavankodu. Females.
1	2	3	16	17	18	19	20	21
E. Commerce, Transport and Storage.	54	Money-lenders and pawn-brokers ...	...	...	...	...	...	...
		Bill-discounters ...	...	...	...	...	...	...
		Money changers and testers..	8	8	...	9	9	...
		Total Sub-order 54 ...	8	8	...	9	9	...
	55	General merchants ...	3,782	1,917	1,865	3,826	1,837	1,989
		Merchants' clerks, accountants, &c. ..	14	8	6	...	...	...
		Total Sub-order 55 ...	3,796	1,925	1,871	3,826	1,837	1,989
	56	Shopkeepers' clerks ...	...	...	...	...	...	...
		Shopkeepers' servants ...	...	...	...	...	...	...
		Shopkeepers unspecified ...	602	278	324	369	173	196
		Total Sub-order 56 ...	602	278	324	369	173	196
	57*a*	Brokers, agents and dubash...	...	...	...	7	4	3
		Auctioneers and Appraisers...	28	12	16	...	...	...
		Total Sub-order 57(*a*) ...	28	12	16	7	4	3
	57*b*	Farmers of tolls ...	...	...	...	2	1	1
		Farmers of liquor ...	...	...	...	8	8	...
		Contractors unspecified ...	5	2	3	...	...	...
		Total Sub-order 57(*b*) ...	5	2	3	10	9	1

XVII.

(State Distribution)—(*Continued*).

—(*Continued*).

Neyattankara.			Trivandram.			Nedumangadu.		
Total.	Males.	Females.	Total.	Males.	Females.	Total.	Males.	Females.
22	23	24	25	26	27	28	29	30
...	...	...	59	31	28	...	...	...
...	...	...	25	23	2	...	...	...
...	...	...	30	26	4	...	...	...
...	...	...	114	80	34	...	...	...
4,042	1,811	2,231	8,080	4,118	3,962	1,932	978	954
...	...	...	307	178	129	...	...	...
4,042	1,811	2,231	8,387	4,296	4,091	1,932	978	954
...	...	...	7	5	2	...	...	...
...	...	...	19	12	7	...	...	...
1,088	500	588	4,176	1,987	2,189	1,176	522	654
1,088	500	588	4,202	2,004	2,198	1,176	522	654
...	...	...	14	9	5	...	...	...
...	...	...	25	13	12	...	...	...
...	...	...	39	22	17	...	...	...
...	...	...	...	...	...	...	...	...
20	13	7	...	...	...	...	...	...
...	...	...	14	8	6	...	...	...
20	13	7	14	8	6	...	...	...

TABLE

Occupations, Part B.—

Class.	Group.	Occupation.	Sirayinkil. Total.	Sirayinkil. Males.	Sirayinkil. Females.	Kottarakkara. Total.	Kottarakkara. Males.	Kottarakkara. Females.
1	2	3	31	32	33	34	35	36
E. Commerce, Transport and Storage.	54	Money-lenders and pawn-brokers ...	15	9	6	...	...	...
		Bill-discounters ...	...	...	...	...	...	...
		Money changers and testers...	...	...	...	...	...	...
		Total Sub-order 54 ...	15	9	6	...	...	...
	55	General merchants ...	4,212	1,998	2,214	1,811	942	869
		Merchants' clerks, accountants, &c. ...	...	...	...	...	...	...
		Total Sub-order 55 ...	4,212	1,998	2,214	1,811	942	869
	56	Shopkeepers' clerks ...	...	...	...	...	...	...
		Shopkeepers' servants ...	...	...	...	...	...	...
		Shopkeepers unspecified ...	1,482	696	786	811	349	462
		Total Sub-order 56 ...	1,482	696	786	811	349	462
	57*a*	Brokers, agents and dubash...	6	4	2	...	...	...
		Auctioneers and Appraisers...	...	...	...	...	...	...
		Total Sub-order 57(*a*) ...	6	4	2	...	...	...
	57*b*	Farmers of tolls ...	...	...	...	...	...	...
		Farmers of liquor ...	24	19	5	...	...	...
		Contractors unspecified ...	...	...	...	...	...	...
		Total Sub-order 57(*b*) ...	24	19	5	...	...	...

XVII.

(State Distribution)—(*Continued*).

—(*Continued*).

Pattanapuram.			Shenkotta.			Quilon.		
Total.	Males.	Females.	Total.	Males.	Females.	Total.	Males.	Females.
37	38	39	40	41	42	43	44	45
...	...	...	...	...	...	60	36	24
...	...	...	...	...	...	10	10	...
...	...	...	4	4	...	12	12	...
...	...	...	4	4	...	82	58	24
1,047	462	585	770	318	452	6,164	2,988	3,176
...	...	...	15	8	7	160	87	73
1,047	462	585	785	326	459	6,324	3,075	3,249
...	...	...	...	...	...	3	3	...
...	...	...	...	...	...	9	4	5
297	125	172	418	219	199	2,486	1,134	1,352
297	125	172	418	219	199	2,498	1,141	1,357
...	...	...	...	...	...	...	...	...
...	...	...	...	...	...	...	...	...
...	...	...	...	...	...	...	...	...
...	...	...	...	...	...	...	...	...
7	7	...	...	...	...	9	9	...
...	...	...	8	5	3	...	...	...
7	7	...	8	5	3	9	9	...

TABLE

Occupations, Part B.—

Class.	Group.	Occupation.	Taluqs: Kunnattur. Total.	Kunnattur. Males.	Kunnattur. Females.	Karunagappalli. Total.	Karunagappalli. Males.	Karunagappalli. Females.
1	2	3	46	47	48	49	50	51
E. Commerce, Transport and Storage.	54	Money-lenders and pawn-brokers ...	...	...	...	31	13	18
		Bill-discounters ...	...	...	...	...	...	...
		Money changers and testers ..	...	...	...	14	14	...
		Total Sub-order 54 ...	...	...	...	45	27	18
	55	General merchants ...	2,623	1,269	1,354	5,767	2,789	2,978
		Merchants' clerks, accountants, &c. ...	...	...	...	93	48	45
		Total Sub-order 55 ...	2,623	1,269	1,354	5,860	2,837	3,023
	56	Shopkeepers' clerks ...	...	...	...	...	...	...
		Shopkeepers' servants ...	...	...	...	...	...	...
		Shopkeepers unspecified ...	217	119	98	1,418	736	682
		Total Sub-order 56 ...	217	119	98	1,418	736	682
	57*a*	Brokers, agents and dubash...	...	...	...	...	...	...
		Auctioneers and Appraisers...	...	...	...	...	...	...
		Total Sub-order 57(*a*) ...	...	...	...	...	...	...
	57*b*	Farmers of tolls ...	...	...	...	...	...	...
		Farmers of liquor ...	...	...	...	...	...	...
		Contractors unspecified ...	...	...	...	...	...	...
		Total Sub-order 57(*b*) ...	...	...	...	...	...	...

XVII.

(State Distribution)—(*Continued*).

—(*Continued*).

Kartigappalli.			Mavellikkara.			Chenganur.		
Total.	Males.	Females.	Total.	Males.	Females.	Total.	Males.	Females.
52	53	54	55	56	57	58	59	60
...	...	...	...	...	...	...	...	...
...	...	...	...	...	...	...	...	...
8	8	...	...	...	...	...	...	...
8	8	...	...	...	...	...	...	...
3,878	1,814	2,064	3,921	1,934	1,987	4,492	2,136	2,356
4	4	...	...	...	...	...	...	...
3,882	1,818	2,064	3,921	1,934	1,987	4,492	2,136	2,356
...	...	...	...	...	...	...	...	...
...	...	...	...	...	...	...	...	...
834	438	396	733	319	414	506	231	275
834	438	396	733	319	414	506	231	275
...	...	...	...	...	...	...	...	...
...	...	...	...	...	...	...	...	...
...	...	...	...	...	...	...	...	...
...	...	...	...	...	...	...	...	...
8	8	...	...	...	...	...	...	...
...	...	...	...	...	...	...	...	...
8	8	...	...	...	...	...	...	..

TABLE

Occupations, Part B.—

Class.	Group.	Occupation.	Taluqs					
			Tiruvalla.			Ambalappula.		
			Total.	Males.	Females.	Total.	Males.	Females.
1	2	3	61	62	63	64	65	66
E. Commerce, Transport and Storage.	54	Money-lenders and pawn-brokers ...	...	...	...	50	23	27
		Bill-discounters ...	...	...	...	...	...	...
		Money changers and testers..	...	...	...	9	9	...
		Total Sub-order 54 ...	...	...	...	59	32	27
	55	General merchants ...	4,691	2,274	2,417	5,749	3,215	2,534
		Merchants' clerks, accountants, &c. ...	5	5	...	48	26	22
		Total Sub-order 55 ...	4,696	2,279	2,417	5,797	3,241	2,556
	56	Shopkeepers' clerks ...	...	...	...	...	...	...
		Shopkeepers' servants ...	...	...	...	2	2	...
		Shopkeepers unspecified ...	1,069	438	631	2,868	1,386	1,482
		Total Sub-order 56 ...	1,069	438	631	2,870	1,388	1,482
	57*a*	Brokers, agents and dubash..	...	...	...	...	...	...
		Auctioneers and Appraisers...	...	...	...	...	...	...
		Total Sub-order 57(*a*) ...	...	...	...	...	...	...
	57*b*	Farmers of tolls ...	...	...	...	...	...	...
		Farmers of liquor ...	...	...	...	21	13	8
		Contractors unspecified ...	3	3	...	...	...	...
		Total Sub-order 57(*b*) ...	3	3	...	21	13	8

XVII.

(State Distribution)—(*Continued*).

—(*Continued*).

Sherttala.			Vykkam.			Ettumanur.		
Total.	Males.	Females.	Total.	Males.	Females.	Total.	Males.	Females.
67	68	69	70	71	72	73	74	75
...	...	...	...	...	...	...	...	...
...	...	...	...	...	...	...	...	...
...	...	...	5	5	...	...	...	...
...	...	..	5	5	...	...	...	...
5,052	2,385	2,667	9,019	4,758	4,261	3,878	1,979	1,899
...	...	...	...	...	...	...	...	...
5,052	2,385	2,667	9,019	4,758	4,261	3,878	1,979	1,899
...	...	...	...	...	...	...	...	...
...	...	...	...	...	...	...	...	...
521	216	305	422	198	224	689	317	372
521	216	305	422	198	224	689	317	372
...	...	...	...	...	...	...	...	...
...	...	...	...	...	...	...	...	...
...	...	...	...	...	...	...	...	...
...	...	...	...	...	...	...	...	...
...	...	...	8	8	...	...	...	...
...	...	...	...	...	...	...	...	...
...	...	...	8	8	...	...	...	...

TABLE

Occupations, Part B.—

Class.	Group.	Occupation.	Taluqs: Kottayam. Total.	Kottayam. Males.	Kottayam. Females.	Changanacheri. Total.	Changanacheri. Males.	Changanacheri. Females.
1	2	3	76	77	78	79	80	81
E. Commerce, Transport and Storage.	54	Money-lenders and pawn-brokers ...	15	6	9	...	...	...
		Bill-discounters ...	...	...	...	...	...	...
		Money changers and testers..	8	8	...	11	11	...
		Total Sub-order 54 ...	23	14	9	11	11	...
	55	General merchants ...	3,905	1,930	1,975	4,568	2,047	2,516
		Merchants' clerks, accountants, &c. ...	75	43	32	57	31	26
		Total Sub-order 55 ..	3,980	1,973	2,007	4,620	2,078	2,542
	56	Shopkeepers' clerks ...	...	...	...	...	...	...
		Shopkeepers' servants ...	...	...	...	...	...	...
		Shopkeepers unspecified ...	2,026	996	1,030	1,365	634	731
		Total Sub-order 56 ...	2,026	996	1,030	1,365	634	731
	57*a*	Brokers, agents and dubash...	3	3	...	8	6	2
		Auctioneers and Appraisers...	...	...	...	...	...	...
		Total Sub-order 57(*a*) ...	3	3	...	8	6	2
	57*b*	Farmers of tolls ...	...	...	...	...	...	...
		Farmers of liquor ...	28	16	12	...	...	...
		Contractors unspecified ...	...	...	...	...	...	...
		Total Sub-order 57(*b*) ...	28	16	12	...	...	...

XVII.

(State Distribution)—(Continued).

—(*Continued*).

Meenachal.			Muvattupula.			Todupula.		
Total.	Males.	Females.	Total.	Males.	Females.	Total.	Males.	Females.
82	83	84	85	86	87	88	89	90
...	...	...	...	...	...	...	...	...
...	...	...	...	...	...	...	...	...
...	...	...	...	...	...	...	...	...
...	...	...	...	...	...	...	...	...
3,371	1,612	1,759	1,824	900	924	984	409	575
...	...	...	...	...	...	...	...	...
3,371	1,612	1,759	1,824	900	924	984	409	575
...	...	...	...	...	...	...	...	...
...	...	...	...	...	...	...	...	...
273	148	125	560	318	242	215	109	106
273	148	125	560	318	242	215	109	106
...	...	...	...	...	...	...	...	...
...	...	...	...	...	...	...	...	...
...	...	...	...	...	...	...	...	...
...	...	...	...	...	...	...	...	...
21	13	8	...	...	...	...	...	...
...	...	...	...	...	...	...	...	...
21	13	8	...	...	...	...	...	...

TABLE

Occupations, Part B.—

Class.	Group.	Occupation.	Taluqs: Kunnattunadu. Total.	Kunnattunadu. Males.	Kunnattunadu. Females.	Alangadu. Total.	Alangadu. Males.	Alangadu. Females.
1	2	3	91	92	93	94	95	96
E. Commerce, Transport and Storage.	54	Money-lenders and pawn-brokers ...	...	...	...	...	...	...
		Bill-discounters ...	...	...	...	...	...	...
		Money changers and testers...	...	...	...	...	...	...
		Total Sub-order 54 ...	...	...	...	...	...	...
	55	General merchants ...	3,174	1,485	1,689	2,733	1,265	1,468
		Merchants' clerks, accountants, &c. .	...	...	...	...	...	...
		Total Sub-order 55 ...	3,174	1,485	1,689	2,733	1,265	1,468
	56	Shopkeepers' clerks ...	...	...	...	...	...	...
		Shopkeepers' servants ...	..	...	...	...	...	...
		Shopkeepers unspecified ...	533	236	297	184	86	98
		Total Sub-order 56 ...	533	236	297	184	86	98
	57*a*	Brokers, agents and dubash...	...	...	...	...	...	...
		Auctioneers and Appraisers ...	...	...	...	...	...	...
		Total Sub-order 57(*a*) ...	...	...	...	...	...	...
	57*b*	Farmers of tolls ...	...	...	...	...	...	...
		Farmers of liquor ...	5	5	...	...	...	...
		Contractors unspecified ...	...	...	...	...	...	...
		Total Sub-order 57(*b*) ...	5	5	...	..	...	...

XVII.

(State Distribution)—(*Continued*).

—(*Continued*).

Parur.			Cardamom Hills.			Periyar & Thekkadi.		
Total.	Males.	Females.	Total.	Males.	Females.	Total.	Males.	Females.
97	98	99	100	101	102	103	104	105
...	...	...	...	...	...	...	...	...
...	...	...	...	...	...	...	...	...
...	...	...	...	...	...	...	...	...
...	...	...	...	...	...	...	...	...
3,215	1,498	1,717	552	403	149	21	16	5
21	13	8	...	...	...	...	...	...
3,236	1,511	1,725	552	403	149	21	16	5
...	...	...	...	...	...	...	...	...
...	...	...	...	...	...	...	...	...
2,470	1,194	1,276	103	58	45	63	52	11
2,470	1,194	1,276	103	58	45	63	52	11
...	...	...	...	...	...	...	...	...
...	...	...	...	...	...	...	...	...
...	...	...	...	...	...	...	...	...
...	...	...	...	...	...	...	...	...
...	...	...	...	...	...	...	...	...
...	...	...	...	...	...	...	...	...
...	...	...	...	...	...	...	...	...

TABLE

Occupations, Part B.—

OCCUPATION AND CLASS.			STATE TOTAL.		
CLASS.	GROUP.	OCCUPATION.	Total.	Males.	Females.
1	2	3	4	5	6
E. Commerce, Transport and Storage.	58*b*	Drivers, firemen ...	*29*	10	19
	59*a*	Cart drivers and carting agents ...	*1,682*	1,483	199
		Palki bearers ...	*27*	17	10
		Total Sub-order 59(*a*) ...	1,709	1,500	209
	59*b*	Elephant owners and drivers ...	*2*	2	...
	60*a*	Boat owners ...	*6*	5	1
	60*b*	Ships' officers, mariners, firemen, &c.	*261*	215	46
		Boat and barge men ...	*5,874*	3,716	2,158
		Pilots ..	*10*	7	3
		Harbour service ...	*291*	202	89
		Total Sub-order 60(*b*) ...	6,436	4,140	2,296
	61*a*	Post and Anchel masters and clerks..	*204*	112	92
		Post and Anchel messengers and runners ...	*562*	341	221
		Messengers unspecified ...	*49*	18	31
		Total Sub-order 61(*a*) ...	815	471	334
	61*b*	Telegraph officers and clerks ...	*4*	3	1
		Telegraph signallers and messengers.	*4*	4	...
		Total Sub-order 61(*b*) ...	8	7	1
	62	Ware-house service ...	*199*	93	106
		Porters ...	*1,272*	663	609
		Watchmen (not village) ...	*10*	8	2
		Total Sub-order 62 ...	1,481	764	717
		Total Class E. ...	*163,967*	*81,789*	*82,178*

XVII.

(State Distribution)—(*Continued*).

TALUQS.

Tovala.			Agastiswaram.			Eranial.		
Total.	Males.	Females.	Total.	Males.	Females.	Total.	Males.	Females.
7	8	9	10	11	12	13	14	15
...	...	...	...	...	...	...	...	...
75 ...	62 ...	13 ...	109 ...	95 ...	14 ...	147 15	126 9	21 6
75	62	13	109	95	14	162	135	27
...	...	...	...	...	...	..	...	...
...	...	...	...	...	...	...	...	...
... ...	... ...	... ...	... ...	... ...	... ...	50 3	37 3	13 ... ...
...	...	...	...	...	...	53	40	13
2 8 ...	2 5 ...	... 3 ...	15 30 ...	9 18 ...	6 12 ...	7 19 ...	4 10 ...	3 9 ...
10	7	3	45	27	18	26	14	12
... ...	... ...	... ...	... ...	... ...	... ...	1 ...	1 ...	... ...
...	..	...	...	...	...	1	1	...
... ...	... ...	... ...	... 88 ...	... 46 ...	... 42 ...	199 63 ...	93 33 ...	106 30 ...
...	...	...	88	46	42	262	126	136
1,343	636	707	6,042	2,846	3,196	6,371	3,331	3,040

TABLE

Occupations, Part B.—

Class.	Group.	Occupation.	Kalkulam. Total.	Kalkulam. Males.	Kalkulam. Females.	Vilavankodu. Total.	Vilavankodu. Males.	Vilavankodu. Females.
1	2	3	16	17	18	19	20	21
E. Commerce, Transport and Storage.	58*b*	Drivers, firemen, &c. ...	...	...	...	...	...	...
	59*a*	Cart drivers & carting agents.	100	96	4	120	120	...
		Palki bearers ...	...	...	...	...	...	...
		Total Sub-order 59(*a*) ...	100	96	4	120	120	...
	59*b*	Elephant owners and drivers.	...	...	...	...	...	...
	60*a*	Boat owners ...	...	...	...	...	...	...
	60*b*	Ships' officers, mariners, firemen, &c. ...	...	...	...	...	...	...
		Boat and barge men ...	...	...	...	13	8	5
		Pilots ...	...	...	...	...	...	...
		Harbour service ...	...	...	...	...	...	...
		Total Sub-order 60(*b*) ...	...	...	...	13	8	5
	61*a*	Post and Anchel masters and clerks ...	2	2	...	8	4	4
		Post and Anchel messengers and runners ...	12	7	5	15	9	6
		Messengers unspecified ...	...	...	...	...	...	...
		Total Sub-order 61(*a*) ...	14	9	5	23	13	10
	61*b*	Telegraph officers and clerks.	...	...	...	...	...	...
		Telegraph signallers and messengers ...	...	...	...	...	...	...
		Total Sub-order 61(*b*) ...	...	...	...	...	...	...
	62	Ware-house service ...	...	...	...	...	...	...
		Porters ...	...	...	...	...	...	...
		Watchmen (not village) ...	...	...	...	...	...	...
		Total Sub-order 62 ...	...	...	...	...	...	...
		Total Class E. ...	4,553	2,330	2,223	4,377	2,173	2,204

XVII.

(State Distribution)—(*Continued*).

—(*Continued*).

Neyattankara.			Trivandram.			Nedumangadu.		
Total.	Males.	Females.	Total.	Males.	Females.	Total.	Males.	Females.
22	23	24	25	26	27	28	29	30
...	...	...	...	...	...	...	...	...
97	97	...	241	222	19	60	53	7
...	...	...	12	8	4	...	...	...
97	97	...	253	230	23	60	53	7
...	...	...	2	2	...	...	...	...
...	...	...	...	...	...	...	...	...
...	...	...	...	...	...	...	...	...
18	11	7	308	202	106	...	...	...
...	...	...	...	...	...	...	...	...
...	...	...	...	...	...	...	...	...
18	11	7	308	202	106	...	...	...
4	3	1	22	13	9	5	2	3
29	15	14	55	29	26	6	4	2
...	...	...	30	10	20	...	...	...
33	18	15	107	52	55	11	6	5
...	...	...	2	1	1	...	...	...
...	...	...	1	1	...	...	...	...
...	...	...	3	2	1	...	...	...
...	...	...	...	..	...	...	...	...
...	...	...	228	113	115	...	...	...
...	...	...	...	...	...	...	...	...
...	...	...	228	113	115	...	...	..
5,298	2,450	2,848	13,657	7,011	6,646	3,179	1,559	1,620

TABLE

Occupations, Part B.—

Class.	Group.	Occupation.	Taluqs: Sirayinkil. Total.	Sirayinkil. Males.	Sirayinkil. Females.	Kottarakkara. Total.	Kottarakkara. Males.	Kottarakkara. Females.
1	2	3	31	32	33	34	35	36
E. Commerce, Transport and Storage.	58*b*	Drivers, firemen, &c. ...	...	...	...	...	...	...
	59*a*	Cart drivers & carting agents.	88	83	5	49	43	6
		Palki bearers ..	...	...	...	...	...	...
		Total Sub-order 59(*a*) ...	88	83	5	49	43	6
	59*b*	Elephant owners and drivers.	...	...	...	...	...	...
	60*a*	Boat owners ...	...	...	...	...	...	...
	60*b*	Ship's officers, mariners, firemen, &c. ...	...	...	...	...	...	...
		Boat and barge men ...	332	213	119	1	1	...
		Pilots ...	...	...	...	...	...	...
		Harbour service ...	...	...	...	...	...	...
		Total Sub-order 60(*b*) ...	332	213	119	1	1	...
	61*a*	Post and Anchel masters and clerks ...	1	1	...	5	3	2
		Post and Anchel messengers and runners ...	22	13	9	12	8	4
		Messengers unspecified ...	...	...	...	...	...	...
		Total Sub-order 61(*a*) ...	23	14	9	17	11	6
	61*b*	Telegraph officers and clerks.	...	...	...	...	...	...
		Telegraph signallers and messengers ...	...	...	...	...	...	...
		Total Sub-order 61(*b*) ...	...	...	...	...	...	...
		Ware-house service ...	...	...	...	...	...	...
		Porters ...	...	...	...	...	...	...
		Watchmen (not village) ...	...	...	...	...	...	...
		Total Sub-order 62 ...	...	...	...	...	...	...
		Total Class E. ...	6,182	3,036	3,146	2,689	1,346	1,343

XVII.

(State Distribution)—(*Continued*).

—(*Continued*).

Pattanapuram.			Shenkotta.			Quilon.		
Total.	Males.	Females.	Total.	Males.	Females.	Total.	Males.	Females.
37	38	39	40	41	42	43	44	45
...	...	...	...	...	...	...	..	...
21	21	...	73	42	31	109	84	25
...	...	...	...	...	...	...	...	...
21	21	...	73	42	31	109	84	25
...	...	...	...	...	...	...	...	...
...	...	...	...	...	...	6	5	1
...	...	...	...	...	...	116	98	18
76	54	22	...	...	...	983	665	318
...	...	...	...	...	...	7	4	3
...	...	...	...	...	...	121	86	35
76	54	22	...	...	...	1,227	853	374
3	2	1	2	2	...	15	8	7
14	9	5	11	8	3	23	13	10
...	...	...	...	...	...	19	8	11
17	11	6	13	10	3	57	29	28
...	...	...	...	...	...	1	1	...
...	...	...	...	...	...	1	1	...
...	...	...	...	...	...	2	2	...
...	...	...	...	...	...	...	...	...
..	...	...	21	13	8	163	89	74
...	...	...	...	...	...	...	...	...
...	..	..	21	13	8	163	89	74
1,465	680	785	1,322	619	703	10,477	5,345	5,132

TABLE

Occupations, Part B.—

Class.	Group.	Occupation.	Taluqs: Kunnattur. Total.	Kunnattur. Males.	Kunnattur. Females.	Karunagappalli. Total.	Karunagappalli. Males.	Karunagappalli. Females.
1	2	3	46	47	48	49	50	51
E. Commerce, Transport and Storage.	58*b*	Drivers, firemen, &c. ...	...	...	...	...	...	...
	59*a*	Cart drivers & carting agents.	...	...	...	5	5	...
		Palki bearers ...	...	...	...	...	...	...
		Total Sub-order 59(*a*) ...	...	...	...	5	5	...
	59*b*	Elephant owners and drivers..	...	...	...	...	...	...
	60*a*	Boat owners ...	...	...	...	...	...	...
	60*b*	Ships' officers, mariners, firemen, &c. ...	...	...	...	...	...	...
		Boat and barge men ...	15	10	5	991	600	391
		Pilots ...	...	...	...	...	...	...
		Harbour service ...	...	...	...	...	...	...
		Total Sub-order 60(*b*) ...	15	10	5	991	600	391
	61*a*	Post and Anchel masters and clerks ...	1	1	...	8	3	5
		Post and Anchel messengers and runners ...	15	9	6	21	13	8
		Messengers unspecified ...	...	...	...	...	...	...
		Total Sub-order 61(*a*) ...	16	10	6	29	16	13
	61*b*	Telegraph officers and clerks..	..	...	...	...	...	...
		Telegraph signallers and messengers ...	...	...	...	...	...	...
		Total Sub-order 61(*b*) ...	...	...	...	...	...	...
	62	Ware-house service ...	...	...	...	...	...	...
		Porters ...	23	14	9	62	34	28
		Watchmen (not village) ...	...	...	...	...	...	...
		Total Sub-order 62 ...	23	14	9	62	34	28
		Total Class E. ...	2,894	1,422	1,472	8,410	4,255	4,155

XVII.

(State Distribution)—(*Continued*).

—(*Continued*).

Kartigappalli.			Mavellikkara.			Chenganur.		
Total.	Males.	Females.	Total.	Males.	Females.	Total.	Males.	Females.
52	53	54	55	56	57	58	59	60
...	...	...	...	...	...	...	...	...
8 ...	8 ...	... ...	6 ...	6 ...	... ...	8 ...	8 ...	... ...
8	8	..	6	6	...	8	8	...
...	...	...	...	...	...	...	...	...
...	...	...	...	...	...	...	...	...
... 387	... 191	... 196	... 129	... 71	... 58	... 126	... 84	... 42 ... ...
387	191	196	129	71	58	126	84	42
7 12 ...	4 8 ...	3 4 ...	13 14 ...	7 9 ...	6 5 ...	9 22 ...	5 13 ...	4 9 ...
19	12	7	27	16	11	31	18	13
... ...	... ...	... ...	... ...	... ...	... ...	... ...	... ...	... ...
...	...	...	...	...	...	...	...	...
... 20 ...	... 13 ...	... 7 ...	... ...	... ...	... ...	... ...	... ...	... ...
20	13	7	...	...	...	...	...	...
5,166	2,496	2,670	4,816	2,346	2,470	5,163	2,477	2,686

TABLE

Occupations, Part B.—

Class.	Group.	Occupation.	Taluqs: Tiruvalla. Total.	Tiruvalla. Males.	Tiruvalla. Females.	Ambalappula. Total.	Ambalappula. Males.	Ambalappula. Females.
1	2	3	61	62	63	64	65	66
E. Commerce, Transport and Storage.	58*b*	Drivers, firemen, &c. ...	...	...	...	...	...	...
	59*a*	Cart drivers & carting agents.	18	18	...	...	...	...
		Palki bearers ...	...	...	...	...	...	...
		Total Sub-order 59(*a*) ...	18	18	...	...	...	...
	59*b*	Elephant owners and drivers..	...	...	...	...	...	...
	60*a*	Boat owners ...	...	...	...	...	...	...
	60*b*	Ships' officers, mariners, firemen, &c ...	...	...	...	95	80	15
		Boat and barge men ...	...	...	...	758	466	292
		Pilots ...	...	...	...	3	3	...
		Harbour service ...	...	...	...	167	113	54
		Total Sub-order 60(*b*) ...	...	...	...	1,023	662	361
	61*a*	Post and Anchel masters and clerks ...	7	4	3	13	7	6
		Post and Anchel messengers and runners ...	31	19	12	36	22	14
		Messengers unspecified ...	...	...	...	...	...	...
		Total Sub-order 61(*a*) ...	38	23	15	49	29	20
	61*b*	Telegraph officers and clerks.	...	...	...	...	...	...
		Telegraph signallers and messengers ...	...	...	...	1	1	...
		Total Sub-order 61(*b*) ...	...	...	...	1	1	...
	62	Ware-house service ...	...	...	...	...	...	...
		Porters ...	43	24	19	289	153	136
		Watchmen (not village) ...	...	...	...	...	...	...
		Total Sub-order 62 ...	43	24	19	289	153	136
		Total Class E. ...	5,867	2,785	3,082	10,109	5,519	4,590

XVII.

(State Distribution)—(*Continued*).

—(*Continued*).

Sherttala.			Vykkam.			Ettumanur.		
Total.	Males.	Females.	Total.	Males.	Females.	Total.	Males.	Females.
67	68	69	70	71	72	73	74	75
...	...	...	...	...	...	...	...	...
...	...	...	...	...	...	21	21	...
...	...	...	...	...	...	...	...	...
...	...	...	...	...	...	21	21	...
...	...	...	...	...	...	...	...	...
...	...	...	...	...	...	...	...	...
...	...	...	...	...	...	...	...	...
1,056	697	359	125	66	59	80	38	42
...	...	...	...	...	...	...	...	...
...	...	...	...	...	...	...	...	...
1,056	697	359	125	66	59	80	38	42
2	2	...	5	2	3	7	3	4
9	6	3	13	9	4	15	8	7
...	...	...	...	...	...	...	...	...
11	8	3	18	11	7	22	11	11
...	...	...	...	...	...	...	...	...
...	...	...	...	...	...	...	...	...
...	...	...	...	...	...	...	...	...
...	...	...	...	...	...	...	...	...
...	...	...	48	29	19	...	...	...
...	...	...	..	...	.	...	...	...
...	...	...	48	29	19	...	...	...
6,640	3,306	3,334	9,645	5,075	4,570	4,690	2,366	2,324

TABLE

Occupations, Part B.—

Class.	Group.	Occupation.	Taluqs: Kottayam. Total.	Kottayam. Males.	Kottayam. Females.	Changanacheri. Total.	Changanacheri. Males.	Changanacheri. Females.
1	2	3	76	77	78	79	80	81
E. Commerce, Transport and Storage.	58b	Drivers, firemen, &c. ...	...	...	...	...	...	...
	59a	Cart drivers & carting agents.	101	85	16	74	54	20
		Palki bearers ..	...	...	...	...	...	...
		Total Sub-order 59(a) ...	101	85	16	74	54	20
	59b	Elephant owners and drivers.	...	...	...	...	...	...
	60a	Boat owners ...	...	...	...	...	...	...
	60b	Ships' officers, mariners, firemen, &c. ...	...	...	...	...	...	...
		Boat and barge men ...	160	106	54	97	67	30
		Pilots ...	...	...	...	...	...	...
		Harbour service ...	..	...	...	...	...	...
		Total Sub-order 60(b) ...	160	106	54	97	67	30
	61a	Post and Anchel masters and clerks ...	13	6	7	5	2	3
		Post and Anchel messengers and runners ...	36	17	19	13	9	4
		Messengers unspecified ...	...	...	...	...	...	...
		Total Sub-order 61(a) ...	49	23	26	18	11	7
	61b	Telegraph officers and clerks.	...	...	...	...	...	...
		Telegraph signallers and messengers ...	1	1	..	...	...	...
		Total Sub-order 61(b) ...	1	1	...	...	...	...
	62	Ware-house service ...	...	...	...	...	...	...
		Porters ...	85	49	36	89	34	55
		Watchmen (not village) ...	...	...	...	...	...	...
		Total Sub-order 62 ...	85	49	36	89	34	55
		Total Class E. ...	6,456	3,266	3,190	6,282	2,895	3,387

XVII.

(State Distribution)—(*Continued*).

—(*Continued*).

Meenachal.			Muvattupula.			Todupula.		
Total.	Males.	Females.	Total.	Males.	Females.	Total.	Males.	Females.
82	83	84	85	86	87	88	89	90
...	...	...	...	...	...	...	...	...
34	26	8	...	...	...	...	...	...
...	...	...	...	...	...	...	...	...
34	26	8	...	...	...	...	...	...
...	...	...	...	..	...	...	...	...
...	...	...	...	...	...	...	...	...
...	...	...	...	...	...	...	...	...
13	8	5	2	2	...	...	...	...
...	...	...	...	...	...	...	...	...
...	...	...	...	...	...	...	..	...
13	8	5	2	2	...	...	..	...
5	3	2	9	4	5	2	...	2
10	8	2	19	13	6	8	5	3
...	...	...	...	...	...	...	...	...
15	11	4	28	17	11	10	5	5
...	...	...	...	...	...	...	...	...
...	...	...	...	...	...	...	...	...
...	...	...	...	...	...	...	...	...
...	...	...	...	...	...	...	...	...
	...	...	...	...	...	...	...	...
...	...	...	...	...	...	...	...	...
...	...	...	...	...	...	...	...	...
3,727	1,818	1,909	2,414	1,237	1,177	1,209	523	866

TABLE

Occupations, Part B.—

Class.	Group.	Occupation.	Kunnattunadu. Total.	Males.	Females.	Alangadu. Total.	Males.	Females.
1	2	3	91	92	93	94	95	96
E. Commerce, Transport and Storage.	58*b*	Drivers, firemen, &c. ...	...	...	...	...	...	...
	59*a*	Cart drivers & carting agents.	10	10	...	...	...	...
		Palki bearers ...	...	...	..	...	...	...
		Total Sub-order 59(*a*) ...	10	10	...	...	...	...
	59*b*	Elephant owners and drivers.	...	...	..	...	...	...
	60*a*	Boat owners ...	...	...	...	...	...	...
	60*b*	Ships' officers, mariners, firemen, &c. ...	...	...	...	...	...	...
		Boat and barge men ...	76	52	24	18	13	5
		Pilots ...	...	...	...	...	...	...
		Harbour service ...	...	...	...	...	...	...
		Total Sub-order 60(*b*) ...	76	52	24	18	13	5
	61*a*	Post and Anchel masters and clerks ...	...	...	...	2	2	...
		Post and Anchel messengers and runners ...	10	8	2	12	9	3
		Messengers unspecified ...	...	...	...	...	...	...
		Total Sub-order 61(*a*) ...	10	8	2	14	11	3
	61*b*	Telegraph officers and clerks.	...	...	...	...	...	..
		Telegraph signallers and messengers ...	...	...	...	...	...	...
		Total Sub-order 61(*b*) ..	...	...	..	...	...	...
	62	Ware-house service ...	...	...	...	...	...	...
		Porters ...	...	...	...	11	4	7
		Watchmen (not village) ...	...	...	...	...	...	...
		Total Sub-order 62 ...	..	...	...	11	4	7
		Total Class E. ...	3,808	1,796	2,012	2,960	1,379	1,581

XVII.

(State Distribution)—(*Continued*).

—(*Continued*).

Parur.			Cardamom Hills.			Periyar and Thekkadi.		
Total.	Males.	Females.	Total.	Males.	Females.	Total.	Males.	Females.
97	98	99	100	101	102	103	104	105
..	...	...	...	...	...	29	10	19
...	...	...	...	...	...	108	98	10
...	...	..	...	...	...	...	...	...
...	...	...	...	...	...	108	98	10
...	...	...	...	...	...	...	...	...
...	...	...	...	...	...	...	...	...
..	...	...	...	...	...	...	...	...
103	84	19	...	...	...	7	7	...
...	...	...	...	...	...	...	...	...
...	...	...	...	...	...	...	...	...
103	84	19	...	...	..	7	7	...
4	1	3	1	1	...	...	...	...
7	5	2	3	3	...	...	...	...
...	...	...	...	...	...	...	...	...
11	6	5	4	4	...	...	...	...
...	...	...	...	...	...	...	...	...
...	...	...	...	...	...	...	...	...
...	...	...	...	...	...	...	...	...
...	...	...	...	...	...	...	...	...
37	13	24	...	...	...	2	2	...
...	...	...	...	...	...	10	8	2
37	13	24	...	...	...	12	10	2
5,857	2,808	3,049	659	465	194	240	193	47

TABLE

Occupations, Part B.—

Class.	Group.	Occupation.	Total.	Males.	Females.
1	2	3	4	5	6
F. Professions.	63*a*	Priests, ministers, preachers, missionaries, &c. ...	*8,380*	4,354	4,026
		Catechists, readers, &c. ...	*518*	253	265
		Exorcists, hail-averters, amulettiers, &c. ...	*1,203*	737	466
		Total Sub-order 63(*a*) ...	**10,101**	**5,344**	**4,757**
	63*b*	Religious mendicants, inmates of convents, &c. ..	*24*	23	1
		Church, temple, pagoda, masjid, &c., services ...	*13,677*	7,667	6,010
		Total Sub-order 63(*b*) ...	**13,701**	**7,690**	**6,011**
	64	Administrative and inspecting officials ...	*82*	43	39
		Principals, professors and teachers in colleges, &c. ...	*899*	626	273
		Clerks, &c., on educational establishments, schools, &c. ...	*4*	1	3
		Total Sub-order 64 ...	**985**	**670**	**315**
	65	Editors and ballad makers ...	*19*	15	4
		Private secretaries and clerks ...	*73*	38	35
		Public Scribes ...	*999*	637	362
		Total Sub-order 65 ...	**1,091**	**690**	**401**
	66	Advocates and pleaders ...	*4,221*	2,055	2,166
		Mukhtiars ...	*2*	2	...
		Lawyer's clerks ...	*234*	201	33
		Stamp vendors ...	*40*	18	22
		Petition writers ...	*76*	65	11
		Total Sub-order 66 ...	**4,573**	**2,341**	**2,232**

XVII.

(State Distribution)—(*Continued*).

—(*Continued*).

Tovala.			Agastiswaram.			Eranial.		
Total.	Males.	Females.	Total.	Males.	Females.	Total.	Males.	Females.
7	8	9	10	11	12	13	14	15
184	96	88	633	296	337	354	198	156
...	...	...	59	28	31	...	...	...
...	...	...	...	...	...	26	19	7
184	96	88	692	324	368	380	217	163
...	...	...	...	...	...	4	4	...
209	117	92	713	348	365	461	234	227
209	117	92	713	348	365	465	238	227
...	...	...	7	3	4	...	..	...
8	5	3	51	33	18	23	18	5
...	...	...	...	...	...	...	...	...
8	5	3	58	36	22	23	18	5
...	...	...	3	2	1	...	...	...
...	...	...	...	...	...	...	...	...
44	26	18	55	31	24	78	46	32
44	26	18	58	33	25	78	46	32
22	12	10	230	113	117	81	36	45
...	...	...	...	...	...	...	...	...
...	...	...	29	24	5	...	...	...
...	...	...	5	2	3	5	2	3
...	...	...	...	...	...	...	...	...
22	12	10	264	139	125	86	38	48

TABLE

Occupations, Part B.—

Class.	Group.	Occupation.	Taluqs: Kalkulam. Total.	Kalkulam. Males.	Kalkulam. Females.	Vilavankodu. Total.	Vilavankodu. Males.	Vilavankodu. Females.
1	2	3	16	17	18	19	20	21
F. Professions.	63a	Priests, ministers, preachers, missionaries, &c. ...	138	67	71	100	46	54
		Catechists, readers, &c. ...	22	12	10	...	...	...
		Exorcists, hail-averters, amulettiers, &c. ...	36	23	13	...	...	...
		Total Sub-order 63(a) ...	196	102	94	100	46	54
	63b	Religious mendicants, inmates of convents, &c. ...	...	...	...	...	...	...
		Church, temple, pagoda, masjid, &c., services ...	756	386	370	326	188	138
		Total Sub-order 63(b) ...	756	386	370	326	188	138
	64	Administrative and inspecting officials ...	3	2	1	...	...	...
		Principals, professors and teachers in colleges, &c. ...	45	29	16	27	18	9
		Clerks, &c., on educational establishments, schools, &c.	...	...	..	...	...	...
		Total Sub-order 64 ...	48	31	17	27	18	9
	65	Editors and ballad makers ...	...	...	...	...	...	...
		Private secretaries and clerks.	...	...	...	...	...	...
		Public Scribes ...	25	16	9	31	19	12
		Total Sub-order 65 ..	25	16	9	31	19	12
	66	Advocates and pleaders ...	123	59	64	41	18	23
		Mukhtiars ...	...	...	...	...	...	...
		Lawyer's clerks ...	3	3	...	...	...	...
		Stamp vendors ...	...	...	...	7	3	4
		Petition writers ...	2	2	...	5	4	1
		Total Sub-order 66 ...	128	64	64	53	25	28

XVII.

(State Distribution)—(*Continued*).

—(*Continued*).

Neyattankara.			Trivandram.			Nedumangadu.		
Total.	Males.	Females.	Total.	Males.	Females.	Total.	Males.	Females.
22	23	24	25	26	27	28	29	30
230	125	105	845	456	389	65	37	28
..	..	...	88	46	42	...	...	...
32	18	14	10	8	2	...	...	...
262	143	119	943	510	433	65	37	28
...	...	...	6	5	1	...	...	...
359	234	125	1,384	770	614	212	123	89
359	234	125	1,390	775	615	212	123	89
7	3	4	22	14	8	...	...	...
43	31	12	179	137	42	21	15	6
...	...	...	4	1	3	...	...	...
50	34	16	205	152	53	21	15	6
...	...	...	8	5	3	...	...	...
...	...	...	37	20	17	...	...	...
34	21	13	90	51	39	9	6	3
34	21	13	135	76	59	9	6	3
33	15	18	1,180	600	580	19	10	9
...	...	...	2	2	...	...	...	
3	3	...	57	45	12	...	...	...
...	...	...	5	2	3	...	...	...
...	...	...	10	8	2	...	...	...
36	18	18	1,254	657	597	19	10	9

TABLE

Occupations, Part B.—

Class.	Group.	Occupation.	Taluqs: Sirayinkil. Total.	Sirayinkil. Males.	Sirayinkil. Females.	Kottarakkara. Total.	Kottarakkara. Males.	Kottarakkara. Females.
1	2	3	31	32	33	34	35	36
F. Professions.	63*a*	Priests, ministers, preachers, missionaries, &c. ...	71	39	32	183	96	87
		Catechists, readers, &c. ..	...	...	...	...	...	...
		Exorcists, hail-averters, amulettiers, &c. ..	30	14	16	30	19	11
		Total Sub-order 63(*a*) ...	101	53	48	213	115	98
	63*b*	Religious mendicants, inmates of convents, &c. ...	2	2	...	...	...	...
		Church, temple, pagoda, masjid, &c., services ...	417	246	171	308	196	112
		Total Sub-order 63(*b*) ...	419	248	171	308	196	112
	64	Administrative and inspecting officials ...	1	1	...	...	...	...
		Principals, professors and teachers in colleges, &c. ...	28	19	9	27	16	11
		Clerks, &c., on educational establishments, schools, &c.	...	...	...	...	...	...
		Total Sub-order 64 ...	29	20	9	27	16	11
	65	Editors and ballad makers ..	...	...	...	...	...	...
		Private secretaries and clerks.	...	...	...	...	...	...
		Public Scribes ...	24	16	8	34	24	10
		Total Sub-order 65 ...	24	16	8	34	24	10
	66	Advocates and pleaders ...	108	55	53	60	26	34
		Mukhtiars ...	...	...	...	...	...	...
		Lawyer's clerks ...	2	2	...	...	...	...
		Stamp vendors ...	...	...	...	...	...	...
		Petition writers ...	5	5	...	...	...	...
		Total Sub-order 66 ...	115	62	53	60	26	34

XVII.

(State Distribution)—(*Continued*).

—(*Continued*).

Pattanapuram.			Shenkotta.			Quilon.		
Total.	Males.	Females.	Total.	Males.	Females.	Total.	Males.	Females.
37	38	39	40	41	42	43	44	45
115	64	51	39	24	15	401	214	187
...	..	...	...	...	...	85	38	47
61	38	23	77	50	27	10	6	4
176	102	74	116	74	42	496	258	238
...	...	...	...	...	...	5	5	...
285	158	127	294	163	131	386	227	159
285	158	127	294	163	131	391	232	159
...	...	...	...	...	...	8	4	4
14	9	5	21	13	8	76	49	27
...	...	...	...	...	...	...	...	...
14	9	5	21	13	8	84	53	31
...	...	...	...	...	...	4	4	...
...	...	...	...	...	...	14	8	6
19	14	5	...	...	...	37	23	14
19	14	5	...	...	...	55	35	20
18	8	10	19	8	11	321	169	152
...	...	...	...	...	...	...	...	...
...	...	...	...	...	...	53	46	7
...	...	...	...	...	...	5	2	3
...	...	...	3	3	...	24	16	8
18	8	10	22	11	11	403	233	170

TABLE

Occupations, Part B.—

Class.	Group.	Occupation.	Taluqs — Kunnattur. Total.	Kunnattur. Males.	Kunnattur. Females.	Karunagappalli. Total.	Karunagappalli. Males.	Karunagappalli. Females.
1	2	3	46	47	48	49	50	51
F. Professions.	63*a*	Priests, ministers, preachers, missionaries, &c. ...	50	28	22	64	34	30
		Catechists, readers, &c. ...	...	...	...	...	...	...
		Exorcists, hail-averters, amulettiers, &c. ...	66	37	29	23	15	8
		Total Sub-order 63(*a*) ...	116	65	51	87	49	38
	63*b*	Religious mendicants, inmates of convents, &c. ..	...	...	...	...	...	...
		Church, temple, pagoda, masjid, &c., services ...	323	189	134	319	199	120
		Total Sub-order 63(*b*) ...	323	189	134	319	199	120
	64	Administrative and inspecting officials ...	...	...	...	4	2	2
		Principals, professors, and teachers in colleges, &c. ...	12	8	4	34	21	13
		Clerks, &c., on educational establishments, schools, &c..	...	...	...	...	...	...
		Total Sub-order 64 ...	12	8	4	38	23	15
	65	Editors and ballad makers ...	...	...	...	...	...	...
		Private secretaries and clerks.		...	...	...	...	...
		Public Scribes ...	29	19	10	47	32	15
		Total Sub-order 65 ...	29	19	10	47	32	15
	66	Advocates and pleaders ...	33	14	19	107	50	57
		Mukhtiars ...	...	...	...	...	...	...
		Lawyer's clerks ...	...	...	...	...	...	...
		Stamp vendors ...	...	...	...	...	...	...
		Petition writers ...	...	...	...	5	5	...
		Total Sub-order 66 ...	33	14	19	112	55	57

XVII.

(State Distribution)—(*Continued*).

—(*Continued*).

Kartigappalli.			Mavellikkara.			Chenganur.		
Total.	Males.	Females.	Total.	Males.	Females.	Total.	Males.	Females.
52	53	54	55	56	57	58	59	60
602	314	288	139	78	61	94	54	40
...	...	...	...	...	...	...	...	...
26	16	10	22	13	9	23	15	8
628	330	298	161	91	70	117	69	48
...	...	...	...	...	...	...	...	...
457	269	188	436	237	199	461	247	214
457	269	188	436	237	199	461	247	214
6	3	3	...	...	...	5	2	3
25	19	6	24	17	7	17	14	3
...	...	...	...	...	...	...	...	...
31	22	9	24	17	7	22	16	6
...	...	...	...	...	...	...	...	...
...	...	...	...	...	...	...	...	...
30	21	9	12	8	4	27	19	8
30	21	9	12	8	4	27	19	8
101	49	52	54	25	29	62	29	33
...	...	...	...	...	...	...	...	...
...	...	...	...	...	...	6	6	...
...	...	...	...	...	...	...	...	...
...	...	...	...	...	...	...	...	...
101	49	52	54	25	29	68	35	33

TABLE

Occupations, Part B.—

Class.	Group.	Occupation.	Taluqs: Tiruvalla. Total.	Tiruvalla. Males.	Tiruvalla. Females.	Ambalappula. Total.	Ambalappula. Males.	Ambalappula. Females.
1	2	3	61	62	63	64	65	66
F. Professions.	63a	Priests, ministers, preachers; missionaries, &c. ...	259	145	114	557	289	268
		Catechists, readers, &c. ...	42	18	24	67	32	35
		Exorcists, hail-averters, amulettiers, &c. ...	129	78	51	150	89	61
		Total Sub-order 63(*a*) ...	430	241	189	774	410	364
	63b	Religious mendicants, inmates of convents, &c. ...	...	...	...	...	...	...
		Church, temple, pagoda, masjid, &c., services ...	569	334	235	523	313	210
		Total Sub-order 63(*b*) ...	569	334	235	523	313	210
	64	Administrative and inspecting officials ...	5	3	2	...	...	...
		Principals, professors and teachers in colleges, &c. ...	29	21	8	36	24	12
		Clerks, &c., on educational establishments, schools, &c.	...	...	...	...	...	...
		Total Sub-order 64 ...	34	24	10	36	24	12
	65	Editors and ballad makers ...	...	...	...	...	...	...
		Private secretaries and clerks.	...	...	...	12	5	7
		Public Scribes ...	47	31	16	21	14	7
		Total Sub-order 65 ...	47	31	16	33	19	14
	66	Advocates and pleaders ...	184	89	95	612	284	328
		Mukhtiars ...	...	...	...	...	...	...
		Lawyer's clerks ...	37	33	4	...	...	...
		Stamp vendors ...	...	...	...	7	4	3
		Petition writers ...	...	...	...	9	9	...
		Total Sub-order 66 ...	221	122	99	628	297	331

XVII.

(State Distribution)—(*Continued*).

—(*Continued*).

Sherttala.			Vykkam.			Ettumanur.		
Total.	Males.	Females.	Total.	Males.	Females.	Total.	Males.	Females.
67	68	69	70	71	72	73	74	75
57	36	21	94	58	36	201	117	84
...	...	...	...	...	...	...	...	...
27	16	11	18	12	6	95	59	36
84	52	32	112	70	42	296	176	120
...	...	..	...	...	...	...	...	..
343	228	115	572	364	208	490	298	192
343	228	115	572	364	208	490	298	192
...	...	...	5	2	3	...	...	...
12	8	4	26	21	5	25	19	6
...	...	...	...	...	...	...	...	...
12	8	4	31	23	8	25	19	6
...	...	...	...	...	...	...	...	...
...	...	...	...	...	...	...	...	...
8	8	...	31	20	11	55	34	21
8	8	...	31	20	11	55	34	21
144	68	76	51	23	28	39	18	21
...	...	...	...	...	...	...	...	...
...	...	...	...	...	...	...	...	...
...	...	...	...	...	...	...	...	...
...	...	...	...	...	...	...	...	..
144	68	76	51	23	28	39	18	21

TABLE

Occupations, Part B.—

Class.	Group.	Occupation.	Taluqs: Kottayam. Total.	Kottayam. Males.	Kottayam. Females.	Changanacheri. Total.	Changanacheri. Males.	Changanacheri. Females.
1	2	3	76	77	78	79	80	81
F. Professions.	63*a*	Priests, ministers, preachers, missionaries, &c. ...	1,162	569	593	728	337	391
		Catechists, readers, &c. ...	93	45	48	54	31	23
		Exorcists, hail-averters, amulettiers, &c. ...	76	48	28	64	39	25
		Total Sub-order 63(*a*) ...	1,331	662	669	846	407	439
	63*b*	Religious mendicants, inmates of convents, &c. ...	6	6	...	...	...	...
		Church, temple, pagoda, masjid, &c., services ...	571	325	246	330	159	171
		Total Sub-order 63(*b*) ...	577	331	246	330	159	171
	64	Administrative and inspecting officials ...	9	4	5	...	...	...
		Principals, professors and teachers in colleges, &c. ...	18	14	4	15	9	6
		Clerks, &c., on educational establishments, schools, &c.	...	...	...	...	...	...
		Total Sub-order 64 ...	27	18	9	15	9	6
	65	Editors and ballad makers ...	4	4	...	...	...	...
		Private secretaries and clerks.	10	5	5	...	...	...
		Public Scribes ...	37	24	13	19	13	6
		Total Sub-order 65 ...	51	33	18	19	13	6
	66	Advocates and pleaders ...	262	128	134	70	33	37
		Mukhtiars ...	...	...	...	...	...	...
		Lawyer's clerks ...	26	21	5	...	...	...
		Stamp vendors ...	6	3	3	...	...	...
		Petition writers ...	8	8	...	...	...	...
		Total Sub-order 66 ...	302	160	142	70	33	37

XVII.

(State Distribution)—(*Continued*).

—(*Continued*).

Meenachal.			Muvattupula.			Todupula.		
Total.	Males.	Females.	Total.	Males.	Females.	Total.	Males.	Females.
82	83	84	85	86	87	88	89	90
87	49	38	195	104	91	43	24	19
...	...	...	8	3	5	...	...	...
24	10	14	67	43	24	1	1	...
111	59	52	270	150	120	44	25	19
1	1	...	...	...	...	...	...	...
275	133	142	431	246	185	159	78	81
276	134	142	431	246	185	159	78	81
...	...	...	...	...	...	...	...	...
9	5	4	9	7	2	8	3	5
...	...	...	...	...	...	...	...	...
9	5	4	9	7	2	8	3	5
...	...	...	...	...	...	...	...	...
...	...	...	...	...	...	...	...	...
46	31	15	17	12	5	10	8	2
46	31	15	17	12	5	10	8	2
14	6	8	64	30	34	5	2	3
...	...	...	...	...	...	...	...	...
...	...	...	...	...	...	...	...	...
...	...	...	...	...	...	...	...	...
...	...	...	...	...	...	...	...	...
14	6	8	64	30	34	5	2	3

TABLE

Occupations, Part B.—

Class.	Group.	Occupation.	Taluqs: Kunnattunadu. Total.	Kunnattunadu. Males.	Kunnattunadu. Females.	Alangadu. Total.	Alangadu. Males.	Alangadu. Females.
1	2	3	91	92	93	94	95	96
F. Professions.	63*a*	Priests, ministers, preachers, missionaries, &c. ...	105	55	50	126	64	62
		Catechists, readers, &c. ...	...	...	...	...	...	...
		Exorcists, hail-averters, amulettiers, &c. ...	38	22	16	42	29	13
		Total Sub-order 63(*a*) ...	143	77	66	168	93	75
	63*b*	Religious mendicants, inmates of convents, &c. ...	...	...	...	...	...	...
		Church, temple, pagoda, masjid, &c., services ...	393	227	166	411	198	213
		Total Sub-order 63(*b*) ...	393	227	166	411	198	213
	64	Administrative and inspecting officials ...	...	...	...	...	...	...
		Principals, professors and teachers in colleges, &c. ...	2	2	...	12	8	4
		Clerks, &c., on educational establishments, schools, &c.	...	...	...	...	...	...
		Total Sub-order 64 ...	2	2	...	12	8	4
	65	Editors and ballad makers ...	...	...	...	...	...	...
		Private secretaries and clerks.	...	...	...	...	...	...
		Public Scribes ...	26	16	10	26	15	11
		Total Sub-order 65 ...	26	16	10	26	15	11
	66	Advocates and pleaders .	17	8	9	27	12	15
		Mukhtiars ...	...	...	...	...	...	...
		Lawyer's clerks ...	...	...	...	...	...	...
		Stamp vendors ...	...	...	...	...	...	...
		Petition writers ...	...	...	...	...	...	...
		Total Sub-order 66 ...	17	8	9	27	12	15

XVII.

(State Distribution)—(*Continued*).

—(*Continued*).

Parur.			Cardamom Hills.			Periyar and Thekkadi.		
Total.	Males.	Females.	Total.	Males.	Females.	Total.	Males.	Females.
97	98	99	100	101	102	103	104	105
402	210	192	51	27	24	6	4	2
...	...	...	...	...	...	...	...	...
...	...	...	...	...	...	...	...	...
402	210	192	51	27	24	6	4	2
...	...	...	...	...	...	...	...	...
503	232	271	1	1	...	...	...	...
503	232	271	1	1	...	...	...	...
...	...	...	...	...	...	...	...	...
23	14	9	...	...	...	...	...	...
...	...	...	...	...	...	...	...	...
23	14	9	...	...	...	...	...	...
...	...	...	...	...	...	...	...	...
...	...	...	...	...	...	...	...	...
31	19	12	...	...	...	...	...	...
31	19	12	...	...	...	...	...	...
120	58	62	...	...	...	...	...	...
...	...	...	...	...	...	...	...	...
18	18	...	...	...	...	...	...	...
...	...	...	...	...	...	...	...	...
5	5	...	...	...	...	...	...	...
143	81	62	...	...	...	...	...	...

TABLE

Occupations, Part B.—

Class.	Group.	Occupation.	Total.	Males.	Females.
1	2	3	4	5	6
F. Professions.	67*a*	Administrative and Inspecting staff...	*2*	1	1
		Practitioners by diploma ...	*28*	21	7
		Practitioners without diploma (Native Physicians) ...	*5,489*	2,800	2,689
		Oculists ...	*12*	9	3
		Vaccinators ...	*50*	21	29
		Midwifery ...	*1*	..	1
		Total Sub-order 67(*a*) ...	**5,582**	**2,852**	**2,730**
	67*b*	Hospital and Asylum Assistants and Apothecaries ...	*126*	76	50
		Compounders and Hospital menials...	*30*	15	15
		Total Sub-order 67(*b*) ...	**156**	**91**	**65**
	68*a*	Administrative and Inspecting staff...	*2*	1	1
		Civil Engineers and Architects ...	*51*	30	21
		Revenue Surveyors and Survey Superintendents ...	*28*	20	8
		Total Sub-order 68(*a*) ...	**81**	**51**	**30**
	68*b*	Draughtsmen, &c., in Survey Offices and Overseers, &c. ...	*47*	15	32
		Clerks, &c., in Engineering and Survey Offices ...	*417*	274	143
		Total sub-order 68(*b*) ...	**464**	**289**	**175**
	69*b*	Astrologers and horoscope-casters ...	*3,778*	1,545	2,233
		Almanac makers and sellers ...	*7*	4	3
		Diviners (selectors of wells and house sites) ...	*2*	2	...
		Total Sub-order 69(*b*) ...	**3,787**	**1,551**	**2,236**

XVII.

(State Distribution)—(*Continued*)

Taluqs.								
Tovala.			Agastiswaram.			Eranial.		
Total.	Males.	Females.	Total.	Males.	Females.	Total.	Males.	Females.
7	8	9	10	11	12	13	14	15
...	...	...	...	...	...	...	...	...
...	...	...	2	2	...	...	...	...
54	26	28	166	86	80	424	215	209
..	...	...	...	...	...	...	...	...
..	...	...	7	3	4	...	...	...
...	...	...	...	...	...	...	...	...
54	26	28	175	91	84	424	215	209
...	...	...	7	4	3	1	1	...
...	...	...	...	..	...	...	..	...
...	...	...	7	4	3	1	1	...
...	...	...	...	...	...	...	...	...
...	...	...	11	6	5	...	...	...
...	...	...	...	...	...	...	...	...
...	...	...	11	6	5	...	...	...
...	...	...	6	2	4	...	...	...
...	...	...	21	13	8	6	4	2
...	...	...	27	15	12	6	4	2
19	7	12	141	52	89	47	19	28
...	...	...	...	...	...	...	...	...
...	...	...	...	...	...	...	...	...
19	7	12	141	52	89	47	19	28

TABLE

Occupations, Part B.—

Class.	Group.	Occupation.	Kalkulam. Total.	Kalkulam. Males.	Kalkulam. Females.	Vilavankodu. Total.	Vilavankodu. Males.	Vilavankodu. Females.
1	2	3	16	17	18	19	20	21
F. Professions	67*a*	Administrative and Inspecting staff ...	...	...	...	...	...	...
		Practitioners by diploma ...	...	...	...	...	...	...
		Practitioners without diploma (Native Physicians) ...	29	18	11	71	39	32
		Oculists ..	9	6	3	...	...	...
		Vaccinators ...	...	...	...	...	...	...
		Midwifery ...	...	...	...	...	.	...
		Total Sub-order 67(*a*) ...	38	24	14	71	39	32
	67*b*	Hospital & Asylum Assistants and Apothecaries ...	4	2	2	...	...	..
		Compounders and Hospital menials ...	..	..		...	...	...
		Total Sub-order 67(*b*) ..	4	2	2	...	...	...
	68*a*	Administrative and Inspecting staff ..	...	...	...	...	...	...
		Civil Engineers & Architects.	...	...	...	...	...	...
		Revenue Surveyors and Survey Superintendents ...	...	...	...	...	...	...
		Total Sub-order 68(*a*) ...	...	...	...	...	...	...
	68*b*	Draughtsmen, &c., in Survey Offices and Overseers, &c....	...	...	...	...	...	...
		Clerks, &c., in Engineering and Survey Offices ...	10	6	4	...	..	...
		Total Sub-order 68(*b*) ...	10	6	4	...	...	...
	68*b*	Astrologers and horoscope-casters ...	44	19	25	37	16	21
		Almanac makers and sellers.	...	...	...	...	...	..
		Diviners (selectors of wells and house sites) ...	...	...	...	...	...	...
		Total Sub-order 69(*b*) ...	44	19	25	37	16	21

XVII.

(State Distribution)—(*Continued*).

—(*Continued*).

Neyattankara.			Trivandram.			Nedumangadu.		
Total.	Males.	Females.	Total.	Males.	Females.	Total.	Males.	Females.
22	23	24	25	26	27	28	29	30
...	...	...	2	1	1	...	...	...
...	...	...	20	13	7	...	...	...
181	95	86	1,309	615	694	77	38	39
...	...	...	3	3	...	...	...	...
...	...	...	27	13	14	...	...	...
...	...	...	1	...	1	...	...	...
181	95	86	1,362	645	717	77	38	39
3	3	...	44	25	19	..	...	...
...	...	...	23	12	11	...	...	...
3	3	...	67	37	30	...	...	...
...	...	...	2	1	1	...	...	...
...	...	...	17	9	8	...	...	...
...	...	...	16	12	4	...	...	...
...	...	...	35	22	13	...	...	...
...	...	...	21	4	17	...	...	...
15	8	7	183	110	73	...	...	...
15	8	7	204	114	90	...	...	...
235	98	137	229	94	135	106	50	56
...	...	...	7	4	3	...	...	...
...	...	...	...	...	...	...	...	...
235	98	137	236	98	138	106	50	56

TABLE

Occupations, Part B.—

Class.	Group.	Occupation.	Taluqs — Sirayinkil. Total.	Sirayinkil. Males.	Sirayinkil. Females.	Kottarakkara. Total.	Kottarakkara. Males.	Kottarakkara. Females.
1	2	3	31	32	33	34	35	36
F. Professions.	67*a*	Administrative and Inspecting staff ...	...	...	...	...	...	...
		Practitioners by diploma ...	...	...	...	...	...	...
		Practitioners without diploma Native Physicians) ...	527	269	258	45	25	20
		Oculists ...	...	...	...	...	...	...
		Vaccinators ...	...	...	...	...	...	...
		Midwifery ...	...	...	...	...	...	...
		Total Sub-order 67(*a*) ...	527	269	258	45	25	20
	67*b*	Hospital & Asylum Assistants and Apothecaries ...	...	...	...	5	2	3
		Compounders and Hospital menials ...	...	...	...	...	...	...
		Total Sub-order 67(*b*) .	...	...	...	5	2	3
	68*a*	Administrative and Inspecting staff ..	...	...	...	...	...	...
		Civil Engineers & Architects.	...	...	...	...	...	...
		Revenue Surveyers and Survey Superintendents ...	...	...	..	2	2	...
		Total Sub-order 68(*a*) ...	...	...	...	2	2	...
	68*b*	Draughtsmen, &c., in Survey Offices and Overseers, &c....	...	...	...	...	...	...
		Clerks, &c., in Engineering and Survey Offices ...	6	4	2	6	3	3
		Total Sub-order 68(*b*) ...	6	4.	2	6	3	3
	69*b*	Astrologers and horoscope-casters ...	308	127	181	254	100	154
		Almanac makers and sellers..	...	...	...	...	...	...
		Diviners (selectors of wells and house sites) ...	2	2	...	...	...	...
		Total Sub-order 69(*b*) ...	310	129	181	254	100	154

XVII.

(State Distribution)—(*Continued*).

—(*Continued*).

Pattanapuram.			Shenkotta.			Quilon.		
Total.	Males.	Females.	Total.	Males.	Females.	Total.	Males.	Females.
37	38	39	40	41	42	43	44	45
...	...	...	...	...	...	...	...	...
...	...	...	...	...	...	4	4	...
24	14	10	41	22	19	282	145	137
...	...	...	...	...	...	...	...	...
...	...	...	...	...	...	16	5	11
...	...	...	...	...	...	...	...	...
24	14	10	41	22	19	302	154	148
...	...	...	3	1	2	13	8	5
...	...	...	...	...	...	7	3	4
...	...	...	3	1	2	20	11	9
...	...	...	...	...	...	...	...	...
...	...	...	...	...	...	8	5	3
...	...	...	...	...	...	...	...	...
...	...	...	...	...	...	8	5	3
...	...	...	...	...	...	7	3	4
...	...	...	2	2	...	19	13	6
...	...	...	2	2	...	26	16	10
213	90	123	57	20	37	206	87	119
...	...	...	...	...	...	...	...	...
...	...	...	...	...	...	...	...	...
213	90	123	57	20	37	206	87	119

TABLE

Occupations, Part B.—

Class.	Group.	Occupation.	Taluqs: Kunnattur. Total.	Kunnattur. Males.	Kunnattur. Females.	Karunagappalli. Total.	Karunagappalli. Males.	Karunagappalli. Females.
1	2	3	46	47	48	49	50	51
F. Professions.	67a	Administrative and Inspecting staff ...	...	...	...	...	...	...
		Practitioners by diploma ...	...	...	...	...	...	...
		Practitioners without diploma (Native Physicians) ...	117	61	56	184	95	89
		Oculists ...	...	...	...	...	...	...
		Vaccinators ...	...	...	...	...	...	...
		Midwifery ..	...	...	...	...	..	...
		Total Sub-order 67(a) ...	117	61	56	184	95	89
	67b	Hospital & Asylum Assistants and Apothecaries ...	...	...	..	5	2	3
		Compounders and Hospital menials ...	...	...	...	...	...	...
		Total Sub-order 67(b) ...	...	...	...	5	2	3
	68a	Administrative and Inspecting staff ..	...	...	...	...	...	...
		Civil Engineers & Architects..	...	...	...	...	...	...
		Revenue Surveyors and Survey Superintendents ...	...	...	...	...	...	...
		Total Sub-order 68(a) ..	...	...	...	...	...	...
	68b	Draughtsmen, &c., in Survey Offices and Overseers, &c. ...	...	...	...	...	...	...
		Clerks, &c., in Engineering and Survey Offices ...	...	...	...	...	...	...
		Total Sub-order 68(b) ...	...	...	...	...	...	...
	69b	Astrologers and horoscope-casters ...	77	31	46	...	...	...
		Almanac makers and sellers..	...	...	...	...	...	...
		Diviners (selectors of wells and house sites) ...	...	...	...	...	...	...
		Total Sub-order 69(b) ...	77	31	46	...	...	...

XVII.

(State Distribution)—(*Continued*).

—(*Continued*).

Kartigappalli.			Mavellikkara.			Chenganur.		
Total.	Males.	Females.	Total.	Males.	Females.	Total.	Males.	Females.
52	53	54	55	56	57	58	59	60
...	...	...	...	...	...	...	...	...
...	...	...	...	...	...	...	..	...
169	88	81	183	93	90	264	139	125
...	...	...	...	...	...	...	...	...
...	...	...	...	..	...	...	...	...
...	...	...	...	...	...	...	...	...
169	88	81	183	93	90	264	139	125
9	4	5	...	...	...	5	3	2
...	...	...	..	...	...	...	...	...
9	4	5	...	...	...	5	3	
...	...	...	...	..	...	...	...	..
...	...	...	...	...	...	...	...	...
...	...	...	...	...	...	...	...	...
...	...	...	...	...	...	...	...	...
...	...	...	...	...	...	...	...	...
...	...	...	8	3	5	...	...	...
...	...	...	8	3	5	...	...	...
...	...	...	184	80	104	245	103	142
...	...	...	...	...	...	...	...	...
...	...	...	...	...	...	...	...	...
...	...	...	184	80	104	245	103	142

TABLE

Occupations, Part B.—

Class.	Group.	Occupation.	Taluqs: Tiruvalla. Total.	Tiruvalla. Males.	Tiruvalla. Females.	Ambalappula. Total.	Ambalappula. Males.	Ambalappula. Females.
1	2	3	61	62	63	64	65	66
F. Professions.	67a	Administrative and Inspecting staff ...	...	...	...	..	...	...
		Practitioners by diploma ...	...	...	...	2	2	...
		Practitioners without diploma (Native Physicians) ...	208	111	97	372	193	179
		Oculists ...	...	...	...	...	...	...
		Vaccinators ...	...	...	...	...	...	...
		Midwifery ...	...	...	...	...	...	..
		Total Sub-order 67(a) ...	208	111	97	374	195	179
	67b	Hospital & Asylum Assistants and Apothecaries ...	3	2	1	7	4	3
		Compounders and Hospital menials ...	...	...	...	...	...	...
		Total Sub-order 67(b) ...	3	2	1	7	4	3
	68a	Administrative and Inspecting staff ...	...	...	...	...	...	...
		Civil Engineers & Architects.	...	...	...	...	...	...
		Revenue Surveyors and Survey Superintendents ...	...	...	...	10	6	4
		Total Sub-order 68(a) ...	...	...	...	10	6	4
	68b	Draughtsmen, &c., in Survey Offices and Overseers, &c....	...	...	...	...	...	...
		Clerks, &c., in Engineering and Survey Offices ...	...	...	...	17	14	3
		Total Sub-order 68(b) ...	...	...	...	17	14	3
	69b	Astrologers and horoscope-casters ...	209	94	115	150	67	83
		Almanac makers and sellers...	...	...	...	...	...	...
		Diviners (selectors of wells and house sites) ...	...	...	...	...	..	...
		Total Sub-order 69(b) ...	209	94	115	150	67	83

XVII.

(State Distribution)—(*Continued*).

—(*Continued*).

Sherttala.			Vykkam.			Ettumanur.		
Total.	Males.	Females.	Total.	Males.	Females.	Total.	Males.	Females.
67	68	69	70	71	72	73	74	75
...	...	...	..	...	...	...	...	...
...	...	...	...	...	...	...	...	...
67	37	30	112	58	54	77	41	36
...	...	...	...	...	...	...	...	...
...	...	...	...	...	...	...	...	...
...	...	...	...	...	...	...	...	...
67	37	30	112	58	54	77	41	36
...	...	...	...	...	...	...	...	...
...	...	...	...	...	...	...	...	...
..	...	...	...	...	...	...	...	...
...	...	...	...	...	...	...	...	...
6	3	3	...	...	...	...	...	...
...	...	...	...	...	...	...	...	...
6	3	3	...	...	...	...	...	...
...	...	...	...	...	...	...	...	..
...	...	...	...	...	...	...	...	...
...	...	...	...	..	...	...	...	...
154	58	96	206	74	132	114	48	66
...	...	...	...	...	...	...	...	...
...	...	...	...	...	...	...	...	...
154	58	96	206	74	132	114	48	66

TABLE
Occupations, Part B.—

Class.	Group.	Occupation.	Taluqs: Kottayam. Total.	Kottayam. Males	Kottayam. Females.	Changanacheri. Total.	Changanacheri. Males.	Changanacheri. Females.
1	2	3	76	77	78	79	80	81
F. Professions.	67*a*	Administrative and Inspecting staff ...	...	...	...	..	...	...
		Practitioners by diploma ...	...	...	...	...	...	...
		Practitioners without diploma (Native Physicians) ...	106	57	49	91	49	42
		Oculists ...	...	..	...	...	...	...
		Vaccinators ...	...	...	...	...	...	...
		Midwifery ...	...	...	...	...	...	...
		Total Sub-order 67(*a*) ...	106	57	49	91	49	42
	67*b*	Hospital & Asylum Assistants and Apothecaries ...	8	6	2	2	2	...
		Compounders and Hospital menials ...	...	...	...	...	...	...
		Total Sub-order 67(*b*) ..	8	6	2	2	2	...
	68*a*	Administrative and Inspecting staff ...	...	...	...	...	...	...
		Civil Engineers & Architects.	...	..	...	...	...	...
		Revenue Surveyors and Survey Superintendents ...	...	...	...	...	...	...
		Total Sub-order 68(*a*) ...	...	...	...	...	...	...
	68*b*	Draughtsmen, &c., in Survey Offices and Overseers, &c...	...	...	...	...	...	...
		Clerks, &c., in Engineering and Survey Offices ...	62	49	13	15	13	2
		Total Sub-order 68(*b*) ...	62	49	13	15	13	2
	69*b*	Astrologers and horoscope-casters ...	121	59	62	110	41	69
		Almanac makers and sellers...	...	...	...	..	...	...
		Diviners (selectors of wells and house sites) ...	...	...	...	...	...	...
		Total Sub-order 69(*b*) ...	121	59	62	110	41	69

XVII.

(State Distribution)—(Continued).

—(Continued).

Meenachal.			Muvattupula.			Todupula.		
Total.	Males.	Females.	Total.	Males.	Females.	Total.	Males.	Females.
82	83	84	85	86	87	88	89	90
...	...	...	..	...	...	...	...	...
...	...	...	...	...	...	...	...	...
33	19	14	14	8	6	...	...	...
...	...	...	...	...	...	...	...	...
...	...	...	...	...	..	...	...	...
...	...	...	...	...	...	...	...	...
33	19	14	14	8	6	...	...	...
...	...	...	1	1	...	..	...	...
...	...	...	...	...	...	...	...	...
...	...	...	1	1	...	...	...	...
...	...	...	...	...	...	...	...	...
...	...	...	7	5	2	...	...	...
...	...	...	...	...	...	...	...	...
...	...	...	7	5	2	...	...	...
...	...	...	...	...	...	...	...	...
...	...	...	...	...	...	.	...	...
...	...	...	...	...	..	...	...	...
41	13	28	67	24	43	14	5	9
...	...	...	...	...	...	..	...	...
...	...	...	...	...	...	...	...	...
41	13	28	67	24	43	14	5	9

TABLE

Occupations, Part B.—

Class.	Group.	Occupation.	Taluqs: Kunnattunadu. Total.	Kunnattunadu. Males.	Kunnattunadu. Females.	Alangadu. Total.	Alangadu. Males.	Alangadu. Females.
1	2	3	91	92	93	94	95	96
F. Professions.	67*a*	Administrative and Inspecting staff ...	...	...	...	...	...	...
		Practitioners by diploma ..	...	...	...	...	...	...
		Practitioners without diploma (Native Physicians) ...	145	79	66	10	6	4
		Oculists ...	...	...	...	...	...	...
		Vaccinators ...	...	...	...	...	...	...
		Midwifery ...	...	...	...	...	...	...
		Total Sub-order 67(*a*) ...	145	79	66	10	6	4
	67*b*	Hospital & Asylum Assistants and Apothecaries ...	2	2	...	...	...	...
		Compounders and Hospital menials ...	...	...	...	...	...	...
		Total Sub-order 67(*b*) ...	2	2	...	...	...	...
	68*a*	Administrative and Inspecting staff ...	...	...	...	...	...	...
		Civil Engineers & Architects.	...	...	...	...	...	...
		Revenue Surveyors and Survey Superintendents ...	...	...	...	...	...	...
		Total Sub-order 68(*a*) ...	...	...	...	...	...	...
	68*b*	Draughtsmen, &c., in Survey Offices and Overseers, &c....	...	...	...	...	...	...
		Clerks, &c., in Engineering and Survey Offices ...	...	...	...	...	...	...
		Total Sub-order 68(*b*) ...	...	...	...	...	...	...
	69*b*	Astrologers and horoscope-casters ...	41	14	27	59	21	38
		Almanac makers and sellers...	...	...	...	...	...	...
		Diviners (selectors of wells and house sites) ...	...	...	...	...	...	...
		Total Sub-order 69(*b*) ...	41	14	27	59	21	38

XVII.

(State Distribution)—(*Continued*).

—(*Continued*).

Parur.			Cardamom Hills.			Periyar & Thekkadi.		
Total.	Males.	Females.	Total.	Males.	Females.	Total.	Males.	Females.
97	98	99	100	101	102	103	104	105
...	...	...	...	...	...	...	...	...
...	...	...	...	...	...	...	...	...
107	59	48	...	...	...	...	...	...
...	...	...	...	...	...	...	...	...
...	...	...	...	...	...	...	...	...
...	...	...	...	..	...	...	...	...
107	59	48	...	...	...	...	...	...
4	4	...	...	...	...	...	...	...
...	...	...	...	...	...	...	...	...
4	4		...	...	..	...	...	...
...	...	...	...	...	..	...	...	...
...	...	...	...	...	...	2	2	...
...	...	..	...		...	...	...	...
...	...	...	...	...	...	2	2	...
...	...	...	...	...	...	13	6	7
...	...	...	...	...	...	47	32	15
..	...	...	...	...	...	60	38	22
90	34	56	...	...	...	...	...	...
...	...	...	...	...	...	...	...	...
..	...	...	...	...	...	...	...	...
90	34	56	...	...	...	...	...	...

TABLE

Occupations, Part B.—

Class.	Group.	Occupation.	Total.	Males.	Females.
		Occupation and Class.	State Total.		
1	2	3	4	5	6
F. Professions.	70	Painters and Superintendents of Schools of Arts, &c.	*776*	393	383
		Sculptors ...	*101*	13	88
		Photographers ...	*9*	6	3
		Total Sub-order 70 ...	**886**	**412**	**474**
	71	Music composers and teachers ...	*270*	207	63
		Band-masters, &c. (not military) ...	*394*	230	164
		Actors, singers, dancers and their accompanists ...	*1,442*	917	525
		Total Sub-order 71 ..	**2,106**	**1,354**	**752**
	72	Shikaris and bird catchers ...	*61*	33	28
	73*a*	Exhibitors of trained animals (bulls, snakes, monkeys, &c.) ...	*31*	14	17
		Circus players ...	*23*	17	6
		Cock and pigeon fanciers ...	*5*	4	1
		Total Sub-order 73(*a*) ...	**59**	**35**	**24**
	73*b*	Buffoons ...	*22*	13	9
		Story and ballad reciters ...	*20*	10	10
		Conjurors and fortune tellers ...	*27*	14	13
		Total Sub-order 73(*b*) ...	**69**	**37**	**32**
	73*c*	Acrobats and rope-dancers ...	*255*	104	151
	73*d*	Tennis and racquet court service ...	*11*	6	5
		Total Class F. ...	*43,968*	*23,550*	*20,418*

XVII.

(State Distribution)—(*Continued*).

TALUQS.

Tovala.			Agastiswaram.			Eranial.		
Total.	Males.	Females.	Total.	Males.	Females.	Total.	Males.	Females.
7	8	9	10	11	12	13	14	15
7	3	4	116	57	59	146	72	74
...	...	...	37	4	33	...	...	...
...	...	...	...	...	...	...	...	...
7	3	4	153	61	92	146	72	74
...	...	...	29	23	6	...	...	...
...	...	...	...	...	...	9	5	4
28	18	10	41	27	14	20	12	8
28	18	10	70	50	20	29	17	12
...	...	...	...	...	...	...	...	...
7	3	4	...	...	...	10	5	5
...	...	...	9	6	3	...	...	...
...	...	...	...	...	...	...	...	...
7	3	4	9	6	3	10	5	5
...	...	...	...	...	...	...	...	...
...	...	...	..	...	...	...	...	...
...	...	...	11	5	6	...	...	...
...	...	...	11	5	6	...	...	...
...	...	...	16	7	9	12	4	8
...	...	...	...	...	...	...	...	...
582	313	269	2,405	1,177	1,228	1,707	894	813

TABLE
Occupations, Part B.—

Class.	Group.	Occupation.	Taluqs: Kalkulam. Total.	Kalkulam. Males.	Kalkulam. Females.	Vilavankodu. Total.	Vilavankodu. Males.	Vilavankodu. Females.
1	2	3	16	17	18	19	20	21
F. Professions.	70	Painters and Superintendents of Schools of Arts, &c. ...	20	9	11	12	5	7
		Sculptors ...	...	...	...	...	...	...
		Photographers ...	...	...	...	...	...	...
		Total Sub-order 70 ...	20	9	11	12	5	7
	71	Music composers & teachers..	...	...	...	7	5	2
		Band-masters, &c. (not military) ...	9	6	3	...	...	...
		Actors, singers, dancers and their accompanists ...	48	33	15	69	42	27
		Total Sub-order 71 ...	57	39	18	76	47	29
	72	Shikaris and bird catchers ...	...	...	...	7	4	3
	73*a*	Exhibitors of trained animals (bulls, snakes, monkeys, &c.)	...	...	...	...	...	...
		Circus players ...	6	4	2	...	...	...
		Cock and pigeon fanciers ...	...	...	...	...	...	...
		Total Sub-order 73(*a*) ...	6	4	2	...	...	...
	73*b*	Buffoons ...	...	...	...	...	...	...
		Story and ballad reciters ...	...	...	...	...	...	...
		Conjurors and fortune tellers.	...	...	...	...	...	...
		Total Sub-order 73(*b*) ...	...	...	..	...	...	..
	73*c*	Acrobats and rope-dancers...	27	12	15	...	...	..
	73*d*	Tennis and racquet court service ...	..	...	...	...	...	...
		Total Class F. ...	1,359	714	645	740	407	333

XVII.

(State Distribution)—(*Continued*).

—(*Continued*).

Neyattankara.			Trivandram.			Nedumangadu.		
Total.	Males.	Females.	Total.	Males.	Females.	Total.	Males.	Females.
22	23	24	25	26	27	28	29	30
29	14	15	176	94	82	...	...	...
...	...	...	64	9	55	...	...	...
...	...	...	9	6	3	...	...	...
29	14	15	249	109	140	...	...	...
...	...	...	97	84	13	...	...	...
15	8	7	154	88	66	5	3	2
45	31	14	189	93	96	13	8	5
60	39	21	440	265	175	18	11	7
...	...	...	...	...	...	...	...	...
...	...	...	9	4	5	...	...	...
...	...	...	8	7	1	...	...	...
...	...	...	5	4	1	...	...	...
...	...	...	22	15	7	...	...	...
...	...	...	7	4	3	...	...	...
...	...	...	7	3	4	...	...	...
...	...	...	7	4	3	...	...	...
...	...	...	21	11	10	...	...	...
...	...	...	29	12	17	...	...	...
...	...	...	7	4	3	...	...	...
1,264	707	557	6,599	3,502	3,097	527	290	237

TABLE

Occupations, Part B.—

Class.	Group.	Occupation.	Taluqs: Sirayinkil. Total.	Sirayinkil. Males.	Sirayinkil. Females.	Kottarakkara. Total.	Kottarakkara. Males.	Kottarakkara. Females.
1	2	3	31	32	33	34	35	36
F. Professions.	70	Painters and Superintendents of Schools of Arts, &c. ...	...	...	...	...	...	...
		Sculptors ...	...	..	...	...	...	...
		Photographers ...	...	...	...	...	...	...
		Total Sub-order 70 ...	...	...	...	...	...	...
	71	Music composers & teachers...	8	5	3	...	...	...
		Band-masters, &c. (not military) ...	...	...	...	11	6	5
		Actors, singers, dancers and their accompanists ...	68	42	26	62	39	23
		Total Sub-order 71 ...	76	47	29	73	45	28
	72	Shikaris and bird catchers ...	...	...	...	...	...	...
	73*a*	Exhibitors of trained animals (bulls, snakes, monkeys, &c.)	5	2	3	...	...	...
		Circus players ...	...	...	...	...	...	...
		Cock and pigeon fanciers ...	...	...	...	...	...	...
		Total Sub-order 73(*a*) ...	5	2	3	...	...	...
	73*b*	Buffoons ...	...	...	...	...	...	...
		Story and ballad reciters ...	...	...	...	...	...	...
		Conjurors and fortune tellers.	...	...	...	...	...	...
		Total Sub-order 73(*b*) ...	...	...	...	...	...	...
	73*c*	Acrobats and rope-dancers ...	...	...	...	...	...	...
	73*d*	Tennis and racquet court service ...	...	...	...	...	...	...
		Total Class F. ...	1,612	850	762	1,027	554	473

XVII.

(State Distribution)—(*Continued*).

—(*Continued*).

Pattanapuram.			Shenkotta.			Quilon.		
Total.	Males.	Females.	Total.	Males.	Females.	Total.	Males.	Females.
37	38	39	40	41	42	43	44	45
...	...	...	14	6	8	56	29	27
...	...	...	...	...	...	...	...	...
...	..	...	...	...	...	...	...	...
...	...	...	14	6	8	56	29	27
...	...	...	10	6	4	...	...	...
8	4	4	..	...	...	32	20	12
26	16	10	38	24	14	47	32	15
34	20	14	48	30	18	79	52	27
17	8	9	...	...	...	...	...	...
...	...	...	...	...	...	...	...	...
...	...	...	...	...	...	...	...	...
...	...	...	...	...	...	...	...	...
...	...	...	...	...	...	...	...	...
...	...	...	...	...	...	...	...	...
...	...	...	...	...	...	...	...	...
...	...	...	...	...	...	...	...	...
...	...	...	...	...	...	..	...	...
	...	...	...	..	...	37	16	21
...	...	...	...	...	...	4	2	2
800	423	377	618	342	276	2,167	1,183	984

TABLE

Occupations, Part B.—

Class.	Group.	Occupation.	Taluqs: Kunnattur. Total.	Kunnattur. Males.	Kunnattur. Females.	Karunagappalli. Total.	Karunagappalli. Males.	Karunagappalli. Females.
1	2	3	46	47	48	49	50	51
F. Professions.	70	Painters and Superintendents of Schools of Arts, &c. ...	...	...	..	11	5	6
		Sculptors ...	...	...	...	...	...	...
		Photographers ...	...	...	...	...	...	...
		Total Sub-order 70 ...	...	...	...	11	5	6
	71	Music composers and teachers	...		...	...	...	...
		Band-masters, &c. (not military) ...	15	9	6	21	13	8
		Actors, singers, dancers and their accompanists ...	32	21	11	61	38	23
		Total Sub-order 71 ...	47	30	17	82	51	31
	72	Shikaris and bird catchers ...	6	4	2	...	...	...
	73*a*	Exhibitors of trained animals (bulls, snakes, monkeys, &c.)	...	...	...	...	...	...
		Circus players ...	...	...	...	...	...	...
		Cock and pigeon fanciers ...	...		...	...	...	...
		Total Sub-order 73(*a*) ...	...	...	...	...	...	...
	73*b*	Buffoons ...	...	...	...	...	...	...
		Story and ballad reciters ...	...	...	...	...	...	...
		Conjurors and fortune tellers.	...	...	...	...	...	...
		Total Sub-order 73(*b*) ...	...	...	...	...	...	...
	73*c*	Acrobats and rope-dancers ...	...	...	...	...	...	...
	70*d*	Tennis and racquet court service ...	...	...	...	...	...	...
		Total Class F. ...	760	421	339	885	511	374

XVII.

(State Distribution)—(*Continued*).

—(*Continued*).

Kartigappalli.			Mavellikkara.			Chenganur.		
Total.	Males.	Females.	Total.	Males.	Females.	Total.	Males.	Females.
52	53	54	55	56	57	58	59	60
...	...	...	...	...	...	5	2	3
...	...	...	...	...	...	...	..	...
...	...	...	...	...	...	...	...	...
...	...	...	...	...	...	5	2	3
22	14	8	5	4	1	...	...	...
15	8	7	8	5	3	...	...	...
33	23	10	27	19	8	71	47	24
70	45	25	40	28	12	71	47	24
...	...	...	...	...	...	...	...	...
...	...	...	...	...	...	...	...	...
...	...	...	...	...	...	...	...	...
...	...	...	...	...	...	...	...	...
..	..	...	...	...	...	...	...	...
...	...	...	...	...	...	...	...	...
...	...	...	...	...	...	...	...	...
...	...	...	...	...	...	...	...	...
...	...	...	...	...	...	...	...	...
...	...	...	20	8	12	42	15	27
...	...	...	...	...	...	...	...	...
1,495	828	667	1,122	590	532	1,327	695	632

TABLE

Occupations, Part B.—

Class.	Group.	Occupation.	Taluqs					
			Tiruvalla.			Ambalappula.		
			Total.	Males.	Females.	Total.	Males.	Females.
1	2	3	61	62	63	64	65	66
F. Professions.	70	Painters and Superintendents of Schools of Arts, &c. ...	37	19	18	55	31	24
		Sculptors ...	...	...	...	...	...	...
		Photographers ...	...	...	...	...	...	...
		Total Sub-order 70 ...	37	19	18	55	31	24
	71	Music composers and teachers	10	8	2	23	16	7
		Band-masters, &c. (not military) ...	22	13	9	15	9	6
		Actors, singers, dancers and their accompanists ...	55	39	16	61	41	20
		Total Sub-order 71 ...	87	60	27	99	66	33
	72	Shikaris and bird catchers ...	...	...	...	...	..	...
	73a	Exhibitors of trained animals (bulls, snakes, monkeys, &c.)	...	...	...	...	...	...
		Circus players ...	...	...	...	...	...	...
		Cock and pigeon fanciers ...	...	...	...	...	...	...
		Total Sub-order 73(*a*) ...	...	...	...	...	...	...
	73b	Buffoons ...	5	3	2	...	...	...
		Story and ballad reciters ...	5	2	3	...	...	...
		Conjurors and fortune tellers	9	5	4	...	...	...
		Total Sub-order 73(*b*) ...	19	10	9	...	...	...
	73c	Acrobats and rope-dancers ...	37	13	24	15	6	9
	73d	Tennis and racquet court service ...	...	...	...	...	...	...
		Total Class F. ...	1,901	1,061	840	2,721	1,452	1,269

XVII.

(State Distribution)—(*Continued*).

—(*Continued*).

Sherttala.			Vykkam.			Ettumanur.		
Total.	Males.	Females.	Total.	Males.	Females.	Total.	Males.	Females.
67	68	69	70	71	72	73	74	75
...	...	...	10	4	6	...	...	...
...	...	...	...	...	...	...	...	...
...	...	...	...	...	...	...	...	...
...	...	...	10	4	6	...	...	...
...	...	...	22	14	8	...	..	...
...	...	...	16	8	8	10	6	4
27	18	9	49	36	13	42	25	17
27	18	9	87	58	29	52	31	21
...	...	...	...	...	...	...	...	...
...	...	...	...	...	...	...	...	...
...	...	...	...	...	...	...	...	...
...	...	...	...	...	...	...	...	...
...	...	...	...	...	...	...	...	...
...	...	...	...	...	...	...	...	...
...	...	...	...	...	...	...	...	...
...	...	...	...	...	...	...	...	...
...	...	...	...	...	...	...	...	...
...	...	...	...	...	...	...	...	...
...	...	...	...	...	...	...	...	...
845	480	365	1,212	694	518	1,148	665	483

TABLE

Occupations, Part B.—

Class.	Group.	Occupation.	Kottayam. Total.	Kottayam. Males.	Kottayam. Females.	Changanacheri. Total.	Changanacheri. Males.	Changanacheri. Females.
1	2	3	76	77	78	79	80	81
F. Professions.	70	Painters and Superintendents of Schools of Arts, &c. ...	41	23	18	17	8	9
		Sculptors ...	...	...	...	...	...	...
		Photographers ...	...	...	...	...	...	...
		Total Sub-order 70 ...	41	23	18	17	8	9
	71	Music composers and teachers	13	8	5	8	5	3
		Band-masters, &c. (not military) ...	...	...	...	...	...	..
		Actors, singers, dancers and their accompanists ...	24	16	8	66	43	23
		Total Sub-order 71 ...	37	24	13	74	48	26
	72	Shikaris and bird catchers ..	24	12	12	...	...	...
	73*a*	Exhibitors of trained animals (bulls, snakes, monkeys, &c.)	...	...	...	...	...	...
		Circus players ..	...	...	...	...	...	...
		Cock and pigeon fanciers ...	...	...	...	...	...	...
		Total Sub-order 73(*a*) ...	...	...	...	...	...	...
	73*b*	Buffoons ...	8	4	4	...	...	...
		Story and ballad reciters ...	8	5	3	...	...	...
		Conjurors and fortune tellers.	...	...	...	...	...	...
		Total Sub-order 73(*b*) ...	16	9	7	...	...	...
	73*c*	Acrobats and rope-dancers ...	7	4	3	13	7	6
	73*d*	Tennis and racquet court service ...	...	...	...	...	...	...
		Total Class F. ...	2,710	1,447	1,263	1,602	789	813

XVII.

(State Distribution)—(*Continued*).

—(*Continued*).

Meenachal.			Muvattupula.			Todupula.		
Total.	Males.	Females.	Total.	Males.	Females.	Total.	Males.	Females.
82	83	84	85	86	87	88	89	90
...	...	...	...	...	...	..	...	...
...	...	...	...	...	...	...	...	...
...	...	...	...	...	...	...	...	...
...	...	...	...	...	...	...	...	...
...	...	...	..	...	...	...	...	...
...	...	...	13	8	5	...	...	...
54	38	16	24	19	5	35	17	18
54	38	16	37	27	10	35	17	18
...	...	...	...	...	...	...	...	...
...	...	...	...	...	...	...	...	...
...	...	...	...	...	...	...	...	...
...	...	...	...	...	...	...	...	...
...	...	...	...	...	...	...	...	...
...	...	...	...	...	...	...	...	...
...	...	...	...	...	...	...	...	...
...	...	...	...	...	...	...	...	...
...	...	...	...	...	...	...	...	...
...	...	...	...	...	...	...	...	...
...	...	...	...	...	...	...	...	...
584	305	279	917	510	407	275	138	137

TABLE

Occupations, Part B.—

Class.	Group.	Occupation.	Taluqs: Kunnattunadu. Total.	Kunnattunadu. Males.	Kunnattunadu. Females.	Alangadu. Total.	Alangadu. Males.	Alangadu. Females.
1	2	3	91	92	93	94	95	96
F. Professions.	70	Painters and Superintendents of Schools of Arts, &c. ...	...	...	...	...	...	...
		Sculptors ...	...	...	...	...	...	...
		Photographers ...	...	...	...	...	...	...
		Total Sub-order 70 ...	...	...	...	...	...	...
	71	Music composers and teachers	7	6	1	...	...	...
		Band-masters, &c. (not military) ...	...	...	...	8	5	3
		Actors, singers, dancers and their accompanists ...	30	21	9	21	14	7
		Total Sub-order 71 ...	37	27	10	29	19	10
	72	Shikaris and bird catchers ...	...	...	...	...	...	...
	73*a*	Exhibitors of trained animals bulls, snakes, monkeys, &c.)	...	...	...	...	...	...
		Circus players ...	...	...	...	...	...	...
		Cock and pigeon fanciers ...	...	...	...	...	...	...
		Total Sub-order 73(*a*) ...	...	...	...	...	...	...
	73*b*	Buffoons ...	...	...	...	...	...	...
		Story and ballad reciters ...	...	...	...	...	...	..
		Conjurors and fortune tellers.	...	...	...	...	...	...
		Total Sub-order 73(*b*) ...	...	...	...	...	...	...
	73*c*	Acrobats and rope-dancers...	...	...	...	...	...	...
	73*d*	Tennis and racquet court service ...	...	...	...	...	...	...
		Total Class F. ...	806	452	354	742	372	370

XVII.

(State Distribution)—(*Continued*).

—(*Continued*).

Parur.			Cardamon Hills.			Periyar & Thekkadi.		
Total.	Males.	Females.	Total.	Males.	Females.	Total	Males.	Females.
97	98	99	100	101	102	103	104	105
24	12	12	...	...	...	...	...	...
...	...	...	...	...	...	...	...	...
...	...	...	...	...	...	...	...	...
24	12	12	...	...	...	...	...	...
9	9	...	...	...	...	...	...	...
8	6	2	...	...	...	...	...	...
36	25	11	...	...	...	...	...	...
53	40	13	...	...	...	...	...	...
...	...	...	2	2	...	5	3	2
...	...	...	...	...	...	...	...	...
...	...	...	...	...	...	...	...	...
...	...	...	...	...	...	...	...	...
...	...	...	...	...	...	...	...	...
2	2	...	...	...	...	...	...	...
...	...	...	...	...	...	...	...	...
...	...	...	...	...	...	...	...	...
2	2	...	...	...	...	...	...	...
...	...	...	...	...	...	...	...	...
...	...	...	...	...	...	...	...	...
1,382	707	675	54	30	24	73	47	26

TABLE

Occupations, Part B.—

Class.	Group.	Occupation.	State Total. Total.	Males.	Females.
1	2	3	4	5	6
G. Indefinite and Independent.	74a	Well sinkers ...	*29*	14	15
		Excavators ...	*2*	2	...
		Road and canal laborers ...	*171*	108	63
		Quarry-men ...	*5,924*	4,143	1,781
		Rice pounders and huskers ...	*2,922*	156	2,766
		Total Sub-order 74(*a*) ...	**9,048**	**4,423**	**4,625**
	74b	General labor ...	*700,807*	345,290	355,517
	75	Undefined means of livelihood ...	*10,315*	644	9,671
	76a	House-rent and other property not being land ...	*22*	11	11
		Allowances from patrons ...	*22*	2	20
		Total Sub-order 76(*a*) ...	**44**	**13**	**31**
	76b	Educational endowments (scholarships) ...	*9*	9	...
		Mendicancy (not religious) ...	*5,161*	2,612	2,549
		Total Sub-order 76(*b*) ...	**5,170**	**2,621**	**2,549**
	77a	Pension, civil services ...	*1,834*	957	877
		Pension, military services ...	*235*	111	124
		Total Sub-order 77(*a*) ...	**2,069**	**1,068**	**1,001**

XVII.

(State Distribution)—(*Continued*).

TALUQS.

Tovala.			Agastiswaram.			Eranial.		
Total.	Males.	Females.	Total.	Males.	Females.	Total.	Males.	Females.
7	8	9	10	11	12	13	14	15
...	...	...	...	..	...	...	...	...
...	...	...	2	2	...	...	...	...
...	...	...	52	32	20	21	12	9
77	46	31	115	73	42	...	...	...
21	2	19	176	7	169	227	9	218
98	48	50	345	114	231	248	21	227
11,339	5,114	6,225	13,804	6,915	6,889	13,917	6,881	7,036
13	4	9	125	59	66	11	4	7
...	...	...	...	...	...	...	...	..
...	...	..	...	...	...	...	...	...
...	...	...	...	...	...	...	...	...
...	...	...	...	...	...	...	...	...
102	44	58	299	174	125	334	175	159
102	44	58	299	174	125	334	175	159
8	3	5	31	19	12	1	1	...
...	...	...	...	...	...	...	...	...
8	3	5	31	19	12	1	1	...

TABLE

Occupations, Part B.—

Class.	Group.	Occupation.	Taluqs: Kalkulam. Total.	Kalkulam. Males.	Kalkulam. Females.	Vilavankodu. Total.	Vilavankodu. Males.	Vilavankodu. Females.
1	2	3	16	17	18	19	20	21
G. Indefinite and Independent.	74a	Well sinkers ...	...	...	..	...	...	...
		Excavators ...	...	...	...	...	...	...
		Road and canal laborers ...	27	16	11	18	12	6
		Quarry-men ...	...	...	...	27	18	9
		Rice pounders and huskers ...	294	5	289	107	11	96
		Total Sub-order 74(a) ...	321	21	300	152	41	111
	74b	General labor ...	12,537	6,153	6,384	7,354	3,577	3,777
	75	Undefined means of livelihood ...	6	2	4	42	19	23
	76a	House-rent & other property not being land ...	...	...	...	...	...	...
		Allowances from patrons ...	10	2	8	3	...	3
		Total Sub-order 76(a) ...	10	2	8	3	...	3
	76b	Educational endowments (scholarships) ...	...	...	...	...	...	...
		Mendicancy (not religious) ...	116	54	62	60	33	27
		Total Sub-order 76(b) ...	116	54	62	60	33	27
	77a	Pension, civil services ...	15	6	9	32	10	22
		Pension, military services ...	...	...	...	...	...	...
		Total Sub-order 77(a) ...	15	6	9	32	10	22

XVII.

(State Distribution)—(*Continued*).

—(*Continued*).

Neyattankara.			Trivandram.			Nedumangadu.		
Total.	Males.	Females.	Total.	Males.	Females.	Total.	Males.	Females.
22	23	24	25	26	27	28	29	30
14	8	6	...	...	...	...	...	...
...	...	...	...	...	...	...	...	...
13	8	5	21	14	7	...	...	...
...	...	...	23	15	8	...	...	...
96	12	84	425	...	425	20	2	18
123	28	95	469	29	440	20	2	18
27,422	13,297	14.125	18,914	8,915	9,999	18,060	8,346	9,714
23	13	10	122	64	58	...	...	...
...	...	...	15	8	7	...	...	...
...	...	...	9	...	9	...	...	...
...	...	...	24	8	16	...	...	...
...	...	...	9	9	...	...	...	...
271	135	136	620	298	322	199	104	95
271	135	136	629	307	322	199	104	95
17	9	8	636	290	346	16	7	9
...	...	...	197	93	104	...	...	...
17	9	8	833	383	450	16	7	9

TABLE

Occupations, Part B.—

Class.	Group.	Occupation.	Sirayinkil. Total.	Sirayinkil. Males.	Sirayinkil. Females.	Kottarakkara. Total.	Kottarakkara. Males.	Kottarakkara. Females.
1	2	3	31	32	33	34	35	36
G. Indefinite and Independent.	74*a*	Well sinkers ...	...	...	...	...	...	...
		Excavators ...	...	...	...	...	...	...
		Road and canal laborers ...	...	...	...	...	...	...
		Quarry-men ...	15	9	6	343	229	114
		Rice pounders and huskers ...	59	5	54	31	...	31
		Total Sub-order 74(*a*) ...	74	14	60	374	229	145
	74*b*	General labor ...	22,188	10,966	11,222	23,163	11,000	12,163
	75	Undefined means of livelihood ...	60	26	34	7	2	5
	76*a*	House-rent & other property not being land ..	...	...	...	...	...	...
		Allowances from patrons ...	...	...	...	...	...	...
		Total Sub-order 76(*a*) ...	...	...	...	...	...	...
	76*b*	Educational endowments (scholarships) ...	...	...	...	...	...	...
		Mendicancy (not religious) ..	281	134	147	96	45	51
		Total Sub-order 76(*b*) ..	281	134	147	96	45	51
	77*a*	Pension, civil services ...	76	44	32	1	1	...
		Pension, military services ...	...		...	...	...	...
		Total Sub-order 77(*a*) ...	76	44	32	1	1	...

Taluqs

XVII.

(State Distribution)—(*Continued*).

—(*Continued*).

Pattanapuram.			Shenkotta.			Quilon.		
Total.	Males.	Females.	Total.	Males.	Females.	Total.	Males.	Females.
37	38	39	40	41	42	43	44	45
...	...	...	15	6	9	...	...	...
...	...	..	...	...	...	...	...	...
...	...	...	...	...	...	19	14	5
...	...	...	...	...	...	728	452	276
18	...	18	70	...	70	114	...	114
18	...	18	85	6	79	861	466	395
12,926	6,612	6,314	11,875	6,089	5,786	21,364	10,250	11,114
...	...	...	23	9	14	44	19	25
...	...	...	...	...	...	7	3	4
...	...	...	...	...	...	...	...	...
...	...	...	...	...	...	7	3	4
...	...	...	...	...	...	...	..	...
211	103	108	66	30	36	273	152	121
211	103	108	66	30	36	273	152	121
3	1	2	1	1	...	100	59	41
...	...	...	...	...	...	38	18	20
3	1	2	1	1	...	138	77	61

TABLE

Occupations, Part B.—

Class.	Group.	Occupation.	Taluqs: Kunnattur. Total.	Kunnattur. Males.	Kunnattur. Females.	Karungappalli. Total.	Karungappalli. Males.	Karungappalli. Females.
1	2	3	46	47	48	49	50	51
G. Indefinite and Independent.	74*a*	Well sinkers ...	...	...	...	...	...	...
		Excavators ...	...	...	...	...	...	...
		Road and canal laborers ...	...	...	...	...	...	...
		Quarry-men ...	173	114	59	...	...	...
		Rice pounders and huskers ...	61	2	59	30	8	22
		Total Sub-order 74(*a*) ...	234	116	118	30	8	22
	74*b*	General labor ...	22,240	11,662	10,578	26,712	12,718	13,994
	75	Undefined means of livelihood ...	...	...	...	7	2	5
	76*a*	House-rent & other property not being land ...	...	...	...	...	...	...
		Allowances from patrons ...	...	...	...	...	...	...
		Total Sub-order 76(*a*) ...	...	...	...	...	...	...
	76*b*	Educational endowments (scholarships) ...	...	...	...	...	...	...
		Mendicancy (not religious) ..	136	67	69	370	187	183
		Total Sub-order 76(*b*) ...	136	67	69	370	187	183
	77*a*	Pension, civil services ...	...	...	...	30	17	13
		Pension, military services ...	...	...	...	...	...	...
		Total Sub-order 77(*a*) ...	...	...	...	30	17	13

XVII.

(State Distribution)—(*Continued*).

—(*Continued*).

Kartigappalli.			Mavellikkara.			Chenganur.		
Total.	Males.	Females.	Total.	Males.	Females.	Total.	Males.	Females.
52	53	54	55	56	57	58	59	60
...	...	...	...	...	...	...	...	...
...	...	...	...	...	...	...	...	...
...	...	...	...	...	...	...	...	...
220	158	62	113	88	25	526	397	129
143	6	137	43	1	42	70	12	58
363	164	199	156	89	67	596	409	187
35,372	17,159	18,213	36,650	17,325	19,325	24,104	11,477	12,627
29	15	14	79	52	27	93	19	74
...	...	...	...	...	...	...	...	...
...	...	...	...	...	...	...	...	...
...	...	...	...	...	...	...	...	...
...	...	...	...	...	...	...	...	...
163	85	78	115	59	56	106	56	50
163	85	78	115	59	56	106	56	50
79	48	31	69	40	29	70	37	33
...	...	...	...	...	...	...	...	...
79	48	31	69	40	29	70	37	33

TABLE

Occupations, Part B.—

Class.	Group.	Occupation.	Taluqs: Tiruvalla. Total.	Tiruvalla. Males.	Tiruvalla. Females.	Ambalappula. Total.	Ambalappula. Males.	Ambalappula. Females.
1	2	3	61	62	63	64	65	66
G. Indefinite and Independent.	74*a*	Well sinkers ...	...	...	...	...	...	...
		Excavators ...	...	...	...	...	...	...
		Road and canal laborers ...	...	...	...	...	...	...
		Quarry-men ...	922	736	186	469	315	154
		Rice pounders and huskers ...	143	14	129	303	16	287
		Total Sub-order 74(*a*) ...	1,065	750	315	772	331	441
	74*b*	General labor ...	38,250	18,486	19,764	30,349	14,916	15,433
	75	Undefined means of livelihood ...	47	23	24	51	21	30
	76*a*	House-rent and other property not being land ...	...	...	...	...	...	...
		Allowances from patrons ...	...	...	...	...	...	...
		Total Sub-order 76(*a*) ...	...	...	...	...	...	...
	76*b*	Educational endowments (scholarships) ...	...	...	...	...	...	...
		Mendicancy (not religious) ...	151	87	64	259	134	125
		Total Sub-order 76(*b*) ...	151	87	64	259	134	125
	77*a*	Pension, civil services ...	43	24	19	77	38	39
		Pension, military services ...	...	...	...	...	...	...
		Total Sub-order 77(*a*) ...	43	24	19	77	38	39

XVII.

(State Distribution)—(*Continued*).

—(*Continued*).

Sherttala.			Vykkam.			Ettumanur.		
Total.	Males.	Females.	Total.	Males.	Females.	Total.	Males.	Females.
67	68	69	70	71	72	73	74	75
...	...	...	...	...	...	...	...	...
...	...	...	...	...	...	...	...	...
...	...	...	...	...	...	...	...	..
...	...	...	475	314	161	153	98	55
27	13	14	54	7	47	29	4	25
27	13	14	529	321	208	182	102	80
32,305	16,309	15,996	26,105	12,380	13,725	30,803	14,940	15,863
3,649	...	3,649	518	13	505	590	...	590
...	...	...	...	...	...	...	...	...
...	...	...	...	...	...	...	...	...
...	...	...	...	...	..	...	...	...
...	...	..	...	...	...	...	...	...
121	64	57	261	106	155	77	38	39
121	64	57	261	106	155	77	38	39
24	10	14	50	28	22	6	2	4
...	...	...	...	...	...	...	...	...
24	10	14	50	28	22	6	2	4

TABLE

Occupations, Part B.—

Class.	Group.	Occupation.	Taluqs: Kottayam. Total.	Kottayam. Males.	Kottayam. Females.	Changanacheri. Total.	Changanacheri. Males.	Changanacheri. Females.
1	2	3	76	77	78	79	80	81
G. Indefinite and Independent.	74a	Well sinkers ...	...	...	...	...	...	...
		Excavators ...	...	...	...	...	...	...
		Road and canal laborers ...	...	...	...	...	...	...
		Quarry-men ..	315	216	99	446	312	134
		Rice pounders and huskers ...	47	7	40	57	...	57
		Total Sub-order 74(a) ...	362	223	139	503	312	191
	74b	General labor ...	20,075	9,953	10,122	26,245	13,014	13,231
	75	Undefined means of livelihood ...	424	...	424	839	28	811
	76a	House-rent and other property not being land ...	...	...	...	...	...	...
		Allowances from patrons ...	...	...	...	...	...	...
		Total Sub-order 76(a) ...	...	...	...	...	...	...
	76b	Educational endowments (scholarships) ...	...	...	...	...	...	...
		Mendicancy (not religious) ...	47	22	25	99	48	51
		Total Sub-order 76(b) ...	47	22	25	99	48	51
	77a	Pension, civil services ...	170	92	78	109	62	47
		Pension, military services ...	...	...	...	...	...	...
		Total Sub-order 77(a) ...	170	92	78	109	62	47

XVII.

(State Distribution)—(*Continued*).

—(*Continued*).

Meenachal.			Muvattupula.			Todupula.		
Total.	Males.	Females.	Total.	Males.	Females.	Total.	Males.	Females.
82	83	84	85	86	87	88	89	90
...	...	...	...	...	...	...	...	...
...	...	...	...	...	...	•.	...	...
...	...	...	...	...	...	...	...	...
..	...	...	343	218	125	...	...	...
19	...	19	58	...	58	22	...	22
19	...	19	401	218	183	22	...	22
9,556	4,593	4,963	27,198	13,076	14,122	5,256	2,467	2,789
104	9	95	204	58	146	178	53	125
...	..	...	...	...	...	...	...	...
...	...	...	...	...	...	...	...	...
...	...	...	...	...	...	...	...	...
...	...	...	...	...	...	...	...	...
58	27	26	46	26	20	12	7	5
53	27	26	46	26	20	12	7	5
45	29	16	1	1	...	8	5	3
...	...	...	...	...	...	...	...	...
45	29	16	1	1	...	8	5	3

TABLE

Occupations, Part B.—

Class.	Group.	Occupation.	Taluqs: Kunnattunadu. Total.	Kunnattunadu. Males.	Kunnattunadu. Females.	Alangadu. Total.	Alangadu. Males.	Alangadu. Females.
1	2	3	91	92	93	94	95	96
G. Indefinite and Independent.	74a	Well sinkers ...	...	...	...	...	...	...
		Excavators ...	...	...	...	...	...	...
		Road and canal laborers ...	...	...	...	...	...	...
		Quarry-men ...	181	116	65	8	5	3
		Rice pounders and huskers ...	58	13	45	38	...	38
		Total Sub-order 74(a) ...	239	129	110	46	5	41
	74b	General labor ...	38,840	20,421	18,419	24,571	11,687	12,884
	75	Undefined means of livelihood ...	1,069	49	1,020	165	65	100
	76a	House-rent and other property not being land ...	...	...	...	...	...	...
		Allowances from patrons ...	...	...	...	...	...	...
		Total Sub-order 76(a) ...	...	...	...	...	...	...
	76b	Educational endowments (scholarships) ...	...	...	...	...	...	...
		Mendicancy (not religious) ...	50	27	23	85	46	39
		Total Sub-order 76(b) ...	50	27	23	85	46	39
	77a	Pension, civil services ...	15	9	6	58	38	20
		Pension, military services ...	...	...	...	...	...	...
		Total Sub-order 77(a) ...	15	9	6	58	38	20

XVII.

(State Distribution)—(*Continued*).

—(*Continued*).

Parur.			Cardamom Hills.			Periyar and Thekkadi.		
Total.	Males.	Females.	Total.	Males.	Females.	Total.	Males.	Females.
97	98	99	100	101	102	103	104	105
...	...	...	...	...	...	...	...	...
...	...	...	...	...	...	...	...	...
...	...	...	...	...	...	...	...	...
249	212	37	...	...	...	3	2	1
62	...	62	...	...	...	...	...	...
311	212	99	...	...	...	3	2	1
24,121	13,799	10,322	4,835	2,904	1,931	2,357	1,889	468
1,770	...	1,770	15	10	5	8	6	2
...	...	...	...	...	...	...	...	...
...	...	...	...	...	...	...	...	...
...	...	...	...	...	...	...	...	...
...	...	...	...	...	...	...	...	...
81	44	37	...	...	...	1	1	...
81	44	37	...	...	...	1	1	...
43	26	17	...	...	...	...	...	...
...	...	...	...	...	...	...	...	...
43	26	17	...	...	...	...	...	...

TABLE

Occupations, Part B.—

Occupation and Class.			State Total.		
Class.	Group.	Occupation.	Total.	Males.	Females.
1	2	3	4	5	6
G. Indefinite and Independent.	77b	Inmates of Asylums, &c. ...	*81*	**55**	**26**
		Prisoners, under trial ...	*115*	**108**	**7**
		Prisoners, for debt ...	*37*	**37**	...
		Prisoners, convicted ...	*591*	**570**	**21**
		Total Sub-order 77(*b*) ...	**824**	**770**	**54**
		Total Class G. ...	*728,277*	*354,829*	*373,448*
		Not stated ...	**821**	**282**	**539**
		Grand Total ...	*2,557,736*	*1,290,415*	*1,267,321*

XVII.

(State Distribution)—(*Continued*).

Taluqs.								
Tovala.			Agastiswaram.			Eranial.		
Total.	Males.	Females.	Total.	Males.	Females.	Total.	Males.	Females.
7	8	9	10	11	12	13	14	15
...		...	...	...	...	...	...	...
...	...	...	3	3	...	6	6	...
...	...	...	4	4	...	...	...	...
...	...	...	13	11	2	...	...	...
...	...	...	20	18	2	6	6	...
11,560	5,213	6,347	14,624	7,299	7,325	14,517	7,088	7,429
...	...	...	...	...	...	65	36	29
29,751	14,489	15,262	87,241	43,226	44,015	105,098	52,883	52,215

TABLE

Occupations, Part B.—

Class.	Group.	Occupation.	Taluqs: Kalkulam. Total.	Kalkulam. Males.	Kalkulam. Females.	Vilavankodu. Total.	Vilavankodu. Males.	Vilavankodu. Females.
1	2	3	16	17	18	19	20	21
G. Indefinite and Independent.	77*b*	Inmates of Asylums, &c. ...	...	...	...	...	...	...
		Prisoners, under trial ...	3	3	...	...	...	...
		Prisoners, for debt ...	...	...	...	...	...	...
		Prisoners, convicted ...	2	2	...	...	...	...
		Total Sub-order 77(*b*) ...	5	5	...	...	...	...
		Total Class G. ...	13,010	6,243	6,767	7,643	3,680	3,963
		Not stated ...	...	...	...	...	...	...
		Grand Total ...	59,474	29,834	29,640	68,521	35,202	33,319

XVII.

(State Distribution)—(*Continued*).

—(*Continued*).

Neyattankara.			Trivandram.			Nedumangadu.		
Total.	Males.	Females.	Total.	Males.	Females.	Total.	Males.	Females.
22	23	24	25	26	27	28	29	30
...	...	...	81	55	26	...	...	...
6	6	...	18	14	4	...	...	...
...	...	...	13	13	...	...	...	...
...	...	...	412	393	19	...	...	...
6	6	...	524	475	49	...	...	...
27,862	13,488	14,374	21,515	10,181	11,334	18,295	8,459	9,836
...	...	...	1	1	...	...	...	...
110,755	56,953	53,802	111,938	56,909	55,029	55,497	27,857	27,640

TABLE

Occupations, Part B.—

Class.	Group.	Occupation.	Taluqs: Sirayinkil. Total.	Sirayinkil. Males.	Sirayinkil. Females.	Kottarakkara. Total.	Kottarakkara. Males.	Kottarakkara. Females.
1	2	3	31	32	33	34	35	36
G. Indefinite and Independent.	77b	Inmates of Asylums, &c. ...	...	...	...	...	...	...
		Prisoners, under trial ...	5	5	...	3	3	..
		Prisoners, for debt ...	...	...	...	...	...	...
		Prisoners, convicted ...	...	...	...	...	...	...
		Total Sub-order 77(b) ...	5	5	...	3	3	...
		Total Class G. ...	22,684	11,189	11,495	23,644	11,280	12,364
		Not stated ...	...	...	...	...	.	...
		Grand Total ...	97,995	48,271	49,724	71,517	36,055	35,462

XVII.

(State Distribution)—(*Continued*).

—(*Continued*).

Pattanapuram.			Shenkotta.			Quilon.		
Total.	Males.	Females.	Total.	Males.	Females.	Total.	Males.	Females.
37	38	39	40	41	42	43	44	45
...	...	...	...	...	...	...	...	...
8	8	...	4	4	...	12	9	3
...	...	...	...	...	...	12	12	...
...	...	...	...	...	...	91	91	...
8	8	...	4	4	...	115	112	3
13,166	6,724	6 442	12,054	6,139	5,915	22,802	11,079	11,723
...	...	...	...	...	...	592	176	416
39,447	19,858	19,589	32,088	15,700	16,388	121,935	60,832	61,103

TABLE

Occupations, Part B.—

Class.	Group.	Occupation.	Taluqs: Kunnattur. Total.	Kunnattur. Males.	Kunnattur. Females.	Karunagappalli. Total.	Karunagappalli. Males.	Karunagappalli. Females.
1	2	3	46	47	48	49	50	51
G. Indefinite and Independent.	77b	Inmates of Asylums, &c. ...	...	...	...	...	...	...
		Prisoners, under trial ...	...	...	...	...	...	...
		Prisoners, for debt ...	...	...	...	...	...	...
		Prisoners, convicted ...	...	...	...	...	...	...
		Total Sub-order 77(b) ...	...	...	...	...	...	...
		Total Class G. ...	22,610	11,845	10,765	27,149	12,932	14,217
		Not stated ...	...	...	...	...	...	...
		Grand Total ...	73,529	37,397	36,132	108,826	52,862	55,964

XVII.

(State Distribution)—(*Continued*).

—(*Continued*).

Kartigappalli.			Mavellikkara.			Chenganur.		
Total.	Males.	Females.	Total.	Males.	Females.	Total.	Males.	Females.
52	53	54	55	56	57	58	59	60
...	...	...	...	...	...	...	...	...
...	...	...	5	5	...	...	...	...
...	...	...	...	...	...	...	...	...
...	...	...	...	...	...	...	...	...
...	...	...	5	5	...	...	...	...
36,006	17,471	18,535	37,074	17,570	19,504	24,969	11,998	12,971
...	...	...	...	...	...	...	...	..
91,950	45,216	46,734	103,619	52,494	51,125	93,960	48,443	45,517

TABLE

Occupations, Part B.—

Class.	Group.	Occupation.	Taluqs — Tiruvalla. Total.	Tiruvalla. Males.	Tiruvalla. Females.	Ambalappula. Total.	Ambalappula. Males.	Ambalappula. Females.
1	2	3	61	62	63	64	65	66
G. Indefinite and Independent.	77b	Inmates of Asylums, &c. ...	...	...	...	...	...	...
		Prisoners, under trial ...	13	13	...	...		...
		Prisoners, for debt ...	...	...	...	8	8	...
		Prisoners, convicted ...	...	...	...	38	38	...
		Total Sub-order 77(b) ...	13	13		46	46	...
		Total Class G. ...	39,569	19,383	20,186	31,554	15,486	16,068
		Not stated ...	...	...	...	...	...	...
		Grand Total ...	122,142	62,514	59,628	94,745	46,909	47,836

XVII.

(State Distribution)—(Continued).

—(Continued).

Sherttala.			Vykkam.			Ettumanur.		
Total.	Males.	Females.	Total.	Males.	Females.	Total.	Males.	Females.
67	68	69	70	71	72	73	74	75
...	...	...	...	...	...	...	...	...
8	8	...	4	4	...	...	...	...
...	...	...	...	...	...	...	...	...
...	...	...	...	...	...	...	...	...
8	8	...	4	4	...	...	...	...
36,134	16,404	19,730	27,467	12,852	14,615	31,658	15,082	16,576
...	...	...	1	1	...	...	...	...
117,261	58,448	58,813	80,628	40,947	39,681	80,823	41,536	39,287

TABLE

Occupations, Part B.—

Class.	Group.	Occupation.	Taluqs: Kottayam. Total.	Kottayam. Males.	Kottayam. Females.	Changanacheri. Total.	Changanacheri. Males.	Changanacheri. Females.
1	2	3	76	77	78	79	80	81
G. Indefinite and Independent.	77b	Inmates of Asylums, &c. ...	...	...	...	...	...	...
		Prisoners, under trial ...	...	...	...	9	9	...
		Prisoners, for debt ...	...	...	...	...	...	...
		Prisoners, convicted ...	25	25	...	...	...	...
		Total Sub-order 77(b) ...	25	25	...	9	9	...
		Total Class G. ...	21,103	10,315	10,788	27,804	13,473	14,331
		Not stated ...	1	1	...	4	4	...
		Grand Total ...	77,094	39,229	37,865	74,722	38,596	36,126

XVII.

(State Distribution)—(*Continued*).

—(*Continued*).

Meenachal.			Muvattupula.			Todupula.		
Total.	Males.	Females.	Total.	Males.	Females.	Total.	Males.	Females.
82	83	84	85	86	87	88	89	90
...	...	...	...	...	...	...	...	...
2	2	...	4	4	...	...	...	...
...	...	...	...	...	...	...	...	...
...	...	...	2	2	...	...	...	...
2	2	...	6	6	...	...	...	...
9,779	4,660	5,119	27,856	13,385	14,471	5,476	2,532	2,944
67	32	35	...	...	...	86	30	56
59,976	30,830	29,146	103,009	51,595	51,414	25,202	12,786	12,416

TABLE

Occupations, Part B.—

Class.	Group.	Occupation.	Taluqs: Kunnattunadu. Total.	Kunnattunadu. Males.	Kunnattunadu. Females.	Alangadu. Total.	Alangadu. Males.	Alangadu. Females.
1	2	3	91	92	93	94	95	96
G. Indefinite and Independent.	77*b*	Inmates of Asylums, &c. ...	...	...	...	...	...	...
		Prisoners, under trial ...	...	...	...	2	2	...
		Prisoners, for debt ...	...	...	...	...	...	...
		Prisoners, convicted ...	...	...	...	...	...	...
		Total Sub-order 77(*b*) ...	...	..	...	2	2	...
		Total Class G. ...	40,213	20,635	19,578	24,927	11,843	13,084
		Not stated ...	...	...	...	...	...	...
		Grand Total ..	114,049	57,216	56,833	70,958	35,944	35,014

XVII.

(State Distribution)—(*Continued*).

—(*Continued*).

Parur.			Cardamom Hills.			Periyar & Thekkadi.		
Total.	Males.	Females.	Total.	Males.	Females.	Total.	Males.	Females.
97	98	99	100	101	102	103	104	105
...	...	...	...	...	..	...	...	...
...	...	...	...	.	...	...	...	...
...	...	...	...	...	...	...	...	...
8	8	...	...	...	...	...	...	...
8	8	...	...	...	..	...	...	...
26,334	14,089	12,245	4,850	2,914	1,936	2,369	1,898	471
...	...	...	...	...	...	4	1	3
59,278	30,082	29,196	11,413	6,714	4,699	3,295	2,588	707

PART II.—STATISTICS (FINAL TABLES).

TABLE I.

Area, Houses and Population.

District or State.	Area.	Number of		Occupied Houses.		
	In square miles.	Towns.	Villages.	Total.	Towns.	Villages.
1	2	3	4	5	6	7
Travancore	6,730	8	247	516,536	21,025	495,511

District or State.	Population.								
	Total.			Males.			Females.		
	Total.	Towns.	Villages.	Total.	Towns.	Villages.	Total.	Towns.	Villages.
1	8	9	10	11	12	13	14	15	16
Travancore	2,557,736	107,693	2,450,043	1,290,415	54,501	1,235,914	1,267,321	53,192	1,214,129

Note. —Areas in British occupation included in the above consisting of the Quilon Cantonment, Regimental lines and Residency Escort, Trivandram.

Occupied Houses	Total Population	Males	Females
717	2,765	1,484	1,281.

TABLE II.

Variation in the Enumerated Population since last Census (February 1881).

District or State.	Total.			Males.			Females.		
	1891.	1881.	Variation.	1891.	1881.	Variation.	1891.	1881.	Variation.
1	2	3	4	5	6	7	8	9	10
Travancore ...	2,557,736	2,401,158	+156,578	1,290,415	1,197,134	+ 93,281	1,267,321	1,204,024	+ 63,297

TABLE III.

Towns and Villages classified by Population.

District or State.	Total number of towns and villages	Total population.	1—199		200—499		500—999		1,000—1,999	
			No.	Population.	No.	Population.	No.	Population.	No.	Population.
1	2	3	4	5	6	7	8	9	10	11
Travancore	255	2,557,736	...	...	...	...	1	716	4	5,583

District or State.	2,000—2,999		3,000—4,999		5,000—9,999		10,000—14,999		15,000—19,999		20,000—49,999		50,000 & over.	
	No.	Population.	No.	Population.	No.	Population.	No.	Population.	No.	Population.	No.	Population.	No.	Population.
1	12	13	14	15	16	17	18	19	20	21	22	23	24	25
Travancore ...	7	18,428	28	121,331	107	823,861	66	790,806	27	453,029	15	343,982	...	...

TABLE IV.

Towns according to Population, compared with the preceding Census.

Town.	District or State.	Municipality Suburbs or Cantonment.	Total Population.			Males.			Females.			Notes. (Change in Areas, &c.)
			1891	1881	Variation.	1891	1881	Variation.	1891	1881	Variation.	
1	2	3	4	5	6	7	8	9	10	11	12	13
Trivandram...	Travancore ...	...	27,661	...	...	14,580	...	...	13,081	...	...	Note.—The figures for 1881 are only approximate, for the towns were not then separately censused and their limits defined as on the present occasion; hence the large variation in the results.
...	...	Residency Escort ...	226	...	...	127	...	...	99	...	...	
		Total ...	27,887	41,173	−13,286	14,707	...	...	13,180	...	...	
Alleppey ...	...	...	22,768	25.754	−2,986	11,286	...	...	11,482	...	...	
Quilon ...	...	...	12,836	...	...	6,514	...	...	6,322	...	...	
...	...	Cantonment..	2,539	...	...	1,357	...	...	1,182	...	...	
		Total ...	15,375	13,588	+1,787	7,871	...	...	7,504	...	...	
Nagercoil ...	...	...	11,187	16,534	−5,347	5,335	...	...	5,852	...	...	
Shenkotta ...	...	...	8,727	7,882	+ 845	4,202	...	...	4,525	...	...	
Vycome ...	...	...	7,769	13,053	−5,284	4,113	...	...	3,656	...	...	
Kottayam ...	...	...	7,090	11,293	−4,203	3,539	...	...	3,551	...	...	
Aripaud ...	...	...	6,890	...	...	3,448	...	...	3,442	...	...	Aripaud was not included as a town in the 1881 census.

TABLE V.

Towns arranged territorially, with Population by Religion.

District or State.	Town.	Total Population.			Hindu.			Mussalman.			Christian.			Jew.		
		Total.	Males.	Females.	Total.	Males.	Females.	Total.	Males.	Females.	Total.	Males.	Females.	Total.	Males.	Females.
1	2	3	4	5	6	7	8	9	10	11	12	13	14	15	16	17
Travancore.	Trivandram ...	27,887	14,707	13,180	24,804	13,243	11,561	1,610	817	793	1,473	647	826	...	...	...
	Alleppey ..	22,768	11,286	11,482	11,304	5,583	5,721	7,470	3,441	4,029	3,994	2,262	1,732	...	...	...
	Quilon ...	15,375	7,871	7,504	7,614	3,948	3,666	3,444	1,806	1,638	4,307	2,112	2,195	10	5	5
	Nagercoil ...	11,187	5,335	5,852	9,632	4,618	5,014	57	33	24	1,498	684	814	...	...	...
	Shenkotta ...	8,727	4,202	4,525	8,402	4,042	4,360	287	140	147	38	20	18	...	...	...
	Vycome ...	7,769	4,113	3,656	6,864	3,610	3,254	90	55	35	815	448	367	...	...	...
	Kottayam ...	7,090	3,539	3,551	4,037	2,021	2,016	197	114	83	2,856	1,404	1,452	...	...	...
	Aripaud ...	6,890	3,448	3,442	5,706	2,872	2,834	240	111	129	944	465	479	...	...	...

TABLE VI.

Religions.

District or State.	Total Population.			Hindu.			Mussalman.		
	Total.	Males.	Females.	Total.	Males.	Females.	Total.	Males.	Females.
1	2	3	4	5	6	7	8	9	10
Travancore ...	2,557,736	1,290,415	1,267,321	1,871,864	941,995	929,869	158,823	81,375	77,448

District or State.	Christian.			Jain.			Parsi.			Jew.			None.		
	Total.	Males.	Females.	Total.	Males.	Females.	Total.	Males.	Females.	Total.	Males.	Females.	Total.	Males.	Females.
1	11	12	13	14	15	16	17	18	19	20	21	22	23	24	25
Travancore ...	526,911	266,969	259,942	10	8	2	1	1	...	125	65	60	2	2	...

TABLE VII.

Ages, by Religions, Part (A)—Total Population.

District or State.	Total Population.			Age Periods.					
				Under 1 year		1 year		2 years	
	Total.	Males.	Females.	Males.	Females.	Males.	Females	Males.	Females.
1	2	3	4	5	6	7	8	9	10
Travancore ...	2,557,736	1,290,415	1,267,321	19,526	23,445	29,500	33,522	34,039	37,031

District or State.	Age Periods—(*Continued*).									
	3 years		4 years		Total 0—4		5—9		10—14	
	Males.	Females.	Males.	Females.	Males.	Females.	Males.	Females.	Males.	Females.
1	11	12	13	14	15	16	17	18	19	20
Travancore ..	39,140	42,180	31,194	32,639	153,399	168,817	158,901	157,960	149,926	137,884

TABLE VII.

Ages, by Religions, Part (A)—Total Population—(*Continued*).

AGE PERIODS—(*Continued*).

15—19		20—24		25—29		30—34		35—39	
Males.	Females.	Males.	Females.	Males.	Females.	Males.	Females.	Males.	Females.
21	22	23	24	25	26	27	28	29	30
119,558	126,727	107,327	117,835	118,359	122,448	100,124	96,089	99,938	81,744

AGE PERIODS—(*Continued*).

40—44		45—49		50—54		55—59		60 and over	
Males.	Females.	Males.	Females.	Males.	Females.	Males.	Females.	Males.	Females.
31	32	33	34	35	36	37	38	39	40
79,920	68,755	58,984	47,983	51,118	47,426	32,417	29,770	60,444	63,883

TABLE VII.

Ages, by Religions, Part (B)—Hindu.

District or State.	Total Hindu.			Age Periods.					
				Under 1 year		1 year		2 years	
	Total.	Males.	Females.	Males.	Females.	Males.	Females.	Males.	Females.
1	2	3	4	5	6	7	8	9	10
Travancore ...	1,871,864	941,995	929,869	14,268	16,989	20,917	23,462	24,082	26,008

District or State.	Age Periods—(*Continued*).									
	3 years		4 years		Total 0—4		5—9		10—14	
	Males.	Females.	Males.	Females.	Males.	Females.	Males.	Females.	Males.	Females.
1	11	12	13	14	15	16	17	18	19	20
Travancore ...	28,029	29,809	22,258	23,068	109,554	119,336	112,681	112,212	106,706	98,250

TABLE VII.

Ages, by Religions, Part (B)—Hindu—(*Continued*).

District or State.	Age Periods—(*Continued*).									
	15—19		20—24		25—29		30—34		35—39	
	Males.	Females.	Males.	Females.	Males.	Females.	Males.	Females.	Males.	Females.
1	21	22	23	24	25	26	27	28	29	30
Travancore ...	87,096	93,409	78,793	87,088	87,893	91,086	74,555	72,076	73,878	61,172

District or State.	Age Periods—(*Continued*).									
	40—44		45—49		50—54		55—59		60 and over	
	Males.	Females.	Males.	Females.	Males.	Females.	Males.	Females.	Males.	Females.
1	31	32	33	34	35	36	37	38	39	40
Travancore ...	59,872	52,225	43,806	35.637	38,256	36,166	23,593	21,875	45,312	49,337

TABLE VII.

Ages, by Religions, Part (C)—Mussalman.

District or State.	Total Mussalman.			Age Periods.					
				Under 1 year		1 year		2 years	
	Total.	Males.	Females.	Males.	Females.	Males.	Females.	Males.	Females.
1	2	3	4	5	6	7	8	9	10
Travancore ...	158,823	81,375	77,448	1,382	1,731	1,893	2,329	2,273	2,527

District or State.	Age Periods—(Continued).									
	3 years		4 years		Total 0—4		5—9		10—14	
	Males.	Females.	Males.	Females.	Males.	Females.	Males.	Females.	Males.	Females.
1	11	12	13	14	15	16	17	18	19	20
Travancore ...	2,524	2,777	2,228	2,366	10,300	11,730	10,671	9,860	9,565	8,487

TABLE VII.

Ages, by Religions, Part (C)—Mussalman—(*Continued*).

District or State.	Age Periods—(*Continued*).									
	15—19		20—24		25—29		30—34		35—39	
	Males.	Females.	Males.	Females.	Males.	Females.	Males.	Females.	Males.	Females.
1	21	22	23	24	25	26	27	28	29	30
Travancore ...	7,577	7,782	6,765	7,121	7,174	7,574	6,099	5,698	6,154	4,825

District or State.	Age Periods—(*Continued*).									
	40—44		45—49		50—54		55—59		60 and over	
	Males.	Females.	Males.	Females.	Males.	Females.	Males.	Females.	Males.	Females.
1	31	32	33	34	35	36	37	38	39	40
Travancore ...	4,827	4,030	3,533	2,635	3,124	2,602	2,003	1,709	3,583	3,395

TABLE VII.
Ages, by Religions, Part (D)—Christian.

District or State.	Total Christian.			Age Periods.					
				Under 1 year		1 year		2 years	
	Total.	Males.	Females.	Males.	Females.	Males.	Females.	Males.	Females.
1	2	3	4	5	6	7	8	9	10
Travancore ...	526,911	266,969	259,942	3,876	4,725	6,689	7,730	7,681	8,495

Age Periods—(*Continued*).

3 years		4 years		Total 0—4		5—9		10—14	
Males.	Females.	Males.	Females.	Males.	Females.	Males.	Females.	Males.	Females.
11	12	13	14	15	16	17	18	19	20
8,585	9,593	6,705	7,202	33,536	37,745	35,540	35,880	33,651	31,138

TABLE VII.

Ages, by Religions, Part (D)—Christian—(*Continued*).

District or State.	Age Periods—(*Continued*).									
	15—19		20—24		25—29		30—34		35—39	
	Males.	Females.	Males.	Females.	Males.	Females.	Males.	Females.	Males.	Females.
1	21	22	23	24	25	26	27	28	29	30
Travancore ...	24,878	25,530	21,763	23,621	23,282	23,775	19,463	18,313	19,898	15,746

Age Periods—(*Continued*).									
40—44		45—49		50—54		55—59		60 and over	
Males.	Females.	Males.	Females.	Males.	Females.	Males.	Females.	Males.	Females.
31	32	33	34	35	36	37	38	39	40
15,217	12,496	11,642	9,709	9,734	8,654	6,819	6,186	11,546	11,149

TABLE VII.

Ages, by Religions, Part (E)—Jain.

District or State.	Total Jain.			Age Periods.															
				Under 1 year		1 year		2 years		3 years		4 years		Total 0—4		5 9		10—14	
	Total.	Males.	Females.	Males.	Females.	Males.	Females.	Males.	Females.	Males.	Females.	Males.	Females.	Males.	Females.	Males.	Females.	Males.	Females.
1	2	3	4	5	6	7	8	9	10	11	12	13	14	15	16	17	18	19	20
Travancore ...	10	8	2	...	...	...	...	...	...	...	...	...	...	...	...	...	...	...	...

District or State.	Age Periods—(*Continued*).																			
	15—19		20—24		25—29		30—34		35—39		40—44		45—49		50—54		55—59		60 & over	
	Males.	Females.	Males.	Females.	Males.	Females.	Males.	Females.	Males.	Females.	Males.	Females.	Males.	Females.	Males.	Females.	Males.	Females.	Males.	Females.
1	21	22	23	24	25	26	27	28	29	30	31	32	33	34	35	36	37	38	39	40
Travancore ...	1	...	1	1	2	1	3	...	1	...	...	...	...	...	...	...	...	...	...	...

TABLE VII.

Ages, by Religions, Part (F)—Parsi.

District or State.	Total Parsi.			Age Periods.															
				Under 1 year		1 year		2 years		3 years		4 years		Total 0—4		5—9		10—14	
	Total.	Males.	Females.	Males.	Females.	Males.	Females.	Males.	Females.	Males.	Females.	Males.	Females.	Males.	Females.	Males.	Females.	Males.	Females.
1	2	3	4	5	6	7	8	9	10	11	12	13	14	15	16	17	18	19	20
Travancore ...	1	1	...	...	...	...	...	...	...	...	...	...	...	...	...	...	...	...	...

District or State.	Age Periods—(*Continued*).																			
	15—19		20—24		25—29		30—34		35—39		40—44		45—49		50—54		55—59		60 & over	
	Males.	Females.	Males.	Females.	Males.	Females.	Males	Females.	Males.	Females.	Males.	Females.	Males.	Females.	Males.	Females.	Males.	Females.	Males.	Females.
1	21	22	23	24	25	26	27	28	29	30	31	32	33	34	35	36	37	38	39	40
Travancore ...	...	...	...	...	...	...	...	...	...	...	...	...	...	...	...	...	1	...	...	...

TABLE VII.

Ages, by Religions, Part (G)—Jew.

District or State.	Total Jew.			Age Periods.															
				Under 1 year		1 year		2 years		3 years		4 years		Total 0–4		5–9		10–14	
	Total.	Males.	Females.	Males.	Females.	Males.	Females.	Males.	Females.	Males.	Females.	Males.	Females.	Males.	Females.	Males.	Females.	Males.	Females.
1	2	3	4	5	6	7	8	9	10	11	12	13	14	15	16	17	18	19	20
Travancore ...	125	65	60	...	...	1	1	3	1	2	1	3	3	9	6	9	8	4	9

District or State.	Age Periods—(*Continued*).																			
	15–19		20–24		25–29		30–34		35–39		40–44		45–49		50–54		55–59		60 & over	
	Males.	Females.	Males.	Females.	Males.	Females.	Males.	Females.	Males.	Females.	Males.	Females.	Males.	Females.	Males.	Females.	Males.	Females.	Males.	Females.
1	21	22	23	24	25	26	27	28	29	30	31	32	33	34	35	36	37	38	39	40
Travancore ...	6	6	5	4	7	12	3	2	7	1	4	4	3	2	4	4	1	...	3	2

TABLE VII.

Ages, by Religions, Part (H)—None.

District or State.	Total None.			Age Periods.															
				Under 1 year		1 year		2 years		3 years		4 years		Total 0—4		5—9		10—14	
	Total.	Males.	Females.	Males.	Females.	Males.	Females.	Males.	Females.	Males.	Females.	Males.	Females.	Males.	Females.	Males.	Females.	Males.	Females.
1	2	3	4	5	6	7	8	9	10	11	12	13	14	15	16	17	18	19	20
Travancore ...	2	2	...	...	...	...	...	...	...	...	...	...	...	...	...	...	...	...	.

District or State.	Age Periods—(*Continued*).																			
	15—19		20—24		25—29		30—34		35—39		40—44		45—49		50—54		55—59		60 and over	
	Males.	Females.	Males.	Females.	Males.	Females.	Males.	Females.	Males.	Females.	Males.	Females.	Males.	Females.	Males.	Females.	Males.	Females.	Males.	Females.
1	21	22	23	24	25	26	27	28	29	30	31	32	33	34	35	36	37	38	39	40
Travancore ...	...	...	...	...	1	...	1	...	...	...	...	...	...	...	...	...	...	...	...	...

TABLE VIII.

Civil Condition by Religion and Age, Part (A)—Total Population.

(1) Unmarried.

District or State.	Total Unmarried.			Age Periods.									
				0—4		5—9		10—14		15—19		20—24	
	Total.	Males.	Females.	Males.	Females.	Males.	Females.	Males.	Females.	Males.	Females.	Males.	Females.
1	2	3	4	5	6	7	8	9	10	11	12	13	14
Travancore...	1,251,140	677,612	573,528	153,397	168,791	158,449	156,724	147,308	124,094	101,864	57,102	52,803	19,010

(1) Unmarried—(*Continued*).

Age Periods—(*Continued*).

25—29		30—34		35—39		40—44		45—49		50—54		55—59		60 and over.	
Males.	Females.	Males.	Females.	Males.	Females.	Males.	Females.	Males.	Females.	Males.	Females.	Males.	Females.	Males.	Females.
15	16	17	18	19	20	21	22	23	24	25	26	27	28	29	30
28,021	12,468	12,187	8,594	7,869	6,866	4,940	5,817	3,044	3,580	2,699	3,782	1,658	2,143	3,373	4,557

TABLE VIII.

Civil Condition by Religion and Age, Part (A)—Total Population.

District or State.	(2) Married.												
	Total Married.			Age Periods.									
				0–4		5–9		10–14		15–19		20–24	
	Total.	Males.	Females.	Males.	Females.	Males.	Females.	Males.	Females.	Males.	Females.	Males.	Females.
1	2	3	4	5	6	7	8	9	10	11	12	13	14
Travancore...	1,119,602	567,088	552,514	2	26	387	1,125	2,519	13,559	17,489	68,970	54,057	96,872

(2) Married—(*Continued*).

Age Periods—(*Continued*).															
25–29		30–34		35–39		40–44		45–49		50–54		55–59		60 and over.	
Males.	Females.	Males.	Females.	Males.	Females.	Males.	Females.	Males.	Females.	Males.	Females.	Males.	Females.	Males.	Females.
15	16	17	18	19	20	21	22	23	24	25	26	27	28	29	30
89,302	105,860	86,100	80,159	89,656	65,590	70,496	45,874	51,486	29,501	41,678	20,694	25,076	11,981	38,840	12,303

TABLE VIII.

Civil Condition by Religion and Age, Part (A)—Total Population.

(3) WIDOWED.

District or State.	Total Widowed.			Age Periods.									
				0—4		5—9		10—14		15—19		20—24	
	Total.	Males.	Females.	Males.	Females.	Males.	Females.	Males.	Females.	Males.	Females.	Males.	Females.
1	2	3	4	5	6	7	8	9	10	11	12	13	14
Travancore...	186,994	45,715	141,279	...	...	65	111	99	231	205	655	467	1,953

(3) WIDOWED—(*Continued*).

AGE PERIODS—(*Continued*).

25—29		30—34		35—39		40—44		45—49		50—54		55—59		60 and over	
Males.	Females.	Males.	Females.	Males.	Females.	Males.	Females.	Males.	Females.	Males.	Females.	Males.	Females.	Males.	Females.
15	16	17	18	19	20	21	22	23	24	25	26	27	28	29	30
1,036	4,120	1,837	7,336	2,413	9,288	4,484	17,064	4,454	14,902	6,741	22,950	5,683	15,646	18,231	47,023

TABLE VIII.

Civil Condition by Religion and Age, Part (B)—Hindu.

(1) UNMARRIED.

District or State.	Total Unmarried.			Age Periods.									
				0—4		5—9		10—14		15—19		20—24	
	Total.	Males.	Females.	Males.	Females.	Males.	Females.	Males.	Females.	Males.	Females.	Males.	Females.
1	2	3	4	5	6	7	8	9	10	11	12	13	14
Travancore...	921,429	500,955	420,474	109,552	119,310	112,497	111,477	105,305	89,861	77,135	45,019	42,878	15,468

(1) UNMARRIED—(*Continued*).

Age Periods—(*Continued*).															
25—29		30—34		35—39		40—44		45—49		50—54		55—59		60 and over.	
Males.	Females.	Males.	Females.	Males.	Females.	Males.	Females.	Males.	Females.	Males.	Females.	Males.	Females.	Males.	Females.
15	16	17	18	19	20	21	22	23	24	25	26	27	28	29	30
23,514	10,292	10,299	7,040	6,695	5,720	4,151	4,828	2,541	2,919	2,244	3,123	1,365	1,694	2,779	3,723

TABLE VIII.

Civil Condition by Religion and Age, Part (B)—Hindu.

District or State.	(2) Married.												
	Total Married.			Age Periods.									
				0—4		5—9		10—14		15—19		20—24	
	Total.	Males.	Females.	Males.	Females.	Males	Females.	Males.	Females.	Males.	Females.	Males.	Females.
1	2	3	4	5	6	7	8	9	10	11	12	13	14
Travancore...	808,310	408 055	400,255	2	26	158	663	1,358	8,241	9,825	47.941	35,622	70,143

(2) Married—(*Continued*).

Age Periods—(*Continued*).															
25—29		30—34		35—39		40—44		45—49		50—54		55—59		60 and over	
Males.	Females.	Males.	Females.	Males.	Females.	Males.	Females.	Males.	Females.	Males.	Females.	Males.	Females.	Males.	Females.
15	16	17	18	19	20	21	22	23	24	25	26	27	28	29	30
63,648	77,686	62,953	59,406	65,425	48,400	52,415	34,028	37,957	21,221	31,051	15,159	18,352	8,385	29,289	8,956

TABLE VIII.
Civil Condition by Religion and Age, Part (B)—Hindu.

District or State.	(3) Widowed. Total Widowed. Total.	Males.	Females.	Age Periods. 0—4 Males.	0—4 Females.	5—9 Males.	5—9 Females.	10—14 Males.	10—14 Females.	15—19 Males.	15—19 Females.	20—24 Males.	20—24 Females.
1	2	3	4	5	6	7	8	9	10	11	12	13	14
Travancore...	142,125	32,985	109,140	...	...	26	72	43	148	136	449	293	1,477

(3) Widowed—(Continued).

Age Periods—(Continued). 25—29 Males.	25—29 Females.	30—34 Males.	30—34 Females.	35—39 Males.	35—39 Females.	40—44 Males.	40—44 Females.	45—49 Males.	45—49 Females.	50—54 Males.	50—54 Females.	55—59 Males.	55—59 Females.	60 & over. Males.	60 & over. Females.
15	16	17	18	19	20	21	22	23	24	25	26	27	28	29	30
731	3,108	1,303	5,630	1,758	7,052	3,306	13,369	3,308	11,497	4,961	17,884	3,876	11,796	13,244	36,658

TABLE VIII.

Civil Condition by Religion and Age, Part (C)—Mussalman.

District or State.	(1) Unmarried.												
	Total Unmarried.			Age Periods.									
				0—4		5—9		10—14		15—19		20—24	
	Total.	Males.	Females.	Males.	Females.	Males.	Females.	Males.	Females.	Males.	Females.	Males.	Females.
1	2	3	4	5	6	7	8	9	10	11	12	13	14
Travancore ..	80,407	43,872	36,535	10,300	11,730	10,605	9,752	9,423	7,621	6,736	3,284	3,542	1,135

(1) Unmarried—(*Continued*).

Age Periods—(*Continued*).															
25—29		30—34		35—39		40—44		45—49		50—54		55—59		60 and over.	
Males.	Females.	Males.	Females.	Males.	Females.	Males.	Females.	Males.	Females.	Males.	Females.	Males.	Females.	Males.	Females.
15	16	17	18	19	20	21	22	23	24	25	26	27	28	29	30
1,682	813	530	551	383	436	192	376	137	224	120	218	69	157	153	238

TABLE VIII.

Civil Condition by Religion and Age, Part (C)—Mussalman.

District or State.	(2) Married.												
	Total Married.			Age Periods.									
				0—4		5—9		10—14		15—19		20—24	
	Total.	Males.	Females.	Males.	Females.	Males.	Females.	Males.	Females.	Males.	Females.	Males.	Females.
1	2	3	4	5	6	7	8	9	10	11	12	13	14
Travancore ...	68,045	34,822	33,223	...	...	55	97	133	835	821	4,422	3,186	5,864

(2) Married—(*Continued*).

Age Periods—(*Continued*).															
25—29		30—34		35—39		40—44		45—49		50—54		55—59		60 and over	
Males.	Females.	Males.	Females.	Males.	Females.	Males.	Females.	Males.	Females.	Males.	Females.	Males.	Females.	Males.	Females.
15	16	17	18	19	20	21	22	23	24	25	26	27	28	29	30
5,418	6,527	5,431	4,712	5,644	3,841	4,376	2,713	3,209	1,690	2,619	1,152	1,591	709	2,339	661

TABLE VIII.

Civil Condition by Religion and Age, Part (C)—Mussalman.

(3) WIDOWED.

District or State.	Total Widowed.			Age Periods. 0—4		5—9		10—14		15—19		20—24	
	Total.	Males.	Females.	Males.	Females.	Males.	Females.	Males.	Females.	Males.	Females.	Males.	Females.
1	2	3	4	5	6	7	8	9	10	11	12	13	14
Travancore...	10,371	2,681	7,690	...	..	11	11	9	31	20	76	37	122

(3) WIDOWED—(*Continued*).

AGE PERIODS—(*Continued*).

25—29		30—34		35—39		40—44		45—49		50—54		55—59		60 and over.	
Males.	Females.	Males.	Females.	Males.	Females.	Males.	Females.	Males.	Females.	Males.	Females.	Males.	Females.	Males.	Females
15	16	17	18	19	20	21	22	23	24	25	26	27	28	29	30
74	234	138	435	127	548	259	941	187	721	385	1,232	343	843	1,091	2,496

TABLE VIII.

Civil Condition by Religion and Age, Part (D)—Christian.

(1) UNMARRIED.

DISTRICT OR STATE.	TOTAL UNMARRIED.			AGE PERIODS. 0—4		5—9		10—14		15—19		20—24	
	Total.	Males.	Females.	Males.	Females.	Males.	Females.	Males.	Females.	Males.	Females.	Males.	Females.
1	2	3	4	5	6	7	8	9	10	11	12	13	14
Travancore...	249,233	132,741	116,492	33,536	37,745	35,338	35,487	32,576	26,604	17,986	8,796	6,378	2,406

(1) UNMARRIED—(*Continued*).

AGE PERIODS—(*Continued*).

25—29		30—34		35—39		40—44		45—49		50—54		55—59		60 and over.	
Males.	Females.	Males.	Females.	Males.	Females.	Males.	Females.	Males.	Females.	Males.	Females.	Males.	Females.	Males.	Females.
15	16	17	18	19	20	21	22	23	24	25	26	27	28	29	30
2,818	1,362	1,356	1,003	790	710	597	613	366	437	335	441	224	292	441	596

TABLE VIII.

Civil Condition by Religion and Age, Part (D)—Christian.

District or State.	(2) Married.												
	Total Married.			Age Periods.									
				0—4		5—9		10—14		15—19		20—24	
	Total.	Males.	Females.	Males.	Females.	Males.	Females.	Males.	Females.	Males.	Females.	Males.	Females.
1	2	3	4	5	6	7	8	9	10	11	12	13	14
Travancore...	243,189	124,180	119,009	...	...	174	365	1,028	4,482	6,843	16,604	15,248	20,861

(2) Married—(*Continued*).															
Age Periods—(*Continued*).															
25—29		30—34		35—39		40—44		45—49		50—54		55—59		60 and over.	
Males.	Females.	Males.	Females.	Males.	Females.	Males.	Females.	Males.	Females.	Males.	Females.	Males.	Females.	Males.	Females.
15	16	17	18	19	20	21	22	23	24	25	26	27	28	29	30
20,234	21,636	17,711	16,040	18,580	13,348	13,701	9,130	10,317	6,588	8,004	4,382	5,131	2,887	7,209	2,686

TABLE VIII.

Civil Condition by Religion and Age, Part (D)—Christian.

(3) WIDOWED.

District or State.	Total Widowed.			Age Periods.									
				0—4		5—9		10—14		15—19		20—24	
	Total.	Males.	Females.	Males.	Females.	Males.	Females.	Males.	Females.	Males.	Females.	Males.	Females.
1	2	3	4	5	6	7	8	9	10	11	12	13	14
Travancore...	34,489	10,048	24.441	...	...	28	28	47	52	49	130	137	354

(3) WIDOWED—(Continued).

Age Periods—(Continued)															
25—29		30—34		35—39		40—44		45—49		50—54		55—59		60 & over.	
Males.	Females.	Males.	Females.	Males.	Females.	Males.	Females.	Males.	Females.	Males.	Females.	Males.	Females.	Males.	Females.
15	16	17	18	19	20	21	22	23	24	25	26	27	28	29	30
230	777	396	1,270	528	1,688	919	2,753	959	2,684	1,395	3,831	1,464	3,007	3,896	7,867

TABLE VIII.

Civil Condition by Religion and Age, Part (E)—Jain.

(1) UNMARRIED.

District or State.	Total Unmarried.			Age Periods. 0—4		5—9		10—14		15—19		20—24	
	Total.	Males.	Females.	Males	Females	Males.	Females.	Males.	Females.	Males.	Females.	Males.	Females
1	2	3	4	5	6	7	8	9	10	11	12	13	14
Travancore ..	3	3	...	...	...	...	...	...	...	1	...	1	...

(1) UNMARRIED—(*Continued*).

AGE PERIODS—(*Continued*).

25—29		30—34		35—39		40—44		45—49		50—54		55—59		60 and over.	
Males.	Females.	Males.	Females.	Males.	Females.	Males.	Females.	Males.	Females.	Males.	Females.	Males.	Females.	Males.	Females.
15	16	17	18	19	20	21	22	23	24	25	26	27	28	29	30
...	...	1	...	...	...	...	...	...	...	...	...	...	...	...	...

TABLE VIII.

Civil Condition by Religion and Age, Part (E)—Jain.

(2) Married.

District or State.	Total Married.			Age Periods. 0–4		5–9		10–14		15–19		20–24	
	Total.	Males.	Females.	Males.	Females.	Males.	Females.	Males.	Females.	Males	Females.	Males.	Females
1	2	3	4	5	6	7	8	9	10	11	12	13	14
Travancore ...	7	5	2	...	..	...	...	...	...	...	..	...	1

(2) Married—(Continued).

Age Periods—(Continued).

25–29		30–34		35–39		40–44		45–49		50–54		55–59		60 and over	
Males.	Females.	Males.	Females.	Males.	Females.	Males.	Females.	Males.	Females.	Males.	Females.	Males.	Females.	Males.	Females.
15	16	17	18	19	20	21	22	23	24	25	26	27	28	29	30
2	1	2	...	1	...	...	...	..	...	...	...	...	...	...	...

TABLE VIII.
Civil Condition by Religion and Age, Part (F)—Parsi.

(2) MARRIED.

District or State.	Total Married.			Age Periods. 0—4		5—9		10—14		15—19		20—24	
	Total.	Males.	Females.	Males.	Females.	Males.	Females.	Males.	Females.	Males.	Females.	Males.	Females.
1	2	3	4	5	6	7	8	9	10	11	12	13	14
Travancore...	1	1	...	...	...	...	...	...	...	...	..	...	...

(2) MARRIED—(Continued).

AGE PERIODS—(Continued).

25—29		30—34		35—39		40—44		45—49		50—54		55—59		60 and over.	
Males.	Females.	Males.	Females.	Males.	Females.	Males.	Females.	Males.	Females.	Males.	Females.	Males.	Females.	Males.	Females.
15	16	17	18	19	20	21	22	23	24	25	26	27	28	29	30
...	...	...	...	...	...	...	...	...	...	...	...	1	...	...	..

TABLE VIII.

Civil Condition by Religion and Age, Part (G)—Jew.

(1) UNMARRIED.

DISTRICT OR STATE.	TOTAL UNMARRIED.			AGE PERIODS.									
				0—4		5—9		10—14		15—19		20—24	
	Total.	Males.	Females.	Males.	Females.	Males.	Females.	Males.	Females.	Males.	Females.	Males.	Females.
1	2	3	4	5	6	7	8	9	10	11	12	13	14
Travancore...	66	39	27	9	6	9	8	4	8	6	3	4	1

(1) UNMARRIED—(*Continued*).

AGE PERIODS—(*Continued*).															
25—29		30—34		35—39		40—44		45—49		50—54		55—59		60 and over	
Males.	Females.	Males.	Females.	Males.	Females.	Males.	Females.	Males.	Females.	Males.	Females.	Males.	Females.	Males.	Females.
15	16	17	18	19	20	21	22	23	24	25	26	27	28	29	30
6	1	...	...	1	...	...	...	...	...	...	...	...	...	...	...

TABLE VIII.

Civil Condition by Religion and Age, Part (G)—Jew.

(2) MARRIED.

DISTRICT OR STATE.	TOTAL MARRIED.			AGE PERIODS.									
				0—4		5—9		10—14		15—19		20—24	
	Total.	Males.	Females.	Males.	Females.	Males.	Females.	Males.	Females.	Males.	Females.	Males.	Females.
1	2	3	4	5	6	7	8	9	10	11	12	13	14
Travancore...	50	25	25	...	...	...	...	...	1	...	3	1	3

(2) MARRIED—(*Continued*).

AGE PERIODS—(*Continued*).

25—29		30—34		35—39		40—44		45—49		50—54		55—59		60 and over	
Males.	Females.	Males.	Females.	Males.	Females.	Males.	Females.	Males.	Females.	Males.	Females.	Males.	Females.	Males.	Females.
15	16	17	18	19	20	21	22	23	24	25	26	27	28	29	30
...	10	3	1	6	1	4	3	3	2	4	1	1	...	3	...

TABLE VIII.

Civil Condition by Religion and Age, Part (G)—Jew.

District or State.	(3) Widowed.												
	Total Widowed.			Age Periods.									
				0—4		5—9		10—14		15—19		20—24	
	Total.	Males.	Females.	Males.	Females.	Males.	Females.	Males.	Females.	Males.	Females.	Males.	Females.
1	2	3	4	5	6	7	8	9	10	11	12	13	14
Travancore...	9	1	8	...	...	...	...	...	...	...	...	...	...

(3) Widowed—(*Continued*).

Age Periods—(*Continued*).															
25—29		30—34		35—39		40—44		45—49		50—54		55—59		60 & over.	
Males.	Females.	Males.	Females.	Males.	Females.	Males.	Females.	Males.	Females.	Males.	Females.	Males.	Females.	Males.	Females.
15	16	17	18	19	20	21	22	23	24	25	26	27	28	29	30
1	1	...	1	...	...	...	1	...	...	...	3	...	...	...	2

TABLE VIII.
Civil Condition by Religion and Age, Part (H)—None.

District or State.	(1) Unmarried.												
	Total Unmarried.			Age Periods.									
				0–4		5—9		10—14		15—19		20—24	
	Total.	Males.	Females.	Males.	Females.	Males.	Females.	Males.	Females.	Males.	Females.	Males.	Females.
1	2	3	4	5	6	7	8	9	10	11	12	13	14
Travancore ..	2	2	...	...	...	...	...	...	...	...	...	...	...

(1) Unmarried—(Continued).															
Age Periods—(Continued).															
25—29		30—34		35—39		40—44		45—49		50—54		55—59		60 and over.	
Males.	Females.	Males.	Females.	Males.	Females.	Males.	Females.	Males.	Females.	Males.	Females.	Males.	Females.	Males.	Females.
15	16	17	18	19	20	21	22	23	24	25	26	27	28	29	30
1	...	1	...	...	...	...	...	...	...	...	...	...	...	...	...

TABLE IX.

Education by Religion and Age, Part (A)—Total Population.

DISTRICT OR STATE.	TOTAL POPULATION.			TOTAL BY EDUCATION.							
				Learning.		Literate.		Illiterate.		Not stated.	
	Total.	Males.	Females.	Males.	Females.	Males.	Females.	Males.	Females.	Males.	Females.
1	2	3	4	5	6	7	8	9	10	11	12
Travancore ...	2,557,736	1,290,415	1,267,321	51,955	9,687	246,557	34,139	991,898	1,223,494	5	1

AGE PERIODS.

0—14

Total.		Learning.		Literate.		Illiterate.		Not stated.	
Males.	Females.	Males.	Females.	Males.	Females.	Males.	Females.	Males.	Females.
13	14	15	16	17	18	19	20	21	22
462,226	464,661	45,911	8,238	15,395	5,713	400,918	450,710	2	...

TABLE IX.

Education by Religion and Age, Part (A)—Total Population—(*Continued*).

District or State.	Age Periods—(*Continued*). 15—24 Total. Males.	Total. Females.	Learning. Males.	Learning. Females.	Literate. Males.	Literate. Females.	Illiterate. Males.	Illiterate. Females.	Not stated. Males.	Not stated. Females.
1	23	24	25	26	27	28	29	30	31	32
Travancore ...	226,885	244,562	4,455	689	60,846	9,381	161,584	234,492	...	...

Age Periods—(*Continued*). 25 and over. Total. Males.	Total. Females.	Learning. Males.	Learning. Females.	Literate. Males.	Literate. Females.	Illiterate. Males.	Illiterate. Females.	Not stated. Males.	Not stated. Females.
33	34	35	36	37	38	39	40	41	42
601,304	558,098	1,589	760	170,316	19,045	429,396	538,292	3	1

TABLE IX.

Education by Religion and Age, Part (B)—Hindu.

District or State.	Total Hindu.			Total by Education.							
				Learning.		Literate.		Illiterate.		Not stated.	
	Total.	Males.	Females.	Males.	Females.	Males.	Females.	Males.	Females.	Males.	Females.
1	2	3	4	5	6	7	8	9	10	11	12
Travancore	1,871,864	941,995	929,869	38,349	6,791	177,474	23,836	726,169	899,241	3	1

Age Periods.

0—14.

Total.		Learning.		Literate.		Illiterate.		Not stated.	
Males.	Females.	Males.	Females.	Males.	Females.	Males.	Females.	Males.	Females.
13	14	15	16	17	18	19	20	21	22
328,941	329,798	33,801	5,761	10,669	3,808	284,469	320,229	2	...

TABLE IX.

Education by Religion and Age, Part (B)—Hindu—(*Continued*).

District or State.	Age Periods—(*Continued*). 15—24									
	Total.		Learning.		Literate.		Illiterate.		Not stated.	
	Males.	Females.	Males.	Females.	Males.	Females.	Males.	Females.	Males.	Females.
1	23	24	25	26	27	28	29	30	31	32
Travancore ...	165,889	180,497	3,398	528	43,597	6,571	118,894	173,398	...	...

Age Periods—(*Continued*). 25 and over.									
Total.		Learning.		Literate.		Illiterate.		Not stated.	
Males.	Females.	Males.	Females.	Males.	Females.	Males.	Females.	Males.	Females.
33	34	35	36	37	38	39	40	41	42
447,165	419,574	1,150	502	123,208	13,457	322,806	405,614	1	1

TABLE IX.

Education by Religion and Age, Part (C)—Mussalman.

District or State.	Total Mussalman.			Total by Education.							
				Learning.		Literate.		Illiterate.		Not stated.	
	Total.	Males.	Females.	Males.	Females.	Males.	Females.	Males.	Females.	Males.	Females.
1	2	3	4	5	6	7	8	9	10	11	12
Travancore ...	158,823	81,375	77,448	1,804	374	11,709	1,280	67,860	75,794	2	...

Age Periods.

0—14

Total.		Learning.		Literate.		Illiterate.		Not stated.	
Males.	Females.	Males.	Females.	Males.	Females.	Males.	Females.	Males.	Females.
13	14	15	16	17	18	19	20	21	22
30,536	30,077	1,537	260	849	266	28,150	29,551	...	...

TABLE IX.

Education by Religion and Age, Part (C)—Mussalman—(*Continued*).

District or State.	Age Periods—(*Continued*). 15—24 Total.		Learning.		Literate.		Illiterate.		Not stated.	
	Males.	Females.	Males.	Females.	Males.	Females.	Males.	Females.	Males.	Females.
1	23	24	25	26	27	28	29	30	31	32
Travancore ...	14, 342	14,903	141	26	2,721	289	11,480	14,588	...	...

Age Periods—(*Continued*). 25 and over. Total.		Learning.		Literate.		Illiterate.		Not stated.	
Males.	Females.	Males.	Females.	Males.	Females.	Males.	Females.	Males.	Females.
33	34	35	36	37	38	39	40	41	42
36,497	32,468	126	88	8,139	725	28,230	31,655	2	...

TABLE IX.

Education by Religion and Age, Part (D)—Christian.

District or State.	Total Christian.			Total by Education.							
				Learning.		Literate.		Illiterate.		Not stated.	
	Total.	Males.	Females.	Males.	Females.	Males.	Females.	Males.	Females.	Males.	Females.
1	2	3	4	5	6	7	8	9	10	11	12
Travancore ...	526,911	266,969	259,942	11,785	2,508	57,335	8,987	197,849	248,447	...	...

Age Periods.

0—14

Total.		Learning.		Literate.		Illiterate.		Not stated.	
Males.	Females.	Males.	Females.	Males.	Females.	Males.	Females.	Males.	Females.
13	14	15	16	17	18	19	20	21	22
102,727	104,763	10,558	2,203	3,877	1,636	88,292	100,924	...	...

TABLE IX.

Education by Religion and Age, Part (D)—Christian—(*Continued*).

District or State.	Age Periods—(*Continued*). 15—24									
	Total.		Learning.		Literate.		Illiterate.		Not stated.	
	Males.	Females.	Males.	Females.	Males.	Females.	Males.	Females.	Males.	Females.
1	23	24	25	26	27	28	29	30	31	32
Travancore ...	46,641	49,151	914	135	14,518	2,512	31,209	46,504	...	...

Age Periods—(*Continued*). 25 and over.									
Total.		Learning.		Literate.		Illiterate.		Not stated.	
Males.	Females.	Males.	Females.	Males.	Females.	Males.	Females.	Males.	Females.
33	34	35	36	37	38	39	40	41	42
117,601	106,028	313	170	38,940	4,839	78,348	101,019	...	...

TABLE IX.

Education by Religion and Age, Part (E)—Jain.

District or State.	Total Jain.			Total by Education.							
				Learning.		Literate.		Illiterate.		Not stated.	
	Total.	Males.	Females.	Males.	Females.	Males.	Females.	Males.	Females.	Males.	Females.
1	2	3	4	5	6	7	8	9	10	11	12
Travancore ...	10	8	2	1	...	3	...	4	2	...	...

Age Periods. 0—14									
Total.		Learning.		Literate.		Illiterate.		Not stated.	
Males.	Females.	Males.	Females.	Males.	Females.	Males.	Females.	Males.	Females.
13	14	15	16	17	18	19	20	21	22
...	...	...	...	...	...	...	...	...	...

TABLE IX.

Education by Religion and Age, Part (E)—Jain—(*Continued*).

DISTRICT OR STATE.	AGE PERIODS—(*Continued*). 15—24									
	Total.		Learning.		Literate.		Illiterate.		Not stated.	
	Males.	Females.	Males.	Females.	Males.	Females.	Males.	Females.	Males.	Females.
1	23	24	25	26	27	28	29	30	31	32
Travancore ...	2	1	1	...	1	...	...	1	...	...

AGE PERIODS—(*Continued*). 25 and over.									
Total.		Learning.		Literate.		Illiterate.		Not stated.	
Males.	Females.	Males.	Females.	Males.	Females.	Males.	Females.	Males.	Females.
33	34	35	36	37	38	39	40	41	42
6	1	...	...	2	...	4	1	...	...

TABLE IX.

Education by Religion and Age, Part (F)—Parsi.

District or State.	Total Parsi.			Total by Education.							
				Learning.		Literate.		Illiterate.		Not stated.	
	Total.	Males.	Females.	Males.	Females.	Males.	Females.	Males.	Females.	Males.	Females.
1	2	3	4	5	6	7	8	9	10	11	12
Travancore ...	1	1	...	...	...	...	...	1	...	...	...

Age Periods. 0—14									
Total.		Learning.		Literate.		Illiterate.		Not stated.	
Males.	Females.	Males.	Females.	Males.	Females.	Males.	Females.	Males.	Females.
13	14	15	16	17	18	19	20	21	22
...	...	...	...	...	...	...	...	...	...

TABLE IX.

Education by Religion and Age, Part (F)—Parsi—(*Continued*).

District or State.	Age Periods—(*Continued*). 15—24 Total. Males.	Total. Females.	Learning. Males.	Learning. Females.	Literate. Males.	Literate. Females.	Illiterate. Males.	Illiterate. Females.	Not stated. Males.	Not stated. Females.
1	23	24	25	26	27	28	29	30	31	32
Travancore ...	...	...	...	...	...	...	...	...	...	...

Age Periods—(*Continued*). 25 and over. Total. Males.	Total. Females.	Learning. Males.	Learning. Females.	Literate. Males.	Literate. Females.	Illiterate. Males.	Illiterate. Females.	Not stated. Males.	Not stated. Females.
33	34	35	36	37	38	39	40	41	42
1	...	...	...	...	...	1	...	...	...

TABLE IX.

Education by Religion and Age, Part (G)—Jew.

District or State.	Total Jew.			Total by Education.							
				Learning.		Literate.		Illiterate.		Not stated.	
	Total.	Males.	Females.	Males.	Females.	Males.	Females.	Males.	Females.	Males.	Females.
1	2	3	4	5	6	7	8	9	10	11	12
Travancore ...	125	65	60	16	14	34	36	15	10	...	...

Age Periods.

0—14									
Total.		Learning.		Literate.		Illiterate.		Not stated.	
Males.	Females.	Males.	Females.	Males.	Females.	Males.	Females	Males.	Females.
13	14	15	16	17	18	19	20	21	22
22	23	15	14	...	3	7	6	...	...

TABLE IX.

Education by Religion and Age, Part (G)—Jew—(Continued.)

District or State.	Age Periods—(Continued). 15—24 Total. Males.	Females.	Learning. Males.	Females.	Literate. Males.	Females.	Illiterate. Males.	Females.	Not stated. Males.	Females.
1	23	24	25	26	27	28	29	30	31	32
Travancore ...	11	10	1	...	9	9	1	1	...	...

Age Periods—(Continued). 25 and over. Total. Males.	Females.	Learning. Males.	Females.	Literate. Males.	Females.	Illiterate. Males.	Females.	Not stated. Males.	Females.
33	34	35	36	37	38	39	40	41	42
32	27	...	...	25	24	7	3	...	...

TABLE IX.

Education by Religion and Age, Part (H)—None.

District or State.	Total None.			Total by Education.							
				Learning.		Literate.		Illiterate.		Not stated.	
	Total.	Males.	Females.	Males.	Females.	Males.	Females.	Males.	Females.	Males.	Females.
1	2	3	4	5	6	7	8	9	10	11	12
Travancore ...	2	2	...	...	...	2	...	...	...	...	...

Age Periods. 0—14									
Total.		Learning.		Literate.		Illiterate.		Not stated.	
Males.	Females.	Males.	Females.	Males.	Females.	Males.	Females.	Males.	Females.
13	14	15	16	17	18	19	20	21	22
...	...	...	...	...	...	...	...	...	...

TABLE IX.

Education by Religion and Age, Part (H)—None—(*Continued*).

District or State.	Age Periods—(*Continued*).									
	15—24									
	Total.		Learning.		Literate.		Illiterate.		Not stated.	
	Males.	Females.	Males.	Females.	Males.	Females.	Males.	Females.	Males.	Females.
1	23	24	25	26	27	28	29	30	31	32
Travancore ...	...	...	...	...	...	...	...	...	...	...

Age Periods—(*Continued*).									
25 and over.									
Total.		Learning.		Literate.		Illiterate.		Not stated.	
Males.	Females.	Males.	Females.	Males.	Females.	Males.	Females.	Males.	Females.
33	34	35	36	37	38	39	40	41	42
2	...	...	...	2	...	...	...	...	...

TABLE X.

Parent Tongue.

District or State.	Total Population.			A. Vernaculars of India.					
				Malayalam.			Saurashtram.		
	Total.	Males.	Females.	Total.	Males.	Females.	Total.	Males.	Females.
1	2	3	4	5	6	7	8	9	10
Travancore ...	2,557,736	1,290,415	1,267,321	2,079,271	1,046,371	1,032,900	720	343	377

A. Vernaculars of India—(*Continued*).

Nagaram.			Tamil.			Telugu.		
Total.	Males.	Females.	Total.	Males.	Females.	Total.	Males.	Females.
11	12	13	14	15	16	17	18	19
103	51	52	448,322	227,668	220,654	5,426	2,967	2,459

TABLE X.

Parent Tongue—(*Continued*).

District or State.	A. Vernaculars of India—(*Continued*).											
	Canarese.			Tulu.			Konkan.			Mahratti.		
	Total.	Males.	Females.	Total.	Males.	Females.	Total.	Males.	Females.	Total.	Males.	Females.
1	20	21	22	23	24	25	26	27	28	29	30	31
Travancore ...	891	534	357	893	652	241	10,697	5,671	5,026	2,205	1,106	1,099

A. Vernaculars of India—(*Continued*).

Hindustani.			Parsi.			Guzaratti.			Cutchi.		
Total.	Males.	Females.	Total.	Males.	Females.	Total.	Males.	Females.	Total.	Males.	Females.
32	33	34	35	36	37	38	39	40	41	42	43
5,455	3,025	2,430	1	1	...	427	245	182	160	84	76

TABLE X.

Parent Tongue—(Continued).

District or State.	A. Vernaculars of India—(Continued).						B. Vernaculars of Asiatic Countries beyond India.		
	Sindhi.			Bengali.			Singalese.		
	Total.	Males.	Females.	Total.	Males.	Females.	Total.	Males.	Females.
1	44	45	46	47	48	49	50	51	52
Travancore ...	11	7	4	5	4	1	3	3	...

B. Vernaculars of Asiatic Countries beyond India—(Continued).

Chinese.			Hebrew.			Syrian.			Arabic.		
Total.	Males.	Females.	Total.	Males.	Females.	Total.	Males.	Females.	Total.	Males.	Females
53	54	55	56	57	58	59	60	61	62	63	64
1	1	...	138	72	66	2	2	...	1,029	531	498

TABLE X.

Parent Tongue—(*Continued*).

District or State.	C. European Languages.											
	Italian.			Spanish.			Portuguese.			French.		
	Total.	Males.	Females.	Total.	Males.	Females.	Total.	Males.	Females.	Total.	Males.	Females.
1	65	66	67	68	69	70	71	72	73	74	75	76
Travancore ...	8	8	...	11	8	3	460	265	195	30	18	12

C. European Languages—(*Continued*).									D.		
German.			English.			Irish.			Not stated.		
Total.	Males.	Females.	Total.	Males.	Females.	Total.	Males.	Females.	Total.	Males.	Females.
77	78	79	80	81	82	83	84	85	86	87	88
2	2	...	1,435	764	671	29	11	18	1	1	...

TABLE XI.

Birth-place.

Birth-place.	Total.	Males.	Females.
A. Within the Province.			
Travancore	2,540,758	1,279,321	1,261,437
Tinnevelly	7,785	4,831	2,954
Madura	2,113	1,464	649
Trichinopoly	499	340	159
Tanjore	507	314	193
South Arcot	69	62	7
Chingleput	28	18	10
Madras	508	296	212
Cochin	1,274	814	460
Malabar	362	258	104
South Canara	271	208	63
Nilgiris	1	1	...
Coimbatore	580	479	101
Salem	11	6	5
North Arcot	173	110	63
Nellore	53	29	24
Cuddappah	13	9	4
Kurnool	20	13	7
Bellary	6	4	2
Ceded Districts	2	1	1
Krishna	22	16	6
Godavari	36	21	15
Vizagapatam	395	209	186
Ganjam	164	118	46
Pondicherry	2	1	1
Total A ...	2,555,652	1,288,943	1,266,709

TABLE XI.

Birth-place—(*Continued*).

Birth-place.	Total.	Males.	Females.
B. In India beyond the Province.			
Mysore	154	88	66
Coorg	1	1	...
North Canara	27	25	2
Goa	11	11	...
Bijapur	3	3	...
Kolhapur	1	1	...
Ratnagiri	20	20	...
Bombay	182	162	20
Hyderabad	227	112	115
Nagpore	10	7	3
Jabbalpore	4	4	...
Central Provinces (Unspecified) ...	102	58	44
Bhopal	1	1	...
Malwa	55	48	7
Bundelkhand	1	1	...
Gwaliar	1	1	...
Baroda	28	13	15
Guzerat	10	10	...
Cutch	66	41	25
Marwar	2	2	...
Jeypore	15	15	...
Delhi	22	20	2
Punjab	2	2	...
Agra	17	15	2
Allahabad	11	10	1
Benares	33	26	7
Oudh	44	40	4
Rohilkund	1	1	...
North-West Provinces (Unspecified) ...	15	14	1
Calcutta	10	8	2
Dacca	1	1	...
Bengal (Unspecified)	54	45	9
Orissa	10	4	6
Nepaul	2	2	...
British Burmah	2	...	2
British India (Unspecified)	539	342	197
Total B ...	1,684	1,154	530

TABLE XI.

Birth-place—(*Continued*).

Birth-place.	Total.	Males.	Females.
C. In Asia beyond India.			
Ceylon	131	107	24
Singapore	1	1	...
Java	1	1	...
China	3	3	...
Afghanistan	9	9	...
Persia	1	1	...
Arabia	93	86	7
Total C. ...	239	208	31
D. In Europe.			
Italy	9	9	...
Spain	9	6	3
France	2	1	1
Germany	3	3	...
Belgium	1	...	1
England	71	42	29
Scotland	16	11	5
Ireland	15	8	7
Wales	2	2	...
Holland	1	1	...
Europe (Unspecified)	21	16	5
Total D. ...	150	99	51
E. In Africa.			
Africa (Unspecified) ... E. ...	2	2	...
F. In America.			
The United States	2	2	...
Canada	5	5	...
America (Unspecified)	2	2	...
Total F. ...	9	9	...
Total ...	2,557,736	1,290,415	1,267,321

TABLE XII.

Insane by Age.

District or State.	Total Afflicted.			Distribution by Age.									
				0—4		5—9		10—14		15—19		20—24	
	Total.	Males.	Females.	Males.	Females.	Males.	Females.	Males.	Females.	Males.	Females.	Males.	Females.
1	2	3	4	5	6	7	8	9	10	11	12	13	14
Travancore...	394	249	145	1	...	4	6	5	4	15	7	27	9

Distribution by Age—(*Continued*).

25—29		30—34		35—39		40—44		45—49		50—54		55—59		60 and over	
Males.	Females.	Males.	Females.	Males.	Females.	Males.	Females.	Males.	Females.	Males.	Females.	Males.	Females.	Males.	Females.
15	16	17	18	19	20	21	22	23	24	25	26	27	28	29	30
34	12	26	16	29	19	35	19	30	18	19	10	11	11	13	14

TABLE XII.-A.

Persons of Unsound Mind by Caste, Tribe or Race.

Class.	Group.	Caste.	Total Afflicted. Total.	Males.	Females.	Religion.
A. Agricultural.	1 Military and Dominant.	Nair	68	46	22	Hindu.
		Marava	1	...	1	,,
		Total group 1 ..	69	46	23	...
	2(a) Other Agricultural land-holding classes.	Pandi Sudra	41	27	14	Hindu.
		Vellāla	7	4	3	,,
		Total group 2(a) ...	48	31	17	...
	2(c) Field-labouring classes.	Kurava	6	4	2	Hindu.
		Pariah	6	2	4	,,
		Pulaya	16	10	6	,,
		Ullāden	1	1	...	,,
		Total group 2(c) ...	29	17	12	...
	4 Forest and Hill tribes...	Malayarien	1	...	1	Hindu.
		Velan	2	1	1	,,
		Total group 4 ...	3	1	2	...
		Total class A. ...	149	95	54	...

TABLE XII.-A.

Persons of Unsound Mind by Caste, Tribe or Race—(*Continued*).

Class.	Group.	Caste.	Total Afflicted. Total.	Males.	Females.	Religion.
B. Professional...	5 Priests ...	Brahmin	11	9	2	Hindu.
		Malayala Brahmin ...	1	1	...	„
		Ilayadu	1	...	1	„
		Total group 5 ...	13	10	3	...
	10 Astrologers, Quack doctors, &c.	Kaniyan	2	1	1	Hindu.
		Total class B. ...	15	11	4	...
C. Commercial ...	14 Traders ...	Chetti	4	2	2	Hindu.
		Jonaka	1	...	1	Mussalman.
		Total group 14 ...	5	2	3	...
		Total class C. ...	5	2	3	...
D. Artisans and Village Menials.	17 Goldsmiths ...	Tattān	4	3	1	Hindu.
	17(*a*) Artisans (general)...	Kammālan	3	1	2	Hindu.
	18 Barbers ...	Kshourakan	1	1	..	Hindu.
		Mārān	3	1	2	„
		Total group 18 ...	4	2	2	...

19 Blacksmiths ...	Kollan	7	3	4	Hindu.
20 Carpenters, Masons and Turners ...	Āsāri	9	7	2	Hindu.
21 Brass & Coppersmiths..	Kannān	1	1	...	Hindu.
22 Tailors ...	Pānān	1	1	...	Hindu.
23 Weavers, calenderers and dyers.	Patnūl	1	...	1	Hindu.
	Sālē	1	1	...	"
	Total group 23 ...	2	1	1	...
24 Washermen ...	Velutadan	1	1	...	Hindu.
26 Shepherds, Wool-weavers, &c. ...	Idaya	2	2	..	Hindu.
27 Oil pressers ...	Chekkāla	3	3	...	Hindu.
	Vāniyan	6	5	1	"
	Total group 27 ...	9	8	1	...
28 Potters ...	Kosavan	1	...	1	Hindu.
31 Lime-burners ...	Paravan	3	1	2	Hindu.
35 Fishermen, Boatmen, Palki-bearers, Water bearers, Cooks, &c. ...	Mukkuvan	5	2	3	Hindu.

TABLE XII.-A.

Persons of Unsound Mind by Caste, Tribe or Race—(*Continued*).

Class.	Group.	Caste.	Total Afflicted.			Religion.
			Total.	Males.	Females.	
D. Artisans and Village Menials —(*Contd*).	36 Distillers and Toddy-drawers.	Īluva	60	31	29	Hindu.
		Chānnān	14	10	4	,,
		Tandān ...	6	4	2	,,
		Total group 36 ...	80	45	35	...
		Total class D. ...	132	78	54	...
E. Vagrant minor Artisans and Performers.	43 Mat-makers, cane splitters, grass-cutters, &c.	Nolaya	1	1	...	Hindu.
	44 Hunters, Fowlers, &c.	Vēdan	1	1	...	Hindu.
	45(*a*) Beggars ...	Sangam Pandāram ...	1	...	1	Hindu.
		Total class E. ...	3	2	1	...
F. Races and Nationalities.	48 Asiatic races of reputed non-Indian descent ...	Mughal	5	4	1	Mussalman.

TABLE XII.-A.

Persons of Unsound Mind by Caste, Tribe or Race—(*Continued*).

	52 Christian converts ...	Native Christian ...	54	29	25	Christian.
		Syrian	2	2	...	,,
		Total group 52 ...	56	31	25	...
		Total class F. ...	61	35	26	...
G. Undefined.	54 Linguistic, territorial and religious names.	Konkani	10	7	3	Hindu.
		Tulukkan	19	19	...	Mussalman.
		Total group 54 ...	29	26	3	...
		Total class G. ...	29	26	3	...
		Grand Total ...	394	249	145	

TABLE XIII.

Deaf-mutes by Age.

District or State.	Total Afflicted.			Distribution by Age.									
				0—4		5—9		10—14		15—19		20—24	
	Total.	Males.	Females.	Males.	Females.	Males.	Females.	Males.	Females.	Males.	Females.	Males.	Females.
1	2	3	4	5	6	7	8	9	10	11	12	13	14
Travancore...	745	435	310	13	5	55	33	51	32	52	29	47	33

Distribution by Age—(*Continued*).

25—29		30—34		35—39		40—44		45—49		50—54		55—59		60 and over.	
Males.	Females.	Males.	Females.	Males.	Females.	Males.	Females.	Males.	Females.	Males.	Females.	Males.	Females.	Males.	Females.
15	16	17	18	19	20	21	22	23	24	25	26	27	28	29	30
38	27	33	32	30	18	27	27	17	16	20	20	11	7	41	31

TABLE XIII.-A.

Deaf-mutes by Caste, Tribe or Race.

Class.	Group.	Caste.	Total Afflicted. Total.	Males.	Females.	Religion.
A. Agricultural.	1 Military and Dominant..	Nair ...	144	87	57	Hindu.
		Kshatriya ...	1	...	1	"
		Marava ...	1	...	1	"
		Sāmantaka ...	1	1	...	"
		Total group 1 ...	147	88	59	...
	2(*a*) Other Agricultural land-holding classes.	Pāndi Sudra ...	31	21	10	Hindu.
		Vellala ...	15	5	10	"
		Total group 2(*a*) ...	46	26	20	...
	2(*c*) Field-labouring classes.	Kurava ...	10	5	5	Hindu.
		Pallan ...	1	1	...	"
		Pariah ...	12	4	8	"
		Pulaya ...	41	20	21	"
		Ullāden ...	3	2	1	"
		Total group 2(*c*) ...	67	32	35	...
	4 Forest and Hill tribes...	Vēlan ...	5	4	1	Hindu.
		Total class A. ...	265	150	115	...

TABLE XIII.-A.

Deaf-mutes by Caste, Tribe or Race—(*Continued*).

Class.	Group.	Caste.	Total Afflicted. Total.	Males.	Females.	Religion.
B. Professional....	5 Priests ...	Foreign Brahmin ...	14	9	5	Hindu.
		Malayala Brahmin ...	1	1	...	"
		Namburi ...	1	1	...	"
		Total group 5 ...	16	11	5	...
	7 Temple servants ..	Ambalavāsi ...	1	1	...	Hindu.
		Krishnanvaga ...	6	4	2	"
		Total group 7 ...	7	5	2	...
	10 Astrologers and Quack-doctors.	Kaniyan ...	8	4	4	Hindu.
		Total class B. ...	31	20	11	...
C. Commercial ...	14 Traders ...	Chetti ...	6	4	2	Hindu.
		Jonaka ...	4	3	1	Mussalman.
		Total group 14 ...	10	7	3	...
		Total class C. ...	10	7	3	...

D. Artisans and Village Menials.	17 Goldsmiths ...	Tattān ...	4	3	1	Hindu.
	17(*a*) Artisans (general)...	Kammālan ...	10	6	4	Hindu.
	18 Barbers ...	Kāvadi ...	1	1	...	Hindu.
		Kshourakan ...	5	3	2	„
		Mārān ...	6	5	1	„
		Total group 18 ...	12	9	3	...
	19 Blacksmiths ...	Kollan ...	12	6	6	Hindu.
	20 Carpenters Masons and Turners.	Ā sāri ...	16	10	6	Hindu.
	21 Brass & Coppersmiths.	Kannān ...	2	2	...	Hindu.
	23 Weavers, calenderers and dyers.	Patnūl ...	1	1	...	Hindu.
		Sālē ...	4	1	3	„
		Total group 23 ...	5	2	3	...
	24 Washermen ...	Velutadan ...	10	7	3	Hindu.
	26 Shepherds and Wool-weavers.	Idaya ...	3	2	1	Hindu.
	27 Oil pressers ...	Chekkāla ...	4	2	2	Hindu.
		Vāniyan ...	11	4	7	„
		Total group 27 ...	15	6	9	...

TABLE XIII.-A.

Deaf-mutes by Caste, Tribe or Race—(*Continued*).

Class.	Group.	Caste.	Total Afflicted.			Religion.
			Total.	Males.	Females.	
D. Artisans and Village Menials—(*Continued*).	28 Potters ...	Kosava ...	4	3	1	Hindu.
	30 Salt workers ...	Ullava ...	1	...	1	Hindu.
	31 Lime-burners ...	Paravan ...	2	2	...	Hindu.
	35 Fishermen, Boatmen, Palki-bearers, Cooks, Water-bearers, &c.	Mukkuva ...	18	9	9	Hindu.
	36 Distillers and Toddy-drawers.	Īluva ...	134	76	58	Hindu.
		Chānnān ...	46	29	17	,,
		Tandān ...	8	4	4	,,
		Total group 36 ...	188	109	79	...
	38 Leather workers ...	Chemmān ...	1	1	...	Hindu.
		Total class D. ...	303	177	126	...
E. Vagrant minor artisans and performers.	44 Hunters, Fowlers, &c...	Vēdan ...	2	2	...	Hindu.
	45(*a*) Beggars ...	Sangam Pandāram ...	7	4	3	Hindu.
		Total class E. ...	9	6	3	...

F. Races and Nationalities.	48 Asiatic races of reputed non-Indian descent ...	Mughal ...	6	4	2	Mussalman.
	52 Christian converts ...	Native Christian ...	79	46	33	Christian.
		Syrian ...	10	10	...	„
		Total group 52 ...	89	56	33	...
		Total class F. ...	95	60	35	...
G. Undefined.	54 Linguistic territorial and religious names ...	Mussalman ...	1	1	...	Mussalman.
		Tulukkan ...	31	14	17	„
		Total group 54 ...	32	15	17	...
		Total class G. ...	32	15	17	...
		Grand Total ...	745	435	310	... ...

TABLE XIV.

Blind by Age.

District or State.	Total Afflicted.			Distribution by Age.									
				0—4		5—9		10—14		15—19		20—24	
	Total.	Males.	Females.	Males.	Females.	Males.	Females.	Males.	Females.	Males.	Females.	Males.	Females.
1	2	3	4	5	6	7	8	9	10	11	12	13	14
Travancore ...	1,017	598	419	20	10	35	16	36	20	40	17	45	29

Distribution by Age—(*Continued*).

District or State.	25—29		30—34		35—39		40—44		45—49		50—54		55—59		60 & over	
	Males.	Females.	Males.	Females.	Males.	Females.	Males.	Females.	Males.	Females.	Males.	Females.	Males.	Females.	Males.	Female.
1	15	16	17	18	19	20	21	22	23	24	25	26	27	28	29	30
Travancore ..	37	33	38	34	54	29	40	28	50	20	54	33	32	32	117	118

TABLE XIV.-A.

Blind by Caste, Tribe or Race.

Class.	Group.	Caste.	Total Afflicted. Total.	Males.	Females.	Religion.
A. Agricultural.	1 Military and Dominant..	Nair	213	119	94	Hindu.
		Kshatriya	1	1	...	„
		Total group 1 ...	214	120	94	...
	2(*a*) Other Agricultural land-holding classes.	Pandi Sudra	67	30	37	Hindu.
		Vellāla	13	10	3	„
		Total group 2(*a*) . .	80	40	40	...
	2(*c*) Field-labouring classes.	Kurava	28	17	11	Hindu.
		Pariah	20	10	10	„
		Pulaya	73	47	26	„
		Ullāden	1	1	...	„
		Total group 2(*c*) ...	122	75	47	...
	4 Forest and Hill tribes...	Malayarien	1	1	...	Hindu.
		Vēlan	1	...	1	„
		Total group 4 ...	2	1	1	...
		Total class A. ...	418	236	182	...

TABLE XIV.-A.

Blind by Caste, Tribe or Race—(*Continued*).

Class.	Group.	Caste.	Total Afflicted.			Religion.
			Total.	Males.	Females.	
B. Professional...	5 Priests ...	Foreign Brahmin... ...	13	7	6	Hindu.
		Malayala Brahmin ...	4	4	...	„
		Potti	1	1	...	„
		Ilayadu	6	3	3	„
		Total group 5 ...	24	15	9	...
	7 Temple servants ...	Ambalavāsi	4	3	1	Hindu.
		Krishnanvāga	2	2	...	„
		Total group 7 ...	6	5	1	...
	10 Astrologers and Quack-doctors.	Kaniyān	1	1	...	Hindu.
		Pulluvan	1	...	1	„
		Total group 10 ...	2	1	1	...
		Total class B. ...	32	21	11	...
C. Commercial.	14 Traders ...	Chetti	13	10	3	Hindu.
		Jonaka	2	1	1	Mussalman.
		Labbai	1	1	...	„
		Total group 14 ...	16	12	4	...
		Total class C. ...	16	12	4	...

Blind by Caste, Tribe or Race—(*Continued*).

D. Artisans and Village Menials.	17 Goldsmiths ...	Tattān	4	4	...	Hindu.
	17(*a*) Artisans (general)...	Kammālan	20	10	10	Hindu.
	18 Barbers ...	Kāvadi	1	1	...	Hindu.
		Kshourakan	3	1	2	,,
		Mārān	5	5	...	,,
		Total group 18 ...	9	7	2	...
	19 Blacksmiths ...	Kollan	5	3	2	Hindu.
	20 Carpenters, Masons & Turners.	Āsāri	21	10	11	Hindu.
	21 Brass & Coppersmiths..	Kannān	8	6	2	Hindu.
	23 Weavers, calenderers and dyers.	Patnūl	1	1	...	Hindu.
		Sālē	3	2	1	,,
		Total group 23 ...	4	3	1	...
	24 Washermen ...	Velutadan	11	7	4	Hindu.
	26 Shepherds, and Wool-weavers.	Idaya	4	2	2	Hindu.
	27 Oil pressers ...	Chekkālā	5	4	1	Hindu.
		Vaniyan	6	3	3	,,
		Total group 27 ...	11	7	4	...
	28 Potters ...	Kosava	4	1	3	Hindu.
	31 Lime-burners ...	Paravan	5	...	5	Hindu.

TABLE XIV.-A.

Blind by Caste, Tribe or Race—(*Continued*).

Class.	Group.	Caste.	Total Afflicted.			Religion.
			Total.	Males.	Females.	
D. Artisans and Village Menials —(*Continued*).	35 Fishermen, Boatmen, Palki-bearers, Cooks, &c.	Mukkuva	10	6	4	Hindu.
	36 Distillers and Toddy-drawers.	Īluva	187	102	85	Hindu.
		Chānnān	47	32	15	,,
		Tandān	9	8	1	,,
		Total group 36 ...	243	142	101	...
		Total class D ...	359	208	151	...
E. Vagrant minor Artisans and Performers.	43 Mat-makers, cane splitters, grass-cutters, &c.	Nolaya	4	2	2	Hindu.
	44 Hunters, Fowlers, &c...	Vēdan	1	1	...	Hindu.
	45(*a*) Beggars ...	Sangam Pandāram ...	7	4	3	Hindu.
		Total class E ...	12	7	5	...
F. Races and Nationalities.	48 Asiatic races of reputed non-Indian descent.	Mughal	6	2	4	Mussalman.
		Sheik	3	2	1	,,
		Total group 48 ...	9	4	5	...

	52 Christian converts ...	Native Christian	117	70	47	Christian.
		Syrian	7	7	...	„
		Total group 52 ...	124	77	47	...
		Total class F ...	133	81	52	...
G. Undefined.	54 Linguistic, territorial and religious names.	Konkani	3	3	...	Hindu.
		Tulukkan	44	30	14	Mussalman.
		Total group 54 ...	47	33	14	...
		Total class G ...	47	33	14	...
		Grand Total ...	1,017	598	419	...

TABLE XV.

Lepers by Age.

District or State.	Total Afflicted.			Distribution by Age.									
				0—4		5—9		10—14		15—19		20—24	
	Total.	Males.	Females.	Males.	Females.	Males.	Females.	Males.	Females.	Males.	Females.	Males.	Females.
1	2	3	4	5	6	7	8	9	10	11	12	13	14
Travancore...	968	684	284	3	5	10	9	20	11	29	21	39	23

Distribution by Age—(*Continued*).

25—29		30—34		35—39		40—44		45—49		50—54		55—59		60 and over	
Males.	Females.	Males.	Females.	Males.	Females.	Males.	Females.	Males.	Females.	Males.	Females.	Males.	Females.	Males.	Females.
15	16	17	18	19	20	21	22	23	24	25	26	27	28	29	30
61	22	76	31	91	28	96	33	79	33	64	30	38	11	78	27

TABLE XV.-A.

Lepers by Caste, Tribe or Race.

Class.	Group.	Caste.	Total Afflicted. Total.	Males.	Females.	Religion.
A. Agricultural.	1 Military and Dominant..	Nair ...	200	135	65	Hindu.
		Kshatriya ...	1	1	...	„
		Sāmantaka ...	1	...	1	„
		Total group 1 ...	202	136	66	...
	2(a) Other Agricultural land-holding classes.	Pandi Sudra ...	32	22	10	Hindu.
		Vellāla ...	14	13	1	„
		Total group 2(a) ...	46	35	11	...
	2(c) Field-labouring classes.	Kurava ...	46	35	11	Hindu.
		Pariah ...	16	12	4	„
		Pulaya ...	76	45	31	„
		Ullāden ...	1	...	1	„
		Total group 2(c) ...	139	92	47	...
	4 Forest and Hill tribes...	Vēlan ...	8	7	1	Hindu.
		Total class A. ...	395	270	125	...

TABLE XV.-A.

Lepers by Caste, Tribe or Race—(*Continued*).

Caste.	Group.	Caste.	Total Afflicted. Total.	Males.	Females.	Religion.
B. Professional ..	5 Priests ...	Foreign Brahmin ...	4	4	...	Hindu.
		Malayala Brahmin ...	2	2	...	"
		Embran ...	1	1	...	"
		Potti ...	1	1	...	"
		Total group 5 ...	8	8	...	...
	6 Devotees ...	Vyravi ...	1	...	1	Hindu.
	7 Temple servants ...	Ambalavasi ..	9	8	1	Hindu.
		Krishnanvaga ...	4	3	1	"
		Total group 7 ...	13	11	2	...
	10 Astrologers and Quack-doctors.	Kaniyan ...	2	2	...	Hindu.
		Total class B. ...	24	21	3	...

TABLE XV.-A.

Lepers by Caste, Tribe or Race—(*Continued*).

C. Commercial ...	14 Traders ...	Chetti	5	4	1	Hindu.
		Jonaka	2	1	1	Mussalman.
		Total group 14 ...	7	5	2	...
		Total class C ...	7	5	2	...
D. Artisans and Village Menials.	17 Goldsmiths ...	Tattān	11	9	2	Hindu.
	17(*a*) Artisans (general) ...	Kammālan	20	13	7	Hindu.
	18 Barbers ...	Kāvadi	1	1	...	Hindu.
		Kshourakan	5	5	...	"
		Mārān	1	1	...	"
		Total group 18 ...	7	7	..	...
	19 Blacksmiths ...	Kollan	8	5	3	Hindu.
	20 Carpenters, Masons & Turners.	Āsāri	27	20	7	Hindu.
	21 Brass and Copper-smiths.	Kannān	3	2	1	Hindu.
	24 Washermen ...	Velutadan	7	6	1	Hindu.
	26 Shepherds and Wool-weavers.	Idaya	2	2	...	Hindu.
	27 Oil pressers ...	Chekkāla	5	2	3	Hindu.
		Vāniyan	7	4	3	"
		Total group 27 ...	12	6	6	...

TABLE XV-.A.

Lepers by Caste, Tribe or Race—(*Continued*).

Caste.	Group.	Caste.	Total Afflicted. Total.	Males.	Females.	Religion.
D. Artisans and Village Menials —(*Continued*).	28 Potters ...	Kosava	9	7	2	Hindu.
	31 Lime-burners ...	Paravan	4	3	1	Hindu.
	35 Fishermen, Boatmen, Palki-bearers, Water-bearers, Cooks, &c.	Mukkuvan	14	7	7	Hindu.
		Pōndan	1	1	...	„
		Total group 35 ...	15	8	7	...
	36 Distillers and Toddy-drawers.	Īluva	228	163	65	Hindu.
		Chānnān	20	18	2	„
		Tandān	13	11	2	„
		Total group 36 ...	261	192	69	...
		Total class D ...	386	280	106	...
E. Vagrant minor Artisans and Performers.	40 Stonemakers and stone-quarriers.	Kallāsāri	3	2	1	Hindu.
	43 Mat-makers, cane splitters, grass-cutters, &c.	Nolaya	2	...	2	Hindu.

E. Vagrant minor Artisans and Performers—(*Continued*).	44 Hunters, Fowlers, &c...	Talavan	1	1	...	Hindu.
		Vēdan	2	2	...	,,
		Total group 44 ...	3	3	...	...
	45(*a*) Beggars ...	Sangam Pandāram ...	7	6	1	Hindu.
		Total class E ...	15	11	4	...
F. Races and Nationalities.	48 Asiatic races of reputed non-Indian descent.	Mughal	4	3	1	Mussalman.
	51 Eurasians ...	East Indian	1	1	...	Christian.
	52 Christian converts ...	Native Christian	82	45	37	Christian.
		Syrian	8	8	...	,,
		Total group 52 ...	90	53	37	...
		Total class F ...	95	57	38	...
G. Undefined.	54 Linguistic, territorial and religious names.	Konkani	1	1	...	Hindu.
		Tulukkan	45	39	6	Mussalman.
		Total group 54 ...	46	40	6	...
		Total class G ...	46	40	6	...
		Grand Total ...	968	684	284	...

TABLE XVI.

Castes, Tribes and Races by Nationality or Traditional Occupation.

Class.	Group.	Caste, &c.	No. of recorded sub-divisions.	State Total. Total.	State Total. Males.	State Total. Females.	Religion.	Strength.
A. Agricultural.	1 Military and Dominant.	1 Nair ...	75	483,725	241,598	242,127	Hindu.	
		2 Ambalakāran ...	...	1	1	...	"	
		3 Kartāvu ...	...	97	55	42	"	
		4 Koiltamburān ...	...	101	58	43	"	
		5 Kshatrya ...	7	1,276	653	623	"	
		6 Mahratta ...	...	93	50	43	"	
		7 Maravar. ...	7	5,642	2,889	2,753	"	
		8 Pandāla ...	...	71	36	35	"	
		9 Rajaput ...	1	20	13	7	"	
		10 Raju ...	1	52	30	22	"	
		11 Sāmantakar ...	...	188	97	91	"	
		12 Tampān ...	...	286	144	142	"	
		13 Tirumulpād ...	...	410	232	178	"	
		14 Unniyādiri ...	...	94	51	43	"	
		15 Vellōdi ...	...	44	18	26	"	
		Total group 1—15 ...	...	492,100	245,925	246,175	...	
	2(*a*) Other Agricultural land-holding classes.	1 Gavarulu ...	...	12	7	5	Hindu.	
		2 Karayālar ...	...	58	27	31	"	
		3 Kattāran ...	...	5	3	2	"	
		4 Kodipattan ...	...	423	210	213	"	
		5 Kuruni ...	...	7	7	...	"	
		6 Lōti ...	...	1	1	...	"	
		7 Mālli ...	...	1	1	...	"	

Castes, Tribes and Races by Nationality or Traditional Occupation—(*Continued*).

A. Agricultural.

Group	Caste, tribe or race		Persons	Males	Females	Religion	
	8 Mudali ...	5	926	437	489	„	
	9 Pāndi Sudra ...	8	5,144	2,511	2,633	„	
	10 Valamalu ...	...	5	2	3	„	
	11 Vellāla ...	14	44,886	22,808	22,078	„	
	Total group 2(*a*)—11 ...	...	51,468	26,014	25,454	...	
2(*c*) Field-labouring classes.	1 Kanakkan ...	...	192	94	98	Hindu.	
	2 Kuravar ...	7	60,377	29,660	30,717	„	
	3 Padayāchi ...	...	4	1	3	„	
	4 Pallan ...	...	5,655	2,811	2,844	„	
	5 Pariah ...	9	71,847	36,463	35,384	{ „ { Christian.	71,786 61
	6 Pulaya ...	5	202,616	103,153	99,463	Hindu.	
	7 Udaya ...	...	7	2	5	„	
	8 Ullādan ...	...	2,873	1,473	1,400	„	
	9 Vettuvan ...	...	87	39	48	„	
	Total group 2(*c*)—9 ...	...	343,658	173,696	169,962	...	
4 Forest and Hill tribes.	1 Irular ...	...	16	7	9	Hindu.	
	2 Kāttar ...	...	39	23	16	„	
	3 Kattilaya ...	...	76	40	36	„	
	4 Kāttu Parisha (forest tribe)..	...	34	23	11	„	
	5 Khond ...	1	10	8	2	„	
	6 Malayarien ...	1	4,809	2,498	2,311	„	
	7 Mariya ...	...	3	3	...	„	
	8 Muduvan ...	...	1,077	545	532	„	
	9 Mynāta ...	...	44	24	20	„	
	10 Nādipanikan ...	...	29	9	20	„	
	11 Pania ...	...	2	...	2	„	
	12 Vēlan ...	2	17,143	8,660	8,483	„	
	Total group 4—12 ...	...	23,282	11,840	11,442	...	
	Total class A. ...	...	910,508	457,475	453,033	...	

TABLE XVI.

Castes, Tribes and Races by Nationality or Traditional Occupation—(*Continued*).

Class.	Group.	Caste, &c.	No. of recorded sub-divisions.	State Total. Total.	State Total. Males.	State Total. Females.	Religion.	Strength.
B. Professional.	5 Priests ...	1 Brahmin ...	...	2,645	1,423	1,222	Hindu.	
		Foreign Brahmin ...	..	3,529	1,961	1,568	,,	
		Aiyengar ...	...	898	479	419	,,	
		Canarese Brahmin ...	...	35	18	17	,,	
		Gouda Brahmin ...	...	77	66	11	,,	
		Hindustani Brahmin ...	...	6	3	3	,,	
		Kannadasta ...	...	9	4	5	,,	
		Kāsi Brahmin ...	...	59	24	35	,,	
		Kēsiar ...	...	67	34	33	,,	
		Mahratta Brahmin ...	...	964	525	439	,,	
		Nambiyān ...	...	214	110	104	,,	
		Survēriya ...	...	1	1	...	,,	
		Tamil Brahmin ...	...	21,899	11,238	10,661	,,	
		Telugu Brahmin ...	...	797	385	412	,,	
		Malayala Brahmin ...	...	3,451	1,866	1,585	,,	
		Akkaradēsi ...	...	25	25	...	,,	
		Bhattadiri ...	...	146	74	72	,,	
		Embrān ...	...	1,938	1,150	788	,,	
		Nambūdiri ...	...	3,750	1,979	1,771	,,	
		Ponmany Gramom ...	...	96	55	41	,,	
		Potti ...	...	2,595	1,421	1,174	,,	
		Tiruvalladēsi ...	...	328	167	161	,,	
		Trippunittoraidēsi ...	...	66	50	16	,,	
		2 Ariapattar ...	1	40	21	19	,,	
		3 Ilayadu ...	4	3,260	1,686	1,574	,,	

Castes, Tribes and Races by Nationality or Traditional Occupation—(*Continued*).

B. Professional.

	4 Tangal ...	...	14	9	5	Mussalman.	
	Total Group 5—4 ...	...	46,909	24,774	22,135	...	
6 Devotees ...	1 Fakkir ...	...	5	4	1	Mussalman.	
	2 Gosains ..	1	61	40	21	Hindu.	
	3 Sanniyāsi ...	...	9	8	1	„	
	4 Vyravi ...	2	712	356	356	„	
	Total group 6 —4 ...	...	787	408	379	...	
7 Temple servants ..	1 Ambalavāsi ...	16	7,469	3,890	3,579	Hindu.	
	2 Krishnanvagā ...	...	6,953	3,394	3,559	„	
	3 Pilāppalli ...	...	69	33	36	„	
	4 Sātāni ...	1	14	7	7	„	
	Total group 7—4 ...	...	14,505	7,324	7,181	...	
8 Genealogists ...	Tākur ...	...	4	3	1	Hindu.	
10 Astrologers and Quack-doctors.	1 Kaniyān ...	1	9,548	4,846	4,702	Hindu.	
	2 Pulluvan ...	...	274	123	151	„	
	Total group 10—2 ...	...	9,822	4,969	4,853	...	
	Total class B. ...	...	72,027	37,478	34,549	...	

TABLE XVI.

Castes, Tribes and Races by Nationality or Traditional Occupation—(*Continued*).

Class.	Group.	Caste, &c.	No. of recorded sub-divisions.	State Total. Total.	Males.	Females.	Religion.	Strength.
C. Commercial.	14 Traders ...	1 Balija ...	11	449	249	200	Hindu.	
		2 Baniya ...	...	62	53	9	{ Hindu. { Jain.	55 7
		3 Chetti ...	28	17,769	9,089	8,680	Hindu.	
		4 Ilavāniyan ...	...	3,311	1,647	1,664	,,	
		5 Jōnakā ...	1	51,791	26,568	25,223	Mussalman.	
		6 Labbai ...	...	361	213	148	,,	
		7 Mēttan ...	1	54,086	27,523	26,563	,,	
		8 Rāwut ...	...	57	30	27	,,	
		9 Vaduka ...	13	2,696	1,427	1,269	Hindu.	
		10 Vaisya ...	...	474	259	215	,,	
		Total group 14—10 ...	...	131,056	67,058	63,998	...	
	15 Pedlars ...	1 Balukar ...	...	6	6	...	Hindu.	
		2 Manikār ...	...	36	22	14	,,	
		Total group 15—2 ...	...	42	28	14	...	
		Total class C. ...	...	131,098	67,086	64,012	...	
	17 Goldsmiths ...	Tattan ...	4	24,698	12,506	12,192	Hindu.	
	17(*a*) Artisans (general).	1 Kammālan ...	4	1,982	985	997	Hindu.	

TABLE XVI.

Castes, Tribes and Races by Nationality or Traditional Occupation—(*Continued*).

D. Artisans and Village Menials.

	2 Kamsāla ...	...	13	7	6	„
	Total group 17(*a*)—2 ...	...	1,995	992	1,003	...
18 Barbers ...	1 Īlavāti ..	...	2,869	1,360	1,509	Hindu.
	2 Kāvadi ...	2	5,267	2,677	2,590	„
	3 Kōmaram ...	...	257	138	119	„
	4 Kshowrakan ...	9	16,130	7,987	8,143	„
	5 Mārān ...	12	15,228	7,456	7,772	„
	6 Ostta ...	2	66	22	44	Mussalman.
	7 Taravan ...	...	455	226	229	Hindu.
	Total group 18—7 ...	...	40,272	19,866	20,406	...
19 Blacksmiths ...	1 Kollan ...	3	26,982	13,903	13,079	Hindu.
	2 Lōhar ...	...	3	3	...	„
	Total group 19—2 ...	...	26,985	13,906	13,079	...
20 Carpenters, Masons and Turners.	Āsāri ...	5	33,641	16,932	16,709	Hindu.
	Tachan ...	1	4,066	2,014	2,052	„
	Total group 20...	...	37,707	18,946	18,761	...
21 Brass and Copper-smiths.	1 Chembutatti ...	...	98	56	42	Hindu.
	2 Kannān ...	3	5,697	2,894	2,803	„
	Total group 21—2 ...	...	5,795	2,950	2,845	...
22 Tailors ...	Pānān ...	3	2,708	1,409	1,299	Hindu.
22(*a*) Grain-parchers and confectioners.	1 Idiyar ...	...	1,266	660	606	Hindu.
	2 Mudayar ...	..	1	1	...	„
	Total group 22(*a*)—2 ..	...	1,267	661	606	...

TABLE XVI.

Castes, Tribes and Races by Nationality or Traditional Occupation—(*Continued*).

Class.	Group.	Caste, &c.	No. of recorded sub-divisions.	State Total. Total.	Males.	Females.	Religion.	Strength.
Village Menials—(*Continued*).	23 Weavers, calenderers and dyers.	1 Kōri ...	...	7	5	2	Hindu.	
		2 Patnūl ...	...	854	393	461	,,	
		3 Sālē ...	5	7,289	3,580	3,709	,,	
		Total group 23—3 ...	...	8,150	3,978	4,172	...	
	24 Washermen ...	1 Ainuttar ...	...	2	1	1	Hindu.	
		2 Dobi ...	...	138	65	73	,,	
		3 Mannān ...	2	7,082	3,509	3,573	,,	
		4 Velutadan ...	6	13,826	6,993	6,833	,,	
		Total group 24—4 ...	...	21,048	10,568	10,480	...	
	26 Shepherds and wool-weavers.	1 Āttidaya ...	...	217	109	108	Hindu.	
		2 Gollalu ...	1	67	36	31	,,	
		3 Idaya ...	9	5,848	2,863	2,985	,,	
		4 Kāngaya ...	...	125	67	58	,,	
		5 Kūttidaya ...	...	105	58	47	,,	
		Total group 26—5 ...	...	6,362	3,133	3,229	...	
	27 Oil-pressers ...	1 Chekkala ...	3	11,592	5,739	5,853	Hindu.	
		2 Vanian ...	3	13,758	7,031	6,727	,,	
		Total group 27—2	...	25,350	12,770	12,580	...	

Castes, Tribes and Races by Nationality or Traditional Occupation—(*Continued*).

16 D. Artisans and

28 Potters ...	Kosava ...	5	6,395	3 269	3,126	Hindu.	
30 Salt, &c., workers.	Alava ...	1	394	206	188	Hindu.	
31 Lime-burners ...	Paravan ...	1	8,172	3,983	4,189	Hindu.	
35 Fishermen, Boatmen, Palki-bearers, Water-bearers, Cooks, &c.	1 Chaluppan ...	...	921	471	450	Hindu.	
	2 Kāhār ...	...	1	1	...	,,	
	3 Marakkān ...	2	5,491	2,639	2,852	{ Mussalman { Christian.	549 4,942
	4 Mukkuvan ...	5	30,354	15,082	15,272	Hindu.	
	5 Pōndan ...	3	1,139	617	522	,,	
	Total group 35—5 ...	...	37,906	18,810	19,096	...	
35(*a*) Personal service.	Chākkār ...	...	565	306	259	Hindu.	
36 Distillers & Toddy-drawers.	1 Īluva ...	7	414,217	206,528	207,689	Hindu.	
	2 Pāshi ...	...	3	3	...	,,	
	3 Chānnān ...	11	136,611	70.001	66,610	,,	
	4 Tandān ...	3	22,614	11,158	11,456	,,	
	Total group 36—4 ...	...	573,445	287,690	285,755	...	
38 Leather workers...	Chemmān ...	6	2,156	1,094	1,062	Hindu.	
39 Scavengers ...	1 Dāss ...	...	10	5	5	Hindu.	
	2 Valluvan ...	1	113	56	57	,,	
	Total group 39—2 ...	...	123	61	62	...	
	Total class D. ...	...	831,493	417,104	414,389	...	

TABLE XVI.

Castes, Tribes and Races by Nationality or Traditional Occupation—(*Continued*).

Class.	Group.	Caste, &c.	No. of recorded sub-divisions.	State Total. Total.	Males.	Females.	Religion.	Strength.
Artisans and Performers.	40 Grind-stone makers and stone-quarriers.	Kallāsāri ...	3	8,138	4,079	4,059	Hindu.	
	41 Earth-workers and stone-dressers.	1 Ottan ... 2 Ottiya ...	... ...	377 25	292 10	85 15	Hindu. „	
		Total group 41—2 ...	...	402	302	100	...	
	43 Mat-makers, cane splitters, grass-cutters, &c.	Nolayan ...	1	2,323	1,260	1,063	Hindu.	
	44 Hunters, Fowlers, &c.	1 Talavan ... 2 Vēdan ... 3 Vettāran ...	... 1 ...	756 6,809 349	371 3,498 178	385 3,311 171	Hindu. „ „	
		Total group 44—3 ...	...	7,914	4,047	3,867	...	
	45 Miscellaneous and disreputable vagrants.	1 Kākkālan ... 2 Passiavan ...	1 ...	897 64	422 35	475 29	Hindu. „	
		Total group 45—2 ...	...	961	457	504	...	
	45(*a*) Beggars ...	Panisivan	...	58	32	26	Hindu.	

TABLE XVI.

Castes, Tribes and Races by Nationality or Traditional Occupation—(*Continued*).

Class	Group	Caste, Tribe or Race		Total	Males	Females	Religion	
E. Vagrant minor		Sangam Pandāram ...	10	10,724	5,416	5,308	„	
		Total group 45(*a*) ...	...	10,782	5,448	5,334	...	
	46 Tumblers and Acrobats.	1 Gopāl	...	4	3	1	Hindu.	
		2 Kūttādi	...	38	17	21	„	
		Total group 46—2 ...	...	42	20	22	...	
	47 Jugglers, snake charmers and animal exhibitors.	Kuluvan	1	73	42	31	Hindu.	
		Total class E. ...	...	30,635	15,655	14,980	...	
F. Races and Nationalities.	48 Asiatic races of reputed non-Indian descent.	1 Arabs ...	2	446	260	186	Mussalman.	
		2 Chinese ...	...	1	1	...	Christian.	
		3 Jew ...	...	125	65	60	Jew.	
		4 Kābūl ..	...	129	84	45	Mussalman.	
		5 Mughal ...	...	582	317	265	„	
		6 Parsi ...	...	1	1	...	Parsi.	
		7 Pathan ...	...	4,353	2,508	1,845	Mussalman.	
		8 Sheik ...	...	414	240	174	„	
		9 Singalese ...	...	29	17	12	Hindu.	
		10 Syed ...	...	232	117	115	Mussalman.	
		Total group 48—10 ...	...	6,312	3,610	2,702	...	
	50 Non-Asiatic races.	European ...	10	361	210	151	{ Christian. { None.	360 1
	51 Eurasians ...	1 East Indian ...	..	2,072	995	1,077	Christian.	
		2 Eurasian ...	...	532	285	247	„	
		Total group 51 ...		2,604	1,280	1,324	...	

TABLE XVI.

Castes, Tribes and Races by Nationality or Traditional Occupation—(*Continued*).

Class.	Group.	Caste, &c.	No. of recorded sub-divisions.	State Total. Total.	Males.	Females.	Religion.	Strength.
F. Races & Nationalities—*Cont.*	52 Christian converts.	1 Native ...	3	221,006	112,489	108,517	Christian.	
		2 Syrian ...	5	297,795	150,395	147,400	„	
		Total group 52 ...	...	518,801	262,884	255,917	...	
		Total class F. ...	...	528,078	267,984	260,094	...	
G. Undefined.	54 Linguistic, territorial and religious names.	1 Bengalese ...	...	3	3	...	Hindu.	
		2 Guzarati ...	...	48	28	20	„	
		3 Jain ...	...	3	3	...	Jain.	
		4 Kannadiyan ...	...	41	19	22	Hindu.	
		5 Konkani ...	3	7,070	3,681	3,389	„	
		6 Kutch ...	3	316	147	169	Mussalman.	
		7 Mussalman ...	1	14,750	7,203	7,547	„	
		8 Tamil ...	...	3	3	...	Hindu.	
		9 Telugu ...	...	20	10	10	„	
		10 Tulukkan ...	...	29,770	15,555	14,215	Mussalman.	
		Total group 54—10 ...	...	52,024	26,652	25,372	...	
	55 Unknown ...	1 Bālāji ...	1	97	77	20	Hindu.	
		2 Bhavarāsi ...	...	11	7	4	„	
		3 Bhujar ...	...	1	1	...	„	
		4 Bhujavar ...	...	1	1	...	„	
		5 Chilambātti ...	...	9	6	3	„	

TABLE XVI.

Castes, Tribes and Races by Nationality or Traditional Occupation—(*Continued*).

G. Undefined.	6 Heathen ...	...	1	1	...	„	
	7 Kadiyan ...	...	3	2	1	„	
	8 Kāmuvar ...	...	2	2	...	„	
	9 Kodayan ...	...	15	3	12	„	
	10 Kūch ...	...	2	1	1	„	
	11 Malayānkaran ...	...	246	146	100	„	
	12 Mustān ...	...	4	1	3	Mussalman.	
	13 Nāgamom ...	...	13	5	8	Hindu.	
	14 Nālikan ...	...	187	104	83	„	
	15 Naralavēlu ...	...	1	1	...	„	
	16 Neriyan ...	...	145	63	82	„	
	17 Nodiyan ...	...	13	10	3	„	
						„	49
	18 Not stated ...	...	192	108	84	Christian.	142
						None.	1
	19 Pāni ...	...	898	425	473	Mussalman.	
	20 Pattōl ...	...	10	5	5	Hindu.	
	21 Sahabiti ...	...	5	1	4	„	
	22 Tāli ...	...	1	1	...	„	
	23 Tāttedam ...	...	10	6	4	„	
	24 Tōlar ...	...	6	4	2	„	
	Total group 55—24 ...	...	1,873	981	892	...	
	Total class G. ...	...	53,897	27,633	26,264	...	
	Grand Total ...	...	2,557,736	1,290,415	1,267,321	...	

TABLE

Occupations by Age, Part (A)—

Class	Group	Occupation	STATE Total. Total.	0—4.	5—14.	15 and over.
1	2	3	4	5	6	7
A. Government.	1	British Resident of Travancore and Cochin ...	2	...	...	2
		Officers ...	8	1	4	3
		Office superintendents and clerical establishments...	198	12	23	163
		Menials and peons, &c. ...	7	...	...	7
		Total Sub-order 1 ...	215	13	27	175
	4	Officers ...	34	1	7	26
		Non-commissioned officers and privates ...	915	88	108	719
		Followers ...	54	2	31	21
		Clerks ...	1	...	...	1
		Total Sub-order 4 ...	1,004	91	146	767
	6	H. H. The Maharajah of Travancore, G.C.S.I. ...	1	...	...	1
		Officers ...	957	115	272	570
		Clerical establishments ...	6,741	876	1,530	4,335
		Menials, &c. ...	40,936	5,236	8,579	27,121
		Total Sub-order 6 ...	48,635	6,227	10,381	32,027
	7	Officers ...	104	3	21	80
		Privates, &c. ...	1,163	40	166	957
		Total Sub-order 7 ...	1,267	43	187	1,037
		Total Class A. ...	51,121	6,374	10,741	34,006

XVII.

Travancore State Summary.

TOTAL.

Males.				Females.			
Total.	0—4.	5—14.	15 and over.	Total.	0—4.	5—14.	15 and over.
8	9	10	11	12	13	14	15
1	...	...	1	1	...	...	1
5	...	4	1	3	1	...	2
144	8	12	124	54	4	11	39
7	...	...	7	...	...	...	...
157	8	16	133	58	5	11	42
23	1	4	18	11	...	3	8
646	45	53	548	269	43	55	171
35	2	24	9	19	...	7	12
1	...	...	1	...	...	...	...
705	48	81	576	299	43	65	191
1	...	...	1	...	...	...	...
540	59	142	339	417	56	130	231
3,667	448	763	2,456	3,074	428	767	1,879
23,369	2,840	4,586	15,943	17,567	2,396	3,993	11,178
27,577	3,347	5,491	18,739	21,058	2,880	4,890	13,288
44	1	2	41	60	2	19	39
765	12	58	695	398	28	108	262
809	13	60	736	458	30	127	301
29,248	3,416	5,648	20,184	21,873	2,958	5,093	13,822

TABLE

Occupations by Age, Part (A)—

Class.	Group.	Occupation.	Town — Total. Total.	Total. 0—4.	Total. 5—14.	Total. 15 and over.
1	2	3	16	17	18	19
A. Government.	1	British Resident of Travancore and Cochin ...	2	...	...	2
		Officers ...	8	1	4	3
		Office superintendents and clerical establishments ...	33	1	6	26
		Menials and peons, &c. ...	4	...	...	4
		Total Sub-order 1 ...	47	2	10	35
	4	Officers ...	34	1	7	26
		Non-commissioned officers and privates ...	915	88	108	719
		Followers ...	44	2	23	19
		Clerks ...	1	...	...	1
		Total Sub-order 4 ...	994	91	138	765
	6	H. H. The Maharajah of Travancore, G.C.S.I. ...	1	...	...	1
		Officers ...	548	76	170	302
		Clerical establishments ...	2,503	382	678	1,443
		Menials, &c. ...	6,375	924	1,619	3,832
		Total Sub-order 6 ...	9,427	1,382	2,467	5,578
	7	Officers ...	104	3	21	80
		Privates, &c ...	1,163	40	166	957
		Total Sub-order 7 ...	1,267	43	187	1 037
		Total Class A. ...	11,735	1,518	2,802	7,415

XVII.

Travancore State Summary—(*Continued*).

—(*Continued*).

Males.				Females.			
Total.	0—4.	5—14.	15 and over.	Total.	0—4.	5—14.	15 and over.
20	21	22	23	24	25	26	27
1	...	...	1	1	...	...	1
5	...	4	1	3	1	...	2
24	1	3	20	9	...	3	6
4	...	...	4	...	...	...	...
34	1	7	26	13	1	3	9
23	1	4	18	11	...	3	8
646	45	53	548	269	43	55	171
25	2	16	7	19	...	7	12
1	...	...	1	...	...	...	...
695	48	73	574	299	43	65	191
1	...	...	1	...	...	...	...
317	46	95	176	231	30	75	126
1,144	164	352	628	1,359	218	326	815
3,205	487	873	1,845	3,170	437	746	1,987
4,667	697	1,320	2,650	4,760	685	1,147	2,928
44	1	2	41	60	2	19	39
765	12	58	695	398	28	108	262
809	13	60	736	458	30	127	301
6,205	759	1,460	3,986	5,530	759	1,342	3,429

TABLE

Occupation by Age, Part (A)—

Class.	Group.	Occupation.	Country — Total. Total.	Country — Total. 0—4.	Country — Total. 5—14.	Country — Total. 15 and over.
1	2	3	28	29	30	31
A. Government.	1	British Resident of Travancore and Cochin ...	...	...	...	...
		Officers ...	...	...	...	...
		Office superintendents and clerical establishments...	165	11	17	137
		Menials and peons, &c. ...	3	...	...	3
		Total Sub-order 1 ...	168	11	17	140
	4	Officers ...	...	...	...	...
		Non-commissioned officers and privates ...	...	...	...	...
		Followers ...	10	...	8	2
		Clerks ...	...	...	...	...
		Total Sub-order 4 ...	10	...	8	2
	6	H. H. The Maharajah of Travancore, G.C.S.I. ...	...	...	...	...
		Officers ...	409	39	102	268
		Clerical establishments ...	4,238	494	852	2,892
		Menials, &c. ...	34,561	4,312	6,960	23,289
		Total Sub-order 6 ...	39,208	4,845	7,914	26,449
	7	Officers ...	...	...	...	...
		Privates, &c. ...	...	...	...	...
		Total Sub-order 7 ...	...	...	...	...
		Total Class A. ...	39,386	4,856	7,939	26,591

XVII.

Travancore State Summary—(*Continued*).

—(*Continued*).

Males.				Females.			
Total.	0—4.	5—14.	15 and over.	Total.	0—4.	5—14.	15 and over.
32	33	34	35	36	37	38	39
...	...	...	...	...	...	...	...
...	...	...	...	...	...	...	...
120	7	9	104	45	4	8	33
3	...	...	3	...	...	...	...
123	7	9	107	45	4	8	33
...	...	...	...	...	...	...	...
...	...	...	...	...	...	...	...
10	...	8	2	...	...	...	...
...	...	...	...	...	...	...	...
10	...	8	2	...	...	...	...
...	...	...	...	...	...	...	...
223	13	47	163	186	26	55	105
2,523	284	411	1,828	1,715	210	441	1,064
20,164	2,353	3,713	14,098	14,397	1,959	3,247	9,191
22,910	2,650	4,171	16,089	16,298	2,195	3,743	10,360
...	...	...	...	...	...	...	...
...	...	...	...	...	...	...	...
...	...	...	...	...	...	...	...
23,043	2,657	4,188	16,198	16,343	2.199	3,751	10,393

TABLE

Occupation by Age, Part (A)—

Class.	Group.	Occupation.	State — Total. Total.	0—4.	5—14.	15 and over.
1	2	3	4	5	6	7
B. Pasture and Agriculture.	8(*a*)	Horse dealers ...	4	...	...	4
		Cattle dealers ...	8	...	2	6
		Herdsmen ...	740	57	259	424
		Buffalo breeders & dealers.	34	6	14	14
		Total Sub-order 8(*a*) ...	786	63	275	448
	8(*b*)	Elephant catchers ...	2	...	...	2
	8(*c*)	Sheep and goat breeders and dealers ...	795	81	157	557
	9(*a*)	Veterinary Surgeons ...	23	3	8	12
		Farriers ..	21	3	7	11
		Horse and elephant breakers and trainers ...	321	46	82	193
		Total Sub-order 9(*a*) ...	365	52	97	216
	10	Land-occupants, not cultivating ...	1,697	251	449	997
		Land-occupants, cultivating ...	37	8	12	17
		Tenants, not cultivating...	48	7	17	24
		Tenants, cultivating ...	3,610	429	789	2,392
		Total Sub-order 10 ..	5,392	695	1,267	3,430
	11	Field-labourers and crop-watchers ...	1,046,071	136,137	248,098	661,836

XVII.

Travancore State Summary—(*Continued*).

TOTAL.

Males.				Females.			
Total.	0—4.	5—14.	15 and over.	Total.	0—4.	5—14.	15 and over.
8	9	10	11	12	13	14	15
4	...	...	4	...	...	...	...
8	...	2	6	...	...	...	...
507	23	201	283	233	34	58	141
16	3	6	7	18	3	8	7
535	26	209	300	251	37	66	148
2	...	...	2	...	...	...	...
547	46	102	399	248	35	55	158
13	2	3	8	10	1	5	4
10	1	4	5	11	2	3	6
211	31	50	130	110	15	32	63
234	34	57	143	131	18	40	73
695	111	207	377	1,002	140	242	620
15	4	4	7	22	4	8	10
30	4	9	17	18	3	8	7
1,712	228	427	1,057	1,898	201	362	1,335
2,452	347	647	1,458	2,940	348	620	1,972
543,540	66,672	130,667	346,201	502,531	69,465	117,431	315,635

TABLE

Occupation by Age, Part (A)—

Class.	Group.	Occupation.	Town — Total. Total.	0—4.	5—14.	15 and over.
1	2	3	16	17	18	19
B. Pasture and Agriculture.	8(*a*)	Horse dealers ...	4	...	...	4
		Cattle dealers ...	2	...	...	2
		Herdsmen ...	21	6	6	9
		Buffalo breeders & dealers.	1	...	...	1
		Total Sub-order 8(*a*) ...	28	6	6	16
	8(*b*)	Elephant catchers ...	...	...	...	...
	8(*c*)	Sheep and goat breeders and dealers ...	17	4	4	9
	9(*a*)	Veterinary Surgeons ...	7	2	2	3
		Farriers ...	7	2	1	4
		Horse and elephant breakers and trainers ...	38	5	12	21
		Total Sub-order 9(*a*) ...	52	9	15	28
	10	Land-occupants, not cultivating ...	158	23	35	100
		Land-occupants, cultivating ...	8	2	2	4
		Tenants, not cultivating...	20	4	5	11
		Tenants, cultivating ...	38	8	10	20
		Total Sub-order 10 ...	224	37	52	135
	11	Field-labourers and crop-watchers ...	21,370	2,547	4,836	13,987

XVII.

Travancore State Summary—(*Continued*).

—(*Continued*).

Males.				Females.			
Total.	0—4.	5—14.	15 and over.	Total.	0—4.	5—14.	15 and over.
20	21	22	23	24	25	26	27
4	...	...	4	...	...	...	...
2	...	...	2	...	...	...	...
12	2	3	7	9	4	3	2
1	...	...	1	...	...	...	...
19	2	3	14	9	4	3	2
...	...	..	...	...	...	...	...
5	2	1	2	12	2	3	7
4	1	1	2	3	1	1	1
4	1	1	2	3	1	...	2
23	3	7	13	15	2	5	8
31	5	9	17	21	4	6	11
82	8	17	57	76	15	18	43
4	1	...	3	4	1	2	1
14	2	4	8	6	2	1	3
18	3	5	10	20	5	5	10
118	14	26	78	106	23	26	57
11,352	1,249	2,642	7,461	10,018	1,298	2,194	6,526

TABLE

Occupations by Age, Part (A)—

Class.	Group.	Occupation.	Country: Total. Total.	Total. 0—4.	Total. 5—14.	Total. 15 and over.
1	2	3	28	29	30	31
B. Pasture and Agriculture.	8(*a*)	Horse dealers ...	...	...	...	...
		Cattle dealers ...	6	...	2	4
		Herdsmen ...	719	51	253	415
		Buffalo breeders & dealers	33	6	14	13
		Total Sub-order 8(*a*) ...	758	57	269	432
	8(*b*)	Elephant catchers ...	2	...	...	2
	8(*c*)	Sheep and goat breeders and dealers ...	778	77	153	548
	9(*a*)	Veterinary Surgeons ...	16	1	6	9
		Farriers ...	14	1	6	7
		Horse and elephant breakers and trainers ..	283	41	70	172
		Total Sub-order 9(*a*) ...	313	43	82	188
	10	Land-occupants, not cultivating ...	1,539	228	414	897
		Land-occupants, cultivating ...	29	6	10	13
		Tenants, not cultivating...	28	3	12	13
		Tenants, cultivating ...	3,572	421	779	2,372
		Total Sub-order 10 ...	5,168	658	1,215	3,295
	11	Field-labourers and crop-watchers ...	1,024,701	133,590	243,262	647,849

XVII.

Travancore State Summary—(*Continued*).

—(*Continued*).

Males.				Females.			
Total.	0—4.	5—14.	15 and over.	Total.	0—4.	5—14.	15 and over.
32	33	34	35	36	37	38	39
...	...	...	...	...	...	...	...
6	...	2	4	...	...	...	...
495	21	198	276	224	30	55	139
15	3	6	6	18	3	8	7
516	24	206	286	242	33	63	146
2	...	...	2	...	...	...	...
542	44	101	397	236	33	52	151
9	1	2	6	7	...	4	3
6	...	3	3	8	1	3	4
188	28	43	117	95	13	27	55
203	29	48	126	110	14	34	62
613	103	190	320	926	125	224	577
11	3	4	4	18	3	6	9
16	2	5	9	12	1	7	4
1,694	225	422	1,047	1,878	196	357	1,325
2,334	333	621	1,380	2,834	325	594	1,915
532,188	65,423	128,025	338,740	492,513	68,167	115,237	309,109

TABLE

Occupations by Age, Part (A)—

Class.	Group.	Occupation.	STATE — Total. Total.	0—4.	5—14.	15 and over.
1	2	3	4	5	6	7
B. Pasture and Agriculture.	12	Tea and coffee planters, managers and assistants.	232	43	45	144
		Cocoanut growers ...	27	7	6	14
		Betel-vine growers ...	204	16	49	139
		Cardamom and pepper growers	127	22	39	66
		Market gardeners (vegetable growers) ...	3,793	548	1,169	2,076
		Gardeners, &c. ...	127	13	27	87
		Manure preparers and sellers ...	78	2	7	69
		Forest officers ...	11	...	...	11
		Forest guards and peons..	253	20	42	191
		Total Sub-order 12 ...	4,852	671	1,384	2,797
	13	Agents and managers of landed estates ...	285	45	64	176
		Total Class B. ...	1,058,548	137,744	251,342	669,462

XVII.

Travancore State Summary—(*Continued*).

TOTAL.

Males.				Females.			
Total.	0—4.	5—14.	15 and over.	Total.	0—4.	5—14.	15 and over.
8	9	10	11	12	13	14	15
150	26	22	102	82	17	23	42
12	3	4	5	15	4	2	9
95	...	29	66	109	16	20	73
66	11	21	34	61	11	18	32
3,220	468	1,005	1,747	573	80	164	329
92	4	21	67	35	9	6	20
41	...	2	39	37	2	5	30
10	...	...	10	1	...	...	1
109	9	17	83	144	11	25	108
3,795	521	1,121	2,153	1,057	150	263	644
169	24	36	109	116	21	28	67
551,274	67,670	132,839	350,765	507,274	70,074	118,503	318,697

TABLE

Occupations by Age, Part (A)—

Class.	Group.	Occupation.	Town: Total. Total.	Total. 0—4.	Total. 5—14.	Total. 15 and over.
1	2	3	16	17	18	19
B. Pasture and Agriculture.	12	Tea and coffee planters, managers and assistants.	19	4	6	9
		Cocoanut growers ...	3	1	...	2
		Betel-vine growers ...	2	...	...	2
		Cardamom and pepper growers ...	...	...	...	...
		Market gardeners (vegetable growers) ...	3	...	...	3
		Gardeners, &c. ...	6	3	1	2
		Manure preparers and sellers ...	...	...	...	...
		Forest officers ...	5	...	...	5
		Forest guards and peons...	13	...	8	5
		Total Sub-order 12 ...	51	8	15	28
	13	Agents and managers of landed estates ...	51	15	10	26
		Total Class B. ...	21,793	2,626	4,938	14,229

XVII.

Travancore State Summary—(*Continued*).

—(*Continued*).

Males.				Females.			
Total.	0—4.	5—14.	15 and over.	Total.	0—4.	5—14.	15 and over.
20	21	22	23	24	25	26	27
12	2	4	6	7	2	2	3
2	1	...	1	1	...	...	1
1	...	...	1	1	...	...	1
...	...	...	...	...	...	...	...
2	...	...	2	1	...	...	1
4	2	1	1	2	1	...	1
...	...	...	...	...	...	...	...
4	...	...	4	1	...	...	1
4	...	2	2	9	...	6	3
29	5	7	17	22	3	8	11
23	3	7	13	28	12	3	13
11,577	1,280	2,695	7,602	10,216	1,346	2,243	6,627

TABLE

Occupations by Age, Part (A)—

Class.	Group.	Occupation.	Country — Total. Total.	0—4.	5—14.	15 and over.
1	2	3	28	29	30	31
B. Pasture and Agriculture.	12	Tea and coffee planters, managers and assistants.	213	39	39	135
		Cocoanut growers ...	24	6	6	12
		Betel-vine growers ...	202	16	49	137
		Cardamom and pepper growers ...	127	22	39	66
		Market gardeners (vegetable growers) ...	3,790	548	1,169	2,073
		Gardeners, &c. ...	121	10	26	85
		Manure preparers and sellers ...	78	2	7	69
		Forest officers ...	6	...	...	6
		Forest guards and peons..	240	20	34	186
		Total Sub-order 12 ...	4,801	663	1,369	2,769
	13	Agents and managers of landed estates ...	234	30	54	150
		Total Class B. ...	1,036,755	135,118	246,404	655,233

XVII.

Travancore State Summary—(*Continued*).

—(*Continued*).

Males.				Females.			
Total.	0—4.	5—14.	15 and over.	Total.	0—4.	5—14.	15 and over.
32	33	34	35	36	37	38	39
138	24	18	96	75	15	21	39
10	2	4	4	14	4	2	8
94	...	29	65	108	16	20	72
66	11	21	34	61	11	18	32
3,218	468	1,005	1,745	572	80	164	328
88	2	20	66	33	8	6	19
41	...	2	39	37	2	5	30
6	...	...	6	...	...	...	...
105	9	15	81	135	11	19	105
3,766	516	1,114	2,136	1,035	147	255	633
146	21	29	96	88	9	25	54
539,697	66,390	130,144	343,163	497,058	68,728	116,260	312,370

TABLE

Occupations by Age, Part (A)—

Class.	Group.	Occupation and Class. / Occupation.	State — Total. Total.	0—4.	5—14.	15 and over.
1	2	3	4	5	6	7
C. Personal Services.	14	Barbers ...	17,395	2,297	4,212	10,886
		Ear-pickers ...	18	1	...	17
		Washermen ...	21,631	2,557	4,972	14,102
		Water-carriers ...	172	25	27	120
		Cooks ...	473	65	105	303
		In-door servants ...	38,842	3,199	8,486	27,157
		Grooms, coachmen, dog-boys, &c. ...	526	79	109	338
		Door-keepers, &c. ...	14	...	6	8
		Total Sub-order 14 ...	79,071	8,223	17,917	52,931
	15	Hotel-keepers, &c. ...	735	77	224	434
		Rest-house keepers ...	2	...	...	2
		Club secretaries	11	...	5	6
		Total Sub-order 15 ...	748	77	229	442
	16	Sanitary officers of Government ...	51	5	14	32
		Sweepers and scavengers..	408	34	130	244
		Total Sub-order 16 ...	459	39	144	276
		Total Class C. ...	80,278	8,339	18,290	53,649

XVII.

Travancore State Summary—(*Continued*).

TOTAL.

Males.				Females.			
Total.	0—4.	5—14.	15 and over.	Total.	0—4.	5—14.	15 and over.
8	9	10	11	12	13	14	15
8,604	1,041	2,169	5,394	8,791	1,256	2,043	5,492
11	1	...	10	7	...	...	7
9,472	1,104	2,250	6,118	12,159	1,453	2,722	7,984
79	3	12	64	93	22	15	56
159	15	37	107	314	50	68	196
10,048	1,081	2,835	6,132	28,794	2,118	5,651	21,025
343	38	67	238	183	41	42	100
10	...	4	6	4	...	2	2
28,726	3,283	7,374	18,069	50,345	4,940	10,543	34,862
254	22	56	176	481	55	168	258
2	...	...	2	...	...	...	...
11	...	5	6	...	...	...	...
267	22	61	184	481	55	168	258
17	1	4	12	34	4	10	20
219	24	57	138	189	10	73	106
236	25	61	150	223	14	83	126
29,229	3,330	7,496	18,403	51,049	5,009	10,794	35,246

TABLE

Occupations by Age, Part (A)—

Class.	Group.	Occupation.	Town — Total. Total.	Town — Total. 0—4.	Town — Total. 5—14.	Town — Total. 15 and over.
1	2	3	16	17	18	19
C. Personal Services.	14	Barbers ...	1,719	299	517	903
		Ear-pickers ...	1	...	...	1
		Washermen ...	1,798	262	480	1,056
		Water-carriers ...	101	17	19	65
		Cooks ...	105	27	37	41
		In-door servants ...	706	88	231	387
		Grooms, coachmen, dog-boys, &c. ...	167	34	60	73
		Door-keepers, &c. ...	2	...	...	2
		Total Sub-order 14 ...	4,599	727	1,344	2,528
	15	Hotel-keepers, &c. ...	175	25	33	117
		Rest-house keepers ...	...	...	...	...
		Club secretaries ...	11	...	5	6
		Total Sub-order 15 ...	186	25	38	123
	16	Sanitary officers of Government ...	51	5	14	32
		Sweepers and scavengers..	51	11	12	28
		Total Sub-order 16 ...	102	16	26	60
		Total Class C. ...	4,887	768	1,408	2,711

XVII.

Travancore State Summary—(*Continued*).

—(*Continued*).

Males.				Females.			
Total.	0—4.	5—14.	15 and over.	Total.	0—4	5—14.	15 and over.
20	21	22	23	24	25	26	27
749	74	189	486	970	225	328	417
1	...	...	1	...	...	...	...
986	125	263	598	812	137	217	458
40	3	7	30	61	14	12	35
59	13	27	19	46	14	10	22
340	43	117	180	366	45	114	207
87	15	24	48	80	19	36	25
1	...	...	1	1	...	...	1
2,263	273	627	1,363	2,336	454	717	1,165
90	14	17	59	85	11	16	58
...	...	...	...	...	...	...	...
11	...	5	6	...	...	...	...
101	14	22	65	85	11	16	58
17	1	4	12	34	4	10	20
29	8	5	16	22	3	7	12
46	9	9	28	56	7	17	32
2,410	296	658	1,456	2,477	472	750	1,255

TABLE

Occupations by Age, Part (A)—

Class.	Group.	Occupation.	Country — Total. Total.	Total. 0—4.	Total. 5—14.	Total. 15 and over.
1	2	3	28	29	30	31
C. Personal Services.	14	Barbers ...	15,676	1,998	3,695	9,983
		Ear-pickers ...	17	1	...	16
		Washermen ...	19,833	2,295	4,492	13,046
		Water-carriers ...	71	8	8	55
		Cooks ...	368	38	68	262
		In-door servants ...	38,136	3,111	8,255	26,770
		Grooms, coachmen, dog-boys, &c. ...	359	45	49	265
		Door-keepers, &c. ...	12	...	6	6
		Total Sub-order 14 ...	74,472	7,496	16,573	50,403
	15	Hotel-keepers, &c. ...	560	52	191	317
		Rest-house keepers ...	2	...	...	2
		Club secretaries ...	...	...	...	...
		Total Sub-order 15 ...	562	52	191	319
	16	Sanitary officers of Government ...	...	...	...	...
		Sweepers and scavengers.	357	23	118	216
		Total Sub-order 16 ...	357	23	118	216
		Total Class C. ...	75,391	7,571	16,882	50,938

XVII.

Travancore State Summary—(*Continued*).

—(*Continued*).

Males.				Females.			
Total.	0—4.	5—14.	15 and over.	Total.	0—4.	5—14.	15 and over.
32	33	34	35	36	37	38	39
7,855	967	1,980	4,908	7,821	1,031	1,715	5,075
10	1	...	9	7	...	...	7
8,486	979	1,987	5,520	11,347	1,316	2,505	7,526
39	...	5	34	32	8	3	21
100	2	10	88	268	36	58	174
9,708	1,038	2,718	5,952	28,428	2,073	5,537	20,818
256	23	43	190	103	22	6	75
9	...	4	5	3	...	2	1
26,463	3,010	6,747	16,706	48,009	4,486	9,826	33,697
164	8	39	117	396	44	152	200
2	...	...	2	...	...	...	...
...	...	...	...	...	...	...	...
166	8	39	119	396	44	152	200
...	...	...	...	...	...	...	...
190	16	52	122	167	7	66	94
190	16	52	122	167	7	66	94
26,819	3,034	6,838	16,947	48,572	4,537	10,044	33,991

TABLE

Occupations by Age, Part (A)—

Class.	Group.	Occupation.	Total.	0—4.	5—14.	15 and over.
		Occupation and Class.	**State** — Total.			
1	2	3	4	5	6	7
D. Preparation and supply of material substances.	17	Cow and buffalo keepers and milk & butter sellers.	709	33	215	461
		Ghee preparers & sellers...	56	7	16	33
		Butchers ...	646	81	91	474
		Fowl and egg sellers ...	47	8	17	22
		Fishermen and fish-curers.	28,885	3,833	6,854	18,198
		Fish dealers ...	26,807	3,074	6,348	17,385
		Total Sub-order 17 ...	57,150	7,036	13,541	36,573
	18	Grain dealers ...	1,084	134	261	689
		Flour preparers & sellers..	53	7	15	31
		Bakers ...	17	...	...	17
		Bran sellers ...	49	6	16	27
		Vegetable sellers ...	351	40	55	256
		Fruit sellers ...	9	4	2	3
		Cocoanut dealers ...	1,230	174	315	741
		Confectioners and sweet-meat makers and sellers and cooks (publique) ...	3,051	343	725	1,983
		Sweet-meat pedlars ...	16	...	3	13
		Total Sub-order 18 ...	5,860	708	1,392	3,760

XVII.

Travancore State Summary—(*Continued*).

TOTAL.

Males.				Females.			
Total.	0—4.	5—14.	15 and over.	Total.	0—4.	5—14.	15 and over.
8	9	10	11	12	13	14	15
224	10	63	151	485	23	152	310
37	3	9	25	19	4	7	8
388	43	25	320	258	38	66	154
29	4	9	16	18	4	8	6
19,132	2,401	4,549	12,182	9,753	1,432	2,305	6,016
10,314	1,091	2,503	6,720	16,493	1,983	3,845	10,665
30,124	3,552	7,158	19,414	27,026	3,484	6,383	17,159
725	91	177	457	359	43	84	232
29	3	8	18	24	4	7	13
13	...	...	13	4	...	...	4
10	2	5	3	39	4	11	24
149	11	20	118	202	29	35	138
6	2	1	3	3	2	1	...
727	92	178	457	503	82	137	284
1,393	169	363	861	1,658	174	362	1,122
13	...	2	11	3	...	1	2
3,065	370	754	1,941	2,795	338	638	1,819

TABLE

Occupations by Age, Part (A)—

Class.	Group.	Occupation.	Town — Total. Total.	Total. 0—4.	Total. 5—14.	Total. 15 and over.
1	2	3	16	17	18	19
D. Preparation and supply of material substances.	17	Cow and buffalo keepers and milk & butter sellers.	130	24	36	70
		Ghee preparers & sellers ..	19	5	5	9
		Butchers ...	259	32	51	176
		Fowl and egg sellers ...	13	2	3	8
		Fishermen & fish-curers...	1,445	312	495	638
		Fish dealers ...	1,413	233	448	732
		Total Sub-order 17 ...	3,279	608	1,038	1,633
	18	Grain dealers ...	486	85	166	235
		Flour preparers & sellers..	22	6	7	9
		Bakers ...	8	...	...	8
		Bran sellers ...	18	5	3	10
		Vegetable sellers ...	90	8	17	65
		Fruit sellers ...	5	2	1	2
		Cocoanut dealers ...	472	56	87	329
		Confectioners and sweet-meat makers and sellers and cooks (publique) ...	555	95	158	302
		Sweet-meat pedlars ...	16	...	3	13
		Total Sub-order 18 ...	1,672	257	442	973

XVII.

Travancore State Summary—(*Continued*).

—(*Continued*).

Males.				Females.			
Total.	0—4.	5—14.	15 and over.	Total.	0—4.	5—14.	15 and over.
20	21	22	23	24	25	26	27
72	4	21	47	58	20	15	23
9	2	3	4	10	3	2	5
114	13	14	87	145	19	37	89
4	1	1	2	9	1	2	6
910	167	315	428	535	145	180	210
822	115	272	435	591	118	176	297
1,931	302	626	1,003	1,348	306	412	630
253	42	86	125	233	43	80	110
8	2	4	2	14	4	3	7
4	...	...	4	4	...	...	4
4	1	...	3	14	4	3	7
10	...	...	10	80	8	17	55
5	2	1	2	...	...	...	...
62	4	12	46	410	52	75	283
435	70	110	255	120	25	48	47
13	...	2	11	3	...	1	2
794	121	215	458	878	136	227	515

TABLE

Occupations by Age, Part (A)—

Class.	Group.	Occupation.	Country: Total. Total.	0—4.	5—14.	15 and over.
1	2	3	28	29	30	31
D. Preparation and supply of material substances.	17	Cow and buffalo keepers & milk and butter sellers...	579	9	179	391
		Ghee preparers & sellers..	37	2	11	24
		Butchers ...	387	49	40	298
		Fowl and egg sellers ...	34	6	14	14
		Fishermen & fish curers...	27,440	3,521	6,359	17,560
		Fish dealers ...	25,394	2,841	5,900	16,653
		Total Sub-order 17 ...	53,871	6,428	12,503	34,940
	18	Grain dealers ...	598	49	95	454
		Flour preparers & sellers.	31	1	8	22
		Bakers ..	9	...	...	9
		Bran sellers ...	31	1	13	17
		Vegetable sellers ...	261	32	38	191
		Fruit sellers ...	4	2	1	1
		Cocoanut dealers ...	758	118	228	412
		Confectioners and sweet-meat makers & sellers & cooks (publique) ...	2,496	248	567	1,681
		Sweet-meat pedlars ...	...	...	...	...
		Total Sub-order 18 ...	4,188	451	950	2,787

XVII.

Travancore State Summary—(*Continued*).

—(*Continued*).

Males.				Females.			
Total.	0—4.	5—14.	15 and over.	Total.	0—4.	5—14.	15 and over.
32	33	34	35	36	37	38	39
152	6	42	104	427	3	137	287
28	1	6	21	9	1	5	3
274	30	11	233	113	19	29	65
25	3	8	14	9	3	6	...
18,222	2,234	4,234	11,754	9,218	1,287	2,125	5,806
9,492	976	2,231	6,285	15,902	1,865	3,669	10,368
28,193	3,250	6,532	18,411	25,678	3,178	5,971	16,529
472	49	91	332	126	...	4	122
21	1	4	16	10	...	4	6
9	...	...	9	...	...	...	...
6	1	5	...	25	...	8	17
139	11	20	108	122	21	18	83
1	...	...	1	3	2	1	...
665	88	166	411	93	30	62	1
958	99	253	606	1,538	149	314	1,075
...	...	...	...	...	...	...	...
2,271	249	539	1,483	1,917	202	411	1,304

TABLE

Occupations by Age, Part (A)—

Class.	Group.	Occupation.	STATE Total. Total.	0—4.	5—14.	15 and over.
1	2	3	4	5	6	7
D. Preparation and supply of material substances.	19	Sharbat preparers and sellers ...	6	...	2	4
		Country-spirits distillers and sellers ...	1,581	240	401	940
		Toddy drawers and sellers.	75,746	10,335	18,047	47,364
		Foreign wine and spirit dealers ...	2	...	...	2
		Tea sellers ...	7	2	2	3
		Coffee preparers & sellers..	131	22	25	84
		Sugar sellers ...	24	2	11	11
		Molasses (jaggery, gur, &c.) makers and sellers.	68,395	9,600	15,764	43,031
		Salt prepares and sellers..	1,207	138	283	786
		Grocers and general condiment dealers ...	508	82	105	321
		Betel leaf and arecanut sellers ..	1,222	136	289	797
		Tobacco and snuff manufacturers and sellers ...	4,026	462	982	2,582
		Opium, &c. sellers ...	9	1	3	5
		Total Sub-order 19 ...	152,864	21,020	35,914	95,930
	20	Oil-pressers and sellers ...	14,071	1,761	3,613	8,697
		Oil sellers ...	2,987	412	751	1,824
		Oil-cake dealers ...	677	100	177	400
		Kerosine oil dealers ...	35	7	10	18
		Matches sellers ...	12	5	3	4
		Lamp and lantern makers and sellers ...	25	2	6	17
		Lamp lighting ...	22	3	1	18
		Total Sub-order 20 ...	17,829	2,290	4,561	10,978

XVII.

Travancore State Summary—(*Continued*).

TOTAL.

Males.				Females.			
Total.	0—4.	5—14.	15 and over.	Total.	0—4.	5—14.	15 and over.
8	9	10	11	12	13	14	15
6	...	2	4	...	...	...	...
469	87	141	241	1,112	153	260	699
40,675	5,102	9,297	26,276	35,071	5,233	8,750	21,088
2	...	...	2	...	...	...	...
7	2	2	3	...	...	...	...
70	10	13	47	61	12	12	37
16	1	8	7	8	1	3	4
38,075	4,732	8,657	24,686	30,320	4,868	7,107	18,345
688	78	155	455	519	60	128	331
423	66	84	273	85	16	21	48
585	54	128	403	637	82	161	394
2,385	249	631	1,505	1,641	213	351	1,077
5	...	1	4	4	1	2	1
83,406	10,381	19,119	53,906	69,458	10,639	16,795	42,024
7,874	849	1,924	5,101	6,197	912	1,689	3,596
1,325	167	340	818	1,662	245	411	1,006
526	72	124	330	151	28	53	70
22	4	3	15	13	3	7	3
8	4	1	3	4	1	2	1
15	1	3	11	10	1	3	6
14	...	1	13	8	3	...	5
9,784	1,097	2,396	6,291	8,045	1,193	2,165	4,687

TABLE

Occupations by Age, Part (A)—

Class.	Group.	Occupation.	Town Total. Total. 16	Total. 0—4. 17	Total. 5—14. 18	Total. 15 and over. 19
1	2	3	16	17	18	19
D. Preparation and supply of material substances	19	Sharbat preparers and sellers ...	2	...	...	2
		Country-spirits distillers and sellers ...	47	9	13	25
		Toddy drawers and sellers.	36	9	10	17
		Foreign wine and spirit dealers ...	2	...	...	2
		Tea sellers ...	7	2	2	3
		Coffee preparers & sellers.	75	13	12	50
		Sugar sellers ...	6	...	2	4
		Molasses (jaggery, gur, &c.) makers and sellers..	347	65	86	196
		Salt preparers and sellers.	64	7	15	42
		Grocers and general condiment dealers ...	112	19	32	61
		Betel-leaf and arecanut sellers ...	148	17	47	84
		Tobacco and snuff manufacturers and sellers ...	665	122	218	325
		Opium, &c., sellers ...	9	1	3	5
		Total Sub-order 19 ...	1,520	264	440	816
	20	Oil-pressers and sellers ...	372	71	101	200
		Oil sellers ...	689	132	225	332
		Oil-cake dealers ...	83	20	26	37
		Kerosine oil dealers ...	18	4	4	10
		Matches sellers ...	9	3	3	3
		Lamp and lantern makers and sellers ...	23	2	5	16
		Lamp lighting ..	22	3	1	18
		Total Sub-order 20 ...	1,216	235	365	616

XVII.

Travancore State Summary—(*Continued*).

—(*Continued*).

Males.				Females.			
Total.	0—4.	5—14.	15 and over.	Total.	0—4.	5—14.	15 and over.
20	21	22	23	24	25	26	27
2	...	...	2	...	...	...	...
24	5	7	12	23	4	6	13
16	5	3	8	20	4	7	9
2	...	...	2	...	...	...	...
7	2	2	3	...	...	...	...
36	5	8	23	39	8	4	27
5	...	2	3	1	...	...	1
195	18	55	122	152	47	31	74
40	4	8	28	24	3	7	14
86	15	24	47	26	4	8	14
74	8	19	47	74	9	28	37
265	49	81	135	400	73	137	190
5	...	1	4	4	1	2	1
757	111	210	436	763	153	230	380
168	29	54	85	204	42	47	115
389	57	110	222	300	75	115	110
45	9	14	22	38	11	12	15
13	2	3	8	5	2	1	2
5	2	1	2	4	1	2	1
13	1	2	10	10	1	3	6
14	...	1	13	8	3	...	5
647	100	185	362	569	135	180	254

TABLE

Occupations by Age, Part (A)—

Class.	Group.	Occupation.	Country — Total. Total.	0—4.	5—14.	15 and over.
1	2	3	28	29	30	31
D. Preparation and supply of material substances.	19	Sharbat preparers and sellers ...	4	...	2	2
		Country-spirits distillers and sellers ...	1,534	231	388	915
		Toddy drawers and sellers.	75,710	10,326	18,037	47,347
		Foreign wine and spirit dealers ...	...	...	...	..
		Tea sellers ...	...	...	...	...
		Coffee preparers & sellers.	56	9	13	34
		Sugar sellers ...	18	2	9	7
		Molasses (jaggery, gur, &c.) makers and sellers..	68,048	9,535	15,678	42,835
		Salt preparers and sellers.	1,143	131	268	744
		Grocers and general condi ment dealers ...	396	63	73	260
		Betel- leaf and arecanut sellers ...	1,074	119	242	713
		Tobacco and snuff manufacturers and sellers ...	3,361	340	764	2,257
		Opium, &c., sellers ...	...	...	...	...
		Total Sub-order 19 ...	151,344	20,756	35,474	95,114
	20	Oil-pressers and sellers ...	13,699	1,690	3,512	8,497
		Oil sellers ...	2,298	280	526	1,492
		Oil-cake dealers ...	594	80	151	363
		Kerosine oil dealers ...	17	3	6	8
		Matches sellers ...	3	2	...	1
		Lamp and lantern makers and sellers ...	2	...	1	1
		Lamp lighting ...	...	...	...	...
		Total Sub-order 20 ...	16,613	2,055	4,196	10,362

XVII.

Travancore State Summary—(*Continued*).

—(*Continued*).

Males.				Females.			
Total.	0—4.	5—14.	15 and over.	Total.	0—4.	5—14.	15 and over.
32	33	34	35	36	37	38	39
4	...	2	2	...	...	...	...
445	82	134	229	1,089	149	254	686
40,659	5,097	9,294	26,268	35,051	5,229	8,743	21,079
...	...	...	...	...	...	...	...
...	...	...	...	...	...	...	...
34	5	5	24	22	4	8	10
11	1	6	4	7	1	3	3
37,880	4,714	8,602	24,564	30,168	4,821	7,076	18,271
648	74	147	427	495	57	121	317
337	51	60	226	59	12	13	34
511	46	109	356	563	73	133	357
2,120	200	550	1,370	1,241	140	214	887
...	...	...	...	...	...	...	...
82,649	10,270	18,909	53,470	68,695	10,486	16,565	41,644
7,706	820	1,870	5,016	5,993	870	1,642	3,481
936	110	230	596	1,362	170	296	896
481	63	110	308	113	17	41	55
9	2	..	7	8	1	6	1
3	2	...	1	...	...	...	...
2	...	1	1	...	...	...	...
...	...	...	...	...	...	...	...
9,137	997	2,211	5,929	7,476	1,058	1,985	4,433

TABLE

Occupations by Age, Part (A)—

Class.	Group.	Occupation.	State — Total. Total.	0—4.	5—14.	15 and over.
1	2	3	4	5	6	7
D. Preparation and supply of material substances.	21	Fire-wood and grass gatherers and sellers ...	71	4	10	57
		Fire-wood contractors and dealers ...	389	35	95	259
		Charcoal burners and dealers ...	50	6	10	34
		Hay dealers ...	23	2	3	18
		Total Sub-order 21 ...	533	47	118	368
	22	Brick and tile burners and sellers ...	56	10	15	31
		Lime, chunam and shell burners and sellers ...	1,265	128	321	816
		Thatch dealers and thatchers ...	174	21	46	107
		Total Sub-order 22 ...	1,495	159	382	954
	23	Building contractors ...	378	42	89	247
		Stone workers ...	5,839	604	1,050	4,185
		Masons ...	1,783	139	265	1,379
		Mud wall & roof-builders..	162	22	36	104
		Glaziers ...	41	8	12	21
		Tilers ...	124	34	42	48
		Total Sub-order 23 ...	8,327	849	1,494	5,984
	25	Cart-makers and sellers...	3	...	...	3
		Palki-makers ...	3	...	1	2
		Total Sub-order 25 ...	6	...	1	5

XVII.

Travancore State Summary—(*Continued*).

TOTAL.

Males.				Females.			
Total.	0—4.	5—14.	15 and over.	Total.	0—4.	5—14.	15 and over.
8	9	10	11	12	13	14	15
8	3	2	3	63	1	8	54
122	10	29	83	267	25	66	176
19	2	1	16	31	4	9	18
13	...	2	11	10	2	1	7
162	15	34	113	371	32	84	255
30	3	9	18	26	7	6	13
642	66	143	433	623	62	178	383
81	11	22	48	93	10	24	59
753	80	174	499	742	79	208	455
219	17	57	145	159	25	32	102
1,171	102	180	889	4,668	502	870	3,296
624	56	127	441	1,159	83	138	938
88	11	21	56	74	11	15	48
26	4	9	13	15	4	3	8
15	4	2	9	109	30	40	39
2,143	194	396	1,553	6,184	655	1,098	4,431
2	...	...	2	1	...	...	1
2	...	1	1	1	...	...	1
4	...	1	3	2	...	...	2

TABLE

Occupations by Age, Part (A)—

Class.	Group.	Occupation.	Town			
			Total.			
			Total.	0—4.	5—14.	15 and over.
1	2	3	16	17	18	19
D. Preparation and supply of material substances.	21	Fire-wood and grass gatherers and sellers ...	5	1	...	4
		Fire-wood contractors and dealers ...	107	18	29	60
		Charcoal burners and dealers ...	...	...	...	...
		Hay dealers ...	8	1	2	5
		Total Sub-order 21 ...	120	20	31	69
	22	Brick and tile burners and sellers ...	15	4	3	8
		Lime, chunam and shell burners and sellers ...	35	5	12	18
		Thatch dealers and thatchers ...	34	5	12	17
		Total Sub-order 22 ...	84	14	27	43
	23	Building contractors ...	48	12	9	27
		Stone workers ...	29	7	8	14
		Masons ...	360	50	95	215
		Mud wall and roof-builders.	28	4	11	13
		Glaziers ...	41	8	12	21
		Tilers ...	32	5	9	18
		Total Sub-order 23 ...	538	86	144	308
	25	Cart-makers and sellers...	3	...	...	3
		Palki-makers ...	3	...	1	2
		Total Sub-order 25 ...	6	...	1	5

XVII.

Travancore State Summary—(*Continued*).

—(*Continued*).

Males.				Females.			
Total.	0—4.	5—14.	15 and over.	Total.	0—4.	5—14.	15 and over.
20	21	22	23	24	25	26	27
2	1	...	1	3	...	...	3
44	5	12	27	63	13	17	33
...	...	...	...	...	...	...	...
4	...	1	3	4	1	1	2
50	6	13	31	70	14	18	38
9	2	2	5	6	2	1	3
26	5	8	13	9	...	4	5
18	3	7	8	16	2	5	9
53	10	17	26	31	4	10	17
29	7	7	15	19	5	2	12
17	4	5	8	12	3	3	6
216	34	61	121	144	16	34	94
17	...	6	11	11	4	5	2
26	4	9	13	15	4	3	8
8	1	2	5	24	4	7	13
313	50	90	173	225	36	54	135
2	...	...	2	1	...	...	1
2	...	1	1	1	...	...	1
4	...	1	3	2	...	...	2

TABLE

Occupations by Age, Part (A)—

Class.	Group.	Occupation.	Country — Total. Total.	Total. 0—4.	Total. 5—14.	Total. 15 and over.
1	2	3	28	29	30	31
D. Preparation and supply of material substances.	21	Fire-wood and grass gatherers and sellers ...	66	3	10	53
		Fire-wood contractors and dealers ...	282	17	66	199
		Charcoal burners and dealers ...	50	6	10	34
		Hay dealers ...	15	1	1	13
		Total Sub-order 21 ...	413	27	87	299
	22	Brick and tile burners and sellers ...	41	6	12	23
		Lime, chunam and shell burners and sellers ...	1,230	123	309	798
		Thatch dealers and thatchers ...	140	16	34	90
		Total Sub-order 22 ...	1,411	145	355	911
	23	Building contractors ...	330	30	80	220
		Stone workers ...	5,810	597	1,042	4,171
		Masons ...	1,423	89	170	1,164
		Mud wall & roof-builders.	134	18	25	91
		Glaziers ...	...	...	...	...
		Tilers ...	92	29	33	30
		Total Sub-order 23 ..	7,789	763	1,350	5,676
	25	Cart-makers and sellers...	...	...	...	...
		Palki-makers ...	...	...	...	...
		Total Sub-order 25 ...	...	...	...	...

XVII.

Travancore State Summary—(*Continued*).

—(*Continued*).

Males.				Females.			
Total.	0—4.	5—14.	15 and over.	Total.	0—4.	5—14.	15 and over.
32	33	34	35	36	37	38	39
6	2	2	2	60	1	8	51
78	5	17	56	204	12	49	143
19	2	1	16	31	4	9	18
9	...	1	8	6	1	...	5
112	9	21	82	301	18	66	217
21	1	7	13	20	5	5	10
616	61	135	420	614	62	174	378
63	8	15	40	77	8	19	50
700	70	157	473	711	75	198	438
190	10	50	130	140	20	30	90
1,154	98	175	881	4,656	499	867	3,290
408	22	66	320	1,015	67	104	844
71	11	15	45	63	7	10	46
...	...	...	...	...	...	...	...
7	3	...	4	85	26	33	26
1,830	144	306	1,380	5,959	619	1,044	4,296
...	...	...	...	...	...	...	...
...	...	...	...	...	...	...	...
...	...	...	...	...	...	...	...

TABLE

Occupations by Age, Part (A)—

Occupation and Class.			State			
			Total.			
Class.	Group.	Occupation.	Total.	0—4.	5—14.	15 and over.
1	2	3	4	5	6	7
D. Preparation and supply of material substances.	26	Shipwrights and boat-builders, &c. ...	142	16	35	91
		Canoe diggers, &c. ...	603	69	161	373
		Total Sub-order 26 ...	745	85	196	464
	27	Paper makers and palm-leaf binders ...	26	6	5	15
		Stationers ...	27	3	13	11
		Total Sub-order 27 ...	53	9	18	26
	28	Press proprietors and printers ...	214	36	66	112
		Book-binders ...	90	20	25	45
		Book-sellers ...	26	...	2	24
		Newspaper proprietors ...	1	...	...	1
		Picture dealers ...	1	...	...	1
		Total Sub-order 28 ...	332	56	93	183
	29	Watch and clock-makers...	34	3	10	21
	30	Wood and ebony carvers...	2	...	...	2
		Ivory carvers ...	168	27	50	91
		Turners ...	1,239	223	406	610
		Engravers ...	99	5	32	62
		Total Sub-order 30 ...	1,508	255	488	765

XVII.

Travancore State Summary—(*Continued*).

TOTAL.

Males.				Females.			
Total.	0—4.	5—14.	15 and over.	Total.	0—4.	5—14.	15 and over.
8	9	10	11	12	13	14	15
79	6	20	53	63	10	15	38
143	11	23	109	460	58	138	264
222	17	43	162	523	68	153	302
17	2	3	12	9	4	2	3
19	2	9	8	8	1	4	3
36	4	12	20	17	5	6	6
103	17	26	60	111	19	40	52
57	5	22	30	33	15	3	15
17	...	2	15	9	...	...	9
1	...	...	1	...	...	...	...
1	...	...	1	...	...	...	...
179	22	50	107	153	34	43	76
18	...	6	12	16	3	4	9
2	...	...	2	...	...	...	...
66	12	22	32	102	15	28	59
733	78	289	366	506	145	117	244
50	2	22	26	49	3	10	36
851	92	333	426	657	163	155	339

TABLE

Occupations by Age, Part (A)—

Class.	Group.	Occupation.	Town — Total. Total.	Total. 0–4.	Total. 5–14.	Total. 15 and over.
1	2	3	16	17	18	19
D. Preparation and supply of material substances.	26	Shipwrights and boat-builders, &c. ...	...	...	...	...
		Canoe diggers, &c. ...	5	...	1	4
		Total Sub-order 26 ..	5	...	1	4
	27	Paper-makers and palm-leaf binders ...	...	...	...	...
		Stationers ...	14	3	7	4
		Total Sub-order 27 ...	14	3	7	4
	28	Press proprietors and printers ...	202	32	63	107
		Book-binders ...	51	7	20	24
		Book-sellers ...	22	...	2	20
		Newspaper proprietors ...	1	...	...	1
		Picture dealers ..	1	...	...	1
		Total Sub-order 28 ..	277	39	85	153
	29	Watch and clock-makers...	34	3	10	21
	30	Wood and ebony carvers...	2	...	...	2
		Ivory carvers ...	56	12	17	27
		Turners ...	314	43	121	150
		Engravers ...	51	5	19	27
		Total Sub-order 30 ...	423	60	157	206

XVII.

Travancore State Summary—(*Continued*).

—(*Continued*).

Males.				Females.			
Total.	0—4.	5—14.	15 and over.	Total.	0—4.	5—14.	15 and over.
20	21	22	23	24	25	26	27
...	...	...	...	...	...	...	...
2	...	...	2	3	...	1	2
2	...	...	2	3	...	1	2
...	...	...	...	...	...	...	...
10	2	5	3	4	1	2	1
10	2	5	3	4	1	2	1
97	15	24	58	105	17	39	49
37	4	18	15	14	3	2	9
15	...	2	13	7	...	..	7
1	...	...	1	...	...	...	...
1	...	...	1	...	...	...	...
151	19	44	88	126	20	41	65
18	...	6	12	16	3	4	9
2	...	...	2	...	...	...	...
26	5	8	13	30	7	9	14
149	18	57	74	165	25	64	76
28	2	12	14	23	3	7	13
205	25	77	108	218	35	80	103

TABLE

Occupations by Age, Part (A)—

Class.	Group.	Occupation.	COUNTRY — Total. Total.	Total. 0—4.	Total. 5—14.	Total. 15 and over.
1	2	3	28	29	30	31
D. Preparation and supply of material substances.	26	Shipwrights and boat-builders, &c. ...	142	16	35	91
		Canoe diggers, &c. ...	598	69	160	369
		Total Sub-order 26 ...	740	85	195	460
	27	Paper makers and palm-leaf binders ...	26	6	5	15
		Stationers ..	13	...	6	7
		Total Sub-order 27 ...	39	6	11	22
	28	Press proprietors and printers ...	12	4	3	5
		Book-binders ...	39	13	5	21
		Book-sellers ...	4	...	...	4
		Newspaper proprietors ...	...	...	...	...
		Picture dealers ...	...	...	...	.
		Total Sub-order 28 ...	55	17	8	30
	29	Watch and clock-makers..	...	...	...	...
	30	Wood and ebony carvers..	...	...	...	...
		Ivory carvers ...	112	15	33	64
		Turners ...	925	180	285	460
		Engravers ...	48	...	13	35
		Total Sub-order 30 ...	1,085	195	331	559

XVII.

Travancore State Summary—(*Continued*).

—(*Continued*).

Males.				Females.			
Total.	0—4.	5—14.	15 and over.	Total.	0—4.	5—14.	15 and over.
32	33	34	35	36	37	38	39
79	6	20	53	63	10	15	38
141	11	23	107	457	58	137	262
220	17	43	160	520	68	152	300
17	2	3	12	9	4	2	3
9	...	4	5	4	...	2	2
26	2	7	17	13	4	4	5
6	2	2	2	6	2	1	3
20	1	4	15	19	12	1	6
2	...	...	2	2	...	...	2
...	...	...	...	...	...	...	...
...	...	...	...	...	...	...	...
28	3	6	19	27	14	2	11
...	...	...	...	...	...	...	...
...	...	...	...	...	...	...	...
40	7	14	19	72	8	19	45
584	60	232	292	341	120	53	168
22	...	10	12	26	...	3	23
646	67	256	323	439	128	75	236

TABLE

Occupations by Age, Part (A)—

Class.	Group.	Occupation.	State — Total. Total.	0—4.	5—14.	15 and over.
1	2	3	4	5	6	7
D. Preparation and supply of material substances.	31	Toy and kite makers and sellers ...	8	2	1	5
	32	Conch dealers and drum makers ...	3	...	...	3
	33	Bangle-sellers in lac ...	16	...	...	16
		Flower garland makers and sellers ...	60	13	17	30
		Sacred thread makers and sellers ...	44	8	10	26
		Total Sub-order 33 ...	120	21	27	72
	34	Upholsterers ...	11	2	4	5
		Furniture makers ...	48	7	14	27
		Looking-glass sellers ...	3	...	...	3
		Total Sub-order 34 ...	62	9	18	35
	35	Whip, goad, &c., makers...	9	1	1	7
	36	Knife and tool makers ...	16	2	5	9
		Knife and tool grinders ...	39	7	10	22
		Mechanic (not Railway)...	22	...	1	21
		Total Sub-order 36 ...	77	9	16	52
	37	Gun makers ...	4	...	...	4
		Ammunition and cap dealers ...	7	2	...	5
		Gunpowder makers and sellers ...	6	1	1	4
		Fire-work makers ...	82	11	18	53
		Sword makers and sellers.	5	...	1	4
		Total Sub-order 37 ...	104	14	20	70

XVII.

Travancore State Summary—(*Continued*).

TOTAL.

Males.				Females.			
Total.	0—4.	5—14.	15 and over.	Total.	0—4.	5—14.	15 and over.
8	9	10	11	12	13	14	15
5	1	1	3	3	1	...	2
3	...	...	3	...	..	...	...
16	...	...	16	...	...	...	...
36	9	11	16	24	4	6	14
22	4	3	15	22	4	7	11
74	13	14	47	46	8	13	25
5	1	1	3	6	1	3	2
23	3	7	13	25	4	7	14
2	...	...	2	1	...	...	1
30	4	8	18	32	5	10	17
7	1	1	5	2	...	...	2
12	1	3	8	4	1	2	1
26	3	9	14	13	4	1	8
18	...	1	17	4	..	...	4
56	4	13	39	21	5	3	13
3	...	...	3	1	...	...	1
7	2	...	5	...	...	...	...
6	1	1	4	...	...	...	...
43	3	10	30	39	8	8	23
3	...	1	2	2	...	...	2
62	6	12	44	42	8	8	26

TABLE

Occupations by Age, Part (A)—

Class.	Group.	Occupation.	Town — Total. Total.	Town — Total. 0—4.	Town — Total. 5—14.	Town — Total. 15 and over.
1	2	3	16	17	18	19
D. Preparation and supply of material substances.	31	Toy and kite makers and sellers ..	8	2	1	5
	32	Conch dealers and drum makers ...	3	...	...	3
	33	Bangle-sellers in lac ...	8	...	...	8
		Flower garland makers and sellers ..	26	7	7	12
		Sacred thread makers and sellers ...	24	7	4	13
		Total Sub-order 33 ...	58	14	11	33
	34	Upholsterers ...	11	2	4	5
		Furniture-makers ...	48	7	14	27
		Looking-glass sellers ...	3	...	...	3
		Total Sub-order 34 ...	62	9	18	35
	35	Whip, goad, &c., makers...	...	...	...	...
	36	Knife and tool makers ...	11	2	4	5
		Knife and tool grinders ...	12	3	2	7
		Mechanic (not Railway) ..	...	...	...	...
		Total Sub-order 36 ...	23	5	6	12
	37	Gun-makers ...	4	...	...	4
		Ammunition and cap dealers ...	7	2	...	5
		Gunpowder makers and sellers ...	6	1	1	4
		Fire-work makers ..	31	6	7	18
		Sword makers and sellers.	5	...	1	4
		Total Sub-order 37 ...	53	9	9	35

XVII.

Travancore State Summary—(*Continued*).

—(*Continued*).

Males.				Females.			
Total.	0—4.	5—14.	15 and over.	Total.	0—4.	5—14.	15 and over.
20	21	22	23	24	25	26	27
5	1	1	3	3	1	...	2
3	...	...	3	...	...	...	...
8	...	...	8	...	...	...	...
16	4	5	7	10	3	2	5
12	3	1	8	12	4	3	5
36	7	6	23	22	7	5	10
5	1	1	3	6	1	3	2
23	3	7	13	25	4	7	14
2	...	...	2	1	...	...	1
30	4	8	18	32	5	10	17
...	...	...	...	...	...	...	...
8	1	2	5	3	1	2	...
6	1	1	4	6	2	1	3
...	...	...	...	...	...	...	...
14	2	3	9	9	3	3	3
3	...	...	3	1	...	...	1
7	2	...	5	...	...	...	...
6	1	1	4	...	...	...	...
11	2	4	5	20	4	3	13
3	...	1	2	2	...	..	2
30	5	6	19	23	4	3	16

TABLE

Occupations by Age, Part (A)—

Class.	Group.	Occupation.	Country: Total. Total.	Country: Total. 0—4.	Country: Total. 5—14.	Country: Total. 15 and over.
1	2	3	28	29	30	31
D. Preparation and supply of material substances.	31	Toy and kite makers and sellers ...	...	...	...	...
	32	Conch dealers and drum makers ...	...	...	...	...
	33	Bangle-sellers in lac ...	8	...	...	8
		Flower garland makers and sellers ...	34	6	10	18
		Sacred thread makers and sellers ...	20	1	6	13
		Total Sub-order 33 ...	62	7	16	39
	34	Upholsterers ...	...	...	...	...
		Furniture-makers ...	...	...	...	...
		Looking-glass sellers ...	...	...	...	...
		Total Sub-order 34 ...	...	...	...	...
	35	Whip, goad, &c., makers...	9	1	1	7
	36	Knife and tool makers ...	5	...	1	4
		Knife and tool grinders ...	27	4	8	15
		Mechanic (not Railway)...	22	...	1	21
		Total Sub-order 36 ...	54	4	10	40
	37	Gun-makers ...	...	...	...	...
		Ammunition and cap dealers ...	...	...	...	...
		Gunpowder makers and sellers ...	...	...	...	...
		Fire-work makers ...	51	5	11	35
		Sword makers and sellers.	...	...	...	...
		Total Sub-order 37 ...	51	5	11	35

XVII.

Travancore State Summary—(*Continued*).

—(*Continued*).

Males.				Females.			
Total.	0—4.	5—14.	15 and over.	Total.	0—4.	5—14.	15 and over.
32	33	34	35	36	37	38	39
...	...	...	...	...	...	...	...
...	...	...	...	...	...	...	...
8	...	...	8	...	...	...	...
20	5	6	9	14	1	4	9
10	1	2	7	10	...	4	6
38	6	8	24	24	1	8	15
...	...	...	...	...	...	...	...
...	...	...	...	...	...	...	...
...	...	...	...	...	...	...	...
...	...	...	...	...	...	...	...
7	1	1	5	2	...	...	2
4	...	1	3	1	...	...	1
20	2	8	10	7	2	...	5
18	...	1	17	4	...	...	4
42	2	10	30	12	2	...	10
...	...	...	...	...	...	...	...
...	...	...	...	...	...	...	...
...	...	...	...	...	...	...	...
32	1	6	25	19	4	5	10
...	...	...	...	...	...	...	...
32	1	6	25	19	4	5	10

TABLE

Occupations by Age, Part (A)—

Class.	Group.	Occupation and Class. — Occupation.	State — Total. — Total.	0—4.	5—14.	15 and over.
1	2	3	4	5	6	7
D. Preparation and supply of material substances.	38	Woollen-cloth dealers ...	6	2	...	4
	39	Silk dealers ...	8	3	3	2
	40	Cotton cleaners and pressers ...	11	5	2	4
		Cotton-carpet sellers ...	3	...	1	2
		Cotton spinners, &c. ...	3,963	458	886	2,619
		Cotton-weavers, mill-owners and managers ...	32,074	3,756	7,950	20,368
		Cotton Factory hands ...	325	31	82	212
		Tape and cotton sellers ...	316	43	95	178
		Total Sub-order 40 ...	36,692	4,293	9,016	23,383
	41	Flax-spinners, weavers and sellers ...	148	27	35	86
		Hemp-rope makers and sellers ...	79	18	16	45
		Net makers and sellers ..	1,766	218	415	1,133
		Coir preparers, manufacturers and sellers ...	26,713	2,414	5,342	18,957
		Total Sub-order 41 ...	28,706	2,677	5,808	20,221
	42	Tailors ...	5,559	708	1,445	3,406
		Hat, cap, turban makers and sellers ...	14	5	2	7
		Turban-binders ...	12	4	2	6
		Umbrella makers and sellers ...	6,471	851	1,863	3,757
		Lace sellers ...	3	...	...	3
		Button sellers ...	1	...	...	1
		Piece-goods dealers ...	2,859	360	663	1,836
		Total Sub-order 42 ...	14,919	1,928	3,975	9,016

XVII.

Travancore State Summary—(*Continued*)

TOTAL.

Males.				Females.			
Total.	0—4.	5—14.	15 and over.	Total.	0—4.	5—14.	15 and over.
8	9	10	11	12	13	14	15
4	2	...	2	2	...	...	2
5	1	3	1	3	2	...	1
6	2	1	3	5	3	1	1
3		1	2	...	...	...	...
1,009	129	297	583	2,954	329	589	2,036
17,664	1,840	4,481	11,343	14,410	1,916	3,469	9,025
158	14	46	98	167	17	36	114
126	11	35	80	190	32	60	98
18,966	1,996	4,861	12,109	17,726	2,297	4,155	11,274
87	17	25	45	61	10	10	41
65	14	13	38	14	4	3	7
923	111	206	606	843	107	209	527
7,368	612	1,442	5,314	19,345	1,802	3,900	13,643
8,443	754	1,686	6,003	20,263	1,923	4,122	14,218
2,466	321	705	1,440	3,093	387	740	1,966
6	2	1	3	8	3	1	4
4	...	1	3	8	4	1	3
3,434	451	921	2,062	3,037	400	942	1,695
2	...	...	2	1	...	...	1
1	...	...	1	...	...	...	...
1,941	231	447	1,263	918	129	216	573
7,854	1,005	2,075	4,774	7,065	923	1,900	4,242

TABLE

Occupations by Age, Part (A)—

Class.	Group.	Occupation.	Town — Total. Total.	Town — Total. 0—4.	Town — Total. 5—14.	Town — Total. 15 and over.
1	2	3	16	17	18	19
D. Preparation and supply of material substances.	38	Woollen-cloth dealers ...	6	2	...	4
	39	Silk-dealers ...	8	3	3	2
	40	Cotton cleaners and pressers ...	11	5	2	4
		Cotton-carpet sellers ...	3	...	1	2
		Cotton spinners, &c. ...	527	103	164	260
		Cotton weavers, mill-owners and managers ...	1,236	295	360	581
		Cotton Factory hands ...	107	22	26	59
		Tape and cotton sellers ...	151	24	31	96
		Total Sub-order 40 ...	2,035	449	584	1,002
	41	Flax-spinners, weavers and sellers ...	57	7	14	36
		Hemp-rope makers and sellers ...	16	6	4	6
		Net-makers and sellers ...	15	3	7	5
		Coir preparers, manufacturers and sellers ...	380	80	127	173
		Total Sub-order 41 ..	468	96	152	220
	42	Tailors ...	551	89	129	333
		Hat, cap, turban makers and sellers ...	9	3	2	4
		Turban-binders ...	7	2	2	3
		Umbrella makers and sellers ...	128	22	43	63
		Lace-sellers ...	3	...	...	3
		Button-sellers ...	1	...	...	1
		Piece-goods dealers ...	631	119	189	323
		Total Sub-order 42 ...	1,330	235	365	730

XVII.

Travancore State Summary—(*Continued*).

—(*Continued*).

Males.				Females.			
Total.	0—4.	5—14.	15 and over.	Total.	0—4.	5—14.	15 and over.
20	21	22	23	24	25	26	27
4	2	...	2	2	...	...	2
5	1	3	1	3	2	...	1
6	2	1	3	5	3	1	1
3	...	1	2	...	...	...	...
287	45	117	125	240	58	47	135
633	127	173	333	603	168	187	248
72	14	17	41	35	8	9	18
83	8	17	58	68	16	14	38
1,084	196	326	562	951	253	258	440
28	3	8	17	29	4	6	19
10	4	3	3	6	2	1	3
7	2	3	2	8	1	4	3
182	42	56	84	198	38	71	89
227	51	70	106	241	45	82	114
214	31	61	122	337	58	68	211
5	2	1	2	4	1	1	2
3	...	1	2	4	2	1	1
65	11	22	32	63	11	21	31
2	...	...	2	1	...	...	1
1	...	...	1	...	...	...	...
360	73	92	195	271	46	97	128
650	117	177	356	680	118	188	374

TABLE

Occupations by Age, Part (A)—

Class.	Group.	Occupation.	Country — Total. Total.	0—4.	5—14.	15 and over.
1	2	3	28	29	30	31
D. Preparation and supply of material substances.	38	Woollen-cloth dealers ...	...	...	...	...
	39	Silk-dealers ...	...	...	...	...
	40	Cotton cleaners and pressers ...	...	...	...	...
		Cotton-carpet sellers ...	...	...	...	...
		Cotton spinners, &c. ...	3,436	355	722	2,359
		Cotton weavers, mill-owners and managers ...	30,838	3,461	7,590	19,787
		Cotton Factory hands ...	218	9	56	153
		Tape and cotton sellers ...	165	19	64	82
		Total Sub-order 40 ...	34,657	3,844	8,432	22,381
	41	Flax-spinners, weavers and sellers ...	91	20	21	50
		Hemp-rope makers and sellers ...	63	12	12	39
		Net-makers and sellers ...	1,751	215	408	1,128
		Coir preparers, manufacturers and sellers ...	26,333	2,334	5,215	18,784
		Total Sub-order 41 .	28,238	2,581	5,656	20,001
	42	Tailors ...	5,008	619	1,316	3,073
		Hat, cap, turban makers and sellers ...	5	2	...	3
		Turban-binders ...	5	2	...	3
		Umbrella makers and sellers ...	6,343	829	1,820	3,694
		Lace-sellers ...	...	...	...	...
		Button sellers ...	...	...	...	...
		Piece-goods dealers ...	2,228	241	474	1,513
		Total Sub-order 42 ...	13,589	1,693	3,610	8,286

XVII.

Travancore State Summary—(*Continued*).

—(*Continued*).

Males.				Females.			
Total.	0—4.	5—14.	15 and over.	Total.	0—4.	5—14.	15 and over.
32	33	34	35	36	37	38	39
...	...	...	...	...	...	...	...
...	...	...	...	...	...	...	...
...	...	...	...	...	...	...	...
...	...	...	...	...	...	...	...
722	84	180	458	2,714	271	542	1,901
17,031	1,713	4,308	11,010	13,807	1,748	3,282	8,777
86	...	29	57	132	9	27	96
43	3	18	22	122	16	46	60
17,882	1,800	4,535	11,547	16,775	2,044	3,897	10,834
59	14	17	28	32	6	4	22
55	10	10	35	8	2	2	4
916	109	203	604	835	106	205	524
7,186	570	1,386	5,230	19,147	1,764	3,829	13,554
8,216	703	1,616	5,897	20,022	1,878	4,040	14,104
2,252	290	644	1,318	2,756	329	672	1,755
1	...	..	1	4	2	...	2
1	...	...	1	4	2	...	2
3,369	440	899	2,030	2,974	389	921	1,664
...	...	...	...	...	...	...	...
...	...	...	...	...	...	...	...
1,581	158	355	1,068	647	83	119	445
7,204	888	1,898	4,418	6,385	805	1,712	3,868

TABLE

Occupations by Age, Part (A)—

Class.	Group.	Occupation.	STATE — Total. Total.	0—4.	5—14.	15 and over.
1	2	3	4	5	6	7
D. Preparation and supply of material substances.	43	Gold and silver dealers ..	346	37	95	214
		Gold and silver workers...	19,140	2,484	4,585	12,071
		Goldsmiths' dust washers.	46	7	15	24
		Enamellers ...	5	...	1	4
		Gold and silver braid makers ...	17	1	5	11
		Diamond polishers and dealers ...	2	...	...	2
		Ruby workers ..	39	7	16	16
		Ruby and emerald, &c., dealers ...	3	...	...	3
		Pearl and other precious stone dealers ...	21	2	2	17
		Coral dealers ...	32	7	9	16
		Total Sub-order 43 ...	19,651	2,545	4,728	12,378
	44	Brass workers and sellers.	23	1	10	12
		Copper workers & sellers..	134	14	36	84
		Bell metal workers and sellers ...	2,634	338	639	1,657
		General workers in brass, copper and bell metal ...	87	11	27	49
		Brass and copper dealers..	3	...	...	3
		Total Sub-order 44 ...	2,881	364	712	1,805

XVII.

Travancore State Summary—(*Continued*).

TOTAL.

Males.				Females.			
Total.	0—4.	5—14.	15 and over.	Total.	0—4.	5—14.	15 and over.
8	9	10	11	12	13	14	15
251	24	78	149	95	13	17	65
10,001	1,183	2,361	6,457	9,139	1,301	2,224	5,614
25	4	7	14	21	3	8	10
2	...	...	2	3	...	1	2
10	...	3	7	7	1	2	4
2	...	...	2	...	...	...	...
20	3	9	8	19	4	7	8
3	...	...	3	...	...	...	...
12	...	...	12	9	2	2	5
24	3	8	13	8	4	1	3
10,350	1,217	2,466	6,667	9,301	1,328	2,262	5,711
15	...	8	7	8	1	2	5
107	12	29	66	27	2	7	18
1,458	151	329	978	1,176	187	310	679
58	4	19	35	29	7	8	14
3	...	...	3	...	...	...	...
1,641	167	385	1,089	1,240	197	327	716

TABLE

Occupations by Age. Part (A)—

Class.	Group.	Occupation.	Town — Total. Total.	Town — Total. 0—4.	Town — Total. 5—14.	Town — Total. 15 and over.
1	2	3	16	17	18	19
D. Preparation and supply of material substances.	43	Gold and silver dealers ...	24	7	5	12
		Gold and silver workers...	1,583	244	386	953
		Goldsmiths' dust washers.	13	4	5	4
		Enamellers ...	5	...	1	4
		Gold and silver-braid makers ...	2	...	...	2
		Diamond polishers and dealers ...	1	...	...	1
		Ruby workers ...	9	2	4	3
		Ruby and emerald, &c., dealers ...	1	...	...	1
		Pearl and other precious stone dealers ...	3	...	...	3
		Coral dealers ...	6	2	2	2
		Total Sub-order 43 ...	1,647	259	403	985
	44	Brass-workers and sellers.	11	1	3	7
		Copper workers & sellers..	48	5	12	31
		Bell-metal workers and sellers ...	360	76	95	189
		General workers in brass, copper and bell metal ...	33	7	6	20
		Brass and copper dealers..	1	...	...	1
		Total Sub-order 44 ...	453	89	116	248

XVII.

Travancore State Summary—*(Continued)*.

—*(Continued)*.

Males.				Females.			
Total.	0—4.	5—14.	15 and over.	Total.	0—4.	5—14.	15 and over.
20	21	22	23	24	25	26	27
14	4	3	7	10	3	2	5
722	157	182	383	861	87	204	570
8	2	3	3	5	2	2	1
2	...	...	2	3	...	1	2
1	...	...	1	1	...	...	1
1	...	...	1	...	...	...	...
5	1	2	2	4	1	2	1
1	...	...	1	...	...	...	...
2	...	...	2	1	...	...	1
4	2	1	1	2	...	1	1
760	166	191	403	887	93	212	582
7	...	2	5	4	1	1	2
25	4	8	13	23	1	4	18
164	29	37	98	196	47	58	91
25	4	3	18	8	3	3	2
1	...	...	1	...	...	...	...
222	37	50	135	231	52	66	113

TABLE

Occupations by Age, Part (A)—

Class.	Group.	Occupation.	Country: Total. Total.	Country: Total. 0—4.	Country: Total. 5—14.	Country: Total. 15 and over.
1	2	3	28	29	30	31
D. Preparation and supply of material substances.	43	Gold and silver dealers ...	322	30	90	202
		Gold and silver workers...	17,557	2,240	4,199	11,118
		Goldsmith's dust washers.	33	3	10	20
		Enamellers ...	...	...	...	...
		Gold and silver-braid makers ...	15	1	5	9
		Diamond polishers and dealers ...	1	...	...	1
		Ruby workers ...	30	5	12	13
		Ruby and emerald, &c., dealers ...	2	...	...	2
		Pearl and other precious stone dealers ...	18	2	2	14
		Coral dealers ...	26	5	7	14
		Total Sub-order 43 ...	18,004	2,286	4,325	11,393
	44	Brass-workers and sellers.	12	...	7	5
		Copper workers & sellers..	86	9	24	53
		Bell-metal workers and sellers ...	2,274	262	544	1,468
		General workers in brass, copper and bell metal ...	54	4	21	29
		Brass and dealers ...	2	...	...	2
		Total Sub-order 44 ...	2,428	275	596	1,557

XVII.

Travancore State Summary—(Continued).

—(Continued).

Males.				Females.			
Total.	0—4.	5—14.	15 and over.	Total.	0—4.	5—14.	15 and over.
32	33	34	35	36	37	38	39
237	20	75	142	85	10	15	60
9,279	1,026	2,179	6,074	8,278	1.214	2,020	5,044
17	2	4	11	16	1	6	9
...	...	...	...	...	...	...	...
9	...	3	6	6	1	2	3
1	...	...	1	...	..	...	...
15	2	7	6	15	3	5	7
2	...	...	2	...	...	...	...
10	...	...	10	8	2	2	4
20	1	7	12	6	4	...	2
9,590	1,051	2,275	6,264	8,414	1,235	2,050	5,129
8	...	6	2	4	...	1	3
82	8	21	53	4	1	3	..
1,294	122	292	880	980	140	252	588
33	...	16	17	21	4	5	12
2	...	...	2	...	...	...	...
1,419	130	335	954	1,009	145	261	603

TABLE

Occupations by Age, Part (A)—

Class.	Group.	Occupation.	State — Total. Total.	0—4.	5—14.	15 and over.
1	2	3	4	5	6	7
D. Preparation and supply of material substances.	45	Tin workers and sellers ...	60	4	12	44
		Tinfoil sellers ...	6	2	2	2
		Zinc workers and sellers. .	13	5	3	5
		Lead and quicksilver workers and sellers ...	91	14	24	53
		General workers in lead and zinc ...	27	7	9	11
		Total Sub-order 45 ...	197	32	50	115
	46	Iron and steel sellers ...	91	5	26	60
		Blacksmiths ...	19,308	2,416	4,859	12,033
		Iron & hardware dealers...	84	15	22	47
		Lock makers and sellers...	4	...	2	2
		Total Sub-order 46 ...	19,487	2,436	4,909	12,142
	47	Bottle dealers ...	9	2	3	4
		Glass and chinaware dealers ...	30	4	11	15
		Total Sub-order 47 ...	39	6	14	19
	48	Potters and pot-makers and sellers ...	5,504	661	1,311	3,532
		Grind-stone, mill-stone, &c., makers and sellers...	6	2	1	3
		Pestle & mortar makers and sellers ...	6	1	2	3
		Total Sub-order 48 ...	5,516	664	1,314	3,538
	49	Timber & bamboo dealers.	693	93	178	422
		Wood-cutters & sawyers...	4,888	659	1,173	3,056
		Carpenters ...	39,534	5,411	9,980	24,143
		Box makers and sellers ...	241	8	105	128
		Total Sub-order 49 ...	45,356	6,171	11,436	27,749

XVII.

Travancore State Summary—(*Continued*).

TOTAL.

Males.				Females.			
Total.	0—4.	5—14.	15 and over.	Total.	0—4.	5—14.	15 and over.
8	9	10	11	12	13	14	15
39	...	9	30	21	4	3	14
4	1	2	1	2	1	...	1
5	1	2	2	8	4	1	3
21	...	3	18	70	14	21	35
18	3	7	8	9	4	2	3
87	5	23	59	110	27	27	56
74	2	22	50	17	3	4	10
10,239	1,204	2,531	6,504	9,069	1,212	2,328	5,529
55	8	14	33	29	7	8	14
4	...	2	2	...	...	...	...
10,372	1,214	2,569	6,589	9,115	1,222	2,340	5,553
5	1	2	2	4	1	1	2
14	3	4	7	16	1	7	8
19	4	6	9	20	2	8	10
2,718	296	667	1,755	2,786	365	644	1,777
4	1	1	2	2	1	...	1
4	1	1	2	2	...	1	1
2,726	298	669	1,759	2,790	366	645	1,779
464	54	100	310	229	39	78	112
2,227	269	556	1,402	2,661	390	617	1,654
20,674	2,551	5,123	13,000	18,860	2,860	4,857	11,143
43	5	12	26	198	3	93	102
23,408	2,879	5,791	14,738	21,948	3,292	5,645	13,011

TABLE

Occupations by Age, Part (A)—

Class.	Group.	Occupation.	Town — Total. Total.	Town — Total. 0—4.	Town — Total. 5—14.	Town — Total. 15 and over.
1	2	3	16	17	18	19
D. Preparation and supply of material substances.	45	Tin workers and sellers ...	32	4	7	21
		Tinfoil sellers ...	6	2	2	2
		Zinc workers and sellers...	7	3	2	2
		Lead and quicksilver workers and sellers ...	43	4	10	29
		General workers in lead and zinc ...	15	4	7	4
		Total Sub-order 45 ...	103	17	28	58
	46	Iron and steel sellers ...	24	3	7	14
		Blacksmiths ..	892	207	264	421
		Iron & hardware dealers.	20	4	7	9
		Lock makers and sellers..	4	...	2	2
		Total Sub-order 46 ...	940	214	280	446
	47	Bottle dealers ...	9	2	3	4
		Glass & chinaware dealers.	10	3	3	4
		Total Sub-order 47 ...	19	5	6	8
	48	Potters and pot-makers and sellers ...	801	160	311	330
		Grind-stone, mill-stone, &c., makers and sellers..	...	...	...	...
		Pestle and mortar makers and sellers ...	...	...	...	...
		Total Sub-order 48 ...	801	160	311	330
	49	Timber & bamboo dealers.	54	8	15	31
		Wood-cutters and sawyers.	293	49	113	131
		Carpenters ...	1,525	284	581	660
		Box-makers and sellers ...	46	6	15	25
		Total Sub-order 49 ...	1,918	347	724	847

XVII.

Travancore State Summary—(*Continued*).

—(*Continued*).

Males.				Females.			
Total.	0—4.	5—14.	15 and over.	Total.	0—4.	5—14.	15 and over.
20	21	22	23	24	25	26	27
24	...	6	18	8	4	1	3
4	1	2	1	2	1	...	1
4	1	2	1	3	2	...	1
16	...	2	14	27	4	8	15
10	2	5	3	5	2	2	1
58	4	17	37	45	13	11	21
20	2	5	13	4	1	2	1
484	110	141	233	408	97	123	188
10	2	4	4	10	2	3	5
4	...	2	2	...	...	...	...
518	114	152	252	422	100	128	194
5	1	2	2	4	1	1	2
5	2	2	1	5	1	1	3
10	3	4	3	9	2	2	5
417	96	167	154	384	64	144	176
...	...	...	...	...	...	...	...
...	...	...	...	...	...	...	...
417	96	167	154	384	64	144	176
30	4	8	18	24	4	7	13
162	19	56	87	131	30	57	44
801	132	297	372	724	152	284	288
30	4	8	18	16	2	7	7
1,023	159	369	495	895	188	355	352

TABLE

Occupations by Age, Part (A)—

Class.	Group.	Occupation.	Country: Total. Total.	0—4.	5—14.	15 and over.
1	2	3	28	29	30	31
D. Preparation and supply of material substances.	45	Tin workers and sellers ...	28	...	5	23
		Tinfoil sellers ...	...	...	...	...
		Zinc-workers and sellers...	6	2	1	3
		Lead and quicksilver workers and sellers ...	48	10	14	24
		General workers in lead and zinc ...	12	3	2	7
		Total Sub-order 45 ...	94	15	22	57
	46	Iron and steel sellers ...	67	2	19	46
		Blacksmiths ...	18,416	2,209	4,595	11,612
		Iron & hardware dealers...	64	11	15	38
		Lock makers and sellers...	...	...	...	...
		Total Sub-order 46 ...	18,547	2,222	4,629	11,696
	47	Bottle-dealers ...	...	...	...	...
		Glass & chinaware dealers..	20	1	8	11
		Total Sub-order 47 ...	20	1	8	11
	48	Potters and pot-makers and sellers ...	4,703	501	1,000	3,202
		Grind-stone, mill-stone, &c., makers and sellers.	6	2	1	3
		Pestle and mortar makers and sellers ...	6	1	2	3
		Total Sub-order 48 ...	4,715	504	1,003	3,208
	49	Timber & bamboo dealers.	639	85	163	391
		Wood-cutters and sawyers.	4,595	610	1,060	2,925
		Carpenters ...	38,009	5,127	9,399	23,483
		Box-makers and sellers ...	195	2	90	103
		Total Sub-order 49 ...	43,438	5,824	10,712	26,902

XVII.

Travancore State Summary—(*Continued*).

—(*Continued*).

Males.				Females.			
Total.	0—4.	5—14.	15 and over.	Total.	0—4.	5—14.	15 and over.
32	33	34	35	36	37	38	39
15	...	3	12	13	...	2	11
...	...	... •	...	...	..	...	... 2
1	...	...	1	5	2	1	
5	...	1	4	43	10	13	20
8	1	2	5	4	2	...	2
29	1	6	22	65	14	16	35
54	...	17	37	13	2	2	9
9,755	1,094	2,890	6,271	8,661	1,115	2.205	5,341
45	6	10	29	19	5	5	9
...	...	...	...	...	...	...	...
9,854	1,100	2,417	6,337	8,693	1,122	2,212	5,359
...	...	...	...	...	...	...	...
9	1	2	6	11	...	6	5
9	1	2	6	11	...	6	5
2,301	200	500	1,601	2,402	301	500	1,601
4	1	1	2	2	1	...	1
4	1	1	2	2	...	1	1
2,309	202	502	1,605	2,406	302	501	1,603
434	50	92	292	205	35	71	99
2,065	250	500	1,315	2,530	360	560	1,610
19,873	2,419	4,826	12,628	18,136	2,708	4,573	10,855
13	1	4	8	182	1	86	95
22,385	2,720	5,422	14,243	21,053	3,104	5,290	12,659

TABLE

Occupations by Age, Part (A)—

Class.	Group.	Occupation.	State — Total. Total.	0—4.	5—14.	15 and over.
1	2	3	4	5	6	7
D. Preparation and supply of material substances.	50	Rattan workers and sellers.	140	9	37	94
		Basket weavers and winnowing fan makers and sellers ...	7,913	1,699	2,343	3,871
		Mat makers and sellers ...	1,145	139	279	727
		Leaf-plate sellers ...	77	16	19	42
		Leaf-fan makers & sellers.	98	4	28	66
		Comb makers and sellers..	50	7	16	27
		Broom sellers ...	23	5	7	11
		Total Sub-order 50 ...	9,446	1,879	2,729	4,838
	51	Wax, honey and general forest produce collectors and sellers ...	39	8	11	20
	52	Druggists ...	131	16	33	82
		Kanku or red-powder preparers and sellers ...	12	1	1	10
		Perfume sellers ...	6	1	...	5
		Total Sub-order 52 ...	149	18	34	97
	53	Tanners, &c. ...	302	59	58	185
		Shoe and boots makers and sellers ...	168	21	59	88
		Leather dyers ...	11	4	2	5
		Hide dealers ...	46	7	11	28
		Grease preparers and sellers ...	18	2	6	10
		Total Sub-order 53 ...	545	93	136	316
		Total Class D. ...	430,756	55,692	103,166	271,898

XVII.

Travancore State Summary—(*Continued*).

TOTAL.

Males.				Females.			
Total.	0—4.	5—14.	15 and over.	Total.	0—4.	5—14.	15 and over.
8	9	10	11	12	13	14	15
60	2	17	41	80	7	20	53
4,002	893	1,308	1,801	3,911	806	1,035	2,070
665	66	176	423	480	73	103	304
40	12	10	18	37	4	9	24
60	1	14	45	38	3	14	21
26	4	9	13	24	3	7	14
7	2	3	2	16	3	4	9
4,860	980	1,537	2,343	4,586	899	1,192	2,495
29	4	10	15	10	4	1	5
119	15	31	73	12	1	2	9
1	...	...	1	11	1	1	9
3	...	...	3	3	1	...	2
123	15	31	77	26	3	3	20
180	26	30	124	122	33	28	61
132	14	48	70	36	7	11	18
3	...	1	2	8	4	1	3
16	4	5	7	30	3	6	21
12	1	4	7	6	1	2	3
343	45	88	210	202	48	48	106
220,214	26,439	52,725	141,050	210,542	29,253	50,441	130,848

TABLE

Occupations by Age, Part (A)—

Class.	Group.	Occupation.	Town — Total. Total.	0—4.	5—14.	15 and over.
1	2	3	16	17	18	19
D. Preparation and supply of material substances.	50	Rattan workers and sellers	46	4	9	33
		Basket weavers and winnowing fan makers and sellers ...	13	6	2	5
		Mat makers and sellers ...	44	10	13	21
		Leaf-plate sellers ...	19	3	4	12
		Leaf fan makers & sellers.	1	...	...	1
		Comb makers and sellers..	3	...	...	3
		Broom sellers ...	14	5	5	4
		Total Sub-order 50 ...	140	28	33	79
	51	Wax, honey and general forest produce collectors and sellers ...	...	...	...	...
	52	Druggists ...	10	3	3	4
		Kanku or red-powder preparers and sellers ...	7	1	1	5
		Perfume sellers ...	3	1	...	2
		Total Sub-order 52 ...	20	5	4	11
	53	Tanners, &c. ...	18	7	3	8
		Shoe and boots makers and sellers ...	36	7	11	18
		Leather dyers ...	4	1	1	2
		Hide dealers ...	10	3	2	5
		Grease preparers and sellers ...	6	2	1	3
		Total Sub-order 53 ...	74	20	18	36
		Total Class D. ...	19,357	3,557	5,820	9,980

XVII.

Travancore State Summary—(Continued).

—(Continued).

Males.				Females.			
Total.	0—4.	5—14.	15 and over.	Total.	0—4.	5—14.	15 and over.
20	21	22	23	24	25	26	27
21	1	2	18	25	3	7	15
8	4	1	3	5	2	1	2
24	3	8	13	20	7	5	8
4	...	...	4	15	3	4	8
1	...	...	1	...	...	...	...
2	..	...	2	1	...	...	1
5	2	1	2	9	3	4	2
65	10	12	43	75	18	21	36
...	...	...	...	...	...	...	...
8	2	3	3	2	1	...	1
1	...	...	1	6	1	1	4
1	...	...	1	2	1	...	1
10	2	3	5	10	3	1	6
10	3	2	5	8	4	1	3
14	3	4	7	22	4	7	11
2	...	1	1	2	1	...	1
5	2	1	2	5	1	1	3
4	1	1	2	2	1	...	1
35	9	9	17	39	11	9	19
10,141	1,732	3,063	5,346	9,216	1,825	2,757	4,634

TABLE

Occupations by Age, Part (A)—

Class.	Group.	Occupation.	Country: Total. Total.	0—4.	5—14.	15 and over.
1	2	3	28	29	30	31
D. Preparation and supply of material substances.	50	Rattan workers & sellers...	94	5	28	61
		Basket weavers and winnowing fan-makers and sellers ...	7,900	1,693	2,341	3,866
		Mat makers and sellers ...	1,101	129	266	706
		Leaf-plate sellers ...	58	13	15	30
		Leaf fan makers & sellers.	97	4	28	65
		Comb makers and sellers..	47	7	16	24
		Broom sellers ...	9	...	2	7
		Total Sub-order 50 ...	9,306	1,851	2,696	4,759
	51	Wax, honey and general forest produce collectors and sellers ...	39	8	11	20
	52	Druggists ...	121	13	30	78
		Kanku or red-powder preparers and sellers ...	5	...	...	5
		Perfume sellers ...	3	...	...	3
		Total Sub-order 52 ...	129	13	30	86
	53	Tanners, &c. ...	284	52	55	177
		Shoe and boots makers and sellers ...	132	14	48	70
		Leather dyers ...	7	3	1	3
		Hide dealers ...	36	4	9	23
		Grease preparers and sellers ...	12	...	5	7
		Total Sub-order 53 ...	471	73	118	280
		Total Class D. ...	411,399	52,135	97,346	261,918

XVII.

Travancore State Summary—(*Continued*).

—(*Continued*).

Males.				Females.			
Total.	0—4.	5—14.	15 and over.	Total.	0—4.	5—14.	15 and over.
32	33	34	35	36	37	38	39
39	1	15	23	55	4	13	38
3,994	889	1,307	1,798	3,906	804	1,034	2,068
641	63	168	410	460	66	98	296
36	12	10	14	22	1	5	16
59	1	14	44	38	3	14	21
24	4	9	11	23	3	7	13
2	..	2	...	7	...	...	7
4,795	970	1,525	2,300	4,511	881	1,171	2,459
29	4	10	15	10	4	1	5
111	13	28	70	10	..	2	8
...	...	...	...	5	...	...	5
2	...	...	2	1	...	...	1
113	13	28	72	16	...	2	14
170	23	28	119	114	29	27	58
118	11	44	63	14	3	4	7
1	...	...	1	6	3	1	2
11	2	4	5	25	2	5	18
8	...	3	5	4	...	2	2
308	36	79	193	163	37	39	87
210,073	24,707	49,662	135,704	201,326	27,428	47,684	126,214

TABLE

Occupations by Age, Part (A)—

Class.	Group.	Occupation.	State — Total. Total.	0—4.	5—14.	15 and over.
1	2	3	4	5	6	7
E. Commerce, Transport and Storage.	54	Money lenders and pawn-brokers ...	271	30	70	171
		Bill discounters ...	43	1	3	39
		Money changers & testers.	156	6	100	50
		Total Sub-order 54 ...	470	37	173	260
	55	General merchants ...	119,907	16,102	30,055	73,750
		Merchants' clerks, accountants, &c. ...	885	78	214	593
		Total Sub-order 55 ...	120,792	16,180	30,269	74,343
	56	Shopkeepers' clerks ...	10	...	5	5
		Shopkeepers' servants ...	30	...	9	21
		Shopkeepers unspecified...	31,845	3,666	7,341	20,838
		Total Sub-order 56 ...	31,885	3,666	7,355	20,864
	57*a*	Brokers, agents & dubash...	52	4	16	32
		Auctioneers & appraisers..	53	5	17	31
		Total Sub-order 57(*a*) ...	105	9	33	63
	57*b*	Farmers of tolls ...	2	...	...	2
		Farmers of liquor ...	178	39	32	107
		Contractors unspecified ...	49	6	9	34
		Total Sub-order 57(*b*) ...	229	45	41	143
	58*b*	Drivers and firemen ...	29	1	9	19
	59*a*	Cart drivers and carting agents ...	1,682	101	235	1,346
		Palki-bearers ...	27	...	6	21
		Total Sub-order 59(*a*) ...	1,709	101	241	1,367

XVII.

Travancore State Summary—(*Continued*).

TOTAL.

Males.				Females.			
Total.	0—4.	5—14.	15 and over.	Total.	0—4.	5—14.	15 and over.
8	9	10	11	12	13	14	15
137	15	47	75	134	15	23	96
41	...	3	38	2	1	...	1
146	2	99	45	10	4	1	5
324	17	149	158	146	20	24	102
58,722	7,663	14,298	36,761	61,185	8,439	15,757	36,989
496	44	111	341	389	34	103	252
59,218	7,707	14,409	37,102	61,574	8,473	15,860	37,241
8	...	5	3	2	...	...	2
18	..	2	16	12	...	7	5
15,099	1,728	3,789	9,582	16,746	1,938	3,552	11,256
15,125	1,728	3,796	9,601	16,760	1,938	3,559	11,263
36	2	14	20	16	2	2	12
25	2	13	10	28	3	4	21
61	4	27	30	44	5	6	33
1	...	...	1	1	...	...	1
133	31	20	82	45	8	12	25
28	1	6	21	21	5	3	13
162	32	26	104	67	13	15	39
10	...	1	9	19	1	8	10
1,483	70	192	1,221	199	31	43	125
17	...	3	14	10	...	3	7
1,500	70	195	1,235	209	31	46	132

TABLE

Occupations by Age, Part (A)—

Class.	Group.	Occupation.	Town — Total. Total.	0—4.	5—14.	15 and over.
1	2	3	16	17	18	19
E. Commerce, Transport and Storage.	54	Money lenders and pawn-brokers ...	20	7	8	5
		Bill discounters ...	15	1	1	13
		Money changers & testers.	22	6	6	10
		Total Sub-order 54 ...	57	14	15	28
	55	General merchants ...	14,757	2,644	4,068	8,045
		Merchants' clerks, accountants, &c. ...	86	7	17	62
		Total Sub-order 55 ...	14,843	2,651	4,085	8,107
	56	Shopkeepers' clerks ...	6	...	2	4
		Shopkeepers' servants ...	...	...	...	...
		Shopkeepers unspecified ...	1,022	146	334	542
		Total Sub-order 56 ...	1,028	146	336	546
	57*a*	Brokers, agents & dubash.	6	2	1	3
		Auctioneers & appraisers.	6	2	1	3
		Total Sub-order 57(*a*) ...	12	4	2	6
	57*b*	Farmers of tolls ..	...	...	...	...
		Farmers of liquor ...	12	3	3	6
		Contractors unspecified ...	30	4	5	21
		Total Sub-order 57(*b*) ...	42	7	8	27
	58*b*	Drivers and firemen ...	...	...	...	...
	59*a*	Cart drivers and carting agents ...	48	12	15	21
		Palki-bearers ...	21	...	5	16
		Total Sub-order 59(*a*) ...	69	12	20	37

XVII.

Travancore State Summary—(*Continued*).

—(*Continued*).

Males.				Females.			
Total.	0—4.	5—14.	15 and over.	Total.	0—4.	5—14.	15 and over.
20	21	22	23	24	25	26	27
13	3	6	4	7	4	2	1
13	...	1	12	2	1	...	1
14	2	5	7	8	4	1	3
40	5	12	23	17	9	3	5
7,396	1,439	1,932	4,025	7,361	1,205	2,136	4,020
29	4	8	17	57	3	9	45
7,425	1,443	1,940	4,042	7,418	1,208	2,145	4,065
4	...	2	2	2	...	...	2
...	...	...	...	...	...	...	...
330	52	100	178	692	94	234	364
334	52	102	180	694	94	234	366
5	2	1	2	1	...	...	1
4	1	1	2	2	1	...	1
9	3	2	4	3	1	...	2
...	...	...	...	...	...	...	...
5	1	1	3	7	2	2	3
17	...	3	14	13	4	2	7
22	1	4	17	20	6	4	10
...	...	...	...	...	...	...	...
20	8	4	8	28	4	11	13
14	...	3	11	7	...	2	5
34	8	7	19	35	4	13	18

TABLE

Occupations by Age, Part (A)—

Class.	Group.	Occupation.	Country — Total. Total.	Total. 0—4.	Total. 5—14.	Total. 15 and over.
1	2	3	28	29	30	31
E. Commerce, Transport and Storage.	54	Money lenders and pawn-brokers ...	251	23	62	166
		Bill discounters ...	28	...	2	26
		Money changers & testers.	134	...	94	40
		Total Sub-order 54 ...	413	23	158	232
	55	General merchants ...	105,150	13,458	25,987	65,705
		Merchants' clerks, accountants, &c. ...	799	71	197	531
		Total Sub-order 55 ...	105,949	13,529	26,184	66,236
	56	Shopkeepers' clerks ...	4	..	3	1
		Shopkeepers' servants ...	30	...	9	21
		Shopkeepers unspecified...	30,823	3,520	7,007	20,296
		Total Sub-order 56 ...	30,857	3,520	7,019	20,318
	57*a*	Brokers, agents & dubash.	46	2	15	29
		Auctioneers & appraisers.	47	3	16	28
		Total Sub-order 57(*a*) ...	93	5	31	57
	57*b*	Farmers of tolls ...	2	..	...	2
		Farmers of liquor ...	166	36	29	101
		Contractors unspecified ...	19	2	4	13
		Total Sub-order 57(*b*) ...	187	38	33	116
	58*b*	Drivers and firemen ...	29	1	9	19
	59*a*	Cart drivers and carting agents ...	1,634	89	220	1,325
		Palki-bearers ...	6	...	1	5
		Total Sub-order 59(*a*) ...	1,640	89	221	1,330

XVII.

Travancore State Summary—(*Continued*).

—(*Continued*).

Males.				Females.			
Total.	0—4.	5—14.	15 and over.	Total.	0—4.	5—14.	15 and over.
32	33	34	35	36	37	38	39
124	12	41	71	127	11	21	95
28	...	2	26	...	...	...	...
132	...	94	38	2	...	...	2
284	12	137	135	129	11	21	97
51,326	6,224	12,366	32,736	53,824	7,234	13,621	32,969
467	40	103	324	332	31	94	207
51,793	6,264	12,469	33,060	54,156	7,265	13,715	33,176
4	...	3	1	...	...	...	...
18	...	2	16	12	...	7	5
14,769	1,676	3,689	9,404	16,054	1,844	3,318	10,892
14,791	1,676	3,694	9,421	16,066	1,844	3,325	10,897
31	...	13	18	15	2	2	11
21	1	12	8	26	2	4	20
52	1	25	26	41	4	6	31
1	...	...	1	1	...	...	1
128	30	19	79	38	6	10	22
11	1	3	7	8	1	1	6
140	31	22	87	47	7	11	29
10	...	1	9	19	1	8	10
1,463	62	188	1,213	171	27	32	112
3	...	...	3	3	...	1	2
1,466	62	188	1,216	174	27	33	114

TABLE

Occupations by Age, Part (A)—

Class.	Group.	Occupation.	State Total. Total.	0—4.	5—14.	15 and over.
1	2	3	4	5	6	7
E. Commerce, Transport and Storage.	59*b*	Elephant owners and drivers ...	2	...	...	2
	60*a*	Boat owners ...	6	...	...	6
	60*b*	Ships' officers, mariners, firemen, &c. ...	261	24	36	201
		Boat and barge men ...	5,874	763	1,394	3,717
		Pilots ...	10	...	...	10
		Harbour service ...	291	13	39	239
		Total Sub-order 60(*b*) ...	6,436	800	1,469	4,167
	61*a*	Post and anchel masters and clerks ...	204	39	49	116
		Post and anchel messengers and runners ...	562	77	112	373
		Messengers unspecified ...	49	4	11	34
		Total Sub-order 61(*a*) ...	815	120	172	523
	61*b*	Telegraph officers and clerks ...	4	...	...	4
		Telegraph signallers and messengers ...	4	...	...	4
		Total Sub-order 61(*b*) ...	8	...	...	8
	62	Ware-house service ...	199	27	43	129
		Porters ...	1,272	130	302	840
		Watchmen (not village)...	10	...	1	9
		Total Sub-order 62 ...	1,481	157	346	978
		Total Class E. ...	163,967	21,116	40,108	102,743

XVII.

Travancore State Summary—(*Continued*).

TOTAL.

Males.				Females.			
Total.	0—4.	5—14.	15 and over.	Total.	0—4.	5—14.	15 and over.
8	9	10	11	12	13	14	15
2	...	...	2	...	...	...	...
5	...	...	5	1	...	...	1
215	14	28	173	46	10	8	28
3,716	424	793	2,499	2,158	339	601	1,218
7	...	...	7	3	...	...	3
202	12	31	159	89	1	8	80
4,140	450	852	2,838	2,296	350	617	1,329
112	18	20	74	92	21	29	42
341	38	63	240	221	39	49	133
18	2	...	16	31	2	11	18
471	58	83	330	344	62	89	193
3	...	...	3	1	...	...	1
4	...	...	4	...	...	...	...
7	...	...	7	1	...	...	1
93	8	23	62	106	19	20	67
663	52	161	450	609	78	141	390
8	...	1	7	2	...	...	2
764	60	185	519	717	97	161	459
81,789	10,126	19,723	51,940	82,178	10,990	20,385	50,803

TABLE

Occupations by Age, Part (A)—

Class.	Group.	Occupation.	Town — Total. Total.	Town — Total. 0—4.	Town — Total. 5—14.	Town — Total. 15 and over.
1	2	3	16	17	18	19
E. Commerce, Transport and Storage.	59b	Elephant owners and drivers ...	...	...	...	...
	60a	Boat owners ...	4	...	...	4
	60b	Ships' officers, mariners, firemen, &c. ...	...	...	...	...
		Boat and barge men ...	...	...	...	...
		Pilots ...	...	...	...	...
		Harbour service ...	1	...	...	1
		Total Sub-order 60(b) ...	1	...	...	1
	61a	Post and anchel masters and clerks ...	43	7	18	18
		Post and anchel messengers and runners ...	22	9	2	11
		Messengers unspecified ...	24	2	10	12
		Total Sub-order 61(a) ...	89	18	30	41
	61b	Telegraph officers and clerks ...	4	...	...	4
		Telegraph signallers and messengers ...	4	...	...	4
		Total Sub-order 61(b) ...	8	...	...	8
	62	Ware-house service ...	22	5	5	12
		Porters ...	16	4	6	6
		Watchmen (not village)	...	...	...	...
		Total Sub-order 62 ...	38	9	11	18
		Total Class E. ...	16,191	2,861	4,507	8,823

XVII.

Travancore State Summary—(*Continued*).

—(*Continued*).

Males.				Females.			
Total.	0—4.	5—14.	15 and over.	Total.	0—4	5—14.	15 and over.
20	21	22	23	24	25	26	27
...	...	...	...	...	...	...	...
3	...	...	3	1	...	...	1
...	..	...	...	...	...	...	...
...	...	...	...	...	...	...	...
...	...	...	...	...	...	...	...
1	...	...	1	...	..	...	...
1	...	...	1	...	...	...	...
23	4	9	10	20	3	9	8
13	4	2	7	9	5	...	4
...	...	...	...	24	2	10	12
36	8	11	17	53	10	19	24
3	...	...	3	1	...	...	1
4	...	...	4	...	...	...	..
7	...	..	7	1	...	...	1
11	4	2	5	11	1	3	7
10	2	5	3	6	2	1	3
...	...	...	...	...	...	...	...
21	6	7	8	17	3	4	10
7,932	1,526	2,085	4,321	8,259	1,335	2,422	4,502

TABLE

Occupations by Age, Part (A)—

Class.	Group.	Occupation.	Country — Total. Total.	Total. 0—4.	Total. 5—14.	Total. 15 and over.
1	2	3	28	29	30	31
E. Commerce, Transport and Storage.	59*b*	Elephant owners and drivers ...	2	...	...	2
	60*a*	Boat owners ...	2	...	...	2
	60*b*	Ships' officers, mariners, firemen, &c. ...	261	24	36	201
		Boat and barge men ...	5,874	763	1,394	3,717
		Pilots ...	10	...	...	10
		Harbour service ...	290	13	39	238
		Total Sub-order 60(*b*) ...	6,435	800	1,469	4,166
	61*a*	Post and anchel masters and clerks ...	161	32	31	98
		Post and anchel messengers and runners ...	540	68	110	362
		Messengers unspecified ...	25	2	1	22
		Total Sub-order 61(*a*) ...	726	102	142	482
	61*b*	Telegraph officers and clerks ..	...	...	...	...
		Telegraph signallers and messengers ...	...	...	...	...
		Total Sub-order 61(*b*) ...	...	...	...	...
	62	Ware-house service ...	177	22	38	117
		Porters ...	1,256	126	296	834
		Watchmen (not village) ...	10	...	1	9
		Total Sub-order 62 ...	1,443	148	335	960
		Total Class E. ...	147,776	18,255	35,601	93,920

XVII.

Travancore State Summary—(*Continued*).

—(*Continued*).

Males. Total.	Males. 0—4.	Males. 5—14.	Males. 15 and over.	Females. Total.	Females. 0—4.	Females. 5—14.	Females. 15 and over.
32	33	34	35	36	37	38	39
2	...	...	2	...	...	...	...
2	...	...	2	...	...	...	...
215	14	28	173	46	10	8	28
3,716	424	793	2,499	2,158	339	601	1,218
7	...	...	7	3	...	...	3
201	12	31	158	89	1	8	80
4,139	450	852	2,837	2,296	350	617	1,329
89	14	11	64	72	18	20	34
328	34	61	233	212	34	49	129
18	2	...	16	7	...	1	6
435	50	72	313	291	52	70	169
...	...	...	...	...	...	...	...
...	...	..	...	...	...	...	...
...	...	...	...	...	...	...	...
82	4	21	57	95	18	17	60
653	50	156	447	603	76	140	387
8	...	1	7	2	...	...	2
743	54	178	511	700	94	157	449
73,857	8,600	17,638	47,619	73,919	9,655	17,963	46,301

TABLE

Occupations by Age, Part (A)—

Class.	Group.	Occupation and Class. Occupation.	State Total. Total.	0—4.	5—14.	15 and over.
1	2	3	4	5	6	7
F. Professions.	63a	Priests, ministers, preachers, missionaries, &c...	8,380	1,090	2,004	5,286
		Catechists, readers, &c. ...	518	56	102	360
		Exorcists, hail-averters, amulettiers, &c. ...	1,203	194	279	730
		Total Sub-order 63(*a*) ...	10,101	1,340	2,385	6,376
	63b	Religious mendicants, inmates of convents, &c.	24	2	5	17
		Church, temple, pagoda, masjid, &c., services ...	13,677	1,466	2,953	9,258
		Total Sub-order 63(*b*) ...	13,701	1,468	2,958	9,275
	64	Administrative and inspecting officials ...	82	10	15	57
		Principals, professors and teachers in colleges, &c. schools, &c. ..	899	93	218	588
		Clerks, &c., on educational establishments ...	4	...	2	2
		Total Sub-order 64 ...	985	103	235	647
	65	Editors and ballad makers.	19	1	6	12
		Private secretaries and clerks ...	73	17	14	42
		Public Scribes ...	999	187	240	572
		Total Sub-order 65 ...	1,091	205	260	626
	66	Advocates and pleaders	4,221	672	1,070	2,479
		Mukhtiars ...	2	...	...	2
		Lawyer's clerks ...	234	28	50	156
		Stamp vendors ...	40	6	9	25
		Petition writers ...	76	7	10	59
		Total Sub-order 66 ...	4,573	713	1,139	2,721

XVII.

Travancore State Summary—(*Continued*).

TOTAL.

Males.				Females.			
Total.	0—4.	5—14.	15 and over.	Total.	0—4.	5—14.	15 and over.
8	9	10	11	12	13	14	15
4,354	484	1,025	2,845	4,026	606	979	2,441
253	29	44	180	265	27	58	180
737	126	172	439	466	68	107	291
5,344	639	1,241	3,464	4,757	701	1,144	2,912
23	2	5	16	1	...	...	1
7,667	641	1,579	5,447	6,010	825	1,374	3,811
7,690	643	1,584	5,463	6,011	825	1,374	3,812
43	1	5	37	39	9	10	20
626	60	132	434	273	33	86	154
1	...	...	1	3	...	2	1
670	61	137	472	315	42	98	175
15	1	6	8	4	...	...	4
38	9	8	21	35	8	6	21
637	128	151	358	362	59	89	214
690	138	165	387	401	67	95	239
2,055	332	470	1,253	2,166	340	600	1,226
2	...	...	2	...	...	...	...
201	25	43	133	33	3	7	23
18	1	6	11	22	5	3	14
65	4	8	53	11	3	2	6
2,341	362	527	1,452	2,232	351	612	1,269

TABLE

Occupations by Age, Part (A)—

Class.	Group.	Occupation.	Town Total. Total.	0—4.	5—14.	15 and over.
1	2	3	16	17	18	19
F. Professions.	63*a*	Priests, ministers, preachers, missionaries, &c. ...	164	18	54	92
		Catechists, readers, &c. ...	223	29	83	111
		Exorcists, hail-averters, amulettiers, &c. ...	47	5	11	31
		Total Sub-order 63 (*a*) ...	434	52	148	234
	63*b*	Religious mendicants, inmates of convents, &c..	17	2	5	10
		Church, temple, pagoda, masjid, &c., services ...	1,757	342	665	750
		Total Sub-order 63(*b*) ...	1,774	344	670	760
	64	Administrative and inspecting officials ...	24	5	5	14
		Principals, professors and teachers in colleges, &c., schools, &c. ...	120	22	36	62
		Clerks, &c., on educational establishments ...	4	...	2	2
		Total Sub-order 64 ...	148	27	43	78
	65	Editors and ballad makers.	8	1	2	5
		Private secretaries and clerks ...	15	4	4	7
		Public Scribes ...	64	12	20	32
		Total Sub-order 65 ...	87	17	26	44
	66	Advocates and pleaders ...	868	132	296	440
		Mukhtiars ...	2	...	...	2
		Lawyer's clerks ...	115	14	29	72
		Stamp vendors ...	16	3	3	10
		Petition writers ...	21	4	7	10
		Total Sub-order 66 ...	1,022	153	335	534

XVII.

Travancore State Summary—(*Continued*).

—(*Continued*).

Males.				Females.			
Total.	0—4.	5—14.	15 and over.	Total.	0—4.	5—14.	15 and over.
20	21	22	23	24	25	26	27
88	10	27	51	76	8	27	41
93	12	38	43	130	17	45	68
29	2	6	21	18	3	5	10
210	24	71	115	224	28	77	119
16	2	5	9	1	...	...	1
1,125	214	427	484	632	128	238	266
1,141	216	432	493	633	128	238	267
10	1	2	7	14	4	3	7
59	14	17	28	61	8	19	34
1	...	...	1	3	...	2	1
70	15	19	36	78	12	24	42
6	1	2	3	2	...	...	2
7	...	3	4	8	4	1	3
38	8	11	19	26	4	9	13
51	9	16	26	36	8	10	18
428	51	120	257	440	81	176	183
2	...	...	2	...	...	...	...
91	12	24	55	24	2	5	17
10	1	2	7	6	2	1	3
17	3	6	8	4	1	1	2
548	67	152	329	474	86	183	205

TABLE

Occupations by Age, Part (A)—

Class.	Group.	Occupation.	COUNTRY Total. Total.	Total. 0—4.	Total. 5—14.	Total. 15 and over.
1	2	3	28	29	30	31
F. Professions.	63a	Priests, ministers, preachers, missionaries, &c. ...	8,216	1,072	1,950	5,194
		Catechists, readers, &c....	295	27	19	249
		Exorcists, hail-averters, amulettiers, &c. ...	1,156	189	268	699
		Total Sub-order 63(a) ...	*9,667*	*1,288*	*2,237*	*6,142*
	63b	Religious mendicants, inmates of convents, &c.	7	...	...	7
		Church, temple, pagoda, masjid, &c., services ..	11,920	1,124	2,288	8,508
		Total Sub-order 63(b) ...	11,927	1,124	2,288	8,515
	64	Administrative and inspecting officials ...	58	5	10	43
		Principals, professors and teachers in colleges, &c., schools, &c. ...	779	71	182	526
		Clerks, &c., on educational estalishments ...	...	...	...	...
		Total Sub-order 64 ...	837	76	192	569
	65	Editors and ballad makers.	11	...	4	7
		Private secretaries and clerks ...	58	13	10	35
		Public Seribs ...	935	175	220	540
		Total Sub-order 65 ...	1,004	188	234	582
	66	Advocates and pleaders...	3,353	540	774	2.039
		Mukhtiars ...	...	...	...	...
		Lawyer's clerks ...	119	14	21	84
		Stamp vendors ...	24	3	6	15
		Petition writers ...	55	3	3	49
		Total Sub-order 66 ...	3,551	560	804	2,187

XVII.

Travancore State Summary—(*Continued*).

—(*Continued*).

Males.				Females.			
Total.	0—4.	5—14.	15 and over.	Total.	0—4.	5—14.	15 and over.
32	33	34	35	36	37	38	39
4,266	474	998	2,794	3,950	598	952	2,400
160	17	6	137	135	10	13	112
708	124	166	418	448	65	102	281
5,134	615	1,170	3,349	4,533	673	1,067	2,793
7	...	...	7	...	...	...	...
6,542	427	1,152	4,963	5,378	697	1,136	3,545
6,549	427	1,152	4,970	5,378	697	1,136	3,545
33	...	3	30	25	5	7	13
567	46	115	406	212	25	67	120
...	...	...	...	...	...	...	...
600	46	118	436	237	30	74	133
9	...	4	5	2	...	...	2
31	9	5	17	27	4	5	18
599	120	140	339	336	55	80	201
639	129	149	361	365	59	85	221
1,627	281	350	996	1,726	259	424	1,043
...	...	...	...	...	...	...	...
110	13	19	78	9	1	2	6
8	...	4	4	16	3	2	11
48	1	2	45	7	2	1	4
1,793	295	375	1,123	1,758	265	429	1,064

TABLE

Occupations by Age, Part (A)—

Class.	Group.	Occupation.	State — Total. Total.	0—4.	5—14.	15 and over.
1	2	3	4	5	6	7
F. Professions.	67*a*	Administrative and inspecting staff ...	2	...	...	2
		Practitioners by diploma ...	28	6	4	18
		Practitioners without diploma (native physicians) ...	5,489	750	1,264	3,475
		Oculists ...	12	1	6	5
		Vaccinators ...	50	10	14	26
		Midwifery ...	1	...	...	1
		Total Sub-order 67(*a*) ...	5,582	767	1,288	3,527
	67*b*	Hospital & asylum assistants and apothecaries ...	126	26	20	80
		Compounders and hospital menials ...	30	3	3	24
		Total Sub-order 67(*b*) ...	156	29	23	104
	68*a*	Administrative and inspecting staff ...	2	...	...	2
		Civil engineers & architects ...	51	5	10	36
		Revenue surveyors and survey superintendents ...	28	...	5	23
		Total Sub-order 68(*a*) ...	81	5	15	61
	68*b*	Draughtsmen, &c., in survey offices and overseers, &c. ...	47	5	15	27
		Clerks, &c., in engineering and survey offices ...	417	73	78	266
		Total Sub-order 68(*b*) ...	464	78	93	293
	69*b*	Astrologers and horoscope-casters ...	3,778	519	888	2,371
		Almanac makers and sellers ...	7	2	2	3
		Diviners (selectors of wells and house sites) ...	2	...	...	2
		Total Sub-order 69(*b*) ...	3,787	521	890	2,376

XVII.

Travancore State Summary—(*Continued*).

TOTAL.

Males.				Females.			
Total.	0—4.	5—14.	15 and over.	Total.	0—4.	5—14.	15 and over.
8	9	10	11	12	13	14	15
1	...	...	1	1	...	...	1
21	4	2	15	7	2	2	3
2,800	345	645	1,810	2,689	405	619	1,665
9	...	5	4	3	1	1	1
21	3	2	16	29	7	12	10
...	...	...	...	1	...	...	1
2,852	352	654	1,846	2,730	415	634	1,681
76	14	10	52	50	12	10	28
15	2	1	12	15	1	2	12
91	16	11	64	65	13	12	40
1	...	...	1	1	...	...	1
30	2	7	21	21	3	3	15
20	...	3	17	8	...	2	6
51	2	10	39	30	3	5	22
15	1	3	11	32	4	12	16
274	63	58	153	143	10	20	113
289	64	61	164	175	14	32	129
1,545	202	380	963	2,233	317	508	1,408
4	1	1	2	3	1	1	1
2	...	..	2	...	...	...	...
1,551	203	381	967	2,236	318	509	1,409

TABLE

Occupations by Age, Part (A)—

Class.	Group.	Occupation.	Town — Total. Total.	0—4.	5—14.	15 and over.
1	2	3	16	17	18	19
F. Professions.	67*a*	Administrative and inspecting staff ...	2	...	...	2
		Practitioners by diploma ...	20	5	4	11
		Practitioners without diploma (native physicians) ...	403	55	133	215
		Oculists ...	5	...	2	3
		Vaccinators ...	9	2	2	5
		Midwifery ...	1	...	...	1
		Total Sub-order 67(*a*) ...	440	62	141	237
	67*b*	Hospital & asylum assistants and apothecaries ...	48	7	15	26
		Compounders and hospital menials ...	15	3	2	10
		Total Sub-order 67(*b*) ...	63	10	17	36
	68*a*	Administrative and inspecting staff ...	2	...	...	2
		Civil engineers & architects ...	42	5	6	31
		Revenue surveyors and survey superintendents ...	19	...	3	16
		Total Sub-order 68(*a*)	63	5	9	49
	68*b*	Draughtsmen, &c., in survey offices and overseers, &c. ...	9	2	2	5
		Clerks, &c., in engineering and survey offices ...	106	16	21	69
		Total Sub-order 68(*b*) ...	115	18	23	74
	69*b*	Astrologers and horoscope-casters ...	73	12	22	39
		Almanac makers and sellers ...	2	...	...	2
		Diviners (selectors of wells and house sites) ...	1	...	...	1
		Tota Sub-order 69(*b*) ...	76	12	22	42

XVII.

Travancore State Summary—(*Continued*).

—(*Continued*).

Males.				Females.			
Total.	0—4.	5—14.	15 and over.	Total.	0—4.	5—14.	15 and over.
20	21	22	23	24	25	26	27
1	...	...	1	1	...	...	1
16	4	2	10	4	1	2	1
208	24	81	103	195	31	52	112
4	...	2	2	1	...	...	1
5	1	1	3	4	1	1	2
...	...	...	...	1	...	...	1
234	29	86	119	206	33	55	118
23	3	7	13	25	4	8	13
11	2	1	8	4	1	1	2
34	5	8	21	29	5	9	15
1	...	...	1	1	...	...	1
25	2	5	18	17	3	1	13
15	...	2	13	4	...	1	3
41	2	7	32	22	3	2	17
4	1	1	2	5	1	1	3
62	12	14	36	44	4	7	33
66	13	15	38	49	5	8	36
37	5	12	20	36	7	10	19
1	...	...	1	1	..	...	1
1	...	...	1	...	...	...	...
39	5	12	22	37	7	10	20

TABLE

Occupations by Age, Part (A)—

Class.	Group.	Occupation.	Country — Total. Total.	Total. 0—4.	Total. 5—14.	Total. 15 and over.
1	2	3	28	29	30	31
F. Professions.	67*a*	Administrative and inspecting staff ...	...	...	...	...
		Practitioners by diploma ...	8	1	...	7
		Practitioners without diploma (native physicians) ...	5,086	695	1,131	3,260
		Oculists ..	7	1	4	2
		Vaccinators ...	41	8	12	21
		Midwifery ...	...	...	...	...
		Total Sub-order 67(*a*) ..	5,142	705	1,147	3,290
	67*b*	Hospital & asylum assistants and apothecaries ...	78	19	5	54
		Compounders and hospital menials ...	15	...	1	14
		Total Sub-order 67(*b*) ...	93	19	6	68
	68*a*	Administrative and inspecting staff ...	...	...	...	...
		Civil engineers & architects ...	9	...	4	5
		Revenue surveyors and survey superintendents ...	9	...	2	7
		Total Sub-order 68(*a*) ...	18	...	6	12
	68*b*	Draughtsmen, &c., in survey offices and overseers, &c. ...	38	3	13	22
		Clerks, &c., in engineering and survey offices ...	311	57	57	197
		Total Sub-order 68(*b*) ...	349	60	70	219
	69*b*	Astrologers and horoscope-casters ...	3,705	507	866	2,332
		Almanac makers and sellers ...	5	2	2	1
		Diviners (selectors of wells and house sites) ...	1	...	...	1
		Total Sub-order 69(*b*) ...	3,711	509	868	2,334

XVII.

Travancore State Summary—(*Continued*).

—(*Continued*).

Males.				Females.			
Total.	0—4.	5—14.	15 and over.	Total.	0—4.	5—14.	15 and over.
32	33	34	35	36	37	38	39
...	...	...	...	...	...	...	...
5	...	...	5	3	1	...	2
2,592	321	564	1,707	2,494	374	567	1,553
5	...	3	2	2	1	1	...
16	2	1	13	25	6	11	8
...	...	...	...	...	...	...	...
2,618	323	568	1,727	2,524	382	579	1,563
53	11	3	39	25	8	2	15
4	...	...	4	11	...	1	10
57	11	3	43	36	8	3	25
...	...	...	...	...	...	...	...
5	...	2	3	4	...	2	2
5	...	1	4	4	...	1	3
10	...	3	7	8	...	3	5
11	...	2	9	27	3	11	13
212	51	44	117	99	6	13	80
223	51	46	126	126	9	24	93
1,508	197	368	943	2,197	310	498	1,389
3	1	1	1	2	1	1	...
1	...	...	1	...	...	...	...
1,512	198	369	945	2,199	311	499	1,389

Class.	Group.	Occupation.	State Total. Total.	State Total. 0—4.	State Total. 5—14.	State Total. 15 and over.
1	2	3	4	5	6	7
F. Professions.	70	Painters and superintendents of schools of arts, &c. ...	776	145	181	450
		Sculptors ...	101	14	19	68
		Photographers ...	9	1	...	8
		Total Sub-order 70 ...	886	160	200	526
	71	Music composers and teachers ...	270	17	96	157
		Bandmasters, &c. (not military) ...	394	36	88	270
		Actors, singers, dancers and their accompanists..	1,442	114	349	979
		Total Sub-order 71 ...	2,106	167	533	1,406
	72	Shikaris and bird catchers.	61	8	20	33
	73*a*	Exhibitors of trained animals (bulls, snakes, monkeys, &c.) ...	31	5	8	18
		Circus players ...	23	1	9	13
		Cock and pigeon fanciers.	5	...	1	4
		Total Sub-order 73(*a*) ...	59	6	18	35
	73*b*	Buffoons ...	22	6	5	11
		Story and ballad reciters..	20	5	6	9
		Conjurors & fortune tellers	27	4	7	16
		Total Sub-order 73(*b*) ...	69	15	18	36
	73*c*	Acrobats and rope-dancers	255	27	53	175
	73*d*	Tennis and racquet court service ...	11	2	4	5
		Total Class F. ...	43,968	5,614	10,132	28,222

XVII.

Travancore State Summary—(*Continued*).

TOTAL.

Males.				Females.			
Total.	0—4.	5—14.	15 and over.	Total.	0—4.	5—14.	15 and over.
8	9	10	11	12	13	14	15
393	60	75	258	383	85	106	192
13	...	...	13	88	14	19	55
6	...	...	6	3	1	...	2
412	60	75	277	474	100	125	249
207	13	70	124	63	4	26	33
230	15	62	153	164	21	26	117
917	60	209	648	525	54	140	331
1,354	88	341	925	752	79	192	481
33	4	9	20	28	4	11	13
14	1	3	10	17	4	5	8
17	...	7	10	6	1	2	3
4	...	1	3	1	...	...	1
35	1	11	23	24	5	7	12
13	2	4	7	9	4	1	4
10	3	2	5	10	2	4	4
14	2	2	10	13	2	5	6
37	7	8	22	32	8	10	14
104	4	22	78	151	23	31	97
6	1	2	3	5	1	2	2
23,550	2,645	5,239	15,666	20,418	2,969	4,893	12,556

TABLE

Occupations by Age, Part (A)—

Class.	Group.	Occupation.	Town — Total. Total.	Town — Total. 0—4.	Town — Total. 5—14.	Town — Total. 15 and over.
1	2	3	16	17	18	19
F. Professions.	70	Painters and superintendents of schools of arts, &c. ...	180	35	47	98
		Sculptors ...	41	12	17	12
		Photographers ...	7	1	...	6
		Total Sub-order 70 ...	228	48	64	116
	71	Music composers and teachers ..	27	3	12	12
		Bandmasters, &c. (not military) ...	31	11	4	16
		Actors, singers, dancers and their accompanists..	107	12	14	81
		Total Sub-order 71 ...	165	26	30	109
	72	Shikaris and bird catchers.	4	1	1	2
	73*a*	Exhibitors of trained animals (bulls, snakes, monkeys, &c.) ...	2	...	...	2
		Circus players ...	6	...	1	5
		Cock and pigeon fanciers..	...	...	...	...
		Total Sub-order 73(*a*) ...	8	...	1	7
	73*b*	Buffoons ...	3	1	...	2
		Story and ballad reciters..	15	1	2	12
		Conjurors & fortune tellers	10	2	3	5
		Total Sub-order 73(*b*) ...	28	4	5	19
	73*c*	Acrobats and rope-dancers	18	3	7	8
	73*d*	Tennis and racquet court service ..	7	2	2	3
		Total Class F. ...	4,680	784	1,544	2,352

XVII.

Travancore State Summary—(*Continued*).

—(*Continued*).

Males.				Females.			
Total.	0—4.	5—14.	15 and over.	Total.	0—4.	5—14.	15 and over.
20	21	22	23	24	25	26	27
92	14	22	56	88	21	25	42
4	...	...	4	37	12	17	8
4	...	...	4	3	1	...	2
100	14	22	64	128	34	42	52
11	2	4	5	16	1	8	7
20	5	1	14	11	6	3	2
57	4	6	47	50	8	8	34
88	11	11	66	77	15	19	43
4	1	1	2	...	...	...	...
2	...	...	2	...	...	...	...
4	...	1	3	2	...	...	2
...	...	...	...	...	...	...	...
6	...	1	5	2	...	...	2
1	...	...	1	2	1	...	1
10	...	1	9	5	1	1	3
4	1	1	2	6	1	2	3
15	1	2	12	13	3	3	7
9	1	4	4	9	2	3	4
3	1	1	1	4	1	1	2
2,659	414	860	1,385	2,021	370	684	967

TABLE

Occupations by Age, Part (A)—

Class.	Group.	Occupation.	Country — Total. Total.	0—4.	5—14.	15 and over.
1	2	3	28	29	30	31
F. Professions.	70	Painters and superintendents of schools of arts, &c. ...	596	110	134	352
		Sculptors ...	60	2	2	56
		Photographers ...	2	...	...	2
		Total Sub-order 70 ...	658	112	136	410
	71	Music composers and teachers ...	243	14	84	145
		Bandmasters, &c. (not military) ...	363	25	84	254
		Actors, singers, dancers and their accompanists...	1,335	102	335	898
		Total Sub-order 71 ...	1,941	141	503	1,297
	72	Shikaris and bird catchers.	57	7	19	31
	73*a*	Exhibitors of trained animals (bulls, snakes, monkeys, &c.) ...	29	5	8	16
		Circus players ...	17	1	8	8
		Cock and pigeon fanciers.	5	...	1	4
		Total Sub-order 73 (*a*) ...	51	6	17	28
	73*b*	Buffoons ...	19	5	5	9
		Story and ballad reciters.	9	3	4	2
		Conjurors & fortune tellers.	13	3	4	6
		Total Sub-order 73(*b*) ...	41	11	13	17
	73*c*	Acrobats and rope-dancers	237	24	46	167
	73*d*	Tennis and racquet court service ...	4	...	2	2
		Total Class F. ...	39,288	4,830	8,588	25,870

XVII.

Travancore State Summary—(*Continued*).

—(*Continued*).

Males.				Females.			
Total.	0—4.	5—14.	15 and over.	Total.	0—4.	5—14.	15 and over.
32	33	34	35	36	37	38	39
301	46	53	202	295	64	81	150
9	...	...	9	51	2	2	47
2	...	...	2	...	...	...	...
312	46	53	213	346	66	83	197
196	11	66	119	47	3	18	26
210	10	61	139	153	15	23	115
860	56	203	601	475	46	132	297
1,266	77	330	859	675	64	173	438
29	3	8	18	28	4	11	13
12	1	3	8	17	4	5	8
13	...	6	7	4	1	2	1
4	...	1	3	1	...	...	1
29	1	10	18	22	5	7	10
12	2	4	6	7	3	1	3
4	2	1	1	5	1	3	1
6	2	1	3	7	1	3	3
22	6	6	10	19	5	7	7
95	3	18	74	142	21	28	93
3	...	1	2	1	...	1	...
20,891	2,231	4,379	14,281	18,397	2,599	4,209	11,589

TABLE

Occupations by Age, Part (A)—

Class.	Group.	Occupation.	State: Total. Total.	0—4.	5—14.	15 and over.
1	2	3	4	5	6	7
G. Indefinite and Independent.	74*a*	Well-sinkers ...	29	7	9	13
		Excavators ...	2	...	...	2
		Road and canal laborers...	171	12	27	132
		Quarry-men ...	5,924	858	1,389	3,677
		Rice-pounders & huskers..	2,922	379	610	1,933
		Total Sub-order 74(*a*) ...	9,048	1,256	2,035	5,757
	74*b*	General labor ...	700,807	84,248	164,663	451,896
	75	Undefined means of livelihood ...	10,315	965	2,283	7,067
	76*a*	House-rent and other property not being land ...	22	3	3	16
		Allowances from patrons..	22	...	1	21
		Total Sub-order 76(*a*) ...	44	3	4	37
	76*b*	Educational endowments (scholarship) ...	9	...	3	6
		Mendicancy (not religious)	5,161	409	1,165	3,587
		Total Sub-order 76(*b*) ...	5,170	409	1,168	3,593
	77*a*	Pension, civil services ...	1,834	211	453	1,170
		Pension, military services.	235	31	73	131
		Total Sub-order 77(*a*) ...	2,069	242	526	1,301

XVII.

Travancore State Summary—(*Continued*).

TOTAL.

Males.				Females.			
Total.	0—4.	5—14.	15 and over.	Total.	0—4.	5—14.	15 and over.
8	9	10	11	12	13	14	15
14	4	2	8	15	3	7	5
2	...	...	2	...	...	...	...
108	6	16	86	63	6	11	46
4,143	505	989	2,649	1,781	353	400	1,028
156	91	40	25	2,766	288	570	1,908
4,423	606	1,047	2,770	4,625	650	988	2,987
345,290	38,728	83,062	223,500	355,517	45,520	81,601	228,396
644	21	81	542	9,671	944	2,202	6,525
11	3	2	6	11	...	1	10
2	...	1	1	20	...	...	20
13	3	3	7	31	...	1	30
9	...	3	6	...	...	...	...
2,612	181	563	1,868	2,549	228	602	1,719
2,621	181	566	1,874	2,549	228	602	1,719
957	94	253	610	877	117	200	560
111	12	43	56	124	19	30	75
1,068	106	296	666	1,001	136	230	635

TABLE

Occupations by Age, Part (A)—

Class.	Group.	Occupation.	Town: Total. Total.	Total. 0—4.	Total. 5—14.	Total. 15 and over.
1	2	3	16	17	18	19
G. Indefinite and Independent.	74a	Well-sinkers ...	6	1	1	4
		Excavators ...	...	...	...	...
		Road and canal laborers...	25	2	7	16
		Quarry-men ...	43	4	13	26
		Rice-pounders & huskers..	385	79	98	208
		Total Sub-order 74(*a*) ...	459	86	119	254
	74b	General labor ...	26,359	4,030	5,206	17,123
	75	Undefined means of livelihood	...	...	...	...
	76a	House-rent and other property not being land ...	13	3	2	8
		Allowances from patrons..	2	...	1	1
		Total Sub-order 76(*a*) ...	15	3	3	9
	76b	Educational endowments (scholarship) ...	9	...	3	6
		Mendicancy (not religious).	133	26	39	68
		Total Sub-order 76(*b*) ...	142	26	42	74
	77a	Pension, civil services ...	501	61	179	261
		Pension, military services.	230	29	72	129
		Total Sub-order 77(*a*) ...	731	90	251	390

XVII.

Travancore State Summary—(*Continued*).

—(*Continued*).

Males.				Females.			
Total.	0—4.	5—14.	15 and over.	Total.	0—4.	5—14.	15 and over.
20	21	22	23	24	25	26	27
2	...	...	2	4	1	1	2
...	...	...	...	...	...	...	...
14	...	4	10	11	2	3	6
23	1	8	14	20	3	5	12
2	...	...	2	383	79	98	206
41	1	12	28	418	85	107	226
12,233	1,552	2,866	7,815	14,126	2,478	2,340	9,308
...	...	...	...	...	...	...	...
5	3	1	1	8	...	1	7
2	...	1	1	...	...	...	...
7	3	2	2	8	...	1	7
9	...	3	6	...	...	...	...
58	9	18	31	75	17	21	37
67	9	21	37	75	17	21	37
239	24	91	124	262	37	88	137
111	12	43	56	119	17	29	73
350	36	134	180	381	54	117	210

TABLE

Occupations by Age, Part (A)—

Class.	Group.	Occupation.	Country: Total. Total.	Total. 0—4.	Total. 5—14.	Total. 15 and over.
1	2	3	28	29	30	31
G. Indefinite and Independent.	74a	Well-sinkers ...	23	6	8	9
		Excavators ...	2	...	...	2
		Road and canal laborers...	146	10	20	116
		Quarry-men ...	5,881	854	1,376	3,651
		Rice pounders & huskers...	2,537	300	512	1,725
		Total Sub-order 74(a) ...	8,589	1,170	1,916	5,503
	74b	General labor ...	674,448	80,218	159,457	434,773
	75	Undefined means of livelihood ...	10,315	965	2,283	7,067
	76a	House-rent and other property not being land ...	9	...	1	8
		Allowances from patrons...	20	...	...	20
		Total Sub-order 76(a) ...	29	...	1	28
	76b	Educational endowments (scholarship) ...	...	...	...	...
		Mendicancy (not religious).	5,028	383	1,126	3,519
		Total Sub-order 76(b) ...	5,028	383	1,126	3,519
	77a	Pension, civil services ...	1,333	150	274	909
		Pension, military services.	5	2	1	2
		Total Sub-order 77(a) ...	1,338	152	275	911

XVII.

Travancore State Summary—(*Continued*).

—(*Continued*).

Males.				Females.			
Total.	0—4.	5—14.	15 and over.	Total.	0—4.	5—14.	15 and over.
32	33	34	35	36	37	38	39
12	4	2	6	11	2	6	3
2	...	...	2	...	...	...	...
94	6	12	76	52	4	8	40
4,120	504	981	2,635	1,761	350	395	1,016
154	91	40	23	2,383	209	472	1,702
4,382	605	1,035	2,742	4,207	565	881	2,761
333,057	37,176	80,196	215,685	341,391	43,042	79,261	219,088
644	21	81	542	9,671	944	2,202	6,525
6	...	1	5	3	...	...	3
...	...	...	...	20	...	...	20
6	...	1	5	23	...	...	23
...	...	...	...	...	...	...	...
2,554	172	545	1,837	2,474	211	581	1,682
2,554	172	545	1,837	2,474	211	581	1,682
718	70	162	486	615	80	112	423
...	...	...	...	5	2	1	2
718	70	162	486	620	82	113	425

TABLE

Occupations by Age, Part (A)—

Class.	Group.	Occupation.	State — Total. Total.	0—4.	5—14.	15 and over.
1	2	3	4	5	6	7
G. Indefinite and Independent.	77b	Inmates of asylums, &c ...	81	...	...	81
		Prisoners under trial ...	115	...	...	115
		Prisoners for debt ...	37	...	...	37
		Prisoners convicted ...	591	4	1	586
		Total Sub-order 77(b) ...	824	4	1	819
		Total Class G. ...	728,277	87,127	170,680	470,470
		Not stated ...	821	210	212	399
		Grand Total ..	2,557,736	322,216	604,671	1,630,849

XVII.

Travancore State Summary—(*Continued*).

TOTAL.

Males.				Females.			
Total.	0—4.	5—14.	15 and over.	Total.	0—4.	5—14.	15 and over.
8	9	10	11	12	13	14	15
55	...	...	55	26	...	...	26
108	...	...	108	7	...	...	7
37	...	...	37	...	..	...	...
570	1	1	568	21	3	...	18
770	1	1	768	54	3	...	51
354,829	39,646	85,056	230,127	373,448	47 481	85,624	240,343
282	127	101	54	539	83	111	345
1,290,415	153,399	308,827	828,189	1,267,321	168,817	295,844	802,660

TABLE

Occupations by Age, Part (A)—

Class.	Group.	Occupation.	Town — Total. Total.	Town — Total. 0—4.	Town — Total. 5—14.	Town — Total. 15 and over.
1	2	3	16	17	18	19
G. Indefinite and Independent.	77*b*	Inmates of asylums, &c...	81	...	...	81
		Prisoners under trial ...	105	...	...	105
		Prisoners for debt ...	37	...	...	37
		Prisoners convicted ...	528	4	1	523
		Total Sub-order 77(*b*) ...	751	4	1	746
		Total Class G. ...	28,457	4,239	5,622	18,596
		Not stated ...	593	160	138	295
		Grand Total ...	107,693	16,513	26,779	64,401

XVII.

Travancore State Summary—(*Continued*).

—(*Continued*).

Males.				Females.			
Total.	0—4.	5—14.	15 and over.	Total.	0—4.	5—14.	15 and over.
20	21	22	23	24	25	26	27
55	...	...	55	26	...	...	26
100	...	...	100	5	...	...	5
37	...	...	37	...	...	...	...
510	1	1	508	18	3	...	15
702	1	1	700	49	3	...	46
13,400	1,602	3,036	8,762	15,057	2,637	2,586	9,834
177	97	59	21	416	63	79	274
54,501	7,706	13,916	32,879	53,192	8,807	12,863	31,522

TABLE
Occupations by Age, Part (A)—

Class.	Group.	Occupation.	Country — Total. Total.	0—4.	5—14.	15 and over.
1	2	3	28	29	30	31
G. Indefinite and Independent.	77*b*	Inmates of asylums, &c. ...	...	...	...	...
		Prisoners under trial ...	10	...	...	10
		Prisoners for debt ...	...	...	...	...
		Prisoners convicted ...	63	...	...	63
		Total Sub-order 77(*b*) ...	73	...	...	73
		Total Class G. ...	699,820	82,888	165,058	451,874
		Not stated ...	228	50	74	104
		Grand Total ...	2,450,043	305,703	577,892	1,566,448

XVI.

Travancore State Summary—(*Continued*).

—(*Continued*).

Males.				Females.			
Total.	0—4.	5—14.	15 and over.	Total.	0—4.	5—14.	15 and over.
32	33	34	35	36	37	38	39
...	...	...	...	...	...	...	...
8	...	...	8	2	...	...	2
...	...	...	...	...	...	...	...
60	...	...	60	3	...	...	3
68	...	...	68	5	...	...	5
341,429	38,044	82,020	221,365	358,391	44,844	83,038	230,509
105	30	42	33	123	20	32	71
1,235,914	145,693	294,911	795,310	1,214,129	160,010	282,981	771,138

TABLE

Occupations combined

Sub-order.	Occupation, &c.	Total Number of persons in Table XVII.-(A).		
		Total.	Males.	Females.
1	2	3	4	5
6	Menials, &c.	40,936	23,369	17,567
14	Barbers	17,395	8,604	8,791
17	Cow and buffalo-keepers and milk and butter sellers	709	224	485
18	Grain dealers	1,084	725	359
19	Molasses (jaggery, gur, &c., makers and sellers	68,395	38,075	30,320
20	Oil pressers and sellers	14,071	7,874	6,197
	Oil cake dealers	677	526	151
42	Piece goods dealers	2,859	1,941	918
43	Gold and silver workers	19,140	10,001	9,139
44	Bell-metal workers and sellers	2,634	1,458	1,176
46	Blacksmiths	4,690	2,249	2,441
55	General merchants	119,907	58,722	61,185
57 (b)	Farmers of liquor	178	133	45
64	Principals, professors and teachers in colleges and schools	894	623	271
66	Advocates and pleaders	4,221	2,055	2,166
67 (a)	Practitioners without diploma (native physicians)	5,489	2,800	2,689
71	Actors, singers, dancers and their accompanists	1,442	917	525
	Total ...	304,721	160,296	144,425

XVII.-(C).

with Agriculture.

PERSONS RETURNED AS COMBINING THE OCCUPATION WITH AGRICULTURE.

Total.			Connection with the land.								
			(a) Owners or occupants.			(b) Tenants.			(c) Farm servants or field labourers.		
Total.	Males.	Females.	Total.	Males.	Females.	Total.	Males.	Females.	Total.	Males.	Females.
6	7	8	9	10	11	12	13	14	15	16	17
194	117	77	7	4	3	63	35	28	124	78	46
1,483	786	697	230	117	113	178	84	94	1,075	585	490
64	28	36	25	13	12	9	4	5	30	11	19
372	168	204	114	46	68	47	31	16	211	91	120
66	24	42	12	5	7	11	4	7	43	15	28
101	43	58	31	11	20	9	3	6	61	29	32
278	135	143	48	29	19	17	9	8	213	97	116
864	345	519	238	134	104	87	43	44	539	168	371
2,149	1,122	1,027	479	245	234	147	72	75	1,523	805	718
49	25	24	12	7	5	13	6	7	24	12	12
3,143	1,478	1,665	438	217	221	147	71	76	2,558	1,190	1,368
13,417	6,464	6,953	3,125	1,718	1,407	1,114	704	410	9,178	4,042	5,136
47	22	25	31	14	17	5	3	2	11	5	6
43	42	1	8	7	1	8	8	...	27	27	...
879	436	443	198	91	107	119	70	49	562	275	287
743	332	411	264	141	123	137	69	68	342	122	220
24	15	9	9	4	5	7	4	3	8	7	1
23,916	11,582	12,334	5,269	2,803	2,466	2,118	1,220	898	16,529	7,559	8,970

TABLE A.

Christians by Sect and Race, Part I.—Sects.

District or State.	Total Christians.			Distribution by Sect. Church of England.							
				Total.		Foreign.		Eurasian.		Native.	
	Total.	Males.	Females.	Males.	Females.	Males.	Females.	Males.	Females.	Males.	Females.
1	2	3	4	5	6	7	8	9	10	11	12
Travancore ...	526,911	266,969	259,942	8,359	8,109	108	75	1	...	8,250	8,034

Distribution by Sect—(*Continued*).

Congregationalist.								Episcopalian.							
Total.		Foreign.		Eurasian.		Native.		Total.		Foreign.		Eurasian.		Native.	
Males.	Females.	Males.	Females.	Males.	Females.	Males.	Females.	Males.	Females.	Males.	Females.	Males.	Females.	Males.	Females.
13	14	15	16	17	18	19	20	21	22	23	24	25	26	27	28
54	59	1	...	4	5	49	54	3	5	3	3	...	...	...	2

TABLE A.

Christians by Sect and Race, Part I.—Sects—(Continued).

DISTRICT OR STATE.	DISTRIBUTION BY SECT—(Continued).															
	LUTHERAN.								METHODIST.							
	Total.		Foreign.		Eurasian.		Native.		Total.		Foreign.		Eurasian.		Native.	
	Males.	Females.	Males.	Females.	Males.	Females.	Males.	Females.	Males.	Females.	Males.	Females.	Males.	Females.	Males.	Females.
1	29	30	31	32	33	34	35	36	37	38	39	40	41	42	43	44
Travancore...	1	1	...	...	...	...	1	1	4	8	4	8	...	...	...	...

DISTRIBUTION BY SECT—(Continued).															
NON-CONFORMIST.								PRESBYTERIAN.							
Total.		Foreign.		Eurasian.		Native.		Total.		Foreign.		Eurasian.		Native.	
Males.	Females.	Males.	Females.	Males.	Females.	Males.	Females.	Males.	Females.	Males.	Females.	Males.	Females.	Males.	Females.
45	46	47	48	49	50	51	52	53	54	55	56	57	58	59	60
1	...	1	...	...	...	...	...	1	...	1	...	...	...	...	...

TABLE A.

Christians by Sect and Race, Part I.—Sects—(*Continued*).

District or State.	Distribution by Sect—(*Continued*).															
	Protestant.								Roman Catholic.							
	Total.		Foreign.		Eurasian.		Native.		Total.		Foreign.		Eurasian.		Native.	
	Males.	Females.	Males.	Females.	Males.	Females.	Males.	Females.	Males.	Females.	Males.	Females.	Males.	Females.	Males.	Females.
1	61	62	63	64	65	66	67	68	69	70	71	72	73	74	75	76
Travancore...	13,238	12,501	38	24	59	57	13,141	12,420	141,604	137,593	43	30	172	167	141,389	137,396

Distribution by Sect—(*Continued*).															
Syrian.								Not Stated.							
Total.		Foreign.		Eurasian.		Native.		Total.		Foreign.		Eurasian.		Native.	
Males.	Females.	Males.	Females.	Males.	Females.	Males.	Females.	Males.	Females.	Males.	Females.	Males.	Females.	Males.	Females.
77	78	79	80	81	82	83	84	85	86	87	88	89	90	91	92
89,371	87,203	...	...	...	...	89,371	87,203	14,333	14,463	10	11	49	18	14,274	14,434

TABLE A.

Christians by Sect and Race, Part II.—Races.

District or State.	Total Christians.			Distribution by Race.										
				A.—Foreign.										
				Total.			Church of England.		Congregationalist.		Episcopalian.		Methodist.	
	Total.	Males.	Females.	Total.	Males.	Females.	Males.	Females.	Males.	Females.	Males.	Females.	Males.	Females.
1	2	3	4	5	6	7	8	9	10	11	12	13	14	15
Travancore ...	526,911	266,969	259,942	360	209	151	108	75	1	...	3	3	4	8

Distribution by Race—(*Continued*).

A.—Foreign—(*Continued*).										B.—Eurasian.						
Non-Conformist.		Presbyterian.		Protestant		Roman Catholic.		Not stated.		Total.			Church of England.		Congregationalist.	
Males.	Females.	Males.	Females.	Males.	Females.	Males.	Females.	Males.	Females	Total.	Males.	Females.	Males.	Females.	Males.	Females.
16	17	18	19	20	21	22	23	24	25	26	27	28	29	30	31	32
1	...	1	...	38	24	43	30	10	11	532	285	247	1	...	4	5

TABLE A.

Christians by Sect and Race, Part II.—Races—(*Continued*).

District or State.	Distribution by Race—(*Continued*).												
	B.—Eurasian—(*Continued*).						C.—Native.						
	Protestant.		Roman Catholic.		Not stated.		Total.			Church of England.		Congregationalist.	
	Males.	Females.	Males.	Females.	Males.	Females.	Total.	Males.	Females.	Males.	Females.	Males.	Females.
1	33	34	35	36	37	38	39	40	41	42	43	44	45
Travancore ...	59	57	172	167	49	18	526,019	266,475	259,544	8,250	8,034	49	54

Distribution by Race—(*Continued*).											
C.—Native—(*Continued*).											
Episcopalian.		Lutheran.		Protestant.		Roman Catholic.		Syrian.		Not stated.	
Males.	Females.	Males.	Females.	Males.	Females.	Males.	Females.	Males.	Females.	Males.	Females.
46	47	48	49	50	51	52	53	54	55	56	57
...	2	1	1	13,141	12,420	141,389	137,396	89,371	87,203	14,274	14,434

TABLE B.

Europeans and Eurasians by Age.

District or State.	Total.			Europeans.											Eurasians.										
				All Ages.			0—14.		15—34.		35—49.		50 and over.		All Ages.			0—14.		15—34.		35—49.		50 and over.	
	Total.	Males.	Females.	Total.	Males.	Females.	Males.	Females.	Males.	Females.	Males.	Females.	Males.	Females.	Total.	Males.	Females.	Males.	Females.	Males.	Females.	Males.	Females.	Males.	Females.
1	2	3	4	5	6	7	8	9	10	11	12	13	14	15	16	17	18	19	20	21	22	23	24	25	26
TRAVANCORE. PART I.—Total Population.	893	495	398	361	210	151	63	42	62	67	59	28	26	14	532	285	247	62	87	124	99	66	46	33	15
PART II.—Persons enumerated in Military limits.	84	42	42	21	11	10	3	4	6	5	2	...	...	1	63	31	32	15	14	7	10	6	5	3	3
PART III.—Persons enumerated outside Military limits.	809	453	356	340	199	141	60	38	56	62	57	28	26	13	469	254	215	47	73	117	89	60	41	30	12

NOTE.—There are no Armenians in this State.

TABLE C.

English Literates by Caste, &c.

Class.	Group.	Caste, &c.	Religion.	Total Strength. Males. Total Males.	Males. Literate. Total.	Males. Literate. English.	Females. Total Females.	Females. Literate. Total.	Females. Literate. English.
A. Agricultural.	1 Military and Dominant.	1 Nair	Hindu	241,598	90,542	572	242,127	16,673	42
		2 Ambalakāran	"	1	1	...	...	...	...
		3 Kartāvu	"	55	12	1	42	2	...
		4 Koiltamburan	"	58	24	6	43	7	...
		5 Kshatrya	"	653	210	11	623	122	1
		6 Mahratta	"	50	8	1	43	...	...
		7 Maravar	"	2,889	433	3	2,753	10	...
		8 Pandāla	"	36	17	2	35	7	...
		9 Rajaput	"	13	5	...	7	2	...
		10 Raju	"	30	9	2	22	5	...
		11 Sāmantakar	"	97	27	3	91	15	...
		12 Tampan	"	144	63	2	142	25	...
		13 Tirumulpād	"	232	106	2	178	51	...
		14 Unniyādiri	"	51	22	1	43	15	...
		15 Vellodi	"	18	4	...	26	1	...
		Total group 1	...	245,925	91,483	606	246,175	16,935	43

A. Agricultural.

2(*a*) Other Agricultural land-holding classes.	1 Gavarulu ...	Hindu ...	7	...	...	5	...	...
	2 Karayālar ...	„ ...	27	5	...	31	...	...
	3 Kattāran ...	„ ...	3	...	...	2	...	...
	4 Kodipattan ...	„ ...	210	2	...	213	...	...
	5 Kuruni ...	„ ...	7	...	...	...	...	...
	6 Lōti ...	„ ...	1	...	...	...	...	...
	7 Mālli ...	„ ...	1	...	...	...	...	...
	8 Mudali ...	„ ...	437	144	12	489	34	...
	9 Pāndi Sudra ...	„ ...	2,511	636	2	2,633	56	...
	10 Valamalu ...	„ ...	2	...	...	3	...	...
	11 Vellāla ...	„ ...	22,808	8,114	313	22,078	781	1
	Total group 2(*a*) ...	...	26,014	8,901	327	25,454	871	1
2(*c*) Field-labouring classes.	1 Karakkan ...	Hindu ...	94	3	...	98	2	...
	2 Kuravar ...	„ ...	29,660	467	...	30,717	107	...
	3 Padayāchi ...	„ ...	1	1	...	3	...	...
	4 Pallan ...	„ ...	2,811	52	...	2,844	4	...
	5 Pariah ...	{ Hindu { Christian	36,463	858	2	35,384	91	...
	6 Pulaya ...	Hindu ...	103,153	4,031	...	99,463	630	...
	7 Udaya ...	„ ...	2	...	...	5	...	...
	8 Ullādan ...	„ ...	1,473	12	...	1,400	2	...
	9 Vettuvan ...	„ ...	39	4	...	48	...	...
	Total group 2(*c*) ...	...	173,696	5,428	2	169,962	836	...
4 Forest and Hill tribes.	1 Iruler ...	Hindu ...	7	...	...	9	...	...
	2 Kāttar ...	„ ...	23	6	...	16	...	...
	3 Kāttilaya ...	„ ...	40	7	...	36	...	...
	4 Kāttu Parisha (forest tribe) ...	„ ...	23	...	...	11	...	...
	5 Khond ...	„ ...	8	1	...	2	...	...
	6 Malayarien ...	„ ...	2,498	60	...	2,311	4	...
	7 Mariya ...	„ ...	3	...	...	...	...	...

TABLE C.

English Literates by Caste, &c.—(Continued).

Class.	Group.	Caste, &c.	Religion.	Total Males.	Males Literate Total.	Males Literate English.	Total Females.	Females Literate Total.	Females Literate English.
A. Agricultural —(Continued).	4 Forest and Hill tribes—(Contd.)	8 Muduvan ...	Hindu ...	545	15	...	532	...	...
		9 Mynāta ...	" ...	24	4	...	20	...	...
		10 Nādipanikan ...	" ...	9	...	...	20	...	...
		11 Pania ...	" ...	...	...	...	2	...	...
		12 Vēlan ...	" ...	8,660	317	...	8,483	71	...
		Total group 4 ...	..	11,840	410	...	11,442	75	...
		Total class A. ...	...	457,475	106,222	935	453,033	18,717	44
B. Profession.	5 Priests ...	1 Brahmin ...	Hindu ...	1,423	793	107	1,222	98	...
		Foreign Brahmin ...	" ...	1,961	1,044	147	1,568	142	1
		Aiyengar ...	" ...	479	244	36	419	61	...
		Canarese Brahmin ...	" ..	18	9	1	17	7	...
		Gouda Brahmin ...	" ..	66	35	...	11	4	...
		Hindustani Brahmin ..	" ...	3	2	2	3	...	...
		Kannadasta ...	" ...	4	2	...	5	1	...
		Kāsi Brahmin ...	" ...	24	17	...	35	3	...
		Kēsiar ...	" ...	34	18	3	33	16	...

TABLE C.

English Literates by Caste, &c.—(*Continued*).

B. Professional.

	Mahratta Brahmin ...	" ...	525	255	36	439	97	1
	Nambiyān ...	" ...	110	32	1	104	9	...
	Surveriya ...	" ...	1	1	...	...	...	...
	Tamil Brahmin ...	" ...	11,238	6,325	498	10,661	472	...
	Telugu Brahmin ...	" ...	385	140	32	412	26	...
	Malayala Brahmin ...	" ...	1,866	914	4	1,585	162	...
	Akkaradēsi ...	" ...	25	9	...	...	...	...
	Bhattadiri ...	" ...	74	50	...	72	5	...
	Embrān ...	" ...	1,150	369	5	788	74	...
	Nambūdiri ...	" ...	1,979	935	1	1,771	107	...
	Ponmany Gramom ...	" ...	55	23	...	41	3	...
	Potti ...	" ...	1,421	643	6	1,174	151	...
	Tiruvalladēsi ...	" ...	167	50	...	161	28	...
	Trippūnittoraidēsi ...	" ...	50	15	...	16	3	...
	2 Āriapattar ...	" ...	21	7	...	19	4	...
	3 Ilayadu ...	" ...	1,686	535	...	1,574	72	...
	4 Tangal ...	Mussalman...	9	2	...	5	...	...
	Total group 5 ..	...	24,774	12,469	879	22,135	1,545	2
6 Devotees ...	1 Fakkir ...	Mussalman ..	4	4	...	1	...	...
	2 Gosains ...	Hindu ...	40	8	...	21	...	...
	3 Sanniyāsi ..	" ..	8	4	...	1	...	...
	4 Vyravi ...	" ...	356	97	...	356	18	...
	Total group 6 ..	...	408	113	...	379	18	...
7 Temple servants.	1 Ambalavāsi ...	Hindu ...	3,890	1,097	8	3,579	183	...
	2 Krishnanvagai ...	" ...	3,394	858	5	3,559	74	...
	3 Pilāppalli ...	" ..	33	14	...	36	2	...
	4 Sātāni ...	" ...	7	1	...	7	1	...
	Total group 7 ...	...	7,324	1,970	13	7,181	260	...
8 Genealogists ...	Tākur ...	Hindu ...	3	...	...	1	..	...

TABLE C.

English Literates by Caste, &c.—(*Continued*).

Class.	Caste and Religion.			Total Strength.					
				Males.			Females.		
	Group.	Caste, &c.	Religion.	Total Males.	Literate. Total.	Literate. English.	Total Females.	Literate. Total.	Literate. English.
B. Profession-al—(*Contd.*)	10 Astrologers and quack doctors.	1 Kaniyān ...	Hindu ...	4,846	1,674	4	4,702	98	...
		2 Pulluvan ...	,, ...	123	...	...	151	...	...
		Total group 10 ...	...	4,969	1,674	4	4,853	98	...
		Total class B. ...	...	37,478	16,226	896	34,549	1,921	2
mercial.	14 Traders ..	1 Balija ...	Hindu ...	249	83	14	200	2	...
		2 Baniya ...	{ Hindu { Jain ...	53	26	2	9	...	...
		3 Chetti ...	Hindu ...	9,089	2,613	35	8,680	184	...
		4 Ilavāniyan ...	,, ...	1,647	255	2	1,664	5	...
		5 Jonaka ...	Mussalman ..	26,568	2,562	...	25,223	153	...
		6 Labbai ...	,, ...	213	41	...	148	13	...
		7 Mettan ...	,, ...	27,523	2,155	7	26.563	145	...
		8 Rāwut ...	,, ...	30	4	...	27	2	...
		9 Vaduka ...	Hindu ...	1,427	501	5	1.269	15	...
		10 Vaisya ...	,, ...	259	18	...	215	...	...
		Total group 14 ...	...	67,058	8,258	65	63,998	519	...

Class	Group	Caste	Religion						
C. Com	15 Pedlars ...	1 Balukar ...	Hindu ...	6	1	...	...	...	...
		2 Manikār ...	,, ...	22	...	...	14	...	...
		Total group 15 ...	...	28	1	...	14	...	...
		Total class C. ...	...	67,086	8,259	65	64,012	519	...
D. Artisans and Village Menials.	17 Goldsmiths ...	Tattan ...	Hindu ...	12,506	4,481	15	12,192	128	...
	17(*a*) Artisans (general).	1 Kammālan ...	Hindu ...	985	205	1	997	19	...
		2 Kamsāla ...	,, ...	7	...	...	6	...	...
		Total group 17(*a*) ...	...	992	205	1	1,003	19	...
	18 Barbers ...	1 Īlavāti ...	Hindu ...	1,360	41	...	1,509	5	...
		2 Kāvadi ...	,, ...	2,677	294	...	2,590	13	...
		3 Kōmaram ...	,, ...	138	5	...	119	...	...
		4 Kshourakan ...	,, ...	7,987	943	6	8,143	44	...
		5 Mārān ...	,, ...	7,456	2,181	3	7,772	316	...
		6 Ostta ...	Mussalman ..	22	2	...	44	...	...
		7 Taravan ...	Hindu ...	226	...	...	229	...	...
		Total group 18 ...	...	19,866	3,466	9	20,406	378	...
	19 Blacksmiths ...	1 Kollan ...	Hindu ...	13,903	1,703	...	13,079	120	...
		2 Lōhar ...	,, ...	3	1	...	...	..	...
		Total group 19 ...	...	13,906	1,704	...	13,079	120	...
	20 Carpenters, masons & turners.	1 Asāri ...	Hindu ...	16,932	4,013	1	16,709	247	...
		2 Tachan ...	,, ...	2,014	334	...	2,052	7	...
		Total group 20 ...	..	18,946	4,347	1	18,761	254	...

TABLE C.

English Literates by Caste, &c.—(*Continued*).

Class.	Caste and Religion.			Total Strength.					
				Males.			Females.		
	Group.	Caste, &c.	Religion.	Total Males.	Literate. Total.	Literate. English.	Total Females.	Literate. Total.	Literate. English.
Village Menials—(*Continued*).	21 Brass and coppersmiths.	1 Chembutatti ...	Hindu ...	56	18	...	42	...	...
		2 Kannān ...	,, ...	2,894	167	...	2,803	1	...
		Total group 21 ...	...	2,950	185	...	2,845	1	...
	22 Tailors ...	Pānān ...	Hindu ...	1,409	169	6	1,299	8	...
	22(*a*) Grain parchers and confectioners.	1 Idiyar ...	Hindu ...	660	69	...	606	4	...
		2 Mudayar ...	,, ...	1	...	...	...	...	...
		Total group 22(*a*) ...	...	661	69	...	606	4	...
	23 Weavers, calenderers and dyers.	1 Kōri ...	Hindu ...	5	1	...	2	...	...
		2 Patnūl ...	,, ...	393	97	...	461	12	...
		3 Sālē ...	,, ...	3,580	825	5	3,709	102	...
		Total group 23 ...	...	3,978	923	5	4,172	114	...

TABLE C.

English Literates by Caste, &c.—(*Continued*).

D. Artisans and

24 Washermen ...	1 Ainuttar ...	Hindu ...	1	...	...	1	...	...
	2 Dōbi ...	" ...	65	11	...	73	...	...
	3 Mannān ...	" ...	3,509	72	...	3,573	...	...
	4 Velutadan ...	" ...	6,993	744	4	6,833	52	...
	Total group 24 ...	...	10,568	827	4	10,480	52	...
26 Shepherds and wool-weavers.	1 Āttidaya ...	Hindu ...	109	9	...	108	1	...
	2 Gollalu ...	" ...	36	9	1	31	...	...
	3 Idaya ...	" ...	2,863	442	7	2,985	29	...
	4 Kāngaya ...	" ...	67	5	...	58	...	...
	5 Kūttidaya ...	" ...	58	2	...	47	...	...
	Total group 26 ...	...	3,133	467	8	3,229	30	...
27 Oil-pressers ...	1 Chekkāla ...	Hindu ...	5,739	784	1	5,853	65	...
	2 Vānian ...	" ...	7,031	995	6	6,727	68	...
	Total group 27 ...	...	12,770	1,779	7	12,580	133	...
28 Potters ...	Kosava ..	Hindu ...	3,269	430	...	3,126	50	...
30 Salt,&c.,workers.	Alava ...	Hindu ...	206	28	...	188	9	...
31 Lime-burners ...	Paravan ...	Hindu ...	3,983	252	...	4,189	28	...
35 Fishermen, boatmen, palki-bearers, water bearers, cooks, &c.	1 Chaluppan ...	Hindu ...	471	20	...	450	...	...
	2 Kāhar ...	" ...	1	...	...	...	...	...
	3 Marakkān ...	Mussalman / Christian...	2,639	314	...	2,852	18	...
	4 Mukkuvan ...	Hindu ...	15,082	931	1	15,272	102	...
	5 Pōndan ...	" ...	617	91	1	522	7	...
	Total group 35 ...	..	18,810	1,356	2	19,096	127	...

TABLE C.

English Literates by Caste, &c.—(*Continued*).

Class.	Group.	Caste, &c.	Religion.	Males: Total Males.	Males: Literate: Total.	Males: Literate: English.	Females: Total Females.	Females: Literate: Total.	Females: Literate: English.
D. Artisans and Village Menials —(*Continued*).	35(*a*) Personal service.	Chākkār ...	Hindu ...	306	...	...	259	...	...
	36 Distillers and toddy-drawers.	1 Īluva ...	Hindu ...	206,528	24,996	30	207,689	1,089	...
		2 Pāshi ..	,, ..	3	...	...	...	...	...
		3 Chānnān ...	,, ...	70,001	3,566	15	66,610	250	...
		4 Tandān ...	,, ...	11,158	317	...	11,456	68	...
		Total group 36 ...	...	287,690	28,879	45	285,755	1,407	...
	38 Leather workers.	Chemmān ...	Hindu ...	1,094	48	...	1,062	5	...
	39 Scavengers ...	1 Dāss ...	Hindu ...	5	...	..	5	...	...
		2 Valluvan ...	,, ..	56	23	3	57	7	...
		Total group 39 ..	...	61	23	3	62	7	...
		Total class D. ...	...	417,104	49,638	106	414,389	2,874	...

E. Vagrant minor Artisans and Performers.

Group	Caste	Religion						
40 Grind-stone makers and stoue quarriers.	Kallāsāri ...	Hindu ...	4,079	38	...	4,059	23	...
41 Earth workers & stone dressers.	1 Ottan ...	Hindu ...	292	16	2	85	...	...
	2 Ottiya ...	,, ...	10	1	...	15	...	...
	Total group 41 ...	...	302	17	2	100	...	...
43 Matmakers, cane splitters, grass-cutters, &c.	Nolayan ...	Hindu ...	1,260	89	...	1,063	2	...
44 Hunters, fowlers, &c.	1 Talavan ...	Hindu ...	371	...	...	385	...	..
	2 Vēdan ...	,, ...	3,498	53	...	3,311	...	...
	3 Vettāran ...	,, ...	178	...	...	171	...	...
	Total group 44 ...	...	4,047	53	...	3,867	...	...
45 Miscellaneous and disreputable vagrants.	1 Kākkālan ...	Hindu ...	422	8	...	475	..	..
	2 Passiavan ...	,, ...	35	...	...	29	...	...
	Total group 45 ...	...	457	8	...	504	...	...
45(*a*) Beggars ...	1 Panisivan ...	Hindu ...	32	...	...	26	...	...
	2 Sangampandāram ...	,, ...	5,416	474	2	5,308	13	...
	Total group 45(*a*) ...	...	5,448	474	2	5,334	13	...
46 Tumblers and acrobats.	1 Gopāl ...	Hindu ...	3	2	...	1	...	...
	2 Kūttādi ...	,, ...	17	13	...	21	...	...
	Total group 46 ...	...	20	15	...	22	...	...

TABLE C.

English Literates by Caste, &c.—(*Continued*).

Class.	Group.	Caste, &c.	Religion.	Males. Total Males.	Males. Literate. Total.	Males. Literate. English.	Females. Total Females.	Females. Literate. Total.	Females. Literate. English.
Vagrant, &c. (*Contd.*)	47 Jugglers, snake charmers and animal exhibitors.	Kuluvan ...	Hindu ...	42	...	...	31	...	...
		Total class E. ...	...	15,655	694	4	14,980	38	...
and Nationalities.	48 Asiatic races of reputed non-Indian descent.	1 Arabs ...	Mussalman ..	260	58	...	186	10	...
		2 Chinese ...	Christian ...	1	1	1	...	...	...
		3 Jew ...	Jew ...	65	34	...	60	36	...
		4 Kābūl ...	Mussalman ..	84	17	...	45	4	...
		5 Mughul ...	" ...	317	78	21	265	20	...
		6 Parsi ...	Parsi ..	1	...	...	...	...	...
		7 Pathān ...	Mussalman ..	2,508	632	24	1,845	165	...
		8 Sheik ...	" ...	240	156	13	174	40	...
		9 Singhalese ...	Hindu ...	17	...	...	12	...	...
		10 Syed ...	Mussalman ..	117	70	5	115	26	1
		Total group 48 ...	...	3,610	1,046	64	2,702	301	1

TABLE C.

English Literates by Caste, &c.—(*Continued*).

Class	Group	Caste, &c.	Religion						
F. Races	50 Non-Asiatic races.	European ...	{ Christian / None }	210	160	149	151	88	72
	51 Eurasians ...	1 East Indian ...	Christian ...	995	435	180	1,077	305	38
		2 Eurasian ...	„ ...	285	203	177	247	140	61
		Total group 51 ...	...	1,280	638	357	1,324	445	99
	52 Christian converts.	1 Native ...	Christian ...	112,489	28,658	310	108,517	4,189	27
		2 Syrian ...	„ ...	150,395	27,555	224	147,400	4,240	39
		Total group 52 ...	...	262,884	56,213	534	255,917	8,429	66
		Total class F. ...	...	267,984	58,057	1,104	260,094	9,263	238
G. Undefined.	54 Linguistic, territorial & religious names.	1 Bengalese ...	Hindu ...	3	3	...	...	...	...
		2 Guzarati ...	„ ...	28	21	...	20	...	...
		3 Jain ...	Jain ...	3	2	...	...	...	...
		4 Kannadiyan ...	Hindu ...	19	...	...	22	...	...
		5 Konkanese ...	„ ...	3,681	1,456	10	3,389	99	...
		6 Kutch ...	Mussalman ..	147	43	2	169	7	...
		7 Mussalman ...	„ ...	7,203	1,368	3	7,547	358	...
		8 Tamil ...	Hindu ...	3	3	...	...	...	...
		9 Telugu ...	„ ...	10	...	...	10	...	...
		10 Tulukkan ...	Mussalman ..	15,555	4,412	8	14,215	301	...
		Total group 54 ...	...	26,652	7,308	23	25,372	765	...

TABLE C.

English Literates by Caste, &c.—(*Continued*).

Class.	Caste and Religion.			Total Strength.					
	Group.	Caste, &c.	Religion.	Males.			Females.		
				Total Males.	Literate. Total.	Literate. English.	Total Females.	Literate. Total.	Literate. English.
...ined—(*Continued*).	55 Unknown ...	1 Bālāji ...	Hindu ...	77	26	2	20	4	...
		2 Bhavarāsi ...	„ ...	7	...	...	4	...	...
		3 Bhujār ...	„ ...	1	...	...	...	...	...
		4 Bhujavar ...	„ ...	1	...	...	...	...	...
		5 Chilambātti ...	„ ...	6	...	...	3	...	...
		6 Heathen ...	„ ...	1	...	...	...	...	...
		7 Kadiyan ...	„ ...	2	...	...	1	...	...
		8 Kāmuvar ...	„ ...	2	...	...	...	...	...
		9 Kodayan ...	„ ...	3	...	...	12	...	...
		10 Kūch ...	„ ...	1	...	...	1	...	...
		11 Malayānkāran ...	„ ...	146	...	...	100	...	...
		12 Mustān ...	Mussalman ..	1	...	...	3	...	...
		13 Nāgamom ...	Hindu ...	5	...	...	8	...	...
		14 Nālikan ...	„ ...	104	...	...	83	..	...
		15 Naralavēlu ...	„ ...	1	...	...	...	...	...
		16 Neriyan ...	„ ...	63	...	...	82	...	...
		17 Nodiyan ...	„ ...	10	...	...	3	...	...

G. Unde								
	18 Not stated ...	Hindu ... / Christian .. / None ...	108	26	2	84	2	...
	19 Pani ...	Mussalman ..	425	97	...	473	36	...
	20 Pattōl ...	Hindu ...	5	2	...	5	...	...
	21 Sahabiti ...	„ ...	1	...	...	4	...	...
	22 Tāli ...	„ ...	1	...	...	...	...	...
	23 Tāttedam ...	„ ...	6	...	...	4	...	...
	24 Tōlar ...	„ ..	4	2	...	2	...	...
	Total group 55 ...	...	981	153	4	892	42	...
	Total class G. ...	...	27,633	7,461	27	26,264	807	...
	Grand Total ...	...	1,290,415	246,557	3,137	1,267,321	34,139	284

TABLE

Castes by

Class.	Group.	Caste, &c.	Religion.	Total Males.	Pupils.
	Caste and Religion.			Total	
				Males	
A. Agricultural.	1 Military and Dominant.	1 Nair ...	Hindu ...	241,598	20,162
		2 Ambalakāran ...	,, ...	1	...
		3 Kartāvu ...	,, ...	55	4
		4 Koiltamburān ...	,, ...	58	7
		5 Kshatrya ...	,, ...	653	77
		6 Mahratta ...	,, ...	50	2
		7 Maravar ...	,, ...	2,889	76
		8 Pandāla ...	,, ...	36	4
		9 Rajaput ...	,, ...	13	1
		10 Raju ...	,, ...	30	2
		11 Sāmantakar ...	,, ...	97	16
		12 Tampān ...	,, ...	144	15
		13 Tirumulpād ...	,, ...	232	19
		14 Unniyādiri ...	,, ...	51	4
		15 Vellodi ...	,, ...	18	1
		Total group 1 ...	...	245,925	20,390
	2(*a*) Other Agricultural land-holding classes.	1 Gavarulu ...	Hindu ...	7	2
		2 Karayālar ...	,, ...	27	...
		3 Kattāran ...	,, ...	3	...
		4 Kodipattan ...	,, ...	210	7
		5 Kuruni ...	,, ...	7	...
		6 Lōti ...	,, ...	1	...
		7 Mālli ...	,, ...	1	...
		8 Mudali ...	,, ...	437	18
		9 Pāndi Sudra ...	,, ...	2,511	74
		10 Valamalu ...	,, ...	2	...
		11 Vellālā ...	,, ...	22,808	1,730
		Total group 2(*a*) ..	...	26,014	1,831
	2(*c*) Field-labouring classes.	1 Kanakkan ...	Hindu ...	94	3
		2 Kuravar ...	,, ...	29,660	119
		3 Padayāchi ...	,, ...	1	...
		4 Pallan ...	,, ...	2,811	8
		5 Pariah ..	{ Hindu ... Christian }	36,463	165

D.

Education.

STRENGTH.

—(*Continued*).			Females.				
Literate.	Illiterate.	Not stated.	Total Females	Pupils.	Literate.	Illiterate.	Not stated.
90,542	130,894	...	242,127	3,897	16,673	221,557	...
1	...	...	...	...	...	...	...
12	39	...	42	1	2	39	...
24	27	...	43	2	7	34	...
210	366	...	623	30	122	471	...
8	40	...	43	...	...	43	..
433	2,380	...	2,753	10	10	2,733	...
17	15	...	35	2	7	26	...
5	7	...	7	...	2	5	...
9	19	...	22	1	5	16	...
27	54	...	91	4	15	72	...
63	66	...	142	2	25	115	...
106	107	...	178	4	51	123	...
22	25	...	43	2	15	26	...
4	13	...	26	...	1	25	...
91,483	134,052	...	246,175	3,955	16,935	225,285	...
...	5	...	5	...	...	5	...
5	22	...	31	...	...	31	...
...	3	...	2	...	...	2	...
2	201	...	213	...	...	213	...
...	7	...	...	...	...	...	...
...	1	...	...	...	...	...	...
...	1	...	...	...	...	...	...
144	275	...	489	9	34	446	...
636	1,801	...	2,633	13	56	2,564	...
...	2	...	3	...	...	3	...
8,114	12,963	1	22,078	251	781	21,046	...
8,901	15,281	1	25,454	273	871	24,310	...
3	88	...	98	...	2	96	...
467	29,074	...	30,717	74	107	30,536	...
1	...	...	3	...	...	3	...
52	2,751	...	2,844	5	4	2,835	...
858	35,440	..	35,384	53	91	35,240	...

TABLE

Castes by

Class.	Caste and Religion. Group.	Caste, &c.	Religion.	Total Males. Total Males.	Total Males. Pupils.
A. Agricultural.	2(*c*) Field-labouring classes —(*Continued*).	6 Pulaya ...	Hindu ...	103,153	3,135
		7 Udaya ...	" ...	2	...
		8 Ullādan ...	" ...	1,473	2
		9 Vettuvan ...	" ...	39	1
		Total group 2(*c*) ...	...	173,696	3,433
	4 Forest and Hill tribes.	1 Iruler ...	Hindu ...	7	...
		2 Kāttar ...	" ...	23	...
		3 Kāttilaya ...	" ...	40	1
		4 Kāttu Parisha (forest tribe) ...	" ...	23	...
		5 Khond ...	" ...	8	...
		6 Malayarien ...	" ...	2,498	12
		7 Mariya ...	" ...	3	...
		8 Muduvan ...	" ...	545	...
		9 Mynāta ...	" ..	24	...
		10 Nādipanikkan ...	" ...	9	...
		11 Pania ...	" ...	...	...
		12 Vēlan ...	" ...	8,660	13
		Total group 4 ...	...	11,840	26
		Total class A. ...	...	457,475	2,6850
B. Professional.	5 Priests.	1 Brahmin ...	Hindu ...	1,423	336
		Foreign Brahmin ...	" ...	1,961	445
		Aiyengar ...	" ...	479	59
		Canarese Brahmin ...	" ...	18	2
		Gouda Brahmin ...	" ...	66	4
		Hindustani Brahmin ...	" ...	3	1
		Kannadasta ...	" ...	4	...
		Kāsi Brahmin ...	" ...	24	1
		Kēsiar ...	" ...	34	7
		Mahratta Brahmin ...	" ...	525	99
		Nambiyān ..	" ...	110	12
		Surveriya ...	" ...	1	...
		Tamil Brahmin ...	" ...	11,238	1,396
		Telugu Brahmin ...	" ...	385	76

D.

Education—(*Continued*).

STRENGTH.

—(*Continued*).			Females.				
Literate.	Illiterate.	Not stated.	Total Females	Pupils.	Literate.	Illiterate.	Not stated.
4,031	95,987	...	99,463	72	630	98,761	...
...	2	...	5	...	...	5	...
12	1,459	...	1,400	...	2	1,398	...
4	34	...	48	...	...	48	...
5,428	164,835	...	169,962	204	836	168,922	...
...	7	...	9	...	...	9	...
6	17	...	16	...	...	16	...
7	32	...	36	...	...	36	...
...	23	...	11	...	...	11	...
1	7	...	2	...	...	2	...
60	2,426	...	2,311	...	4	2,307	...
...	3	...	...	...	...	...	...
15	530	...	532	...	...	532	...
4	20	...	20	...	...	20	...
...	9	...	20	...	...	20	...
...	...	...	2	...	...	2	...
317	8,330	...	8,483	...	71	8,412	...
410	11,404	...	11,442	...	75	11,367	...
106,222	325,572	1	453,033	4,432	18,717	429,884	...
793	294	...	1,222	77	98	1,047	...
1,044	472	...	1,568	86	142	1,340	...
244	176	...	419	13	61	345	...
9	7	...	17	...	7	10	...
35	27	...	11	...	4	7	...
2	...	...	3	...	...	3	...
2	2	...	5	...	1	4	...
17	6	...	35	...	3	32	...
18	9	...	33	2	16	15	...
255	171	...	439	15	97	327	...
32	66	...	104	2	9	93	...
1	...	...	...	...	...	...	...
6,325	3,517	...	10,661	349	472	9,840	...
140	169	...	412	12	26	374	...

TABLE

Caste by

Class.	Caste and Religion. Group.	Caste, &c.	Religion.	Total Males. Total Males.	Total Males. Pupils.
B. Professional.	5 Priests —(*Continued*).	Malayala Brahmin ...	Hindu ...	1,866	11
		Akkaradēsi ...	,, ...	25	4
		Bhattadiri ...	,, ...	74	5
		Embrān ...	,, ...	1,150	178
		Nambūdiri ...	,, ...	1,979	100
		Ponmany Gramom ...	,, ...	55	1
		Pōtti ...	,, ...	1,421	72
		Tiruvalladēsi ...	,, ...	167	17
		Trippūnittoraidēsi ...	,, ...	50	10
		2 Āriapattar ...	,, ...	21	7
		3 Ilayadu ...	,, ...	1,686	55
		4 Tangal ...	Mussalman.	9	...
		Total group 5 ...	...	24,774	2,898
	6 Devotees.	1 Fakkir ...	Mussalman.	4	...
		2 Gosains ...	Hindu. ..	40	...
		3 Sanniyāsi ...	,, ...	8	...
		4 Vyravi ...	,, ...	356	24
		Total group 6 ...	...	408	24
	7 Temple servants.	1 Ambalavāsi ...	Hindu ...	3,890	140
		2 Krishnanvagai ...	,, ...	3,394	184
		3 Pilāppalli ...	,, ...	33	13
		4 Sātāni ...	,, ...	7	...
		Total group 7 ...	...	7,324	337
	8 Genealogists...	Tākur ...	Hindu ...	3	...
	10 Astrologers & quack doctors.	1 Kaniyān ...	Hindu ..	4,846	193
		2 Pulluvan ...	,, ...	123	...
		Total group 10 ...	...	4,969	193
		Total class B. ...	...	37,478	3,452

D.

Education—(*Continued*).

Strength.

—(*Continued*).			Females.				
Literate.	Illiterate.	Not stated.	Total Females	Pupils.	Literate.	Illiterate.	Not stated.
914	941	..	1,585	31	162	1,392	...
9	12	...	...	...	...	...	...
50	19	...	72	3	5	64	...
369	603	...	788	14	74	700	...
935	944	...	1,771	11	107	1,653	...
23	31	...	41	2	3	36	...
643	706	...	1,174	6	151	1,017	...
50	100		161	12	28	121	...
15	25	...	16	1	3	12	...
7	7	...	19	1	4	14	...
535	1,096	...	1,574	10	72	1,492	...
2	7	...	5	...	...	5	...
12,469	9,407	...	22,135	647	1,545	19,943	...
4	...	...	1	...	...	1	...
8	32	...	21	...	...	21	...
4	4	...	1	...	...	1	...
97	235	...	356	9	18	329	...
113	271	...	379	9	18	352	...
1,097	2,653	...	3,579	12	183	3,384	...
858	2,352	...	3,559	6	74	3,479	...
14	6	...	36	1	2	33	...
1	6	...	7	...	1	6	...
1,970	5,017	...	7,181	19	260	6,902	...
...	3	...	1	...	...	1	...
1,674	2,979	...	4,702	10	98	4,594	...
...	123	...	151	...	...	151	...
1,674	3,102	...	4,853	10	98	4,745	...
16,226	17,800	...	34,549	685	1,921	31,943	...

TABLE

Caste by

Class.	Caste and Religion. Group.	Caste, &c.	Religion.	Total Males. Total Males.	Pupils.
C. Commercial.	14 Traders ...	1 Balija ...	Hindu ...	249	32
		2 Baniya ...	Hindu / Jain	53	3
		3 Chetti ...	Hindu ...	9,089	582
		4 Ilavaniyan ...	,, ...	1,647	114
		5 Jonaka ...	Mussalman	26,568	427
		6 Labbai ...	,, ...	213	12
		7 Mēttan ...	,, ...	27,523	343
		8 Rāwut ...	,, ...	30	2
		9 Vaduka ...	Hindu ...	1,427	27
		10 Vaisya ...	,, ...	259	...
		Total group 14 ...	...	67,058	1,542
	15 Pedlars ...	1 Balukar ...	Hindu ...	6	...
		2 Manikar ...	,, ...	22	...
		Total group 15 ...	...	28	...
		Total class C. ...	...	67,086	1,542
D. Artisans and Village Menials.	17 Goldsmiths ...	Tattān ...	Hindu ...	12,506	1,188
	17(a) Artisans (general).	1 Kammālan ...	Hindu ...	985	65
		2 Kamsāla ...	,, ...	7	...
		Total group 17(a) ...	...	992	65
	18 Barbers ...	1 Īlavāti ...	Hindu ...	1,360	38
		2 Kāvadi ...	,, ...	2,677	40
		3 Kōmaram ...	,, ...	138	1
		4 Kshourakan ...	,, ...	7,987	113
		5 Mārān ...	,, ...	7,456	422
		6 Ostta ...	Mussalman	22	1
		7 Taravan	Hindu ...	226	...
		Total group 18 ...	...	19,866	615

D.

Education—(*Continued*).

STRENGTH.

—(*Continued*).			Females.				
Literate.	Illiterate.	Not stated.	Total Females	Pupils.	Literate.	Illiterate.	Not stated.
83	132	2	200	2	2	195	1
26	24	...	9	...	...	9	...
2,613	5,894	...	8,680	75	184	8,421	...
255	1,278	...	1,664	18	5	1,641	...
2,562	23,579	...	25,223	93	153	24,977	...
41	158	2	148	2	13	133	...
2,155	25,025	...	26,563	46	145	26,372	...
4	24	...	27	1	2	24	...
501	899	...	1,269	...	15	1,254	...
18	241	...	215	...	...	215	...
8,258	57,254	4	63,998	237	519	63,241	1
1	5	...	...	...	...	..	...
...	22	...	14	...	...	14	..
1	27	...	14	...	...	14	...
8,259	57,281	4	64,012	237	519	63,255	1
4,481	6,837	...	12,192	19	128	12,045	...
205	715	...	997	3	19	975	...
...	7	...	6	...	...	6	...
205	722	...	1,003	3	19	981	...
41	1,281	...	1,509	2	5	1,502	...
294	2,343	...	2,590	1	13	2,576	...
5	132	...	119	...	...	119	...
943	6,931	...	8,143	11	44	8,088	...
2,181	4,853	...	7,772	63	316	7,393	...
2	19	...	44	...	...	44	...
...	226	...	229	...	...	229	...
3,466	15,785	...	20,406	77	378	19,951	...

TABLE

Caste by

Class.	Group.	Caste, &c.	Religion.	Total Males.	Pupils.
		Caste and Religion.		Total Males	
D. Artisans and Village Menials.	19 Blacksmiths...	1 Kollan ...	Hindu ...	13,903	207
		2 Lōhar ...	,, ...	3	...
		Total group 19 ...	...	13,906	207
	20 Carpenters, masons and turners.	1 Āsāri ...	Hindu ...	16,932	533
		2 Tachan ...	,, ...	2,014	60
		Total group 20 ...	...	18,946	593
	21 Brass & coppersmiths.	1 Chembutatti ...	Hindu ...	56	5
		2 Kannān ...	,, ...	2,894	40
		Total group 21 ...	...	2,950	45
	22 Tailors ...	Pānān ..	Hindu ...	1,409	27
	22(*a*) Grain parchers and confectioners.	1 Idiyar ...	Hindu ...	660	54
		2 Mudayar ...	,, ...	1	...
		Total group 22(*a*) ...	...	661	54
	23 Weavers, calenderers and dyers.	1 Kori ...	Hindu ..	5	...
		2 Patnūl ...	,, ...	393	15
		3 Sālē ...	,, ...	3,580	164
		Total group 23 ...	...	3,978	179
	24 Washermen...	1 Ainuttar ...	Hindu ...	1	...
		2 Dōbi ...	,, ...	65	4
		3 Mannān ...	,, ...	3,509	22
		4 Velutadan ...	,, ...	6,993	73
		Total group 24 ...	...	10,568	99
	26 Shepherds and wool-weavers.	1 Āttidaya ...	Hindu ...	109	4
		2 Gollalu ...	,, ...	36	10

D.

Education—(*Continued*).

Strength.

—(*Continued*).			Females.				
Literate.	Illiterate.	Not stated.	Total Females	Pupils.	Literate.	Illiterate.	Not stated.
1,703	11,993	...	13,079	15	120	12,944	...
1	2	...	...	...	...	...	...
1,704	11,995	...	13,079	15	120	12,944	...
4,013	12,386	...	16,709	59	247	16,403	...
334	1,620	...	2,052	9	7	2,036	...
4,347	14,006	...	18,761	68	254	18,439	...
18	33	...	42	...	...	42	...
167	2,687	...	2,803	...	1	2,802	...
185	2,720	...	2,845	...	1	2,844	...
169	1,213	...	1,299	...	8	1,291	...
69	537	...	606	5	4	597	...
...	1	...	...	...	...	...	...
69	538	...	606	5	4	597	...
1	4	...	2	...	...	2	...
97	281	...	461	...	12	449	...
825	2,591	...	3,709	25	102	3,582	...
923	2,876	...	4,172	25	114	4,033	...
...	1	...	1	...	...	1	...
11	50	...	73	1	...	72	...
72	3,415	...	3,573	...	...	3,573	...
744	6,176	...	6,833	11	52	6,770	...
827	9,642	...	10,480	12	52	10,416	...
9	96	...	108	...	1	107	...
9	17	...	31	2	...	29	...

TABLE

Caste by

Class.	Group. (Caste and Religion.)	Caste, &c.	Religion.	Total Males. (Total — Males)	Pupils.
D. Artisans and Village Menials.	26 Shepherds and wool-weavers —(*Continued*).	3 Idaya ...	Hindu ...	2,863	58
		4 Kāngaya ...	,, ...	67	2
		5 Kūttidaya ...	,, ...	58	1
		Total group 26 ...	...	3,133	75
	27 Oil-pressers...	1 Chekkāla ...	Hindu ...	5,739	182
		2 Vānian ...	,, ...	7,031	148
		Total group 27 ...	...	12,770	330
	28 Potters ...	Kosava ...	Hindu ...	3,269	76
	30 Salt, &c., workers ...	Alava ...	Hindu ..	206	13
	31 Lime-burners.	Paravan ...	Hindu ...	3,983	40
	35 Fishermen, boatmen, palki-bearers, water bearers, cooks, &c.	1 Chaluppan ...	Hindu ...	471	7
		2 Kāhar ...	,, ...	1	...
		3 Marakkan ...	{ Musslmn / Christn. }	2,639	97
		4 Mukkuvan ...	Hindu ...	15,082	210
		5 Pōndan ...	,, ...	617	13
		Total group 35 ...	...	18,810	327
	35(*a*) Personal service.	Chākkār ...	Hindu ...	306	...
	36 Distillers and toddy-drawers.	1 Īluva ...	Hindu ...	206,528	3,173
		2 Pāshi ...	,, ...	3	...
		3 Chānnān ...	,, ...	70,001	949
		4 Tandān ...	,, ...	11,158	54
		Total group 36 ...	...	287,690	4,176

D.

Education—(*Continued*).

STRENGTH.

—(*Continued*).			Females.				
Literate.	Illiterate.	Not stated.	Total Females	Pupils.	Literate.	Illiterate.	Not stated.
442	2,363	...	2,985	2	29	2,954	..
5	60	...	58	...	...	58	...
2	55	...	47	...	...	47	...
467	2,591	...	3,229	4	30	3,195	...
784	4,773	...	5,853	18	65	5,770	...
995	5,888	..	6,727	7	68	6,652	...
1,779	10,661	...	12,580	25	133	12,422	...
430	2,763	...	3,126	9	50	3,067	...
28	165	...	188	3	9	176	...
252	3,691	...	4,189	4	28	4,157	...
20	444	...	450	2	...	448	..
...	1	...	...	...	...	...	...
314	2,228	...	2,852	3	18	2,831	...
931	13,941	...	15,272	58	102	15,112	...
91	513	...	522	4	7	511	..
1,356	17,127	...	19,096	67	127	18,902	...
...	306	...	259	...	...	259	...
24,996	178,359	...	207,689	1,038	1,089	205,562	...
...	3	...	...	...	...	...	...
3,566	65,486	...	66,610	121	250	66,239	...
317	10,787	...	11,456	17	68	11,371	...
28,879	254,635	...	285,755	1,176	1,407	283,172	...

TABLE

Caste by

Class.	Caste and Religion. Group.	Caste, &c.	Religion.	Total — Males — Total Males.	Total — Males — Pupils.
D. Artisans and Village Menials.	38 Leather workers.	Chemmān ...	Hindu ...	1,094	5
	39 Scavengers ...	1 Dass ...	Hindu ...	5	...
		2 Valluvan ...	" ...	56	12
		Total group 39 ...	...	61	12
		Total class D. ...	...	417,104	8,126
E. Vagrant minor Artisans and Performers.	40 Grind-stone makers and stone quarriers.	Kallāsāri ...	Hindu ...	4,079	55
	41 Earth workers and stone dressers.	1 Ottan ...	Hindu ...	292	...
		2 Ottiya ...	" ...	10	...
		Total group 41 ...	...	302	...
	43 Matmakers, cane splitters, grass-cutters, &c.	Nolayan ...	Hindu ...	1,260	23
	44 Hunters, fowlers, &c.	1 Talavan ...	Hindu ...	371	...
		2 Vēdan ...	" ...	3,498	12
		3 Vettāran ...	" ...	178	...
		Total group 44 ...	...	4,047	12
	45 Miscellaneous and disreputable vagrants.	1 Kākkalan ...	Hindu ...	422	6
		2 Passiavan ...	" ...	35	...
		Total group 45 ...	...	457	6
	45(a) Beggars ...	1 Panisivan ...	Hindu ...	32	4
		2 Sangampandaram ...	" ...	5,416	66
		Total group 45(a) ...	...	5,448	70

D.

Education—(*Continued*).

STRENGTH.

—(*Continued*).			Females.				
Literate.	Illiterate.	Not stated.	Total Females.	Pupils.	Literate.	Illiterate.	Not stated.
48	1,041	...	1,062	...	5	1,057	...
...	5	...	5	...	...	5	...
23	21	...	57	4	7	46	...
23	26	...	62	4	7	51	...
49,638	359,340	..	414,389	1,516	2,874	409,999	...
38	3,986	...	4,059	2	23	4,034	...
16	276	...	85	...	...	85	...
1	9	...	15	...	...	15	...
17	285	...	100	...	...	100	...
89	1,148	...	1,063	...	2	1,061	...
...	371	...	385	...	...	385	...
53	3,433	..	3,311	...	...	3,311	...
...	178	...	171	...	...	171	...
53	3,982	...	3,867	...	...	3,867	...
8	408	...	475	...	...	475	...
...	35	...	29	...	...	29	...
8	443	...	504	...	...	504	...
...	28	...	26	...	...	26	...
474	4,876	...	5,308	6	13	5,289	...
474	4,904	...	5,334	6	13	5,315	...

TABLE

Caste by

Class.	Group.	Caste, &c.	Religion.	Total Males.	Pupils.
		Caste and Religion.		Total	
				Males	
E. Vagrant minor Artisans and Performers.	46 Tumblers and acrobats.	1 Gopāl ...	Hindu ...	3	1
		2 Kūttādi ...	,, ...	17	3
		Total group 46 ...	...	20	4
	47 Jugglers, snake charmers and animal exhibitors.	Kuluvan ...	Hindu ...	42	...
		Total class E. ...	...	15,655	170
F. Races and Nationalities.	48 Asiatic races of reputed non-Indian descent.	1 Arabs ...	Mussalman.	260	40
		2 Chinese ...	Christian..	1	...
		3 Jew ...	Jew ...	65	16
		4 Kābūl ...	Mussalman.	84	7
		5 Mughul ...	,, ...	317	12
		6 Parsi ...	Parsi ...	1	...
		7 Pathan ...	Mussalman.	2,508	126
		8 Sheik ...	,, ...	240	45
		9 Singhalese ...	Hindu ...	17	...
		10 Syed ...	Mussalman.	117	12
		Total group 48 ...	...	3,610	258
	50 Non-Asiatic races.	European ...	{ Christian { None ...	} 210	24
	51 Eurasians ...	1 East Indian ...	Christian..	995	158
		2 Eurasian ...	,, ...	285	44
		Total group 51 ...	...	1,280	202
	52 Christian converts.	1 Native ...	Christian..	112,489	5,642
		2 Syrian ...	,, ...	150,395	5,811
		Total group 52 ...	...	262,884	11,453
		Total class F. ...	...	267,984	11,937

D.

Education—(*Continued*).

STRENGTH.

—(*Continued*).			Females.				
Literate.	Illiterate.	Not stated.	Total Females	Pupils.	Literate.	Illiterate.	Not stated.
2	...	..	1	...	...	1	...
13	1	...	21	...	...	21	...
15	1	...	22	...	...	22	...
...	42	...	31	...	...	31	...
694	14,791	...	14,980	8	38	14,934	...
58	162	...	186	4	10	172	...
1	...	...	...	...	...	...	...
34	15	...	60	14	36	10	...
17	60	...	45	...	4	41	...
78	227	...	265	4	20	241	...
...	1	...	...	...	...	...	...
632	1,750	...	1,845	80	165	1,600	...
156	39	...	174	10	40	124	...
...	17	...	12	...	...	12	...
70	35	...	115	1	26	88	...
1,046	2,306	...	2,702	113	301	2,288	...
160	26	...	151	34	88	29	...
435	402	...	1,077	96	305	676	...
203	38	...	247	38	140	69	...
638	440	...	1,324	134	445	745	...
28,658	78,189	...	108,517	1,224	4,189	103,104	...
27,555	117,029	...	147,400	1,108	4,240	142,052	...
56,213	195,218	...	255,917	2,332	8,429	245,156	...
58,057	197,990	...	260,094	2,613	9,263	248,218	...

TABLE

Caste by

Class.	Caste and Religion. Group.	Caste, &c.	Religion.	Total — Males — Total Males.	Total — Males — Pupils.
G. Undefined.	54 Linguistic, territorial and religious names.	1 Bengalese ...	Hindu ...	3	...
		2 Guzerati ...	,, ...	28	...
		3 Jain ...	Jain ...	3	1
		4 Kannadiyan ...	Hindu ...	19	...
		5 Konkani ...	,, ...	3,681	249
		6 Kutch ...	Mussalman.	147	30
		7 Mussalman ...	,, ...	7,203	320
		8 Tamil ...	Hindu ...	3	...
		9 Telugu ...	,, ...	10	...
		10 Tulukken ...	Mussalman.	15,555	402
		Total group 54 ...	...	26,652	1,002
	55 Unknown ...	1 Bālāji ...	Hindu ...	77	11
		2 Bhavarāsi ...	,, ...	7	...
		3 Bhujār ...	,, ...	1	...
		4 Bhujavar ...	,, ...	1	...
		5 Chilambātti ...	,, ...	6	...
		6 Heathen ...	,, ...	1	...
		7 Kadiyan ...	,,	2	...
		8 Kāmuvar ...	,, ...	2	...
		9 Kodayan ...	,, ...	3	...
		10 Kūch ...	,, ..	1	...
		11 Malayánkáran ...	,, ...	146	...
		12 Mustān ...	Mussalman	1	...
		13 Nāgamom ...	Hindu ...	5	...
		14 Nálikan ...	,, ...	104	...
		15 Naralavēlu ...	,, ...	1	...
		16 Neriyan ...	,, ...	63	...
		17 Nodiyan ...	,, ...	10	...
		18 Not stated ...	Christ. None Hindu	108	13
		19 Pani ...	Mussalman	425	21
		20 Pattōl ...	Hindu ...	5	...
		21 Sahabiti ...	,, ...	1	...
		22 Tāli ...	,, ...	1	...
		23 Táttedam ...	,, ...	6	...
		24 Tōlar ...	,, ...	4	1
		Total group 55 ...	...	981	46
		Total class G. ...	...	27,633	1,048
		Grand Total ...	...	1,290,415	51,955

D.

Education—(*Continued*).

STRENGTH.

—(*Continued*).			Females.				
Literate.	Illiterate.	Not stated.	Total Females.	Pupils.	Literate.	Illiterate.	Not stated.
3	...	...	...	...	...	...	...
21	7	...	20	...	...	20	...
2	...	...	...	...	...	...	...
...	19	...	22	...	..	22	...
1,456	1,976	...	3,389	57	99	3,233	...
43	74	...	169	6	7	156	...
1,868	5,515	...	7,547	45	358	7,144	...
3	...	...	...	...	...	...	...
...	10	...	10	...	...	10	...
4,412	10,741	..	14,215	80	301	13,834	...
7,808	18,342	...	25,372	188	765	24,419	...
26	40	...	20	2	4	14	...
...	7	...	4	...	...	4	...
...	1	...	...	...	...	...	...
...	1	...	...	...	...	...	...
...	6	...	3	...	...	3	...
...	1	...	...	...	...	...	...
...	2	...	1	...	...	1	...
...	2	...	...	...	...	...	...
...	3	...	12	...	...	12	...
...	1	...	1	...	...	1	...
...	146	...	100	...	...	100	...
...	1	...	3	...	...	3	...
...	5	...	8	...	...	8	...
...	104	...	83	...	...	83	...
...	1	...	...	...	...	...	...
...	63	...	82	...	...	82	...
...	10	...	3	...	...	3	...
26	69	...	84	4	2	78	...
97	307	...	473	2	36	435	...
2	3	...	5	...	...	5	...
...	1	...	4	...	...	4	...
...	1	...	...	...	...	...	...
...	6	...	4	...	...	4	...
2	1	...	2	...	...	2	...
153	782	...	892	8	42	842	...
7,461	19,124	...	26,264	196	807	25,261	...
246,557	991,898	5	1,267,321	9,687	34,139	1,223,494	1

TABLE E.

Castes, &c., by Civil Condition and Age.

Caste and Religion.				Total Strength.							
				Males.							
				All Ages.				0—9.			
Class.	Group.	Caste, &c.	Religion.	Total.	Un-married.	Married.	Widow-ed.	Total.	Un-married.	Married.	Widow-ed.
1	2	3	4	5	6	7	8	9	10	11	12
A. Agricultural.	1 Military and Dominant.	1 Nair ...	Hindu ...	241,598	132,701	99,463	9,434	55,296	55,296	...	...
		2 Ambalakāran ...	„ ...	1	1	...	...	...	...	...	...
		3 Kartávu ...	„ ...	55	24	23	8	12	12	...	...
		4 Koiltamburán ...	„ ...	58	29	20	9	13	13	...	...
		5 Kshatrya ...	„ ...	653	324	236	93	146	146	...	...
		6 Mahratta ...	„ ...	50	26	21	3	12	12	...	...
		7 Maravar ...	„ ...	2,889	1,507	1,268	114	653	653	...	...
		8 Pandála ...	„ ...	36	16	14	6	8	8	...	...
		9 Rajaput ...	„ ...	13	6	5	2	3	3	...	...
		10 Raju ...	„ ...	30	12	13	5	6	6	...	...
		11 Sāmantakar ...	„ ...	97	47	35	15	20	20	...	...
		12 Tampān ...	„ ...	144	77	45	22	33	33	...	...
		13 Tirumulpád ...	„ ...	232	85	116	31	51	51	...	...
		14 Unniyādiri ...	„ ...	51	27	16	8	12	12	...	...
		15 Vellodi ...	„ ...	18	10	6	2	4	4	...	...
		Total group 1 ...	...	245,925	134,892	101,281	9,752	56,269	56,269	...	...

Castes, &c., by Civil Condition and Age—(*Continued*).

A. Agricultural.

2(*a*) Other Agricultural land-holding classes.	1 Gavarulu ...	Hindu ...	7	4	3	...	2	2	...	...
	2 Karayálar ...	" ...	27	16	10	1	7	7	...	..
	3 Kattāran ...	" ...	3	1	2	...	...	...	...	...
	4 Kodipattan ...	" ...	210	101	86	23	46	46	...	...
	5 Kuruni ...	" ...	7	4	3	...	2	2	...	...
	6 Lōti ...	" ...	1	...	1	...	...	...	...	...
	7 Málli ...	" ...	1	...	1	...	...	...	...	...
	8 Mudali ...	" ...	437	237	169	31	98	98	...	..
	9 Pándi Sudra ...	" ...	2,511	1,451	955	105	551	551	...	...
	10 Valamalu ...	" ...	2	...	2	...	...	...	...	...
	11 Vellāla ...	" ...	22,808	12,750	9,561	497	5,100	5,100	...	...
	Total group 2(*a*).	...	26,014	14,564	10,793	657	5,806	5,806	...	...
2(*c*) Field-labouring classes.	1 Kanakkan ...	Hindu ...	94	48	42	4	22	22	...	...
	2 Kurava ...	" ...	29,660	15,633	13,246	781	7,119	7,119	...	...
	3 Padayáchi ...	" ...	1	1	...	...	...	...	...	...
	4 Pallan ...	" ...	2,811	1,499	1,239	73	685	685	...	...
	5 Pariah ...	{ Hindu { Chrstn. }	36,463	19,264	16,237	962	8,759	8,759	...	...
	6 Pulaya ...	Hindu ...	103,153	54,532	45,840	2,781	25,253	25,253	...	...
	7 Udaya ...	" ...	2	...	2	...	...	...	...	...
	8 Ullādan ...	" ...	1,473	809	628	36	356	356	...	...
	9 Vettuvan ...	" ..	39	21	17	1	10	10	...	...
	Total group 2(*c*).	...	173,696	91,807	77,251	4,638	42,204	42,204	...	...
4 Forest and Hill tribes.	1 Iruler ...	Hindu ...	7	4	3	...	2	2	...	...
	2 Káttar ...	" ...	23	12	11	...	5	5	...	...
	3 Káttilaya ...	" ...	40	23	15	2	11	11	...	...
	4 Káttu Parisha (forest tribe) ...	" ...	23	13	9	1	7	7	...	...
	5 Khond ...	" ...	8	4	4	...	1	1	...	...
	6 Malayarien ...	" ...	2,498	1,280	1,147	71	607	607	...	...
	7 Mariya ...	" ...	3	1	2	...	...	...	...	...

TABLE E.

Castes, &c., by Civil Condition and Age—(Continued).

Class.	Caste and Religion.			Total Strength—(Continued). Males—(Continued).							
	Group.	Caste, &c.	Religion.	10—14.				15—39.			
				Total.	Un-married.	Married.	Widowed.	Total.	Un-married.	Married.	Widowed.
1	2	3	4	13	14	15	16	17	18	19	20
A. Agricultural.	1 Military and Dominant.	1 Nair ...	Hindu ...	26,751	26,551	200	...	107,600	48,249	58,603	748
		2 Ambalakāran ...	„ ...	...	..	...	...	1	1	...	...
		3 Kartāvu ...	„ ...	6	2	4	...	25	10	14	1
		4 Koiltamburān ...	„ ...	6	2	4	...	27	14	12	1
		5 Kshatrya ...	„ ...	71	54	17	...	291	114	164	13
		6 Mahratta ...	„ ...	6	6	...	...	21	7	13	1
		7 Maravar ...	„ ...	320	310	10	...	1,363	500	831	32
		8 Pandāla ...	„ ...	4	1	3	...	16	7	8	1
		9 Rajaput ...	„ ...	1	1	...	...	5	2	3	...
		10 Raju ...	„ ...	4	2	2	...	14	4	9	1
		11 Sāmantakar ...	„ ...	12	5	7	...	44	21	20	3
		12 Tampān ...	„ ...	15	14	1	...	64	29	31	4
		13 Tirumulpād ...	„ ...	24	18	6	...	104	14	85	5
		14 Unniyādiri ...	„ ...	6	3	3	...	25	12	10	3
		15 Vellodi ...	„ ...	1	...	1	...	10	6	4	...
		Total group 1 ...	...	27,227	26,969	258	...	109,610	48,990	59,807	813

TABLE E.

Castes, &c., by Civil Condition and Age—(*Continued*).

2(*a*) Other Agricultural land-holding classes.	1 Gavarulu ...	Hindu ...	1	1	...	...	3	1	2	...
	2 Karayálar ...	„ ...	4	4	...	...	10	4	6	...
	3 Kattāran ...	„ ...	1	1	...	...	1	...	1	...
	4 Kodipattan ...	„ ...	21	16	5	...	97	37	57	3
	5 Kuruni ...	„ ...	1	1	...	...	3	1	2	...
	6 Lōti ...	„ ...	...	...	...	...	...	...	...	...
	7 Málli ...	„ ...	...	...	...	...	1	...	1	...
	8 Mudali ...	„ ...	50	44	6	...	189	81	100	8
	9 Pándi Sudra ...	„ ...	274	243	31	...	1,116	519	568	29
	10 Valamalu ...	„ ...	...	...	...	...	1	...	1	...
	11 Vellála ...	„ ...	2,505	2,445	60	...	10,407	4,429	5,919	59
	Total group 2(*a*) ...	...	2,857	2,755	102	...	11,828	5,072	6,657	99
2(*c*) Field-labouring classes.	1 Kanakkan ...	Hindu ...	10	10	...	...	41	15	25	1
	2 Kurava ...	„ ...	3,290	3,277	13	...	12,716	4,911	7,679	126
	3 Padayáchi ...	„ ..	...	...	...	...	1	1	...	...
	4 Pallan ...	„ ...	316	316	...	...	1,204	467	725	12
	5 Pariah ...	{ Hindu } { Chrstn }	4,030	4,011	19	...	15,662	6,094	9,409	159
	6 Pulaya ...	Hindu ...	11,916	11,906	10	...	42,235	16,182	25,649	404
	7 Udaya ...	„ ...	...	...	...	...	1	...	1	...
	8 Ulládan ...	„ ...	165	165	...	...	665	274	384	7
	9 Vettuvan ...	„ ...	5	5	...	...	16	6	10	...
	Total group 2(*c*) ...	...	19,732	19,690	42	...	72,541	27,950	43,882	709
4 Forest and Hill tribes.	1 Iruler ...	Hindu ...	1	1	...	...	3	1	2	...
	2 Káttar ...	„ ...	3	3	...	...	10	4	6	...
	3 Káttilaya ...	„ ...	5	5	...	...	15	6	8	1
	4 Káttu Parisha (forest tribe) ...	„ ...	3	3		...	8	3	5	...
	5 Khond ...	„ ...	2	2	...	...	4	1	3	...
	6 Malayarien ...	„ ...	273	268	5	...	1,031	375	645	11
	7 Mariya ...	„ ...	...	...	...	...	2	1	1	...

TABLE E.

Castes, &c., by Civil Condition and Age—(*Continued*).

Class.	Caste and Religion.			Total Strength—(*Continued*).							
				Males—(*Continued*).				Females.			
				40 and over.				All Ages.			
	Group.	Caste, &c.	Religion.	Total.	Un-Married.	Married.	Widow-ed.	Total.	Un-Married.	Married.	Widow-ed.
1	2	3	4	21	22	23	24	25	26	27	28
A. Agricultural.	1 Military and Dominant.	1 Nair ...	Hindu ...	51,951	2,605	40,660	8,686	242,127	111,231	102,865	28,031
		2 Ambalakáran ..	" ...	...	...	...	...	...	...	...	...
		3 Kartávu ...	" ...	12	...	5	7	42	13	23	6
		4 Koiltamburán ...	" ...	12	...	4	8	43	13	26	4
		5 Kshatrya ...	" ...	145	10	55	80	623	215	366	42
		6 Mahratta ...	" ...	11	1	8	2	43	19	21	3
		7 Marava ...	" ...	553	44	427	82	2,753	1,272	1,160	321
		8 Pandála ...	" ...	8	...	3	5	35	11	18	6
		9 Rajaput ...	" ...	4	...	2	2	7	3	3	1
		10 Raju ...	" ...	6	...	2	4	22	6	14	2
		11 Sāmantakar ...	" ...	21	1	8	12	91	28	54	9
		12 Tampān ...	" ...	32	1	13	18	142	43	84	15
		13 Tirumulpád ..	" ...	53	2	25	26	178	62	99	17
		14 Unniyádiri ...	" ...	8	...	3	5	43	14	23	6
		15 Vellodi ...	" ...	3	...	1	2	26	9	15	2
		Total group 1 ...	...	52,819	2,664	41,216	8,939	246,175	112,939	104,771	28,465

A. Agricultural.

Group	Caste	Religion								
2(*a*) Other Agricultural land-holding classes.	1 Gavarulu ...	Hindu ...	1	...	1	...	5	1	4	...
	2 Karayálar ...	,, ...	6	1	4	1	31	14	15	2
	3 Kattāran ...	,, ...	1	...	1	...	2	1	1	...
	4 Kodipattan ...	,, ...	46	2	24	20	213	53	125	35
	5 Kuruni ...	,, ...	1	...	1	...	...	...	...	...
	6 Lōti ...	,, ...	1	...	1	...	..	..	..	...
	7 Málli ...	,, ...	...	...	...	...	...	...	...	...
	8 Mudali ...	,, ...	100	14	63	23	489	211	228	50
	9 Pandi Sudra ...	,, ...	570	138	356	76	2,633	1,205	1,127	301
	10 Valamalu ...	,, ...	1	...	1	...	3	...	3	...
	11 Velláia ...	,, ..	4,796	776	3,582	438	22,078	10,141	9,392	2,545
	Total group 2(*a*) ...	...	5,523	931	4,034	558	25,454	11,626	10,895	2,933
2(*c*) Field-labouring classes.	1 Kanakkan ..	Hindu ...	21	1	17	3	98	40	56	2
	2 Kurava ...	,, ..	6,535	326	5,554	655	30,717	14,102	13,059	3,556
	3 Padayáchi ...	,, ...	...	...	...	...	3	...	3	...
	4 Pallan ...	,, ...	606	31	514	61	2,844	1,307	1,207	330
	5 Pariah ...	{ Hindu / Chrstn }	8,012	400	6,809	803	35,384	16,246	15,037	4,101
	6 Pulaya ...	Hindu ...	23,749	1,191	20,181	2,377	99,463	45,687	42,252	11,524
	7 Udaya ...	,, ...	1	...	1	...	5	1	4	...
	8 Ulládan ...	,, ...	287	14	244	29	1,400	645	595	160
	9 Vettuvan ...	,, ...	8	...	7	1	48	19	29	...
	Total group 2(*c*) ...	...	39,219	1,963	33,327	3,929	169,962	78,047	72,242	19,673
4 Forest and Hill tribes.	1 Iruler ...	Hindu ...	1	...	1	...	9	4	5	...
	2 Káttar ...	,, ...	5	...	5	...	16	7	9	...
	3 Kāttilaya ...	,, ...	9	1	7	1	36	22	14	...
	4 Kāttu Parisha (forest tribe) ...	,, ...	5	...	4	1	11	4	7	...
	5 Khond ...	,, ...	1	...	1	...	2	...	2	...
	6 Malayarien ...	,, ...	587	30	497	60	2,311	1,072	970	269
	7 Mariya ...	,, ...	1	...	1	...	...	...	...	...

TABLE E.

Castes, &c., by Civil Condition and Age—(*Continued*).

Class.	Caste and Religion.			Total Strength—(*Continued*). Females—(*Continued*).							
	Group.	Caste, &c.	Religion.	0—9. Total.	0—9. Un-married.	0—9. Married.	0—9. Widow-ed.	10—14. Total.	10—14. Un-married.	10—14. Married.	10—14. Widow-ed.
1	2	3	4	29	30	31	32	33	34	35	36
A. Agricultural.	1 Military and Dominant.	1 Nair ...	Hindu ...	60,500	60,500	...	...	26,609	24,756	1,853	...
		2 Ambalakáran ...	„ ...	...	...	...	...	...	...	...	...
		3 Kartávu ...	„ ...	9	9	...	...	4	4	...	...
		4 Koiltamburán ...	„ ...	9	9	...	...	4	4	...	...
		5 Kshatrya ...	„ ...	151	151	...	...	75	62	13	...
		6 Mahratta ...	„ ...	10	10	...	...	5	5	...	...
		7 Marava ...	„ ...	686	686	...	...	291	273	18	...
		8 Pandála ...	„ ...	7	7	...	...	4	4	...	...
		9 Rajaput ...	„ ...	1	1	...	...	2	2	...	...
		10 Raju ...	„ ...	4	4	...	...	3	2	1	...
		11 Sāmantakar ...	„ ...	21	21	...	...	10	7	3	...
		12 Tampān ...	„ ...	25	25	...	...	18	15	3	...
		13 Tirumulpád ...	„ ...	44	44	...	...	22	16	4	2
		14 Unniyādiri ...	„ ...	10	10	...	...	5	4	...	1
		15 Vellodi ...	„ ...	6	6	...	...	3	3	...	...
		Total group 1 ...	...	61,483	61,483	...	...	27,055	25,157	1,895	3

TABLE E.

Castes, &c., by Civil Condition and Age—(*Continued*).

A. Agricultural.

2(*a*) Other Agricultural land-holding classes.	1 Gavarulu ...	Hindu ...	1	1	...	...	...	...	...	...
	2 Karayálar ...	„ ...	8	8	...	...	3	3	...	...
	3 Kattāran ...	„ ...	1	1	...	...	...	...	...	...
	4 Kodipattan ...	„ ...	48	48	...	...	24	5	19	...
	5 Kuruni ...	„ ...	...	...	...	...	...	...	...	...
	6 Lòti ...	„ ...	...	...	...	...	...	...	...	...
	7 Málli ...	„ ...	...	...	...	...	...	...	...	...
	8 Mudali ...	„ ...	119	117	2	...	52	45	7	...
	9 Pandi Sudra ...	„ ...	652	652	...	...	287	269	18	...
	10 Valamalu ...	„ ...	...	...	...	...	...	...	...	...
	11 Vellāla ...	„ ...	5,512	5,512	...	...	2,424	2,258	166	...
	Total group 2(*a*) ...	...	6,341	6,339	2	...	2,790	2,580	210	...
2(*c*) Field-labouring classes.	1 Kanakkan ...	Hindu ...	24	24	...	...	11	8	3	...
	2 Kurava ...	„ ...	7,676	7,676	...	...	3,378	3,143	235	...
	3 Padayáchi ...	„ ...	...	...	...	...	...	...	...	...
	4 Pallan ...	„ ...	711	711	...	...	312	291	21	...
	5 Pariah ...	Hindu Chrstn	8,842	8,842	...	...	3,890	3,620	270	...
	6 Pulaya ...	Hindu ...	24,866	24,866	...	...	10,939	10,164	775	...
	7 Udaya ...	„ ...	1	1	...	...	...	...	...	...
	8 Ulládan ...	„ ...	350	350	...	...	154	140	14	...
	9 Vettuvan ...	„ ...	11	11	...	...	5	4	1	...
	Total group 2(*c*) ...	...	42,481	42,481	...	...	18,689	17,370	1,319	...
4 Forest and Hill tribes.	1 Iruler ...	Hindu .	2	2	...	...	1	1	...	...
	2 Káttar ...	„ ...	3	3	...	...	1	1	...	...
	3 Káttilaya ...	„ ...	10	10	...	...	4	4	...	...
	4 Káttu Parisha (forest tribe) ...	„ ...	2	2	...	...	1	1	...	...
	5 Khond ...	„ ...	...	...	...	...	...	...	...	...
	6 Malayarien ...	„ ...	587	587	...	...	254	240	14	..
	7 Mariya ...	„ ...	...	...	...	...	...	...	...	...

TABLE E.

Castes, &c., by Civil Condition and Age—(*Continued*).

Class.	Group.	Caste, &c.	Religion.	Females 15—39. Total.	Females 15—39. Un-married.	Females 15—39. Married.	Females 15—39. Widow-ed.	Females 40 and over. Total.	Females 40 and over. Un-married.	Females 40 and over. Married.	Females 40 and over. Widow-ed.
1	2	3	4	37	38	39	40	41	42	43	44
A. Agricultural.	1 Military and Dominant.	1 Nair ...	Hindu ...	104,178	21,903	78,131	4,144	50,840	4,072	22,881	23,887
		2 Ambalakáran ...	,, ...	...	...	...	...	...	...	...	...
		3 Kartávu ...	,, ...	18	...	17	1	11	...	6	5
		4 Koiltamburán ...	,, ...	18	...	18	...	12	...	8	4
		5 Kshatrya ...	,, ...	330	2	321	7	67	...	32	35
		6 Mahratta ...	,, ...	21	4	17	...	7	...	4	3
		7 Marava ...	,, ...	1,189	279	863	47	587	34	279	274
		8 Pandála ...	,, ...	15	...	14	1	9	...	4	5
		9 Rajaput ...	,, ...	3	...	3	...	1	...	...	1
		10 Raju ...	,, ...	10	...	10	...	5	...	3	2
		11 Sāmantakar ...	,, ...	43	...	42	1	17	...	9	8
		12 Tampān ...	,, ...	72	3	67	2	27	...	14	13
		13 Tirumulpād ...	,, ...	88	2	84	2	24	...	11	13
		14 Unniyádiri ...	,, ...	20	...	18	2	8	...	5	3
		15 Vellodi ...	,, ...	13	...	13	...	4	...	2	2
		Total group 1 ...	...	106,018	22,193	79,618	4,207	51,619	4,106	23,258	24,255

Castes, &c., by Civil Condition and Age—(*Continued*).

A. Agricultural.

Group	Caste	Religion								
2(*a*) Other Agricultural land-holding classes.	1 Gavarulu ...	Hindu ...	4	...	4	...	...	...	...	...
	2 Karayálar ...	„ ...	15	3	12	...	5	...	3	2
	3 Kattáran ...	„ ...	1	...	1	...	...	...	...	...
	4 Kodipattan ...	„ ...	96	...	85	11	45	...	21	24
	5 Kuruni ...	„ ...	...	...	...	...	...	...	...	...
	6 Lōti ...	„ ...	...	...	...	...	...	...	...	...
	7 Málli ...	„ ...	...	...	...	...	...	...	.	...
	8 Mudali ...	„ ...	215	42	165	8	103	7	54	42
	9 Pándi Sudra ...	„ ...	1,143	241	861	41	551	43	248	260
	10 Valamalu ...	„ ...	3	...	3	...	...	...	..	...
	11 Vellála ...	„ ...	9,525	2,003	7,145	377	4,617	368	2,081	2,168
	Total group 2(*a*) ...	...	11,002	2,289	8,276	437	5,321	418	2,407	2,496
2(*c*) Field-labouring classes.	1 Kanakkan ...	Hindu ...	44	8	35	1	19	...	18	1
	2 Kurava ...	„ ...	13,218	2,770	9,921	527	6,445	513	2,903	3,029
	3 Padayáchi ...	„ ...	3	...	3	...	...	...	...	...
	4 Pallan ...	„ ...	1,224	258	918	48	597	47	268	282
	5 Pariah ...	Hindu / Chrstn	15,216	3,193	11,419	604	7,436	591	3,348	3,497
	6 Pulaya ...	Hindu ...	42,771	8,988	32,075	1,708	20,887	1,669	9,402	9,816
	7 Udaya ...	„ ...	2	...	2	...	2	...	2	...
	8 Ulládan ...	„ ...	604	130	450	24	292	25	131	136
	9 Vettuvan ...	„ ...	23	4	19	...	9	...	9	...
	Total group 2(*c*) ...	...	73,105	15,351	54,842	2,912	35,687	2,845	16,081	16,761
4 Forest and Hill tribes.	1 Iruler ...	Hindu ...	4	1	3	...	2	..	2	...
	2 Káttar ...	„ ...	10	3	7	...	2	...	2	...
	3 Káttilaya ...	„ ...	19	8	11	...	3	...	3	...
	4 Káttu Parisha (forest tribe) ...	„ ...	6	1	5	...	2	...	2	..
	5 Khond ...	„ ...	2	...	2	...	...	...	...	...
	6 Malayarien ...	„ ...	986	208	739	39	484	37	217	230
	7 Mariya ...	„ ...	...	...	...	...	...	...	...	...

TABLE E.

Castes, &c., by Civil Condition and Age—(*Continued*).

Class.	Caste and Religion.			Total Strength—(*Continued*). Males—(*Continued*).							
	Group.	Caste, &c.	Religion.	All Ages. Total.	Un-married.	Married.	Widow-ed.	0—9. Total.	Un-married.	Married.	Widow-ed.
1	2	3	4	5	6	7	8	9	10	11	12
A. Agricultural—(*Continued*).	4 Forest and Hill tribes—(*Contd.*)	8 Muduvan ...	Hindu ...	545	278	249	18	132	132	...	...
		9 Mynáta ...	„ ...	24	14	10	...	7	7	...	...
		10 Nádipanikkan ...	„ ...	9	4	5	...	2	2	...	...
		11 Pania ...	„ ...	...	...	...	...	...	...	...	...
		12 Vēlan ...	„ ...	8,660	4,610	3,815	235	2,086	2,086	...	...
		Total group 4 ...	...	11,840	6,243	5,270	327	2,860	2,860	...	...
		Total class A. ...	...	457,475	247,506	194,595	15,374	107,139	107,139	...	...
sional.	5 Priests ...	1 Brahmin ...	Hindu ...	1,423	579	708	136	293	290	2	1
		Foreign Brahmin.	„ ...	1,961	800	999	162	438	434	4	...
		Aiyengar ...	„ ...	479	194	203	82	100	85	11	4
		Canarese Brahmn.	„ ...	18	5	9	4	3	3	...	...
		Gouda Brahmin ...	„ ...	66	33	25	8	17	17	...	...
		Hindstni. Brahmn.	„ ..	3	1	2	...	1	1	...	...
		Kannadasta ...	„ ...	4	1	3	...	1	1	...	...
		Kási Brahmin ...	„ ...	24	7	12	5	5	5	...	...
		Kesiar ...	„ ...	34	12	13	9	8	8	...	...

Castes, &c., by Civil Condition and Age—(*Continued*).

	Mahratta Brahmn.	,, ...	525	230	217	78	109	104	4	1
	Nambiyán ...	,, ...	110	49	48	13	25	25	...	...
	Surveriya ...	,, ...	1	...	1	...	...	...	...	...
	Tamil Brahmin ...	,, ...	11,238	4,782	5,616	840	2,519	2,364	135	20
	Telugu Brahmin...	,, ...	385	208	158	19	82	78	4	...
	Malayala Brahmn.	,, ...	1,866	1,123	624	119	437	437	...	...
	Akkaradēsi ...	,, ...	25	17	8	...	7	7	...	...
	Bhattadiri ...	,, ...	74	37	35	2	17	17	...	...
	Embrán ...	,, ...	1,150	591	361	198	237	237	...	...
	Nambūdiri ...	,, ...	1,979	1,170	685	124	445	445	...	...
	PonmanyGramom	,, ...	55	29	21	5	13	13	...	...
	Potti ...	,, ...	1,421	797	505	119	332	332	...	...
	Tiruvalladēsi ...	,, ...	167	69	84	14	18	18	...	...
	Trippunittoraidēsi	,, ...	50	21	22	7	9	9	...	...
	2 Āriapattar ...	,, ...	21	10	11	...	5	5	...	...
	3 Ilayadu ...	,, ...	1,686	836	644	206	358	358	...	...
	4 Tangal ...	Mussalmn.	9	4	4	1	2	2	...	...
	Total group 5 ...	...	24,774	11,605	11,018	2,151	5,481	5,295	160	26
6 Devotees ...	1 Fakkir ...	Mussalmn.	4	1	3	...	1	1	...	...
	2 Gosains ...	Hindu ...	40	21	18	1	10	10	...	...
	3 Sanniyási ...	,, ...	8	4	4	...	2	2	...	...
	4 Vyravi ...	,, ...	356	187	161	8	96	96	...	...
	Total group 6 ...	...	408	213	186	9	109	109	...	...
7 Temple servants.	1 Ambalavási ...	Hindu ...	3,890	2,110	1,326	454	868	868	...	...
	2 Krishnanvagai...	,, ...	3,394	1,825	1,422	147	748	748	...	...
	3 Pilāppalli ...	,, ...	33	15	13	5	8	8	...	...
	4 Sátáni ...	,, ...	7	3	4	...	1	1	...	...
	Total group 7 ...	...	7,324	3,953	2,765	606	1,625	1,625	...	...
8 Genealogists.	Tákur ...	Hindu ...	3	1	2	...	...	...	...	...

TABLE E.

Castes, &c., by Civil Condition and Age—(*Continued*).

Class.	Caste and Religion.			Total Strength—(*Continued*).							
				Males—(*Continued*).							
	Group.	Caste, &c.	Religion.	10–14.				15—39.			
				Total.	Un-married.	Married.	Widowed.	Total.	Un-married.	Married.	Widowed.
1	2	3	4	13	14	15	16	17	18	19	20
A. Agricultural —(*Continued*).	4 Forest and Hill tribes—(*Contd.*)	8 Muduvan ...	Hindu ...	57	57	...	...	213	81	129	3
		9 Mynáta ...	„ ...	3	3	...	...	9	4	5	...
		10 Nádipanikkan ...	„ ...	1	1	...	...	4	1	3	...
		11 Pania ...	„ ...	...	...	...	...	...	...	...	...
		12 Vēlan ...	„ ...	1,005	1,002	3	...	3,591	1,424	2,131	36
		Total group 4 ...	...	1,353	1,345	8	...	4,890	1,901	2,938	51
		Total class A. ...	...	51,169	50,759	410	...	198,869	83,913	113,284	1,672
sional.	5 Priests ...	1 Brahmin ...	Hindu ...	154	144	9	1	684	143	525	16
		Foreign Brahmin.	„ ...	217	187	20	10	870	171	689	10
		Aiyengar ...	„ ...	52	17	28	7	228	85	128	15
		Canarese Brahmin	„ ...	1	...	1	...	10	2	7	1
		Gouda Brahmin...	„ ...	5	2	3	...	34	14	18	2
		Hindstni.Brahmn.	„ ...	...	...	...	...	2	...	2	...
		Kannadasta ...	„ ...	1	...	1	...	2	...	2	...
		Kási Brahmin ...	„ ...	2	...	2	...	11	2	8	1
		Kesiar ...	„ ...	3	1	2	...	14	3	7	4

Castes, &c., by Civil Condition and Age—(*Continued*).

B. Profes										
	Mahratta Brahmn.	,, ...	53	24	28	1	233	97	129	7
	Nambiyán ...	,, ...	12	4	8	...	54	20	34	...
	Surveriya ...	,, ...	...	...	...	...	1	...	1	...
	Tamil Brahmin ...	,, ...	1,248	1,020	208	20	5,054	1,228	3,676	150
	Telugu Brahmin...	,, ...	52	36	14	2	182	81	96	5
	Malayala Brahmn.	,, ..	213	213	...	...	878	432	444	2
	Akkaradēsi ...	,, ...	...	...	..	...	17	9	8	...
	Bhattadiri ...	,, ...	8	7	1	...	34	13	21	...
	Embrán ...	,, ...	119	100	19	...	513	254	252	7
	Nambūdiri ...	,, ...	228	227	1	...	925	469	451	5
	Ponmany Gramom	,, ...	6	6	...	...	25	9	15	1
	Potti ...	,, ...	153	138	15	...	605	298	302	5
	Tiruvalladēsi ...	,, ...	14	12	2	...	74	34	38	2
	Trippunittoraidēsi	,, ...	6	5	1	...	26	7	18	1
	2 Āriapattar ...	,, ...	3	2	1	...	8	3	5	...
	3 Ilayadu ...	,, ...	175	165	10	...	805	301	485	19
	4 Tangal ...	Mussalmn.	1	1	...	...	4	1	3	...
	Total group 5 ...	...	2,726	2,311	374	41	11,293	36,76	7,364	253
6 Devotees ...	1 Fakkir ..	Mussalmn.	...	...	...	...	2	...	2	...
	2 Gosains ...	Hindu ...	5	5	...	...	16	6	10	...
	3 Sanniyási ...	,, ...	1	1	...	...	3	1	2	...
	4 Vyravi ...	,, ...	36	30	6	...	146	57	88	1
	Total group 6 ...		42	36	6	...	167	64	102	1
7 Temple servants.	1 Ambalavási ...	Hindu ...	420	412	8	...	1,772	743	962	67
	2 Krishnanvagai...	,, ...	369	359	10	...	1,499	687	783	29
	3 Pilāppalli ...	,, ...	3	2	1	...	15	5	8	2
	4 Sátáni ...	,, ...	1	1	...	...	3	1	2	...
	Total group 7 ...		793	774	19	...	3,289	1,436	1,755	98
8 Genealogists.	Tákur ...	Hindu ...	1	1	...	...	1	...	1	...

TABLE E.

Castes, &c., by Civil Condition and Age—(*Continued*).

Class.	Group.	Caste, &c.	Religion.	Total Strength—(Continued). Males—(Continued). 40 and over. Total.	Un-married.	Married.	Widow-ed.	Females. All Ages. Total.	Un-married.	Married.	Widow-ed.
1	2	3	4	21	22	23	24	25	26	27	28
A. Agricultural—(*Continued*).	4 Forest and Hill tribes—(*Contd.*)	8 Muduvan ...	Hindu ...	143	8	120	15	532	233	230	69
		9 Mynáta ...	„ ...	5	...	5	...	20	10	10	...
		10 Nádipanikkan...	„ ...	2	...	2	...	20	11	9	...
		11 Pania ...	„ ...	...	...	...	...	2	...	2	...
		12 Vēlan ...	„ ...	1,978	98	1,681	199	8,483	3,868	3,601	1,014
		Total group 4 ...	...	2,737	137	2,324	276	11,442	5,231	4,859	1,352
		Total class A. ...	...	100,298	5,695	80,901	13,702	453,033	207,843	192,767	52,423
sional.	5 Priests ...	1 Brahmin ...	Hindu ...	292	2	172	118	1,222	292	760	170
		Foreign Brahmin.	„ ...	436	8	286	142	1,568	316	986	266
		Aiyengar ...	„ ...	99	7	36	56	419	105	231	83
		Canarese Brahmn.	„ ...	4	...	1	3	17	4	11	2
		Gouda Brahmin...	„ ...	10	...	4	6	11	2	7	2
		Hindstni. Brahmn.	„ ...	...	...	...	...	3	...	3	...
		Kannadasta ...	„ ...	...	...	...	...	5	2	3	...
		Kási Brahmin ...	„ ...	6	...	2	4	35	7	26	2
		Kesiar ...	„ ...	9	...	4	5	33	5	24	4

Castes, &c., by Civil Condition and Age—(*Continued*).

B. Profes										
	Mahratta Brahmn.	„ ...	130	5	56	69	439	95	252	92
	Nambiyán ...	„ ...	19	...	6	13	104	23	68	13
	Surveriya ...	„ ...	...	...	...	...	...	...	...	...
	Tamil Brahmin ...	„ ...	2,417	170	1,597	650	10,661	2,334	6,428	1,899
	Telugu Brahmin...	„ ...	69	13	44	12	412	74	256	82
	Malayala Brahmn.	„ ...	338	41	180	117	1,585	716	668	201
	Akkaradēsi ...	„ ...	1	1	...	...	...	...	...	...
	Bhattadiri ...	„ ...	15	...	13	2	72	28	34	10
	Embrán ...	„ ...	281	...	90	191	788	179	511	98
	Nambūdiri ...	„ ...	381	29	233	119	1,771	977	567	227
	PonmanyGramom	„ ...	11	1	6	4	41	18	18	5
	Potti ...	„ ...	331	29	188	114	1,174	404	618	152
	Tiruvalladēsi ...	„ ...	61	5	44	12	161	50	89	22
	Trippunittoraidēsi	„ ...	9	...	3	6	16	7	6	3
	2 Āriapattar ...	„ ...	5	...	5	...	19	8	11	...
	3 Ilayadu ...	„ ...	348	12	149	187	1,574	616	779	179
	4 Tangal ...	Mussalmn.	2	...	1	1	5	3	2	...
	Total group 5 ...	...	5,274	323	3,120	1,831	22,135	6,265	12,358	3,512
6 Devotees ...	1 Fakkir ...	Mussalmn.	1	...	1	...	1	...	1	...
	2 Gosains ...	Hindu ...	9	...	8	1	21	5	16	...
	3 Sanniyási ...	„ ...	2	...	2	...	1	...	...	1
	4 Vyravi ...	„ ...	78	4	67	7	356	155	161	40
	Total group 6 ...	...	90	4	78	8	379	160	178	41
7 Temple servants.	1 Ambalavási ...	Hindu ...	830	87	356	387	3,579	1,473	1,643	463
	2 Krishnanvagai ...	„ ...	778	31	629	118	3,559	1,634	1,513	412
	3 Pilāppalli ...	„ ...	7	...	4	3	36	14	17	5
	4 Sátáni ...	„ ...	2	...	2	...	7	2	5	...
	Total group 7 ...	...	1,617	118	991	508	7,181	3,123	3,178	880
8 Genealogists.	Tákur ...	Hindu ...	1	...	1	...	1	...	1	...

TABLE E.

Castes, &c., by Civil Condition and Age—(*Continued*).

Class.	Caste and Religion.			Total Strength—(*Continued*).							
				Females—(*Continued*).							
				0—9.				10—14.			
	Group.	Caste.	Religion.	Total.	Un-married.	Married.	Widow-ed.	Total.	Un-married.	Married.	Widow-ed.
1	2	3	4	29	30	31	32	33	34	35	36
A. Agricultural—(*Continued*).	4 Forests and Hill tribes—(*Contd.*)	8 Muduvan ...	Hindu ...	120	120	...	...	59	55	4	...
		9 Mynáta ...	„ ...	6	6	...	...	2	2	...	...
		10 Nádipanikkan ...	„ ...	6	6	...	...	3	3	...	...
		11 Pania ...	„ ...	...	...	...	...	...	...	...	...
		12 Vēlan ...	„ ...	2,117	2,117	...	...	933	869	64	...
		Total group 4 ...	...	2,853	2,853	...	...	1,258	1,176	82	...
		Total class A. ...	...	113,158	113,156	2	...	49,792	46,283	3,506	3
sional.	5 Priests ...	1 Brahmin ...	Hindu ...	268	222	44	2	140	70	68	2
		Foreign Brahmin.	„ ...	348	235	106	7	176	81	75	20
		Aiyengar ...	„ ...	97	91	4	2	47	14	31	2
		Canarese Brahmn	„ ...	4	4	...	...	2	...	2	...
		Gouda Brahmin...	„ ...	2	2	...	...	1	...	1	...
		Hindstni. Brahmn.	„ ...	...	...	...	...	...	...	...	...
		Kannadasta ...	„ ...	2	2	...	...	1	...	1	...
		Kási Brahmin ...	„ ...	8	6	2	...	4	1	3	...
		Kēsiar ...	„ ...	6	4	2	...	3	1	2	...

B. Profes											
	Mahratta Brahmn	„ ...	96	75	20	1	47	20	24	3
	Nambiyán ...	„ ...	29	22	6	1	10	1	9	...
	Surveriya ...	„ ...	...	...	...	...	...	...	...	...
	Tamil Brahmin ...	„ ...	2,363	1,901	413	49	1,183	433	685	65
	Telugu Brahmin..	„ ...	90	60	29	1	45	14	30	1
	Malayala Brahmn.	„ ...	392	384	4	4	201	181	17	3
	Akkaradēsi ...	„ ...	...	...	...	...	...	...	...	...
	Bhattadiri ...	„ ...	17	17	...	...	9	3	6	...
	Embrán ...	„ ...	193	145	47	1	96	34	61	1
	Nambūdiri ...	„ ...	441	441	...	...	222	188	29	5
	PonmanyGramom	„ ...	11	11	...	...	6	4	2	...
	Potti ...	„ ...	292	276	12	4	145	123	22	...
	Tiruvalladēsi ...	„ ...	39	39	...	...	21	10	11	...
	Tripunnittoraidēsi	„ ...	5	5	...	...	3	2	1	...
	2 Āriapattar ...	„ ...	3	3	...	...	1	1	...	...
	3 Ilayadu ...	„ ...	346	346	...	...	174	112	59	3
	4 Tangal ...	Mussalmn.	2	2	...	...	1	1	...	...
	Total group 5 ...	...	5,054	4,293	689	72	2,538	1,294	1,139	105
6 Devotees ...	1 Fakkir ...	Mussalmn.	...	...	...	...	...	...	...	...
	2 Gosains ...	Hindu ...	1	1	...	..	1	...	1	...
	3 Sanniyási ...	„ ...	...	...	...	...	...	...	...	...
	4 Vyravi ...	„ ...	85	85	...	...	39	37	2	...
	Total group 6 ...	...	86	86	...	...	40	37	3	...
7 Temple servants.	1 Ambalavási ...	Hindu ...	807	807	...	...	394	299	95	...
	2 Krishnanvagai ...	„ ..	889	889	...	...	391	363	28	..
	3 Pilāppalli ...	„ ...	9	9	...	...	4	1	3	...
	4 Sátáni ...	„ ...	1	1	...	...	...	...	...	...
	Total group 7 ...	...	1,706	1,706	...	...	789	663	126	...
8 Genealogists.	Tákur ...	Hindu ...	...	...	...	...	...	...	...	...

TABLE E.

Castes, &c., by Civil Condition and Age—(*Continued*).

Class.	Caste and Religion.			Total Strength—(*Continued*). Females—(*Continued*). 15—39.				40 and over.			
	Group.	Caste, &c.	Religion.	Total.	Un-married.	Married.	Widow-ed.	Total.	Un-married.	Married.	Widow-ed.
1	2	3	4	37	38	39	40	41	42	43	44
A. Agricultural —(*Continued*).	4 Forest and Hill tribes—(*Contd.*)	8 Muduvan ...	Hindu ...	234	50	175	9	119	8	51	60
		9 Mynáta ...	„ ...	10	2	8	...	2	...	2	...
		10 Nadipanikkan ...	„ ...	10	2	8	...	1	...	1	...
		11 Pania ...	„ ...	2	...	2	...	...	...	...	...
		12 Vélan ...	„ ...	3,651	771	2,736	144	1,782	111	801	870
		Total group 4 ...	...	4,934	1,046	3,696	192	2,397	156	1,081	1,160
		Total class A. ...	...	195,059	40,879	146,432	7,748	95,024	7,525	42,827	44,672
sional.	5 Priests ...	1 Brahmin ...	Hindu ...	544	...	508	36	270	...	140	130
		Foreign Brahmin.	„ ...	696	...	625	71	348	...	180	168
		Aiyengar ...	„ ...	188	...	154	34	87	...	42	45
		Canarese Brahmn.	„ ...	9	...	8	1	2	...	1	1
		Gouda Brahmin ...	„ ...	4	...	3	1	4	...	3	1
		Hindstni. Brahmn.	„ ...	2	...	2	...	1	...	1	...
		Kannadasta ...	„ ...	1	...	1	...	1	...	1	...
		Kási Brahmin ...	„ ...	16	...	15	1	7	...	6	1
		Kesiar ...	„ ...	16	...	13	3	8	...	7	1

TABLE E.

Castes, &c., by Civil Condition and Age—(*Continued*).

	Mahratta Brahmn.	„ ...	193	...	155	38	103	...	53	50
	Nambiyān ...	„ ...	39	...	37	2	26	...	16	10
	Surveriya ...	„ ...	...	...	...	...	...	...	...	...
	Tamil Brahmin ...	„ ...	4,741	...	4,096	645	2,374	...	1,234	1,140
	Telugu Brahmin..	„ ...	185	...	149	36	92	...	48	44
	Malayala Brahmn.	„ ...	599	148	447	4	393	3	200	190
	Akkaradēsi ...	„ ...	...	...	...	...	...	...	...	...
	Bhattadiri ...	„ ...	29	6	20	3	17	2	8	7
	Embrán ...	„ ...	308	..	306	2	191	...	97	94
	Nambūdiri ...	„ ...	662	297	358	7	446	51	180	215
	PonmanyGramom	„ ...	12	3	9	...	12	...	7	5
	Potti ...	„ ...	441	3	438	...	296	2	146	148
	Tiruvalladēsi ...	„ ...	59	1	58	...	42	...	20	22
	Trippunittoraidēsi	„ ...	2	...	2	...	6	...	3	3
	2 Āriapattar ...	„ ...	12	4	8	...	3	...	3	...
	3 Ilayadu ...	„ ...	708	156	550	2	346	2	170	174
	4 Tangal ...	Mussalmn.	2	...	2	...	...	...	...	...
	Total group 5 ...	...	9,468	618	7,964	886	5,075	60	2,566	2,449
6 Devotees ...	1 Fakkir ...	Mussalmn.	1	...	1	...	...	...	...	...
	2 Gosains ...	Hindu ...	18	4	14	...	1	...	1	...
	3 Sanniyási ...	„ ...	1	...	...	1	...	...	...	...
	4 Vyravi ...	„ ...	156	29	123	4	76	4	36	36
	Total group 6 ...	...	176	33	138	5	77	4	37	36
7 Temple servants.	1 Ambalavási ...	Hindu ...	1,598	331	1,170	97	780	36	378	366
	2 Krishnanvagai ...	„ ..	1,532	322	1,149	61	747	60	336	351
	3 Pilāppalli ...	„ ...	15	3	9	3	8	1	5	2
	4 Sátáni ...	„ ...	6	1	5	...	...	...	...	...
	Total group 7 ...	...	3,151	657	2,333	161	1,535	97	719	719
8 Genealogists.	Tákur ...	Hindu ...	1	...	1	...	...	...	...	...

TABLE E.

Castes, &c., by Civil Condition and Age—(*Continued*).

Class.	Caste and Religion.			Total Strength—(*Continued*). Males. All Ages.				Males. 0—9.			
	Group.	Caste, &c.	Religion.	Total.	Un-married.	Married.	Widow-ed.	Total.	Un-married.	Married.	Widow-ed.
1	2	3	4	5	6	7	8	9	10	11	12
B. Profession-al—(*Contd.*)	10 Astrologers and quack doctors.	1 Kaniyán ...	Hindu ...	4,846	2,562	2,157	127	1,090	1,090	...	...
		2 Pulluvan ...	" ...	123	67	52	4	32	32	...	...
		Total group 10 ...	...	4,969	2,629	2,209	131	1,122	1,122	...	...
		Total class B. ...	...	37,478	18,401	16,180	2,897	8,337	8,151	160	26
meroial.	14 Traders ...	1 Balija ...	Hindu ...	249	122	121	6	61	61	...	...
		2 Baniya ...	{ Hindu / Jain }	53	27	24	2	10	10	...	...
		3 Chetti ...	Hindu ...	9,089	5,056	3,534	499	2,047	2,047	...	...
		4 Ilavániyan ...	" ...	1,647	793	752	102	364	364	...	...
		5 Jonaka ...	Mussalmn.	26,568	14,260	11,479	829	6,661	6,643	14	4
		6 Labbai ...	" ...	213	108	90	15	55	55	...	...
		7 Mēttan ...	" ...	27,523	15,167	11,381	975	7,455	7,435	15	5
		8 Ráwut ...	" ...	30	15	13	2	8	8	...	...
		9 Vaduka ...	Hindu ...	1,427	767	560	100	326	326	...	...
		10 Vaisya ...	" ...	259	133	113	13	65	65	...	...
		Total group 14 ...	...	67,058	36,448	28,067	2,543	17,052	17,014	29	9

TABLE E.

Castes, &c., by Civil Condition and Age—(*Continued*).

Class	Group	Caste	Religion								
C. Com	15 Pedlars ...	1 Balukar ...	Hindu ...	6	4	2	...	2	2	...	...
		2 Manikár ...	„ ...	22	12	10	...	6	6	...	...
		Total group 15 ...	...	28	16	12	...	8	8	...	...
		Total class C. ...	...	67,086	36,464	28,079	2,543	17,060	17,022	29	9
D. Artisans and Village Menials.	17 Goldsmiths.	Tattan ...	Hindu	12,506	6,057	6,056	393	2,839	2.839	...	...
	17(*a*) Artisans (general).	1 Kammála ...	Hindu ...	985	479	447	59	216	216	...	...
		2 Kamsála ...	„ ...	7	4	3	...	2	2	...	...
		Total group 17(*a*).	...	992	483	450	59	218	218	...	...
	18 Barbers ...	1 Īlaváti ...	Hindu ...	1,360	715	606	39	332	332	...	...
		2 Kávadi ...	„ ...	2,677	1,445	1,158	74	653	653	...	...
		3 Komaram ..	„ ...	138	73	61	4	36	36	...	...
		4 Kshourakan ...	„ ...	7,987	4,158	3,606	223	1,795	1,795	...	...
		5 Márán ...	„ ...	7,456	4,128	2,758	570	1,593	1,593	...	...
		6 Ostta ...	Mussalmn.	22	11	11	...	6	6	...	...
		7 Taravan ...	Hindu ...	226	121	99	6	55	55	...	...
		Total group 18 ...	...	19,866	10,651	8,299	916	4,470	4,470	...	...
	19 Blacksmiths.	1 Kollan ...	Hindu ...	13,903	7,071	6,580	252	3,224	3,224	...	...
		2 Lōhar ...	„ ...	3	1	2	...	...	...	...	...
		Total group 19 ...	...	13,906	7,072	6,582	252	3,224	3,224	...	...
	20 Carpenters, masons and turners.	1 Āsári ...	Hindu ...	16,932	9,011	7,507	414	3,801	3,801	...	...
		2 Tachan ...	„ ...	2,014	973	983	58	446	446	...	...
		Total group 20 ...	...	18,946	9,984	8,490	472	4,247	4,247	...	...

TABLE E.
Castes, &c., by Civil Condition and Age—(*Continued*).

Class.	Caste and Religion.			Total Strength—(*Continued*).							
				Males—(*Continued*).							
				10—14.				15—39.			
	Group.	Caste, &c.	Religion.	Total.	Un-married.	Married.	Widow-ed.	Total.	Un-married.	Married.	Widow-ed.
1	2	3	4	13	14	15	16	17	18	19	20
B. Profession-al—(*Contd.*)	10 Astrologers and quack doctors.	1 Kaniyán ...	Hindu ...	521	516	5	...	2,189	904	1,272	13
		2 Pulluvan ...	„ ...	14	14	...	...	53	20	32	1
		Total group 10 ...	...	535	530	5	...	2,242	924	1,304	14
		Total class B. ...	...	4,097	3,652	404	41	16,992	6,100	10,526	366
mercial.	14 Traders ...	1 Balija ...	Hindu ...	31	26	5	...	99	34	64	1
		2 Baniya ...	{ Hindu Jain }	7	7	.	...	24	9	15	...
		3 Chetti ...	Hindu ...	987	913	74	...	4,032	1,830	2,113	89
		4 Ilavániyan ...	„ ...	181	177	4	...	736	236	482	18
		5 Jonaka ...	Mussalmn.	2,966	2,942	21	3	11,598	4,474	6,988	136
		6 Labbai ...	„ ...	24	19	5	...	93	32	58	3
		7 Mēttan ...	„ ...	3,827	3,793	30	4	10,044	3,683	6,234	127
		8 Ráwut ...	„ ...	3	3	...	...	13	4	9	...
		9 Vaduka ...	Hindu ...	154	116	38	...	627	274	318	35
		10 Vaisya ...	„ ...	33	25	6	2	113	41	68	4
		Total group 14 ..	...	8,213	8,021	183	9	27,379	10,617	16,349	413

Castes, &c., by Civil Condition and Age—(*Continued*).

Class	Group	Caste	Religion								
C. Com	15 Pedlars ...	1 Balukar ...	Hindu ...	1	1	...	...	2	1	1	...
		2 Manikár ...	„ ...	3	3	...	...	8	3	5	...
		Total group 15 ...	...	4	4	...	...	10	4	6	...
		Total class C. ...	...	8,217	8,025	183	9	27,389	10,621	16,355	413
D. Artisans and Village Menials.	17 Goldsmiths.	Tattan ...	Hindu ...	1,373	1,334	39	...	5,740	1,719	3,970	51
	17(*a*) Artisans (general).	1 Kammála ...	Hindu ...	106	103	3	...	448	138	299	11
		2 Kamsála ...	„ ...	1	1	...	...	3	1	2	...
		Total group 17(*a*)...	...	107	104	3	...	451	139	301	11
	18 Barbers ...	1 Īlaváti ...	Hindu ...	156	153	3	...	558	214	338	6
		2 Kávadi ...	„ ...	305	305	...	...	1,117	458	647	12
		3 Kōmaram ...	„ ...	16	16	...	...	53	19	33	1
		4 Kshourakan ...	„ ...	868	860	8	...	3,560	1,419	2,105	36
		5 Márán ...	„ ...	812	772	40	...	3,318	1,509	1,771	38
		6 Ostta ...	Mussalmn.	1	1	...	...	12	4	8	...
		7 Taravan ...	Hindu ...	25	25	...	...	95	39	56	...
		Total group 18 ...	...	2,183	2,132	51	...	8,713	3,662	4,958	93
	19 Blacksmiths	1 Kollan ...	Hindu ...	1,489	1,460	29	...	5,961	1,907	4,020	34
		2 Lōhar ...	„ ...	...	...	...	...	2	1	1	...
		Total group 19 .	...	1,489	1,460	29	...	5,963	1,908	4,021	34
	20 Carpenters, masons and turners.	1 Āsári ...	Hindu ...	1,789	1,752	37	...	7,579	2.828	4,669	82
		2 Tachan ...	„ ...	215	211	4	...	903	288	604	11
		Total group 20 ...	...	2,004	1,963	41	...	8,482	3,116	5,273	93

TABLE E.
Castes, &c., by Civil Condition and Age—(*Continued*).

Class.	Caste and Religion.			Total Strength—(*Continued*).							
				Males—(*Continued*).				Females.			
				40 and over.				All Ages.			
	Group.	Caste, &c.	Religion.	Total.	Un-Married.	Married.	Widowed.	Total.	Un-Married.	Married.	Widowed.
1	2	3	4	21	22	23	24	25	26	27	28
B. Professional—(*Contd.*)	10 Astrologers and quack doctors	1 Kaniyān ...	Hindu ...	1,046	52	880	114	4,702	2,157	2,004	541
		2 Pulluvan ...	" ...	24	1	20	3	151	73	63	15
		Total group 10 ...	...	1,070	53	900	117	4,853	2,230	2,067	556
		Total class B. ...	...	8,052	498	5,090	2,464	34,549	11,778	17,782	4,989
mercial.	14 Traders ...	1 Balija ...	Hindu ...	58	1	52	5	200	93	93	14
		2 Baniya ...	{ Hindu / Jain }	12	1	9	2	9	3	6	...
		3 Chetti ...	Hindu ...	2,023	266	1,347	410	8,680	3,958	3,705	1,017
		4 Ilavāniyan ...	" ...	366	16	266	84	1,664	766	706	192
		5 Jonaka ...	Mussalman	5,343	201	4,456	686	25,223	11,957	10,877	2,389
		6 Labbai ...	" ...	41	2	27	12	148	68	63	17
		7 Mēttan ...	" ...	6,197	256	5,102	839	26,563	12,789	11,328	2,446
		8 Rāwut ...	" ...	6	...	4	2	27	11	12	4
		9 Vaduka ...	Hindu ...	320	51	204	65	1,269	433	672	164
		10 Vaisya ...	" ...	48	2	39	7	215	90	95	30
		Total group 14 ...	...	14,414	796	11,506	2,112	63,998	30,168	27,557	6,273

TABLE E.

Castes, &c., by Civil Condition and Age—(*Continued*).

Class	Group	Caste	Religion								
C. Com	15 Pedlars ...	1 Balukār ...	Hindu ...	1	...	1	...	...	...	...	...
		2 Manikar ..	„ ...	5	...	5	...	14	4	10	...
		Total group 15 ...	...	6	...	6	...	14	4	10	...
		Total class C. ...	...	14,420	796	11,512	2,112	64,012	30,172	27,567	6,273
D. Artisans and Village Menials.	17 Goldsmiths.	Tattan ...	Hindu ...	2,554	165	2,047	342	12,192	4,213	7,229	750
	17(*a*) Artisans (general).	1 Kammāla ...	Hindu ...	215	22	145	48	997	354	579	64
		2 Kamsāla ...	„ ...	1	...	1	...	6	2	4	...
		Total group 17(*a*).	...	216	22	146	48	1,003	356	583	64
	18 Barbers ...	1 Īlavāti ...	Hindu ...	314	16	265	33	1,509	858	473	178
		2 Kāvadi ...	„ ...	602	29	511	62	2,590	1,287	1,004	299
		3 Kōmaram ...	„ ...	33	2	28	3	119	55	50	14
		4 Kshourakan ...	„ ...	1,764	84	1,493	187	8,143	3,740	3,461	942
		5 Mārān ...	„ ...	1,733	254	947	532	7,772	2,884	2,755	2,133
		6 Ostta ...	Mussalman	3	...	3	...	44	20	20	4
		7 Taravan ..	Hindu ...	51	2	43	6	229	109	102	18
		Total group 18 ...	...	4,500	387	3,290	823	20,406	8,953	7,865	3,588
	19 Blacksmiths	1 Kollan ...	Hindu ...	3,229	480	2,531	218	13,079	5,918	5,650	1,511
		2 Lōhar ...	„ ...	1	...	1	...	..	...	...	...
		Total group 19 ...	...	3,230	480	2,532	218	13,079	5,918	5,650	1,511
	20 Carpenters, masons, and turners.	1 Āsāri ..	Hindu ...	3,763	630	2,801	332	16,709	7,595	7,173	1,941
		2 Tachan ...	„ ...	450	28	375	47	2,052	901	896	255
		Total group 20 ...	...	4,213	658	3,176	379	18,761	8,496	8,069	2,196

TABLE E.

Castes, &c., by Civil Condition and Age—(*Continued*).

Class.	Caste and Religion.			Total Strength—(*Continued*). Females—(*Continued*). 0—9.				10—14.			
	Group.	Caste, &c.	Religion.	Total.	Un-married.	Married.	Widowed.	Total.	Un-married.	Married.	Widowed.
1	2	3	4	29	30	31	32	33	34	35	36
B. Profession-al—(*Contd.*)	10 Astrologers and quack doctors.	1 Kaniyān ...	Hindu ...	1,172	1,172	...	...	516	481	35	...
		2 Pulluvan ...	„ ...	37	37	...	...	21	20	1	...
		Total group 10 ...	...	1,209	1,209	...	...	537	501	36	...
		Total class B. ...	...	8,055	7,294	689	72	3,904	2,495	1,304	105
mercial.	14 Traders ...	1 Balija ...	Hindu ...	46	46	...	...	22	21	1	...
		2 Baniya ...	{ Hindu / Jain }	2	2	...	...	1	1	...	...
		3 Chetti ...	Hindu ...	2,166	2,166	...	...	947	883	64	...
		4 Ilavāniyan ...	„ ...	416	416	...	...	183	171	12	...
		5 Jonaka ...	Mussalman	7,582	7,538	40	4	2,669	2,409	255	5
		6 Labbai ...	„ ...	40	40	...	...	15	13	2	...
		7 Mēttan ...	„ ...	7,207	7,171	33	3	3,139	2,818	313	8
		8 Rāwut ...	„ ...	7	7	...	...	3	3	...	...
		9 Vaduka ...	Hindu ...	300	300	...	...	134	8	126	...
		10 Vaisya ...	„ ...	51	51	...	...	23	18	5	...
		Total group 14 ...	...	17,817	17,737	73	7	7,136	6,345	778	13

Castes, &c., by Civil Condition and Age—(*Continued*).

C. Com

15 Pedlars ...	1 Balukar ...	Hindu ...	...	...	...	...	...	...	...	...
	2 Manikār ...	„ ...	3	3	...	...	1	1	...	...
	Total group 15 ...	...	3	3	...	...	1	1	...	...
	Total class C. ...	...	17,820	17,740	73	7	7,137	6,346	778	13

D. Artisans and Village Menials.

17 Goldsmiths..	Tattan ...	Hindu ...	3,047	3,047	...	...	1,340	1,043	294	3
17(*a*) Artisans (general).	1 Kammāla ...	Hindu ...	246	246	...	...	108	102	6	...
	2 Kamsāla ...	„ ...	2	2	...	...	...	...	...	...
	Total group 17(*a*).	...	248	248	...	...	108	102	6	...
18 Barbers ...	1 Īlavāti ...	Hindu ...	377	377	...	...	166	159	7	...
	2 Kāvadi ...	„ ...	646	646	...	...	284	268	16	...
	3 Kōmaram ...	„ ...	29	29	...	...	13	13	...	...
	4 Kshourakan ...	„ ...	2,035	2,035	...	...	897	837	60	...
	5 Mārān ...	„ ...	1,738	1,738	...	...	862	617	245	...
	6 Ostta ...	Mussalman	11	11	...	...	4	4	...	...
	7 Taravan ...	Hindu ...	60	60	...	...	26	24	2	...
	Total group 18 ...	...	4,896	4,896	...	...	2,252	1,922	330	...
19 Blacksmiths	1 Kollan ...	Hindu ...	3,268	3,268	...	...	1,438	1,250	188	...
	2 Lōhar ...	„ ...	...	...	...	...	...	...	...	...
	Total group 19 ...	...	3,268	3,268	...	...	1,438	1,250	188	...
20 Carpenters, masons and turners.	1 Āsāri ...	Hindu ...	4,173	4,173	...	...	1,841	1,618	223	...
	2 Tachan ...	„ ...	511	511	...	...	225	211	14	...
	Total group 20 ...	...	4,684	4,684	...	...	2,066	1,829	237	...

TABLE E.

Castes, &c., by Civil Condition and Age—(*Continued*).

Class.	Group.	Caste, &c.	Religion.	Total Strength—(Continued). Females—(Continued). 15—39. Total.	Un-married.	Married.	Widow-ed.	40 and over. Total.	Un-married.	Married.	Widow-ed.
1	2	3	4	37	38	39	40	41	42	43	44
B. Profession-al—(*Contd.*)	10 Astrologers and quack doctors.	1 Kaniyān ..	Hindu ...	2,032	426	1,526	80	982	78	443	461
		2 Pulluvan ...	„ ...	65	15	48	2	28	1	14	13
		Total group 10 ...	...	2,097	441	1,574	82	1,010	79	457	474
		Total class B. ...	...	14,893	1,749	12,010	1,134	7,697	240	3,779	3,678
C. Com-mercial.	14 Traders ...	1 Balija ...	Hindu ...	94	26	67	1	38	...	25	13
		2 Baniya ...	{ Hindu { Jain	5	...	5	...	1	...	1	...
		3 Chetti ...	Hindu ...	3,747	782	2,820	145	1,820	127	821	872
		4 Ilavāniyan ...	„ ...	716	151	537	28	349	28	157	164
		5 Jonaka ...	Mussalmn.	10,675	1,687	8,573	415	4,297	323	2,009	1,965
		6 Labbai ...	„ ...	61	12	47	2	32	3	14	15
		7 Mēttan ...	„ ...	11,524	2,351	8,656	517	4,693	449	2,326	1,918
		8 Rāwut ...	„ ...	11	1	9	1	6	...	3	3
		9 Vaduka ...	Hindu ...	550	106	418	26	285	19	128	138
		10 Vaisya ...	„ ...	90	17	69	4	51	4	21	26
		Total group 14 ...	...	27,473	5,133	21,201	1,139	11,572	953	5,505	5,114

Castes, &c., by Civil Condition and Age—(*Continued*).

Class	Group	Caste	Religion								
C. Com	15 Pedlars ...	1 Balukar ...	Hindu ...	...	...	...	...	...	...	...	...
		2 Manikār ...	„ ...	6	...	6	...	4	...	4	...
		Total group 15 ...	...	6	...	6	...	4	...	4	...
		Total class C. ...	...	27,479	5,133	21,207	1,139	11,576	953	5,509	5,114
D. Artisans and Village Menials.	17 Goldsmiths.	Tattan ...	Hindu ...	5,245	123	5,015	107	2,560	...	1,920	640
	17(*a*) Artisans (general).	1 Kammála ...	Hindu ...	434	6	413	15	209	...	160	49
		2 Kamsála ...	„ ...	4	...	4	...	...	...	...	...
		Total group 17(*a*).	...	438	6	417	15	209	...	160	49
	18 Barbers ...	1 Īlaváti ...	Hindu ...	649	280	329	40	317	42	137	138
		2 Kávadi ...	„ ...	1,117	333	741	43	543	40	247	256
		3 Kōmaram ...	„ ...	53	11	40	2	24	2	10	12
		4 Kshourakan ...	„ ...	3,502	735	2,631	136	1,709	133	770	806
		5 Márán ...	„ ...	3,461	370	1,741	1,350	1,711	159	769	783
		6 Ostta ...	Mussalman	19	3	15	1	10	2	5	3
		7 Taravan ...	Hindu ...	115	23	88	4	28	2	12	14
		Total group 18 ...	...	8,916	1,755	5,585	1,576	4,342	380	1,950	2,012
	19 Blacksmiths	1 Kollan ...	Hindu ...	5,629	1,182	4,223	224	2,744	218	1,239	1,287
		2 Lōhar ...	„ ...	...	...	...	...	...	...	...	...
		Total group 19 ...	...	5,629	1,182	4,223	224	2,744	218	1,239	1,287
	20 Carpenters, masons and turners.	1 Āsári ...	Hindu ...	7,191	1,506	5,398	287	3,504	298	1,552	1,654
		2 Tachan ...	„ ...	884	176	671	37	432	3	211	218
		Total group 20 ...	...	8,075	1,682	6,069	324	3,936	301	1,763	1,872

TABLE E.

Castes, &c., by Civil Condition and Age—(Continued).

Class.	Caste and Religion.			Total Strength—(Continued).							
				Males.							
				All Ages.				0—9.			
	Group.	Caste, &c.	Religion.	Total.	Un-married.	Married.	Widow-ed.	Total.	Un-married.	Married.	Widow-ed.
1	2	3	4	5	6	7	8	9	10	11	12
Village Menials—(Continued).	21 Brass and coppersmiths.	1 Chembutatti ...	Hindu ...	56	25	26	5	12	12	...	...
		2 Kannán ...	„ ...	2,894	1,552	1,217	125	640	640	...	...
		Total group 21 ...	...	2,950	1,577	1,243	130	652	652	...	...
	22 Tailors ...	Pánán ...	Hindu ...	1,409	591	777	41	313	313	...	...
	22(a) Grain parchers and confectioners.	1 Idiyar ...	Hindu ...	660	375	217	68	148	148	...	...
		2 Mudayar ...	„ ...	1	1	...	...	...	...	...	...
		Total group 22(a).	...	661	376	217	68	148	148	...	...
	23 Weavers, calenderers and dyers.	1 Kōri ...	Hindu ...	5	2	3	...	1	1	...	...
		2 Patnūl ...	„ ...	393	180	185	28	88	88	...	...
		3 Sálē ...	„ ...	3,580	1,902	1,507	171	796	796	...	...
		Total group 23 ...	...	3,978	2,084	1,695	199	885	885	...	...

Castes, &c., by Civil Condition and Age—(*Continued*).

D. Artisans and

Group	Caste	Religion								
24 Washermen.	1 Ainuttar ...	Hindu ...	1	...	1	...	...	...	...	...
	2 Dōbi ...	„ ...	65	34	28	3	16	16	...	...
	3 Mannān ...	„ ...	3,509	1,907	1,508	94	840	840	...	...
	4 Velutadan ...	„ ...	6,993	3,770	2,945	278	1,575	1,575	...	...
	Total group 24 ...	...	10,568	5,711	4,482	375	2,431	2,431	...	...
26 Shepherds and wool-weavers.	1 Āttidaya ...	Hindu ...	109	53	46	10	27	27	...	...
	2 Gollalu ...	„ ...	36	20	13	3	7	7	...	...
	3 Idaya ...	„ ...	2,863	1,387	1,383	93	623	623	...	...
	4 Kángaya ...	„ ...	67	31	32	4	14	14	...	...
	5 Kūttidaya ...	„ ...	58	27	26	5	13	13	...	..
	Total group 26 ...	...	3,133	1.518	1,500	115	684	684	...	..
27 Oil-pressers	1 Chekkála ...	Hindu ...	5,739	3,056	2,524	159	1,308	1,308	...	...
	2 Vánian ...	„ ...	7,031	3,783	2,987	261	1,552	1,552	...	...
	Total group 27 ...	...	12,770	6,839	5,511	420	2,860	2,860	...	...
28 Potters ...	Kosava ...	Hindu ...	3,269	1,759	1,383	127	735	735	...	...
30 Salt, &c., workers.	Alava ...	Hindu ...	206	105	95	6	51	51	...	...
31 Lime-burners.	Paravan ...	Hindu ...	3,983	2,122	1,756	105	989	989	...	...
35 Fishermen, boatmen, palki-bearers, water bearers, cooks, &c.	1 Chaluppan ...	Hindu ...	471	255	183	33	105	105	...	...
	2 Káhar ...	„ ...	1	1	...	...	...	..	...	...
	3 Marakkān ...	{ Mslmn. { Christn.	2,639	1,322	1,207	110	681	680	1	...
	4 Mukkuva ...	Hindu ...	15,082	7,966	6,730	386	3,830	3,830	...	...
	5 Pōndan ...	„ ...	617	318	244	55	138	138	..	...
	Total group 35 ...	...	18.810	9,862	8,364	584	4,754	4.753	1	...

TABLE E.

Castes, &c., by Civil Condition and Age—(*Continued*).

Class.	Caste and Religion.			Total Strength—(*Continued*).							
				Males—(*Continued*).							
	Group.	Caste, &c.	Religion.	10—14.				15—39.			
				Total.	Un-married.	Married.	Widow-ed.	Total.	Un-married.	Married.	Widow-ed.
1	2	3	4	13	14	15	16	17	18	19	20
Village Menials—(*Continued*).	21 Brass and coppersmiths.	1 Chembutatti ...	Hindu ...	6	5	1	...	25	8	17	...
		2 Kannán ...	„ ...	310	306	4	...	1,250	558	672	20
		Total group 21 ...	...	316	311	5	...	1,275	566	689	20
	22 Tailors ...	Pánán ...	Hindu ...	129	124	5	...	644	150	482	12
	22(*a*) Grain parchers and confectioners.	1 Idiyar ...	Hindu ...	73	68	5	...	304	144	153	7
		2 Mudayar ...	„ ...	...	...	...	...	1	1	...	...
		Total group 22(*a*).	...	73	68	5	...	305	145	153	7
	23 Weavers, calenderers and dyers.	1 Kōri ...	Hindu ...	...	...	...	...	3	1	2	...
		2 Patnūl ...	„ ...	43	42	1	...	180	40	133	7
		3 Sálē ...	„ ...	391	380	11	...	1,600	610	959	31
		Total group 23 ...	...	434	422	12	...	1,783	651	1,094	38

Castes, &c., by Civil Condition and Age—(*Continued*).

D. Artisans and

24 Washermen.	1 Ainuttar ...	Hindu ...	...	..	...	...	1	...	1	...
	2 Dōbi ...	„ ...	7	7	...	...	26	10	15	1
	3 Mannān ...	„ ...	395	388	7	...	1,500	605	879	16
	4 Velutadan ...	„ ...	742	721	21	...	3,171	1,292	1,808	71
	Total group 24 ...	...	1,144	1,116	28	...	4,698	1,907	2,703	88
26 Shepherds and wool-weavers.	1 Āttidaya ...	Hindu ...	11	8	3	...	49	18	28	3
	2 Gollalu ...	„ ...	3	2	1	...	17	11	5	1
	3 Idaya ...	„ ...	308	279	29	...	1,261	465	779	17
	4 Kángaya ...	„ ...	7	5	2	...	28	9	17	2
	5 Kūttidaya ...	„ ...	6	4	2	...	25	10	14	1
	Total group 26 ...	...	335	298	37	...	1,380	513	843	24
27 Oil-pressers.	1 Chekkála ...	Hindu ...	627	611	16	...	2,633	1,071	1,539	23
	2 Vánian ...	„ ...	790	778	12	...	3,100	1,201	1,866	33
	Total group 27 ...	...	1,417	1,389	28	...	5,733	2,272	3,405	56
28 Potters ...	Kosava ..	Hindu ...	356	346	10	...	1,467	607	814	46
30 Salt, &c., workers.	Alava ...	Hindu ...	24	22	2	..	83	30	52	1
31 Lime-burners.	Paravan ..	Hindu ...	437	433	4	...	1,691	657	1,017	17
35 Fishermen, boatmen, palki-bearers, water bearers, cooks, &c.	1 Chaluppan ...	Hindu ..	50	50	...	...	213	83	120	10
	2 Káhar ...	„ ...	...		...	...	1	1	...	...
	3 Marakkán ...	Mslmn. / Christn.	323	312	11	...	1,117	303	795	19
	4 Mukkuva ...	Hindu ...	1,666	1,660	6	...	6,424	2,368	3,992	64
	5 Pōndan ...	„ ...	66	66	...	...	278	102	167	9
	Total group 35 ...	...	2,105	2,088	17	...	8,033	2,857	5,074	102

TABLE E.

Castes, &c., by Civil Condition and Age—(*Continued*).

Class.	Caste and Religion.			Total Strength—(*Continued*).							
				Males—(*Continued*).				Females.			
				40 and over.				All Ages.			
	Group.	Caste, &c.	Religion.	Total.	Un-Married.	Married.	Widow-ed.	Total.	Un-Married.	Married.	Widow-ed.
1	2	3	4	21	22	23	24	25	26	27	28
Village Menials—(*Continued*).	21 Brass and coppersmiths.	1 Chembutatti ...	Hindu ...	13	...	8	5	42	13	27	2
		2 Kannán ...	" ...	694	48	541	105	2,803	859	1,778	166
		Total group 21 ...	...	707	48	549	110	2,845	872	1,805	168
	22 Tailors ...	Pànán ...	Hindu ...	323	4	290	29	1,299	579	572	148
	22(*a*) Grain parchers and confectioners.	1 Idiyar ...	Hindu ...	135	15	59	61	606	138	383	85
		2 Mudayar ...	" ...	...	...	...	...	...	...	...	...
		Total group 22(*a*).	...	135	15	59	61	606	138	383	85
	23 Weavers, calenderers and dyers.	1 Kōri ...	Hindu ...	1	...	1	...	2	...	2	...
		2 Patnūl ...	" ...	82	10	51	21	461	209	198	54
		3 Sálē ...	" ...	793	116	537	140	3,709	1,697	1,580	432
		Total group 23 ...	...	876	126	589	161	4,172	1,906	1,780	486

Castes, &c., by Civil Condition and Age—(*Continued*).

24 Washermen.	1 Ainuttar ...	Hindu ...	...	...	...	...	1	...	1	...
	2 Dōbi ...	„ ...	16	1	13	2	73	26	39	8
	3 Mannán ...	„ ...	774	74	622	78	3,573	1,642	1,503	428
	4 Velutadan ...	„ ...	1,505	182	1,116	207	6,833	3,116	2,921	796
	Total group 24 ...	...	2,295	257	1,751	287	10,480	4,784	4,464	1,232
26 Shepherds and wool-weavers.	1 Āttidaya ...	Hindu ...	22	...	15	7	108	51	47	10
	2 Gollalu ...	„ ...	9	...	7	2	31	11	20	...
	3 Idaya ...	„ ...	671	20	575	76	2,985	1,337	1,309	339
	4 Kangaya ...	„ ...	18	3	13	2	58	23	28	7
	5 Kūttidaya ...	„ ...	14	...	10	4	47	22	21	4
	Total group 26 ...	...	734	23	620	91	3,229	1,444	1,425	360
27 Oil-pressers.	1 Chekkála ...	Hindu ...	1,171	66	969	136	5,853	2,687	2,488	678
	2 Vánian ...	„ ...	1,589	252	1,109	228	6,727	3,090	2,854	783
	Total group 27 ...	...	2,760	318	2,078	364	12,580	5,777	5,342	1,461
28 Potters ...	Kosava ...	Hindu ...	711	71	559	81	3,126	1,448	1,317	361
30 Salt, &c., workers.	Alava ...	Hindu ...	48	2	41	5	188	84	85	19
31 Lime-burners.	Paravan ...	Hindu ...	866	43	735	88	4,189	1,934	1,790	465
35 Fishermen, boatmen, palki-bearers, water bearers, cooks, &c.	1 Chaluppan ...	Hindu ...	103	17	63	23	450	201	194	55
	2 Káhar ...	„ ...	...	...	...	...	...	...	...	...
	3 Marakkan ...	{ Muslmn. Chrstn. }	518	27	400	91	2,852	1,229	1,092	531
	4 Mukkuva ...	Hindu ...	3,162	108	2,732	322	15,272	7,012	6,493	1,767
	5 Pōndan ...	„ ...	135	12	77	46	522	229	229	64
	Total group 35 ...	...	3,918	164	3,272	482	19,096	8,671	8,008	2,417

TABLE E.

Castes, &c., by Civil Condition and Age—(*Continued*).

Class.	Caste and Religion.			Total Strength—(*Continued*). Females—(*Continued*).							
	Group.	Caste, &c.	Religion.	0—9. Total.	0—9. Un-married.	0—9. Married.	0—9. Widow-ed.	10—14. Total.	10—14. Un-married.	10—14. Married.	10—14. Widow-ed.
1	2	3	4	29	30	31	32	33	34	35	36
Village Menials—(*Continued*).	21 Brass and coppersmiths.	1 Chembutatti ...	Hindu ...	9	9	...	...	4	4	...	...
		2 Kannán ...	„ ...	699	699	...	...	307	149	158	...
		Total group 21 ...	...	708	708	...	...	311	153	158	...
	22 Tailors ...	Pánán ...	Hindu ...	323	323	...	...	143	120	23	...
	22(*a*) Grain parchers and confectioners.	1 Idiyar ...	Hindu ...	134	134	...	...	69	4	65	...
		2 Mudayar ...	„ ...	...	...	...	...	...	...	...	...
		Total group 22(*a*).	...	134	134	...	...	69	4	65	...
	23 Weavers, calenderers and dyers.	1 Kori ...	Hindu ...	...	...	...	...	...	...	...	...
		2 Patnūl ...	„ ...	115	115	...	...	50	46	4	...
		3 Sálē ...	„ ...	923	923	...	...	406	379	27	...
		Total group 23 ...	...	1,038	1,038	...	...	456	425	31	...

D. Artisans and

24 Washermen.	1 Ainuttar ...	Hindu ...	...	...	...	...	...	...	...	...
	2 Dōbi ...	,, ...	18	18	...	...	8	1	7	...
	3 Mannān ...	,, ...	892	892	...	...	394	368	26	...
	4 Velutadan ...	,, ...	1,702	1,702	...	...	748	697	51	...
	Total group 24 ...	...	2,612	2,612	...	...	1,150	1,066	84	...
26 Shepherds and wool-weavers.	1 Āttidaya ...	Hindu ...	26	26	...	...	14	14	...	...
	2 Gollalu ...	,, ...	7	7	...	...	4	4	...	...
	3 Idaya ...	,, ...	742	742	...	...	328	307	21	...
	4 Kāngaya ...	,, ...	13	13	...	...	6	6	...	...
	5 Kūttidaya ...	,, ...	12	12	...	...	5	5	...	...
	Total group 26 ...	...	800	800	...	...	357	336	21	...
27 Oil-pressers	1 Chekkāla ...	Hindu ...	1,462	1,462	...	...	643	600	43	...
	2 Vāniyan ...	,, ...	1,681	1,681	...	...	738	688	50	...
	Total group 27 ...	...	3,143	3,143	...	...	1,381	1,288	93	...
28 Potters ...	Kosava ...	Hindu ...	780	780	...	...	352	331	21	...
30 Salt, &c., workers.	Alava ...	Hindu ...	44	44	...	...	21	20	1	...
31 Lime-burners.	Paravan ...	Hindu ...	1,050	1,050	...	...	462	430	32	...
35 Fishermen, boatmen, palki-bearers, waterbearers, cooks, &c.	1 Chaluppan ...	Hindu ...	112	112	...	...	49	47	2	...
	2 Kāhar ...	,, ...	...	...	...	...	...	...	...	...
	3 Marakkān ...	{ Musslmn. Christian }	743	743	...	...	353	303	47	3
	4 Mukkuva ...	Hindu ...	3,820	3,820	...	...	1,677	1,552	125	...
	5 Pōndan ...	,, ...	128	128	...	...	56	55	1	...
	Total group 35 ...	...	4,803	4,803	...	...	2,135	1,957	175	3

TABLE E.

Castes, &c., by Civil Condition and Age—(*Continued*).

Class.	Caste and Religion.			Total Strength—(*Continued*).							
				Females—(*Continued*).							
				15—39.				40 and over.			
	Group.	Caste, &c.	Religion.	Total.	Un-married.	Married.	Widow-ed.	Total.	Un-married.	Married.	Widow-ed.
1	2	3	4	37	38	39	40	41	42	43	44
Village Menials—(*Continued*).	21 Brass and coppersmiths.	1 Chembutatti ...	Hindu ...	22	...	21	1	7	...	6	1
		2 Kannán ...	„ ...	1,205	11	1,168	26	592	...	452	140
		Total group 21 ...	...	1,227	11	1,189	27	599	...	458	141
	22 Tailors ...	Pánán ...	Hindu ...	563	116	426	21	270	20	123	127
	22(*a*) Grain parchers, and confectioners.	1 Idiyar ...	Hindu ...	268	...	253	15	135	...	65	70
		2 Mudayar ...	„ ...	...	...	...	...	...	...	...	...
		Total group 22(*a*).	...	268	...	253	15	135	...	65	70
	23 Weavers, calenderers and dyers.	1 Kōri ...	Hindu ...	2	...	2	...	...	...	...	...
		2 Patnūl ...	„ ...	200	42	150	8	96	6	44	46
		3 Sálē ...	„ ...	1,596	335	1,199	62	784	60	354	370
		Total group 23 ...	...	1,798	377	1,351	70	880	66	398	416

TABLE E.

Castes, &c., by Civil Condition and Age—(*Continued*).

D. Artisans and

24 Washermen.	1 Ainuttar ...	Hindu ...	1	...	1	...	...	...	...	...
	2 Dōbi ...	„ ...	34	6	27	1	13	1	5	7
	3 Mannān ...	„ ...	1,547	326	1,157	64	740	56	320	364
	4 Velutadan ...	„ ...	2,953	611	2,229	113	1,430	106	641	683
	Total group 24 ...	...	4,535	943	3,414	178	2,183	163	966	1,054
26 Shepherds and wool-weavers.	1 Āttidaya ...	Hindu ...	49	10	37	2	19	1	10	8
	2 Gollalu ...	„ ...	16	...	16	...	4	...	4	...
	3 Idaya ...	„ ...	1,297	257	989	51	618	31	299	288
	4 Kángaya ...	„ ...	26	4	21	1	13	...	7	6
	5 Kuttidaya ...	„ ...	21	5	15	1	9	...	6	3
	Total group 26 ...	...	1,409	276	1,078	55	663	32	326	305
Oil-pressers ...	1 Chekkála ...	Hindu ...	2,517	527	1,892	98	1,231	98	553	580
	2 Vaniyan ...	„ ...	2,895	608	2,170	117	1,413	113	634	666
	Total group 27 ...	...	5,412	1,135	4.062	215	2,644	211	1,187	1,246
28 Potters ...	Kosava ...	Hindu ...	1,346	292	1,005	49	648	45	291	312
30 Salt, &c., workers.	Alava ...	Hindu ...	84	18	63	3	39	2	21	16
31 Lime-burners.	Paravan ...	Hindu ...	1,790	376	1,343	71	887	78	415	394
35 Fishermen, boatmen, palki-bearers, water bearers, cooks, &c.	1 Chaluppan ...	Hindu ...	195	40	148	7	94	2	44	48
	2 Káhar ...	„ ...	...	...	...	...	...	...	...	...
	3 Marakkan ...	{ Musalmn { Chrstn... }	1,175	150	748	277	581	33	297	251
	4 Mukkuva ...	Hindu ...	6,572	1,386	4,928	258	3,203	254	1,440	1,509
	5 Pōndan ...	„ ...	228	44	179	5	110	2	49	59
	Total group 35 ...	...	8,170	1,620	6,003	547	3,988	291	1,830	1,867

TABLE E.

Castes, &c., by Civil Condition and Age—(*Continued*).

Class.	Group.	Caste, &c.	Religion.	Total Strength—(Continued). Males. All Ages. Total.	Un-married.	Married.	Widow-ed.	0—9. Total.	Un-married.	Married.	Widow-ed.
1	2	3	4	5	6	7	8	9	10	11	12
D. Artisans and Village Menials—(*Continued*).	35(*a*) Personal service.	Chākkār ...	Hindu ...	306	154	142	10	74	74	...	...
	36 Distillers and toddy-drawers.	1 Īluva ...	Hindu ...	206,528	107,324	92,414	6,790	50,294	50,294	...	..
		2 Pāshi ...	" ...	3	2	1	...	...	...	...	...
		3 Chānnān ...	" ...	70,001	38,202	29,881	1,918	17,140	17,140	...	...
		4 Tandān ...	" ...	11,158	5,943	4,913	302	2,768	2,768	...	...
		Total group 36 ...	...	287,690	151,471	127,209	9,010	70,202	70,202	...	...
	38 Leather workers.	Chemmān ...	Hindu ...	1,094	542	499	53	252	252	...	...
	39 Scavengers	1 Dāss ...	Hindu ...	5	4	1	...	1	1	...	...
		2 Valluvan ...	" ...	56	30	25	1	14	14	...	...
		Total group 39 ...	...	61	34	26	1	15	15	...	...
		Total class D. ...	...	417,104	218,992	184,776	13,336	100,043	100,042	1	...

E. Vagrant minor Artisans and Performers.

40 Grind-stone makers and stone quarriers.	Kallāsāri ...	Hindu ...	4,079	1,941	1,980	158	899	899	...	...
41 Earth workers and stone dressers.	1 Ottan ...	Hindu ...	292	151	131	10	73	73	...	...
	2 Ottiya ...	„ ...	10	5	5	...	3	3	...	...
	Total group 41 ...	...	302	156	136	10	76	76	...	...
43 Matmakers, cane splitters, grass cutters, &c.	Nolayan ...	Hindu ...	1,260	680	545	35	307	307	...	...
44 Hunters, fowlers, &c.	1 Talavan ...	Hindu ...	371	202	157	12	89	89	...	...
	2 Vēdan ...	„ ...	3,498	1,842	1,559	97	840	840	...	...
	3 Vettāran ...	„ ...	178	89	84	5	42	42	...	...
	Total group 44 ...	...	4,047	2,133	1,800	114	971	971	...	...
45 Miscellaneous and disreputable vagrants.	1 Kākkālan ...	Hindu ...	422	213	197	12	101	101	...	...
	2 Pāssiavan ...	„ ...	35	18	15	2	8	8	...	...
	Total group 45 ...	...	457	231	212	14	109	109	...	...
45(*a*) Beggars..	1 Panisivan ...	Hindu ...	32	17	14	1	7	7	...	...
	2 Sangampandāram.	„ ...	5,416	2,898	2,336	182	1,218	1,218	...	...
	Total group 45(*a*).	...	5,448	2,915	2,350	183	1,225	1,225	...	...
46 Tumblers and acrobats.	1 Gopāl ...	Hindu ...	3	2	1	...	1	1	..	...
	2 Kūttādi ...	„ ...	17	9	8	...	4	4	...	...
	Total group 46 ...	...	20	11	9	...	5	5	...	...

TABLE E.

Castes, &c., by Civil Condition and Age—(*Continued*).

Class.	Group.	Caste, &c.	Religion.	Total Strength—(Continued). Males—(Continued). 10—14. Total.	Un-married.	Married.	Widow-ed.	15—39. Total.	Un-married.	Married.	Widow-ed.
1	2	3	4	13	14	15	16	17	18	19	20
D. Artisans and Village Menials—(*Continued*).	35(*a*) Personal service.	Chákkār ...	Hindu ...	34	34	...	...	124	42	80	2
	36 Distillers and toddy-drawers.	1 Īluva ...	Hindu ...	24,837	24,810	27	...	82,468	29,703	51,908	857
		2 Pāshi ...	,, ...	1	1	...	...	2	1	1	...
		3 Chānnān ...	,, ...	8,038	8,017	21	...	28,708	12,241	16,186	281
		4 Tandán ...	,, ...	1,226	1,223	3	...	4,672	1,828	2,796	48
		Total group 36 ...	...	34,102	34,051	51	...	115,850	43,773	70,891	1,186
	38 Leather workers.	Chemmān ...	Hindu ...	110	105	5	...	506	173	304	29
	39 Scavengers.	1 Dāss ...	Hindu ...	2	2	...	...	2	1	1	...
		2 Valluvan ...	,, ...	6	6	...	...	23	9	14	...
		Total group 39 ...	...	8	8	...	...	25	10	15	...
		Total class D. ...	...	48,180	47,808	372	...	172,946	64,897	106,139	1,910

E. Vagrant minor Artisans and Performers.

40 Grind-stone makers and stone quarriers.	Kallásári ...	Hindu ...	443	428	15	...	1,870	527	1,309	34
41 Earth workers and stone dressers.	1 Ottan ..	Hindu ...	36	36	...	...	113	38	73	2
	2 Ottiya ...	„ ...	1	1	...	...	4	1	3	...
	Total group 41 ...	...	37	37	...	...	117	39	76	2
43 Matmakers, cane splitters, grass-cutters, &c.	Nolayan .	Hindu ...	144	144	...	...	536	216	314	6
44 Hunters, fowlers, &c.	1 Talavan ...	Hindu ...	49	49	...	...	149	59	87	3
	2 Vēdan ...	„ ...	401	399	2	...	1,457	563	879	15
	3 Vettáran ...	„ ...	18	18	...	...	81	27	53	1
	Total group 44 ...	...	468	466	2	...	1,687	649	1,019	19
45 Miscellaneous and disreputable vagrants.	1 Kákkálan ...	Hindu ...	46	44	2	...	178	64	112	2
	2 Passiavan ...	„ ...	5	5	...	...	15	5	9	1
	Total group 45 ...	...	51	49	2	...	193	69	121	3
45(*a*) Beggars.	1 Panisivan ...	Hindu ...	4	4	...	...	14	6	8	...
	2 Sangampandáram	„ ...	578	565	13	...	2,549	1,045	1,454	50
	Total group 45(*a*).	...	582	569	13	...	2,563	1,051	1,462	50
46 Tumblers and acrobats.	1 Gopál ...	Hindu ...	...	...	...	...	2	1	1	...
	2 Kūttádi ...	„ ...	2	2	...	...	8	3	5	...
	Total group 46 ...	...	2	2	...	...	10	4	6	...

TABLE E.

Castes, &c., by Civil Condition and Age—(*Continued*).

Class.	Group.	Caste, &c.	Religion.	Males—(Continued). 40 and over. Total.	Un-married.	Married.	Widow-ed.	Females. All Ages. Total.	Un-married.	Married.	Widow-ed.
1	2	3	4	21	22	23	24	25	26	27	28
D. Artisans and Village Menials—(*Continued*).	35(*a*) Personal service.	Chákkár ...	Hindu ...	74	4	62	8	259	114	114	31
	36 Distillers and toddy-drawers.	1 Īluva ...	Hindu ...	48,929	2,517	40,479	5,933	207,689	95,795	87,762	24,132
		2 Páshi ...	„ ...	...	...	..	...	...	...	...	...
		3 Chánnán ...	„ ...	16,115	804	13,674	1,637	66,610	32,149	26,852	7,609
		4 Tandán ...	„ ...	2,492	124	2,114	254	11,456	5,266	4,863	1,327
		Total group 36 ...	...	67,536	3,445	56,267	7,824	285,755	133,210	119,477	33,068
	38 Leather workers.	Chenmán ..	Hindu ...	226	12	190	24	1,062	465	472	125
	39 Scavengers.	1 Dáss ...	Hindu ...	...	...	...	...	5	1	4	...
		2 Valluvan ...	„ ...	13	1	11	1	57	24	27	6
		Total group 39 ..	...	13	1	11	1	62	25	31	6
		Total class D. ...	...	95,935	6,245	78,264	11,426	414,389	189,387	176,461	48,541

E. Vagrant minor Artisans and Performers.

Group	Caste	Religion								
40 Grind-stone makers and stone quarriers.	Kallásári ...	Hindu ...	867	87	656	124	4,059	1,454	2,150	455
41 Earth workers and stone dressers.	1 Ottan ...	Hindu ...	70	4	58	8	85	37	44	4
	2 Ottiya ...	„ ...	2	...	2	...	15	6	9	...
	Total group 41 ...	...	72	4	60	8	100	43	53	4
43 Matmakers, cane splitters, grass-cutters, &c.	Nolayan ...	Hindu ...	273	13	231	29	1,063	479	450	134
44 Hunters, fowlers, &c.	1 Talavan ...	Hindu ...	84	5	70	9	385	172	167	46
	2 Vēdan ...	„ ...	800	40	678	82	3,311	1,507	1,418	386
	3 Vettáran ...	„ ...	37	2	31	4	171	70	73	28
	Total group 44 ...	...	921	47	779	95	3,867	1,749	1,658	460
45 Miscellaneous and disreputable vagrants.	1 Kákkálan ...	Hindu ...	97	4	83	10	475	218	200	57
	2 Passiavan ...	„ ...	7	...	6	1	29	12	16	1
	Total group 45 ...	...	104	4	89	11	504	230	216	58
45(*a*) Beggars.	1 Panisivan ...	Hindu ...	7	...	6	1	26	9	14	3
	2 Sangampandāram.	„ ...	1,071	70	869	132	5,308	2,427	2,269	612
	Total group 45(*a*).	...	1,078	70	875	133	5,334	2,436	2,283	615
46 Tumblers and acrobats.	1 Gopál ...	Hindu ...	...	...	...	...	1	...	1	...
	2 Kūttádi ...	„ ...	3	...	3	...	21	9	11	1
	Total group 46 ...	...	3	...	3	...	22	9	12	1

TABLE E.

Castes, &c., by Civil Condition and Age—(*Continued*).

Class.	Caste and Religion.			Total Strength—(*Continued*).							
				Females—(*Continued*).							
	Group.	Caste, &c.	Religion.	0—9.				10—14.			
				Total.	Un-married.	Married.	Widow-ed.	Total.	Un-married.	Married.	Widow-ed.
1	2	3	4	29	30	31	32	33	34	35	36
D. Artisans and Village Menials—(*Continued*).	35(*a*) Persona service.	Chákkár ...	Hindu ...	62	62	...	...	30	26	4	...
	36 Distillers and toddy-drawers.	1 Īluva ...	Hindu ..	52,107	52,107	...	...	18,780	17,870	910	...
		2 Páshi ...	„ ...	...	...	...	...	...	...	...	...
		3 Chánnán ...	„ ...	16,645	16,645	...	...	7,326	7,273	53	...
		4 Tandán ...	„ ...	2,863	2,863	...	...	1,268	1,178	90	...
		Total group 36 ...	...	71,615	71,615	...	...	27,374	26,321	1,053	...
	38 Leather workers.	Chemmán ...	Hindu ...	264	264	...	...	112	106	6	...
	39 Scavengers.	1 Dáss ...	Hindu ...	1	1	...	...	...	...	...	...
		2 Valluvan ...	„ ...	14	14	...	...	7	5	2	...
		Total group 39 ...	...	15	15	...	...	7	5	2	...
		Total class D. ...	...	103,534	103,534	...	...	41,564	38,734	2,824	6

Castes, &c., by Civil Condition and Age—(*Continued*).

E. Vagrant minor Artisans and Performers.

Group	Caste	Religion								
40 Grind-stone makers and stone quarriers.	Kallāsāri ...	Hindu ...	1,013	1,013	...	...	447	383	64	...
41 Earth workers and stone dressers.	1 Ottan ...	Hindu ...	21	21	...	...	9	8	1	...
	2 Ottiya ...	,, ...	4	4	...	...	1	...	1	...
	Total group 41 ...	...	25	25	...	...	10	8	2	...
43 Matmakers, cane splitters, grass-cutters, &c.	Nolayan ...	Hindu ...	265	265	...	...	116	109	7	...
44 Hunters, fowlers, &c.	1 Talavan ...	Hindu ...	90	90	...	...	42	40	2	...
	2 Vēdan ...	,, ...	827	827	...	...	349	326	23	...
	3 Vettāran ...	,, ...	35	35	...	...	20	18	2	...
	Total group 44 ...	...	952	952	...	...	411	384	27	...
45 Miscellaneous and disreputable vagrants.	1 Kākkālan ...	Hindu ...	117	117	...	...	54	52	2	...
	2 Passiavan ...	,, ...	7	7	...	...	3	3	...	...
	Total group 45 ...	...	124	124	...	...	57	55	2	...
45(*a*) Beggars.	1 Panisivan ...	Hindu ...	6	6	...	...	2	2	...	...
	2 Sangampandāram.	,, ...	1,320	1,320	...	...	578	540	38	...
	Total group 45(*a*).	...	1,326	1,326	...	...	580	542	38	...
46 Tumblers and acrobats.	1 Gopál ...	Hindu ...	...	...	...	...	...	...	...	...
	2 Kūttádi ...	,, ...	5	5	...	...	2	2	...	...
	Total group 46 ...	...	5	5	...	...	2	2	...	...

TABLE E.
Castes, &c., by Civil Condition and Age—(*Continued*).

Class.	Caste and Religion.			Total Strength—(*Continued*). Females—(*Continued*). 15—39.				40 and over.			
	Group.	Caste, &c.	Religion.	Total.	Un-married.	Married.	Widow-ed.	Total.	Un-married.	Married.	Widow-ed.
1	2	3	4	37	38	39	40	41	42	43	44
D. Artisans and Village Menials—(*Continued*).	35(*a*) Personal service.	Chákkár ...	Hindu ...	109	22	83	4	58	4	27	27
	36 Distillers and toddy-drawers.	1 Īluva ...	Hindu ...	93,619	20,847	69,099	3,673	43,183	4,971	17,753	20,459
		2 Pāshi ...	" ...	...	...	...	...	...	...	...	...
		3 Chānnān ...	" ...	28,662	7,017	20,504	1,141	13,977	1,214	6,295	6,468
		4 Taudān ...	" ...	4,927	1,034	3,695	198	2,398	191	1,078	1,129
		Total group 36 ...	...	127,208	28,898	93,298	5,012	59,558	6,376	25,126	28,056
	38 Leather workers.	Chemmān ...	Hindu ...	462	73	369	20	224	22	97	105
	39 Scavengers.	1 Dāss ...	Hindu ...	4	...	4	...	...	...	...	...
		2 Valluvan ...	" ...	25	5	19	1	11	...	6	5
		Total group 39 ...	...	29	5	23	1	11	...	6	5
		Total class D. ...	...	182,713	38,910	135,269	8,534	86,578	8,209	38,368	40,001

E. Vagrant minor Artisans and Performers.

40 Grind-stone makers and stone quarriers.	Kallāsāri ...	Hindu ...	1,748	56	1,621	71	851	2	465	384
41 Earth workers and stone dressers.	1 Ottan ...	Hindu ...	37	7	29	1	18	1	14	3
	2 Ottiya ...	„ ...	7	2	5	...	3	...	3	...
	Total group 41 ...	...	44	9	34	1	21	1	17	3
43 Matmakers, cane splitters, grass-cutters, &c.	Nolayan ...	Hindu ...	459	96	344	19	223	9	99	115
44 Hunters, fowlers, &c.	1 Talavan ...	Hindu ...	174	36	130	8	79	6	35	38
	2 Vēdan ...	„ ...	1,432	301	1,077	54	703	53	318	332
	3 Vettāran ...	„ ...	64	13	49	2	52	4	22	26
	Total group 44 ...	..	1,670	350	1,256	64	834	63	375	396
45 Miscellaneous and disreputable vagrants.	1 Kākkālan ...	Hindu ...	198	42	150	6	106	7	48	51
	2 Passiavan ...	„ ...	13	2	11	...	6	...	5	1
	Total group 45 ...	...	211	44	161	6	112	7	53	52
45(*a*) Beggars.	1 Panisivan ...	Hindu ...	11	1	10	...	7	...	4	3
	2 Sangampandāram.	„ ...	2,296	482	1,730	84	1,114	85	501	528
	Total group 45(*a*).	...	2,307	483	1,740	84	1,121	85	505	531
46 Tumblers and acrobats.	1 Gopāl ...	Hindu ...	1	...	1	...	...	...	...	...
	2 Kūttādi ...	„ ...	10	2	8	...	4	...	3	1
	Total group 46 ...	...	11	2	9	...	4	...	3	1

TABLE E.

Castes, &c., by Civil Condition and Age—(*Continued*).

Class.	Group.	Caste, &c.	Religion.	Males. All Ages. Total.	Males. All Ages. Un-married.	Males. All Ages. Married.	Males. All Ages. Widow-ed.	Males. 0—9. Total.	Males. 0—9. Un-married.	Males. 0—9. Married.	Males. 0—9. Widow-ed.
1	2	3	4	5	6	7	8	9	10	11	12
Vagrant, &c.—(*Contd.*)	47 Jugglers, snake charmers and animalexhibitors.	Kuluvan ...	Hindu ...	42	22	19	1	10	10	...	...
		Total class E. ...	...	15,655	8,089	7,051	515	3,602	3,602	...	...
and Nationalities.	48 Asiatic races of reputed non-Indian descent.	1 Arab ...	Musalmn..	260	132	119	9	64	63	1	...
		2 Chinese ...	Christian..	1	...	1	...	...	...	...	...
		3 Jew ...	Jew ...	65	39	25	1	18	18	..	...
		4 Kābūl ...	Musalmn..	84	44	33	7	21	21	...	...
		5 Mughal ...	„ ...	317	170	133	14	86	86	...	...
		6 Parsi ...	Parsi ...	1	...	1	...	...	...	...	...
		7 Pathán ...	Musalmn..	2,508	1,317	1,119	72	617	615	2	...
		8 Sheik ..	„ ...	240	119	101	20	61	61	...	...
		9 Singhalese ...	Hindu ...	17	9	8	...	5	5	...	...
		10 Syed ...	Musalmn..	117	62	48	7	30	30	...	...
		Total group 48 ...	...	3,610	1,892	1,588	130	902	899	3	...

TABLE E.

Castes, &c., by Civil Condition and Age—(*Continued*).

F. Races	50 Non-Asiatic races.	European ...	{ Chrstn / None }	210	95	105	10	44	44	...	...
	51 Eurasians...	1 East Indian ...	Christian..	995	588	369	38	332	332	...	...
		2 Eurasian ...	„ ...	285	95	179	11	41	41	...	...
		Total group 51 ...	...	1,280	683	548	49	373	373	...	...
	52 Christian converts.	1 Native ...	Christian..	112,489	58,246	50,362	3,881	30,268	30,166	88	14
		2 Syrian ...	„ ...	150,395	72,421	71,968	6,006	37,722	37,623	85	14
		Total group 52 ...	...	262,884	130,667	122,330	9,887	67,990	67,789	173	28
		Total class F. ...	...	267,984	133,337	124,571	10,076	69,309	69,105	176	28
G. Undefined.	54 Linguistic, territorial and religious names.	1 Bengalese ...	Hindu ...	3	1	2	...	...	...	...	...
		2 Guzerati ...	„ ...	28	15	11	2	7	7	...	...
		3 Jain ...	Jain ...	3	2	1	...	...	...	...	...
		4 Kannadiyan ..	Hindu ...	19	11	8	...	6	6	...	...
		5 Konkani ...	„ ...	3,681	2,120	1,324	237	795	795	...	...
		6 Kutch ...	Musalmn..	147	76	56	15	38	38	...	...
		7 Mussalman ...	„ ...	7,203	3,814	3,171	218	1,805	1,801	4	...
		8 Tamil ...	Hindu ...	3	1	2	...	...	...	...	...
		9 Telugu ...	„ ...	10	5	5	...	3	3	...	...
		10 Tulukkan ...	Musalmn..	15,555	8,271	6,825	459	3,915	3,894	19	2
		Total group 54 ...	...	26,652	14,316	11,405	931	6,569	6,544	23	2

TABLE E.

Castes, &c., by Civil Condition and Age—(*Continued*).

Class.	Caste and Religion.			Total Strength—(*Continued*). Males—(*Continued*).							
				10—14.				15—39.			
	Group.	Caste, &c.	Religion.	Total.	Un-married.	Married.	Widow-ed.	Total.	Un-married.	Married.	Widow-ed.
1	2	3	4	13	14	15	16	17	18	19	20
Vagrant, &c.—(*Contd.*)	47 Jugglers, snake charmers and animal exhibitors.	Kuluvan ...	Hindu ...	6	6	...	...	15	5	10	...
		Total class E. ...	...	1,733	1,701	32	...	6,991	2,560	4,317	114
and Nationalities.	48 Asiatic races of reputed non-Indian descent.	1 Arab ...	Musalmn..	28	25	3	...	115	42	71	2
		2 Chinese ...	Christian..	...	...	...	...	1	...	1	...
		3 Jew ...	Jew ...	4	4	...	...	28	17	10	1
		4 Kābūl ...	Musalmn..	9	9	...	...	37	13	23	1
		5 Mughal ...	,, ...	35	31	4	...	128	50	72	6
		6 Parsi ...	Parsi ...	...	...	...	...	...	...	...	...
		7 Pathān ...	Musalmn..	259	248	11	...	1,122	435	673	14
		8 Sheik ...	,, ...	26	20	6	...	95	36	57	2
		9 Singhalese ...	Hindu ...	2	2	...	...	7	2	5	...
		10 Syed ...	Musalmn..	14	14	...	...	50	17	32	1
		Total group 48 ...	...	377	353	24	...	1,583	612	944	27

Castes, &c., by Civil Condition and Age—(*Continued*).

Class	Group	Caste	Religion								
F. Races	50 Non-Asiatic races.	European ...	{ Chrstn / None }	19	19	...	...	99	28	67	4
	51 Eurasians...	1 East Indian ...	Christian..	153	149	4	...	327	94	227	6
		2 Eurasian ..	,, ...	21	20	1	...	153	32	119	2
		Total group 51 ...	...	174	169	5	...	480	126	346	8
	52 Christian converts.	1 Native ...	Christian..	14,716	14,232	462	22	43,847	12,849	30,585	413
		2 Syrian ...	,, ...	18,422	17,845	552	25	63,760	16,035	46,829	896
		Total group 52 ...	...	33,138	32,077	1,014	47	107,607	28,884	77,414	1,309
		Total class F. ...	...	33,708	32,618	1,043	47	109,769	29,650	78,771	1,348
G. Undefined.	54 Linguistic, territorial and religions names.	1 Bengalese ...	Hindu ...	...	..	...	...	2	1	1	...
		2 Guzerati ...	,, ...	4	4	...	...	11	4	6	1
		3 Jain ...	Jain ...	...	...	...	...	3	2	1	...
		4 Kannadiyan ...	Hindu ...	2	2	...	...	7	3	4	...
		5 Konkani ...	,, ...	395	371	24	...	1,690	852	810	28
		6 Kutch ...	Musalmn..	17	17	...	...	61	20	35	6
		7 Mussalman ...	,, ..	740	722	17	1	3,176	1,234	1,905	37
		8 Tamil ...	Hindu ...	...	...	...	...	2	1	1	...
		9 Telugu ...	,, ...	1	1	...	...	4	1	3	...
		10 Tulukkan ...	Musalmn..	1,556	1,526	29	1	6,964	2,731	4,176	57
		Total group 54 ...	...	2,715	2,643	70	2	11,920	4,849	6,942	129

TABLE E.

Castes, &c., by Civil Condition and Age—(*Continued*).

Class.	Caste and Religion.			Total Strength—(*Continued*).							
				Males—(*Continued*).				Females.			
				40 and over.				All Ages.			
	Group.	Caste, &c.	Religion.	Total.	Un-Married.	married.	Widow-ed.	Total.	Un-married.	Married.	Widow-ed.
1	2	3	4	21	22	23	24	25	26	27	28
Vagrant, &c. (*Contd.*)	47 Jugglers, snake charmers and animal exhibitors.	Kuluvan ...	Hindu ...	11	1	9	1	31	15	15	1
		Total class E. ...	...	3,329	226	2,702	401	14,980	6,415	6,837	1,728
and Nationalities.	48 Asiatic races of reputed non-Indian descent.	1 Arab ...	Musalmn...	53	2	44	7	186	85	80	21
		2 Chinese ...	Christian..	...	...	...	...	...	...	...	...
		3 Jew ...	Jew ...	15	...	15	...	60	27	25	8
		4 Kābūl ...	Musalmn...	17	1	10	6	45	19	20	6
		5 Mughal ...	„ ...	68	3	57	8	265	119	114	32
		6 Parsi ...	Parsi ...	1	...	1	...	...	...	...	...
		7 Pathān ...	Musalmn...	510	19	433	58	1,845	836	795	214
		8 Sheik ...	„ ...	58	2	38	18	174	80	73	21
		9 Singhalese ...	Hindu ...	3	...	3	...	12	4	8	...
		10 Syed ...	Musalmn...	23	1	16	6	115	51	50	14
		Total group 48 ...	...	748	28	617	103	2,702	1,221	1,165	316

Castes, &c., by Civil Condition and Age—(*Continued*).

Class	Group	Caste	Religion								
F. Races	50 Non-Asiatic races.	European ...	{ Chrstn None }	48	4	38	6	151	59	71	21
	51 Eurasians...	1 East Indian ...	Christian..	183	13	138	32	1,077	479	497	101
		2 Eurasian ...	„	70	2	59	9	247	109	108	30
		Total group 51 ...	...	253	15	197	41	1,324	588	605	131
	52 Christian converts.	1 Native ...	Christian..	23,658	999	19,227	3,432	108,517	49,178	49,830	9,509
		2 Syrian ...	„	30,491	918	24,502	5,071	147,400	65,586	67,536	14,278
		Total group 52 ...	...	54,149	1,917	43,729	8,503	255,917	114,764	117,366	23,787
		Total class F. ...	...	55,198	1,964	44,581	8,653	260,094	116,632	119,207	24,255
G. Undefined.	54 Linguistic, territorial and religious names.	1 Bengalese ...	Hindu ...	1	...	1	...	...	...	...	...
		2 Guzerati ...	„ ...	6	...	5	1	20	8	12	...
		3 Jain ...	Jain ...	...	...	...	...	...	...	...	...
		4 Kannadiyan ...	Hindu ...	4	...	4	...	22	9	13	...
		5 Konkani ...	„ ...	801	102	490	209	3,389	791	2,047	551
		6 Kutch ...	Musalmn...	31	1	21	9	169	73	73	23
		7 Mussalman ...	„ ...	1,482	57	1,245	180	7,547	3,416	3,243	888
		8 Tamil ...	Hindu ...	1	...	1	...	...	...	...	...
		9 Telugu ...	„ ...	2	...	2	...	10	3	7	...
		10 Tulukkan ...	Musalmn...	3,120	120	2,601	399	14,215	6,614	6,101	1,500
		Total group 54 ...	...	5,448	280	4,370	798	25,372	10,914	11,496	2,962

TABLE E.

Castes, &c., by Civil Condition and Age—(*Continued*).

Class.	Caste and Religion.			Total Strength—(*Continued*). Females—(*Continued*).							
	Group.	Caste, &c.	Religion.	0—9. Total.	0—9. Un-married.	0—9. Married.	0—9. Widow-ed.	10—14. Total.	10—14. Un-married.	10—14. Married.	10—14. Widow-ed.
1	2	3	4	29	30	31	32	33	34	35	36
Vagrant, &c. (*Contd.*)	47 Jugglers, snake charmers and animal exhibitors.	Kuluvan ...	Hindu ...	8	8	...	...	3	3	...	...
		Total class E. ...	...	3,718	3,718	...	...	1,626	1,486	140	...
and Nationalities.	48 Asiatic races of reputed non-Indian descent.	1 Arab ...	Musalmn.	47	47	...	...	22	20	2	...
		2 Chinese ...	Christian..	...	...	...	...	...	...	...	...
		3 Jew ...	Jew ...	14	14	...	...	9	8	1	...
		4 Kábūl ...	Musalmn.	12	12	...	...	5	4	1	...
		5 Mughal ...	„ ...	68	68	...	...	29	26	3	...
		6 Parsi ...	Parsi ...	...	...	...	...	...	...	...	...
		7 Pathān ...	Musalmn.	497	494	3	...	195	176	19	...
		8 Sheik ...	„ ...	45	45	...	...	18	16	2	...
		9 Singhalese ...	Hindu ...	4	4	...	...	...	...	...	...
		10 Syed ...	Musalmn.	31	31	...	...	11	10	1	...
		Total group 48 ...	...	718	715	3	...	289	260	29	...

TABLE E.

Castes, &c., by Civil Condition and Age—(*Continued*).

F. Races	50 Non-Asiatic races.	European ...	{ Chrstn { None }	29	29	...	...	13	13	...	...
	51 Eurasians...	1 East Indian ...	Christian..	291	291	...	...	141	122	19	...
		2 Eurasian ...	,, ...	55	55	...	...	32	28	4	...
		Total group 51 ...	...	346	346	..	...	173	150	23	...
	52 Christian converts.	1 Native ...	Christian..	32,019	31,819	182	18	12,206	10,375	1,809	22
		2 Syrian ...	,, ...	40,568	40,375	183	10	18,426	15,791	2,605	30
		Total group 52 ...	...	72,587	72,194	365	28	30,632	26,166	4,414	52
		Total class F. ...	...	73,680	73,284	368	28	31,107	26,589	4,466	52
G. Undefined.	54 Linguistic, territorial and religious names.	1 Bengalese ...	Hindu ...	...	...	...	...	...	...	...	..
		2 Guzerati ...	,, ...	4	4	...	...	2	2	...	...
		3 Jain ...	Jain ...	...	...	...	...	...	...	...	...
		4 Kaunadiyan ...	Hindu ...	6	6	...	...	2	2	...	...
		5 Konkani ...	,, ...	757	757	...	...	376	34	305	37
		6 Kutch ...	Musalmn..	44	44	..	...	17	15	2	...
		7 Mussalman ...	,, ...	1,947	1,939	8	...	767	687	78	2
		8 Tamil ...	Hindu ...	...	...	...	...	...	...	...	...
		9 Telugu ...	,, ...	2	2	...	...	1	1	...	...
		10 Tulukkan ...	Musalmn..	3,817	3,802	11	4	1,498	1.344	148	6
		Total group 54 ...	...	6,577	6,554	19	4	2,663	2,085	533	45

TABLE E.
Castes, &c., by Civil Condition and Age—(*Continued*).

Class.	Caste and Religion.			Total Strength—(*Continued*).							
				Females—(*Continued*).							
				15—39.				40 and over.			
	Group.	Caste, &c.	Religion.	Total.	Un-married.	Married.	Widow-ed.	Total.	Un-married.	Married.	Widow-ed.
1	2	3	4	37	38	39	40	41	42	43	44
Vagrant, &c.—(*Contd.*)	47 Jugglers, snake charmers and animal exhibitors.	Kuluvan ...	Hindu ...	14	4	10	...	6	...	5	1
		Total class E. ...	...	6,464	1,044	5,175	245	3,172	167	1,522	1,483
and Nationalities.	48 Asiatic races of reputed non-Indian descent.	1 Arab ...	Musalmn.	80	14	61	5	37	4	17	16
		2 Chinese ...	Christian..	...	...	...	...	...	...	...	...
		3 Jew ...	Jew ...	25	5	18	2	12	...	6	6
		4 Kábúl ...	Musalmn.	19	2	15	2	9	1	4	4
		5 Mughal ...	„ ...	113	23	85	5	55	2	26	27
		6 Parsi ...	Parsi ...	...	...	...	...	...	...	...	...
		7 Pathán ...	Musalmn.	783	154	594	35	370	12	179	179
		8 Sheik ...	„ ...	71	15	53	3	40	4	18	18
		9 Singhalese ...	Hindu ...	8	...	8	...	...	...	...	...
		10 Syed ...	Musalmn.	47	7	37	3	26	3	12	11
		Total group 48 ...	...	1,146	220	871	55	549	26	262	261

TABLE E.

Castes, &c., by Civil Condition and Age—(*Continued*).

Class	Group	Caste, &c.	Religion								
F. Races	50 Non-Asiatic races.	European ...	{ Chrstn / None }	74	16	52	6	35	1	19	15
	51 Eurasians...	1 East Indian ...	Christian.	438	57	366	15	207	9	112	86
		2 Eurasian ...	„ ...	123	24	86	13	37	2	18	17
		Total group 51 ...	...	561	81	452	28	244	11	130	103
	52 Christian converts.	1 Native ...	Christian.	45.698	6,116	37,739	1,843	18,594	868	10,100	7,626
		2 Syrian ...	„ ..	59,612	7,946	49,597	2,069	28,794	1,474	15,151	12,169
		Total group 52 ...	...	105,310	14,062	87,336	3,912	47,388	2,342	25,251	19,795
		Total class F. ...	...	107,091	14,379	88,711	4,001	48,216	2,380	25,662	20,174
G. Undefined.	54 Linguistic, territorial and religious names.	1 Bengalese ...	Hindu ...	...	...	...	...	...	...	...	...
		2 Guzerati ...	„ ..	11	2	9	...	3	...	3	...
		3 Jain ...	Jain ...	...	...	...	...	...	...	...	...
		4 Kannadiyan ...	Hindu ...	11	1	10	...	3	...	3	...
		5 Konkani ...	„ ...	1,507	...	1,381	126	749	...	361	388
		6 Kutch ...	Musalmn.	70	13	53	4	38	1	18	19
		7 Mussalman ..	„ ...	3,176	654	2,380	142	1,657	136	777	744
		8 Tamil ...	Hindu ..	...	...	...	...	...	...	...	...
		9 Telugu ...	„ ...	5	...	5	...	2	...	2	...
		10 Tulukkan ...	Musalmn.	5,984	1,208	4,511	265	2,916	260	1,431	1,225
		Total group 54 ...	...	10,764	1,878	8,349	537	5,368	397	2,595	2,376

TABLE E.

Castes, &c., by Civil Condition and Age—(*Continued*).

Class.	Caste and Religion.			Total Strength—(*Continued*). Males—(*Continued*). All Ages.				0—9.			
	Group.	Caste, &c.	Religion.	Total.	Un-married.	Married.	Widow-ed.	Total.	Un-married.	Married.	Widow-ed.
1	2	3	4	5	6	7	8	9	10	11	12
fined.	55 Unknown ...	1 Báláji ...	Hindu ...	77	44	30	3	19	19	...	...
		2 Bhavarási ...	„ ...	7	4	3	...	2	2	...	...
		3 Bhujār ...	„ ...	1	...	1	...	...	...	...	...
		4 Bhujavar ...	„ ...	1	...	1	...	...	...	...	...
		5 Chilambātti ...	„ ...	6	4	2	...	2	2	...	...
		6 Heathen ..	„ ...	1	...	1	...	...	...	...	...
		7 Kadiyan ...	„ ...	2	...	2	...	...	...	...	...
		8 Kámuvar ...	„ ...	2	1	1	...	...	...	...	...
		9 Kodayan ...	„ ...	3	1	2	...	...	...	...	...
		10 Kūch ...	„ ...	1	...	1	...	...	...	...	...
		11 Malayānkāran...	„ ...	146	72	69	5	36	36	...	...
		12 Mustān ...	Musalmn..	1	...	1	...	...	...	...	...
		13 Nágamom ...	Hindu ...	5	2	3	...	1	1	...	...
		14 Nálikan ...	„ ...	104	51	49	4	26	26	...	...
		15 Naralavēlu ...	„ ...	1	1	...	...	...	...	...	...
		16 Neriyan ...	„ ...	63	36	26	1	15	15	...	...
		17 Nodiyan ...	„ ...	10	6	4	...	2	2	...	...

TABLE E.

Castes, &c., by Civil Condition and Age—(*Continued*).

18 Not stated ...	Hindu / Chrstn / None	108	54	50	4	26	26	...	...
19 Pani ...	Musalmn.	425	223	176	26	108	108	...	...
20 Pattōl ...	Hindu ...	5	2	3	...	1	1	...	...
21 Sahabiti ...	" ...	1	...	1	...	...	...	...	...
22 Táli ...	" ...	1	1	...	...	..	...	...	...
23 Táttedam ...	" ...	6	3	3	...	2	2	...	...
24 Tōlar ...	" ...	4	2	2	...	1	1	...	...
Total group 55 ...	...	981	507	431	43	241	241	...	...
Total class G. ...	...	27,633	14,823	11,836	974	6,810	6,785	23	2
Grand Total ...	...	1,290,415	677,612	567,088	45,715	312,300	311,846	389	65

TABLE E.
Castes, &c., by Civil Condition and Age—(*Continued*).

Class.	Group.	Caste, &c.	Religion.	Total Strength—(Continued). Males—(Continued). 10–14. Total.	Un-married.	Married.	Widow-ed.	15–39. Total.	Un-married.	Married.	Widow-ed.
1	2	3	4	13	14	15	16	17	18	19	20
	55 Unknown ...	1 Báláji ...	Hindu ...	10	10	...	...	29	14	15	...
		2 Bhavarási ...	" ...	1	1	...	...	3	1	2	...
		3 Bhujār ..	" ...	...	...	...	...	...	...	...	...
		4 Bhujavar ...	" ...	...	...	...	...	1	...	1	...
		5 Chilambátti ..	" ...	1	1	...	...	2	1	1	...
		6 Heathen ...	" ...	...	...	...	...	1	...	1	...
		7 Kadiyan ...	" ...	...	...	...	...	1	...	1	...
		8 Kámuvar ...	" ...	...	...	...	...	1	1	...	...
		9 Kodayan ...	" ...	...	...	...	...	2	1	1	...
		10 Kūch ...	" ...	...	...	...	...	1	...	1	...
		11 Malayánkáran...	" ...	17	17	...	...	60	17	42	1
		12 Mustān ...	Musalmn.	...	...	...	...	1	...	1	...
		13 Nágamom ...	Hindu ...	...	...	...	...	3	1	2	...
		14 Nālikan ...	" ...	12	12	...	...	41	11	29	1
		15 Naralavēlu ...	" ...	...	...	...	...	1	1	...	...
		16 Neriyan ...	" ...	7	7	...	...	33	14	19	...
		17 Nodiyan ...	" ...	3	3	...	...	4	1	3	...
fined.											

TABLE E.

Castes, &c., by Civil Condition and Age—(*Continued*).

G. Unde

	Caste	Religion								
	18 Not stated ...	Hindu / Chrstn / None	12	12	...	...	47	15	31	1
	19 Pani ...	Musalmn.	44	39	5	...	189	72	114	3
	20 Pattōl ...	Hindu ...	...	...	...	...	3	1	2	...
	21 Sahabiti ...	„ ...	...	...	...	...	1	...	1	...
	22 Táli ...	„ ...	...	...	...	...	1	1	...	...
	23 Táttedam ...	„ ...	...	...	...	...	3	1	2	...
	24 Tōlar ...	„ ...	...	...	..	...	2	1	1	...
	Total group 55 ...	...	107	102	5	...	430	154	270	6
	Total class G. ...	...	2,822	2,745	75	2	12,350	5,003	7,212	135
	Grand Total ...	...	149,926	147,308	2,519	99	545,306	202,744	336,604	5,958

TABLE E.

Castes, &c., by Civil Condition and Age—(*Continued*).

Class.	Caste and Religion.			Total Strength—(*Continued*).							
	Group.	Caste, &c.	Religion.	Males—(*Continued*). 40 and over.				Females. All Ages.			
				Total.	Un-married.	Married.	Widow-ed.	Total.	Un-married.	Married.	Widow-ed.
1	2	3	4	21	22	23	24	25	26	27	28
	55 Unknown ...	1 Báláji ...	Hindu ...	19	1	15	3	20	14	5	1
		2 Bhavarási ...	„ ...	1	...	1	...	4	1	3	...
		3 Bhujár ...	„ ...	1	...	1	...	...	...	...	...
		4 Bhujavar ...	„ ...	...	...	...	...	...	...	...	...
		5 Chilambātti ...	„ ...	1	...	1	...	3	...	3	...
		6 Heathen ...	„ ...	...	...	...	...	...	...	...	...
		7 Kadiyan ...	„ ...	1	...	1	...	1	...	1	...
		8 Kámuvar ...	„ ...	1	...	1	...	...	...	...	...
		9 Kodayan ...	„ ...	1	...	1	...	12	4	8	...
		10 Kūch ...	„ ...	...	...	...	...	1	...	1	...
		11 Malayánkáran...	„ ...	33	2	27	4	100	44	44	12
		12 Mustán ...	Musalmn...	...	...	...	...	3	1	2	...
		13 Nágamom ...	Hindu ...	1	...	1	...	8	3	5	...
		14 Nálikan ...	„ ...	25	2	20	3	83	37	37	9
		15 Naralavēlu ...	„ ...	...	...	...	...	...	...	...	...
		16 Neriyan ...	„ ...	8	...	7	1	82	35	37	10
fined.		17 Nodiyan ...	„ ...	1	...	1	...	3	2	1	...

G. Unde

18 Not stated ...	Hindu / Chrstn / None	23	1	19	3	84	33	45	6
19 Pani ...	Musalmn...	84	4	57	23	473	205	198	70
20 Pattōl ...	Hindu ...	1	...	1	...	5	3	2	...
21 Sahabiti ...	„ ...	...	...	...	...	4	3	1	...
22 Táli ...	„ ...	...	...	...	...	...	...	...	...
23 Táttedam ...	„ ...	1	...	1	...	4	...	4	...
24 Tōlar ...	„ ...	1	...	1	...	2	2	...	...
Total group 55 ...	...	203	10	156	37	892	387	397	108
Total class G. ...	...	5,651	290	4,526	835	26,264	11,301	11,893	3,070
Grand Total ...	...	282,883	15,714	227,576	39,593	1,267,321	573,528	552,514	141,279

TABLE E.

Castes, &c., by Civil Condition and Age—(*Continued*).

Class.	CASTE AND RELIGION.			TOTAL STRENGTH—(*Continued*). Females—(*Continued*). 0—9.				10—14.			
	Group.	Caste, &c.	Religion.	Total.	Un-married.	Married.	Widow-ed.	Total.	Un-married.	Married.	Widow-ed.
1	2	3	4	29	30	31	32	33	34	35	36
	55 Unknown ...	1 Báláji ...	Hindu ...	6	6	...	...	1	1	...	...
		2 Bhavarāsi ...	„ ...	1	1	...	...	...	...	...	...
		3 Bhujár ...	„ ...	...	...	...	...	...	...	...	...
		4 Bhujavar ...	„ ...	...	...	...	...	...	...	...	...
		5 Chilambátti ...	„ ...	...	...	...	...	...	...	...	...
		6 Heathen ...	„ ...	...	...	...	...	...	...	...	...
		7 Kadiyan ...	„ ...	...	...	...	...	...	...	...	...
		8 Kámuvar ...	„ ...	...	...	...	...	...	...	...	...
		9 Kodayan ...	„ ...	3	3	...	...	1	1	...	...
		10 Kūch ...	„ ...	...	...	...	...	...	...	...	...
		11 Malayánkáran...	„ ...	25	25	...	...	11	10	1	...
		12 Mustán ...	Musalmn..	1	1	...	...	...	...	...	...
		13 Nágamom	Hindu ...	2	2	...	...	1	1	...	...
		14 Nálikan ...	„ ...	21	21	...	...	9	8	1	...
		15 Naralavēlu ...	„ ...	...	...	...	...	...	...	...	...
		16 Neriyan ...	„ ...	20	20	...	...	9	9	...	...
fined.		17 Nodiyan ...	„ ...	2	2	...	...	...	...	...	...

G. Unde

120

18 Not stated ...	Hindu / Chrstn / None	20	20	...	..	10	9	1	...
19 Pani ...	Musslmn ..	126	126	...	...	49	37	5	7
20 Pattōl ...	Hindu ...	3	3	...	...	...	.	...	...
21 Sahabiti ...	,, ...	3	3	...	...	...	...	..	...
22 Táli ...	,, ...	...	...	...	...	...	...	...	...
23 Táttedam ...	,, ...	...	...	...	...	...	...	...	...
24 Tōiar ...	,, ...	2	2	...	...	...	...	...	...
Total group 55 ...	...	235	235	...	...	91	76	8	7
Total class G. ...	...	6,812	6,789	19	4	2,754	2,161	541	52
Grand Total ...	...	326,777	325,515	1,151	111	137,884	124,094	13,559	231

TABLE E.

Castes, &c., by Civil Condition and Age—(*Continued*).

Class.	CASTE AND RELIGION.			TOTAL STRENGTH—(*Continued*).							
				Females—(*Continued*).							
	Group.	Caste, &c.	Religion.	15—39.				40 and over.			
				Total.	Un-married.	Married.	Widow-ed.	Total.	Un-married.	Married.	Widow-ed.
1	2	3	4	37	38	39	40	41	42	43	44
	55 Unknown ...	1 Bālāji ...	Hindu ...	9	7	2	...	4	...	3	1
		2 Bhavarāsi ...	,, ...	3	...	3	...	...	...	...	...
		3 Bhujār ...	,, ...	...	...	...	...	...	...	...	...
		4 Bhujavar ...	,, ...	...	...	...	...	...	...	...	...
		5 Chilambātti ...	,, ...	3	...	3	...	...	...	...	...
		6 Heathen ...	,, ...	...	...	...	...	...	...	...	...
		7 Kadiyan ...	,, ...	1	...	1	...	...	...	...	...
		8 Kāmuvar ...	,, ...	...	...	...	...	...	...	...	...
		9 Kodayan ...	,, ...	6	...	6	...	2	...	2	...
		10 Kūch ...	,, ...	1	...	1	...	...	...	...	...
		11 Malayānkāran ...	,, ...	43	8	34	1	21	1	9	11
		12 Mustān ...	Musslmn...	2	...	2	...	...	...	...	...
		13 Nāgamom ...	Hindu ...	4	...	4	...	1	...	1	...
		14 Nālikan ...	,, ...	38	7	29	2	15	1	7	7
		15 Naralavēlu ...	,, ...	...	...	...	...	...	...	...	...
		16 Neriyan ...	,, ...	34	5	28	1	19	1	9	9
		17 Nodiyan ...	,, ...	1	...	1	...	...	...	...	...
fined.											

Castes, &c., by Civil Condition and Age—(*Continued*).

G. Unde

18 Not stated ...	Hindu / Chrstn / None	42	4	36	2	12	...	8	4
19 Pani ...	Musslmn...	186	37	141	8	112	5	52	55
20 Pattōl ...	Hindu ...	2	...	2	...	...	...	...	...
21 Sahabiti ...	" ...	1	...	1	...	...	...	...	...
22 Tāli ...	" ...	...	...	...	...	...	...	...	...
23 Tāttedam ...	" ...	4	...	4	...	...	...	...	...
24 Tōlar ...	" ...	...	...	...	...	...	...	...	...
Total group 55 ...	...	380	68	298	14	186	8	91	87
Total class G. ...	...	11,144	1,946	8,647	551	5,554	405	2,686	2,463
Grand Total ...	...	544,843	104,040	417,451	23,352	257,817	19,879	120,353	117,585

PART III.—MISCELLANEOUS INFORMATION.

PART III.—MISCELLANEOUS INFORMATION.

[NOTE.—The following summary of the census results was submitted to the Dewan on the 23rd April 1891, soon after the Final Census was taken and was published as a Gazette Supplement. The figures given in it will not quite tally with the results of the final tabulation. For the Quilon Cantonment and the Trivandram Residency Escort figures were received subsequently from Madras and were added to the totals of those towns. The figures for Melagudalore, which had found their way by mistake into our returns, and which had been included in Periyar aud Thekkadi, were, since the summary was written, struck off our books. To these changes are due, therefore, any difference between the figures given here and the final results as shown in the body of the Report. The general conclusions, however, arrived at in the summary remain unaffected. They are in no wise different from those deduced in the Report itself.]

CENSUS CENTRAL OFFICE,
CAMP TRIVANDRAM, 23*rd April* 1891.

A.—The Census of Travancore—February 1891.

1. The results of the recent census will be briefly summarised. Our final enumeration was synchronous with that of the whole of the Indian Empire.

2. The final census was taken partly on the night of the 26th February and partly on the morning of the 27th idem—an arrangement carried out with the approval of the Madras Government, conveyed in their G.O., dated the 12th August 1890, No. 648. I had represented that the night census of the house population was specially difficult in Travancore for reasons shown in my letter to you, No. 10, dated the 18th July 1890, from which I quote the following :—

"I have the honour to inform you that I have carefully considered para. 2 of G.O., No. 402, dated 4th June 1890, Revenue, forwarded with your letter, No. $\frac{2957}{\text{M. 1267}}$, dated the 11th instant.

"Travancore comes in the class of 'Special tracts' in which a night enumeration will be impossible, on account of the wildness of the country and the peculiarly isolated condition of the bulk of our houses.

"We have in Travancore about 500,000 houses according to the census of 1881, of which more than 80 per cent. are houses situated *within enclosures*. These enclosures are generally made of strong mud or masonry walls or high fences, and access to them is by an only outer door, which, in most cases, is several yards distant from the door of the house. In the case of the well-to-do classes, the enclosure around the house covers an area of 4 or 5 acres. The inmates shut the outer door after night-fall, and in the case of the labouring population, they come home at about 6 P.M., take warm conjee and go to sleep at about 7 or even earlier. It would be impossible for the enumerator to get at either of these two classes of people referred to above, and the result will be that he may not be able to see the house-holder or talk to him on the census night. I fear the *night* census of the bulk of the Travancore population may fail. If we persist, the results will be anything but accurate.

"The system to be adopted on this occasion should be the same as that adopted in the censuses of 1875 and 1881, and which is explained in page 27 of my Census Report for 1881 thus:—

'Instruction No. 22. The final enumeration will take place at day-light on the $\frac{\text{17th February 1881}}{\text{7th Masy 1056}}$ (with one exception, which will be noticed below)'............... ..

'Instruction No. 29. It has been stated that there is an exception to the rule that the final census is to begin at day-light on the $\frac{\text{17th February 1881}}{\text{7th Masy 1056}}$. It is in the case of chatrams, ambalams, ootupurahs, inns, matams, dâk bungalows, hotels, shops, cutcherries, encampments, pagodas, churches, school-houses, cartstands, backwater stations, &c., the enumerator must proceed to these with loose forms at 8 P.M. on the night of the $\frac{\text{16th February}}{\text{6th Masy}}$ and fill them up by 12 o'clock with entries of persons found there. Travellers on the roads within the enumerator's block should also be included. Care must be taken that no canoe, boat, &c., is reckoned twice.'

"The success of both the former censuses were, I think, mostly due to this convenient arrangement.

"I am very anxious on this point, and unless Government see the real difficulties of the case, I fear the next census of February 1891 may give trouble and hardships of a kind unknown on the Madras coast. It would be a different thing if, as there, the houses are situated in clusters, called villages, and the access to each door is directly from the open street or road.

"I request you will place this information before the Madras Government and get the final enumeration of Travancore altered to the morning of the 27th February, the results being those of the previous night."

3. The order of Government, on the above, ran thus:—

"The Resident will be informed through the Political Department that under the circumstances represented a night census in Travancore will not be insisted upon. The arrangements proposed by the Dewan are approved.

(True Extract.)

(Signed) C. A. GALTON,

Secretary to Government."

4. The census commenced with a Regulation passed by H. H. the Maha Rajah on the 1st of November 1890.

5. This is the *third* systematic enumeration of the people of Travancore ordered by His Highness' Government within the memory of the present generation. The former two enumerations were in February 1875 and February 1881.

6. The night census included the enumeration of:—

(*a*) All travellers, &c., who were found at chatrams, ambalams, ootupurahs, inns, matams, dâk bungalows, hotels, shops, cutcherries, encampments, pagodas, churches, school-houses, cartstands, landing ghats and other such public places.

(*b*) Persons travelling by road on the night of the $\frac{\text{16th Masy 1066}}{\text{26th February 1891}}$ and the houseless poor.

(*c*) Passengers in ships, pathamars, &c., in dock-yards.

The morning census included the enumeration of all houses.

Rule 20 of the Final Census Instructions thus indicated the enumerator's duty on the census morning:—"On the morning of the $\frac{\text{17th Masy}}{\text{27th February}}$ the enumerator will proceed from house to house as rapidly as possible with the enumeration book previously filled up during the preliminary enumeration, summon the chief member of each family residing in the house, and read over to him the entries made for his family in the schedule. He will strike out the entries for persons who have been absent the night before, or have died since the first enumeration, and fill up the form for any person who was in the house during the night previous, but who was not there when the first visit was made, such as guests, infants newly born and others. He is to consider as having been present the night before all living in or taking their meals from the house, even though any of them may have been out fishing or watching in the fields or at a shop, &c., for the night."

7. By way of preparation for the final census, the census work was divided into three parts:—

(1) A house numbering which was taken between the $\frac{\text{10th Alpasi}}{\text{25th October}}$ and $\frac{\text{10th Kartigay 1066}}{\text{24th Novr. 1890}}$.

(2) A register of miscellaneous buildings taken between the $\frac{\text{11th and the 25th Kartigay 1066}}{\text{25th Novr. and 9th Decr. 1890}}$.

(3) And a thorough preliminary enumeration, leisurely and accurately made, between the $\frac{\text{5th Margaly 1066}}{\text{18th Decr. 1890}}$ and $\frac{\text{5th Tye 1066}}{\text{17th January 1891}}$; in some places the work continuing to $\frac{\text{20th Tye 1066}}{\text{1st February 1891}}$.

These Preliminaries were carefully and leisurely carried out with a view to the satisfactory accomplishments of the final synchronous enumeration of the whole State.

8. The whole country was divided into 12,668 blocks, over every one of which an enumerator was appointed for the final census day.

9. The British cantonment of Quilon was censused by the Officer Commanding Quilon, in accordance with the Resident's letter to you, dated Quilon, 13th December 1890, in which the Resident observed :—

"The Officer Commanding Quilon has represented to me that there are no Cantonment funds available for the census expenses in the Quilon Cantonment, and he has asked me to relieve him of the work; this I am unable to do entirely, as the Government have laid down that the census of the population in military cantonments is to be taken by military authorities. I have however arranged with him that he shall take the census *within* the boundaries shown in the enclosed sketch, and I would be much obliged if you will kindly arrange for the taking of the census outside those limits. The Officer Commanding will render your officer every assistance in his power."

The Residency escort at Trevandrum was also censused by British Officers, the Assistant Resident writing to us on the 22nd December 1890 :—

"In reference to the instructions issued by the British Resident, that the census within military limits be taken by military authorities in concert with civil authorities, I shall feel obliged by your kindly deputing an official to meet (during my absence from Trevandrum) the manager of the Resident's office, to assist him in determining the Resident's escort limits within which the census of the escort will be taken by me, so that all other limits may be censused by the Sircar officials."

So also were the people of the Periyar Project works censused by the Chief Engineer, Periyar Project, according to the Resident's letter, No. 1347, dated Trevandrum, 22nd November 1890, in which the Resident wrote :—

"The Madras Government proposes that the Chief Engineer, Periyar Project, shall, as a matter of convenience, take the census of the British camps at Periyar and Thekkadi, the schedules being subsequently transmitted to the Travancore authorities. I presume that His Highness' Government will have no objection to the proposal which will be so convenient to both parties."

10. The census schedules of these three localities named above were forwarded to the Madras Government. I have now got back those for the Periyar Project works from the Madras Census Superintendent.

11. In the hill tracts of Travancore, including most part of the Cardamom Hills' region, only a preliminary enumeration was required,

and this was satisfactorily done. Mr. Maltby, the Superintendent and Magistrate of the Cardamom Hills, writes in his letter, No. 127, dated Coomily, 7th March 1891 :—

"I have the honour to inform you that the census work is now finished, with the exception of that undertaken by the 3rd class Magistrate of Peermade, about which I have not yet had a final report; but as the work is being supervised by the supervisor you were good enough to depute to assist Mr. Beale, I feel confident that it will now be satisfactory."

12. The 3rd class Magistrate of Peermade, Mr. Beale, reported completion of his work on the 26th February 1891. With regard to a portion of his charge, he thought fit to enumerate it on the final census day, and this also was done in time, of which he reported later on thus :—

"In continuation of my letter of the 26th ultimo, I beg to report that the final census enumeration was completed yesterday, and the Forms No. III. in connection therewith have this day been despatched."

13. There was some correspondence with regard to the schedule to be adopted for this census. The one ordered by the Government of India was more complicated and contained columns for fuller details of the people than either of the forms we had adopted before. And I suggested a less ambitious schedule in the interests of an economical census; but Mr. Stuart strongly recommended the adoption of the British Indian schedule, which was subsequently agreed to by His Highness' Government on the ground pointed out by him, that it was "most desirable that the statistics relating to the population of Travancore should be uniform with those compiled for the rest of India."

14. We printed our own schedules and provided our own paper, not indenting upon the British Government for them, though they had kindly offered to supply us with the same.

15. The final census gives the following results :—

Houses	545,213
Males	1,289,012
Females	1,266,062
Total Population ...	2,555,074

This gives to every house 4·69 souls on an average, as against 4·56 souls in 1875 and 4·57 souls in 1881.

On the final census day 515,859 houses were 'occupied' and 29,354 were found 'unoccupied.' The occupied houses form 94·62 per cent. of the total.

The total population of Travancore was found thus distributed on the final census day :—

In houses	2,537,451
Travellers by road	4,414
Travellers by canal	1,985
Sea-going population	423
In public places and miscellaneous buildings	10,801
Total ...	2,555,074

99·7 per cent. of the total population were found within doors on the census night, only 6,822 persons, or 3 in a thousand, having been seen travelling.

16. On an average each enumerator's block contained 43 houses and 202 persons.

17. There are 31 taluqs in Travancore; on an average each taluq has 17,587 houses and 82,422 persons.

18. Fifteen taluqs have a population exceeding this average. The most thickly peopled taluq is Tiruvella, which has 122,142 persons, according to the census. Sherttala stood first on the occasion of the 1881 enumeration, but there have been changes in the territorial limits of taluqs since then. Some thickly-peopled villages have been transferred to the Tiruvalla taluq from Chenganur, and hence the alteration in the relative positions of the two taluqs. Quilon stands second, having a total population of 119,396. Sherttala comes third, with a population of 117,261. There are 10 taluqs in Travancore with a population of more than 100,000 in each. According to the previous census there were 8 taluqs, having each a population exceeding 100,000, while in 1875 there were only 5 such taluqs.

19 Totalling the figures for the Divisions, the results stand thus:—

Name of the Division.	Area in square miles.	Number of houses.	Total population.
Padmanabhapuram	648	79,458	350,085
Trevandrum	795	79,787	375,959
Quilon	2,607	201,548	951,219
Kottayam	2,680	184,420	877,811
Total for 4 Divisions ...	6,730	545,213	2,555,074

20. The areality of the whole State is 379 per square mile, against 343 in 1875 and 356 in 1881. Compared to other parts of India, the areality of Travancore is much greater. In the Madras Presidency it is only 248 per square mile. If we exclude from calculation the lakes, mountains and rivers and the uninhabitable and unimprovable hill tracts, the average density for Travancore comes to 609 per square mile, a state of things justifying Mr. Baines' remark that there is "very considerable congestion in the highly cultivated tracts."

21. The subjoined table gives the increases since the last census :—

Year.	Houses.	Males.	Females.	Total.
1891	545,213	1,289,012	1,266,062	2,555,074
1881	524,950	1,197,134	1,204,024	2,401,158
Increase...	20,263	91,878	62,038	153,916
Percentage of Increase..	3·85	7·67	5·15	6·41

22. The following figures show the proportion of the sexes :—

Per 1,000 *of population.*

Males	Females
504	496 ;

or for every 100 males there are 98·41 females in Travancore.

23. House-accommodation has increased by 3·8 per cent., while the total population has increased by 6·4 per cent. in 10 years. The increase in both instances is nothing abnormal. In my last Census Report (page 92) I wrote :—

" The result of the census of the Provinces and States of the British Indian Empire, where the present census is not the first, showed an increase of 12¾ millions on a population of 218 millions, *i.e.*, 6·2 per cent. on the numbers of 1871. Our census shows an increase of nearly 4 per cent. in 6 years, or which will, at that rate of increase, give 6·2 per cent. for 10 years. This is, I think, about the best proof that can be given of the accuracy of our result."

Judged by that standard, I find that the present result is accurate. The rates of increase tally so well. Considering that the increase is confined to the natural law of fecundity, and not to any appreciable influence of immigration, I think the result may be taken as quite trustworthy. There has also been increase in both the sexes, though the females seem to have increased only by 5·1 per cent. against 7·6 per cent. among males. The rates of increase do not, however, seem to be so uniform in the Madras districts. The population has increased by 4½ per cent. in Tanjore ; 13 per cent. in Madura ; 19 per cent. in South Arcot ; and 23 per cent. in Salem.

24. It was arranged that the totals were to be made up by the enumerators, and an abstract submitted in the form given in Rule

31* of the Final Enumeration Instructions; but I found that these abstracts were not reliable, as they had all been prepared in a hurry, the enumerators (most of whom were Sircar servants) having been ordered back to their permanent work the next day after the census. The foregoing results have therefore been arrived at by a tabulation of the census schedules themselves.

---

* When the work is done the enumerator will, after firmly stitching all the forms in the same book, submit them to the supervisor with a short abstract prepared in the following form. On the top of each form the enumerator should write his own name; and on the outside of the book the supervisor must write his own name. The abstract should first be prepared by the enumerator on a loose paper which should be handed to the supervisor. The supervisor should keep the paper with him and give the book to some other enumerator and tell him to prepare an abstract in the same way. On receiving the book back from him, he should himself prepare an abstract, and if all the three agree, the result may be accepted as correct. If they do not agree, all three should be carefully worked again until agreement is obtained. He will, after testing the books, forward them the same day with the abstracts to the Tahsildar for despatch to the Census Central Office.

N.B.—The supervisor will not take charge of the enumeration books until he has certified the enumerator's abstract to be correct.

Form of Enumerator's Abstract.

Proverty.	Block number.	Houses.			Other buildings.	Persons.								
						Residents.			Floating population.			Total.		
		Occupied.	Empty.	Total.		Males.	Females.	Total.	Males.	Females.	Total.	Males.	Females.	Total.

(Signed)

Enumerator.

Re-added by { (*a*) Enumerator of Block No.
(*b*) Enumerator of Block No.

Certified to have been tested and the total found correct.

(Signed)

Supervisor.

25. The filled-in schedule-books reached the Census Central Office by the 7th Panguni 1066 / 19th March 1891, *i.e.*, the 20th day after the final enumeration. The records were arranged and the total results were abstracted from them, in 17 days thereafter.

26. The results thus tabulated were telegraphed to the Imperial Census Commissioner, Simla, to the British Resident, and to the Census Superintendent of Madras, on the 6th and 7th April 1891, *i.e.*, within 37 days after the final census.

27. The rough totals summarised from the enumerators' abstracts had already been telegraphed to them on the 23rd and 25th March last, *i.e.*, within 24 days after the final enumeration.

The Census Commissioner remarked in his letter to the Government of India on the recent census that the rough totals for the whole of the Indian Empire were ready in 5 weeks after the final census.

28. With regard to the enumerators' abstracts, Mr. Baines writes :—

"The above is the system of communication prescribed, but whether it was in all cases duly observed, I am, of course, unable to say.

"Neither the Provincial Superintendents nor I myself have as yet had an opportunity of testing these summaries, but I have no reason to think that their accuracy is impaired by the speed with which they were compiled."

29. The number of columns in the schedule of 1875 A.D was 10; of 1881, 8; and of 1891 is 14.

30. No obstacles are reported to have occurred in the taking of the census.

31. No part of Travancore was, on any account, omitted from the enumeration.

32. No person was punished under the Census Regulation.

33. More than 5,500 schedules were filled in by the householders themselves and handed over to the enumerators. These were carefully checked.

34. This is the first time that we have been able to census the principal towns of Travancore as such. The limits of each town

were defined, in time, and enumerators were appointed for them, separately; on this point I remarked in my last Census Report (page 276) :—

"Since the census, an attempt has been made to distinguish in the schedules, those for the principal towns from the rest. Our towns have no defined limits, and therefore for census purposes, the taluqs and the revenue divisions thereof, known as Proverties and Karas, were adopted. The Kara was taken as the unit of census operations. All the statistics tabulated are for these minute sub-divisions, Karas. It was ascertained from local officers, what Karas and portions of Karas were comprised in the principal towns, and the figures so totalled were submitted to the Imperial Census Commissioner, for 7 towns in Travancore."

We have now been able to cure this defect of the former census. In deciding what were towns, for census purposes, we followed the dictum laid down by Mr. McIver, in para. 720 of his Census Report that "size, compactness, and certain architectural, commercial or industrial features are all considerations which would go to make up the definition of a town."

35. Two statements (Forms A. and B.) sent to the Census Commissioner and the Census Superintendent are subjoined for your information.

36. The work of tabulation commenced a month ago and is being vigorously pushed on. 105 clerks have already been entertained as tabulators. I expect the whole work of abstraction, tabulation and compilation to be finished in about 3 months.

(Signed) V. NAGAM AIYA,
Dewan Peishcar and Census Commissioner,
Travancore.

FORM A.

CENSUS OF INDIA, 1891.

Total of results tabulated from census schedules.

District (State of Travancore).

Name of town or cantonment.	Occupied houses.	Population. Total.	Males.	Females.	Remarks :—(*E.g.*, extension or decrease of town or district limits since 1881, &c.)
1	2	3	4	5	6
Trivandram ...	4,712	27,661	14,580	13,081	
Alleppey ...	4,505	22,768	11,286	11,482	
Quilon ...	2,259	12,836	6,514	6,322	
Quilon Cantonment*	—	—	—	—	
Nagercoil ...	2,475	11,187	5,335	5,852	
Shenkotta ...	2,121	8,727	4,202	4,525	
Vykkam ...	1,493	7,769	4,113	3,656	
Kottayam ...	1,310	7,090	3,539	3,551	
Aripaud ...	1,433	6,890	3,448	3,442	
A. Total Urban area.	20,308	104,928	53,017	51,911	
B. Total Rural area ..	495,551	2,450,146	1,235,995	1,214,151	
Grand Total ...	515,859	2,555,074	1,289,012	1,266,062	

* This cantonment has been censused by the Regimental Officers and the schedules sent by them to the Madras Census Office through the British Resident. That result is therefore not included here.

Despatched on the 17th April 1891.

(Signed) V. NAGAM AIYA,
Census Commissioner for Travancore.

FORM B.

CENSUS OF INDIA, 1891.

District (State of Travancore).

Taluq.	Name of town, cantonment, &c., and total of rural areas.	Occupied houses.	Persons.		
			Males.	Females.	Total.
Tovala ...	*Towns* ...	...	...	...	...
	Total, *Rural area*..	7,084	14,489	15,262	29,751
	Total, Taluq ...	7,084	14,489	15,262	29,751
Agastiswaram ..	*Town*, Nagercoil.	2,475	5,335	5,852	11,187
	Total, *Rural area*..	17,172	37,891	38,163	76,054
	Total, Taluq ...	19,647	43,226	44,015	87,241
Eranial ...	*Towns* ...	...	...	...	...
	Total, *Rural area*..	22,208	52,883	52,215	105,098
	Total, Taluq ...	22,208	52,883	52,215	105,098
Kalkulam ...	*Towns* ...	...	...	...	...
	Total, *Rural area*..	12,561	29,834	29,640	59,474
	Total, Taluq ...	12,561	29,834	29,640	59,474
Vilavankodu ...	*Towns* ...	...	...		...
	Total, *Rural area*..	13,036	35,202	33,319	68,521
	Total, Taluq ...	13,036	35,202	33,319	68,521
Neyattankara...	*Towns* ...	...	...	...	...
	Total, *Rural area*..	22,266	56,953	53,802	110,755
	Total, Taluq ...	22,266	56,953	53,802	110,755
Trivandram ...	*Town*, Trivandram...	4,712	14,580	13,081	27,661
	Total, *Rural area*..	16,769	42,202	41,849	84,051
	Total, Taluq ...	21,481	56,782	54,930	111,712
Nedumangadu..	*Towns* ...	...	...	...	...
	Total, *Rural area*..	11,633	27,857	27,640	55,497
	Total, Taluq ...	11,633	27,857	27,640	55,497

FORM B.

CENSUS OF INDIA, 1891—(*Continued*).

District (State of Travancore).

Taluq.	Name of town, cantonment, &c., and total of rural areas.	Occupied houses.	Persons. Males.	Persons. Females.	Persons. Total.
Sirayinkil ...	*Towns* ...	...	...	...	...
	Total, *Rural area*..	19,612	48,271	49,724	97,995
	Total, Taluq ...	19,612	48,271	49,724	97,995
Kottarakkara....	*Towns* ...	...	...	...	...
	Total, *Rural area*..	13,684	36,055	35,462	71,517
	Total, Taluq ...	13,684	36,055	35,462	71,517
Pattanapuram ..	*Towns* ...	...	...	...	...
	Total, *Rural area*..	7,915	19,858	19,589	39,447
	Total, Taluq ...	7,915	19,858	19,589	39,447
Shenkotta ...	*Town*, Shenkotta.	2,121	4,202	4,525	8,727
	Total, *Rural area*..	5,572	11,498	11,863	23,361
	Total, Taluq ...	7,693	15,700	16,388	32,088
Quilon ...	Town, Quilon...	2,259	6,514	6,322	12,836
	Cantonment do.*..	...	...	...	...
	Total, *Town*...	2,259	6,514	6,322	12,836
	Total, *Rural area*..	19,921	52,961	53,599	106,560
	Total, Taluq ...	22,180	59,475	59,921	119,396
Kunnattur ...	*Towns* ...	..	...	...	...
	Total, *Rural area*..	14,789	37,397	36,132	73,529
	Total, Taluq ...	14,789	37,397	36,132	73,529
Karunagappalli.	*Towns* ...	...	...	...	...
	Total, *Rural area*..	23,223	52,862	55,964	108,826
	Total, Taluq ...	23,223	52,862	55,964	108,826

* This cantonment has been censused by the Regimental Officers and the schedules sent by them to the Madras Census Office through the British Resident. That result is therefore not included here.

FORM B.

CENSUS OF INDIA, 1891—(*Continued*).

District (State of Travancore).

TALUQ.	Name of town, cantonment, &c., and total of rural areas.	Occupied houses.	PERSONS.		
			Males.	Females.	Total.
Kartigappalli...	*Town*, Aripaud...	1,433	3,448	3,442	6,890
	Total, *Rural area*..	16,873	41,768	43,292	85,060
	Total, Taluq ...	18,306	45,216	46,734	91,950
Mavellikkara ...	*Towns* ...	...	...	...	...
	Total, *Rural area*..	21,718	52,494	51,125	103,619
	Total, Taluq ...	21,718	52,494	51,125	103,619
Chenganur ...	*Towns* ...	...	...	...	...
	Total, *Rural area*..	18,605	48,443	45,517	93,960
	Total, Taluq ...	18,605	48,443	45,517	93,960
Tiruvalla ...	*Towns* ...	...	...	...	...
	Total, *Rural area*..	24,247	62,514	59,628	122,142
	Total, Taluq ...	24,247	62,514	59,628	122,142
Ambalappula...	*Town*, Alleppey ..	4,505	11,286	11,482	22,768
	Total, *Rural area*..	14,215	35,623	36,354	71,977
	Total, Taluq ...	18,720	46,909	47,836	94,745
Sherttala ...	*Towns* ...	...	...	...	...
	Total, *Rural area*..	28,571	58,448	58,813	117,261
	Total, Taluq ...	28,571	58,448	58,813	117,261
Vykkam ...	*Town*, Vykkam...	1,493	4,113	3,656	7,769
	Total, *Rural area*..	16,086	36,834	36,025	72,859
	Total, Taluq ...	17,579	40,947	39,681	80,628
Ettumanur ...	*Towns* ...	...	...	...	...
	Total, *Rural area*..	15,580	41,536	39,287	80,823
	Total, Taluq ...	15,580	41,536	39,287	80,823

FORM B.

CENSUS OF INDIA, 1891—(*Continued*).

District (State of Travancore .

Taluq.	Name of town, cantonment, &c., and total of rural areas.	Occupied houses.	Persons.		
			Males.	Females.	Total.
Kottayam ...	*Town*, Kottayam.	1,310	3,539	3,551	7,090
	Total, *Rural area*..	13,695	35,690	34,314	70,004
	Total, Taluq ...	15,005	39,229	37,865	77,094
Changana-cheri.	*Towns* ...	...	...	...	...
	Total, *Rural area*..	14,658	38,596	36,126	74,722
	Total, Taluq ...	14,658	38,596	36,126	74,722
Meenachal ...	*Towns* ...	...	...	...	...
	Total, *Rural area*..	11,420	30,830	29,146	59,976
	Total, Taluq ...	11,420	30,830	29,146	59,976
Muvattupula ...	*Towns* ...	...	...	...	...
	Total, *Rural area*..	20,387	51,595	51,414	103,009
	Total, Taluq ...	20,387	51,595	51,414	103,009
Todupula ...	*Towns* ...	...	...	...	...
	Total, *Rural area*..	5,025	12,786	12,416	25,202
	Total, Taluq ...	5,025	12,786	12,416	25,202
Kunnattunadu..	*Towns* ...	...	...	...	...
	Total, *Rural area*..	20,702	57,216	56,833	114,049
	Total, Taluq ...	20,702	57,216	56,833	114,049
Alangadu ...	*Towns* ...	...	...	...	...
	Total, *Rural area*..	13,183	35,944	35,014	70,958
	Total, Taluq ...	13,183	35,944	35,014	70,958
Paravoor ...	*Towns* ...	...	...	...	...
	Total, *Rural area*..	10,729	30,082	29,196	59,278
	Total, Taluq ...	10,729	30,082	29,196	59,278

FORM B.

CENSUS OF INDIA, 1891—(*Concluded*).

District (State of Travancore).

TALUQ.	Name of town, cantonment, &c., and total of rural areas.	Occupied houses.	PERSONS.		
			Males.	Females.	Total.
Cardamom Hills.	*Towns* ...	...	...	...	...
	Total, *Rural area*..	1,754	6,714	4,699	11,413
	Total ...	1,754	6,714	4,699	11,413
Periyar and Thekkadi.	*Towns* ...	..	...	...	...
	Total, *Rural area*..	658	2,669	729	3,398
	Total ...	658	2,669	729	3,398
Grand Total...	*Towns* ..	20,308	53,017	51,911	104,928
	Rural tracts ...	495,551	1,235,995	1,214,151	2,450,146
	Total ...	515,859	1,289,012	1,266,062	2,555,074

N.B.—The Cardamom Hills and the Periyar works were separately censused and not by the Taluq authorities; hence they are separately shown in the foregoing table.

20th April 1891.

(Signed) V. NAGAM AIYA,
Census Commissioner for Travancore.

B.—CASTE INDEX.

The following castes are included in the accompanying Index :—

Number.	Caste, &c.	No. of recorded subdivisions.	Group.
1	Ainuttar	...	24
2	Aiyengar	2	5
3	Akkaradési	...	5
4	Alava	1	30
5	Ambalakaran	...	1
6	Ambalavāsi	16	7
7	Arabs	2	48
8	Ariapattar	1	5
9	Āsári	5	20
10	Āttidaya	...	26
11	Báláji	1	55
12	Balija	11	14
13	Balukar	...	15
14	Baniya*	...	14
15	Bengalese	...	54
16	Bhattadiri	...	5
17	Bhavarāsi	...	55
18	Bhujār	...	55
19	Bhujavar	...	55
20	Brahmin	...	5
21	Canarese Brahmin	...	5
22	Chákkár	...	35a
23	Chaluppan	...	35
24	Chānnān	11	36
25	Chekkála	3	27
26	Chembutatti	...	21
27	Chemmán	6	38
28	Chetti	28	14
29	Chilambátti	...	55
30	Chinese	...	48
31	Dáss	...	39
32	Dhoby	...	24
33	East Indian	...	51
34	Embrán	2	5
35	Eurasian	...	51
36	European	10	50
37	Fakkir	...	6
38	Foreign Brahmin	...	5
39	Gavarulu	...	2a
40	Gollalu	1	26
41	Gopāl	...	46
42	Gosains	1	6
43	Gouda Brahmin	4	5
44	Guzaratti	...	54
45	Heathens	...	55
46	Hindustani Brahmin	...	5
47	Idaya	9	26
48	Idiyar	...	22a
49	Ilavāniyan	...	14
50	Ílavati	...	18
51	Ilayadu	4	5
52	Īluva	7	36
53	Iruler	...	4
54	Jain	...	54
55	Jonaka	1	14
56	Jew	...	48
57	Kábúl	...	48
58	Kadiyan	...	55
59	Káhár	...	35
60	Kákkálan	1	45
61	Kallásári	3	40
62	Kammālan	4	17a
63	Kamsála	...	17a
64	Kámuvur	...	55
65	Kanakkan	...	2c
66	Kāngaya	...	26
67	Kaniyán	1	10
68	Kannadasta	...	5
69	Kannadiyan	...	54
70	Kannān	3	21
71	Karayalar	...	2a
72	Kartavu	...	1
73	Kāsi Brahmin	...	5
74	Káttar	...	4
75	Kattaran	...	2a
76	Kattilaya	...	4
77	Kattu Parisha (Forest tribe)	...	4

* Belong partly to the Hindus and partly to the Jains.

Number.	Caste, &c.	No. of recorded subdivisions.	Group.	Number.	Caste, &c.	No. of recorded subdivisions.	Group.
78	Kávadi ...	2	18	120	Mussalman ...	1	54
79	Kēsiar ...	...	5	121	Mustán ...	...	55
80	Khond ...	1	4	122	Mynáta ...	...	4
81	Kodayan ...	...	55				
82	Kodipattan ...	...	2a	123	Nádipanikan ...	...	4
83	Koiltamburan ...	...	1	124	Nágamom ...	...	55
84	Kollan ...	3	19	125	Nair ...	75	1
85	Kómaran ...	...	18	126	Nālikan ...	...	55
86	Konkanese ...	8	54	127	Nambiyán ...	...	5
87	Kóri ...	...	23	128	Nambudiri ...	3	5
88	Kosava ...	5	28	129	Naralavēlu ...	...	55
89	Krishnanvagá ...	...	7	130	Native Christian ...	3	52
90	Kshatriya ...	7	1	131	Neriyan ...	...	55
91	Ksbourakan ...	9	18	132	Nodiyan ...	..	55
92	Kúch ...	...	55	133	Nolayan ...	1	43
93	Kuluvan ...	1	47	134	Not stated† ..	...	55
94	Kuravar ...	7	2c				
95	Kuruni ...	...	2a	135	Ostta ...	2	18
96	Kutch ...	3	54	136	Ottan ...	...	41
97	Kúttádi ...	...	46	137	Ottiya ...	...	41
98	Kūttidaya ...	..	26				
				138	Padayáchi ...	...	2c
99	Labbai ...	...	14	139	Pallan ...	...	2c
100	Lōhar ...	...	19	140	Pānān ...	3	22
101	Lōti ...	...	2a	141	Pandala ...	...	1
				142	Pāni ...	...	55
102	Mahratta ...	...	1	143	Pania ...	...	4
103	Mahratta Brahmin ...	2	5	144	Pandi Sudra ...	8	2a
104	Malayala Brahmin ...	...	5	145	Panisivan ...	...	45a
105	Malayánkáran ...	...	55	146	Paravan ...	1	31
106	Malayarien ...	1	4	147	Pariah‡ ...	9	2c
107	Malli ...	...	2a	148	Parsi ...	...	48
108	Manikár ...	..	15	149	Pashi ...	...	36
109	Maṇṇan ...	2	24	150	Pássiavan ...	...	45
110	Marakkán* ...	2	35	151	Pathán ...	...	48
111	Márán ...	12	18	152	Patnúl ...	...	23
112	Maravar ...	7	1	153	Pattōl ...	...	55
113	Mariya ...	...	4	154	Pilappalli ...	...	7
114	Méttan ...	1	14	155	Pōudan ...	8	35
115	Mudali ...	5	2a	156	Poumany Gramom ...	...	5
116	Mudayar ...	...	22a	157	Pôtti ...	4	5
117	Muduvan ...	...	4	158	Pulaya ...	5	2c
118	Mughul ...	...	48	159	Pulluvan ...	...	10
119	Mukkuvan ..	5	35	160	Rajaput ...	1	1

* Partly Mussalman and partly Christian.

† To be found among the Hindus, Christians and those of no religion.

‡ Belong partly to the Hindu and partly to the Christian religions.

Number.	Caste, &c.	No. of recorded subdivisions.	Group.	Number.	Caste, &c.	No. of recorded subdivisions.	Group.
161	Rāju ...	1	1	185	Táttedam ...	...	55
162	Ráwut ...	...	14	186	Telugu ...	..	54
				187	Telugu Brahmin ...	4	5
163	Sahabiti ...	...	55	188	Tirumulpád ...	...	1
164	Sále ...	5	23	189	Tiruvalládesi ...	...	5
165	Sámantakar ...	...	1	190	Tólar ...	...	55
166	Sangom Pandáram ...	10	45*a*	191	Trippunittoraidési ...	...	5
167	Sanniyási ...	...	6	192	Tulukkan ...	...	54
168	Sátáni ...	1	7				
169	Sheik ...	...	48	193	Udaya ...	...	2*c*
170	Singálese ...	...	48	194	Ulládan ..	...	2*c*
171	Surveriya ...	...	5	195	Unniyádiri ...	...	1
172	Syed ...	...	48				
173	Syrian ...	5	52	196	Vaduka ...	13	14
				197	Vaisya ...	...	14
174	Tachan ...	1	20	198	Valamalu ...	...	2*a*
175	Tákur ...	...	8	199	Valluvan ...	1	39
176	Talavan ...	..	44	200	Vánian ...	3	27
177	Tāli ...	...	55	201	Védan ...	1	44
178	Tamil ...	...	54	202	Vélan ...	2	4
179	Tamil Brahmin ...	17	5	203	Vellálá ..	14	2*a*
180	Tampān ...	...	1	204	Vellōdi ...	...	1
181	Tańdán ...	3	36	205	Velutadan ...	6	24
182	Tangal ...	...	5	206	Vettáran ...	...	44
183	Taravan ...	...	18	207	Vettuvan ...	...	2*c*
184	Tattān ...	4	17	208	Vyravi ...	2	6

LIST OF CASTE NAMES IN TRAVANCORE.

Serial No.	Caste.	Serial No.	Subdivisions.	Numbers of important subdivisions.
1	Ainuttar.			
2	Aiyengar ...	1	Tengalay ...	309
		2	Vedagalay ...	289
3	Akkaradési.			
4	Alava ...	3	Uppalava.	
5	Ambalakáran.			
6	Ambalavasi ...	4	Adiyodi.	
		5	Āládi.	
		6	Brahmani.	
		7	Chákkiyár ...	63
		8	Daivampádi.	
		9	Kurukkal ...	812
		10	Mūthathu ...	516
		11	Nambidi.	
		12	Nambiyár ...	960
		13	Pattarunni ...	297
		14	Psharodi ...	345
		15	Puduvál.	
		16	Pushpakan ...	669
		17	Tīyattunni.	
		18	Unni ...	487
		19	Várriar ...	2,434
7	Ariapattar ...	20	Túthen.	
8	Āsári ...	21	Kadasakkáran.	
		22	Malayala Āsári ..	8,277
		23	Marapanikkan.	
		24	Pándi Āsári ...	2,119
		25	Sudra Āsári ...	300
9	Āttidaya.			
10	Bālāji ...	26	Gentu.	
11	Balija ...	27	Gazulu.	
		28	Golla Balija.	
		29	Horagzoa.	
		30	Kamma.	
		31	Kappu.	
		32	Kavarachetti.	
		33	Rawut.	
		34	Saharia.	
		35	Sindhulu.	
		36	Vádu.	
		37	Yahaba.	
12	Balukar.			
13	Baniya.			
14	Bengalese.			
15	Bhattadiri.			
16	Bhavarasi.			
17	Bhujār.			

Serial No.	CASTE.	Serial No.	Subdivisions.	Numbers of important subdivisions.
18	Bhujavar.			
19	Brahmin.			
20	Canarese Brahmin.			
21	Chākkár.			
22	Chaluppan.			
23	Chánnán ...	38	Ilaya chánnän.	
		39	Kavaluda chánnán.	
		40	Kavara chànnán.	
		41	Kiriyattu channán ...	563
		42	Mútta chánnán.	
		43	Nádán ...	721
		44	Pēragathu chánnàn.	
		45	Periyanáttu chánnán.	
		46	Tiruppáppur chànnān ...	327
		47	Udayāda chánnán.	
		48	Valankaiuyarvu kondón.	
24	Chekkāla ...	49	Āttáchekkala.	
		50	Pulva.	
		51	Sudra chekkála.	
25	Chembutatti.			
26	Chemmán ...	52	Chakkiliyan ...	644
		53	Tugal chemmán.	
		54	Urakáran.	
		55	Vilkollan.	
		56	Vilkuruppu.	
		57	Villásān ...	622
27	Chetti ...	58	Beri chetti.	
		59	Chozhia.	
		60	Kala chetti ...	499
		61	Kalavánibha chetti.	
		62	Karnádattár.	
		63	Karuman chetti.	
		64	Kavara chetti ...	428
		65	Komatti.	
		66	Konaka chetti ...	402
		67	Kosa chetti.	
		68	Kudumi chetti ...	2,038
		69	Mahrashtra chetti.	
		70	Malayala chetti ...	1,063
		71	Mallika chetti.	
		72	Nánjanád chetti.	
		73	Náttukótta chetti ...	304
		74	Núl chetti ...	466
		75	Pandi chetti.	
		76	Pattaria chetti.	
		77	Pāttra chetti.	
		78	Sátriya.	
		79	Sripandára chetti ...	851
		80	Sudra chetti ...	1,051
		81	Tamil.	

Serial No.	Caste.	Serial No.	Subdivisions.	Numbers of important subdivisions.
		82	Telugu chetti.	
		83	Tēvángu chetti.	
		84	Vellala.	
		85	Vellala chetti	1,647
28	Chilambātti.			
29	Dass.			
30	Dhoby.			
31	Embrān ...	86	Murukunād.	
		87	Tulunád.	
32	Foreign Brahmin.			
33	Gavarulu.			
34	Gollalu ...	88	Allagollalu.	
35	Gopāl.			
36	Gosains ...	89	Ládan.	
37	Gouda Brahmins ...	90	Cawnporian.	
		91	Kanoujian.	
		92	Pancha gouda.	
		93	Rajaput.	
38	Guzaratti.			
39	Heathens.			
40	Hindustani Brahmin.			
41	Idaya	94	Ādimámunivar.	
		95	Angámmālaparisha.	
		96	Kónan.	
		97	Nambi Idaya.	
		98	Nandagopa.	
		99	Vadukidaya.	
		100	Vala Idaya.	
		101	Yádavan.	
		102	Yadavan Tengala.	
42	Idiyar.			
43	Ilavaniyan.			
44	Īlaváti.			
45	Ilayadu ...	103	Kovilitti.	
		104	Nambiyādi ...	578
		105	Onnámparisha.	
		106	Randāmparisha.	
46	Īluva ...	107	Chērillom.	
		108	Chónigom.	
		109	Chóvan ...	10,241
		110	Mūttilom.	
		111	Pándi Iluva ...	2,457
		112	Panikkan.	
		113	Tīyan ...	559
47	Iruler. ...			
48	Kadiyan.			
49	Káhár.			
50	Kákkálan ...	114	Kákkān.	
51	Kallásāri ...	115	Kallan.	
		116	Pandi Kallásári.	
		117	Silpásári.	

Serial No.	Caste.	Serial No.	Subdivisions.	Numbers of important subdivisions.
52	Kammála ...	118	Kuruppu Kammála.	
		119	Pandi Kammala.	
		120	Pitcha Kannala.	
		121	Sudra Kammála.	
53	Kamsála.			
54	Kámuvar.			
55	Kanakkan.			
56	Kangaya.			
57	Kaniyán ...	122	Kanikuruppu.	
58	Kannadasta.			
59	Kannadiyan.			
60	Kannán ...	123	Musári ...	733
		124	Pandi Kannán.	
		125	Sudra Kannán.	
61	Karayalar.			
62	Kartávu.			
63	Kási Brahmin.			
64	Kāttar.			
65	Kattáran.			
66	Káttilaya.			
67	Káttuparisha (Forest tribe).			
68	Kavadi ...	126	Kiriyattu kávadi.	
		127	Pránópakari.	
69	Késiar.			
70	Khond ...	128	Khondan káppil.	
71	Kodayan.			
72	Kodipattan.			
73	Koiltamburan.			
74	Kollan ...	129	Panakáran.	
		130	Pándi kollan.	
		131	Sudra kollan.	
75	Kómaram.			
76	Konkani ...	132	Kási.	
		133	Konkana Brahmin ...	5,010
		134	Pattar.	
77	Kóri.			
78	Kosava ...	135	Kulāla.	
		136	Ōdan.	
		137	Saliyaváhana.	
		138	Vélán ...	3,587
		139	Viswa brahma	
79	Krishnanvaga.			
80	Kshatriya ...	140	Kásibát.	
		141	Kodam.	
		142	Koil Adhikari.	
		143	Kudumbi.	
		144	Nārai.	
		145	Rajavamsom.	
		146	Somavamsom.	
81	Kshourakan ...	147	Ambattan ...	427

Serial No.	Caste.	Serial No.	Subdivisions.	Numbers of important subdivisions.
		148	Hajám.	
		149	Idanásuvan.	
		150	Katti.	
		151	Kudimakan.	
		152	Náviten.	
		153	Pandi Kshourakan.	
		154	Pranópakári	1,410
		155	Vilakkitalavan.	
82	Kúch.			
83	Kuluvan	156	Tottian.	
84	Kurava	157	Arikurava.	
		158	Kākkakurava	236
		159	Kundakurava.	
		160	Malakurava.	
		161	Malayámkurava.	
		162	Nádikurava.	
		163	Nánjikurava.	
85	Kuruni.			
86	Kūttádi.			
87	Kūttidaya.			
88	Lóhar.			
89	Lōti.			
90	Mahratta.			
91	Mahratta Brahmin	164	Desasth.	
		165	Row.	
92	Malayala Brahmin.			
93	Malayánkáran.			
94	Malayarien	166	Arayan	1,632
95	Malli.			
96	Manikār.			
97	Mannān	167	Alakkuvélan.	
		168	Padiyan	900
98	Márán	169	Karivelamārán.	
		170	Kosamárán.	
		171	Kuruppu.	
		172	Mangalliyam	535
		173	Nambi kuruppu.	
		174	Ochan	231
		175	Pandi Ochan.	
		176	Pársaiva.	
		177	Pulikkapanikkan.	
		178	Sītikan	558
		179	Vádiyakkáran.	
		180	Vádiyapanikkan.	
99	Marava	181	Cherutáliketti.	
		182	Kallen.	
		183	Kondaketti	840
		184	Kondayankáttan.	
		185	Kottáli.	
		186	Tevan.	

Serial No.	Caste.	Serial No.	Subdivisions.	Numbers of important Sub-divisions.
		187	Vanniya Tēvan.	
100	Mariya.			
101	Mudali ...	188	Kaikkalava ...	414
		189	Paradesa Mudali.	
		190	Tondamandalam.	
		191	Vadadesa Mudali.	
		192	Vellala Mudali.	
102	Mudayar.			
103	Muduvan.			
104	Mukkuvan ...	193	Chavalakkāran ...	1,785
		194	Kattikkāran.	
		195	Marakkan. ...	10,053
		196	Valakkaran.	
		197	Vālen ...	11,935
105	Mynāta.			
106	Nadipanikkan.			
107	Nagamom.			
108	Nair ...	198	Alanáttu Nair.	
		199	Chekkála Nair ...	5,312
		200	Chérákuruppu.	
		201	Chérillattu Nair.	
		202	Ettuvīdan.	
		203	Guru Nair.	
		204	Idashéri Nair ...	18,083
		205	Ilayidam.	
		206	Illattu Nair ...	256,527
		207	Kalarikuruppu.	
		208	Karichān Nair.	
		209	Karivélattu Nair ...	4,464
		210	Kiriyattu Nair ...	30,448
		211	Kochillattu Nair.	
		212	Kokkara Nair.	
		213	Kólattu Nair.	
		214	Kūlappara Nair.	
		215	Kuruppu Nair.	
		216	Kykkara Kuruppu.	
		217	Kymmal.	
		218	Kyppalli Nair.	
		219	Mádambi.	
		220	Mala Nair.	
		221	Malayala Sudra.	
		222	Malayáttūr Nair.	
		223	Māmpalli vátti.	
		224	Manamangalattu Nair.	
		225	Mangalattu Nair.	
		226	Manigramom.	
		227	Maniillattunair.	
		228	Menone.	
		229	Nallūr Nair.	
		230	Nanduni Kuruppu.	

Serial No.	Caste.	Serial No.	Subdivisions.	Numbers of important subdivisions.
		231	Nanduni Nair.	
		232	Nanduni panikkar.	
		233	Neduvaliswarúpattu Nair.	
		234	Neduvila Nair.	
		235	Neduvilaswarúpattu Nair.	
		236	Otti Nair.	
		237	Pādamangalam ...	3,632
		238	Pada Nair.	
		239	Pallichán Nair ...	2,432
		240	Panakkel Nair.	
		241	Pandári.	
		242	Pándiillom.	
		243	Panikkar.	
		244	Paravurswarūpattu Nair.	
		245	Parisapanikkar.	
		246	Pariyapádu Nair.	
		247	Pattáli Nair.	
		248	Pattukáppu Nair.	
		249	Pattu vīdan.	
		250	Periyanáttillattu Nair.	
		251	Perungáli Nair.	
		252	Pérur Nair.	
		253	Párurswarupattu Nair.	
		254	Ponnarapanikkar.	
		255	Pulikka Nair ...	1,810
		256	Pūppada Kuruppu.	
		257	Puttúr Nair.	
		258	Sripadattuillom.	
		259	Sudra.	
		260	Swarupam ...	88,482
		261	Talippan Nair.	
		262	Tamilpádam ...	901
		263	Tunjattu Náir.	
		264	Unnittán.	
		265	Vadakattu Nair.	
		266	Valikka Nair.	
		267	Vandikkáran.	
		268	Vátti.	
		269	Veliyattu Nair.	
		270	Velùlr Nair.	
		271	Venchanattuswarùpùm.	
		272	Vikkala Kuruppu.	
109	Nálikan.			
110	Nambiyán.			
111	Nambudiri. ...	273	Āddiyan.	
		274	Ōthu.	
		275	Yāthrakkali ...	163
112	Naralavélu.			
113	Neriyan.			
114	Nodiyan.			

Serial No.	Caste.	Serial No.	Subdivisions.	Numbers of important subdivisions.
115	Nolayan ...	276	Arayan.	
116	Not stated.			
117	Ottan.			
118	Ottiya.			
119	Padayachi.			
120	Pallan.			
121	Pánán	277	Tayyápánán.	
		278	Tunnal.	
		279	Tūsi vellála.	
122	Pandala.			
123	Pándi Sudra ...	280	Dási ...	1
		281	Devadásan ...	52
		282	Devaradiyál ...	19
		283	Madamudalikurukkal.	
		284	Nánjanád Sudra ...	444
		285	Nattuvan ...	183
		286	Paradesa Sudra.	
124	Pania.			
125	Panisivan ...	287	Pūsari.	
126	Paravan ...	288	Chunnambu paravan.	
127	Pariah ...	289	Chámban.	
		290	Chandāla ...	674
		291	Kiriyattu pariah.	
		292	Kollā pariah.	
		293	Kolliyan.	
		294	Pándi pariah.	
		295	Perum pariah.	
		296	Thīnda pariah.	
		297	Vempariah.	
128	Pashi.			
129	Passiavan.			
130	Patnul.			
131	Pattól.			
132	Pilappalli.			
133	Póndan ...	298	Bogi.	
		299	Pallichān.	
		300	Palli Sévugan.	
134	Ponmany Gramom.			
135	Pótti ...	301	Karnátaka.	
		302	Srīvalli.	
		303	Tulunád.	
		304	Vellan.	
136	Pulaya ...	305	Kákkapulaya.	
		306	Kaluttanattu Kúttam.	
		307	Muttathi Kúttam ...	13,110
		308	Palli Kūttam	
		309	Pullen.	
137	Pulluvan.			
138	Rajaput ...	310	Singh.	
139	Raju ...	311	Konda Raju.	

Serial No.	Caste.	Serial No.	Subdivisions.	Numbers of important subdivisions.
140	Sahabiti.			
141	Salé ...	312	Kaichaliyan.	
		313	Kaikkalava.	
		314	Kudumicháliyan ...	852
		315	Pattakachāliyan ..	1,047
		316	Pattárien.	
142	Samantakar.			
143	Sangompandáram ...	317	Bhikshapandáram.	
		318	Chettipandáram.	
		319	Madapatipandáram.	
		320	Naickenpandáram.	
		321	Pallipandáram.	
		322	Pandáram ...	6,017
		323	Paradési.	
		324	Parppadakapandáram.	
		325	Táthanpandáram.	
		326	Vyravi pandáram.	
144	Sanniyási.			
145	Sátáni ...	327	Satani tengala.	
146	Singálese.			
147	Surveriya.			
148	Tachan ...	328	Kóltachan.	
149	Tákur.			
150	Talavan.			
151	Táli.			
152	Tamil.			
153	Tamil Brahmin.	329	Aiyer.	
		330	Ashtasahasrom ...	1,460
		331	Brahacharanom ...	3,345
		332	Chóladésom ...	527
		333	Dravida Brahmin ...	3,854
		334	Kolakkátan.	
		335	Margathu.	
		336	Mukkāni ...	637
		337	Sankéthi ...	1,024
		338	Sozhia.	
		339	Talavukár.	
		340	Tannodathár.	
		341	Vadama ...	9,999
		342	Vajasanaiyer.	
		343	Vallanád.	
		344	Vatadésom.	
		345	Váttima.	
154	Tampán.			
155	Tandán ...	346	Ettáli.	
		347	Tandá Kuruppu.	
		348	Uráli ...	10,053
156	Taravan.			
157	Tattàn ...	349	Kiriyattu tattan.	
		350	Malayala tattan ...	2,979

Serial No.	Caste.	Serial No.	Subdivisions.	Numbers of important subdivisions.
		351	Pándi tattan ...	3,475
		352	Sudra tattan.	
158	Táttédam.			
159	Telugu.			
160	Telugu Brahmin ...	353	Karnakammalu.	
		354	Murianád.	
		355	Niyogi.	
		356	Vallanád.	
161	Tirumulpád.			
162	Tiruvalládési.			
163	Tólar.			
164	Trippunittoraidési.			
165	Udaya.			
166	Ulládan.			
167	Unniyádiri.			
168	Vaduka ...	357	Kappu.	
		358	Katchi Naicken.	
		359	Kavara Naicken.	
		360	Kavara Naidu.	
		361	Kavundan.	
		362	Muttukáppu.	
		363	Naicken ...	176
		364	Naidu ...	1,421
		365	Pantakāppu.	
		366	Reddi ...	196
		367	Reddikáppu.	
		368	Telugukàppu.	
		369	Tottakkàran.	
169	Vaisya.			
170	Valamalu.			
171	Valluvan ...	370	Tiruvalluvan.	
172	Vanian ...	371	Múppan.	
		372	Pandi Vánian ...	1,034
		373	Sudra Vánian.	
173	Védan ...	374	Kána Védan.	
174	Vélan ...	375	Kánikkáran ...	180
		376	Malavélan ...	1,313
175	Vellála ...	377	Akampadi.	
		378	Asaivaka.	
		379	Choliya.	
		380	Karakkáttu vellála ...	323
		381	Karalár.	
		382	Kondakettu.	
		383	Kurukkapandáram.	
		384	Linga vellala.	
		385	Mámsom.	
		386	Nanjanád pillai.	
		387	Nanjanád vellála ...	9,505
		388	Pándi vellála ...	3,200
		389	Saiva vellála.	

Serial No.	Caste.	Serial No.	Subdivisions.	Numbers of important subdivisions.
		390	Tondamán.	
176	Vellódi.			
177	Velutadan ...	391	Cháyakkáran ...	2,365
		392	Īrankolli.	
		393	Kaludaivannán.	
		394	Rejakan.	
		395	Uvar.	
		396	Vannán ...	1,301
178	Vettáran.			
179	Vettuvan.			
180	Vyravi ...	397	Bhairági.	
		398	Yogīswaran.	

Christian.

Serial No.	Caste.	Serial No.	Subdivisions.	Numbers of important subdivisions.
1	Chinese.			1
2	East Indian.			2,072
3	Eurasian.			532
4	European ...	1	American ...	5
		2	Anglo-Indian ...	4
		3	Dutch ...	1
		4	English ...	61
		5	French ...	1
		6	German ...	1
		7	Irish ...	4
		8	Portuguese ...	5
		9	Scotch ...	13
		10	Spanish ...	1
5	Marakkán ...	11	Margom ...	930
		12	Thuppoyee ...	259
6	Native Christian ...	13	Christian ...	3,730
		14	Hindu Bhrishtu.	
		15	Portuguese ...	924
7	Syrian ...	16	Calcutta Syrian.	
		17	Moplah ...	5,196
		18	Nasrani ...	68,472
		19	Palayakūr ...	121,965
		20	Puthenkūr ...	40,790

Jain.

Jew.

Serial No.	Caste.	Serial No.	Subdivisions.	Numbers of important subdivisions.
	Mussalman.			
1	Arabs ...	1	Islam.	
		2	Rawut.	
2	Fakkir.			
3	Jonaka ...	3	Mappilla ...	345
4	Kábúl.			
5	Kutch ...	4	Chīntikkár.	
		5	Kutchi Seit.	
		6	Seit.	
6	Labbai.			
7	Mettan ...	7	Rawut.	
8	Mughal.			
9	Mussalman ...	8	Mahomed ...	2,356
10	Mustan.			
11	Ostta ...	9	Kshourakan.	
		10	Ostta Kshouraken.	
12	Páni.			
13	Pathán.			
14	Rawut.			
15	Sheik.			
16	Syed.			
17	Tangal.			
18	Tulukkan.			
	Parsi.			

C.—NAMES OF KARAS.

[NOTE.—The names of Karas are given here as stated in page 289 of the Report. These are minute subdivisions of the Taluqs used for revenue and other purposes of administration.]

Number and Taluq.	Number and Proverty.	Number.	Name of Kara.
1. Tovala.	1. Mélpidáka.	1	Thittuvilachavalakára Kudiyiruppu.
		2	Vembadikara.
		3	Bhoothappándi.
		4	Thittuvilaperiatheruvoo.
		5	Īsánthimangalam Kīlūr
		6	Pidárankuli.
		7	Thittuvilatheruvoo.
		8	Āndythōppu.
		9	Isánthimangalam Mēlavūr.
		10	Vilaparachēri.
		11	Chiramatom.
		12	Thuvarankádu.
		13	Thittuvilapallitheruvoo.
		14	Do. Chithentheruvoo.
		15	Iluppayadi.
		16	Puliyadishērry.
		17	Ilanthayadi.
		18	Marthanda Nalloor.
		19	Vilānkádu Mēlūr.
		20	Nángandishērry.
		21	Mángulamshērry.
		22	Naduváshērry.
		23	Pudushērry.
1. Tovala—(*Continued*).	1. Mélpidāka—(*Continued*).	24	Chēnákulam.
		25	Kulathūr.
		26	Gōvindapuram.
		27	Mulayanallūr.
		28	Thekkarasankuli.
		29	Cháttupudūr.
		30	Pannikuli.
		31	Vádakkarasankuli.
		32	Pákkinēri.
		33	Kalumkadisherry.
		34	Suchukuli.
		35	Maṇattitta.
		36	Vilāmkádu Kīlūr.
	2. Naduppidaka.	37	Kílēdersanamkōppu.
		38	Malampradēsam.
		39	Maṇṇadisherry.
		40	Kēsavanēri.
		41	Thellánthichánnákudi.
		42	Mudanganvila.
		43	Udayadisherry.
		44	Anthirapuram.
		45	Kaluvanthittusherry.

Number and Taluq.	Number and Proverty.	Number.	Name of Kara.
—(*Continued*).	2. Naduppidaka—(*Continued*).	46	Vembadisherry.
		47	Kukkavilákamshērry.
		48	Kandalavushērry.
		49	Sankilianpára.
		50	Kandakulicherry.
		51	Pilávadiyur Īlakkudi.
		52	Mēlēdersanamkōppu.
		53	Puliyadisherry.
		54	Kollamthiruthusherry.
		55	Mathiyur.
		56	Jnánam Ur.
		57	Vīravanalloor.
		58	Arumanalloor.
		59	Ambuliconamsherry.
		60	Chekkadisherry.
		61	Puduchērry.
		62	Eluthalampadusherry.
		63	Jnanampuliadisherry.
		64	Perumálpattusherry.
	puram.	65	Malampradēsam.
		66	Ulakudisherry.
		67	Panayadikkónam.
		68	Āladikkōnam.
		69	Thirattumala.
		70	Kadambākulam.
		71	Kēsavanéri.
		72	Kadukkara.
		73	Idayankōṇam.

Number and Taluq.	Number and Proverty.	Number.	Name of Kara.
—(*Continued*).	5. Tōválappidaka.	107	Chōlapuram.
		108	Sivajnanapuram.
		109	Thiāgasoundariyapuram.
		110	Perumālpuram Alakiasherry.
		111	Villacherry.
		112	Tōvála.
		113	Kurishadi.
		114	Poyyamanachērri.
		115	Chembakarámanpudūr.
		116	Kōvilakudi.
		117	Kumārapuram.
		118	Mādhavaláyam.
		119	Perumālpuram.
		120	Krishnanpudur.
		121	Aramboly.
		122	Chenthanāthapuram.
		123	Ādithyapuram.
		124	Veeramārtāndanpudūr.
		125	Missionkudiyiruppu.
		126	Thānumālayanpudūr.
	kudi.	127	Thalakkudi.
		128	Ramanāthapuram.
		129	Kandanmettucherry.
		130	Poolānkuli.
		131	Ponnamuppanpana.
		132	Bheemanagari.
		133	Vembattoor.
		134	Parvathipudūr.

Taluk	Division	No.	Name
1. Tovala—	3. Ananta	74	Chettikkōṇam.
		75	Malapilámkōṇam.
		76	Panandiram Vilákam.
		77	Sáranvali.
		78	Iravipudár.
		79	Nainánthōppu.
		80	Veerakeralanpudūr.
		81	Ananthapuram.
	4. Alakiapandipuram.	82	Brāhmanankōṇam.
		83	Kēsavanpudūr.
		84	Chembakarámanpudūr.
		85	Alakiapándipuram.
		86	Do. gramom.
		87	Mēlekkara.
		88	Ettamadasherry.
		89	Ettāmada.
		90	Madavilákam.
		91	Kaniyánpára.
		92	Chenthiparashērry.
		93	Velavakkal Kadaniankuli.
		94	Pudu kudiyiruppu.
		95	Idamalakkōnam.
		96	Keeramkulam.
		97	Kurathiyara.
		98	Vadakkupēyōda.
		99	Chemmanvila.
		100	Thekkupēyōda.
		101	Marukalthala.
		102	Idakkōdu.
		103	Malampradēsam.
		104	Kannanpudūr.
		105	Ādichanpudūr.
		106	Bálamārtándanpudūr.

Taluk	Division	No.	Name
Tovala	6. Tálak	135	Ananthapadmanabhapuram.
		136	Tiruppadisārom Kilūr.
		137	Chemmankulamshērry.
		138	Vilāmkōttushērry.
		139	Thálakkudikīlchērry.
		140	Thondákkuli.
		141	Thálakkudimēlparachērri.
		142	Sripadmanabhanalloor.
		143	Vēmbadichērry.
		144	Tirupadisárom.
		145	Pulikkurithoppu.
		146	Kundukal Vallakuli.
		147	Periapana.
2. Agastiswaram.	7. Kottarpidaka.	148	Vadivīswarompavuthi thekku theru vīthi.
		149	East of the Old Road.
		150	Īluvakkuditheruvu.
		151	Vákayadi Vadakku theruvu vīthi.
		152	Do. Vániyakkudi.
		153	Do. do.
		154	Do. Īluvakkudi.
		155	Do. Veeramanichettiar theruvu.
		156	Do. Mēla theruvu vīthi.
		157	Do. Mēttu theruvu.
		158	Do. Patnūl Street North of the Public Road.
		159	Do. Patnūl Street. West of the Old Road.
		160	Do. do. do.
		161	Ramaswamy koil theruvu.
		162	Do. both sides of the Old Road.
		163	Do. Neerāli theruvu.
		164	Do. Kilakke theruvu.
		165	Vákayadi theru kusa theruvu.
		166	Do. Vellāmkudi.

Number and Taluq.	Number and Proverty.	Number.	Name of Kara.
—(*Continued*).	—(*Continued*).	167	Pattalianvila.
		168	Ēlakaram grámom.
		169	Lane North of the Vákayadi theru village.
		170	Chendadisavánthan kudiyiruppu.
		171	Kilmaravanvila kudiyiruppu.
		172	Konnanpilávila kudiyiruppu.
		173	Western Irulappapuram kudiyiruppu.
		174	Eastern do. do.
		175	Vadalivila kudiyiruppu.
		176	Chavalatheruvu.
		177	Kathikkārakkudi.
		178	Vannákkudi.
		179	Kottar Chettia theruvu.
		180	Idalákkudi near Ānapālam.
		181	Chayakkárakudi. do.
		182	Chaluppa theruvu. do.
		183	Idalákkudi Pattani theruvu.
		184	Do. Puthu theruvu.
		185	Ilamkada theruvu.
		186	Patnūl street South of the Public Road.
		187	Kachappara theruvu.
		188	Ilamkada.
		189	Vyālivila theruvu.
		190	Perumalkulam theruvu.
		191	Vyálivila kudiyiruppu.
		192	Idalakudi pattanikudi.
		193	Vēmbadi theruvu.
		194	Kammánkudi theruvu Idalákudi.
		195	Kykkala theruvu.

Number and Taluq.	Number and Proverty.	Number.	Name of Kara.
—(*Continued*).	—(*Continued*).	230	Vadiveeswaram Madathucherry.
		231	Do. Kadayicherry.
		232	Do. Savayamkulamcherry.
		233	Thattánvila.
		234	Nagercoil pakuthy thōppu Vániyakkudi.
		235	Vadiveeswaram pakuthy Ilamkadacherry.
		236	Do. Mela Maravanvila.
		237	Mela Vaṇṇánvila.
		238	Nagercoil pakuthy Ramen Puthūr.
		239	Vadiveeswaram pakuthy Náyakkenvila.
		240	Do. Keelavaṇṇan vila kudiyiruppu.
		241	Nagercoil Bungalow Ady.
		242	Vadiveeswaram pakuthy Karuppu Kōttucherry.
		243	Nagercoil pakuthy Theyranputhoor Īlaver kudiyiruppu.
		244	Do. Chavalakkárakudi
		245	Do. Potti Matam.
		246	Do. Idakkudi theruvu.
		247	Vadiveeswaram pakuthy Oottuvá Matamchērry.
		248	Nagercoil pakuthy Olukinachērry gramom.
		249	Do. Kothichapilla Ur.
		250	Do. Keelramenpudur.
		251	Do. Īromkudi.
		252	Do. Mudaliar vilavattam.
		253	Do. Thērāputhūr Ur.
		254	Do. Keelakkōnam.

2. Agastiswaram	7. Kottarpidaka	196	Palli theruvu Idalákudi.
		197	Vēdakkora kudiyiruppu.
		198	Sankaranvila.
		199	Idalákkudi chandi theruvu.
		200	Do. Arippu theruvu.
		201	Kariyamanikkapuram.
		202	Nagercoil pakuthy Part I.
		203	Do. Part II.
		204	Do Iluvakkudi.
		205	Do. Idakkudi.
		206	Kottar Chetty theruvu gramom.
		207	Vadiveeswaram Kavara theruvu gramom.
		208	Do. Kániyála theruvu.
		209	Vadiveeswaram Ur.
		210	Kottar Kammála theruvu.
		211	Do. Paravakkudi.
		212	Do. Kurun theruvu.
		213	Kottar Kambōlam.
		214	Do. Pánán theruvu.
		215	Vadiveeswaram mēla theruvu.
		216	Kottar Sáliá theruvu.
		217	Vadiveeswaram Ur Thekku theruvu.
		218	Do. Palla theruvu gramom.
		219	Do. Keela theruvu Ur.
		220	Do. Nadu theruvu.
		221	Mīnákshipuram.
		222	Vadiveeswaram Dalavá theruvu gramom.
		223	Do. Kalmada theruvu.
		224	Do. Periya theruvu gramom.
		225	Do. Mettu theruvu.
		226	Vyalivila pallakkudi.
		227	Do. Kannankulanchērry.
		228	Do. Kalasam Irakky Kudiyiruppu.
		229	Do. Mallan Kumāravila.

2. Agastiswaram	7. Kottarpidaka	255	Vadalivilavattom.
		256	Nagercoil Vaṇṇákkudi.
		257	Do. Gramom.
		258	Do. Thēráputhūr Kosakkudi.
		259	Do. Chemmákudi.
		260	Do. Puravu Sherry Ur.
		261	Do. Punnakkātvattom.
		262	Do. ThathiyámkulamKeelachēry.
		263	Kūttamkát Vilavattom.
		264	Nagercoil pakuthy thēráputhur Kythadichān tope.
		265	Do. Dalavápuram
		266	Do. Idakkudi.
		267	Do. Matathuvilavattom.
		268	Do. Cháthen Chettyvila.
		269	Do Mēlakōnam.
		270	Do. Thathiyānkulam Mēlacherry.
		271	Do. Káttuvila.
		272	Do. Màda theruvu.
		273	Olukinacherry Ur.
		274	Do. Tōppuvāniyakudi Keela Ur.
		275	Do. Cháthen Chetty vilayil puliyenvila.
		276	Do. Tōppu vániyakudi (1).
		277	Do. Periyavila vattam.
		278	Do. Tōpu vániyakudi (2).
		279	Do. do. (3).
		280	Do. Kannákkudi.
		281	Do. Kothichapilla gramom.
		282	Do. Kanniya Madamcherry.
		283	Tamarakulam pakuthy pūvū kudiyiruppu.
		284	Do. Karumbāttuvila kudiyiruppu.
		285	Do. kudiyiruppu.

Number and Taluq.	Number and Proverty.	Number.	Name of Kara.
—(*Continued*).	pidaka.	286	Tamarakulam Karkarampottachēry.
		287	Do. Visayanēry.
		288	Do. Attakulamchéry.
		289	Do. Īttankádu.
		290	Támarakulam.
		291	Alakulamchéry.
		292	Kottayadi kudiyiruppu.
		293	Tamarakulam pakuthy puliyamkulamchéry.
		294	Do. Chettyvila kudiyiruppu.
		295	Do. Theyrivila.
		296	Do. Kumáraperumavila.
		297	Do. Sástánkoil vila kudiyiruppu.
		298	Do. Chotta panikken theruvila.
		299	Do. Idayenvila.
		300	Do. Chetty kudiyiruppu.
		301	Do. Punnayadi.
		302	Do. Káttuvila.
		303	Do. Christope vattam Támarakulam kudiyiruppu.
		304	Do. Āndyvila kudiyiruppu.
		305	Do. Chittan kudiyiruppu.
		306	Do. Chembakarámen puthenthura.
		307	Do. Mukiliyan kudiyiruppu.
		308	Do. Īchavila kudiyiruppu.
		309	Do. Vellayenvila kudiyiruppu.
		310	Do. Kumáraperumal kudiyiruppu

Number and Taluq.	Number and Proverty.	Number.	Name of Kara.
—(*Continued*).	pidaka—(*Continued*).	334	Agastiswaram pakuthy Nariyanvila kudiyiruppu.
		335	Do. Kulasekharapuram pakuthy Veppa Vilachēry.
		336	Do. Mayilady.
		337	Do. Avarivila.
		338	Do. Vanbanvila.
		339	Do. Payilakulam.
		340	Do. Pottayadi.
		341	Do. Karambavila.
		342	Do. Kanpāthapothachery.
		343	Do. Coilvila.
		344	Do. Puthuvūr.
		345	Do. Chálaputhuvur Kandēry
		346	Do. do. Parachēry.
		347	Do. Kuruchy.
		348	Do. Kulasekharapuram kara.
		349	Do. Lakshmi kudiyiruppu.
		350	Do. Lakshmikulam parachery.
		351	Do. Kottàram.
		352	Do. Malayenvila kudiyiruppu.

		No.		
2. Agastiswaram	8. Agastiswaram	311	Do.	Terivila kudiyiruppu.
		312	Do.	Valakáren tope.
		313	Do.	Matathuvaka kudiyiruppu.
		314	Do.	Alattil.
		315	Do	Kallarivilachen kudiyiruppu.
		316	Kiınikaınuvila.	
		317	Agastiswaram pakuthy	Taruvakara vattavila kudiyiruppu.
		318	Do.	Agastiswaramkara.
		319	Do.	Pandára tope kudiyiruppu.
		320	Do.	Vadukampattu kudiyiruppu.
		321	Do.	Vilakkanákulam.
		322	Do.	Kovakulam.
		323	Do.	Ettukuditheruvila.
		324	Do.	Ēlusattuppattu kudiyiruppu.
		325	Do.	Josephvila kudiyiruppu.
		326	Do	Chetty kudiyiruppu.
		327	Do.	Ilanthayadi kudiyiruppu.
		328	Do.	Ponnaravila kudiyiruppu.
		329	Do.	Paracherryvila kudiyiruppu.
		330	Do.	Agastiswaram.
		331	Do.	Mádukathvila kudiyiruppu.
		332	Do.	Ramenputhūr kudiyiruppu.
		333	Do.	Kōmbavila kudiyiruppu.
2. Agastiswaram	8. Agastiswaram	353	Do.	Peruma matom kudiyiruppu.
		354	Kanniyakumári pakuthy	Mahádánapuram.
		355	Do.	Cape Comorin.
		356	Do.	Vàriyūr.
		357	Do.	Alakappapuram.
		358	Do.	Pottakulam.
		359	Do.	Bhagavathipuram pallakudi.
		360	Do.	Lakshmipuram.
		361	Do.	James Town.
		362	Do.	Picha kudiyiruppu.
		363	Do.	Bhagavathipuram.
		364	Do.	Chembakarámapuram.
		365	Do.	Sivarámapuram.
		366	Do.	Mettu kudiyiruppu.
		367	Do.	Ālivila kudiyiruppu.
		368	Do.	Ālivila kudiyiruppu alias Restákádu.
		369	Do.	Kanakappapuram.
		370	Do.	Kánimatam.
		371	Do.	Prándanēry
		372	Agastiswaram pakuthy	Āvanom kudiyiruppu
		373	Kanniyakumári pakuthy	Vattakotta.
		374	Do.	Mahárájapuram
		375	Do.	Kumärapuram.
		376	Do.	Punnákulam.
		377	Do.	Váriyūr Allom.
		378	Do.	Ottayalvila.
		379	Do.	Kalluvila Ur.

Number and Taluq.	Number and Proverty.	Number.	Name of Kara.	Number and Taluq.	Number and Proverty.	Number.	Name of Kara.
—(*Continued*).	8. Agastiswarampidaka—(*Contd.*)	380	Kanniyákumári pakuthy Pálam road	—(*Continued*).	—(*Continued*).	441	Kalladivila.
			sherry.			442	Pallathuramukhom.
		381	Do. Leepuram Ur.			443	Ilanthavila.
		382	Agastiswaram pakuthy Achenkulam.			444	Nainaputhoor.
		383	Do. Kavakulam kudiyiruppu.			445	Mala ananjan kudiyiruppu.
		384	Do. Manthánamputhūr.			446	Vadakkutharyvila.
		385	Do. Terivila kudiyiruppu.			447	Puthalam Channar kudiyiruppu.
		386	Do. Chenthayadi kudiyiruppu.			448	Do. Alavar kudiyiruppu.
		387	Do. Periyavila.			449	Panomkottánvila.
		388	Do. Idayenvila kudiyiruppu.			450	Manakkudi thura.
		389	Kanniyakumári pakuthy			451	Kuroonjalianvila.
			Tekku Kundal.			452	Ariyaperumalvila.
		390	Do. Chundaparambu Ur.			453	Tekkutheruvila.
		391	Do. Vadakkukundal Ur.			454	Kaniyanvila.
		392	Do. Anjettuvila.			455	Kádettuchéry.
		393	Agastiswaram pakuthy Devakulam sherry.			456	Palcoolamchery.
		394	Kilmana kudiyiruppu.			457	Madusūdanapuram.
		395	Vellamkudi.			458	Vandy kudiyiruppu.
		396	Chukkupara thērivila.			459	Alisankádu.
						460	Oodayappan kudiyiruppu.
	pidaka.	397	Parakka pakuthy Kēsavanputhúr.			461	Mookilanvila.
		398	Kāttádithattoo			462	Pulloovila.
		399	Pulavila.			463	Vyravila.
		400	Kannambivila.			464	Mottayan kudiyiruppu.
		401	Panavila.			465	Coonjanvila.
		402	Mēla puthúr.			466	Parappavila.
		403	Keela puthūr.			467	Vellálanvila.
		404	Do. Vániakudi.			468	Perumkolam.
		405	Ilandayadi thattu.			469	Manikettipottanvila.

Taluk	Pakuthi	No.	Name
2. Agastiswaram	9. Parakka	406	Tekku Churankudi Cháṇṇákudi.
		407	Chúrankudi.
		408	Vellam oadivila.
		409	Kadaka muttyvila.
		410	Eathamoly kudiyiruppu.
		411	Nariyenvila.
		412	Thikkilamvila.
		413	Kodikkálchery.
		414	Keerivila.
		415	Mankávila.
		416	Periyakáttu thura.
		417	Kallaveeriyanvila.
		418	Dharmapuram Ur.
		419	Periyavila.
		420	Polykara thura.
		421	Nadu theruvu.
		422	Parakkay Nadu theruvu.
		423	Vadakku theruvu.
		424	Kannankulam Mēla theruvu.
		425	Mangamaṇaválan perun theruvu.
		426	Tengumputhuvur.
		427	Paṇikken kudiyiruppu.
		428	Mēla parachery.
		429	Keela parachery.
		430	Tekku theruvu.
		431	Kaṇṇankulam keela theruvu.
		432	Ancha kudiyiruppu.
		433	Valapullikal.
		434	Oyaravila.
		435	Chothavila.
		436	Panavila.
		437	Aruthakudivila.
		438	Pethaperumaul kudiyiruppu.
		439	Sámiyapuram.
		440	Maṇakudi kudiyiruppu.

Taluk	Pakuthi	No.	Name
2. Agastiswaram	9. Parakkapidaka	470	Anantaswamipuram.
		471	Pullayāpuram.
		472	Kovilvila.
		473	Kaṇṇakulamcherry.
		474	Puthen thura.
		475	Keelakátvila.
		476	Mēlakátvila.
		477	Ramen puthuvūr.
		478	Attikáttuvila.
		479	Chemban kara.
		480	Vallom kudiyiruppu.
		481	Chinnananjanvila.
		482	Keelakrishnan puthūr.
		483	Mēlakrishnan puthūr.
		484	Thamarakudivila.
		485	Kōttavila.
		486	Vadakku churankudi.
		487	Mūkkan kādu.
		488	Nankūranpilāvila.
		489	Pàlkinattinvila.
	10. Suchindrumpidaka.	490	Luchindrum Akkara kara.
		491	Do. Kadayil chērry.
		492	Do. Asramom gramom.
		493	Do. do. Ur.
		494	Do. Kákka moor.
		495	Do. Kulothu chērry.
		496	Iraviputhūr.
		497	Do. Vishnupuram gramom.
		498	Thànu malayan puthūr.
		499	Chēmbakaraman puthur kudiyiruppu.
		500	Kithadi parachéry.
		501	Vorisadi parachéry.
		502	Kuttikal parachéry.
		503	Kudiluséri.

Number and Taluq.	Number and Proverty.	Number.	Name of Kara.
—(Continued).	10. Suchindrumpidaka—(Continued).	504	Ilayanayinarkulam shērry.
		505	Nainakulam sherry.
		506	Manavila kudiyiruppu.
		507	Karayán kuli.
		508	Kaniyánkulamvila.
		509	Kalkáttu kannala theruvu.
		510	Suchindrum Tekkai theruvu gramom.
		511	Tekkumon Ur.
		512	Vadakkai theruvu gramom.
		513	Nadu theruvu Ur.
		514	Mēla theruvu gramom.
		515	Therppakulathu gramom.
		516	Mela theruvu Ur.
		517	Thekkumon gramom.
		518	Pērambala theruvu gramom.
		519	Kottayarnedu theruvu.
		520	Sannadi theruvu.
		521	Kalkat chavalakara theruvu.
		522	Do. Ilavakudi Mela theruvu.
		523	Do. Do. Keela theruvu.
		524	Do. parachery.
		525	Paraputhurvila kudiyiruppu.
		526	Cheriya Mettuvila kudiyiruppu.
	pidaka.	527	Vadasēri pakuthy Krishnankoil gramom.
		528	Do. do. Keela theruvu.
		529	Do. do. Mela theruvu.

Number and Taluq.	Number and Proverty.	Number.	Name of Kara.
—(Continued).	11. Padappattu pidaka—(Continued).	558	Iracha kulam Mangakulam chēry.
		559	Do. Nambiyánkulam chēry.
		560	Govindapuram Īlavakudi.
		561	Do. Ambalam Thuruthu chēry.
		562	Do. Āttumkara Thekkum, Vadakum chēry.
		563	Do. Chavalakárakudi Ilakudi Channakudi.
		564	Do. Ur gramom, &c.
		565	Do. Veeránamangalam Ur, &c.
		566	Do. Nāvakát gramom, &c
		567	Do. Melaputtery gramom, &c.
		568	Do. Attu patti chēry.
		569	Do. Parayadi chēry.
		570	Do. Puthery Īluvakudi.
		571	Do. Kalungudi Mēla chēry.
		572	Do. Kalungadi Neduva chēry
		573	Do. Chettykulam chery.
		574	Do. Kalungadi Keela chēry.
		575	Do. Keela puthēry Ur.
	pidaka.	576	Tērūr pakuthy Bánanthitta gramom.
		577	Do. Thekkūr.
		578	Do. Vadakkūr.
		579	Do. Vadakara chēry.
		580	Do. Puthupara chēry.
		581	Do. Uthirappatti chēry.
		582	Do. Karuppu kōtta.

Taluk	Pakuthy	No.	Name
2. Agastiswaram	11. Padappattu	530	Do. Chetti theruvu.
		531	Do. Idakkudi.
		532	Do. Vaniya theruvu.
		533	Do. Kammānkudi.
		534	Do. Kudiyiruppu Arivuvila Chānná-kudi.
		535	Do. Kudiyiruppu.
		536	Do. Anju theruvu Kudumbasēri theruvu.
		537	Do. Kykkala theruvu, &c.
		538	Do. Thaliyapuram Ramavarman Nəgercoil Thānumālayen theruvu.
		539	Do. Vanchi Martandan theruvu, &c.
		540	Do. Gramom.
		541	Do. Ur.
		542	Do. Chetty theruvu.
		543	Do. Chayakkara theruvu, &c.
		544	Do. Pārvathipuram.
		545	Do. Vāniyakudi, &c.
		546	Do. Chōlapuram.
		547	Do. Kunnavala chēry.
		548	Do. Kammānkudi.
		549	Do. Attakulam chēry.
		550	Do. Vishnupuram chēry.
		551	Do. Puliyadi chēry.
		552	Do. Kaniyákulam Ilandayadi chēry, &c.
		553	Do. Kadayanvila.
		554	Do. Sáyakaren parampuvila.
		555	Do. Kilavadi chēry and Chadaya-puram chēry.
		556	Irachakulam pakuthy Thekku putten chēry.
		557	Do. Vechakulam chēry.
2. Agastiswaram	12. Thēr	583	Kulasekaram puthūr pakuthy Āvanam kolam kudiyiruppu.
		584	Do. Thandanáyakam Kōnam.
		585	Do. Chadayamkulam chēry.
		586	Do. Poothu grámom Vadakku chēry.
		587	Do. Pallakudi.
		588	Do. Poothu gramom Thekku chēry.
		589	Do. Kaṇṇan chēry pallakudi.
		590	Do. Saṅkaram Puthūr.
		591	Do. Kothankulam chēry.
		592	Do. Kōttavila kudiyiruppu.
		593	Do. Kurandi Īlavakudi.
		594	Do. Chettiyakulam chēry.
		595	Do. Mángulam chēry.
		596	Devakulam.
		597	Kurandi parachēry.
		598	Do. Mánkulam.
		599	Do. Thirukurandi chēry.
		600	Do Kulasēkhara puthūr.
		601	Do. Attikulam chēry.
		602	Do. Pudu gramom Īlavakudi.
		603	Do. do. Thekkūr.
		604	Do. do. Vadakkūr.
		605	Do. Kurandi.
		606	Do. Rāmapuram.
		607	Nallūr pakuthy Lakshmipuram.
		608	Do. Marukāl Thala chēry.
		609	Do. Alakanapuram.
		610	Do. Kōnavila chēry.
		611	Do. Nalloor.
		612	Do. Attāni Markulam chēry.
		613	Do. Thiruvanchi nallūr.
		614	Do. Attiyadi chēry.

Number and Taluq.	Number and Proverty.	Number.	Name of Kara.
2. Agastiswaram —(Continued).	12. Thērpidaka —(Continued).	615	Nallūr Marunkūr.
		616	Do. Periyakulam chēry.
		617	Do. Vallabharōyan Kōttuvila kudiyiruppu.
		618	Do. Vanchimartanda nallūr.
		619	Do. Chundavila kudiyiruppu.
		620	Do. Raman Ādichen puthūr.
		621	Do. Kumarapuram tope kudiyiruppu.
		622	Do. Thēr parachēry.
		623	Do. Panayadi chēry.
	13. Kadiapattanam.	624	First Munnila.
		625	Second do.
		626	Third do.
		627	Fourth do.
		628	Fifth do.
		629	Sixth do.
		630	Seventh do.
		631	Eighth do.
		632	Ninth do.
		633	Tenth do.
	14. Thiruvithankodu.	634	Karukkankuli.
		635	Puthūr.
		636	Thiruvithancode.
		637	Gramom.
nial.		638	Punkara.

Number and Taluq.	Number and Proverty.	Number.	Name of Kara.
—(Continued).	17. Eranial —(Continued).	671	Sixth Munnila.
		672	Seventh do.
		673	Eighth do.
		674	Ninth do.
		675	Tenth do.
		676	Eleventh do.
		677	Twelfth do.
		678	Thirteenth do.
		679	Fourteenth do.
		680	Kattimamkodu.
		681	Kodupakuli.
	18. Colachel.	682	Murukankodu.
		683	Neyyūr Keela chēry.
		684	Manavila.
		685	Kokkodu.
		686	Irimbilakote muri.
		687	Do. Karumpana.
		688	Chathamkara pandakasála.
		689	Do. Thuramukhom.
		690	Do. Parakudi.
		691	Do. Pattara.
		692	Do. Kilakkum kara.
		693	Do. Mēl kara.
		694	Do. Pulayanvila.
		695	Irumbili.
		696	Kariyara.
		697	Chatham kara pidaka.
		698	Colachel kada pidaka.

Taluk	Pakuthi	No.	Village
3. Eranial	15. Nattálam.	639	Thengankuli.
		640	Thachakōde.
		641	Kánjirakōte kara.
		642	Perumbūli.
		643	Nelvēly Mekum kara.
		644	Nattálam.
		645	Nelvēly Kilakum kara.
	16. Killiyūr.	646	Keelkulam North.
		647	Do. East.
		648	Do. South.
		649	Poottētti North.
		650	Do. West.
		651	Do. South.
		652	Vēnkōdu
		653	Kunjankódu.
		654	Tholikkodu.
		655	Valukodu.
		656	Chemmuthal.
		657	Perály North.
		658	Do. South.
		659	Killiyur South.
		660	Poottētti East.
		661	Thippra Mala East.
		662	Do. do. West.
		663	Palūr pidaka.
		664	Thalakote kōnam.
		665	Neduvila.
	17. Eranial.	666	First Munnila.
		667	Second do.
		668	Third do.
		669	Fourth do.
		670	Fifth do.
3. Eranial		699	Keela kara pidaka.
	19. Midalam.	700	Mēla midálam.
		701	Keela midálam.
		702	Thēvy kodu.
		703	Irukalampádu.
		704	Perumakuli.
		705	Alinjikodu.
		706	Pálapallom.
		707	Vaikalkara.
		708	Kurándi.
		709	Ālamūdu.
		710	Tholukkada.
	20. Neendakara.	711	Rajakkamangalam.
		712	Melakurandi.
		713	Kōthavila Ur.
		714	Kūthavila Ur.
		715	Sūrappallam.
		716	Mēlakánjiravila.
		717	Thekkurichi.
		718	Maniyan kudiyiruppu.
		719	Palaya kada.
		720	Mampattuvila.
		721	Alakkalvila.
		722	Manna Ur.
		723	Murungavila.
		724	Ālamvila.
		725	Rajakkamangalam Thura.
		726	Kákka tope.
		727	Thiruvikōdu.
		728	Pallom.
		729	Káravila.
		730	Anantanadan kudiyiruppu.
		731	Sankaran Kuli.

Number and Taluq.	Number and Proverty.	Number.	Name of Kara.
—(*Continued*).	—(*Continued*).	732	Alikkal Thura.
		733	Palla tope Thura.
		734	Kanakkuruchiyil Vellamōdi.
		735	Do. Dalavapuram.
		736	Do. Pattomvila.
		737	Do. Kaṇṇakulam.
		738	Vadakku Kannakuruchi.
		739	Puthu Matom Ūr.
		740	Kannakurichi Puthūr.
		741	Do. Minchiravila.
		742	Do. Koippuram.
		743	Do. Paravanvila.
		744	Do. Āruthenguvila.
		745	Do. Keela Ūr.
		746	Do. Mēla Ūr.
		747	Do. Naduvūr.
		748	Do. Kaṇṇakurichi.
		749	Pillayarvila.
		750	Chattuvan tope.
		751	Pulluvila.
		752	Tháravila.
		753	Thammathu Kōnam.
		754	Erumbukadu.
		755	Mudamkanvila.
		756	Mávila.
		757	Ammacharvila.
		758	Villivila.
		759	Ādēravila.
		760	Vyrávi kudiyiruppu.

Number and Taluq.	Number and Proverty.	Number.	Name of Kara.
—(*Continued*).		795	Iravipuram pidaka.
		796	Vilavūr pidaka.
	22. Brahmapuram.	797	Brahmapuram.
		798	Tenkara.
		799	Choliarkōnam.
		800	Kollamvila.
		801	Kuttakkara.
		802	Sattamangalam.
		803	Kuluma kara.
		804	Kumarakovil.
		805	Appattuvila.
		806	Chadayamangalam.
	23. Kappiara.	807	Karunkal pidaka.
		808	Páttramangalam.
		809	Kappiara West.
		810	Do. East.
		811	Kilakkey kulikot pidaka.
		812	Maruthūrkuruchi.
		813	Mekkey kulikōde.
		814	Kaviyallūr.
		815	Palliyadi.
		816	Thittimēlkōnam.
	Āttūr.	817	Cherukōl.
		818	Thamanūr.
		819	Tholichal.
		820	Ettuvakodu.

Taluk	Pakuthi	No.	Name
8. Eranial	20. Neendakara	761	Kidankaravila.
		762	Puthu kudiyiruppu.
		763	Palavila.
		764	Mantakādu.
		765	Sūramkudi.
		766	Vallivila.
		767	Násuvanvila.
		768	Chundappattivila.
		769	Pettaperumál kudiyiruppu.
		770	Kosavanvila.
		771	Pūchi vilākam.
		772	Karinjan kōdu.
		773	Parachēry.
		774	Thottiakōdu.
		775	Peruvila.
		776	Pambanvila.
		777	Veeráni.
		778	Ālūr
		779	Vembannoor.
		780	Āsárippallam.
		781	Perinjavila.
		782	Keelakorandi.
4. Kalkulam.	21. Kalkulam.	783	Ūrakom pidaka.
		784	Mudukulam pidaka.
		785	Thakkala pidaka.
		786	Kakkuruchi.
		787	Keralapuram pidaka.
		788	Chárakōdu.
		789	Parakottu pidaka.
		790	Muthalakurichi.
		791	Kuttikāt pidaka.
		792	Puliyurkuruchi.
		793	Maruvurkōnam pidaka.
		794	Mūlachel pidaka.
4. Kalkulam	24.	821	Mekkin kara.
		822	Kannannūr.
		823	Kilakkum kara.
		824	Elichel.
		825	Āttūr.
	25. Thiruvattár.	826	Kollōle.
		827	Charūr.
		828	Thumpōde.
		829	Viyalur.
		830	Kāmūr.
		831	Kodalachimala.
		832	Kaduvachanimala.
		833	Vettimala.
		834	Thiruvattár.
		835	Thirunanthi kara.
		836	Chēkkal.
		837	Panayakode.
		838	Vadakotkonam.
		839	Kuruvikodu.
		840	Perinkattu konam.
		841	Vadapidaka thachamala.
		842	Tripparappu.
	26. Mekkodu.	843	Perinchakonam.
		844	Pūvankode.
		845	Kallankudi.
		846	Mekkodu.
		847	Máthanu pidaka.
		848	Chemkodi East.
		849	Do. South.
		850	Do. North.
		851	Muthalāru pidaka.
		852	Āttur konam.
		853	Mārānkanam.

Number and Taluq.	Number and Proverty.	Number.	Name of Kara.
(*Continued*).	27. Kothanallūr.	854	Káttalá.
		855	Gramom.
		856	Valikkalompádu.
		857	Kanjirathukonam.
		858	Perinjilampu.
		859	Ittavila
		860	Kumárapuram.
		861	Manalikkara.
		862	Muttakádu.
		863	Kottikōdu.
		864	Kythakōdu.
	mana.	865	Máthur.
		866	Chelappavūr.
		867	Ayakkōdu.
		868	Vendalikodu.
		869	Kolacha vilakam.
		870	Cheruthikonam.
		871	Moliyadi mala.
		872	Ambittanchona mala.
		873	Vattam vila mala.
		874	Akattu mala.
		875	Kaduvāvettimala.
		876	Kamala mala.
		877	Ariyanpakkavila.
		878	Márikōnam.
		879	Churulakkōdu.
		880	Velumūttu mala.
		881	Vekkálimūttu mala.

Number and Taluq.	Number and Proverty.	Number.	Name of Kara.
—(*Continued*).	32. Eludēsapattu.	912	Neerodithura.
		913	Pallittōttam.
		914	Anukottu Desom.
		915	Madathuvilákattu munnila.
		916	Kovilvilakam munnilayil pana vilagam Desom
		917	Martandanthura.
		918	Chūlál Dēsom.
		919	Kollamkot Dēsom.
		920	Do. Thura.
		921	Mēlavankanji Desom.
		922	Thōttachel.
		923	Mungithōttam.
		924	Mukkádu.
		925	Kuravenkōdu.
		926	Kanjiravila.
		927	Pengadu.
	dēsapattu.	928	Pirakodu.
		929	Kulappiram.
		930	Kulivila.
		931	Aienkámom.
		932	Āthamkodu.
		933	Pávara.
		934	Chathenkodu.
		935	Mekkádu.
		936	Mankádu.
		937	Karukkan thōttam.

Taluk	Pakuthi	No.	Name
4. Kalkulam	28. Pon	882	Andūr.
		883	Pullayil.
		884	Ānavattam.
		885	Pannikottu pidaka.
		886	Ponmana pidaka.
		887	Villattūr.
		888	Kuru mala.
		889	Kythaōōttu.
		890	Valluvamkallu mala.
5. Vilavankodu.	29. Vilavankodu.	891	Karumáttūr.
		892	Vilavankodu.
		893	Meenachel.
		894	Madichel.
		895	Palukal.
		896	Ērattu.
		897	Vanniyūr.
	30. Kunnathūr.	898	Nallūr.
		899	Kodumkulam.
		900	Payanam.
		901	Kulivila
		902	Puduvidu.
		903	Chalachakōnam.
		904	Mélangalam Dēsom.
	31. Pynkulam.	905	Pynkulam.
		906	Ālamkulam.
		907	Kottáram.
		908	Anantamangalam.
		909	Puthukkada.
		910	Pattanam.
		911	Amasi.
5. Vilavankodu	33. Āru	938	Ettupara.
		939	Parthivapuram.
		940	Palliyil.
		941	Kollal.
		942	Virivila.
	34. Pakodu.	643	Kulitora.
		944	Pakodu.
		945	Kadamakkodu.
		946	Mēlpiram.
		947	Vilasēri.
		948	Idakkodu.
		949	Andukodu.
		950	Mēlpála.
		951	Do. Ramavurman chira.
		952	Málakkodu.
	35. Arumana.	953	Alakal.
		954	Kulichel.
		955	Máráppadi.
		956	Nallakara.
		957	Kōttakkakom.
		958	Ávayil.
		959	Chuthūrkonam.
		960	Thumpakkodu.
		961	Vellamkodu.
		962	Chithral mēkkum kara.
		963	Do. Kilakkum kara.
		964	Arumana.
		965	Thachūrkōnam.
		966	Nallurkōnam.
		967	Kāvumkonam.
		968	Padappachakonam.
		969	Mathūr kónam.
		970	Mannūr.

Number and Taluq.	Number and Proverty.	Number.	Name of Kara.
kodu—(*Continued*).	35. Arumana—(*Continued*).	971	Kuruvūr.
		972	Kokkodu.
		973	Chūlál.
		974	Mulukkodu.
		975	Kythakam.
		976	Viravel.
		977	Károde.
	lial.	978	Kiráthūr.
		979	Kalial.
		980	Kadayal.
		981	Karinjilli.
		982	Arakanád.
		983	Kannumāmudu.
		984	Kattachal.
		985	Nedumara.
		986	Pichipara mala.
		987	Cheruvullūr.
		988	Puliyūrchala.
		989	Mánkōdu.
		990	Vellingappara mala.
		991	Parandavilakam.
		992	Thūlivilakam.
		993	Viratti mala.
		994	Adakkádu.
		995	Vēlivilakathu mala.
		996	Karuppiyathu mala.
		997	Kanjirampara mala.
		998	Mannakal.

Number and Taluq.	Number and Proverty.	Number.	Name of Kara.
—(*Continued*).	39. Marukil.	1031	Kulumom.
		1032	Pēvarathala.
		1033	Mūmkode.
		1034	Īrachodu.
		1035	Karippu vila.
		1036	Vettamom.
		1037	Kattara.
		1038	Keelakád.
	40. Kunnattukāl.	1039	Ānavūr.
		1040	Vellarida.
		1041	Ēráthumunnila.
		1042	Thálattumunnila.
		1043	Kovallūr.
		1044	Cheriyakolla.
	layil.	1045	Aromkarathala.
		1046	Kuliyattukonam.
		1047	Karakulam kara.
		1048	Kulan kara.
		1049	Pilámthōttam.
		1050	Thōttattingal.
		1051	Kuttarakkel.
		1052	Ārayūr.
		1053	Palavompalli.
		1054	Mēkkē Ashárūr.
		1055	Vettikád.
		1056	Thattán Vilákam.

Taluk	Pakuthi	No.	Name
5. Vilavan	36. Ka	999	Maruthunpara.
		1000	Thalakku mala.
		1001	Karumattu.
		1002	Mēvattivila.
		1003	Perum mala.
		1004	Pattukani.
6. Neyattankara.	37. Neyattankara.	1005	Manappalangi.
		1006	Puthuvīdu.
		1007	Āmbalvilāgam.
		1008	Perumbaluthūr.
		1009	Perunthōttam.
		1010	Māmbalakara.
		1011	Kavungal.
		1012	Chittrampalanji.
		1013	Pāttakudi.
		1014	Kōttarakōnam.
		1015	Valuthur.
		1016	Maruthathūr.
		1017	Vattappalinji Irumbil.
		1018	Manjadithala.
		1019	Valavilakom.
		1020	Vadakode.
	38. Vilappil.	1021	Chevullūr.
		1022	Karōde.
		1023	Kurishumuttom.
		1024	Thuruttumūla.
		1025	Punnathánom.
		1026	Vilavūrkal.
		1027	Kalattil.
		1028	Kannankodu.
		1029	Perumallūr.
		1030	Valiaveedu.
6. Neyattankara	41. Kol	1057	Kulathara matom.
		1058	Ārukál.
		1059	Tempulimūdu.
		1060	Kilakke Āshárūr.
		1061	Valiya Veedu.
		1062	Īrāttu.
		1063	Vettivilakom.
		1064	Padapparathala.
		1065	Neythalāru.
	42. Kulathur.	1066	Kárkodu.
		1067	Vaduvūrkōnam.
		1068	Vadakkē puthuveedu.
		1069	Kōttakkakam.
		1070	Perumpalanji.
		1071	Kulippalanji.
		1072	Mullashēri.
		1073	Kánthallūr.
		1074	Muthushēri.
		1075	Kottūrkónam.
		1076	Nallūrvattam.
		1077	Pallathu.
		1078	Venkadambu.
		1079	Puthupurakal.
		1080	Cherunelpalanji.
		1081	Kávuvilákam.
		1082	Punniruttal.
	43. Parachala.	1083	Cheruvárakōnom.
		1084	Keelathōttam.
		1085	Pullūrkōnam.
		1086	Muriyathōttam.
		1087	Kōttakakom.
		1088	Mēlakkōnam.

Number and Taluq.	Number and Proverty.	Number.	Name of Kara.
—(Continued).	davila.	1089	Karumánūr.
		1090	Muriyam kara.
		1091	Āyail.
		1092	Thathiyūr.
		1093	Vada kara.
		1094	Kunnunádu.
		1095	Chēmbur.
		1096	Āttúr.
		1097	Mylachel.
		1098	Ālattúr.
		1099	Idapala.
		1100	Kuravara.
		1101	Válicode.
		1102	Válichel.
		1103	Perumkadavila.
		1104	Neykuppukáni.
		1105	Valamalakáni.
		1106	Kaliyattukáni.
		1107	Chembomkavukáni.
		1108	Púthakalkáni.
		1109	Meenattukáni.
		1110	Nirappilakáni.
		1111	Viláthukáni.
		1112	Karuthakelkáni.
		1113	Veymalakkáni.
		1114	Myladikáni.
		1115	Puravimalakáni.

Number and Taluq.	Number and Proverty.	Number.	Name of Kara.
6. Neyattan-kara—(Contd.)	46. Nēmom.	1149	Páppanamkodu.
		1150	Kalliyúr.
		1151	Perunkodu.
		1152	Kuthámom.
		1153	Ponnumangalam.
		1154	Idakōdu.
		1155	Idavilakam.
dram.	47. Vanchiyúr.	1156	Palavangádi.
		1157	Tekkumbhakam.
		1158	Vanchiyúr.
		1159	Páthirikari.
		1160	Kunnukuli.
		1161	Ārennúr.
		1162	Chengalashēri.
	48. Palkulamkara.	1163	Kadakompalli.
		1164	Vyyámúla.
		1165	Pulli.
		1166	Iravipērúr.
		1167	Perunthánni.
		1168	Palkulam kara.
		1169	Karikkakam.
		1170	Théttumkeel.
	yúrkavu.	1171	Anchámada.
		1172	Ārámada.
		1173	Rendámada.

Taluk	Pakuti	No.	Name
6. Neyattankara	44. Perumka	1116	Annithuthikáni.
		1117	Āmalakáni.
		1118	Kuruvikōttukáni.
		1119	Muthiyappárakáni.
		1120	Arakeelakáni.
		1121	Thommalakáni.
		1122	Kuranja mankáni.
		1123	Vellayilkáni.
		1124	Vilangumalakáni.
		1125	Mūnnara.
		1126	Ottasēkhara mangalam.
		1127	Máráyamuttom.
		1128	Pilámpalanji.
		1129	Pūlanádu.
		1130	Kuttiyánikkád.
		1131	Chilampara.
		1132	Chulliyúr.
	45. Kōttukál.	1133	Páchalúr.
		1134	Kanikudithala.
		1135	Venniyúr.
		1136	Puthalam.
		1137	Muriyathōttam.
		1138	Nágashēri.
		1139	Kodithara.
		1140	Válatope.
		1141	Piravilakam.
		1142	Anthiyúr.
		1143	Tiruvallam.
		1144	Koliyathōttam.
		1145	Velláni.
		1146	Thittavēli.
		1147	Tenkarathalakkel.
		1148	Nēmom.

Taluk	Pakuti	No.	Name
7. Trivan	49. Vatti	1174	Mūthada.
		1175	Puthichakōnam.
		1176	Thuruthumúla.
		1177	Mudavaram.
	50. Kalak-kúttam.	1178	Airupára.
		1179	Alinēra.
		1180	Vadakumbhágam.
		1181	Tekkumbhágam.
		1182	Uthiyaramùla.
		1183	Páttavilakam.
		1184	Kari.
	51. Thonakknal.	1185	Pillaveedu.
		1186	Puliveedu.
		1187	Ālappád.
		1188	Pattom.
		1189	Idavilákam.
		1190	Punnakunnam.
		1191	Mundakkel.
		1192	Thachapalli.
		1193	Kallúr
	52. Nellamon.	1194	Kōttakkakam.
		1195	Chala.
		1196	Muttathura A Division.
		1197	Do. B do.
		1198	Anchámtengu.
		1199	Viruthivilakam.
		1200	Do. A Division.
		1201	Do. B do.
		1202	Nadakkara A do.
		1203	Do. B do.
		1204	Tekkéveedu.
		1205	Ayikaraveedu.
		1206	Ilamthōttam.

Number and Taluq.	Number and Proverty.	Number.	Name of Kara.
—(*Continued*).	53. Pattam.	1207	Cheriyamannara.
		1208	Valayila.
		1209	Páthiripalli.
		1210	Panayara.
		1211	Kinavoor.
		1212	Tekkéveedu.
		1213	Chettivilakam.
		1214	Nedumpara.
		1215	Kurungánúr.
		1216	Valluveedu.
		1217	Madathuvilākam.
		1218	Cherukara.
	54. Ullúr.	1219	Vayalariam.
		1220	Mēluliyathura.
		1221	Chembalunthi.
		1222	Chenchéri.
		1223	Ālamkodu.
		1224	Mávarathalakónam.
		1225	Srikáriyam.
		1226	Karipparathala.
		1227	Parakkottukónam.
		1228	Pérúr.
	lattúr.	1229	Kulattúr.
		1230	Vayakkalam.
		1231	Āttuppara.
		1232	Kamu kara.
		1233	Mēnamkulam.

Number and Taluq.	Number and Proverty.	Number.	Name of Kara.
—(*Continued*).	59. Vembáikunnam.	1264	Āmballúr.
		1265	Theepukal.
		1266	Mánikkal.
		1267	Vettinād.
		1268	Kuttiyāni.
		1269	Kilakkum kara.
		1270	Tholuttum kara.
		1271	Maluvadi.
		1272	Tōppu kara.
		1273	Idattara.
		1274	Neduvēli.
		1275	Nedumpalli.
	60. Vamana-puram.	1276	Nellanád.
		1277	Mánikkel.
		1278	Vámanapuram.
		1279	Ānakudi.
		1280	Kilchēri.
		1281	Mudakkel.
		1282	Kottukunnam.
	61. Neduman-kádu.	1283	Véttampalli.
		1284	Vadakkum kara.
		1285	Tekkum kara.
		1286	Arasaparambu.
		1287	Chellamkode.
		1288	Karipuram.
		1289	Ānāttu kara.

Taluk	Pakuthi	No.	Name
7. Trivandram	55. Ku	1234	Cheruvakkal.
		1235	Kunnathu.
		1236	Pēdikadu.
	56. Pallippuram.	1237	Tekkaivila.
		1238	Pallichaveedu
		1239	Andúrkōnam.
		1240	Vellūr.
		1241	Idathara.
		1242	Mannara.
		1243	Valiyaveedu.
		1244	Kadinamkulam.
8. Nedumangadu.	57. Karakulam.	1245	Panthapilavu.
		1246	Chekkakónam.
		1247	Karakulam.
		1248	Kalunād.
		1249	Nedumon.
		1250	Idachēri.
		1251	Tholuthuvilākam.
		1252	Ēnik kara.
		1253	Irumpayil.
		1254	Kalattukal.
		1255	Vēruvukkónam.
	58. Kulat-tummēl.	1256	Kollode.
		1257	Mulavamkode.
		1258	Etturuthi.
		1259	Kulan kara.
		1260	Parachel.
		1261	Āmachel.
		1262	Puthuveedu.
		1263	Nannattukāvu.

Taluk	Pakuthi	No.	Name	
8. Nedumangadu	62. Ulamalakkal.	1290	Eliyavúr.	
		1291	Punalal.	
		1292	Vellanád.	
		1293	Kokkothamangalam.	
		1294	Valiyara.	
		1295	Chittuveedu.	
		1296	Changail.	
		1297	Puthukulam kara.	
	63. Ārianád.	1298	Kōttakkakam.	
		1299	Kokkudi.	
		1300	Mannúk kara.	
		1301	Palayatheruvu.	
		1302	Kōttakkakam	1st part.
		1303	Do.	2nd part.
		1304	Do.	3rd part.
		1305	Do.	4th part.
	64. Perum-kulam.	1306	Kadambanád.	
		1307	Kulakkanád.	
		1308	Ānákōdu	
		1309	Púnjánkōde.	
		1310	Thōttampa kara.	
		1311	Kōniyúr.	
		1312	Veeranákávu.	
	65. Navai-kulam.	1313	Thekkē Bhagam.	
		1314	Vadakké Bhagam.	
		1315	Navaikulam.	
		1316	Karavarom.	
		1317	Parakulam.	
		1318	Vadakkéveedu.	

Number and Taluq.	Number and Proverty.	Number.	Name of Kara.
	66. Kadak-kavúr.	1319	Muthuvangal.
		1320	Āyikudi.
		1321	Pálakkel.
		1322	Ayikkaravilakam.
		1323	Kovilalikam.
	67. Edak-kōde.	1324	Mudakkal.
		1325	Panayara.
		1326	Kōnattu.
		1327	Cheruvalli.
		1328	Ayilattu.
		1329	Perukōnam.
yinkil.	68. Āttinkal.	1330	Mēvarkala.
		1331	Valúr.
		1332	Kottiyodu.
		1333	Āttukunnam.
		1334	Chittayil.
		1335	Idavakondolivu.
		1336	Kandolivumulla.
		1337	Thōttaváram.
		1338	Kodumon.
		1339	Kulimonvilagam.
		1340	Mattam.
		1341	Idamattam.
		1342	Kuruchi.

Number and Taluq.	Number and Proverty.	Number.	Name of Kara.
9. Sirayinkil—(*Continued*).	73. Sirayinkil.	1374	Pallivilakam.
		1375	Pálavila.
		1376	Puttúr
		1377	Polunilalikónam.
		1378	Kélachanalikam.
		1379	Koikkaveedu.
		1380	Chelambu.
		1381	Vayaluveedu.
		1382	Madapponn.
		1383	Panachavilakam.
	74. Warkkala.	1384	Vettúr.
		1385	Chemmaruthi.
		1386	Ayirúr.
		1387	Ōdetti.
		1388	Vemkulam.
		1389	Kurakkanni.
		1390	Idava.
		1391	Ilakamon.
		1392	Panayara.
		1393	Warkkala.
	Madavúr.	1394	Pallikkel.
		1395	Kilakkenila.
		1396	Pyvely.
		1397	Naduvathéla.
		1398	Pilávarakōnam.
		1399	Kilpérúr.

Taluk	Pakuti	No.	Name
9. Sira	69. Kilimanúr.	1343	Palayakunnumēl.
		1344	Chúttayil.
		1345	Vēlikad.
		1346	Kulivély.
	70. Kūnthallúr.	1347	Adiyikkalam.
		1348	Chirambayil.
		1349	Kulattiralikom.
		1350	Kytharaveedu.
		1351	Mulluvila.
		1352	Parambil.
		1353	Púvenvilákam.
		1354	Ilavilakam.
		1355	Kodumon.
		1356	Kadayara.
		1357	Kurusikode.
	71. Manambur.	1358	Kannam kara.
		1359	Onampalli.
		1360	Cherunniyúr.
		1361	Ilanjimonkōnam.
		1362	Mullaramkōde.
		1363	Ottúr.
		1364	Mudiyakōde.
		1365	Tencharikōnam.
	72. Nagarur.	1366	Kottakkel.
		1367	Koduvalannur.
		1368	Pulimáttu.
		1369	Pulla.
		1370	Nagarúr.
		1371	Karode.
		1372	Kallingal.
		1373	Kāruvilakam.
	75.	1400	Mudaven mulla.
		1401	Vellallúr.
10. Kottarakkara.	76. Veliyam.	1402	Kilakké kara.
		1403	Padinjáré kara.
		1404	Nelliparambu.
		1405	Kannannúr.
		1406	Ōyúr.
		1407	Káyila.
		1408	Kōttara.
		1409	Cheppara.
		1410	Muttara.
		1411	Vyyakōde.
		1412	Málayil.
		1413	Mylōdu.
		1414	Ōdanávuttam.
		1415	Nedumon.
		1416	Maruthamonpalli.
		1417	Puyappalli.
		1418	Kōlikkodu.
		1419	Kudavettúr.
		1420	Chenkulam.
		1421	Kattayil.
	77. Ummannúr.	1422	Ilammāttu.
		1423	Cheriya Velunallúr.
		1424	Páramkode.
		1425	Arakannur.
		1426	Nellikunnam.
		1427	Meeyána.
		1428	Marankáttukōnam.
		1429	Chōkkúr.
		1430	Venkúr.
		1431	Kála Vayalu.

Number and Taluq.	Number and Proverty.	Number.	Name of Kara.
—(Continued).	77. Ummannúr—(Continued).	1432	Āttukōnam.
		1433	Mekkulam kara.
		1434	Ukkiramkunnu.
		1435	Tévannur.
		1436	Undúr.
		1437	Vilayannur
		1438	Nettayattu.
		1439	Karingannúr.
		1440	Ummannur.
		1441	Tudantala.
		1442	Cheruvakkal.
		1443	Vilanga kara.
		1444	Āyúr.
		1445	Polikōde.
		1446	Vayakkal.
		1447	Neduvely.
		1448	Valakam.
	78. Chadayamangalam.	1449	Chadayamangalam.
		1450	Thudayannúr.
		1451	Kythōdu.
		1452	Kottukal.
	rakkara.	1453	Kilakké kara.
		1454	Paċinjattan kara.
		1455	Trikkannamkode.
		1456	Neduvattúr.
		1457	Vallattumuri.

Number and Taluq.	Number and Proverty.	Number.	Name of Kara.
—(Continued).	81. Elukone—(Continued).	1491	Neduvankávu.
		1492	Kákkakōttumuri.
		1493	Chittankottumuri.
		1494	Karuvély.
		1495	Kolannumuri.
		1496	Yéttuvákkodu.
		1497	Pavithréswarattumuri.
		1498	Idakkadattumuri.
		1499	Do. Thālattu.
		1500	Kulimathikkadu.
		1501	Chōvallúr.
		1502	Vakkanad.
	82. Kulakkada.	1503	Kulakkada East.
		1504	Do. Thālattu.
		1505	Yérattu Kulakkada.
		1506	Āttuparachēri.
		1507	Poovattu West.
		1508	Do. East.
		1509	Perumkulattu.
		1510	Vénkáttu.
		1511	Puthúrmunnilayil.
		1512	Do. Mylamkulam.
		1513	Do. Chunkom.
	vala.	1514	Karrikka muttam.
		1515	Padinjatta kara.

Taluk	Pakuthi	No.	Name
10. Kottarakkara	79. Kotta	1458	Kōttarattala.
		1459	Ānakōttumuri.
		1460	Tēvalapurattu padinjaru.
		1461	Do. kilakku.
		1462	Santúr.
		1463	Tekkumpuram.
		1464	Kulikkel Idavakayil Karikkel.
		1465	Do. do. Tálattu.
		1466	Do. Tekkumchēri.
		1467	Do. Cherumangadu.
	80. Kummil.	1468	Kadakkelmuri.
		1469	Muthayilmuri.
		1470	Kummilmuri.
		1471	Cheru karamuri.
		1472	Chittúrmuri.
		1473	Ilappalannur.
		1474	Mangattumuri.
		1475	Tachakōnam.
		1476	Idattara.
		1477	Muthiramuri.
		1478	Madatharakani.
	81. Elukone.	1479	Tiruppilalikom.
		1480	Pilākode.
		1481	Elukōne.
		1482	Kythakōde.
		1483	Kanjirakode.
		1484	Puthushērikonam.
		1485	Maranātmuri.
		1486	Idavattom.
		1487	Irumbanankadu.
		1488	Kariprathalavukōnam.
		1489	Idakōttumuri.
		1490	Madathōttu kara.
10. Kottarakkara	83. Vettikka	1516	Mannātmuri.
		1517	Uliyanātmuri.
		1518	Nadukkannumuri.
		1519	Irannúrmuri.
		1520	Panavély.
		1521	Ayippellúr.
		1522	Irundur.
		1523	Thettiyodu.
		1524	Mēlila West.
		1525	Do. East.
		1526	Villúr.
		1527	Chengamanādu.
		1528	Chettādi.
		1529	Chekkumpurakkel.
		1530	Talachira.
11. Pattanapuram.	84. Anchal.	1531	Deverthōttattumuri.
		1532	Thalamēlmuri.
		1533	Valiyālamuri.
		1534	Mathirapparamuri.
		1535	Parattakātmuri.
		1536	Trikoikkelmurī.
		1537	Tuppalumuri.
		1538	Yērattumuri.
		1539	Pullomkottumuri.
		1540	Murukkomkotmuri.
		1541	Tumbottumuri.
		1542	Vayakkalmuri.
		1543	Vadamonmuri.
		1544	Agastiyakottumuri.
		1545	Ayilammuri.
		1546	Peringalloormuri.
		1547	Panayanchērimuri.

Number and Taluq.	Number and Proverty.	Number.	Name of Kara.
—(*Continued*).	84. Anchal—(*Continued*).	1548	Idamulakkalmuri.
		1549	Yarúrmuri.
		1550	Alayamonmuri.
		1551	Chōranatmuri.
		1552	Thadikáttilmuri.
		1553	Vālakattumuri.
		1554	Kambamkōttumuri.
		1555	Āyurmuri.
		1556	Padinjáttum kara.
		1557	Kokkáttumuri.
		1558	Márúrmuri.
		1559	Pálcolattumuri.
		1560	Perumannūmuri.
		1561	Malamélmuri.
		1562	Arakkelmuri.
		1563	Chembakarámanallúrmuri.
		1564	Múnkottumuri.
		1565	Kulattúpulamuri.
		1566	Do. malampurathu.
	puram.	1567	Kilakkaymuri.
		1568	Pidavúrmuri.
		1569	Arivittaramuri.
		1570	Neduvannurmuri.
		1571	Kamukanchērimuri.
		1572	Idamon.
		1573	Ottakkallu.
		1574	Chāliyak kara.

Number and Taluq.	Number and Proverty.	Number.	Name of Kara.
11. Pattanapuram—(*Contd.*)		1606	Pándithitta.
		1607	Naduttéri.
		1608	Manjakkála.
	89. Pattālidésom.	1609	Yérattu North.
		1610	Málūr.
		1611	Pantapilavu.
		1612	Meenattumuri.
		1613	Kannimel.
		1614	Kundayam.
		1615	Nadutēri.
		1616	Marathakam Desam.
		1617	Tálattu North.
		1618	Thekkéthary.
kotta.	90. Karkudi.	1619	Karkudi.
		1620	Káttála kudiyiruppu.
		1621	Vēppom parachēri.
		1622	Kēsavapuram.
	91. Ilattúr.	1623	Ilattūr.
		1624	Natarájapuram parachēri.
		1625	Āthankala parachēri.
		1626	Kīla parachéri.
	bah.	1627	Pantanadheeswaram kovil mala.
		1628	Oonchakketti mala.
		1629	Shenkōtta.

11. Pattanapuram		
85. Pattana	1575	Manchallúr.
	1576	Páthirikkal.
	1577	Karimbállúr.
	1578	Punnala.
	1579	Nadukkunnu.
86. Mylam.	1580	Mylam.
	1581	Pulamon.
	1582	Thāmarakkudi
	1583	Kalayapuram.
	1584	Anthamon.
	1585	Īnchakāt Thálattu.
	1586	Pallikkel.
	1587	Do. East.
	1588	Do. Perumkulattu.
	1589	Īnchakát Ērattu.
	1590	Kòttarattala East
	1591	Do. West.
87. Vilakkudi.	1592	Karaválúrmuri.
	1593	Punalúrmuri.
	1594	Venchémbu.
	1595	Máttara.
	1596	Vilakkudimuri.
	1597	Kuttikōttumuri.
	1598	Āvaneeswaram.
	1599	Vadakkum kara.
	1600	Elambanmuri.
	1601	Kariyaramuri.
	1602	Ārampunnamuri.
88. Tha-lavúr.	1603	Vadakóttumuri.
	1604	Kurāmuri.
	1605	Gnarakattumuri.

12. Shen		
92. Kas	1630	Mélavúr.
	1631	Kálám kara.
	1632	Tavana kara.
	1633	Púlám kudiyiruppu.
	1634	Lala kudiyiruppu.
	1635	Mukkada kurichi mala.
	1636	Kannimá kovil mala.
	1637	Teertha kara mala.
93. Klánkad.	1638	Varadayyangramom.
	1639	Klánkádu.
	1640	Mártándapuram.
	1641	Lāndappachēri.
	1642	Chember parachēri.
	1643	Vayakattu parachēri.
94. Shámbúr-vadakara.	1644	Mēlavúr.
	1645	Kīlavúr.
	1646	Mattuchinnánpalasa.
	1647	Vintallúr.
	1648	Muttammápuram.
	1649	Lakshmipuram.
95. Āyikkudi.	1650	Panavili.
	1651	Āyikkudi.
	1652	Kámákshipuram.
	1653	Tirumalayápuram.
	1654	Puthu kudiyiruppu.
	1655	Balasubrahmanniyapuram.
	1656	Anantapuram.
	1657	Kōthavarmmapuram.
96. Siva-nallúr.	1658	Sivanshērirayer thōttam.
	1659	Valukkapāra thōttam.
	1660	Panomkykáni thōttam.

Number and Taluq.	Number and Proverty.	Number.	Name of Kara.
kotta—(*Continued*).	96. Sivanallur (*Continued*).	1661	Punniamuttu thōttam.
		1662	Mádamuthu thōttam.
		1663	Achemputhúr.
		1664	Sivanallúr.
		1665	Párvathipuram.
		1666	Mék kara.
	ara.	1667	Sadásivapuram.
		1668	Tiruváriyapuram.
		1669	Kōtta theruvu.
		1670	Puliyara.
		1671	Mylappapuram.
		1672	Iravivarmapuram.
		1673	Kēsavapuram.
		1674	Tirumalayāpuram.
		1675	Korangannādu.
		1676	Puthuvūr.
		1677	Thekkumēttubhagavathipuram.
		1678	Āriyenkāvu.
		1679	Arakka parachēri.
		1680	Āriyenkavumala.
		1681	Nedumpāramala.
		1682	Kaludayuruttimala.
		1683	Ānachāvidi.
		1684	Eanasikkimala.
		1685	Arivikkaramala.
		1686	Vadakkumudukkupattu.
		1687	Thēnpàra.

Number and Taluq.	Number and Proverty.	Number.	Name of Kara.
—(*Continued*).	puram—(*Continued*).	1720	Mullu vila.
		1721	Tekkumbhagom.
		1722	Umayanullur Desam Āyirom Tengu.
		1723	Do. Naduvilay kara.
		1724	Do. Válattengil.
		1725	Do. Tekkum kara shēri.
		1726	Mayyanádu shéri.
		1727	Panthrendumuri.
		1728	Manakkádu.
		1729	Vadakkumkara East.
		1730	Keelavūr.
		1731	Párakōnattu.
		1732	Pērēyattu.
		1733	Punthalathálattu.
		1734	Kannóly.
		1735	Thattárkōnam.
		1736	Naduvile kara.
		1737	Chenthāppúr.
		1738	Thrikkovilvattom.
		1739	Cheriya Yēla.
		1740	Chérikōnam.
		1741	Vadakkamylakādu.
		1742	Vettilythálattu.
		1743	Kurumannara.
		1744	Thaluttala.
		1745	Kayyálakkel.
		1746	Umayanallúr Desam thálattu.
		1747	Vadakkambhágattu.
		1748	Vadakkumkara West.

District	Taluk	No.	Name
12. Shen	97. Puliy	1688	Pandiyanpārakadavumala.
		1689	Āriyenkávukōttavásal.
		1690	Mēlavúrkōnam.
		1691	Kilavūrkōnam.
		1692	Mūnkilthondu.
13. Quilon.	98. Kollam.	1693	Punnatala.
		1694	Manayikulam kara.
		1695	Tiruvallavārattu.
		1696	Thēvalli.
		1697	Ōlayil.
		1698	Kōttakkakom.
		1699	Vadakkumbhagam.
		1700	Kuriyippula.
		1701	Meenattu.
		1702	Sakthikulan kara.
		1703	Āsrámattu shēri.
		1704	Uliyakōlil shēri.
		1705	Andamukkam shēri.
		1706	Kannimēl shēri.
		1707	Kykulangara shēri.
		1708	Valia kada shéri.
		1709	Pallithōttattu shēri.
	99. Iravipuram.	1710	Pattathánattu.
		1711	Ayattil.
		1712	Manuluvilappirom.
		1713	Puthuchira.
		1714	Myláppūr.
		1715	Pálattara.
		1716	Vadakkai vila.
		1717	Karpūram.
		1718	Pinakkel.
		1719	Thattamala.

District	Taluk	No.	Name
13. Quilon	99. Iravi	1749	Udayamārtandapuram.
		1750	Arunallūr Tekké vila.
		1751	Amirthakulamgara.
		1752	Kadakattu Tekké vila.
	100. Paravur.	1753	Varinjattu shéri.
		1754	Nadakel shéri.
		1755	Kilakkenēla.
		1756	Kadambakāt shéri.
		1757	Velavurkōnattu shéri.
		1758	Kottam kara.
		1759	Mémanakōnam.
		1760	Karumbalúr kónam.
		1761	Vélamánúr
		1762	Chirakkarakulattúr kónam.
		1763	Ilankulam Tálattu.
		1764	Chirakara Idavattattu.
		1765	Tekkumbhágom.
		1766	Kōttappirom.
		1767	Kúnayil shéri.
		1768	Kurumanda shēri.
		1769	Púthakkulam.
		1770	Nellētti shéri.
		1771	Kalakkōdu.
		1772	Chirakkara Tálattu.
		1773	Kongál.
		1774	Polikkara.
		1775	Cháttanúr mámpallikunnom.
		1776	Uliyanättu shéri.
		1777	Cháttannúr Tālattu shéri.
		1778	Do. Ērattu shéri.
		1779	Koippáttu shéri.
		1780	Edanáttu shéri.
		1781	Meenattu.

Number and Taluq.	Number and Proverty.	Number.	Name of Kara.
—(*Continued*). nád.	101. Kilikollúr.	1782	Pérúr shéri.
		1783	Mangáttu shéri.
		1784	Karikōttu shēri.
		1785	Kannimél shéri.
		1786	Kilikollúr shéri.
		1787	Arunūttimangalattu shéri.
		1788	Perumbala shéri.
		1789	Punukonnúrvani shéri.
		1790	Kottamkara shēri.
		1791	Kundara.
		1792	Punukonnūr Ilanju vely.
		1793	Prákkulam.
		1794	Ashtamudi.
		1795	Peruvom West.
		1796	Do. Turuttu.
		1797	Ambala véli.
		1798	Panayattu Vadakay shéri.
		1799	Kōttakakam.
		1800	Chárukádu.
		1801	Tekkékara shéri.
		1802	Vadakke shéri.
		1803	Naduviléy shéri.
		1804	Chittattu shéri.
		1805	Neerambil shéri.
		1806	Peruvomkilakké shéri.
		1807	Murunta shéri.
		1808	Mulavana shéri.
		1809	Idavattattu shéri.

Number and Taluq.	Number and Proverty.	Number.	Name of Kara.
		1843	Valangāla.
		1844	Pilākkadu.
		1845	Mayilakádu.
		1846	Nedumpanakel.
	105. Padin-jarékallada.	1847	Naduvilé kara.
		1848	Valiapádom.
		1849	Koikkalbhagom.
		1850	Kōthapurathu.
		1851	Tekké kara.
		1852	Vadakké kara.
nattúr.	nattúr.	1853	Iverkala Pidinjarékkara Tekku.
		1854	Do. Vadakku.
		1855	Do. Naduvil.
		1856	Do. Kilakkékara Tekkúmuri.
		1857	Do. Kilakkémuri.
		1858	Do. Vadakkémuri.
		1859	Kadambanat Vadakké kara.
		1860	Do. Tekké kara.
		1861	Thuvayúr South.
		1862	Kunnathúr Padinjarrum kara.
		1863	Do. Kilakké kara.
		1864	Do. Naduvil kara.
		1865	Mánámbila.
		1866	Thurutti kara.
		1867	Mannadiyil Padinjáru Thalattu.
		1868	Do. Kilakkémuri.

Taluk	Pakuthi	No.	Name
13. Quilon	102. Peru	1810	Pérayom.
		1811	Chirumuttil shéri.
		1812	Chemmakkáttu shéri
		1813	Kuliyattu shéri.
		1814	Gnárakkel.
		1815	Chōnam Chira.
		1816	Kurippila shéri.
		1817	Panayattu shéri.
		1818	Mámpali shéri.
		1819	Cháttanámkulattu shéri.
		1820	Kandara shéri.
		1821	Īnchavila.
		1822	Kadavūr.
		1823	Mathilil shéri.
	103. Kilakkékal-lada.	1824	Palayattumuri.
		1825	Kōttavilamuri.
		1826	Munrothurthu.
		1827	Ūppukūttumuri.
		1828	Koikkelmuri.
		1829	Maravūrmuri.
		1830	Tekkaimuri.
		1831	Thálattumuri.
	104. Ādichanallūr.	1832	Ādichanallūr.
		1833	Kundumon.
		1834	Yelavu shēri.
		1835	Puliyila shēri.
		1836	Mieyyannúr shēri.
		1837	Kummallur shēri.
		1838	Pallimon shēri.
		1839	Kythakkuli shēri.
		1840	Nallilá shéri.
		1841	Muttukávil.
		1842	Thaluttala.
14. Kun	106. Kun	1869	Do. Kilakku Kálaikku padinjáré-muri.
		1870	Do. Kilakkummukhommuri.
		1871	Do. Naduviléy.
		1872	Do. Mémannādi.
		1873	Do. Kálaikku kilakku.
		1874	Thōttathil.
	107. Pórvaly.	1875	Naduvilay.
		1876	Vadakkum kara.
		1877	Ambalattubhagom.
		1878	Kambaladi.
		1879	Muthupilákádu East.
		1880	Do. West.
		1881	Peruvēlik kara.
		1882	Idakád.
		1883	Pallichérikkal.
		1884	Palliyil.
		1885	Panappatti.
		1886	Karinthōttuva.
		1887	Manak kara.
	108. Súranád.	1888	Ānayadi.
		1889	Páthirikkel.
		1890	Naduviley.
		1891	Súranád South.
		1892	Īnchakkádu.
		1893	Āyikkunnam.
		1894	Trikkunnapulay South.
		1895	Do. North.
		1896	Kidangayam North.
		1897	Pulikkulam.
		1898	Padinjáthum kara.
		1899	Kilakkum kara.

Number and Taluq.	Number and Proverty.	Number.	Name of Kara.
—(*Continued*).	108. Súranád—(*Continued*).	1900	Idappanarayara.
		1901	Kidangayon Naduvil
		1902	Do. Kannimél.
		1903	Tháleerádi.
		1904	Iravichira East.
		1905	Do. West.
		1906	Do. Naduvil.
		1907	Pandrendumuri.
		1908	Kyppalli.
	109. Pallikkal.	1909	Pallikkal.
		1910	Thottuvāmuri.
		1911	Kythakkel.
		1912	Cherukunnom.
		1913	Thengamathumuri.
		1914	Ilampalli.
		1915	Palakulattināl.
		1916	Do. East.
		1917	Meloottumuri.
		1918	Peringanatmundappalli.
		1919	Do. Thekkummuri.
		1920	Pōttadimuri.
		1921	Cherupūncha.
		1922	Kunnatturkaramuri.
		1923	Malamékkaramuri.
		1924	Amānthakaramuri.
		1925	Karuvattamuri.

Number and Taluq.	Number and Proverty.	Number.	Name of Kara.
14. Kunnattūr—(*Continued*).	113. Enádimangalam.	1960	Kúdalil.
		1961	Kalangūr.
		1962	Kunnida.
		1963	Kurumpa kara.
		1964	Márúr.
		1965	Pūtham kara.
		1966	Ilamannúr.
		1967	Parampil.
		1968	Mangāttu.
		1969	Nedumonnur.
		1970	Ilamangalam
		1971	Arukálikkel West.
		1972	Elamkulam.
		1973	Ēnáttu.
		1974	Kadika.
		1975	Arukálikkel East.
gappalli.	114. Krishnapuram.	1976	Krishnapuram.
		1977	Payanakattukaranmamuri.
		1978	Kottampalli.
		1979	Gnakkanámuri.
		1980	Káppi kilakkummuri.
		1981	Do. Mékkummuri.
		1982	Mémanamuri.
		1983	Matattilkaranma.
		1984	Pullikanakku.
		1985	Cherávalli.
		1986	Chokkadavumuri.

Taluk	Village	No.	Name
14. Kunnattur	110. Adūr.	1926	Múnnālammuri.
		1927	Konnamonkaramuri.
		1928	Kannankōttumuri.
		1929	Parakkottu.
		1930	Pannipila.
		1931	Ayyankoikkel.
		1932	Vellakulangaramuri.
		1933	Kottanallūr.
		1934	Cháttannúrpila.
		1935	Puthuchērybhāgom.
		1936	Vayala.
		1937	Yérathu.
		1938	Chúrakkodu.
		1939	Thuvayur North.
	111. Vallikōdu.	1940	Vallikodu.
		1941	Válamuttom.
		1942	Kōttayattu.
		1943	Piramádom.
		1944	Madūr.
		1945	Valomchuly.
		1946	Málamárur.
		1947	Vettūr.
		1948	Mannombhágom.
		1949	Ilakollúr.
		1950	Kudamukku.
		1951	Kyppattūr.
		1952	Nariyarommuri.
		1953	Vayala Vadakké kara.
	112. Kodu-mon.	1954	Channanapalli.
		1955	Angádikkel South.
		1956	Do. North.
		1957	Idathittu.
		1958	Aykkádu.
		1959	Kodumon.

Taluk	Village	No.	Name
15. Karuna	115. Puthuppalli.	1987	Pirayáttu Vadakku.
		1988	Váyikuli.
		1989	Changenkulangara.
		1990	Puthuppallithekku.
		1991	Kláppana.
		1992	Puthuppalli Vadakkukochumuri.
		1993	Do. Govindamuttom.
		1994	Do. Tekkukochumuri.
		1995	Vára vila.
		1996	Pirayāttu Tekku.
		1997	Sráyikattu Thura.
		1998	Puthuppalli North.
		1999	Alikkel Thura.
		2000	Valiya Kulangara.
	116. Chavara.	2001	Mámukkil Naduvattu shēri.
		2002	Málibhagammuri.
		2003	Neendakaramuri.
		2004	Mámukkil Tekkumbhágom.
		2005	Do. Vadakkumbhágom.
		2006	Putukkattumuri.
		2007	Kulamgarabhágom.
		2008	Madappallimuri.
		2009	Mukundapuram.
		2010	Kōttakkakom.
		2011	Cherushéribhágom
		2012	Chavaramuri.
		2013	Pattathánam.
		2014	Kōlithōttattu Thura.
		2015	Pandárathuruthu.
		2016	Karithura.
		2017	Vellanáthuruthu Thura.
		2018	Putten Sankétam.
		2019	Koyi vila.

—(*Continued*).

Number and Taluq.	Number and Proverty.	Number.	Name of Kara.
	117. Tēvalakkara.	2020	Mottakkel.
		2021	Pālakkel.
		2022	Padinjāthum kara.
		2023	Kōvūr.
		2024	Arumallūr.
		2025	Naduviley kara.
		2026	Kadappara.
		2027	Tekken mynagappalli.
		2028	Northern do.
		2029	Vengail.
	118. Panmana.	2030	Vayalōttumuri.
		2031	Manayilmuri.
		2032	Mēkkummuri.
		2033	Kilakkummuri.
		2034	Kollakamuri.
		2035	Palliyātmuri.
		2036	Kōlattumuri.
		2037	Mékāttumuri.
		2038	Panmanamuri.
		2039	Chittūrmuri.
	lava.	2040	Tekkummuri Padinjattum kara.
		2041	Pāvumpāmuri.
		2042	Todiyilmunnila.
		2043	Manappalli Vadakkummuri.
		2044	Do. Tekkummuri.
		2045	Puliyūrvanchi Vadakkummuri.
		2046	Péngaramuri.
		2078	Kolikottu Kilakkummuri.
		2079	Plánnu Pallilmuri.
	122. Kumara-puram.	2080	Erikkavu kara.
		2081	Thámallarakkil North.
		2082	Pōthappalli South.
		2083	Thámallarakil South.
		2084	Pōthappalli North.
		2085	Karuvátta South.
		2086	Kuruvátta North.
	123. Aripad.	2087	Thulānparampu Thekkummuri.
		2088	Ānádimuri.
		2089	Āyáparampu.
		2090	Cheruthana Thekkummuri.
		2091	Do. Vadakkummuri.
		2092	Tulámparampu Naduvathumuri.
		2093	Do. Vadakkummuri.
palli.	124. Pathiyur.	2094	Padinjáray kara.
		2095	Eruvayil.
		2096	Kāyenkulam.
		2097	Thōttommuri.
		2098	Kilakkummuri.
		2099	Ēvūr Tekke kara.
		2100	Kálāk kara.
		2101	Pathiyūr.
		2102	Eruva.

Taluk	Village	No.	Name
15. Karunagappalli	119. Tha	2047	Tekkummuri Kilakku.
		2048	Puliyūrvanchi Tekkummuri.
		2049	Kaduttúrmuri.
		2050	Kallélibhágom.
		2051	Vadakkummuri Kilakku.
		2052	Do. Padinjattu.
		2053	Mulangōdimuri.
	120. Kulasékharapuram.	2054	Āuthináttu Vadakkummuri Kilakku.
		2055	Do. Thekkumuri Kilakku.
		2056	Do. Vadakku Kōttakkupuram.
		2057	Do. Nielikkulam.
		2058	Do. Thekkummuri.
		2059	Kurungom Palli.
		2060	Āuthináttu Vadakkummuri Mékku.
		2061	Páyel Kadavuthura.
		2062	Kadathūr.
		2063	Āulappáttu Thura.
		2064	Punnakulam.
		2065	Kulithura.
		2066	Āuthinattu Vadakkummuri Mekku Kottakkupurathu.
	121. Karunagappalli.	2067	Kōlikottu Mékkummuri.
		2068	Maruthookulamkara Vadakkummuri.
		2069	Do. Cheriyalikkaltura.
		2070	Ālappáttunumpurkālámuri.
		2071	Pulipramuri.
		2072	Padináyarkulamkara Vadakkummuri.
		2073	Ālappáttumuri.
		2074	Ayanu Vélikulamkara Kesavapuram.
		2075	Do. Thekkummuri.
		2076	Do. Vadakkummuri.
		2077	Padanayarkulamkara Thekkummuri.

Taluk	Village	No.	Name
16. Kartigap	125. Muthukulam.	2103	Kádáshēri Munnila.
		2104	Mangalam Tura.
		2105	Kallikkattu Tura.
		2106	Valia alikkel Tura.
		2107	Tarayil Kadavu Tura.
		2108	Perumpalli Tura.
		2109	Rámanshēri Tura.
		2110	Padachál Tura.
		2111	Nallánikkal Tura.
		2112	Cherutōttathil Munnila.
		2113	Tekkum muriyil Vārūr Munnila.
		2114	Ārattupoola.
		2115	Chēppáttu Kannimél.
		2116	Tekkummuriyil Válappalli Munnila.
		2117	Máyampurakkal Munnila.
	126. Chēppád.	2118	Kánjoor Chēppád.
		2119	Malamēl Kottumuri.
		2120	Kānjoormuri.
		2121	Nangayárkulam kara.
		2122	Palaya Karanmamuri.
		2123	Valliakūlimuri.
		2124	Muttathumuri.
		2125	Parimanathumuri.
		2126	Kilakkummuri.
		2127	Ēvoor Vadakkupadinjāttumuri.
		2128	Do. Vadakku Kilakkummuri.
		2129	Kanichanalloormuri.
	127. Pallippád.	2130	Pallipāttu Vettuvanni.
		2131	Vadakkekkara Kilakku.
		2132	Pullam pádom.
		2133	Neendoor.
		2134	Valutānam.
		2135	Nangayár Kulankaramuri.

Number and Taluq.	Number and Proverty.	Number.	Name of Kara.
—(*Continued*).	127. Pallippád-(*Contd.*)	2136	Tekkummuri.
		2137	Kōttakkakommuri.
		2138	Naduvattammuri.
		2139	Marangáttu Vilamuri.
		2140	Tekkekara Kilakku.
	128. Keerikkád.	2141	Kandalloor North.
		2142	Do. South.
		2143	Putiavila Vadakkumuri.
		2144	Rámapurammuri.
		2145	Chēruvallibhágom.
		2146	Tekkummuri.
		2147	Malamélbhágommuri.
		2148	Karuváttumkulimuri.
		2149	Kannampallibhágommuri.
		2150	Putia Vila South.
	129. Tirukkunnappula.	2151	Kilakkēkara Tekku.
		2152	Pathiyám kara.
		2153	Pallippádu.
		2154	Vallanamuri.
		2155	Vánūr.
		2156	Kilakkékkara Vadakku.
		2157	Kōttayilmuri.
	palli.	2158	Vettuvenni.
		2159	Āyikkádu.
		2160	Kánjūr Kottakkakom.
		2161	Mátevikkádu.

Number and Taluq.	Number and Proverty.	Number.	Name of Kara.
—(*Continued*).	133. Thamarakulam —(*Continued*).	2194	Támarakulam East.
		2195	Vallikkunnom.
		2196	Védarvila.
		2197	Iluppakulam kara.
		2198	Káránma.
		2199	Kaduvinál.
		2200	Kannanákuli.
		2201	Kaduvumkal.
		2202	Padinjáru.
		2203	Meenathu.
	134. Pallikkal.	2204	Manjáditara.
		2205	Káránma.
		2206	Vettikkodu.
		2207	Karimulakkal.
		2208	Bharanikkávu South.
		2209	Chunakkara Naduvil.
		2210	Pallikkal Naduvil.
		2211	Pántikkulam.
		2212	Bharanikkavu North.
		2213	Kattánam.
		2214	Kattachira.
		2215	Iluppakkulam.
		2216	Chunakkara North.
		2217	Kōmallūr.
	kara.	2218	Pongaladi.
		2219	Māmpilály.
		2220	Mulampila.

Taluk	Village	No.	Name
16. Kartigappalli	130. Kartigap	2162	Nangayárkulam kara.
		2163	Putukkandathu.
		2164	Chingōli North.
		2165	Do. South.
	131. Kilakkékkara.	2166	Viyyapurammuri.
		2167	Piláppala Tekkummuri.
		2168	Mélpattommuri.
		2169	Vellomkulomkaramuri.
		2170	Páyippáttumuri.
		2171	Piláppila Vadakkummuri.
		2172	Kárichálmuri.
17. Mavellikkara.	132. Mavellikkara.	2173	Kunnam.
		2174	Eravom kara.
		2175	Arunoothimangalam.
		2176	Mavellikkara.
		2177	Kottárukávu.
		2178	Kalli Mēl.
		2179	Vettiyáthu Vadakku.
		2180	Talak kara.
		2181	Putiakávu.
		2182	Ākkanáttu kara.
		2183	Vettiyáttu Tekku.
		2184	Kottakkakam.
		2185	Kandiyūr.
		2186	Manakkadu.
		2187	Práyik kara.
		2188	Valuvádi.
	133. Thamarakulam.	2189	Tekkēk kara.
		2190	Pērū Káránma.
		2191	Kannimél
		2192	Válappalli.
		2193	Chattiyara.
17. Mavellikkara	135. Panthalom Tekkek	2221	Párakkara.
		2222	Idamáli.
		2223	Perumpulikkal.
		2224	Padikkottukkal.
		2225	Muduyūrkonam.
		2226	Thōnnalloor.
		2227	Naduvil.
		2228	Mangárom.
		2229	Kadakkádu.
		2230	Poolikkádu.
		2231	Bhagavatikkum Padinjáru.
		2232	Mallika.
		2233	Vayalinum Padinjáru.
		2234	Kurumpála.
		2235	Muttattu.
		2236	Thōttakkonam.
	136. Thekkékkara.	2237	Cherukunnam.
		2238	Pónáttu.
		2239	Pallikkal kilakké kara.
		2240	Perungála.
		2241	Vadakké Manguli.
		2242	Īrēlu.
		2243	Impirukkádu.
		2244	Kurathikkadu South.
		2245	Do. North.
		2246	Ménompalli.
		2247	Nadakkavu.
		2248	Varēnikkal.
		2249	Ponnēla.
		2250	Vallárimangalam.
		2251	Nadakkavu Kákkanáttu Koppally Káránna.
		2252	Tekke Mankuli.

Number and Taluq.	Number and Proverty.	Number.	Name of Kara.
—(*Continued*).	137. Kannamangalam.	2253	Kannamangalam North.
		2254	Kyta South.
		2255	Ānjilipra.
		2256	Kannamangalam South.
		2257	Īrēlu North.
		2258	Pōla.
		2259	Kyta North.
		2260	Mattam North.
		2261	Do. South.
		2262	Kadavúr.
	Nooranad.	2263	Ulavakád.
		2264	Pálamél.
		2265	Mutukkattu kara.
		2266	Tatha Mannu.
		2267	Paniyil.
		2268	Idakkunnam.
		2269	Putuppalli Kunnam.
		2270	Naduvil.
		2271	Erumakkuli.
		2272	Vayyanalloor.
		2273	Pallikkal.
		2274	Kodachanádu.
		2275	Ātukkadu.
		2276	Āttuva.
		2277	Cherumukhom.
		2278	Váttúr.
		2279	Idappone.

Number and Taluq.	Number and Proverty.	Number.	Name of Kara.
—(*Continued*).	141. Ala.	2312	Idavákkádu.
		2313	Kóttukulangi.
		2314	Āla North.
		2315	Cheruvalloor.
		2316	Kurandippalli.
		2317	Gnaranjukádu.
		2318	Thuruthi Mēl.
		2319	Ariyunni shéri.
		2320	Mampara.
		2321	Athimon shēri.
		2322	Āla South.
		2323	Edamuri.
		2324	Kadayikkádu.
		2325	Neduváromcodu.
		2326	Mandapariyárom.
		2327	Moolikkodu
	Chenganur.	2328	Peringáliprom South.
		2329	Do. North.
		2330	Ilangi Mēl Vadakkummuri.
		2331	Kadamboor.
		2332	Ulundiyil.
		2333	Grámom.
		2334	Puliyūr Muri.
		2335	Ennakkādu.
		2336	Tayyúr.
		2337	Buthannoor West.
		2338	Ilangi Mēl Thekkummuri.
		2339	Thōnnakkādu.

Taluk	Pakuthi	No.	Village
17. Mavellikkara	138.	2280	Pulimél.
		2281	Valinikkonam.
		2282	Kidangathu.
		2283	Nedukkulangi.
	139. Chennithala.	2284	Kilakké Vali.
		2285	Cheruköle.
		2286	Káránma East.
		2287	Puttenkottakkakom.
		2288	Káránma West.
		2289	Oriprom.
		2290	Tirperunthúr.
		2291	Tekkummuri.
		2292	Padinjárē Vali.
		2293	Eramathúr.
18. Chenganur.	140. Pauthalam Vadakke Kara.	2294	Thumpamon tháláthu.
		2295	Maluvéli.
		2296	Venmoni West.
		2297	Parampoor.
		2298	Ulakkádu.
		2299	Márámannu.
		2300	Mántu kara.
		2301	Gnattúr.
		2302	Venmani East.
		2303	Do. Thálattura.
		2304	Ilavunthittu.
		2305	Pūnthalathālathu.
		2306	Venmanithālathu.
		2307	Kōttukulanji Kárōdu.
		2308	Pūntala Ērathu.
		2309	Kyppala.
		2310	Vennūkkara South.
		2311	Do. North.
18. Chenganur	142.	2340	Buthannoor East.
		2341	Perinjádu.
		2342	Pērecherimuri.
	143. Vadakkēkkara.	2343	Ullannoor.
		2344	Puthen Kāvu.
		2345	Mulakkula.
		2346	Mundan Kávu.
		2347	Mangalom.
		2348	Idanádu
		2349	Kottayam.
		2350	Thittamēl.
		2351	Virala shēri.
		2352	Kárakkádu.
		2353	Panavātuk kara.
		2354	Eramalli kara.
		2355	Pándanadu West.
		2356	Koluvalloor.
		2357	Prayáru.
		2358	Ariyi kara.
		2359	Nannattumuri.
		2360	Angádikkal.
		2361	Vanmali.
		2362	Thiruvom Mundoor.
		2363	Umayáthum kara.
		2364	Kōleduthu shéri.
		2365	Piramattak kara.
		2366	Válárumangalom.
		2367	Kilachery Mēl.
		2368	Láka shéri.
		2369	Peringāla.
		2370	Malukeeru Mél.
		2371	Mutavali.
		2372	Kilavanmali.
		2373	Malukeerukeel.
		2374	Pāndanadu East.

Number and Taluq.	Number and Proverty.	Number.	Name of Kara.
—(*Continued*).	144. Ranni.	2375	Kumarampērūr.
		2376	Vadasheri kara
		2377	Perunādu.
		2378	Angādi.
		2379	Kakkādu.
		2380	Ayittala.
		2381	Thōttamon.
		2382	Mēkkoloor.
		2383	Idakkolum.
		2384	Noovakkádu.
		2385	Chēnnakkal.
		2386	Kunnom.
		2387	Vengálik kara.
		2388	Mylapra.
		2389	Putuseri Mala.
		2390	Mundappula.
		2391	Vykkam.
		2392	Perumpula.
		2393	Pullupram.
		2394	Varavoor.
		2395	Karikkulam.
		2396	Cherukulangi.
		2397	Mamkuli.
		2398	Mádavom.
		2399	Palavangádi kara.
	lūr.	2400	Válamuttam.
		2401	Chennikkara.
		2402	Muttattu Kōnam.

Number and Taluq.	Number and Proverty.	Number.	Name of Kara.
18. Chenga-nur—(*Contd.*)	146. Kumba-la—(*Contd.*)	2436	Vettoor.
		2437	Elathūr Kilakkummuri.
		2438	Kumbala.
		2439	Kandome kara.
		2440	Malayálappula Thálattu.
		2441	Nannavakkadu.
	147. Mánnar.	2442	Pavūk kara.
		2443	Kurattikád.
		2444	Iramathúr kara.
		2445	Kuratti shéri.
		2446	Vadashéri kara.
		2447	Kulangi Kárámma.
		2448	Kuttanpérur South.
		2449	Vishavár shéri.
		2450	Kuttanpērur North.
valla.	oor.	2451	Mēlúkkaramuri.
		2452	Nárangánom.
		2453	Vayalattala.
		2454	Karthaviyam.
		2455	Punnakkádu.
		2456	Káràm Vēli.
		2457	Kānjira Vēli.
		2458	Pérappoor.
		2459	Kulikkála.
		2460	Keelak kara.
		2461	Kadavanamuri.
		2462	Ontheikkáttumuri.

Taluk	Pakuthy	No.	Name
18. Chenganur	145. Ōmal	2403	Prakkánom.
		2404	Manjaṇi kara.
		2405	Parayanálimuri.
		2406	Panniyálimuri.
		2407	Āttarikom.
		2408	Mullanikkáttumuri.
		2409	Iymáli Mekkummuri.
		2410	Do. Kilakkummuri.
		2411	Chīkkanál.
		2412	Mannár Moolamuri.
		2413	Ērathu.
		2414	Mēloottubhágom.
		2415	Pyvallibhágom.
		2416	Puthenpeedicamuri.
	146. Kumbala.	2417	Pariyárom.
		2418	Pathanamthitta.
		2419	Vettiprom.
		2420	Kōttamthara.
		2421	Malayálappila Nalloor.
		2422	Valanchuly.
		2423	Malayálappila Ērattu.
		2424	Kulasekharapathi.
		2425	Atchencoil.
		2426	Kōnniayiramom.
		2427	Konniyūr Thalattu
		2428	Kallély.
		2429	Elantúr Mēkkummuri.
		2430	Aruváppálom.
		2431	Konnimangárom.
		2432	Alúr.
		2433	Malayalappula Idanadu.
		2434	Chittūr.
		2435	Madhura.
19. Tiru	148. Air	2463	Kōlam shéri.
		2464	Kadmathitta.
		2465	Káttūr kara.
		2466	Kōttáthūr .
		2467	Cherukole kara.
		2468	Káttū pēttah.
		2469	Thadiyúr.
		2470	Vellira.
		2471	Mallapila shéri.
		2472	Njūlu kara.
		2473	Pēroor.
		2474	Vanchitara.
		2475	Airoor kara.
		2476	Kánjittu kara.
		2477	Idappávoor kara.
		2478	Keelakoloor.
		2479	Kythakkodi.
		2480	Kunnattu kara.
		2481	Pákku kara.
		2482	Kurunthåru.
		2483	Mūkkannoo kara.
	149. Āranmula.	2484	Pannipravåru.
		2485	Neerulákom.
		2486	Nellikkal.
		2487	Pullāttu kara.
		2488	Kuruchi muttom.
		2489	Vallana.
		2490	Kōttakkara.
		2491	Nadukāttu kara.
		2492	Idayāran mula.
		2493	Thōttappila shéri.
		2494	Nedumprayāru.
		2495	Kuriyannūr.
		2496	Kōipprom.

Number and Taluq.	Number and Proverty.	Number.	Name of Kara.
—(*Continued*).	149. Āranmula—(*Continued*).	2497	Pālakkādu.
		2498	Kidangannūr.
		2499	Mārāmannu kara.
		2500	Mālak kara.
		2501	Kadappra.
		2502	Ārāttupula.
		2503	Parayannūr.
		2504	Idasheri mala.
		2505	Trikkannapuram.
		2506	Lákom.
	150. Kalluppára.	2507	Thēvan kara.
		2508	Muttathumannu.
		2509	Pariyārom.
		2510	Keelavāyipúr.
		2511	Vennikkulom.
		2512	Kavungen parayāru.
		2513	Kottāngāl kara.
		2514	Kulattūr.
		2515	Putushēri.
		2516	Thurittikkadu.
		2517	Ānikkāttu muri.
		2518	Madattumbhāgom.
		2519	Válamkaramuri.
		2520	Chákkōmbhágom.
		2521	Váyippūr kara.
		2522	Kallūr kara.
		2523	Mallappalli.

Number and Taluq.	Number and Proverty.	Number.	Name of Kara.
—(*Continued*).	152. Nedumpirom.	2556	Kilakkékaramuri.
		2557	Maruthōnbhágom.
		2558	Murinjachirabhágom.
		2559	Kochárimukkom.
		2560	Peringara.
		2561	Naduvilēmuri.
		2562	Kulivēlippurom.
		2563	Máttenkari.
		2564	Kálakkal.
		2565	Amichakari.
		2566	Padinjáthummuri.
		2567	Vettiyakkonam.
		2568	Mēlpra.
		2569	Padinjárē kara.
		2570	Kallumkalbhágom.
	Kaviyūr.	2571	Padinjarēthara.
		2572	Morani.
		2573	Tymávum kara.
		2574	Iravipēroor kara.
		2575	Thalattu kara.
		2576	Padinjáttum shéri.
		2577	Kottur kara.
		2578	Thelliyūr.
		2579	Punnamattom.
		2580	Thōlbhágom.
		2581	Kunnanthanom.
		2582	Punnavēli.
		2583	Kunnam.

Taluk	Division	No.	Name
19. Tiruvalla		2524	Vēttuveerabhágom.
		2525	Ampáttubhágom.
	151. Tiruvalla.	2526	Naduvilē chirą.
		2527	Kattur kara.
		2528	Kuluvellipuram.
		2529	Kilakkamuttoor.
		2530	Perumthuruttoo.
		2531	Idinjillom.
		2532	Ālamthuruttu.
		2533	Peringole.
		2534	Aliyadattu chira.
		2535	Váriyakkádu
		2536	Chalakkuli.
		2537	Muttūr kara.
		2538	Valiya kara.
		2539	Káttur kara.
		2540	Muliyennūr kara.
		2541	Āmallūr kara.
		2542	Vengal kara.
		2543	Vámanapuram.
		2544	Chumathara.
		2545	Meentala kara.
		2546	Tiruvámpádi.
		2547	Kávumbhágom.
		2548	Matilbhágom.
		2549	Tukala shéri.
		2550	Iruvalliprom.
		2551	Mannam kara chira.
		2552	Vempála.
		2553	Tengēli.
		2554	Nágacheri.
		2555	Punnakkunnom.

Taluk	Division	No.	Name
19. Tiruvalla	153.	2584	Perimpadi.
		2585	Elumattūr.
		2586	Vallamala.
		2587	Ānjilithánom.
		2588	Kilakkenotara.
		2589	Vallomkulom.
		2590	Thōttabhágom.
		2591	Talayáru.
		2592	Kuttūr kara.
	154. Kadappira.	2593	Mánnáru.
		2594	Vadakkumbhágom.
		2595	Tekkumbhāgom.
		2596	Kadappira.
		2597	Padinjāttummuri.
		2598	Kilakkummuri.
		2599	Parumala.
		2600	Valanja Vattom.
20. Ambalappula.	155. Ky-nakari.	2601	Palláturuttu.
		2602	Āttuváttala.
		2603	Thōttuvattala.
		2604	Kuttamangalam.
	156. Pirak-kádu.	2605	Kēlamangalam.
		2606	Chekkadikkadu.
		2607	Karūr.
		2608	Thōttappalli.
		2609	Pirakkádu.

Number and Taluq.	Number and Proverty.	Number.	Name of Kara.
—(*Continued*).	157. Kōli-mukku.	2610	Changomkari.
		2611	Patchayil.
		2612	Idattuva.
		2613	Táyankari.
		2614	Pándamkari.
		2615	Tekkēmuri.
	158. Thala-vadi.	2616	Neerodippurom.
		2617	Tekkēmuri.
		2618	Kárikkuli
		2619	Ānaprōmbal Vadakku.
		2620	Naduvilémuri.
		2621	Ānaprōmbal Tekku.
	159. Ne-dumudi.	2622	Tekkēmuri.
		2623	Thōttuváthala.
		2624	Āttuváthala.
		2625	Chēnnomkari.
		2626	Pongayil.
	160. Karu-mádi.	2627	Padinjarēmuri.
		2628	Kilakkémuri.
		2629	Āmayidamuri.
	válam.	2630	Tekkumbhágommuri.
		2631	Kannádi Kilakkēmuri.
		2632	Vadakkumbhágommuri.
		2633	Padinjarē Kunnumēl.

Number and Taluq.	Number and Proverty.	Number.	Name of Kara.
20. Ambalappula—(*Continued*).	165. Ālappula—(*Contd.*)	2664	Ālappula mullakkel.
		2665	Paravūr.
		2666	East of the Alleppey Jail.
		2667	North of the Alleppey Vāda.
		2668	Chembakasheri in Alleppey.
		2669	Palláthuruthu.
		2670	Tiruvámbádi.
		2671	Vandánommuri.
		2672	Kallerkode.
		2673	West of the school road.
		2674	West of the Kutwal bridge.
	166. Champak-kulom.	2675	Amichakari.
		2676	Nadubhágom.
		2677	Kōttupunnom.
		2678	Vysiumbhágom.
		2679	Oorikari.
		2680	Chembumpuram.
		2681	Pudukari.
tala.	167. Shert-tala.	2682	Kokkothamangalam Vadakkum kara.
		2683	Do. Kilakkummuri Thekkumbhágom.
		2684	Thekkummuri.
		2685	Vadakkummuri.
	Ariyadu.	2686	Mannancheri.
		2687	Vadakkan Āriyádu.
		2688	Thekkan do.
		2689	Thumpoo valli.

Taluk	Pakuti	No.	Name
20. Ambalappula	161. Ká	2634	Kilakkē Kunnumēl.
		2635	Kannádi Padinjattumuri.
		2636	Do. Vadakkēmuri.
		2637	Ākkákottu Punnamuri.
		2638	Veliyanádu.
	162. Takali.	2639	Vadakárom West.
		2640	Kandomkari.
		2641	Vadakárom East.
		2642	Chirayakom.
		2643	Tennadi.
		2644	Pullangádi.
		2645	Thakali.
		2646	Kunnumēl.
	163. Pulim-kunnu.	2647	Pulimkunnu.
		2648	Kōttabhágommuri.
		2649	Chaturttiakari.
		2650	Punnakkunnammuri.
		2651	Tekkēmuri.
	164. Amba-lappula.	2652	Kákkálam.
		2653	Kōmana.
		2654	Ambalappula.
		2655	Kanjipádom.
		2656	Neerkunnam.
	165. Ālappula.	2657	Vádakkal.
		2658	Alappula.
		2659	Punnappuram.
		2660	Kythavana.
		2661	Alleppey from Chaniyáttukavu to Putten tope.
		2662	Do. West of Cutcherry.
		2663	Do. South of the palace road.

Taluk	Pakuti	No.	Name
21. Shert	168.	2690	Póla.
		2691	Kánjirom chira.
		2692	Perumthurithi.
	169. Va-yalaru.	2693	Ooluva.
		2694	Pattana kadu.
		2695	Vayaláru.
		2696	Kadakkarappalli.
	170. Má-rárikulam.	2697	Káttoormuri.
		2698	Márárikulam.
		2699	Chettikattumuri.
		2700	Perunnērmangalom.
	171. Thanneer-mukkam.	2701	Váranom.
		2702	Perunthuruthu.
		2703	Cháramangalom.
		2704	Thanneermukkam.
		2705	Cheruváranom.
		2706	Maruthorevattom.
		2707	Chirikkandamangalom.
	172. Aroor.	2708	Yelupunna.
		2709	Yeramalloor.
		2710	Chanthiroor.
		2711	Aroor.
	173. Thuravoor.	2712	Kōdamthuruthu.
		2713	Padinjáthumkara Vadakkum kara.
		2714	Yelupunna Thekku.
		2715	Valamangalam Thekku.
		2716	Do. Vadakku.
		2717	Padinjáthumkara Thekku kadaprom.
		2718	Do. Thekkumanakodammuri.
		2719	Do. Thekkummuri.

Number and Taluq.	Number and Proverty.	Number.	Name of Kara.
	174. Vykkam.	2720	Padinjáttumcherimēl Thekkēmuri.
		2721	Kannakottu shéri.
		2722	Pallippurathu shēri.
		2723	Padinjáttumchērimēl Vadakkummuri.
		2724	Kilakkumchērimēl Vadakkēmuri.
		2725	Do. Thekkēmuri.
		2726	Moothēdathukávu.
		2727	Vallakommuri.
		2728	Kilakkumcherimēl Naduvilēmuri.
		2729	Chemmanom.
		2730	Padinjāttumcherimél Padinjattummuri.
	175. Vadayáru.	2731	Adiyommuri.
		2732	Vada kara.
		2733	Keevalloor.
		2734	Midáyikkunnom.
		2735	Mēvalloor.
		2736	Talayolaparampu.
		2737	Vadakkumbhágom.
		2738	Kalampūr.
		2739	Kilakkē kara.
		2740	Pōthi.
		2741	Irumbiom.
		2742	Thōnnalloor.
		2743	Parikkamkunnu.
kam.	nam.	2744	Brahmmamangalom.
		2745	Uthiyompēroor.
		2746	Chēmbu kara.

Number and Taluq.	Number and Proverty.	Number.	Name of Kara.
22. Vykkam—(*Contd.*)	180. Mulakkulam.	2777	Vattakkunnuppula.
		2778	Tekkē kara.
		2779	Vadakkē kara.
		2780	Mūlikkolē.
		2781	Keeloor.
		2782	Arunoottimangalom.
		2783	Kunnuppalli.
		2784	Peruvak kara.
		2785	Amarumák kara.
		2786	Káricode.
	181 Ettumanur.	2787	Mánnánommuri.
		2788	Sreekundhamangalom.
		2789	Pēroor kara.
		2790	Kilakkumbhágom.
		2791	Punnattara.
		2792	Kālicávu.
		2793	Thellámcávu.
		2794	Kadappūr.
		2795	Kānākali.
		2796	Kōlák kara.
		2797	Kuruvilangádu.
		2798	Kurumulloor.
		2799	Padinjáthumbhágom.
		2800	Kalattūr kara.
manur.	pila.	2801	Perumpōikāttu shéri.
		2802	Mariyaturuttu.
		2803	Kyppila.

		No.	Name
22. Vyk	176. Manakkun	2747	Paravoor.
		2748	Kandanádu.
		2749	Thuruttummēl.
		2750	Idavattom.
		2751	Káttūr kara.
		2752	Maravan Turuttu.
		2753	Vadakkumbhágom.
		2754	Thekkumbhágom.
		2755	Kádikkunnoo.
		2756	Yenádi.
	177. Kulasekhara-mangalam.	2757	Turuttummēl.
		2758	Kulasekharamangalom.
		2759	Padinjárē kara.
		2760	Vadakkémuri.
		2761	Padinjárémuri.
		2762	Irumbooli kara.
		2763	Vykkamprayarumuri.
		2764	Thekkémuri.
	178. Pána-vallí.	2765	Chēláttubhágom.
		2766	Mattattilbhāgom.
		2767	Perumbalom.
		2768	Turuttibhágom.
		2769	Pánávalli.
	179. Pallipprom.	2770	Dēvaruvattom.
		2771	Ulavyppumuri.
		2772	Tirunalloor.
		2773	Nadubhágom.
		2774	Pallippurom.
		2775	Chennamppallipurom.
		2776	Tykkáttu shēri.

		No.	Name
23. Ettu	182. Kyp-	2804	Mudiyūr.
		2805	Kodamāloor.
		2806	Ārpoor kara.
	183. Vetchúr.	2807	Kuda Vetchūr.
		2808	Idayálom.
		2809	Talayálam.
		2810	Oollala.
		2811	Thóttakom.
		2812	Kutavara.
		2813	Kallara.
		2814	Perunthuruthoo.
	184. Mánjoor.	2815	Oamalloor.
		2816	Kurumalloor.
		2817	Kótanalloor.
		2818	Oanamthuruthu.
		2819	Maymuri.
		2820	Neendūr.
		2821	Iravimangalom.
		2822	Manjoor Kilakkumbhágom.
		2823	Káttálpakku.
		2824	Mánjoor Thekkumbhágom.
		2825	Do. Vadakkumbhágom.
	185. Kaduthuruthi.	2826	Putuchery kara.
		2827	Yelumáthurutti.
		2828	Iravimangalom.
		2829	Mánnāru.
		2830	Kulasekharapuram.
		2831	Kaduthuruthi.
		2832	Madhuravēli.
		2833	Yerumathuruthu.
		2834	Āyamkudi.
		2835	Vellom shéri.

Number and Taluq.	Number and Proverty.	Number.	Name of Kara.
23. Ettumanur—(*Continued*)	185. Kaduthuruthi—(*Continued*).	2836	Pálak kara.
		2837	Kátom Kuli.
		2838	Pálūturuthu.
		2839	Kavakkádu.
		2840	Páláchira.
		2841	Kánjira Mattom.
		2842	Marangóli.
		2843	Tiruvámpádi.
		2844	Njeeloo kara.
		2845	Pampra.
	186. Kidangoor.	2846	Máriyidom.
		2847	Vadakké Peringorakoil.
		2848	Mayvida.
		2849	Kidangoor.
		2850	Chembilávu.
		2851	Kummannoor.
		2852	Tekkē Peringorakoil.
		2853	Pirayároo.
		2854	Pullappalli.
		2855	Pantha Tala.
tayam.	Kumarakom.	2856	Kilakkumbhágom.
		2857	Kummanom.
		2858	Thattumkal.
		2859	Teruvu.
		2860	Tekkumbhágom.
		2861	Padinjarēbhágom.

Number and Taluq.	Number and Proverty.	Number.	Name of Kara.
	190. Vijayapuram.	2895	Chumkom.
		2896	Mángánom.
		2897	Muttampalom.
		2898	Panayakkuli.
		2899	Pärampula.
		2900	Vadavádoor.
		2901	Kulippurayidom.
		2902	Vijayapuram.
		2903	Manakkādu.
		2904	Amayannūr.
		2905	Ariparambu.
		2906	Ayerkkunnom.
		2907	Málom.
		2908	Parampu kara.
		2909	Thiruvanchūr' kara.
		2910	Nettā shéri.
		2911	Theerikádu.
		2912	Ārumánoor.
		2913	Punnathara.
		2914	Kongándūr.
		2915	Kūdalloor.
		2916	Pariyármangalom.
—(*Continued*).	Kottayam.	2917	Cháliakunnu.
		2918	Govindapuram.
		2919	Kōdimatha.
		2920	Thirunak kara.
		2921	Kottayam.
		2922	Vēlloor.

Taluk	Pakuthi	No.	Village
24. Kot	187.	2862	Chengalom.
		2863	Kumaragom Vadakkumbhágom.
	188. Aimanon.	2864	Parippu kara.
		2865	Oolasa kara.
		2866	Aimanom.
		2867	Valliyāttu kara.
		2868	Kummanom kara.
		2869	Mariyáturuthu.
		2870	Malloo shēri.
		2871	Nattá shēri.
		2872	Párampula.
	189. Nattakom.	2873	Āulappula.
		2874	Pallom.
		2875	Mávilangu.
		2876	Chingavanom.
		2877	Parathara Muttam.
		2878	Kuli Mattom.
		2879	Panachikkádu.
		2880	Muttom.
		2881	Mariyappalli.
		2882	Mulankula.
		2883	Kākkūr.
		2884	Moolavattom.
		2885	Muppayikkādu.
		2886	Punnakkel.
		2887	Kunnappalli.
		2888	Kollanádu.
		2889	Malamēlkávu.
		2890	Pooventhuruttu.
		2891	Choliakádu.
		2892	Chánnánikádu.
		2893	Pákku.
		2894	Velloo thuruttu.

Taluk	Pakuthi	No.	Village
24. Kottayam	191.	2923	Kārāppila.
		2924	Kiliroor.
		2925	Thiruvārppu.
		2926	Changalom.
	192. Pāmpády.	2927	Meenatom.
		2928	Pámpádi.
		2929	Velloor.
		2930	Kothala.
		2931	Mādappádu.
		2932	Kurōppada.
		2933	Pangada.
		2934	Idakkáttoor.
	193. Akalakkunnam.	2935	Idamula.
		2936	Panamattom.
		2937	Ilomkulom.
		2938	Ilompalli.
		2939	Kárkkulom Mallika shéri.
		2940	Yelikkulam.
		2941	Oorulakunnom.
		2942	Matta kara.
		2943	Ānikkādu.
25. Changanacheri.	194. Velianadu.	2944	Veliyanádu.
		2945	Kumarom kari.
		2946	Kadanjoor.
		2947	Kunnam kari.
	195. Neelampērūr.	2948	Neelampēroor.
		2949	Chakkachompākku.
		2950	Tekkeera.
		2951	Vadakkeera.
		2952	Váladi.

Number and Taluq.	Number and Proverty.	Number.	Name of Kara.
—(*Continued*).	195. Neelampérūr —(*Contd.*)	2953	Nárakatara.
		2954	Kynady.
		2955	Cheru kara.
		2956	Vyattupākku.
		2957	Chēnnomkari.
	196. Manchadikara.	2958	Válappalli Kilakkumbhágom.
		2959	Do. Pandinjáttumbhágom.
		2960	Kurichi kara.
		2961	Ithithānam.
		2962	Péroor kara.
		2963	Thuruthi.
	197. Changanacheri.	2964	Perunnayil Padinjáttumbhágom.
		2965	Do. Kilakkumbhāgom.
		2966	Mādappalli.
		2967	Kurumpanēdom.
		2968	Trikkodittánom.
		2969	Pilavátur.
		2970	Váyippádu.
	Puthuppalli.	2971	Puthuppalli.
		2972	Yérikkádu.
		2973	Vákattánom.
		2974	Champa kara.
		2975	Thōttukādu.
		2976	Iravinalloor.
		2977	Tirkōthamangalom.

Number and Taluq.	Number and Proverty.	Number.	Name of Kara.
chal.	201. Lálom.	3010	Vellápádu.
		3011	Keelathadiyūr.
		3012	Nechipulūr.
		3013	Karūr.
		3014	Pōnádu.
		3015	Vayappattu.
		3016	Anthinādu.
		3017	Kadappāttūr.
	Kondūr.	3018	Kondúr.
		3019	Mélāmpāra.
		3020	Keelámpára.
		3021	Mēlucávu.
		3022	Irumápra.
		3023	Válakom.
		3024	Veerakkádu.
		3025	Kōlati.
		3026	Thittanādu.
		3027	Īráttupēttah.
		3028	Thalappálom.
		3029	Peermade.
		3030	Vadakkekkara in Poonjattu Idavagai.
		3031	Mávady mala do.
		3032	Perunnilom do.
		3033	Nadakkal do.
		3034	Thekkē kara do.
		3035	Mannom do.
		3036	Kunnunno do.
		3037	Adakkâ mala do.

Taluk	Pakuthy	No.	Name	
25. Changanacheri	198.	2978	Kádamuri.	
		2979	Pariyárom.	
		2980	Nedumkunnom.	
	199. Muttár.	2981	Manalády.	
		2982	Rāmankari.	
		2983	Mámbalakari.	
		2984	Muttáru.	
		2985	Mittrakari.	
		2986	Vélapra.	
	200. Kanjirappalli.	2987	Cheru Valli.	
		2988	Koovathalattu Kilakkumbhāgom.	
		2989	Kanjula.	
		2990	Páloor.	
		2991	Chénappadi.	
		2992	Manimala.	
		2993	Kulattūr.	
		2994	Peerimade.	
		2995	Do. Aluthayil thottam.	
		2996	Do. Annapoornéswari thottom.	
		2997	Yedakkunnom.	
		2998	Kánjirappalli.	
		2999	Tambalakádu.	
		3000	Vada kara.	
		3001	Ērathu Vada kara.	
		3002	Ālappura.	
		3003	Eruméli.	
		3004	Kuratti.	
		3005	Peruvanthánam.	
		3006	Koovathála Idabhágom.	
		3007	Do. Vadakkumbhágom.	
		3008	Lálom.	
		3009	Pálá.	
26. Meena	202.	3038	Cháthapiláppalli	do.
		3039	Mutta mala	do.
		3040	Mundappalli	do.
		3041	Chénnadu	do.
		3042	Teekoi kara	do.
		3043	Mattu mala	do.
		3044	Velláni	do.
		3045	Mánkompu	do.
		3046	Pilappalli	do.
		3047	Njarákadu	do.
		3048	Adivāram	do.
		3049	Idamala	do.
		3050	Mangalom mala	do.
		3051	Choppoor mala	do.
		3052	Kurinjilla	do.
		3053	Thalanádu	do.
	203. Rámapuram.	3054	Rámapuram.	
		3055	Velliláppalli.	
		3056	Kadanádu.	
		3057	Ēlaracheri.	
		3058	Pilaku.	
		3059	Ayimkompu.	
		3060	Marangādu.	
		3061	Maytiri.	
		3062	Neeloor.	
		3063	Keelthiri.	
		3064	Koodappulom.	
		3065	Idakkoli.	
		3066	Amana kara.	
		3067	Kurinji.	
		3068	Kondāttu.	
		3069	Puliyennūr.	
		3070	Vallichira.	

Number and Taluq.	Number and Proverty.	Number.	Name of Kara.
26. Meenachal—(*Continued*).	204. Puliennur.	3071	Pulavúrmuri.
		3072	Aranápuram.
		3073	Neyyoor.
		3074	Keelpankolom.
		3075	Tekkummuri.
		3076	Padinjáttummuri.
		3077	Kāniyakādu.
		3078	Idanādu.
		3079	Murikkanádu-
		3080	Kodakkachiramuri.
	205. Meenachal.	3081	Meenachel.
		3082	Púvarani.
		3083	Párappalli.
		3084	Pálakádu.
		3085	Idamattom.
		3086	Velliyappalli.
		3087	Keelparayáru.
		3088	Vilakkumadom.
	206. Bharananganom.	3089	Bharananganom.
		3090	Idappādi.
		3091	Aravakkulom.
		3092	Ullanádu.
		3093	Alanádu.
		3094	Choondacheri.
		3095	Pélangananom.
		3096	Pravithānom.
		3097	Kypoor.

Number and Taluq.	Number and Proverty.	Number.	Name of Kara.
—(*Continued*).	208. Ilakkádu—(*Continued*).	3132	Ulavoomuri.
		3133	Mothippalli.
		3134	Nellithanattumuri.
		3135	Marangáttupalli.
		3136	Perunthánom.
		3137	Aundúr.
		3138	Karunochi.
		3139	Poovakkulom.
		3140	Veliyannoor.
		3141	Mutakkanādu.
		3142	Puthuvēli.
		3143	Ariyi kara
		3144	Thāmarakádu.
	galam.	3145	Kóthamangalom.
		3146	Do. Angádi.
		3147	Karūr.
		3148	Chēladu.
		3149	Pendimana.
		3150	Karinjula.
		3151	Ilavanādu.
		3152	Nagara Mudi.
		3153	Nēriyamangalom.
		3154	Keelakkunnom.
		3155	Kallādu.
		3156	Ayiroor.
		3157	Āmala.
		3158	Perumannoor.
		3159	Malayinkeel.

Taluk	Pakuti	No.	Name
27. Muvattupula.	207. Iramallūr.	3098	Ilampra.
		3099	Tankalom.
		3100	Cheruvēttoor.
		3101	Mulavoor.
		3102	Páyipra.
		3103	Mánádi.
		3104	Rākkádu.
		3105	Kunnakkála.
		3106	Cheriya Oorayom.
		3107	Peechādu.
		3108	Válavom.
		3109	Koikkadu.
		3110	Mékadambu.
		3111	Kadáthy.
		3112	Punnōppadi.
		3113	Mudavūr.
		3114	Válappalli.
		3115	Kávum kara.
		3116	Velloorkunnom.
		3117	Polakkāppalli.
		3118	Tirkkalattūr.
		3119	Iramallūr.
		3120	Kuttilanji.
		3121	Nellikuli.
		3122	Idanádu.
		3123	Chiraládu.
		3124	Tirkáriyūr.
		3125	Perumattom.
	208. Ilakkádu.	3126	Vayalāmuri.
		3127	Kuriyanádu.
		3128	Mannakanádu.
		3129	Kurichithánom.
		3130	Ilakkádu.
		3131	Pálakkádu.
27. Muvattupula.	209. Kōtaman	3160	Kavalangádu.
		3161	Pymattom.
		3162	Rámalloor.
		3163	Máramangalom.
		3164	Kadakkavu.
		3165	Náducáni.
		3166	Karukadani.
		3167	Pattáshéri.
		3168	Puthupádi.
		3169	Máthirippalli.
		3170	Váripra.
		3171	Venduvaly.
		3172	Kottapadi.
		3173	Āyicádu.
		3174	Nakom shéri.
		3175	Irumala.
	210. Ēnánalloor.	3176	Ēnánalloor.
		3177	Āyavana.
		3178	Puttoor
		3179	Karimattom.
		3180	Nettám shéri.
		3181	Padinjarē Punnamattom.
		3182	Kadampidi.
		3183	Kálámpūr.
		3184	Parampa shéri.
		3185	Pulinthanom.
		3186	Pothánicádu.
		3187	Elangamom.
		3188	Vārappatti.
		3189	Kakkáttoor.
		3190	Myloor.
		3191	Vettithara.
		3192	Inchoor.

Number and Taluq.	Number and Proverty.	Number.	Name of Kara.
—(*Continued*).	210. Ēnanalloor—(*Continued*).	3193	Kōlippalli.
		3194	Madiyūr.
		3195	Pidayūr.
		3196	Vullārimangalom.
		3197	Āyam.
		3198	Vangattoor.
		3199	Neduvāikādu.
		3200	Cháthamattom.
		3201	Kāvakādu.
		3202	Kulapirom.
		3203	Vadakké Punnamattom.
		3204	Kadavoor.
		3205	Tekké Punnamattom.
		3206	Pana kara.
		3207	Gnarakádu.
	Kūthattukolam.	3208	Pámpákkuda.
		3209	Kákkūr.
		3210	Piramádom.
		3211	Idayáru.
		3212	Keelakombu.
		3213	Ōnakūru.
		3214	Vadakara Paittakulam.
		3215	Kōlippilli.
		3216	Maraya kara.
		3217	Pálakkula.
		3218	Mannattūr.
		3219	Tiruvámbádi.

Number and Taluq.	Number and Proverty.	Number.	Name of Kara.
27. Muvattupula—(*Continued*).	214. Rámangalom—(*Continued*).	3251	Vettithara.
		3252	Káyanádu.
		3253	Neerkuli.
		3254	Vechoor.
		3255	Maymukhom.
		3256	Keelamuri.
		3257	Karukúr.
		3258	Mámala shéri.
		3259	Ēlakkaranádu.
pula.	215. Todupula.	3260	Todupula.
		3261	Cheriya Todupula.
		3262	Olamattom.
		3263	Kánjiramattom.
		3264	Kōláni.
		3265	Karimkunnom.
		3266	Ottalloor.
		3267	Prála.
		3268	Thattárathráttu.
		3269	Vettayanádu.
		3270	Puthi chira.
		3271	Kadayatti chira.
		3272	Muthalakódam.
	kádu.	3273	Mēlpirappila.
		3274	Moonnupeedica.
		3275	Nediyála (Pannikuli).
		3276	Vengáloor.
		3277	Arikkula.

Taluk	Division	No.	Name
27. Muvattupula	211.	3220	Oaliaprom.
		3221	Kootthattookulom.
	212. Muvattupula.	3222	Kávana.
		3223	Āvōli.
		3224	Tekké Márádi.
		3225	Vadakkam Márádi.
		3226	Perumballoor.
		3227	Pandappulli.
		3228	Keel Madangu.
		3229	Mél Madangu.
		3230	Ārakkula.
		3231	Thottak kara.
		3232	Nadu kara.
		3233	Randāroo.
		3234	Peringula.
		3235	Muvattupula.
		3236	Ātikadu.
		3237	Rámangalom.
	213. Piravom.	3238	Piravom.
		3239	Kakkāttu kara.
		3240	Pálūr.
		3241	Vethiyappirom.
		3242	Ālappurom.
		3243	Perumpadavom.
		3244	Ilanji.
		3245	Muthalapurom.
	214. Rá-mangalom.	3246	Ūrayom.
		3247	Mēmuri.
		3248	Pámpira.
		3249	Rámangalom.
		3250	Maniyittu kara.
28. Todu	216. Manak	3278	Puthupariyárom.
		3279	Periyámparambu.
		3280	Viralimattom.
		3281	Manakkádu.
		3282	Chūralloor.
		3283	Kuninji.
		3284	Keelpirappila.
		3285	Chittoor.
		3286	Talamattom.
	217. Kumaramangalom.	3287	Kappu.
		3288	Vengalloor.
		3289	Kallookádu.
		3290	Mudappannoor.
		3291	Ilaloor.
		3292	Perumbilli chira.
		3293	Manjalloor.
		3294	Thaluvarakunnom.
		3295	Kalloor kara.
		3296	Nirompila.
		3297	Nágappila.
		3298	Mylakkombu.
		3299	Kumáramangalom.
		3300	Válakkulom.
		3301	Kalavúr.
		3302	Vadacodu.
	218. Kárikkodu.	3303	Káricode.
		3304	Thōndikkula.
		3305	Muttom.
		3306	Thudanganadu.
		3307	Tekkumbhāgom.
		3308	Idavetti.
		3309	Keerikodu.
		3310	Elumuttom.

Number and Taluq.	Number and Proverty.	Number.	Name of Kara.
— (*Continued*).	218. Kárikkodu—(*Continued*).	3311	Annáyikannan.
		3312	Changarapalli.
		3313	Ilom désom.
		3314	Perumattom.
		3315	Irikodu.
		3316	Velliyāmattom.
		3317	Āulakodu.
		3318	Kudattūr.
		3319	Arakulam.
		3320	Keettila.
		3321	Thalayanádu.
		3322	Moarkádu.
		3323	Kōlappira.
	mannúr.	3324	Nedumattom.
		3325	Kurumpālamattom.
		3326	Pandamattom.
		3327	Vellánthánom.
		3328	Chilavu.
		3329	Tondi.
		3330	Vadakōdu.
		3331	Nériamangalom.
		3332	Pálanádu.
		3333	Kunnakadu.
		3334	Mannoorkádu.
		3335	Chélakádu.
		3336	Peringá shéri.
		3337	Arumannoor.
		3338	Idamaruku.

Number and Taluq.	Number and Proverty.	Number.	Name of Kara.
—(*Continued*).	223. Idappalli Thekkumbhāgom.	3370	Kalloor.
		3371	Punnuruthi.
		3372	Pennala.
		3373	Pálarivattom.
		3374	Chalikkavattom.
		3375	Vádivattom.
		3376	Mámangalom.
		3377	Yelamak kara.
	224. Trikkakkara.	3378	Tengōdu.
		3379	Vadakōdu.
		3380	Gnālakom.
		3381	Pettayakunnom.
		3382	Peringala.
		3383	Vellilāra.
		3384	Vīdakkula.
		3385	Trikkā kara.
		3386	Kákkanádu.
		3387	Thutiyūr.
		3388	Kundannoor.
		3389	Cherumattapila.
		3390	Palliprom.
		3391	Putupalliprom.
	voor.	3392	Vengōla.
		3393	Iringōle.
		3394	Okkel.
		3395	Perumpavūr.

Taluk	Pakuthi	No.	Name
28. Todupula	219. Kari	3339	Vannoor.
		3340	Mannapirom.
		3341	Kurukkanádu.
		3342	Oliyirippu
		3343	Pallikkel.
		3344	Oodumbanoor.
		3345	Neyya shēri.
		3346	Kodikulom.
		3347	Karimannoor.
29. Kunnattunadu.	220. Asamannūr.	3348	Asamannoor.
		3349	Noolēli.
		3350	Panachiyara.
		3351	Punnayara.
		3352	Váyik kara.
		3353	Vayyál.
		3354	Cherukunnom.
		3355	Rāyimangalom.
		3356	Mudakiráye.
		3357	Maythala.
		3358	Yekkunnom.
		3359	Keelillom.
		3360	Pulluvali.
	221. Válak-kulam.	3361	Vadakkē Yeliprom.
		3362	Thekkē do.
		3363	Palliprom.
		3364	Vadakkē Válakkulom.
		3365	Thekke do.
	222. Idappalli Vadakkum-bhágom.	3366	Chuttuppádu.
		3367	Pōnai.
		3368	Pīliyádu.
		3369	Vadakkumbhágom.
29. Kunnattunadu	225. Pe-rumpá-	3396	Kánjirakōdu.
		3397	Kárāttuvalli.
		3398	Vallom.
		3399	Chīlámattom.
	226. Chēránallūr.	3400	Pralayakkádu.
		3401	Pulukkádu.
		3402	Turuthi.
		3403	Nedungapra.
		3404	Vendūr.
		3405	Yelamvagappalli.
		3406	Ayimudi.
		3407	Mudakkula.
		3408	Kōdanádu.
		3409	Kurichilakōdu.
		3410	Thottuva.
		3411	Chēránalloor.
		3412	Yedavūr.
		3413	Palliprom.
		3414	Kudālappādu.
		3415	Koovappadi.
		3416	Kurompa shēri.
		3417	Akanádu.
	227. Aikkaranádu.	3418	Padayompādi.
		3419	Kottom Chathapalli.
		3420	Pannikuli.
		3421	Puliyanjūr.
		3422	Tammánimattom.
		3423	Kadamattom.
		3424	Venkilá.
		3425	Monappalli.
		3426	Cherukunnom.
		3427	Marangáttoor.
		3428	Yēliprom.

Number and Taluq.	Number and Proverty.	Number.	Name of Kara.
—(*Continued*).	ranádu—(*Continued*).	3429	Valavoor.
		3430	Kadayirippu.
		3431	Palomthottam.
		3432	Rámalloor.
		3433	Kutta.
		3434	Káninádu.
		3435	Pámkodu.
		3436	Vadakodu.
		3437	Chemmanádu.
		3438	Marangáttupalli.
		3439	Thiruvánoor.
		3440	Véloor.
		3441	Kodinjoor.
		3442	Kuliyara.
		3443	Kokkarappalli.
		3444	Kodumpoor.
		3445	Muriyamangalom.
		3446	Tonnikka kara.
		3447	Pariyárom.
		3448	Pūttūr kara.
		3449	Kinginimuttom.
		3450	Karucappalli.
		3451	Elamkulom.
		3452	Peringóle.
		3453	Kulikkódu.
		3454	Brahmapuram.
		3455	Mutta kara.
		3456	Kollimuttom.
		3457	Adoor.

Number and Taluq.	Number and Proverty.	Number.	Name of Kara.
29. Kunnattunadu—(*Continued*).	229. Maluvannūr.	3491	Thirkkalattūr.
		3492	Kunnakuradi.
		3493	Kadakkanádu.
		3494	Valampoor.
		3495	Vadakkē Maluvannúr.
		3496	Yeliprom.
		3497	Nelládu.
		3498	Veettūr.
		3499	Kuluroor.
		3500	Mannoor.
	230. Manjapra.	3501	Vadakkumbhágom.
		3502	Naduvattom.
		3503	Neeleeswarom.
		3504	Thótta kara.
		3505	Nénampalli.
		3506	Mánikkamángalom.
		3507	Panayēli.
		3508	Mekkáladi.
		3509	Káladi.
		3510	Mattoor.
		3511	Veerároor.
		3512	Dēvarmatom.
		3513	Kuttili.
gadu.	va.	3514	Chálayakkal.
		3515	Yedathala.
		3516	Kákkanadu.
		3517	Nechivēli.

29. Kunnattunadu	227. Aikka	3458	Mattakuli.
		3459	Puttumánur.
		3460	Venmani.
		3461	Varikkoli.
		3462	Kákkádu.
	228. Kunnattunadu.	3463	Parakkōdu.
		3464	Morkála.
		3465	Vempilli.
		3466	Palli kara.
		3467	Peringála.
		3468	Pinarumundu.
		3469	Punnūrkōdu.
		3470	Valampūr.
		3471	Kythakádu.
		3472	Gnáralloor.
		3473	Eramēli.
		3474	Chittanádu.
		3475	Palanganadu.
		3476	Chengara.
		3477	Choorakōdu.
		3478	Kunmanodu.
		3479	Chēlakulom.
		3480	Vilangu kara.
		3481	Kárakulom.
		3482	Mákkini kara.
		3483	Malayidam Turuthu.
		3484	Ambunádu.
		3485	Oorkádu.
		3486	Kalukkampalom.
		3487	Poriyakkunnom.
		3488	Thāmarachālprom.
		3489	Ayirápurom.
		3490	Maluvannur.

30. Alan	231. Ālu	3518	Yerumathála.
		3519	Muttom.
		3520	Choornni kara.
		3521	Thaikádu.
		3522	Alwaye.
		3523	Thóttumukhom.
		3524	Kuduma shēri.
		3525	Kunnukuly.
		3526	Keelamattu.
	232. Pu-then-chira.	3527	Vadakkummuri.
		3528	Thekkummuri.
		3529	Kilakkummuri.
	233. Alangadu.	3530	Thiruvāloor.
		3531	Karingáturuthu.
		3532	Padinjare Kodungaloor.
		3533	Kuttikáttutara.
		3534	Yēlu kara.
		3535	Uliyanádu.
		3536	Neerikódu.
		3537	Yeramom.
		3538	Mēthanom.
		3539	Chirayam.
		3540	Kayanti kara.
		3541	Muppatadom.
		3542	Idayároo.
		3543	Kilakke Kodaungaloor.
		3544	Kongápalli.
		3545	Ulanādu.
		3546	Kotuvalanji.
		3547	Thóttakkádu.
		3548	Kónjini kara.
		3549	Kōttapuram.
		3550	Pánáyikulam.

Number and Taluq.	Number and Proverty.	Number.	Name of Kara.
—(*Continued*).	234. Airūr.	3551	Veliyettunádu.
		3552	Mánjáli.
		3553	Adūthuruthu.
		3554	Ayiroor.
		3555	Vayalu kara.
		3556	Vadakku Aduva shēri.
		3557	Karumáloor.
		3558	Tekke Aduva shēri.
		3559	Kunna kara.
	235. Chengamanadu.	3560	Chengamanadu.
		3561	Rāyimmal.
		3562	Thuruthu kara.
		3563	Thuruthu shēri.
		3564	Pāppala shēri.
		3565	Maykávu.
		3566	Avuparambu.
		3567	Maykádu.
		3568	Malloo shēri.
		3569	Parampu shēri.
		3570	Nedumpara shēri.
		3571	Kapra shēri.
		3572	Āvanom kodu.
		3573	Keelapariyárom.
		3574	Neduvannoor.
		3575	Prayáru.
		3576	Putuvá shēri.
		3577	Poyikāttu shēri.

Number and Taluq.	Number and Proverty.	Number.	Name of Kara.
30. Alangadu —(*Contd.*)	237. Pārakka-davu(*Contd.*)	3612	Poovattu shéri.
		3613	Mallu shēri.
		3614	Kunnappalli shēri.
		3615	Kuratti.
		3616	Mampra.
		3617	Yelavur.
	238. Puthenvelikkara.	3618	Puttenvēli kara.
		3619	Padinjarēpuliyamthuruttu.
		3620	Vellōttumpurom.
		3621	Thuruttūr.
		3622	Cheriyathēkkánom.
		3623	Cháthóttupurom.
		3624	Kilakképulayamthuruttu.
		3625	Elanthi kara.
		3626	Kuttiyathottam.
		3627	Chálakkak kara.
		3628	Tēlaturuttu.
		3629	Cheriyakadaprom.
		3630	Āttupurom.
rur.	Paravūr.	3631	Paravuthara
		3632	Pallenthuruttu.
		3633	Valiapallenthuruttu.
		3634	Kidámangalom.
		3635	Neendoor.
		3636	Perumpadangu.
		3637	Maravanthuruttu.
		3638	Parayakádu.

Taluk	Village	No.	Name
30. Alangadu	236. Kōdakulangara.	3578	Peecháni kádu.
		3579	Mukkannoor.
		3580	Keetoor.
		3581	Náyathōdu.
		3582	Idayáttūr.
		3583	Kárikōdu.
		3584	Karayámparambu.
		3585	Vyttala.
		3586	Vāloor.
		3587	Kodakulangara.
		3588	Vendoor.
		3589	Cheruválūr.
		3590	Yerayamkudi.
		3591	Paloo shēri.
		3592	Annamanada.
		3593	Thuravoor.
		3594	Kidangūr.
		3595	Ālattūr.
		3596	Ankamāli.
		3597	Āla kara.
		3598	Champannoor.
		3599	Kalloor.
		3600	Kumbidi kara.
		3601	Vennoor.
		3602	Maylettūr.
		3603	Kurukukkuti.
	237. Pārakkadavu.	3604	Karuma shēri.
		3605	Kannomkuli shēri.
		3606	Moolikulam.
		3607	Puliyanom.
		3608	Kottūr shēri.
		3609	Chettikulam.
		3610	Karippā shēri.
		3611	Párakkadavu.

Taluk	Village	No.	Name
31. Pa	239.	3639	Nanthiyáttukunnom.
		3640	Kūttakádu.
		3641	Thottu kara.
	240. Vadakkekara.	3642	Teeyathuruthu.
		3643	Chittáttu kara.
		3644	Pooyappalli.
		3645	Pattanom.
		3646	Ālamthuruthu.
		3647	Máchānthuruthu.
		3648	Kunjithy.
		3649	Valiyathuruthu.
		3650	Kattathuruthu.
		3651	Thuruthipurom.
		3652	Onattukádu.
		3653	Chárakádu.
		3654	Oavathuruthu.
		3655	Pávakádu.
		3656	Madapilathuruthu.
		3657	Perumanom Desavaliyil Pōrannoor.
		3658	Do. Palliprom.
		3659	Do Kodannoor.
		3660	Do. Vattakkádu.
		3661	Do. Chakkiarkádu.
		3662	Do. Yelāttu kara.
		3663	Do. Vendini shēri.
		3664	Do. Vattuvomkoor.
		3665	Do. Perum shēri.
		3666	Munampumuri.
		3667	Máliam kara.
		3668	Chettikádu.
		3669	Moothakunnu.
		3670	Kóttuvallikódu.
		3671	Thurithiprom.
		3672	Kottaprom.

Number and Taluq.	Number and Proverty.	Number.	Name of Kara.
31. Parur—(*Continued*).		3673	Gothunthuruthu.
	241. Kōttu-valli.	3674	Kōttuvalli kara.
		3675	Kythárom.
		3676	Vallupalli.
		3677	Thathapalli.
		3678	Kilakkēprom.
	242. Elikkara.	3679	Palliyākkel.
		3680	Thekkumbhágom.
		3681	Vadakkumbhāgom.
		3682	Kadak kara.
		3683	Nedungádu.
		3684	Manjanakādu.
		3685	Púkkádu.
		3686	Elankunnappula.
		3687	Ōchenthuruthu.
		3688	Vysrákkel.
		3689	Vallárupádattu.
	pula.	3690	Idampādom.
		3691	Kóthavoor kara.
		3692	Varáppula.
		3693	Válom.
		3694	Moolampally.
		3695	Chennoor.
		3696	Chēránalloor.
		3697	Mannonthuruthu.
		3698	Chirakkakom.
	244. Pūn-játtu Ida-vaka.	3706	Pūnjáttu Idavaka.
	245. Cardamom Hills.	3707	Anjunattutharachivayel.
		3708	Anjunáttu kara.
		3709	Anjunattukeelannoor.
		3710	Kánthalloor.
		3711	Anjunattil Puthoor.
		3712	Do. Perumala.
		3713	Chilanthe Ārumalavūr.
		3714	Kōttákūmbavūr.
		3715	Vattapadavoor.
		3716	Anjanáttumekottukudi.
		3717	Udumpancholaparakada Chira.
		3718	Pooppára Amina pachapullu pradēsom.
		3719	Ilayakadu amina.
		3720	Miláppára amina.
		3721	Vandomvettupāra.
		3722	Ránnikaramala (in Chenganur).
		3723	Pathinarakomkāni (in Todupula).
		3724	Nēriyamangalom.
		3725	Kumily.
		3726	Udampanchóla.

243. Varáp-	3699	Dēvarkādu.	246. Periyar.	3727	Periar.
	3700	Puttenpalli.	247. Thekkadi.	3728	Tékkadi.
	3701	Kilakkumbhāgom.			
	3702	Manjummel.			
	3703	Ēloor Vadakkumbhāgom.			
	3704	Do. Thekkumbhágom.			
	3705	Thuruthikadāvu.			

V. NAGAM AIYA,
Settlement Dewan Peishcar and
Census Commissioner, Travancore.